REFUGEES, BORDERS AND IDENTITIES

This book examines the impact of Partition on refugees in East and Northeast India and their struggle for identity, space and political rights. In the wake of the legalisation of the Citizenship Amendment Act in 2019, this region remains a hotbed of identity and refugee politics.

Drawing on extensive research and in-depth fieldwork, this book discusses themes of displacement, rehabilitation, discrimination and politicisation of refugees that preceded and followed the Partition of India in 1947. It portrays the crises experienced by refugees in recreating the socio-cultural milieu of the lost motherland and the consequent loss of their linguistic, cultural, economic and ethnic identities. The author also studies how the presence of the refugees shaped the conduct of politics in West Bengal, Assam and Tripura in the decades following Partition.

Refugees, Borders and Identities will be indispensable for scholars and researchers of refugee studies, border studies, South Asian history, migration studies, Partition studies, sociology, anthropology, political studies, international relations and refugee studies, and for general readers of modern Indian history.

Anindita Ghoshal is Associate Professor of History at Diamond Harbour Women's University, Kolkata, India. Her research interests include Partition and refugee studies, with special emphasis on eastern/northeastern India and Bangladesh. She has been the recipient of a Major Project Grant by OKDISCD-ICSSR (2017–18), Charles Wallace Trust Fellowship (2015), Academic and Foreign Travel Grant from the Indian Council of Historical Research (ICHR) (Cardiff University, UK, 2013), Gautam Chattopadhyay Memorial Prize by Itihas Samsad (2013), Research-Writing Fellowship from MCRG (2012), UGC-MRP (2010) and a Short-Term Scholarship from the Asiatic Society of Bangladesh, Dhaka (2009). She has published various articles in reputed journals, as well as chapters in edited volumes. She has also presented her research in seminars/conferences in India and abroad. Currently, she works as co-investigator on a research project at the University of Manchester, UK, funded by AHRC (2018–2021).

Based on meticulous archival research, this book sheds light on the aftermath of Partition and refugee influx in Assam and Tripura—a region neglected in the extant Partition literature. It should therefore be an essential reading for those interested in the long history of Partition.
  —**Professor Sekhar Bandyopadhyay**, *Director, New Zealand India Research Institute, Victoria University of Wellington, New Zealand*

The available narrative about the Partition-displaced has been about their struggle for home and security. Anindita Ghoshal's book demonstrates that coeval to such struggle was an another narrative about refusal of the refugees to be the 'victims' of politics anymore and as new 'arbiter' of their destiny how they actually shaped the contour of politics in the host country which was, contrary to popular belief, often hostile. Fascinating.
  —**Professor Sajal Nag**, *Department of History, Assam University, Silchar, India*

REFUGEES, BORDERS AND IDENTITIES

Rights and Habitat in East and Northeast India

Anindita Ghoshal

LONDON AND NEW YORK

First published 2021
by Routledge
2 Park Square, Milton Park, Abingdon, Oxon OX14 4RN

and by Routledge
52 Vanderbilt Avenue, New York, NY 10017

Routledge is an imprint of the Taylor & Francis Group, an informa business

© 2021 Anindita Ghoshal

The right of Anindita Ghoshal to be identified as author of this work has been asserted by her in accordance with sections 77 and 78 of the Copyright, Designs and Patents Act 1988.

All rights reserved. No part of this book may be reprinted or reproduced or utilised in any form or by any electronic, mechanical, or other means, now known or hereafter invented, including photocopying and recording, or in any information storage or retrieval system, without permission in writing from the publishers.

Trademark notice: Product or corporate names may be trademarks or registered trademarks, and are used only for identification and explanation without intent to infringe.

British Library Cataloguing-in-Publication Data
A catalogue record for this book is available from the British Library

Library of Congress Cataloging-in-Publication Data
Names: Ghoshal, Anindita, author.
Title: Refugees, borders and identities : rights and habitat in east and northeast India / Anindita Ghoshal.
Description: Abingdon, Oxon ; New York, NY : Routledge, 2021. | Includes bibliographical references and index.
Identifiers: LCCN 2020012628 (print) | LCCN 2020012629 (ebook)
Subjects: LCSH: Refugees—India, Northeastern—Social conditions. | Internally displaced persons—India, Northeastern—Social conditions. | Refugees—Government policy—India. | Internally displaced persons—Government policy—India. | Migration, Internal—India, Northeastern. | India—History—Partition, 1947—Influence.
Classification: LCC HV640.4.I4 G56 2021 (print) | LCC HV640.4.I4 (ebook) | DDC 305.9/0691409541—dc23
LC record available at https://lccn.loc.gov/2020012628
LC ebook record available at https://lccn.loc.gov/2020012629

ISBN: 978-0-367-32265-6 (hbk)
ISBN: 978-0-367-32266-3 (pbk)
ISBN: 978-0-429-31762-0 (ebk)

Typeset in Bembo
by Apex CoVantage, LLC

To my parents
Professor Ashim Kumar Ghoshal
and
Smti. Aparajita Ghoshal

CONTENTS

Foreword by Professor Peter Gatrell   *ix*
Preface   *xi*
Acknowledgements   *xix*
List of abbreviations   *xxv*

    Introduction   1

1   Encountering the 'refugee': crafting the policies   42

2   Dealing with the refugees: rehabilitation, variation, discrimination   81

3   Creating a new refugee domain: Assam and Tripura   118

4   Becoming political: politicisation of refugees in West Bengal   161

5   Politics as defence: activation of refugees in Assam and Tripura   200

    Epilogue   244

Select glossary   *256*
Bibliography   *260*
Index   *295*

FOREWORD

Refugee history has come of age, thanks to the work of scholars such as Pamela Ballinger, Joya Chatterji, Daniel Cohen, Ilana Feldman, Katy Long, Laura Madokoro, Uditi Sen, Caroline Shaw, Pippa Virdee, Benjamin Thomas White, Vazira Zamindar and others, who have followed in the footsteps of pioneers such as Gil Loescher, Tony Kushner and Katharine Knox, Michael Marrus and Claudena Skran. The latest scholarship has been inspired or at least provoked by the interdisciplinary field of refugee studies, to which pioneers such as Howard Adelman, Dawn Chatty, B.S. Chimni, Barbara Harrell-Bond, Renée Hirschon, Peter Loizos, Liisa Malkki, Roger Zetter and Aristide Zolberg made a lasting contribution.

To this growing literature we can now add this valuable and wide-ranging new book by Anindita Ghoshal. As she explains, the mass population displacement in West Bengal that preceded and followed the Partition of India in 1947 was multi-faceted. Her monograph illuminates many aspects of this protracted, difficult and complex process, beginning with the various motives and considerations of those caught up in these often bewildering events: for some of those 'on the move', displacement was a pure ordeal; for others, it might represent an opportunity. Dr Ghoshal proceeds to disclose the assorted vocabulary that circulated at the time, as Governments, refugees and the host population attempted to make sense of events. She contributes a nuanced perspective to the ongoing debates around the identity of those deemed to be 'refugees'.

Dr Ghoshal demonstrates how the presence of refugees in Assam, Tripura and West Bengal shaped the conduct of politics in these states over the course of three decades, often in unexpected ways. She carefully delineates the contours of interaction between the newcomers and the indigenous population in each state. She reflects in compelling fashion on refugees' experiences and aspirations, without losing sight of the overarching and shifting social, political and economic contexts in which refugees found themselves, and to which they contributed their own perspectives according to variables of class, age, gender, religion and ethnicity. She is as insightful on the often-painful emotional dimensions of displacement as she is on its material impact.

In these ways, Anindita Ghoshal's book makes an original and insightful contribution to refugee history and to the history of India at a critical juncture in its post-independence incarnation. I recommend it unreservedly.

Professor Peter Gatrell
School of Arts, Languages and Cultures
University of Manchester
United Kingdom

PREFACE

The creation of refugees is inherent in the logic of the making of nation-states. Nations are notorious for displacing their own people in bids to ensure their homogenous existence; but search for homogeneity is like peeling of an onion, an unending process (Nag 2001: 47–59). The forced migrants are unnecessary or discarded elements for a nation-state which obviously had to take shelter somewhere else. The rise of neo-liberal state has conceived the idea of sheltering displaced people by creating a new political category named the 'refugees'. The idea of 'taking refuge in a foreign country or land' and the emergence of a brand-new term 'refugee' in South Asia was a direct outcome of a similar endeavour of making two nation-states by separating an undivided one. The Indian Partition of 1947 had witnessed mass displacement and relocation of communities on a huge scale not experienced before. Certain journalists have often used the word 'surgery' as a metaphor in describing Partition that was imposed on the Indian subcontinent, when in reality, the borders were implemented through two provinces, Bengal in the east and Punjab in the west. The Radcliffe Award, or the 'notional' border, was imposed in dividing each into two different states. The event unleashed untold miseries and seamless tragedy in the whole subcontinent. Thus, the romanticism of Jawaharlal Nehru in his midnight speech of 15 August 1947, wherein he had declared 'India was born at the stroke of the midnight hour . . . to life and freedom' from its 'tryst with destiny' was only one side of the canvas.[1] 'The other face of freedom' had unfolded many narratives of the ceaseless human sufferings in both the fractured ends of Punjab and Bengal. Partition was not just a division of territories; it was indeed a massive human tragedy of post-colonial South Asia.

The most bitter, prolonged and debilitating fallouts of the Partition were the many issues arising out of and relating to the unfortunate refugees. Thus, in the history of India's Partition, the 'refugee' is central—rather almost a mythical figure without which the national history of India and Pakistan can hardly be told. The process of Partition became particularly palpable when viewing or narrating from the lives of the poor ordinary people, the refugees, though they were a proud part of the so-called struggle of independence, experienced violence and homelessness, and faced persistent resistance from the respective host states in India (Kaur 2009: 429). Their process of rehabilitation had emerged to be an arduous task of nation building, along with the consolidation and stabilisation of the newfound independence. Refugees flowed from the partitioned provinces of Punjab and Bengal, and some other provinces that were transferred to either Pakistan or India also experienced waves of refugee exodus. For the refugees, it became a long agonising struggle of rehabilitating themselves not just territorially, but politically, economically, culturally and psychologically. The migration to the new nation was neither smooth, nor was the reception in this part of the 'utopia' as welcoming as was hoped. The Partition-displaced refugees, who lost their ancestral home and hearth, century-old occupation and subsistence, suddenly realised that they were nobody's children—they were the proverbial nowhere people. They had no patrons, no sponsors and no allies. In their struggle, they were all alone. Most problematically, soon the refugees felt that there was hostility, discrimination and gross apathy towards them and to their settlement. They had to struggle, from pillar to post, for every meal, every concession. Home remained like a distant dream; even rehabilitation had to be fought for. Therefore, it was a long struggle before they could compel the Indian state to accommodate, rehabilitate and resettle them, both spatially and economically.

Perhaps the root of the complexity in this particular scope/area of research lay in the regional identity of refugees and difference in the nature of refugee movement along the eastern and western borders since 1947. In this tragedy, Punjabi refugees proved to be fortunate in getting rehabilitation, as they were offered state protection and care compared to the Bengali refugees, who were not granted equal help and assistance. The official position was that refugee exodus was expected in the Punjab sector, but for the Bengal sector, the leadership did not expect major cross migration, as they thought that the Bengalis were too strong a cultural community to be affected by communal mobilisation. Thus, while refugee arrangement in the western borders, primarily in Punjab, was determined by the policy of exchange, migration in the eastern borders was based on the Delhi Pact (1950).[2] Again, the refugee influx in Punjab was a one-time flush. But on the eastern border, it was continuous in nature. There was very little preparation, a scarcity of resources and a feeling of antagonism by certain classes to accommodating them in the new-born nation. Yet in reality, the uninterrupted trail of Hindu Bengali refugees (and some displaced tribals) from East Bengal to eastern and northeastern bordering states of India continued until the 1970s, without any stable settlement plan or a proper relief and rehabilitation policy. The refugees were initially refused settlement in the major refugee-absorbent states along the newly created Bengal borderlands and were denied a legal identity in the provinces they chose to migrate to. At the regional level, the general attitude of the then Central Government (Centre) towards the refugee-absorbed states like West Bengal, Assam and Tripura was astonishingly discriminatory. The Bengali refugees have often projected as not like an authentic type of refugees within the state discourse that was fashioned after the Punjab experience of violence and movement. After Partition, lasting more than seven decades, the portrayal of the Bengali refugees remained confusing, partly pitiful and partly heroic; they often discursively located out of the orbit of authentic 'refugee-ness' (Kaur 2009: 429). But they proved themselves as a different type of masses, who could create their own agency, portrayed an image of a different 'human tragedy of Partition' within a fold of their unique type of 'refugee-dom'.

The aftermath of Partition not only affected the geophysical structure of a state; it permanently damaged the psychological and cultural matrix of the people. Some popular colloquial terms like refugee, *udbastu*, *sharanarthi*, *bastuhara*, *bangal*, *bhogonia*, *bohiragoto*, *bideshi*, *malaun* and *wansa* became part of daily vocabulary in the refugee-absorbent states. Interestingly, the refugees had soon discovered the issue of identity as being rather complex and multiple, than simple and singular. The Bengali refugees, generally categorised by religious faith, had to embrace many other identities in colloquial terms, like *haghore bangal*, poor Bengali Hindu, Bengali lower-caste Hindu, *rifu* or *refu*, and *muhajir*, undoubtedly adding layers to their singular religious identities. And, in the process of transformation, the concept of 'self' often shifted from religious to linguistic, cultural and economic, whereby political space and the identity of the refugees became complex and multi-layered. A general tendency among the historians and political and social scientists was to look at the Partition either from perspectives of two states or simply two types of refugees, Punjabi and Bengali. They often ignored the problems related to major differences within a single geographical area. This book critiques this perspective and asserts that the 'refugee identity' needs to be defined within a particular state system and culture. The other problematic angle in refugee studies lies in the issue that the refugees have always been labelled as a monolithic group. Other identities based on their class, caste, linguistic attachment and ethnicity often remained insignificant. The categorisations of refugees were made either as a 'political or economic block' or a 'religious community', which had negated both the complexity of their compositions and the historical contexts of the locations and their experience of 'refugee-hood'. So, the problem of 'regionalisation', or the idea of 'multiple layers' within the 'identity of refugees', was seldom raised or questioned by the historians and political and social scientists in the first three decades after Partition. Issues like 'transformation of self' or 'diversity in identity' has drawn little attention in India. It has rather had a better handling in Bangladesh because of the language movement of 1952 and the ultimate birth of a state, which indicated a linguistic identity that overwhelmed the religious identity of the people, which had included the refugees since 1947. Interestingly enough, the marginality of Bengali refugees has always been seen either with the background of Partition or from a religious perspective. Hence, limited academic attention was paid to the inception of the identities of refugees and how they evolved into the complex and multi-layered 'other' in various regions of the post-Partition India.

But despite this monolithic approach, there were instances of different ways of looking at the refugees in the historiography of the refugee studies in India. Disparity, vulnerability and variability in the nature of their migration, divergent treatments towards them and structuring respective policies based on the needs of different regions influenced historical works and writing literary texts on them. In the existing historical works on Partition and refugees in this subcontinent, a clear disparity could be observed in addressing the refugee concerns in the western and eastern borders. Distinct approaches became important to position them and delineate their identities. The historians, political scientists and social scientists comparatively explored well-documented refugee movements across the western borders more, in which the problem of creation of the refugees (as aftereffects of Partition) had either been discussed at length or how the state was dealing with the refugee got focused. But in those scopes of analysis, refugees were seen just as an en masse or as unitary groups; parameters got fixed by putting them into a comparative framework, where the problem of their 'multiple layers' of identity and regional variety (in east-west paradigm) were often ignored. The available works on the Partition of 1947 and the refugees also do not generally provide comparative perspectives between three Hindu Bengali-speaking refugee-absorbent states in eastern and northeastern India like West Bengal, Assam and Tripura. This book goes beyond the frontier of Bengal and examines other frontier areas like the then-Assam and Tripura, which too were very popular and important destinations of the Bengali Hindu refugees from East Pakistan. It explores within a comparative parameter, the multi-stranded absorption process of the Bengali refugees in the post-Partition Indian states of West Bengal, Assam and Tripura. The book argues that though the refugees crossed borders on religious grounds and sought refuge in the neighbouring areas of erstwhile East Pakistan, they faced many types of resistances from all the different dominant host communities in diverse states, during which they gradually became aware of their multiple identities, including linguistic, cultural, economic and ethnic. It delineates the role of various political parties in the rehabilitation process in these states and how some of the parties had soon turned into 'refugee parties', which in turn transformed their electoral fortune, but eventually, these parties also changed their attitude towards the problems of the refugees. Refugees were turned into a political football whereby they were kicked from place to place by the same political parties which refused to settle them amidst their kinsmen.

This particular book proposes to understand the conditions of the Bengali-speaking Hindu refugees within the time frame of 1946–1977. It focuses on tracing the multi-stranded absorption process experienced in those states and tries to deal with the patterns of behaviour of refugees along the eastern borderlands. The book starts with the pre-Partition riots and politics, stating them as the core reason behind the influx of refugees, and comes to an end in 1977 to show how the refugee-related issues had entirely transformed the social environment, or political situation, in the eastern and northeastern states like West Bengal, Assam and Tripura. While the Janata Party Government in 1977 had replaced the ruling power at the Centre,

West Bengal and Tripura experienced a similar change in the state scenarios. The Left Front Government came into power in both of the states, chiefly with the support of refugee vote banks. Assamese subnationalism finally came out on the streets after 1977, with revenge to protest against illegal immigration, as well as an outcome of a de facto policy of enfranchisement of so-called 'non-citizens'. This book enquires, how within 30 years of Partition, the nature of living of the refugees had changed drastically according to the local environment and by the changed sociopolitical-economic conditions in these states. The book chiefly tries to portray that there are major differences even within the single geographical area, where a tendency surfaced to define the assertion of 'refugee identity' within a particular state system or culture. It tries to bring out how refugees by their numerical dominance often determined or reshaped the politics of the regional state formation, particularly in the northeast, largely by a linguistic reorganisation of the Indian polity.

While working on the refugee situation in eastern borders, West Bengal was an example of a relatively better context for refugee absorption and resettlement by the Government initiatives. Under the leadership of various leftist refugee organisations from 1948 onwards, the refugees started using *satyagraha* as an essential strategy, which had a connotation of Gandhian inclination. The continuous influx from the early 1950s hardened the state's attitude towards the refugee community, where their permanent presence was soon perceived as a threat to scarce livelihood resources, chiefly during the food scarcity from the mid-1950s. The discontent with the refugee policies propounded by both the Central and State Governments led to a culture of camp/colony politics. It also created an environment and rather a tradition of refugee political movements to embrace the leftist orientation as their political ideology. The refugee perception of their economic distress led them to take side with those parties for dealing with class politics, not to acquire power. It was evident from the 1960s as the leftist parties incorporated rehabilitation issues by granting ownership rights to those properties already held by the refugees, in their respective agendas. The refugee migration situation in Assam was different from that in West Bengal. The tradition of regular inter-district migration with East Bengal was encouraged from the 1900s to balance the adverse land and man ratio. It changed drastically after Partition, when the indigenous people of the Brahmaputra valley sharply reacted against the Bengali refugee settlements, fearing dominance of one linguistic community. It however consolidated the regionalist politics in greater Assam, as was evident in the Official Language Movement of 1960 and the Medium of Instruction Movement of 1972, which were based on the 'Assam for Assamese' ideology. The Bengalis of Barak valley had protested against it. They had formed their own political organisations to fight against the initiative of cultural hegemony by the so-called domiciles of the Brahmaputra valley. The story of Tripura differed yet further from these two aforementioned states, as the Bengali refugees completely transformed the demographic structure of the province and turned it into a Bengali Hindu refugee majority state. The educational backwardness, the absence of knowledge for plough cultivation and professional skills on the part of the original inhabitants of Tripura, the tribals, limited their space for social escalation compared to the Bengali refugees. With support from the state administration, the deluge of refugees gradually overturned Tripura's economy, culture and society. From the mid-1960s, the Central and State Governments sheltered another bunch of Chakma refugees migrating from Chittagong Hill Tracts that continued up to the Liberation War of 1971. The *Tripura Upajati Juva Samiti* (TUJS), with other tribal political parties, brought that issue into focus about discriminatory nature of the rehabilitation between the Bengali and tribal refugees. Therefore, by situating refugee experiences in these three states along the eastern borderlands, this book tries to make a comparative study on their settlement patterns, and also raises questions about issues related to identity and citizenship of a diverse group clustered as refugees in contemporary India.

This book attempts to interrogate the dominant historiography of the construction of the term 'refugee' in the post-colonial times. It asks questions like: What were the measures that the nation-state adopted to tackle the trauma of the refugees. What initiatives were taken to provide security and stability to the refugees? What were the issues and crises of their respective identities in different states? Addressing the problem of the multiple identities of refugees and their impact on the state system, this book has adopted a comparative perspective with three different states falling in a single region. It has attempted to extend the boundaries of historical studies by incorporating new dimensions through the use of varied, diverse primary and secondary materials that include vernacular and literary sources, mixed with oral narratives. It targets locating interesting stages of transformation of the refugee identities over decades where the migrants moved from communal outlooks to adopt multiple new identities according to the socio-political and cultural requirements of the then host societies. The book tries to contribute to the larger body of literature of socio-cultural–political history of Partition, along with the contemporary trends in refugee studies. This book has thus derived its inspiration from the post-positivist philosophy that assigns priority to the subjective understandings of human experiences, to have a focus on the total history of the past under this particular area of study. It has therefore followed both qualitative and interpretative methods with comparative parameters, to attain and accomplish the necessary understanding of modern trends in writing history. By incorporating narratives and other forms of oral sources/histories in a hermeneutical method (the art of interpretation of subjective experiences of individuals), to contextualise the refugee crises in the partitioned nations, it has tried to explain the behavioural pattern of the refugees, as well as the nature of their protests. This interpretative approach allows the understanding of the implications of expressions of fear, trauma, displacement and pain of up-rootedness during the Partition and afterwards. Thus, diverse types of sources and models of research have been used in this study to classify several patterns of displacements and categorise constraints of the Hindu Bengali refugees and displaced tribals in five chapters, defined and discussed thematically, culminating in an epilogue. To delineate a trajectory and provide comparative understanding along the main arguments, the experience of 'refugee-hood' of the migrants through field investigation has been used to frame the main hypothesis of this work.

This book is about the long impact of Partition on clusters of ethnic groups mainly on enormous uprooted Hindu Bengali populace who migrated to and from the Bengal borderland. The decision to leave a country overnight with a small bag packed in a great hurry, taking oneself away from home and homeland, assets and properties, and friends and relatives was an unfathomable loss for members of countless families. It was a journey from security to insecurities, to an area of strangers without a source of income and not knowing how and from where to start a new life, especially to make a new address (Bhabnani 2014: xi). While moving out from one country to find a new home, experiences of upper-caste and upper-class migrants (who flew safely with their household belongings and bank accounts transferred through official means) hardly matches with popular narratives built around experiences of urban poor and rural folk, even with middle-class families. Thus, the Partition migrants in the popular accounts often appear united in their experiences of misfortunes. Nevertheless, to answer the question 'what happened during the Partition?', narratives were never monochromic across caste, social classes and gendered experiences. The tension behind their 'differing' experiences in diverse regions and states, efforts to compare between them, challenges standardisation and simplification of the accounts of migration, which has been seldom explored. It is interesting to note that the Bengalis became the 'refugees'; chiefly, they became the victim of their Hindu identity, for which they were compelled to migrate from East Bengal. They thought this identity would save their lives and provide them with a respectable living in India. They expected that it would certainly be a major factor in getting a warm welcome, which would ensure them safety, security, relief or rehabilitation and a new address in the land meant apparently for the Hindus. But in reality, after settling down in West Bengal, Assam, Tripura or other rehabilitation areas like Andaman, Bihar, Orissa and Dandakaranya, this particular identity could not even save them from diverse layers of miseries. On the contrary, they faced continuous resistance everywhere on different grounds from the domiciles, locals or tribals. In West Bengal, they faced a strange type of 'otherness', which not only signified the regional differences, but also was tinged with a typical notion of class differences. The West Bengalis imposed a brand-new identity named *bangal* on them, to portray them as rustic, deprived and unsophisticated, who were again always *hagore* (eternally hungry or greedy), ready to grab any opportunity, accept all the privileges or every advantage from the society, polity and economy. In Assam, their linguistic identity became problematic and the key issue of conflict arose with the Assamese domiciles, both Hindus and Muslims, which continues more vehemently these days. In Tripura, the Bengali refugees were categorised as 'non-tribals'—potential enemies or a genuine persistent threat to the traditional ethnic society. The socio-political, cultural, religious and linguistic problems derived from their numerical dominance has given birth to the recent *Tipraland* movement. So when, with the help of their religious identity, the refugees dreamt of surviving in this country with a healthy living with wealth, honour and a kind of due or deserving respect, they painfully discovered more than one identity as refugees in the bordering states of eastern and northeastern India. So, they realised the necessity to give up their passivity and turn political to be able to wrest home and subsistence from an irresponsible state. This book is an attempt to expound their fight against all odds in each state. It aims to tell the tone of their many histories, tries to give voice to their diverse stories and narrates how they could finally embrace new identities in different regions and amidst diverse problems that derived from their identity issues, which was layered by nature and often reflected the complex and multiple dimension of the refugee entity. Thus, this book is about the struggle of the 'nowhere people', the refugees, to fight against the tide and earn their rightful place under the sun, which is continuing until this date.

Notes

1 Text of Pandit Jawaharlal Nehru's speech at the Meeting of the Constituent Assembly for the Assumption of Power at Midnight on 14–15 August 1947. *AICC Papers*, File No. G-5/ 1947–48, NMML.
2 The Nehru-Liaquat Ali Khan Pact, more popularly known as the Delhi Pact, was signed on 8 April 1950 in New Delhi. The basic idea was to create such conditions in both the countries where the minorities would not feel insecure and not think of migrating to the other country. In fact, it was hoped that those who had come would go back. This was to be taken as a measure of success of the pact. 'The Nehru-Liaquat Ali Khan Agreement' dated 8 April 1950. File No. P (PIV) 125 (62)/65, MEA-Pak-II, P IV, NAI.

ACKNOWLEDGEMENTS

The development of a doctoral dissertation into a book, I am afraid, is an ambitious task, involving a tiring and time-consuming process for a researcher. However, writing an acknowledgement at the end is the most relieving as well as enriching one, when the researcher-cum-author gets a chance to revisit and cherish the memories of a long journey through it. For me, the memories are full of turns and twists, but a process to explore some lifetime experiences, primarily through numerous field trips. I still can fondly remember that a 'very young, shy and confused myself', and her first arrival in Dhaka to check out the potential of her research ideas. Benazir Bhutto, the former Prime Minister of Pakistan was shot dead and everything got closed immediately, only after a few hours of my arrival in a new country, Bangladesh. I still can visualise that stranger who helped me to come back to life when I fell into a roadside open drain after a heavy shower in Guwahati, Assam. I can even feel my insecurities within me, as I fell sick after taking a sip of local liquor made by the tribals, as pressed upon me by their *Sardar* (village headman) and to pay respect to their traditional practice and custom. My desire was to hear their versions, arguments and stories in Sabroom, Tripura. Yet the scariest one was personal, when I heard that my father was admitted in a hospital in Kolkata, and I was in *Kalashkathi* village of Barishal, four long rivers away even from Dhaka. Yet, such incidents could not make me panicked, fearful, lethargic or indifferent conducting further ethnographical research. On the contrary, it encouraged me to come out from a safe, protected life, enquire into complex issues derived out of migration or mobility of people, variant nature of the marginality and helplessness of the ethnic, linguistic and religious communities and to understand the minority psyche within the downtrodden classes that reside in eastern/north-eastern India and Bangladesh. The journey has been a blessed odyssey to rediscover a different world and to explore an adventurous entity within me. These experiences guided me further and acted as a driving force in my work. My struggles with harsh realities just made my convictions stronger, reaffirming that there are very many trustworthy, helpful, nice and simple people around us who can extend their hands anytime to kindly help others. This journey has impacted me positively, made me compassionate towards the world and helped me become more humane with moral values. As such, I am truly grateful to those little known or unknown faces, as they inspired me to work harder and contributed to increasing my passion for research.

First, I wish to thank my supervisor, Dr Urvi Mukhopadhyay, for compelling me to write several versions of the doctoral thesis, pushing me to the edge every time to come out with perhaps better-quality drafts, in term of interpretation, analyses or well-argued narratives. My debts to her for trusting my work are indeed enormous from the day I approached her with a structured research proposal. I am equally indebted to Professor Sajal Nag for guiding me untiringly at every stage for many years, by drawing my attention to relevant sources, clarifying doubts and providing insight into my queries related to the north-eastern part of India. He has always been a friend, philosopher and guide in my life. Professor Peter Gatrell, the mentor of my post-doctoral project at the University of Manchester, UK, was immensely helpful by providing suggestions and encouraging me towards the revision and subsequent publication of this work. He graciously agreed to write the Foreword for this book. I fail to choose my words to properly express my gratitude to him. Dr Nandini Bhattacharyya helped me in many ways for almost a decade and contributed both emotionally and intellectually. Irrespective of her busy schedule, she read the final draft of the book, edited and corrected the manuscript thoroughly. I am extremely lucky to have them all in this sphere of my life.

Some fellowships, sponsoring agencies and academic affiliations from research organisations helped me in consulting diverse source materials in different libraries and archives, both in India and abroad, and in conducting fieldworks in diverse and difficult places to do justice to the basic requirement of the research. The post-doctoral project in which I am now working at the University of Manchester (2018–2021) has provided me with a wonderful opportunity to consult some new documents simultaneously related to this book. A major Project Grant (2017) funded by the Omeo Kumar Das Institute of Social Change and Development, Guwahati, Assam, helped me in filling up the gaps that were required to convert the thesis into a book, chiefly related to northeast India. The generous Charles Wallace India Trust offered me its fellowship to work in various libraries and archives in the UK (2014). The Indian Council of Historical Research (ICHR) was kind enough to grant me an Academic and Foreign Travel Grant for presenting a paper in the Department of English, University of Cardiff, Wales, UK (2013), but I could manage to work in the India Office Library and Records, London, and the Centre for South Asian Studies, Cambridge with some portions of the grant. The Mahanirban Calcutta Research Group offered a Research-Writing Fellowship for conducting fieldwork-based research in Tripura (2012). The UGC-Minor Research Project Grant for a project titled 'Communal Politics and Refugee Movement in West Bengal (1946–1967)' was useful to consult primary sources in archives and libraries of New Delhi (2009–2010). An Academic Affiliation with Scholarship provided by the Asiatic Society of Bangladesh, Dhaka, was like a blessing, for apart from allowing me to consult useful materials in Archives and libraries in Dhaka, it gave a timely exposure to a different culture and mentality of a community for a fresh researcher like me (2008).

For consulting materials in the UK, I am grateful to Professor Ian Talbot for guiding me to locate documents in archives and libraries. Professor Yasmin Khan, a member of the trustee board of the Charles Wallace India Trust, was more elaborate regarding how to utilise my stay in the UK and make my study trip more significant. Dr Spencer Austin Leonard helped me in explaining logistics (where to find which material) and how to use a well-equipped digital library. With his support, I could work extensively in the Regenstein Library, University of Chicago, probably the best one to consult huge numbers of Bengali books under one roof. In Bangladesh, my first academic interaction was with the legendary Professor Sirajul Islam, who introduced me to the academic circle of Dhaka to get proper insights and helped me to reach the sources in different libraries there. Professor Sharif Uddin Ahmed genuinely turned out to be my mentor and local guardian in Dhaka. Among many others, Tanvir Mokammel, a reputed documentary filmmaker of Bangladesh, made my work meaningful and living comfortable by providing all necessary support. He helped me in real understanding of the local culture, for bringing clarity in my thought, exposed me to the old Dhaka city (*purano Dacca*), accompanied me in fieldwork to ensure my safety and became a wonderful host in later trips to Bangladesh. In India, Professor Samir Kumar Das helped me in seeing refugee politics from larger perspectives. The discussion with him on how the state handled new social agents in eastern and northeastern India was like an eye-opener for me. Professor Bhupen Sarmah was kind enough to offer me academic stay in the OKDISCD, Guwahati. He helped me in arranging field trips in Assam. It was needful in the last phase of my research. Our evening discussions over cups of tea were enriching to get answers of some grey areas related to Assam. Dr Mallarika Sinha Roy's valuable ideas and critical comments helped me to write the final epilogue of this book.

Consulting primary, secondary and literary sources, censuses, official records, Government reports, newspaper reports, microfilms and other documents in many archives and libraries were truly helpful. In the UK, apart from the records kept in the India Office Library and Records, London, SOAS library and library at the Centre for South Asian Studies, Cambridge, the main library at the University of Manchester and my access to the library's e-resources was of great help. In New Delhi, I worked in National Archives of India, Nehru Memorial Museum and Library, Library of the Jawaharlal Nehru University and Delhi School of Economics, where the staff were prompt in providing materials and professional in providing answers to my queries. In West Bengal, the staff of the West Bengal State Archives, Police Archives, National Library-Kolkata, Centre for Studies in Social Sciences (CSSSC), Ramakrishna Mission Library-Golpark, Secretariat Library, Muzaffar Ahmed Pathagar, Bangiya Sahitya Parishad and Central library of Jadavpur University rendered utmost assistance possible. I wish to thank the Director of the State Archives of Assam and the librarian of the Legislative Assembly Library of Assam for their kind permission to arrange to make photocopies of some relevant portions, when I was running out of time. In Guwahati, the staff at the library of the ICHR Regional Centre, K. K. Handique Library-Gauhati University, District Library and Department of Historical and Antiquarian Studies were also generous. In Tripura, I consulted documents in Tripura State Archives, Secretariat Record Room, Tribal Research Institute, State Central Library, Tripura State Museum, Legislative Assembly library, the Central library of Tripura University, Office of the Land and Settlement Department, Census Office and MBB College library. Two personal collections of late Ramaprasad Dutta named *Ramaprasad Gabesanagar* and Jiten Pal, a leftist refugee leader and editor of the newspapers, *Janakalyan* and *Jagaran*, was of immense help. In Dhaka, my experience of working in the Asiatic Society Library, National Archives of Bangladesh, National Library, Sahitya Academy Library, the Rare Book Section of the Central Library, Dhaka University and Public Library was enriching. In Sylhet, the Muslim Sahitya Sansad library was extremely rich to collect documents on Assam.

As my area of research includes the whole of Bengal, both East and West, I tried to conduct interviews with different types of Bengali refugees, targeted categories like incoming Hindus and outgoing Muslims, to and from Bengal, other minorities and displaced tribals in both the nation-states and from diverse classes and caste groups. Most of my respondents reacted spontaneously to my unstructured interviews, unburdening their stories of panic and uncertainty, family histories of relocation, experience of refugee-hood, issues related to minority crisis, the nature of politics of respective states and their respective political stands. Their encounter with Partition is still very much alive in the world of the first, second and third generations of refugee families, which I felt so many times in villages of Barishal, Rajshahi, Bagura and Sylhet, and in interiors of West Bengal, Assam and Tripura. The refugees who migrated from East Bengal to states along the Bengal borderland, talked to me unhesitatingly and shared stories of their migration routes, the narrative of miseries in camps/colonies, change in their social status or political affiliations. There were too many layers of differences in the process of creation of their new identities, which at the end helped me in reaching a hypothesis and make my own argument. Getting thought-provoking questions from the esteemed audiences of numerous conference/seminar presentations helped me in filling up major gaps. Criticism and feedback of some published research articles and essays, 'op-ed articles' in *Anandabazar Patrika*, a reputed Bengali daily, encouraged to push me into greater depths of some conflicts within my area of research.

My friends and colleagues were always very supportive. They cooperated and contributed to my research pursuits. I am grateful to Dr Elisa T. Bertuzzo, Dr Kakali Mukherjee and Didhiti Das for being steadfast friends; we actually grew up together within our respective areas of interests. While Sugata Sarkar, Amitava Mukherjee and Sanhita Sen initially contributed to my learning of how to write the findings of fieldworks, Dr Nirmal Bandyopadhyay helped me in collecting important vernacular materials. Dr Pallavi Chakravarty Ghosal was supportive in finding materials in Delhi, and Manas/Nabanita Mahanta became companions in Guwahati. Pintu Roy worked hard for me in locating materials, arranged to send photocopies from Guwahati. Dr Samujjal Bhattacharyya handed over to me some institutional documents related to the All Assam Students' Union (AASU) that helped me in understanding their ideological stand and transformation in the nature of their movements. The experience of working in Tripura was informal and less stressful. K. B. Jamatia, the Director of Tribal Research Institute, opened a new world to me for understanding the tribal culture and its mentality, primarily what tribal members expect from the state, their lifestyles and thought processes. My dear friends Parthasarathi Chakrabarty, Chhanda Bhusan, Pranabrata Nandi and Prasenjit Debnath helped me in working in Tripura with much joy and vigour. During the course of my research in Bangladesh, Professor Ahmed A. Jamal, Professor Atful Hye Shibly, Muhammad Hossain Murad, Sanjida Hussain, Rezaul Karim Lotus and their families became my extended family, helped me in every possible way and added some more fun there. My dear friend Ratnadip Acharya was always there to help me throughout. My discussions with Dr Pallab Majumdar of Nottingham University, UK, helped me in understanding the nature of the insecurities of the refugees and states' initiative for their care and rehabilitation from a global perspective. Professor Surojit Mohan Gupta of the University of Hawaii was of huge help when I was editing and articulating my final manuscript. I am extremely grateful to all of them, along with many others.

I do not know how to thank my family for standing by my side as a solid support base and tolerating an unending journey of writing this book. My elder sister Arpita Bhaduri motivated me to approach life positively; she indeed is a pillar of strength. My niece Iipsha Bhaduri was always sure of the publication of her 'Chhomma r boi'. I could feel the warmth of the support of my brother-in-law Indranil Bhaduri when he handed over to me a rare book named *Inside Pakistan* on a cold winter evening from a very old bookstore at Shimla Mall. Rupa used to hate shabby book covers, but carried them happily to my room every time. My father was the very first one to suggest to me to view the crisis of the refugees and consequent social unrest from the top and place their crises on a wide canvas. I would not have started, pursued and completed the work without the encouragement and support of my mother, who means the world to me. As such, this work is dedicated to both of my parents.

Siladitya Sen of the *Anandabazar Patrika* has always been a dear friend, and without his enormous help and support, it would have been impossible to locate a proper cover photo for this book. Further, the concern and care from Saktidas Roy, the Chief Librarian of the ABP Pvt. Ltd., merits a special mention, for helping me in rigorous searching and by providing me with necessary permission to use the illustration as a cover photo. I am grateful to two anonymous proposal reviewers of this book and chiefly to the manuscript reviewer for reading the whole manuscript meticulously with a critical mind. The anonymous third reviewer has given me wonderful suggestions to make the book relevant and indeed a timely publication.

My experience of working with Anvitaa Bajaj from Routledge India has been an extremely enriching experience. I'm truly grateful to Kate Fornadel, not only for her commendable ability to scrutinise my manuscript and provide insightful suggestions, but also for her great help and support, especially when my laptop suddenly stopped working during the lockdown. The gratitude I owe to Dr Shashank S. Sinha, the Publishing Director of Routledge (South Asia), Taylor and Francis Group is limitless, as he bestowed his complete trust on my work from the beginning, even when he did not know me.

Last but not least, I acknowledge the contribution of my best friend (now my husband), Biplab, in this journey. He did so much, like taking all troubles about logistics, arranging my tickets and stays in different states, dropping and picking me up in very early mornings or late nights, accompanying me even on some field trips, being always just a phone call away. I do not know how to thank him enough.

ABBREVIATIONS

AASU	All Assam Students' Union
ADC	Autonomous District Council
AICC	All India Congress Committee
AISF	All India Student Federation
APCC	Assam Pradesh Congress Committee
APHLC	All Party Hill Leaders Conference
ASA	The Assam State Archives
BNA	Bangladesh National Archives
BPCC	Bengal Provincial Congress Committee
BPML	Bengal Provincial Muslim League
BPSF	Bengal Provincial Students Federation
CHT	Chittagong Hill Tracts
CPI	Communist Party of India
CPIM	Communist Party of India (Marxist)
DKSBS	Dakshin Kalikata Bastuhara Sangram Parishad
FB	Forward Block
IB	Intelligence Branch of Bengal Police
IDP	Internally Displaced Persons
IOR	India Office Library and Records
ITA	Indian Tea Association
KPP	Krishak Praja Party
MARS	Mahila Atmaraksha Samity
MNF	Mizo National Front
NAI	National Archives of India
NEIHA	Proceedings of North East India History Association (NEIHA)
NMML	Nehru Memorial Museum and Library
NRC	National Register of Citizens

NVBKP	Nikhil Vanga Bastuhara Karma Parishad
NWFP	North-West Frontier Province
PSP	Praja Socialist Party
PTCA	Plain Tribes Council of Assam
PWP	Peasants and Workers Party
RCPI	Revolutionary Communist Party of India
RCRC	Refugee Central Rehabilitation Council
RERC	Refugee Eviction Resistance Committee
RSP	Revolutionary Socialist Party
SB	Special Branch of Calcutta Police
SP	Socialist Party
SRC	States Reorganization Commission
SRP	Socialist Republican Party
TE	Tripura Era
TNV	Tripura National Volunteer
TSA	Tripura State Archives
TSA	Tripura Secretariat Archives
TSF	Twipra Student Federation
TUJS	Tripura Upajati Jubo Samity
UCRC	United Central Refugee Council
WBSA	West Bengal State Archives

INTRODUCTION

Bengal was a region at the eastern fringe of the subcontinent with essentially agrarian inhabitants and very slim record of migration until the 18th century. In order to bring stability to the underdeveloped eastern frontier, the Mughals conquered Bengal in the late 16th century but their 'alienation from the land was accompanied by feelings of superiority or condescension towards its people' (Eaton 2000: 250–63). The Mughals had introduced tax-free tenures of land to individuals to bring into cultivation and became conscious about its agrarian stability. They started treating the region like a political and socio-economic frontier. When such political cataclysm was taking place, another significant development had silently developed. Islam, as a faith, spread throughout the length and breadth of rural Bengal, converting at least half of its population into the new faith. It acquired a syncretic face by borrowing generously from local religious and cultural traditions (Ahmed 1996: 134–35). Richard Eaton argues that, as the frontiers of cultivation expanded between the 16th and 18th centuries in eastern Bengal away from the core of Brahmanic civilisation, Islam spread as the 'religion of the plough' by incorporating local people residing at the peripheries into its fold (Eaton 1993: 14). The colonial scholars have seen Islam as a militaristic religion. Eaton put emphasis on conversions of marginal lower-caste Hindus through the preaching of Sufi *pirs*. He has viewed the spread of Islam in Bengal by the means of word, not by sword; hence, the masses got attracted towards this idea of equality. The new faith had not changed the cultural fabric of the society. The common language spoken in a common habitat had bound people into a community, by imbibing huge Persian and Arabic elements into the language (Sarkar 1970: 473).

In the 17th and 18th centuries, the numbers of *ashrafs*, or elite Muslims, were negligible in the delta. The lower orders, or *ajlafs*, were dominating the population trend (Mamoon 2012: 19). The peasant cultivators from the eastern frontier got accommodated with the local people of the peripheral region. Islam in

Bengal could not identify itself with the concept of 'political Islam'. The process of assimilation involved agriculture used to relate with other metaphors. Simultaneously, the Mughal representatives like the *Baro-Bhunias* were also not political elites. They could relate themselves with the mainstreams. The syncretic culture in Bengal 'expanded' across space, time and social classes in process of assimilating people from all strata of society (Eaton 2000: 273). H. H. Risley suggests that the Bengali Muslim converts were aborigine; their manners, customs, physical appearances and caste differentiations were hardly different (Risley 1981: 20). The variety of Hinduism practised in the eastern frontier was lax and variant. What polarised the community was the ideology of Brahmanism and the practice of casteism. It had facilitated the spread of Islam but stratified the remaining Hindus into many small communities of castes (Mukherjee 1972: 265–66). The 'Hindus' and 'Muslims' were different in their religious practices, in form of using certain terms in languages and diverse taste in art interests, yet an essence of 'composite culture' was always there.[1] Eaton remarked:

> Islam in rural Bengal absorbed so much local culture and became so profoundly identified with the delta's long-term process of agricultural expansion, the cultivating classes never regarded it as foreign, even though some Muslim and Hindu literati and foreign observers did.
>
> *(Eaton 2000: 274)*

The deltaic Bengal emerged as a fertile region with a huge network of rivers that supported the inhabitants in transportation and helped to maintain an inner-region network. The settled populations carried out wetland cultivation of rice and other food-crops in the riverine valley (Siddiqui 2007: 13). It solidified to create a regional identity 'enhanced degree of communal cooperation' (Eaton 1993: 5). In the traditional settings, a syncretistic cultural identity developed over centuries under various rulers and their customs. It fabricated a unique community relation in Bengal. It had ascendency over processes of Sanskritisation among the Hindus, involving social emulation of higher castes by the lower. The Bengali Muslims were 'chiefly converts from Hinduism' and they 'still observed many Hindu customs and institutions'.[2] Hence, the community relationship also followed patterns of changes; the way demographic and geographical mapping of this region was altering.

The colonial system prepared the ground for a communal division of the country through the prism of 'colonial modernity' (Mohanty 2001: 2). The colonial rulers patronised the Hindus from the time of the Permanent Settlement and showed sympathy towards the Muslims in the post-1857 period. The predicament of Muslim peasants under Hindu zamindars and the depiction of the image of the Muslim community in colonial literature was contradictory. Thus, colonialism played a vital role in creating certain casualties and boundaries within socio-political-religious structures and their structured morals.[3] It brought in a new idea of community-based power politics that ultimately broadened the rift, while Hindus and Muslims produced syncretic religious symbols and practised it through centuries of cohabitation. Driven by the social vices like intolerance, untouchability, non-intermingling of elite classes and insignificant factors like contrasting food habits prepared grounds for community division (Ghatak 1991: vi–vii). Interestingly, the portrayal of the two communities as 'binary opponents' by the colonial engineering encouraged riots and helped question the idea of Bengali identity.[4] They classified the internal politics as fatal bludgeon of political economy of riots derived from the 'communitarian ideology' (Bandyopadhyay 2004b: 270). The leaders of communal brigades desperately tried to deny heterogeneity of communities, upheld a notion of the past, attuned to their claim of creating community identity-based nation-states. Both Hindu and Muslim leaders encouraged the notion of identity-centric historical interpretation, regardless of their political affiliations at the time of dominant communal political culture (Mukhopadhyay 2008: 63). The growing social and cultural divide persuaded the notion of 'identity as culture' that, in the end, led to the political division in Bengal (Sinha 2007: 32–33).

This introductory chapter is significant as it tries to look into many facets. But broadly, it attempts to connect two major frameworks: the genesis of the community or communal divide, and the politics of migration in East Bengal. It enquires on the crystallisation of social cleavages and poses questions like why the culture of assimilation worked well in Bengal, when Muslims were discriminated and lived in a margin of society, despite being the numerical majority (Khan 1985: 836). It, however, questions, why the tradition of harmony in Bengal could not sustain after the emergence of nationalist politics and how people were receptive to communal ideas and how the mass mobilisation, creation of fear or trauma of becoming the 'other' led to some ghettoised habitation. The idea of different territories for diverse communities started developing gradually. It tries to explore the changing nature of riots and transformation of community psyche from pre-Partition to post-1947 days to premise the exodus of people from the 1940s to 1971. The type of relocation of refugees shifted categories from displacement to migration.[5] The emergence of major political parties like the Congress, Hindu Mahasabha and Muslim League, and their ideological backgrounds, became decisive in explaining the roles of communities. Their stands were based on individual facets, distinctiveness in political gains and creating unique attributes of communities with some particular layers.[6] This introductory chapter thus tries to analyse how the political and geographical division on communal lines changed the fate of millions of refugees and led to a transformation in the demographic patterns and history of South Asia.

Colonial perception of the communities

During the age of transformation, the most crucial factor that changed the socio-cultural equation was the transfer of political power/control from the Muslim zamindars of the Mughal system to the Hindu elites in the British era. The composition of the non-Muslim elites had changed after Bengal transferred from the hands of Nawabs to the Europeans. The transformation of Hindus from *babus* to *bhadraloks* started with their adoption of Western education. They got prominence in a structure based on an alliance of colonial trade and collection of taxes. The Permanent Settlement cemented the bonding more and this phase witnessed the rise of the Hindu elites. The groups who were in a position to pay handsome liquid cash were favoured by the colonial rulers. The impact of the Permanent Settlement was so decisive that it was not confined as an experiment with land-related issues; it also contributed to determining the socio-economic and demographic changes (Hunter 1872: 175). The Settlement touched the political establishments too. The administration, judiciary and police were integral parts of the Settlement, as designed by Cornwallis. The nature of the village economy altered with changes in zamindaris and intermediary classes became beneficiaries. It had given rise to small towns with establishment of courts and administrative buildings.[7] The Settlement had changed the cultural matrix of rural Bengal. Previously the land tenure system used to support the middle-class and landed gentry simultaneously. But the Raj was looking for collaborators who could be a right replacement in making of powerful socio-political elites (Ghatak 1991: vi–vii). So, the Hindu zamindars were granted the state patronage, as the British were suspicious of Muslims. The land resources were handed over to them by reducing the number of Muslim *jagirdars* and traditional Muslim gentry (*ashrafs*) class. This system contributed in turn to the emergence of a class of absentee Hindu landlords in rural areas and led to the creation of Hindu elites in Bengal.

The shift of agricultural wealth from the grip of Muslim agriculturists and transfer of power from the Muslim *jotedars* or rural intermediaries (who had influence over poorer Muslim cultivators) to the *naebs* (finance officers) of the exploitative Hindu absentee landlords changed the agrarian equations. The Muslim middle-class was eager in acquiring a social position in the growing hierarchy under the Settlement, by acquiring rights of superior *ryots* (peasants) (Shah 1996: 1–7). The overall impact of the *bandabasta* (Settlement) impacted ground level community relationships in Bengal. The resumption procedure affected both the Hindu and Muslim ruling classes, but not in the same way. The lands passed to the hands of affluent merchants and service classes. Abu Jafar Samsuddin, in his autobiography *Atmasmriti*, remembered how his grandfather lost his *taluk* (estate) because of the clauses of the sunset law under the Settlement (Samsuddin 1989: 3). Akhtaruzzaman Elias, in his novel *Khoabnama*, pointed out that the Settlement had dramatically altered the ownership of land. It helped the Hindu zamindars to take possession of cultivable lands and lower-class Muslims became either sharecroppers of wastelands or day labourers under a new hierarchical structure (Elias 1998: 134). An urban Hindu Bengali middle-class had emerged after the creation of employment opportunities by it. They were Western-educated, wished to be professionals and were eager to make good use of the colonial connections (Mitra 1990: 2441). Such re-arrangement of the economic and class order altered the power structure of the Bengali society.

The British administrators pointed out the impact of the Permanent Settlement, 'Here for the first time in Oriental history, was seen the spectacle of a foreign ruler . . . almost creating a new race of landlords' (Hunter and Garret 1925: 87). It was not an issue of class interest anymore; Muslim zamindars, *jotedars* and peasantry were rather united in the struggle against Hindu landlord classes that became reflected in the electoral politics of Bengal in later decades (Umor 1978: 8–11). Rajat Ray and Ratna Ray argued 'it was basically a conflict between zamindars and *jotedars* of East Bengal' and 'it constantly fed the Muslim separatist movement in the Province as a whole', which led to the division (Ray and Ray 1975: 97–101). The Settlement changed the zamindar-peasant relationship in adverse ways; a section of Bengali Muslim literati vehemently reacted against it. While Muhamed Ibrahim, in his book *Banglar Krishak*, pleaded for the necessity of protecting the interest of peasantry, Khondkar Mohomed Badiuzzaman, in *Banger Zamindar*, directly criticised zamindars with the allegation of misusing their power and exploiting the peasantry (Ibrahim 1923: 3–16).[8] Qazi Nazrul Islam was vocal in rousing peasant's consciousness and he ventilated due grievances and demands of the peasantry through the mouthpiece *Langal*.[9]

Theoretically, the British united India under one government, though it left them into two separate social agencies, groups and identities. After the British Government had taken over the Company rule, it had to redefine its legitimisation in India. The British became critical about the Muslim rule and tried to portray the post-1830s phase as a 'dark age'. The supremacy of the pre-colonial Muslim elites had started declining, and they became suspects in the eyes of the colonial state, especially after 1858 (Khan 1985: 836). A discriminatory attitude had developed in their administrative policies to proclaim special community status, and it led to the particular need for a reserve share of power. They perceived India as 'a society of different religious communities', which emerged as an instrument for the formulation of separatist politics (Robinson 1993: xxv–1). Sekhar Bandyopadhyay commented, some sub-categories as 'relational community' and 'ideological community' started falling into sections like 'communitarian ideology' in Bengal (Bandyopadhyay 2004b: 270). Almost in every write-up on Indian history from the 19th century, the Raj had perceived India as a bounded entity inhabited by two religiously defined communities, rather than as a unified nation (Metcalf 1995: 953).

> British historians imagined Hindus as the original inhabitants and Muslims rather as they . . . imagined themselves: as foreign rulers, as imperial rulers, who arrived as successful conquerors. Muslims served as a foil against which the British defined themselves: by saying that Muslims were oppressive, incompetent, lascivious, and given to self-indulgence: the colonial British could define precisely what they imagined themselves to be, namely, enlightened, competent, disciplined and judicious.
>
> *(Hunter 1872: 175)*

Concern over the 'backwardness' of the Muslims was framed in terms of the relative 'advancement' of the Hindus.

W. W. Hunter provides a useful example of the construction of social categories between the Hindus and Muslims in *The Indian Mussalmans* (1872). To define religious amalgamation, he argued, 'all Muslims in British India could fit into a single noun phrase' and he made a single set of social identities by mentioning, Muslims were a 'monolithic national community' (Hunter 1872: 170–72). The deconstructive analysis of his book is visible in its subtitle: *Are They Bound in Conscience against the Queen*? The book denotes 'the celebration of syncretism actually served as a strategy of establishing domination over those who otherwise might owe their preliminary allegiance to a monolithic national community'.[10] He argued that Muslims had been slow in taking advantage of Western education and as a result, had fallen behind in the competition for jobs and economic advancement, discriminated against by the British (Robinson 2000: 211). After the publication of Hunter's report, education became the battleground for competing claims on Muslim identity. The effects of their initiative to send lower-class Bengali Muslims to English schools became apparent between the censuses of 1871 and 1901 (Anisuzzaman 1969: 26–30). And, he mentioned reasons behind Muslim separatism 'Almost everywhere it was found that the Hindu population seized with avidity on the opportunities afforded by State education or bettering themselves in life; while the Mohammedan community, excepting in certain localities, failed as a whole to do so' (Metcalf 1995: 953). Hunter's study concerns 'the rebel camp on our frontier', and it was his inquiry into 'grievances of the Muhammadans' (Metcalf 1995: 953). He blamed the British attitude of 'neglect of their education' and pointed out how it was important 'to insure that educated Muslims did not feel an obligation to oppose British rule, and to counter those advocating rebellion by establishing Muslim schools throughout Bengal' (Gossman 1999: 24–25). The British administration helped the development of educated middle-classes among the Muslims along with the Hindus, but it could not satisfy their demands and ambitions. The government was convinced to act on Hunter's recommendations to foster a Muslim leadership capable of counterbalancing what it saw as the 'forces of treason' within the Muslim population. They carried on separate policies for both the communities and allowed conflicts between them to maintain their own identity.

Bengal's varied exposure in the colonial period led to certain vulnerabilities in the socio-cultural scenario, too. Interestingly, the Raj first sketched out the region, outlined communities into economic groups and characterised agencies of social leadership. The first 'modern' aspect introduced by the British Raj was a fundamental innovation, the technique of measurements, which they gifted to Indian society. Dipesh Chakrabarty remarked, from surveys of lands and crop output to prospects of minerals and from measuring Indian bodies and brains or to understand the length and breadth of the country, its culture and society, general features and nature of communities, the British not only mapped everything, but classified and quantified it in detail (Chakrabarty 1995: 3375). The major premise of colonial cognition of Indian society was the theme of 'differentiation' that was traced, mapped and itemised through various official ethnographic studies, finally shaped as decennial Indian censuses in 1872.[11] The census in colonial India had a different purpose altogether. The desire of the colonial government to learn all came out of the idea that it could help them be aware of the people and land under its control. It was the key reason behind census exercises. A few years before the first census of colonial India in 1872, Hunter started the work on gazetteers. Both the Imperial Gazetteers of India and census reports covered large numbers of subjects, but neither public opinion nor any representative institutions existed to limit the subjects investigated, either in gazetteers or in census reports. As a result, the census had played different roles in the social and political life of the people in home and colonies. The census was a secular institution in the collection and presentation of data in Great Britain. After the introduction of the colonial census in India, the question on religion, caste and race became an essential category (Bhagat 2001: 4352).

The census report published in 1872 first revealed that 48 per cent of the total populations in Bengal were Muslims who 'lived in the low-lying marshy lands of eastern, northern and central parts of the Province' (Ahmed 1996: 1–2, 113). There were ethical elements of the lowland population of Bengal (Hunter 1872: 88). They ignored internal divisions like Shia and Sunnis within their fold. In the first all India Census of 1881, the enumerators found the Muslims numbered only 19.7 per cent of the population (Hasan 1998: 19). But it had also stated, 90 per cent of the Muslims belonged to 'agricultural or lowly service group[s]' (Mondal 1994: 147–48). Although Muslims were numerically in a stronger position in Bengal, the power and status in the Bengali society rested with the Hindus. The census of 1909 showed that Muslims formed a large part of the agricultural population of Bengal; most of them were tenants rather than landlords.[12] 'The general feeling among the people was strongly adverse to the Census', as pointed out by Hunter, censuses of 1872–1901 were not methodically perfect (Choudhury 1994: vi). 'Communities divided into religious lines and their precise characteristic feature' was the first and foremost point mentioned by the British historians. It was an observation to formulate surveillance about colonial India in official accounts and written documents (Hunter 1872: 88). A strange but strong sense of community consciousness was inculcated and formation of identity politics developed under the realm of colonial policies (Umor 1470: 13–15). Unlike its British predecessors, the Indian colonial census made religion a fundamental ethnographic category for classifying demographic and developmental data.

In the British censuses, the religious identity was optional. Kenneth W. Jones argued that the idea of census was purely a British import in India, and came only in the 19th century, though they initiated it in their country from 1801. Before the British officials published the full Indian census, the East India Company started designing regional censuses from 18th century onwards when amateur historians portrayed India as a society weakened by its internal divisions into various religions and castes (Jones 1981: 73–74). The British began to include religion and castes while counting the Hindus, Muslims, Sikhs and untouchables in India. It had grave political implications. They tried to justify it with the idea of representation in the Legislative bodies. The leading communities were exposed to the concepts of communalism and racism. Finally, it appeared that there was 'a community within a community' under particular religious groups (treatment of 'untouchables' as diverse 'community' separate from the 'Hindus') even if diversifications were in terms of professional groups, classes or occupational castes for a group of people. Apart from these social classifications in the census, the British administrators formed new categories by creating figures in the electoral representation (Datta 1993: 1305). As a result of the census taxonomy, a unique concept of 'religion as a community' came out and it no longer meant just 'a set of ideas', it became a 'formal official definition' of communities (Bandyopadhyay 2004b: 263–64). The census included new categories. It asked questions related to community identities and made side-by-side comparisons. The Bengali Muslims began to identify themselves more with these categories (Anisuzzaman 1969: 24–35). It seems, the projection of cleavages within colonial society was essential for sustaining colonial rule, at the cost of strained communal relationship or politics in India' (Bhagat 2001: 4352).

Muslims: a community into politics

From the late 19th century, Muslims were by no means a homogenous community. The community consisted of considerable regional variations, yet the population distribution and social categorisation became issues behind the majority and minority debates. In the United Provinces (UP), the Muslims constituted a minority, being slightly more than 13 per cent of the population (Seal 1968: 26). In Punjab, they were a majority, accounting for slightly more than 51 per cent of the population. Francis Robinson has shown that Muslims of North India constituted a privileged minority (because of the Mughal legacy). They divided into many lines in the colonial period, tried to adjust in the social realities of rule and became 'more a multiplicity of interests than a community' (Robinson 1993: 23, 46). The UP Muslims had organised themselves as 'Muslims for politics' to preserve a position by the elites. They pressed forward the Muslim identity in politics at different times (Robinson 1993: xxv–4). There were differences between the condition of Muslims in UP and Bengal. Scholars of Muslim separatism in India focused on the mobilisation of the Muslims in UP. While 28 per cent of UP Muslims lived in towns, only 4 per cent of Bengali Muslims did. They were not worse off than their Hindu counterparts (Ahmed 1996: 140). Lack of Muslim participation in higher education was a direct consequence of 'preponderance of the poorer classes in the Muslim population', particularly tenant cultivators and landless labourers (Sen 1976: 11; Gossman 1999: 25). The formation of the Central National Muhammadan Association and other elite groups gave the urban Muslims a voice, but it largely was made up by the non-Bengali Muslims from UP or elsewhere in North India who resided in Calcutta, yet they had little contact with Muslims in rural East Bengal (Robinson 1993: xxiii). There was little link between the Bengali Muslim masses and the kind of leadership represented by few organisations 'whose immediate object was to obtain for themselves a larger share in Government jobs and higher education' (Ahmed 1996: 36; Gossman 1999: 27).

A section of the Muslims 'began to see themselves through the colonial lens of being unified, cohesive and segregated from the Hindus' from the last half of the 19th century.[13] They tried homogenising myths to construct Muslim community identity, enlarged into Muslim nationhood (Bandyopadhyay 2004b: 263). Christopher Bayly draws attention to:

> incidences of communal conflict in India during the period 1700 to 1860' and he denied the claim that the nature and frequency of communal conflicts 'decisively increased after 1860 . . . as a result of colonial policy, religious revivalism or the extension of new types of representative Government.
> *(Bayly 1985: 201–2)*

Francis Robinson stated that Bayly helped in realising that 'there were distinct social formations, expressing themselves in different cultural idioms and operating in sharply differentiated contexts' and 'the one was to become increasingly the sustainer of an Islamic high culture, the other of a Hindu high culture' (Robinson 2000: 214). Many of the early conflicts like 'land wars' were no more or less 'communal', and it also had 'a very close resemblance to the riots of the later colonial period' (Pandey 1990: 15). The Raj rendered enough effort to increase coherence within the Muslim politics of division to trigger resentment among the progressive Hindu community (Shah 1996: 27). The Hindu-Muslim conflict was explained in the lack of cohesion between two religious groups, an issue liable to increase by outside pressure.[14] The political mobilisation of the Bengali Muslims was lagging behind that of the Hindus. They were treating them as a 'coherent force', which posed further challenge to Muslims for acquiring definite socio-political-religious community identity in particular provinces. A sense of mobility at the ground level was emerging. It helped various agencies like urban elite Muslim *Mullahs, Bahas* (religious meetings) to carry on urban message to the countryside. The *Anjumans* (a Persian word meaning association) were active as a social force in every district and subdivisional town in East Bengal. Apart from imparting religious and moral education to the Muslims, they made representations to the government lobbying for more jobs and communal representation (Rashid 1987: 1). Thus, the Islamic reformist movement and political mobilisation to strengthen the argument for separate Muslim interests under the influence of the rich gentry leadership led to rising contradictions between the two in religious terms. It also led to the rejection of the earlier syncretism by lower orders or *ajlafs*. Gyanendra Pandey argued, 'In Bengal with its predominantly Hindu elite, there was not quite the same need to articulate nationalism in terms of Hindu plus Muslim until a somewhat later date' (Pandey 1990: ix–x).

The polarisation of the Muslims could easily be plausible from the tone of Sir Syed Ahmed Khan in the Madras session of the Indian National Congress, 1887. He mentioned, 'It is imagined by some persons that all, or almost all, the Mussalmans of India, are against the Congress movement. That is not true. Indeed, by far the largest part do not know what the Congress movement is' (Zaidi 1987:

52). The whole issue became so sensitive that the Muslims perceived 'it is against their religion to join the Congress, as by joining the Congress, they will be joining the Hindus who are not Mussalmans', and:

> it is against their religion to join the Congress, as by joining the Congress, they will be joining a movement opposed to Government, a thing which is opposed to their religion, which directs obedience and loyalty to Government, albeit Government may not be treating them properly.
>
> *(Zaidi 1987: 56)*

The Muslim press described the phrase 'communalism' as the state of being attached to one's own community. In an editorial of *The Mussalman*, the argument was placed as the 'Indians belonging to any particular religious community might be nationalists in the true sense of the term and at the same time might maintain their communal individuality'.[15] The attitude towards the Congress was reflected in the fortnightly report of *Asr-e-Jadid*, as 'there were 'senseless', 'regrettable' and 'mischievous' attempts to create a split among the Bengal Muslims by those who had made themselves tools in the hands of the leaders of the Congress—an organisation whose goal was to disrupt the national strength of the Muslims by setting them against one another'.[16]

At the beginning of the 20th century, two incidents helped the Bengali Muslims to institutionalise their identities (*Banglapedia* 2003: 43–44). The establishment of new capital for a new province in 1905 and the foundation of the Muslim League (1906) as a political party for the Muslims encouraged them to place demands on the colonial government, though the voice of the Bengali Muslims could not be heard much in it. Francis Robinson noticed, 'In 1906, a large number of Muslims from UP flocked to Dacca for the establishment of the All India Muslim League' (Robinson 1993: 4). Still, the Partition scheme officially encouraged creating foothold of the Muslims in the polity, society and economy of Bengal and Assam.[17] The change in attitude and modification of policies of the colonial rulers further enhanced the political aspiration of the Muslims for creating a separate identity. They became keener to participate in the administration and aspired to attain right for modern education (Sarkar 2011: 8–9). Sir Stuart Mitford Fraser, Risley and George Nathaniel Curzon tried to convey that it was their responsibility to formulate a scheme for larger readjustment in East Bengal.[18] Bengal's boundary revival showcased political considerations on communal basis were not their primary focus. Curzon made an official tour in East Bengal for understanding public opinion and in his speech at Dacca on 18 February 1904, he targeted the community sentiment of the Muslims directly (Sen 1976: 33). The creation of a Muslim-majority province of 'Eastern Bengal and Assam' made an emotional appeal in society (Sinha 2007: 32–33). The agitation against the Bengal division of 1905 meant the 'Swadeshi' movement for the Hindus, the Muslims started terming it as their effort towards the 'anti-Partition' movement.[19]

The growing ethos, lack of secular approaches to political issues and absence of cohesive 'sense of national crises' sharpened the feelings of 'otherness' within them (Sarkar 2011: 15–16). It also led them to a sense of alienation from nationalist movements. H. H. Risley wrote to Sir Arthur Godley that 'Mohammedans sympathies with Hindus is false' and so, 'Partition should be maintained as most advantageous to Mohammedans'.[20] Sir Bampfylde Fuller, the first Lieutenant Governor of East Bengal and Assam, in his *Studies in Indian Life and Sentiment* (1910) described Indian Muslims as natural allies of the British Raj. His iteration is noteworthy 'by their religion and political ideas . . . they are less disposed than the Hindus to dissent from assumptions which lie at the root of imperial authority' (Nanda 2014: 27). Such complexities in the inter-communal crises worsened community relations so much that the two major organisations, the Mohammedan Literary Society and Central National Mohammedan Association, forbade the Muslims to join the anti-Partition movement (Zakaria 1970: 100–1). They celebrated the anniversary of the new province on 16 October 1906 as 'a day to rejoice'. It resented the way boycott was imposed upon them by Hindu landlords (Prasad 2001: 98–99). They protested against acceptance of Fuller's resignation by the pressure groups headed by the Hindus, as it was 'a great injustice' for the Muslim community (Sen 1976: 35–36). Nawab Salimullah wrote to the Commissioner of Eastern Bengal and Assam that 'The Mohammedans have up to now relying on the good faith of the Government . . . but they have no intention of re-considering the question of the partition'.[21] The old agrarian tensions between Hindu landlords and Muslim tenants had transformed into new power equations. The focus revolved around the aspiration for better social positions and participation in political decisionmaking. It also stimulated competitions between Hindu and Muslim elite groups by negotiation with the British administrators. The Partition plan and its complex reaction broadened the gulf wider between the two communities by involving political identity in the individual belief system. It intensified the religious and class-consciousness in every possible way.

Hindus and Muslims as 'blocks': politics of representation

The Bengal renaissance, the conviction of the triumph of '*nava yuga*' (new age) and ideas of alternative modernity had contributed in defining the cultural process of 19th century Bengal (Ray 2001: 29). By shaping up the concept of Hindu identities and patterns of political mobilisation, it led to other identity formation and political articulations (Bandyapadhyay 2001: 27–28). By enforcing reformations among the Bengalis, it forged strong Hindu symbols. Anisuzzaman tried to locate the root causes of trouble behind the creation and adoption of the cultural heritage. Mentioning the differences in the mentality to look at British rule or taking favours, he argued, the renaissance was one of the key reasons in building up differentiation in their belief system, ideological world and in case of treatment afterwards (Anisuzzaman 2001: 18–19). The British constructed a polarised community consciousness during 1905 days, and the consequent Swadeshi Movement isolated the Muslims more. Apart from initiating reform movements, the agitations made explicit of potential for using religious symbols to mobilise the masses (Chaudhury 1946: 5). Economic divisions were sharp in the eastern province, where the Hindu minority made up the entire landlord class. For the political mobilisation of the Muslims, the elite groups formed an untenable alliance with religious leaders to frame appeals. The impoverishment of the Bengali Muslim peasants became a symbol of their 'backwardness'. It helped persuade the colonial authorities to promote Muslim interest. Both the educated *ashraf* and *maulvis* framed protests of the anti-Partition activities as 'anti-peasant and anti-Muslim' (Gossman 1999: 20–21). The act of redrawing the boundary provided occasions for a number of actors like the political elites, religious reformers and British administrators. It re-formulated the Bengali Muslim political identity, and it was used as a catalyst by political organisers to mobilise the majority communities on both sides of the new order around religious and economic symbols.

The Bengali Muslim leaders found the Partition of Bengal to be a 'watershed', which stimulated fears of the Muslim middle-class. The creation of a Muslim-majority province was like opening new vistas of education, employment or prosperity for the Muslim middle-class (Nanda 2014: 15). The Partition's repeal in 1911 provided equal opportunities for the Muslims to exploit betrayal of the colonial administration (Gossman 1999: 19). The *Islam Pracharak* described Swadeshi movement as 'the movement of the Hindus', and it complained 'Bengali Hindu nationalists have begun to oppress the poor and innocent Muslims for not practicing Swadeshi'.[22] Communal wrangling of the press was also symbolic. It stimulated the sentiment by inscribing Hindu religious symbols like image of the Hindu Goddess in crests, and by the question of whether to accept '*bande mataram*' as a national song (Shah 1996: 33). Muzaffar Ahmed has given different picture, which challenged the popular perception of Muslims that they had accepted 1905 in a positive way, as benefitting in terms of jobs and respectable social positions. He argued that the essence of mixed culture yet prevailed. He remembered how the Bengalis from both the Bengals treated it as a blow to their culture. He criticised the pro-Hindu Congress leaders and blamed that they never thought how Muslims would react to the use of Hindu symbols in time of the Swadeshi movement (Ahmed 2003: 26–29). The middle-class Hindus were concerned whether the division led to the withdrawal of the clauses of the Permanent Settlement. The socialist critics opined that they did not initiate leadership to struggle against the Bengal Partition. The political ideology and organisational expertise of Congress started blooming in Bengal from the time of Swadeshi. In their perceived idea of Indian nationalism, the Hindu elements were predominating (De 1974: 243–45). When moderate Congress leaders floated the idea of Swadeshi, their followers found it fascinating and enormously favoured it, too.[23]

The nationalist political leadership put forward the idea of 'composite patriotism' in Bengal. The concept of mass nationalism had been altered by the alliance of Hindu-Congress-elite leadership (Sinha 2007: 22–24). The community conflicts arose in Bengal as the zamindars and upper classes happened to be Hindus, and the economically suppressed populaces were Muslims.[24] The peasant question was never predominating. Bankim Chandra Chatterjee was one of the leading spokesmen of neo-Hinduism. The tone of his novel *Anandamath* could be a prism to understand the Hindu psyche. The central part of the novel is about a band of *sanyasis* called the *santanas*, united to rescue their motherland from the Muslim rulers for setting up a Hindu state and bringing back prosperity to the land. *Rajshingha*, *Sitaram* and *Durgeshnandini* portrayed victories won against Muslim forces by the superior Hindus.[25] Rabindranath Tagore wrote in *Kalantar* in 1333 *Bongabda* (Bengali year) that, 'Hindu and Muslim communities in the past were not conscious of their differences' (Hasan and Asaduddin 2000: 7). He acknowledged that the Hindu literature distorted Muslim religious teachings and history. He blamed the British writers, as they had a tremendous influence on the Hindu historians and novelists.[26] He preferred using Muslim characters and egalitarian principles of Islam to highlight, by means of contrast, the constraints and injustices inherent in the Hindu class system. Sarat Chandra Chatterjee weaves the essence of inter-community life with a highlight on the peasant life in Bengal (Hasan and Asaduddin 2000: 8–9). A feeling of confusion and change in the previous equation of community relationship started after the merger period of the Partition of 1905–1911, in which the nature of the power relationship in the socio-cultural and political arena of Bengal had gone through a sea change.

After phases of complexities to be dominant in power and politics, Bengali Hindus adopted a new brand of agitational politics. The Muslim elite groups were in stages of 'administrative politics' by traditional means.[27] The educated Bengali Muslims became aware of the danger of political passivity in India. They were challenged politically and frightened by the power of Hindu 'agitational politics' in the form of 'protests' (Chattopadhyay 1993: 17). The idea to uplift the living pattern of mass Muslims had been already set by Sir Syed Ahmed Khan. The Muslim middle-classes paved the way to participate in public life, which impacted the politics of Bengal (Ahmed 1974: 288–89). Nawab Salimullah thought of a solution to place firm demands of separate representations through the platform of All India Muslim League. The ideological background was prepared by then, but there were groups, sub-groups, hierarchies and disagreement in opinions within the Muslims, as a community and in their political strategies (Mokammel 1397: 6–7). In 1906, M. A. Jinnah spoke about equal stand in common platforms; yet there was confusion at every level. Nawab Khaja Atikulla conveyed:

> it is not correct that the Muslims of Eastern Bengal, as a body, are in favour of the Partition of Bengal. It is true that Salimullah has given his support to the Partition but that does not prove that the Khaja family is with him in this respect.
>
> (Zaidi 1987: 396–97)

Between 1907 and 1909, the provincial Muslim Leagues were formed and reforms of 1909 gave solidarity towards the demand for constitutional representation.

Bengali Muslims enjoyed considerable advantages in the fields of education and employment during the short span of six years when the Partition had been in force.[28] The spirit of 'Muslim nationalism' was established on a solid rationale. As per the British version, the annulment had come out of the desire to end the continuing political unrest in Bengal (Hardinge 1948: 36–37). The shock of its withdrawal was so profound for the Muslims, a provincial Branch League was established as a 'single body' for the whole of Bengal.[29]

The politics of separation had given birth to new-fangled connotations like 'majority' and 'minority', and it became popular in the representational form of politics. The Morley-Minto reforms (1909) conceded principles of separate electorates for Muslims at all levels.[30] The All-India Muslim League insisted, 'separate electorates should assign status of a constitutional minority, conceded by the British' (Nanda 2014: 17–19). The reforms were to seriously affect the course of Indian politics. The objective of Lord Minto was to win over the Muslim community and prevent it from going the Congress way. The separate electorates had effectively advanced class-consciousness in the name of a religious community (Jalal 2000: 160). By the end of the 19th century, Muslims began to express their existence firmly in societies and politics. The principles of Muslim separateness were implemented in every constitutional change from 1909 (Robinson 1993: 1). The introduction of electorates made the provinces 'the centre of political actions' (Bandyapadhyay 1417: 31). Very few initiatives were taken on all-India level for the signing of a joint scheme of reforms like the Lucknow Pact of 1916 or proposed council reforms of 1917. The year 1919 marked a turning point in development of Hindu nationalism, as the Montague-Chelmsford Reforms further provoked:

> By widening the functions of local Government bodies in municipalities and the rural areas, which were to be chosen by the same voters who elected the new provincial councils, they linked the politics of localities more closely to the politics of the province.[31]

Some favours were shown to the Muslims in order to redress the balance. They perceived British policies with certain solidarity. This reform extended franchise to the affluent sections of the rural areas. It was meant to be a beginning of major threats to the hegemony of the dominant urban Hindus (Chatterji 1995: 173–79).

The reforms of 1909 and 1919 sectionalised political activity by barring Hindus from electing Muslims, and vice versa, in legislatures (Khan 1986: 35). The clamour for nationalism and use of religion to make a definite community identity became vital in the new format of 'representational' politics. Congress was compelled to accept the Muslim demand for separate electorates immediately (Bandyapadhyay 2009: 71). The Hindu *bhadraloks*, who were dominant in Congress, realised the trend of holding representation in Bengal Legislative Assembly; their method of acquiring power through a percentage of the population was fatal in Bengal. They could feel that the majority-minority bottom-line was becoming thin, and it was in favour of the Muslims. The nature of negotiation or conciliation towards other parties was different (Bhagavan 2008: 39–40). Yet, the definition of the term 'representative and responsible Government' changed time and again from the perspective of the Raj. The parameter of soliciting 'separate electorates' was challenged in different reform proposals over the decades.[32] Congress always argued that the Muslims were in a distinct category. They even admitted that Congress should make efforts to incorporate them into their organisation. Congress was compelled to take this kind of a stand, as the British often used to reject its claim to speak on behalf of the whole country, repeatedly describing it as 'representative of only a microscopic minority' on the ground, as there was lack of Muslim participation in Congress (Nehru 2004: 422). A visible form of radicalisation and creation of groups within the party was Congress's another concern (Chatterji 1995: 140–42). The argument of the Muslim leaders towards the separate electorates was that it might reduce chances of communal conflicts. Under this system, rival communities would not have to fight against one another for the same seats. Thus, a small but vocal minority Muslim group developed in the regional level with the active participation of the Bengali Muslims (Shah 1996: 20). Cultural differences between the Bengalis and non-Bengali Muslims functioned as basis of their identity. Abul Mansur Ahmed had aptly commented:

> Hindus and Muslims in India are not one nation; their culture is not the same also . . . but are the Muslims or the Hindus a nation? . . . Religion and culture are not the same. Religion can cross the geographical boundaries, but culture cannot do so. Culture rather grows in a geographical boundary . . . that is how the inhabitants of East Pakistan are different from the inhabitants of the rest of the Indian Nation.
>
> *(Ahmed 1944: 439)*

Transforming social cleavage into political chasm

Bengal in the 1920s turned out to be the most crucial decade to witness the changing matrix between social relationships of Hindus and Muslims. The Muslim middle-classes were not educated enough to rationalise things easily and understand the undertones of politics. The backward Muslim peasants were not literate and united. As Abu Jafar Samsuddin recalled in *Atmasmriti*, there were hardly any literate members in Muslim families. The first matriculation pass out from the Muslim communities in his village happened in 1921. The upper classes were trying to articulate themselves on political lines, interrogated chiefly by the British. The lowest level was free from ill feeling between communities and the tradition of cultural exchange prevailed, exactly the way it used to prevail before. (Samsuddin 1989: 11). But the social environment became sensitive from the 1920s; incidents of conflicts were often treated, claimed or reported as communal conflicts.[33] Gour Kishore Ghosh depicted pictures of growing contradictions right from the early 20th century within the communities in *Jal Pare Pata Nore*, the first novel of his epic trilogy. He portrayed how Hindu chauvinism compelled the Muslims to aspire for better social positions, which ended up in encounters. The design of cultural differences to glorify distinctiveness were created more by the Hindus, chiefly when some Muslims acquired higher positions in jobs or earned respect by competing with others (Ghosh 1997a: 12). In *Prem Nei*, the central character, Fatik, did not get a permanent appointment to the post of headmaster in a local school, as he was a Muslim and the school was founded by a Hindu zamindar. The discriminations continued even in his next job as his students assaulted him on the instructions of a Hindu Brahmin absentee teacher, as he dared to teach Sanskrit and Bengali classes. The author argued that the change in community relationship developed acute distrusts between two numerically strong communities of Bengal (Ghosh 1997b: 277).

Mushirul Hasan remarked that the definition of 'Muslim identity' was integrally related with relevant issues like economic discontent, escalating violence, projection of the political area, new social groups with higher levels of consciousness and greater stakes in power structures, which led to 'community based strategies' (Hasan 1998: 23). Asim Roy pointed out, 'The entire process of identity formation' of the Bengali Muslims:

> on one hand underlines the seminal role of the elite, spurred into action by the changed historical circumstances of their position, their inner divergences and conflicts underlying their differential response, their manipulation of symbols of group identification for the optimal participation and mobilisation of the masses.[34]

The Muslim League expressed its stand by declaring that the community should eschew negotiation, as Muslims must hold on to 'those rights that have already been conceded to them'.[35] Some Muslim periodicals reacted against the assumption of cultural superiority by the Hindus and grievances that lay deep in the heart of the Muslims. Stressing on the need for Hindu-Muslim amity, the *Kohinoor*, a monthly magazine, expressed in a liberal tone that 'the Hindu authors were sowing the seeds of distrust and hatred. If the Hindus were not aware of its consequences, the cordial relationships between the two communities would never be possible' (Chakraborty 2002: 107). Sheikh Osman Ali, a reformer and political leader, stated:

> Hindus might be advanced and cultured, but not all of them were. Similarly, though many Muslims might be backward and illiterate, not all of them were. Therefore there is no reason to regard Muslims as contemptible inferiors; I hope every Hindu brother, instead of regarding us with contempt or dislike, will embrace us with genuine brotherly love.[36]

Some enlightened Muslim groups like the *Muslim Sahitya Samaj* (founded in Dacca in 1926) launched parallel movements against such communal positions. The *Buddhir Mukti Andolon* (movement for the emancipation of the intellect) tried to connect the idea of Muslim identity with the concept of 'Pan-Indian identity' through its mouthpiece *Siksha*. Kazi Abdul Wadud, one of its leading members, argued, a 'Bengali Muslim is a human being first by the right of his birth, then a Bengali by being made of the soil of Bengal, and then a Muslim, and a Bengali Muslim last' (Shah 1996: 21). *Bulbul* stressed, 'Hindu-Muslim antagonism in real life became so complex that grouping on the basis of class-consciousness could not be developed as a solution to communal problem'.[37] The counter-argument on the eclectic culture of the Hindu middle-classes was placed by Nirad C. Chaudhuri, 'in the good graces of the ruling order, they wanted positions in the administrative system, and they aimed at social prestige by imitating the ways of the dominant power', but their:

> instability was due to the motive of expediency on which it was founded. The Hindu middle-class wore Muslim clothes, learned Persian, and affected Muslim ways because all these suited their interest. The continuance of the Islamic elements in the culture of the Hindu middle-class accordingly depended on the continued existence of Muslim rule.
>
> *(Chaudhuri 1951: 472)*

For him, Bengali thinkers or reformers spent their whole life on the formula of a synthesis of Hindu and European cultures, while the Muslims stood there as 'external proletariat' (Chaudhuri 1951: 226–27).

The political changes in urban and rural Bengal altered socio-economic and cultural equations between communities. From the 1920s, the tradition of 'participation' politics transformed into 'institutionalised' politics, as peasants and other marginal groups 'entered' into politics. They were finally brought into fold of parties and elections or centrally organised 'agitational' movements.[38] In the new structure of politics, called the 'dyarchy', the legislatures were constituted on the basis of separate electorates based on population (Bandyopadhyay 2004b: 283). It brought further competition and rivalry, as the centre of politics shifted to Muslim-majority areas. Having tasted power, the Muslims commanded a domineering position in Bengal politics. An effort at constructing a common history of the communities started after mobilisation of constituencies and politics on symbols of separate religious identities. The enlightened leaders from both the communities tried to create possibilities of a shared future.[39] There were initiatives to arrange joint electorates offered by Abul Hashim, in accordance with the C. R. Das Formula under the 'Bengal Pact' of 1923 (Ghosh 1997b: 88–90). The clauses of the pact impacted the society so enormously that it was mentioned in every contemporary novel and autobiography. Their attempt was for accommodating differences to forge a greater unity. C. R. Das thought, 'a Bengali cultural identity would keep the different religious communities together' (Bhattacharya 2014: 7). He tried to raise the 'myth of Bengali cultural identity' and conveyed it to the political audience, 'The Bengali cannot forget that he is a Bengali first and last . . . he has a distinct character' (Azad 2012: 24). The pact incorporated a clause for recruitment of Hindus (eight) and Muslims (25) in the Calcutta Corporation and promised to implement these clauses in provincial Legislative councils.[40] He could feel that the communal division would make the Bengalis a minority in Bengal. In Sirajganj Sammelani, Das could win support of the Muslims and kept their trust afterwards. He returned that respect by treating both the communities alike, by providing employment and rendering social recognition.

The Muslim collaborators treated it like 'a new deal' and the Bengali Muslims viewed it as an attempt to undo erroneous clauses under the Lucknow Pact. The Bengal Pact proved to be a weapon of the diplomatic victory for Muslims of the minority provinces. He dreamt of the 'independent and sovereign Bengal' as remedy against communal forces.[41] But, the worsening situation of journalistic confrontations had taken shape with stories of past exploits. There were cases of working compromises like initiatives of *'desh-bondhu'* Chitta Ranjan Das. He attempted to mediate crises, but passed away in 1925. Muzaffar Ahmed described how the members of Congress and other allied parties acted vehemently to work against the Bengal Pact (Ahmed 2012: 199). After the death of Das, hardly any initiative had been taken to unite the Hindu-Muslim causes and political parties (Rana 2005: 15). The Swarajya Party and 'Das was the last chance of the old system'.[42] The identification of the communities was easy in Bengal because of the correlation between political, economic and religious identities. Congress was dominated by urban Hindus, while the concentration of Muslims was mostly among the rural poor. Geographical concerns and differences of residing in town or countryside accentuated the division. Even when the Muslim middle-class was comparatively decisive in numbers, there were fewer educated Muslims than there were educated Hindus (Shah 1996: 229–30). The Gandhian style of mass movements had popularised into political strategy of Congress (Gandhi 2012: 489). Gandhian trend meant for a type of freedom to take shape from an ethical and moral transformation of policies by social service, self-help and a village-based economy (Bandyapadhyay 2009: 71). He tried to incorporate communities beneath the larger ideology of Congress, and treated Khilafat as an opportunity to unite them, in which it was lagging behind.[43]

The 1930s: a decade of contradiction

As eventualities unfolded, diverse casualties and shifts in community relationships led to a change in the nature of politics and demands of political parties. It made the 1930s a decisive decade for Bengal. Some of the Hindu and Muslim accounts started writing 'staying together is difficult', yet at the local level, the tradition and practice of syncretism or a kind of mixed culture between the Hindu and Muslim families in both the wings of Bengal continued. Regardless of layers of differences at many levels between these two communities, the communitarian feeling was not strong enough to act as hindrance in the regular life of Bengal. The literatures, biographies, autobiographies and other literary sources portray an essence of composite culture even in colonial urban and rural Bengal. Bipin Chandra Pal, in his memoir *Sattor Bachhar*, remembered the Hindus used to offer *shinni* (a liquid sweet dish made of rice-milk) in *Dargahs* and Muslims promised to offer something in temples if wishes got fulfilled (Swadeshi 2015: 191–92). Abu Jafar Samsuddin, in *Atmasmriti*, has given two interesting accounts in the early 1920s. He wrote that both Hindu and Muslim aristocratic or educated families were comparatively liberal. The exchange of vegetables and other raw ingredients between women in the *andarmahal* (inner households) was a normal affair. But both the lower-classes suffered from maltreatment by the rich classes (like not being offered a seat while visiting a zamindari house), which had given rise to a rift in the community relations in Bengal. Still, festivals were truly meant for all and distribution of *bhog* (cooked food) was for everyone. He remembered that villagers consisting of different classes always used to unite in cases of land disputes, financial matters and law pursuits against *mahajans* and zamindars. The professional *lathial bahinis* of villages were equally supportive towards the peasants in land wars, regardless of class, caste or religion (Samsuddin 1989: 21–25).

The tradition of syncretic culture not only enriched the community relations, but also developed a liberal atmosphere around it to support education and job opportunities. Anisuzzaman remembered in his memoir, *Kal Nirabadhi*, that his grandfather used to stay with the family of Radhamadhab Basu, a Brahmo zamindar, to pursue his higher studies. From that family, he felt, his grandfather inherited a liberal mind that continued spreading for generations in his own family (Anisuzzaman 2003: 15–16). The liberal environment in their Park Circus house left a permanent mark in their lives and orientation. He aptly remembered how his father accompanied him every time to attend the *halkhata utsab* in *Naba-barsha* (Bengali New Year), and described the way elders always inspired younger generation to take active part in organising *Saraswati Puja*, exactly the way they participated in *Milad Mehfil*. The feeling of religious separation and otherness was never dominant in their self. Dipesh Chakraborty commented, 'The Muslims participated in the Hindu festivals and thus were narratively absorbed into the image of the eternal Bengali folk' (Chakrabarty 1996: 2149). Sunanda Sikdar, in her autobiography *Doyamoyee Katha*, described how the Hindus and Muslims were comfortable in staying together in East Bengal with cultural differences. She recalled the rural artistes and professional classes collaborated for village fairs (Sikdar 2012: 98–99). Interestingly, the traditional Hindu god *Satyanarayan* used to be often worshipped by the lower-strata people of both the communities in Bengal, again with a common belief that he would protect them from any kind of trouble. When the Hindus offered him a *puja* by performing some elaborate rituals for the Muslims, his identity changed as *Satya-Pir*, an essential connotation of Sufism.[44]

Asim Roy tried to analyse the issues of creating separate identities of communities with a background of composite culture from different perspectives. He argued that the late 19th century census records of Bengal often offered a picture of the process of Sanskritisation among Hindus involving social emulation of the higher dominant castes by the lower. The exaggerating importance of their alien origin penetrated the Muslim society, and the whole community fell as a logical victim to its own myth. In Bengal, when a Hindu was categorised as a 'Bengali', a Muslim was simply identified as a 'Mussalman'. Hence, a predominantly Hindu locality was always termed as *Bengali-para* (the Bengali quarter), whereas Muslim quarters were described as *Mussalman-para* (the Muslim quarter).[45] Within the traditional fold, the Hindu elites initiated to portray themselves as 'wealthy, educated and respectable' in the Bengali society, which gave the Muslims a feeling of 'otherness' and it acted as a factor in Muslim polarisation.[46]

These were probably major reasons for which both the communities slowly got attracted to the two terms, 'nationalism' and 'communalism', which were colonial in origin (Ray 2003: 25–26). The ideological construction of 'nationalism' had changed into 'communalism' for Hindu groups, political strategies were adopted in shorter durations, unlike prior Congress approaches.[47] The Hindu communalism therefore came strongly to the forefront in Bengal's provincial politics from the 1930s (Roy 1999: 86–87). Annada Shankar Roy, a retired IAS (Indian Administrative Service) officer described in his autobiography, *Jibon-Jouban*, issues of rifts that emerged in communities from the 1930s. The reflection of animosity was visible in every insignificant incidence, whenever they interacted professionally. Joya Chatterji remarked 'The province's complex edifice of Zamindari rights, debt-collecting and rent interests, already weakened, now collapsed'.[48] Comparatively better off Bengali Muslim tenants started taking advantage of the chaotic situation in rural Bengal to assume power. The announcement of Ramsay MacDonald's Communal Award (1932) had drastically changed the position of the Muslims in India, Bengali Muslim elites in particular. It led to dramatic reversal in the balance of power between Hindus and Muslims by reducing Hindus to a minority of 80 in the Assembly, while Muslims were given 119 places. The *Gazette of India* revised the population as per the last census. The total population was 50,122,550, of which Hindus were 21,537,921; Buddhists 315,801; Muslims 27,530,321; and Christians 180,572 in 1932.[49] Congress 'has neither accepted nor rejected' the Award . . . they viewed the issues of 'majority' and 'minority' by defining 'a community which is nearly 45 per cent of the total population of a province is not a "minority"; it would not be called a "minority" anywhere in the world'.[50]

'A shameless surrender to the communalists' was the way they termed it, where 'the claims of Hindus have been ignored completely and perhaps deliberately' (Chatterji 1995: 24–27). The JPC Report mentioned 'This Assembly accepts the Communal Award so far as it goes until a substitute is agreed upon by the various communities concerned' (Chatterji 1995: 24–27). The award reduced the Bengali *Bhadralok* to an impotent minority in the Legislative Assembly, and outraged them more, and they lost hope to be dominant in the provincial autonomy.[51] Congress opted for a revision from London; though it remained unchanged. Religious identity as a demographic category became the singular factor in determining the distribution of governmental power under the constitutional reforms of 1935 (Ray and Ray 1975: 97–101). It was a crucial juncture in the rise of Muslim intelligentsia. It provided them with voting rights in the legislature. The Krishak Praja Party (KPP) that was established by Fazlul Huq in July 1936 involved both *ashrafs* (elites) and *ajlafs* (non-elites) in their fold and captured the non-*ashrafs* vote bank. KPP initiated the last attempt to forge a political alliance with Congress, rendering practical beneficiaries to both the communities (Kabir 1943: 99–100). They tried to create more job opportunities and raised issues for agricultural reforms (Tenancy Amendment Bill), yet divulged deep divergence of class interests (Sen Gupta 2001: 397–98). The KPP had the appearance of a Muslim party 'on account of predominant membership of the community and the confinement of leadership almost exclusively among them'.[52] Because of the Congress's refusal to enter into a coalition, Krishak Praja Party was compelled to form the first provincial government with the Muslim League,[53] and the basic ideological conflicts between the two allied parties (KPP and Muslim League in Bengal) remained unaltered (Bhattacharya 2014: 8–9).

The Pakistan movement had virtually no presence in Bengal before 1937 (Ahmed 2013: 94). The Hindu Mahasabha affirmed their stand and ideology as 'they wished to work only for the Hindu folk'.[54] They benefitted from the concept of hegemony and dominance in the political culture of Bengal.[55] The special characteristics of Bengal politics declined with the decision of making the Coalition Government, Huq-Muslim League (Ahmed 2006: 128–30). Fazlul Huq commented once:

> It is not a civil war in the Muslim community but it is a fight in which people of Bengal are divided on purely economic issues . . . the problem of *dal* and *bhat* and some kind of coarse cloth is the problem of problems which stares us in the face and which must be solved immediately.
>
> *(Ghosh 2012: 98–99)*

Abandoning the Bengal Provincial Muslim League, Huq attempted to create a separate League. But it seemed to be a 'deplorable split among the Mussalmans of Bengal' Gossman 1999: 136–39). The communalist 'quota system' politics had messed up the ideology of liberal groups within the Muslim League. The dream of making the 'educated Muslim middle-class' was far off from the reality (Roychoudhury 2007a: 129–30). The engulfing social division between the Hindus and Muslims had provoked political segregation more. Anisuzzaman remembered how the elders of his family strongly perceived that 'the Hindus are not treating the Muslims well or equally', and they lamented why talented Bengali Muslim personalities like Maulana Abul Kalam Azad and Humayun Kabir have joined Congress (Anisuzzaman 2003: 75). The Hindu middle-class reacted immensely when job facilities were enacted more for the Muslims, as an essential British administrative policy. In effect, both the communities became bigoted.[56] The Hindus became more conservative to keep their culture and tradition clean from the state administration during the reign of Muslim League in Bengal from 1937. Sunil Gangapadhyay, in his novel *Aka Ebong Koyekjon*, argued that the situation had given rise to a liberal political movement at least one decade before Partition (Gangapadhyay 1997: 338–39).

The 1940s: the formidable divide

The political trends in Bengal and manifestation of ideas started changing from the 1940s. The percentage of population became so important in the new structure of representative politics; the growth, rise and decline of community population had started to become de facto in Bengal politics.[57] The clashes of interests between non-Bengali and Bengali Muslim leaders were reflected in the Lahore Resolution of 1940. It started from the ideological difference between Fazlul Huq and Moulana Akram Khan. The League under instigation of the non-Bengali leaders voiced 'independent states' for Muslims (Ghosh 2002: 277). The unrest between communities was even visible in the census of 1941. Probably the reason behind the sudden decline of Muslim percentage and growth of Hindu population in the 1941 census was due to the fact that the untouchables did not mention their sub-castes in this census like that of 1931 (De 1975: 14). The nature of national politics was quite abominable. In the Presidential address at the Madras session of the All-India Muslim League in April 1941, Jinnah observed, 'If the Government wants the whole-hearted co-operation of the Muslims of India, they must place their cards on the table' (Bahadur 1988: 223). The 'concept of different land' was reflected in another address: 'The Muslim League has given you a goal which in my judgment is going to lead you to the Promised Land where we shall establish our Pakistan' (Bahadur 1988: 223).

In Bengal, the resignation of Fazlul Huq (from the Working Committee and Council in 1941) on ideological grounds expanded the perplexity more, as it modified the political equations between parties and future plans of this province.[58] His next attempt to keep Bengal united with diverse communities had taken shape of the 'Progressive Coalition Party' with fresh collaborations (Biswas 1966: 384). Significantly, the 'Bose group' of Congress, Hindu Mahasabha and Independent Schedule Caste Party joined hands to form the 'Shyama-Huq' Ministry (Hashim 1978: 35). Yet, 'the second Ministry of Fazlul Huq could not outline any real change in the policy, or the tone of administration'.[59] The leftist-socialist ideas started nurturing within the Muslims, outlined by liberal section of leaders. They left the tag of community identity for organisational affairs of state.[60] The endeavour to accelerate activities of a 'dead organisation' like the Bengal Provincial Muslim League (BPML) had passed on to the hands of Huseyn Shaheed Suhrawardy, the last Premier of the undivided Bengal. He was English educated and politically alert, though sometimes lacked proficiency in Bengali (Chatterji 1995: 81–83). Jinnah tried hard for the mass acceptance of Muslim League as the sole party for Muslims, primarily to make his dream of creating Pakistan into a reality.[61] Suhrawardy's base was largely confined to the urban Muslims of Calcutta. Jinnah managed to push Suhrawardy on Nazimuddin's side and utilised them against Fazlul Huq, as he had a strong hold on the Muslims outside Calcutta (Sen 1976: 126–31). This group compelled Fazlul Huq to tender the resignation of the Ministry. The decline of KPP helped the rise of BPML to take over the hold of Bengal politics, which was surprising and puzzling.[62] From 1944, the League made ample room for all, the extreme right to progressive KPP men; it meant 'everything to everybody'.[63] On account of Jinnah's 'progressive' pronouncements against exploitation and theocracy, many 'radical' Muslims joined the League before the election of 1946.[64]

Muslims of both Bengals trusted and were bent on the political equation, strategy and implementation blueprinted by the League (Biswas 1996: 396). Suhrawardy formed the ministry in 1946 and brought back *mofussil* essences in all India platforms. Unlike Nazimuddin and Fazlul Huq, he did not bother to keep parity in numbers of the Muslim-Hindu ministers. He offered only three Hindu ministers to be part of his Ministry, whereas two of them were scheduled castes (Sen 1976: 203–23). The final attempt of BPML to attract public support to their side was the idea of launching the scheme of 'Sovereign independent State for undivided Bengal', with the consent of left-wing Congress leader Sarat Chandra Bose.[65] He always dreamt of the 'Sovereign socialist republic of Bengal' (Hashim 2006: 147). Being a strong believer of the 'Congress idea of composite Nationalism', Sarat Chandra Bose wrote to Jinnah: 'At the meetings of the members of the two parts of the Legislative Assembly sitting separately and empowered to vote whether or not the province should be partitioned, to vote solidly against partition' (Bose 1968: 7). He stated, 'I do not say that Bengal should remain outside the Union. What I say is that only a Free Bengal can decide her relations with the rest of India' (Misra 1996: 141).[66] Kiran Shankar Roy supported Bose for ideological reasons. Bose and Roy negotiated with Suhrawardy and Hashim without official authorisation by the Congress (Hosen 1990: 16–17). The terms of the 'Suhrawardy-Bose-Roy Agreement' had never been placed before the Bengal Provincial Congress Committee.[67] The Hindu Mahasabha and Congress leaders rejected the scheme straight away, as they were afraid of the League's effort of 'Pakistanisation' of the whole province.[68] Gandhi was the only one in favour of the scheme (Das 1972: 49–50).

The Congress High Command believed that Partition of Bengal would not be of 'long duration', as East Bengal alone was not an imperative, either economically or geopolitically. Jawaharlal Nehru was against it. Sardar Patel never believed Bengal would be benefitted, 'by isolating itself from the rest of India'.[69] When Bengal was about to divide, Suhrawardy and Hashim failed to deploy control over the provincial government and freed themselves as the loyal agents of Jinnah (Sengupta 1995: 5). They hoped to win the support of the Hindus. As Joya Chatterji has opined, after incidents like famine and the Great Calcutta Killing, Hindus were left with almost no reason to trust Suhrawardy again. Chatterji tried to look at the whole phenomenon from different perspectives. She perceived ushering far-reaching changes in the political fortunes or developments of the 1940s as a 'decline, revival and fall of the Bengali *bhadralok* classes'.[70] The social elites dominated the politics and public life of Bengal in the 19th century, then experienced reverses in the 20th century by losing grip over the power. She argued that their loss, in a way, turned out as a gain for the Muslim elites, they steadily enhanced or consolidated their power or position in a Muslim-majority province. The Congress High Command, according to Chatterji, was responsible for Partition, as the Bengali *bhadralok*s rallied behind a cry for Partition to preserve a stronghold in Hindu majority western and central districts of Bengal. Partition became only feasible option to save them from being minorities or fall into a predicament of being perpetually subjected to Muslim domination. Out of such narrow political drives, Bengali *bhadraloks* could be relegated to the fringes of the power structure, as a passive political partner of the North Indian centric Congress politics. But, contradicting this point, Partha Chatterjee argued, 'by the standard of mass agitation of the time' the 1947 campaigns for and against partitioning Bengal 'involved small numbers of people'.[71]

Emergence of the idea of homelands

Throughout the process of politics of identity formation in the late colonial period, the idea of the nation as a 'supra-religious territorial concept' had emerged which had resulted in 'endless unfolding of different configurations in politics' (Bandyapadhyay 2001: 27–28). The depth of the notion of 'staying together for Hindus and Muslims is difficult' left a profound mark in literature. It was a complex phase of mixed psyche. The insecurity began with the idea of separatism, and was reflected in dress or maintaining social customs as per community rules. Prafulla Roy, in *Bhagabhagi*, dealt with the growing differences between 'them' and 'us'. Some liberal leaders in Bengal were participating in Bengali festivals like *Durgapuja* or *Milad*, simultaneously organising processions for Congress or political meetings for the League. The author portrayed a few nationalist Muslim characters, who were afraid of their position in the society at that time, if Pakistan really happened in due course (Roy 2003: 30). The Muslim experience in the traditional Bengali society was infuriating. The social divisions first instigated community clashes and had finally taken shape of boundary making. This notion of territorial division prepared ground from the pre-Partition days when poor, peasant and downtrodden Muslims were treated as the lower-classes. Priobala Gupta's *Smritimonjusha* has thrown light on the *andarmahals* of the Hindu families. She recalled that Hindu society norms were so conservative and strict on narrowly based behavioural norms that servants or domestic helps were forbidden to clean up utensils used by the Muslims (Sikdar 2005: 48). Mahmudul Huq, in *Kalo Borof*, mentioned that middle-class Hindus were critical of Muslim form of religious practices; they used abusive comments to make fun of them (Huq 1992: 36–37). Jibanananda Das has shown, in *Basmatir Upakhyan*, that the word *Mussalman* is itself used with a derogatory connotation. It meant 'inferior community' with whom the educated, enlightened and elite Hindu families seldom had interaction (Sikdar 2005: 49).

Gour Kishore Ghosh, in his novel *Pratibesi*, with innate sensitivity portrayed how water tanks in stations and glasses to drink water used to be different in sizes for Hindus and Muslims. These social and economic discriminations impacted both the communities, and by the late 1940s, it was evident that Hindus and Muslims needed different lands to survive. The Congress, Muslim League and Hindu Mahasabha—all the parties—had given nod to it (Ghosh 1997b: 94–95). Akhtaruzzaman Elias tried to locate reasons behind the sudden consent towards social division. In his novel *Khoabnama*, he argued that Hindus captured respectable positions for centuries and the Muslims were convinced of their inferior condition. Kader, one of the central characters posed the question why, if Hindus were so eager to separate everything from the Muslims, they were opposing the division of the country (Elias 1992: 122–24). The protest against the upper-class Hindus or zamindars started with an alliance between the lower-class Hindus and Muslims in the form of the *Praja* movement. The actual essence of class conflict turned out in the form of communal conflict.

The complex structure of the *Praja* movement was not easy to understand for the uneducated poor Muslim tenants, untouchables and downtrodden peasants who were exploited by the zamindars of *taluks* over generations (Sikdar 2005: 49–50). Communal division sounded more convincing even to the rational Muslim thinkers. The leaders convinced the Muslims that Pakistan would be a country for the poor Muslims. Ashoke Mitra, later an economist by profession, was a student of Dacca University in the pre-Partition period. In his autobiography, *Apila-Chapila*, he remarked that Bengal was divided as the Congress joined hands with Hindu Mahasabha in the last phase. He remembered that Hindu students had protested against Shyama Prasad Mookerjee's public address in Dacca and were tortured by the police of the Muslim League Government. Partition pushed students of Jagannath Hall and Dacca Hall to unite with students of Sallimullah Muslim Hall and Fazlul Huq Hall to continue with the students' solidarity (Mitra 2012: 5455). The Mahasabha had stressed popularising Hindu symbols; Abu Jafar Samsuddin remembered that he had to collect and wear a white dhoti and shirt (which was supposed to be worn according to the proper Hindu way of wearing clothes) to attend lectures by two Mahasabha leaders, because of their political stand and to understand their line of arguments in the National Medical School, Dhaka (Raghavan 1983: 595; Samsuddin 1989: 103).

Political economy of riots

The riots of the 1940s were explosive by nature. Yet the 'Great Calcutta Killing' of 1946 overshadowed all previous techniques, modes, reasons, politics, participations and manifestations of riots in Bengal.[72] It culminated through stages of fusion between nationalism and class-consciousness. The Muslim League decided to 'bid good-bye to the constitutional methods' and had taken a programme of 'direct action for the achievement of Pakistan' for accomplishing a separate land for the Muslims (Sen 1976: 209). Jinnah said in the press conference, 'I am not going to discuss ethics'.[73] The whole of India was aware of the declaration by the Muslim League. As reported previously by other political parties, Suhrawardy and his administration would be in favour of the Muslims on 16 August 1946.[74] Nazimuddin misguided the League followers by saying Jinnah asked for action against the Hindus (Basu 1987: 20). Anticipation of devastation was already there, though nobody had a clear idea what type of catastrophe might happen (Mitra 1407: 226–27). In the end, it proved to be an organised genocide (Bandyapadhyay 1399: 54–55). It became a '*jehad*' against everyone who did not accept Pakistan'.[75]

The absolute decline of law and order; reports of looting, stabbing and rioting by the social agents; mutual hatred; and lack of confidence of other communities created panic in Calcutta and all over Bengal (Bandyapadhyay 1992: 26–27). The vernacular press deliberately published provocative pictures of their brethren. The headline of the *Morning News* was 'Recrudescence of Disturbances in Calcutta: Twenty Four killed and 51 Injured: Panic and Tension in the City', whereas the official version was that, in the very first day, at least 5,000–6,000 people were murdered in Calcutta.[76] It aggravated tensions and instigated both communities to organise revenge in neighbourhoods. Contemporary memoirs depicted shocking evidences that made Calcutta 'a horror city'. Transformation was 'like a nightmare' (Sen 2004: 48). Jyoti Basu opined that the police administration of Calcutta had operated on communal lines. He wrote, when the situation went out of control, 'only then did the British rulers deploy the army and suddenly try and project themselves as guardians of peace and friends of India', and he lamented: 'They did succeed in their ultimate mission though; the genesis of Partition was sown by the riots' (Basu 2010: 37–38).

Sheikh Mujibur Rahman, in *Asamapta Atmajibani*, contradicted such opinion. He wrote in his memoir in 1947 that Jinnah instructed the League to observe a 'Direct Action Day' peacefully to achieve Pakistan. He gave Suhrawardy a clean chit by saying that Abul Hashim guided members to visit Hindu and Muslim *mohallas* (areas) to convey that it was not a movement against the Hindus, but was meant for the British. He argued that Congress and Hindu Mahasabha were responsible for spreading communal sentiments and conducting mass killings. He wrote that Muslims were not prepared for the riot and Hindus were first to attack Muslims, even before the League started its meeting in Maidan (Rahman 2012: 63–67). Ispahani confirmed the press, 'there was no preparation'.[77] Badruddin Umor, on the contrary, firmly condemned the attack, blamed and counter blamed Suhrawardy for having arranged the Calcutta riot, and for literally instructing from the Lalbazar control room.[78] Begum Shayesta, Suhrawardy's sister, described how her brother tried to work against the mob in those riot days with vivid illustration of his basic nature and morals (Ahmed 1997: 110). The experience of communities and description of incidents in the Calcutta riot were almost identical in research writings and literary sources. The tone of representation is somewhat different. Anisuzzaman himself attended the meeting organised by the League in Maidan on 16 August. He wrote, their school turned out as a shelter for Muslims and he along with other young Muslim youth organised two groups in mid-August, a defence party and a medical team (Anisuzzaman 2003: 88–95). Witnessing Muslim atrocity in roads and streets, Anisuzzaman blamed the League for the organised Hindu killing.[79] Manikultala Sen wrote that both the communities were expecting some violence, after clarion call given by the League. The Hindus were quite prepared to handle crisis in their *padas* (Sen 2003: 170–71).

There was a highly charged communal feeling visible in general during the Calcutta riot. All political parties were keen to establish ideologies and political stands with vigour. Government employees, administrative officials and police largely acted as per their religious instincts, lost their sense of duty and responsibility to act (Ali 2013: 91). Muzaffar Ahmed stated that they were shocked to notice the change in mass behaviour. He mentioned a newspaper called *Sultan*, which stopped being published long before, suddenly survived by spreading rumours of communal riots (Ahmed 2012: 197). Kazi Nazrul had never experienced a riot situation before. He reacted vehemently against the way Hindu and Muslim presses were spreading communal malice. Nazrul criticised the religious preachers for their refusal to analyse religion on its rationale, which would keep the society 'static in lieu if helping it to be dynamic'.[80] Communal politics affected the human psyche and touched everyone, even in *mofussil* and rural areas, and tore family values. Prakash Karmakar in his memoir described how he, along with his father, participated in the killing of a Muslim man when in his teenage years. Sunil Gangapadhyay, in *Aka Ebong Koyekjon*, wrote such occurrences had impact on dimensions of human relationships. The physical appearance of Hindus and Muslims became so crucial that *Surjya*, the central character, was compelled to cut his beard to protect himself (Gangapadhyay 1997: 374–76).

Muslims were panicky after the first major day of rioting, and thought they might be finished off in Calcutta, so many left the city (Chakravarty 2013: 15). Anisuzzaman saw a Hindu, who was a milk seller by profession in their Park Circus area for decades, killed by Muslims.[81] Mizanur Rahman opined that largely non-Bengali Muslims like Hindi-speaking Biharis and North Indians participated actively in the riot. His family was saved by a Hindu neighbour (Rahman 2012: 251–53). Nobendu Ghosh, in his novel *Fears Lane*, portrayed pictures of assimilation in a particular lane that comprised heterogeneous characters. The planned riot by the residents completely changed those lives (Ghosh 2001: 193). Manik Bondyopadhyay mentioned in *Swadhinatar Swad* the ways in which politics divided the masses; involved downtrodden classes in riots and the socio-economic impact of those incidents (Bondyopadhyay 1974: 387).

The Noakhali-Tipperah disturbance came as a multiplier effect, a direct repercussion of the Calcutta Killings. The intensive communal propaganda played a vital role and was used as catalyst to create rapid rupture in the peasant society.[82] The damage to homesteads, huts and instances of murder were reflected in the reports of E. S. Simpson and R. Gupta, though the government never published it (Batabyal 2005: 273–74). There were reports of hooligans, burning down of Hindu houses and mass conversions in many personal accounts of the eyewitnesses. Ashoka Gupta wrote in her diary, 22 Hindu houses out of 25 in the village Lakshmipur were burnt out.[83] The native Muslims brought with them exaggerated stories of their Muslim brethren suffering in Calcutta. It vitiated the already tense situation created by rumours.[84] Mohandas Karamchand Gandhi, popularly known as Mahatma Gandhi in Indian politics, stayed in Noakhali with his disciples to work for the riot victims and to resume peace against incidents of communal violences there. He collaborated with the Red Cross in providing medical facilities, along with other organisations.[85] Suhasini Das, in her diary *Noakhali: 1946*, has given an intricate description of her experience while working with Gandhiji. She wrote that the Muslim League Government controlled the press by not allowing them to publish reports at least for a week. Dipankar Mahanta, the editor of the diary mentioned, Noakhali became a place of revenge after news of Calcutta riots poured into villages through working classes (Mahanta 2004: 11). It started as a personal rift between local Muslim leaders with two Hindu zamindars, Rajendralal Basu and Suren Basu of Narayanpur.[86] The Rai Saheb of Noakhali, popularly known as *Sanyasi*, was their prime target. The slogans of the Leaguers were '*Sarwar jindabad*' (long live Sarwar), '*Hindur rakta chai*' (want Hindu blood), '*Rai Sahaber matha chai*' (want the head of Rai Sahib), '*Sanyasir matha chai*' (want the head of Sanyasi), 'Calcutta retaliation', etc.[87] They, under the leadership of Golam Sarwar, decided to boycott the Hindus. The indifference and negligent attitude of the administration made the situation worse.[88] Gandhiji saw Hindu dead bodies lying on the wayside even after the first few days of emergency (Mahanta 2004: 12–13).

Saibal Kumar Gupta remembered in his autobiography *Kichhu Smriti Kichhu Katha* that Mahatma Gandhi was confident of bringing back the peace again. Gandhiji believed that if he was successful in Noakhali, he might influence the decision of Partition (Gupta 1994: 80–82). The Noakhali Relief Committee was formed under leadership of Neli Sengupta. They started working among the abducted, raped and converted Hindu women (Gupta 1999: 11). The Bengal Provincial Congress Committee, Hindu Mahasabha, Marwari Relief Committee, Bharat Sevak Sangha and Kashi Biswanath Seva Samity set up a joint organisation with help of local Hindus named the Noakhali Rescue Relief Rehabilitation Committee (Choudhury 2009: 193–95). The burning situation accelerated in some cases where compromise and negotiation with the prevailing forces became a compulsion. Rama Debnath, in *Smriti-Bismritir Atmakathan*, described how the elders of her family were compelled to negotiate with the League leaders with a lump sum amount so that their house would not be destroyed. Yet, the goons did not spare their family; they forced the family members to convert to Islam. The arrival of Mahatma Gandhi with Sucheta Kripalini saved their lives, and they somehow could migrate to India (Chakraborty 1419: 160–61).

These riots decided relations between Hindus and Muslims in Bengal for decades. 'In the eastern part, gory violence was more localised' as Jayanti Basu has opined, 'certain places including Noakhali, Dhaka and specific pockets of Khulna being the most affected' (Basu 2013: 4). The forced conversion of the Hindus in Noakhali and Tipperah created an environment of utter distrust (Sen 1976: 217). Both the communities got involved in this riot, and were attacked by each other. Bihar had experienced the same traumatic saga of tragedies of pain, horror and anxiety, as a whole in the acts of brutality.[89] While Nehru made a detailed statement in the Central Assembly that 'the Bihar situation was brought completely under control after a week and was quiet now', the Muslim League was determined not to allow Bihari Muslims 'to go back unless strong pockets of the minority community are created in Bihar'.[90] Bibhutibhusan Mukhopadhyay described the horrors of the riots in 1946 in his novel *Kolikata-Noakhali-Bihar*. He had denounced the state-systems and questioned how one can distrust a Minister who was expected to make beneficial policies and save people from atrocities. He lamented that people guided by the communities' morale, dependent on social security services and relying upon state policies could not survive in the end.[91] Prabodh Kumar Sanyal, in *Hasubanu*, had shown the change in layers of identities in the time of the riot period. The author portrays how a local riot changed the entire dimension of human lives. While raising issues like 'why the mutual respect between two communities suddenly went in vain', Hasnu, the protagonist of *Hasubanu*, pointed out crude practical facts like how the leaders misguided the Muslims peasants when negotiating for Pakistan. The peasants thought of occupying Hindu lands, or they were hoping to get rights over lands that had been previously occupied by the Hindu zamindars. But in reality, they lost jobs of a daily labour and were not in a position to earn after the Hindus left.[92]

Popular perception of riots, migration and Partition

The masses used to stay in a communitarian environment in both the wings of Bengal. They never seemed too spontaneous to participate in riots, even when the awareness level was comparatively low.[93] The political parties started injecting masses with communal ideas and divided them along community lines, while the negotiation process for Partition was in full swing. Spreading hatred about each other's communities was the most effective tool in planning to snatch their demands for separate territory. This affected the human minds profoundly, and the members of communities staying together for generations became conscious about their religious identities and incompatibility. The social divisions were clear. Both the Hindu and Muslim leaders were preparing as to how to bargain best to benefit from it. The violence dominated the politics of Bengal and signalled successful polarisations of Hindus and Muslims. And 'the triumph of leaders who used these incidents of violence to stake their party's claim as the sole body capable of protecting not just Muslim or Hindu interests, but Muslim and Hindu lives' (Gossman 1999: 137). The moral fibre of such clashes had grown over the years by both of the political groups. Migration was the only option left for the minorities in East Bengal to escape from any minor incident of assault or huge riot situations. The psychological fear to live in a declared Muslim state affected the educated and politically empowered professional Hindus in such ways that they started treating every single incident with suspicion. The regionalisation and possessiveness to establish the community identity enhanced the rift, which had already made ground through the social and cultural divide.[94]

Creative literature of Bengal had innumerable descriptions of Partition experiences. Repeated references to rioting, violence and victimhood had portrayed a powerful analogy for oral history accounts and other dependable testimonials for understanding the history of the time from a humane lens. Here the depiction of womanhood received serious attention, as the riots followed by Partition had violated her honour and challenged her traditional security at the abode of home. Loss of homeland meant loss of centuries-old seclusion and a sense of security or protection that a woman in traditional household was supposed to enjoy. Tarashankar Bondyapadhyay, in his novel *Uttorayan*, dealt with the mental world of the riot victim women, especially the central character Arati.[95] He portrayed rational sides of them, how they negotiated later with the worst experiences they faced, their expectations from life and from previous relationships. A similar, heart-wrenching narrative of rape of a Hindu maiden by Muslims amidst the Dacca riot of 1946, followed by abject denouncement by her own family, had been portrayed in the character Jhhinuk in Prafulla Roy's novel *Keya Patar Nouka*. Her molested, bruised and tormented entity had merged with the condition of the land where she suffered. The relatives in India, the so-called 'safest place', suggested she stay in a government home in Calcutta, meant for these girls (Roy 2007: 414). There were several such stories written with same emotion, feeling of emptiness and erosion of humanity at a moment of all-around insecurity and degeneration. Jyotirmoyee Debi situated her novel *Epar Ganga Opar Ganga* after one decade of the riots of 1946 in East Bengal. The chief focus was on changed identity and life of the central character Sutara. The failure of her family to accept Sutara (as she stayed with her Muslim neighbours) was conjoined with feeling of loss that continued to dominate the rest of her life (Roychoudhury 2001: 122). Romapada Choudhury, in a short story *Korunkanya*, shows Arundhati, the central character, opting to live her life with a husband who forced her to be with him during the riot, because of the social pressure and mass mentality.[96]

Partition-borne riots not only impacted the women, but their whole psychological world was altered. Hasan Azizul Huq, in his novel *Agunpakhi*, portrayed how from the 1950s the majority community tried hard to find the right excuse to traumatise minorities, so that they could encroach upon properties, looting all material assets including Hindu women (Huq 2008: 130–35). Literary works on Partition addressed issues other than women's tragic plight. Banaful (pen name of Balaichand Mukhopadhyay) placed the characters of his novel *Panchaparba* in Noakhali, West Bengal and Bihar to portray how the migrants coped with the changed environment in different states (Mukhopadhyay 1982: 559). The question of 'community identity' rose in the mind of young Mizanur Rahman. He went to visit his school for the last time, while they were ready to migrate to their 'promised land'. He surprisingly noticed that the Hindus and Muslims were shaking hands, celebrating joys of freedom together, but they would never come back here again. Sankha Ghosh expressed this irony in the poem *Supuribaner Sari*. He wrote 'Nilu is going back to his *desh* for the last time, as he would never be able to visit his birthplace or motherland again'.[97] The Hindus and Muslims from East and West Bengal never thought of being refugees or migrating to another country. In pre-Partition days, Kalikrishna Guha remembered in *Tirpurni* that his grandfather was against the idea of leaving everything. The mass psyche of facing humiliation and loss of family prestige created a fear that compelled them to relocate to another country (Sikdar 2012: 45). There were inter-communal rifts at personal and local levels. The regional identity was dominant in them, over their religion. None of the educated middle-class families thought of losing their age-old neighbours.

Kapil Krishna Thakur, in *Ujantolir Upakatha*, wrote that Hindu and Muslim families were shocked to face such crises and did forbid the members to leave the village, though they failed to convince them in most cases (Thakur 1412: 202–3).

Creating contexts and pretext for riots

The post-Partition riots were designed primarily with local issues. Rumours played a major role across borders. Sheikh Mujibur Rahman mentioned that the riot of 1950 started in Barishal with a rumour that Sher-e-Bangla Fazlul Huq had been murdered in Calcutta by Hindus. The communication system was poor at that point in time. Thus, by the time that confirmation was declared of his well-being, Hindu killing had touched a record in Barishal and Dhaka. Calcutta also experienced Muslim killings as a counter-reaction (Rahman 2012: 170). The riot of 1950 was the dreadful event, but surprisingly, minorities in both the Bengals heard that it started with a cause (unknown to others) in other side of the border (Anisuzzaman 2003: 149). Newspapers of both countries played chief roles in reporting communal news against humanity. Riots against Hindus had been taking place in district towns like Sylhet, Barishal, Dinajpur and Rajshahi. *Namasudras* and others from lower strata became prime targets in 1950 killings.[98] Caste and community politics played significant role in the riot experiences scattered in sensitive pockets for over a year.[99] The Muslim peasants in suburbs were neither politically alert nor economically well-off. Their position was determined by their class position, rather than the caste-identities (Das 1368: 63). Their intention was to snatch every piece of land available along the evacuated Hindu houses (Kamra 2000: 62–65). State policies were against the interests of the minorities (Kamal 2009: 50–51). The Muslim League and its ancillary organisations like *Ansar Bahini*, or Muslim National Guard, enhanced the confidence of the Muslim peasants and sharecroppers for encroaching lands from the poor Hindu peasants.[100] The deliberate creation of an atmosphere charged with mistrust was such that a slight stroke led to virulent atrocities. The minorities had an idea that temporary migration might prove a feasible solution to keep their '*dhon-pran-man*' (wealth-life-respect) (Bandyapadhyay 1970: 15). Some of them were preparing to sell off their properties, and in the process became 'easy targets' for conducting 'soft violence' (Basu 2010: 21). The fear of losing superiority and scare of revenge were two psychological rationales behind the mass departure of landed, propertied and educated Hindus from East Pakistan (Roychoudhury 2007b: 98). The majoritarian community were more conscious about their newly acquired religious dissimilarities, privileges and power than some of their neighbours (Halder 2003: 24–25). Creating a riot situation was the easiest option left for them to snatch their movable and immovable properties (Sengupta 2013: 144–46).

The politics in East Pakistan was temporarily transformed during the time of the 'Language Movement of 1952' as the communitarian feeling showed stronger commitment towards the identity of language (Nag 2006: 5185). The refusal to grant Bengali status as the national language by West Pakistan was based on the extension of same separatist political discourse. 'Bengali was chiefly the language of the Hindus', as it was believed to be 'a Brahminical creation, highly Sanskritised' by the Pakistan authorities from the West.[101] This was not taken well by the Bengali Muslims. The Hindu-Muslim polarisation was shifted to Bengali vs non-Bengali after alteration of power equation (Akhtar Mukul 2001: 17–18). The anti-Hindu attitude of the state was reflected in headlines made by few press reports, ideologically connected to the West Pakistanis or funded by them. *Morning News* reported, 'Dhotis roaming in the street', which meant the language movement initiated or designed only by the Hindus (Semanti Ghosh 2008: 45). The general attitude of the press was reflected in the report of the Ministry of External Affairs. It stated: 'The Morning News made open attacks on the minority community which was alleged to have taken a leading part in attempts to disrupt communications and 'to sabotage the national life of the country'.[102] The context of the 1964 riot was designed by the sudden disappearance of a holy relic from Kashmir's sacred Hazratbal mosque, so rumours gained ground amongst Muslims of the whole subcontinent that the desecration was a deliberate Hindu act. Serious violence towards Hindus and Buddhists started in 1964 and it affected the districts of Khulna, and Jessore the most, provoked by anti-India policies of the Government of Pakistan (Das 2000: 289–90). Media became vigorous, and propaganda was spread by newspapers by describing the situation on the other side of the border.[103] The Hindu press had stressed how the Muslims were never influenced by the notion of geographical unity of Bengal; they had dreamt of establishing pan-Islamisation.[104] Rumours spread by the press played a vital role in spreading communal feeling and occurrences of violence in Bengal. Nurjahan Bose, who survived in both the wings of Pakistan in this particular phase, remembers in her memoir how a group of people used to wait in the steamer *ghat* of Khulna, with swords and other weapons, for arrival of daily newspapers from India during the riot of 1964. It would generally be delivered every evening and she noticed an absolute change in human behaviour at that point in time. For them, it became a daily routine to attack and assault Hindus after they finished reading newspapers, as a revenge for their Muslim brethren, suffering in India (Bose 2011: 30). Radio became another source of getting news from the other country. It often induced fresh spirit to the ongoing debate on the same animosity. Both Hindus and Muslims were panicky and confused about state policies and their future (Ghatak 2012: 28).

Shamsur Rahman, in his autobiography *Kaler Dhulae Lekha*, described how they suddenly read in the newspapers in 1964 that the majority communities in India had killed more than 400 Muslims. Communal propaganda was like an infectious disease in which rationale got affected first. It consequently made the communities vengeful and vindictive (Rahman 2004: 159). The Deputy High Commissioner of Pakistan in Calcutta, along with his officials, frequented Muslim areas, spreading communal feeling amongst their co-religionists.[105] The Government of India set up a Commission of Enquiry 'to enquire into the exodus of the minorities of East Pakistan into India'.[106] The purpose behind the setting up of a Commission was 'to determine the causes of the influx of the refugees' (*udbastu agomonr karon nirdharon kora*),[107] but that report never saw daylight.[108] Testimonials preserved in the Ashoka Gupta Archives point that the fear of the Hindus were real and they were systematically squeezed in East Bengal. In reality, migration was the only option left for the minorities to escape everything from minor incidents to huge riot situations. The incident of 1971 had witnessed an outright different form of holocaust against the Hindus (Tathagata Roy 2007: 284–85). It was the last attempt to shove Hindu Bengalis. The nature of internal politics during the Liberation War was designed to identify and kill them (Roy 2001: 33–35). The Hindus were treated as anti-nationalists and became the prime target of the Pakistani military. The concept of Bengali nationalism and changing definition of nationhood led to the steady rise of the Awami League. Nationalist leaders like Maulana Bhasani, Mujibur Rahman and Taj-uddin Ahmed had shaped emotions of the Bengali masses (Banerjee 1969: 52–55). Kanai Lal Chakraborty, a doctor by profession, writes that he never thought of leaving his motherland East Bengal permanently like many others, but the Liberation War compelled his family to leave the country (Chakraborty 2013: 28–31).

Partition as temporary solution: common understanding of 1947

Trauma resulting from being persecuted or threats to life became major factors that dominated the emotional world of minorities in East Pakistan. It compelled them to leave their motherland, cross the border and settle down in an unknown geographical location. The transformed nature of traumas and layers of insecurities were depicted profoundly or treated sensitively in memoirs and literary works. Asrukumar Sikdar wrote about three villages in Barishal in which hardly any Muslim families resided. But all Hindu families left those villages after the Partition to avoid insecurity and humiliation of their women by the 'others' (Sikdar 2005: 52). Trauma of belonging to a minority community became problematic. Parents of school-goers always used to remind their children not to become involved in any argument with Muslim classmates. The police and administration were against the minorities. Complaints against the Muslims were considered as crime in the new state system. The feeling of loss was deep-rooted, which continued through common memories and formulated general perceptions affecting generations of sufferers. Sirshendu Mukhopadhyay, in his novel *Parapar*, depicted the story of a grown-up boy named Lalit in post-1947 Calcutta. He had never been to East Bengal, and had only heard stories of violence and social rejection from his mother. He often dreamt of similar incidents and became insecure out of that fear (Mukhopadhyay 2000: 242). Sabitri Roy described in her novel *Swaralipi*, how Pritwi felt traumatised seeing flood of refugees literally bleeding from communal attack in Barishal Express (Sabitri Roy 2010: 95–97). Sandip Bandyopadhyay had portrayed a similar devastating picture of entering an empty train in the Sealdah station, where all the passengers had been stabbed to death while crossing the Bhairab bridge of Mymensingh. Those incidents made Darshana and Benapole, the two gateways to India, to appear as a sign of security and relief for the Hindu migrants.

The women used to make cheerful sounds, *uludhwani* (a typical whistling performed during religious rituals) and perform pious rituals after crossing borders. The idea of safety used to dawn in sceptical minds as they could cross the border and touch the soil of the other side. The notion of safety was now identified with the particular lands (Bandyopadhyay 2013: 7678).

The Bengali Hindus used to believe that the migration would be temporary, trusting the statements of Jawaharlal Nehru and Maulana Abul Kalam Azad. Nehru once said to Leonard Mosley that 'Partition would be temporary'. Abul Kalam Azad also commented in one of the sessions of AICC, 'it is going to be a short-lived Partition' (Sikdar 2005: 43–44). In the first phase, the high-caste/class Hindus decided to settle down in West Bengal temporarily, left properties with neighbours, subordinates or sharecroppers. After the 1950s, the situation had changed and minorities had no other options except migrating to India (Das 2012: 56–61). As Gopal Chandra Moulik described, his family members put their home under lock and key while leaving at night and kept the keys with care for long with a false hope of plausible return. The elders had strong belief they would definitely go back someday to the *jonmabhumi* (motherland) (Moulik 2011: 140–41). The idea of temporariness was in both the Bengals. When Anisuzzaman's family decided to migrate to Pakistan, instead of going to Dhaka they settled down in Khulna, because of its proximity to Calcutta (Anisuzzaman 2003: 111). The wishful thinking was such as if someday the Partition would be null and void, Pakistan would be declared a failed state and they would come back again.[109] Sunil Gangapadhyay portrayed beliefs and expectations of the masses of a partitioned country in his two novels. In *Arjun*, the family had to beg in course of leaving their *desh*, while waiting for the steamer. His elder brother and father used to think refugee-hood would be a temporary affair. So, it would not affect their lives permanently (Gangapadhyay 2003: 185). In *Purba-Paschim*, the central character Bhabodeb Majumdar was a disciple of Sri Arabinda. He had a strong belief that India-Pakistan would become one again and the same country after ten years of temporary split. His conviction was so strong that he stuck to his idea of not migrating to India. He even bought Hindu houses and lands at the cheapest rate, with a condition that he would return their property at this price, if they decided to come back (Gangapadhyay 2013: 10).

Yet, the idea of relating religious identities to rights of possession over lands actually began after the post-Partition era. Communities firmly started linking one's identity to the land. A strange way of distinguishing 'my land' and 'your land' (often rather 'my land' vs 'your land') began to emerge. Though it was initially like an idea of creation of two dominions out of one land, later, both the countries conveyed the message to religious minorities that they should move out to a land which was meant for them (Thakur 1412: 162–63). The Hindu families residing in East Pakistan started a trend of sending educated and professionally trained family members to purchase land or houses in India. Others would try to sell off properties secretly before migration. Mihir Sengupta described a similar pattern of staying back of some family members in his novel *Bishadbriksha*. He described how this tendency had grown further up after 1950. The minorities were psychologically weakened; many of them were planning where/when/how to leave East Pakistan (Sengupta 2013: 58, 74). Though to keep communal harmony, slogan from the Hindu side was '*Hindu-Muslim bhai*' (Hindus and Muslims are brothers). Yet, this conscious utterance itself implied the sublime apprehension and brewing tension of the community under duress. This slogan also signified that the Hindus were no more taken for granted as the sons of the soil of East Pakistan. Their identity had shifted to another land. Narayan Sanyal in *Bolmik* compared the refugee exodus to a gigantic snake moving to find some food and reach for a destination (Sikdar 2005: 38). Adhir Biswas recollected in *Mogurar Smriti* that his mother always wished to settle down in India. The reason was not that their life would be more comfortable there. But she thought if they could manage to migrate to West Bengal, they might not have to change the country again in future, as India was meant for the Hindus.[110]

But the idea of separated land did not cut off the refugees from their place of origin. Shankar Ghosh, in *Hastantar* wrote, generally neighbours of a whole Hindu village or *pada* used to migrate together with hope of again resettling in a new land. The refugees attempted to recreate a bit of their *desh* in the other side of the border. Shahidulla Kaysar in *Sangsaptak* described some Hindu villages that suddenly fell vacant. He mentioned that the Muslim neighbours betrayed chiefly to occupy their properties. In *Kagabogabitika*, Mahasweta Devi elaborated the wish of *Mahini* to bring back social custom and habits of East Bengal, whereas Pratibhamoyee, the central character in the story *Dambandha*, tried to recreate the old essence through an old radio that used to broadcast news of Khulna in a pure Khulna accent with intricate details.[111] Asrukumar Sikdar mentioned a poet in *Bhanga Bangla o Bangla Sahitya* who migrated and settled down in Calcutta long back with his family, but he misses the sound of *azan* in the early morning as in his *desh*, as his nostalgia embraced with that particular lyrics and sound. *Chhere Asa Gram*, edited by Dakshinaranjan Basu, is a perfect example of such feeling. The *Jugantar Patrika* had taken an initiative to publish memoirs of ordinary refugees, who left their villages after Partition. While describing their departures or absence from the motherland, their feeling of loss, choosing of expressions, usage of words echo a strange common voice of pain and pathos-as though a collective melancholy and nostalgia over the loss (Basu 1975: Introduction).

Desh/bastu and 'Othering' the territory

The idea of possessing own lands and a home (*vastu*) was the strong notion of identity and essential in the agrarian mindset of Bengal. Being *Udbastu* (somebody who is homeless) or uprooted from the *vastu* came as a shock to those families. *Bastubhite* (in Bengali colloquial language), or 'the site or foundation of a house', was always integral to their identity.[112] In Bengali, there are many different conceptions of house and home. For example, *bastu* means ancestral home, located in a rural area and inhabited by *bastusap* (snakes which guard the family property). *Basha* implies more temporary or a rented house, located in an urban area. *Bari* is somewhere in between, a permanent and personally owned house. The relationship between a spatial form and social process is subsumed in the distinctiveness entailed in the connotation of 'house' and 'home'. Whereas 'house' was a physical structure of residence for the Bengali refugees, a 'home' denoted a 'particular social relations both inside and outside the physical structure, relations which link residents to other families, to communities and the state'.[113] They had their own sets of ideals, morals, values and strange belief systems, including superstitions. Kapil Krishna Thakur has portrayed the continuation of the 'Hindu' value system by defining the concept of *pap* and *punnyo* percolating down the subconscious of the East Bengali mindset. He described in his novel *Ujantolir Upokatha* how a family rebuked another family for rearing chicken, as it might cause anger or *ovisap* (curse) of the *bastu-Thakur*. For that, the old headman of a family suggested them to conduct a *bastu-pujo* in redemption during pre-Partition days (Thakur 1412: 59). From this example only, one can understand the intense emotional attachment with the home or *bastu* in an agrarian society. That was the primary reason why the educated Hindu Bengalis of East Bengal could never accept their uprooted being, their degraded status as the 'refugees'. Previously, most of them actually perceived pre-1947 political events as struggle for their independence and then Partition came as a blow, in which others usurped their own land and home (Das 2008: 112).

The concept of 'home' or a spatial attachment occupies significance in refugee narratives. 'Refugee' was itself a difficult word to define, and even more difficult for them to identify with the image of being uprooted from their motherland or *matribhumi* and compromise in their accented dialect or terms of mother tongue or *matribhasa*.[114] So, refugees during a period in exile (in camps), they often stayed together based on ties to the homeland, what they called their *desh*, which often meant their root or origin, in a more lucid way, where they were basically from. Refugees associate memories and a bond with 'home' and continue to strengthen such ties in exile, essentially in case of further matrimonial relationships in arranged marriages. Simultaneously, many people could never identify themselves as refugees, even though they fled from their homelands as a result of political and religious persecution.[115] The experience of dispossession and nostalgia for their homesteads (*bhitabari*) has been constantly pronounced and glorified in their writing. For the *bhadralok*, the *kuldebata* has long been the focus for the religious life of the household. The *kuldebata* was typically treated as a member of the family. He was 'the eternal head of the family', who was responsible for the protection and prosperity of the lineage and he was supposed to protect the family's land and assets, the 'ancestral estate' (Ghosh 1998: 38–39). There were examples of some other common traits, like an almost identical feeling of loss or similar complaints, such as references of the rivers were often portrayed as a significant symbol in separating communities from their own motherland that reflected in memoirs and films. Apart from legendary works of Rwitik Ghatak, a film called *Notun Ihudi* (*The New Jews*) by Salil Sen depicted the crises and condition of homelessness of thousands of refugees. Nemai Ghosh's film *Chhinnomool* (*The Uprooted*) portrayed emotions of an old woman who was not convinced to leave the ancestral home (*bastu*).

The emergence of two nation-states out of one and making separate homelands for Hindus-Muslims, and their consequent displacement, resulted in a human tragedy of refugee-hood. Before the division, both the Hindus and Muslims dreamt of living in their own promised utopia, India or Pakistan. But within the utopia, the nation-seekers unfortunately did not plan anything concrete for them, especially on how to resettle and rehabilitate them properly. In pre-Partition Bengal, river Padma was a marker to define *epar Bangla* and *opar Bangla* (east and west Bengal). But after the official implementation of the division, the newly created international border became the marker to denote two sides of Bengal (Shamshad 2017: 439). In East Bengal, some of the families had taken the decision to migrate almost overnight, primarily those who were directly or indirectly hit by any one of the communal uprisings. But for most of the families, the decision of migration was deliberated slowly, and they shifted in many waves within the circle of the family.[116] There were many apparently insignificant, simple, secret desires and expectations left with them for the rest of their lives, which remained unfulfilled, regarding their homes, material and emotional assets or a just fond memory related to it. Anjali Neogi, a retired schoolteacher by profession, often mourned about some old books, which she had left in her *desh er bari* (ancestral home). In pre-Partition days when she was a kid, she could not manage to get permission to read quite a few books that were marked as '*boroder boi*' (books meant for the elders). She had sent to India with the first batch of the family migration and naturally lost control over that bookrack, which she always dreamt to inherit.[117] The migration of the uprooted refugee families was primarily for seeking refuge and a national identity. The landscape—through which the refugees passed and tried to rebuild a home, a new life and another identity—was a refuge for them. Therefore, in reality, they constituted a heterogeneous group on the other side of the borderland. The pieces of wastelands on which they built camps and colonies became a part of the city's post-colonial landscape (Sengupta 2016: 20). But most of the refugees from all strata of society lived their afterlives with some kind of emotional deficits and even died with the hope that someday their soul would fly again back to their motherland and they would reunite again by ignoring the artificial border and boundary. It was impossible for them to negotiate with their uprooted self in the wretched life of the rescue camps or in a refugee colony of a new country. Their concept of home, which used to conjure up images of family, warmth, security, emotion and stability for them, vanished forever.

Notes

1 Interview with Anisuzzaman, a retired professor, writer and an intellectual of Bangladesh, taken on 30 December 2014 in Dhaka, Bangladesh.
2 *The Moslem Chronicle*, 28 January 1905, Calcutta, p. 193.
3 Harun-or Rashid. 2007. 'A Move for United Independent Bengal'. In *History of Bangladesh 1704–1971*, ed. Sirajul Islam, 315. Dhaka: Asiatic Society of Bangladesh.
4 Interview with Satyajit Choudhury, a retired professor and former editor of *Banga-Darshan*, taken on 13 February 2014 in Naihati, West Bengal.

5 Interview with Bamacharan Mukherjee, a refugee from East Bengal and former councillor in the Shahidnagar Colony area, taken on 26 November 2010 in Kolkata, West Bengal.
 6 Bani Prasanna Misra. 2012. 'Jodi, Kintu o Sutorang Deshbhager kathakatha'. *Ninth Colounm-Deshbhag-Deshtyag: Prasanga Uttar-Purbo Bharat* 12 (10): 3–5.
 7 Sirajul Islam. 2009. 'Chirasthayi Bandabaster Uddesya o Folafol'. In *Chirasthayi Bandabasta o Bangali Samaj*, ed. Muntasir Mamoon, 155–56. Dhaka: Mawla Brothers.
 8 Khondkar Mohomed Badiuzzaman. 1332 BS. *Banglar Zamindar* 6–18.
 9 *Langal*, 16 December 1925.
10 David Lalyveld. 2005. 'The Colonial Context of Muslim Separatism: From Sayyid Ahmad Bareli to Sayyid Ahmed Khan'. In *Living Together Separately: Cultural India in History and Politics*, ed. Mushirul Hasan and Asim Roy, 405–7. New Delhi: Oxford University Press.
11 Bernard S. Cohn. 1986. 'The Command of Language and the Language of Command'. *Subaltern Studies: Writings on South Asian History and Society*, ed. Ranajit Guha, Vol. 4, 284. New Delhi: Oxford University Press.
12 *Report of the Census of India*. 1901. Vol. VI, 484.
13 Mushirul Hasan. 1996. 'The Myth of Unity: Colonial and National Narratives'. In *Making India Hindu: Religion, Community and the Politics of Democracy in India*, ed. David Ludden, 193. New Delhi: Oxford University Press.
14 Kazi Abdul Wadud. 1935. 'Hindu-Mussalmaner Birodh'. Nizam Lectures, First Speech, Bisvabharati Studies No. 6. 1.
15 Editorial. 'Nationalism vs. Communalism'. *The Mussalman*, 28 April 1932.
16 *Asr-e-Jadid*. Fortnightly report: Provincial Press Adviser's Report on the Press for the Second half of July 1941. 4.
17 File No. L/PJ/6/732, File 2640: 27 August 1905 (No. 28, Government of India, Home Department, Shimla, 3 August 1905), IOR.
18 File No. L/PJ/6/732, File 2695: 30 August 1905, IOR.
19 File No. PJ/6/734, File 3034: 14 September 1905, IOR.
20 File No. L/PJ/6/788, File 4020: 15 November 1906, IOR.
21 File No. L/PJ/6/796, No. 4 of 1907, IOR.
22 Ebne Maaz. 1314 BS. 'Bharoter Bartaman Rajnaitik Abastha o Mussalman'. *Islam Pracharak*.
23 Partha Chatterjee. 1997. 'The Second Partition of Bengal'. In *Reflection of Partition in the East*, ed. Ranabir Samaddar, 37–38. New Delhi: Vikas-Calcutta Research Group.
24 *Ganabani*, 19 May 1927.
25 T. W. Clark. 1967. 'The Role of Bankim Chandra in the Development of Nationalism'. In *Historians of India, Pakistan and Ceylon*, ed. C. H. Phillips, 439–40. New Delhi: Oxford University Press.
26 Imdadul Huq. 1310 BS. 'Hindu Mussalman o Bangla Sahitya'. *Bharati* 27.
27 John R. Maclane. 2007. 'Partition of Bengal 1905: A Political Analysis'. In *History of Bangladesh 1704–1971*, ed. Sirajul Islam, 129–31. Dhaka: Asiatic Society of Bangladesh.
28 David Ludden. 2010. 'Rethinking 1905: Spatial Inequity, Uneven Development and Nationalism'. Distinguish Lecture Series 2, Mahanirban Calcutta Research Group, Kolkata, 24–25.
29 *League Documents*, No. 1, 235.
30 *League Documents*, No. 1, 67.
31 John Gallagher. 1973. 'Congress in Decline: Bengal, 1930 to 1939'. In *Locality, Province and Nation: Essay's on Indian Politics (1870 to 1940)*, ed. John Gallagher, Gordon Johnson and Anil Seal, 269. Reprint from Modern Asian Studies. Cambridge: Cambridge University Press.
32 'Note on the Muslim Communal Question'. *AICC Papers*, Subject File No. G-36/1946, NMML.
33 *Langal*, 15 April 1926.

34 Asim Roy. 2001. 'Being and Becoming a Muslim: A Historical Perspective on the Search for Muslim Identity in Bengal'. *Bengal: Rethinking History-Essays in Historiography*, ed. Sekhar Bandyapadhyay, 187–88. New Delhi: Manohar.
35 *Resolution of the Muslim League on the Communal Award*, 25–26 November 1933, 57–58. All-India Muslim League Resolutions, 1924–36.
36 Sheikh Osman Ali. 1311 BS. 'Satyai Ki Mussalman Ghrinar Patra'. *Islam Pracharak*.
37 Kartik. 1344 BS. *Bulbul*.
38 Partha Chatterjee. 2001. 'Bengal Politics and the Muslim Masses, 1920–47'. In *India's Partition: Process, Strategy and Mobilisation*, ed. Mushirul Hasan, 258–59. New Delhi: Oxford University Press.
39 David Lalyveld. 2005. 'The Colonial Context of Muslim Separatism: From Sayyid Ahmad Bareli to Sayyid Ahmed Khan'. In *Living Together Separately: Cultural India in History and Politics*, ed. Mushirul Hasan and Asim Roy, 405. New Delhi: Oxford University Press.
40 Asok Mitra. April 1997. 'Dubte Raji Achhi'. Deshbhager Panch Dashak. *Ananda Bazar Patrika* 9.
41 Asok Mitra. 2008. 'Tanr Samay Ar Elo Na'. In *Abul Hashim: Tanr Jibon o Samay*, ed. Saiyad Mansur Ahmed, 165–67. Dhaka: Jatiya Sahitya Prakash.
42 John Gallagher. 1973. 'Congress in Decline: Bengal, 1930 to 1939'. In *Locality, Province and Nation: Essay's on Indian Politics (1870 to 1940)*, ed. John Gallagher, Gordon Johnson and Anil Seal, 275. Reprint from Modern Asian Studies. Cambridge: Cambridge University Press.
43 Mushirul Hasan. 1985. 'Religion and Politics in India: The Ulema and the Khilafat Movement: Communal and Revivalist Trends in Congress'. In *Communal and Pan-Islamic Trends in Colonial India*, ed. Mushirul Hasan, 24. New Delhi: Manohar.
44 Interview with Ranjan Sen, taken on 24 March 2019 in Kolkata, West Bengal.
45 Asim Roy. 2001. 'Being and Becoming a Muslim: A Historical Perspective on the Search for Muslim Identity in Bengal'. *Bengal: Rethinking History-Essays in Historiography*, ed. Sekhar Bandyopadhyay, 190. New Delhi: Manohar.
46 Interview with Kamal Lohani, a refugee migrated from West Bengal and leftist activist, taken on 27 December 2014 in Dhaka, Bangladesh.
47 *S. P. Mookerjee Papers*, II–IV Instalments, Speeches and Writings by Him, No. 10, NMML.
48 Joya Chatterji. 2001. 'The Decline, Revival and Fall of Bhadralok Influence in the 1940s: A Historiographical Review'. In *Bengal: Rethinking History-Essays in Historiography*, ed. Sekhar Bandyopadhyay, 300. New Delhi: Manohar.
49 *The Hindustan Times*, 9 September 1932.
50 'Political Comments by an Indian Observer', *The Hindu*, 5 July 1936.
51 *AICC Papers*, Pkt. No. 69, File No. 4, NMML.
52 Humayun Kabir. 'Among the Bengal Peasants'. *The Hindustan Times*, Sunday (Magazine Section), 20 May 1945, 4.
53 *The Telegraph*, 26 August 2014.
54 'Is Mahasabha Communal?' Draft of a Lecture by L. B. Bhopatkar, *Ashutosh Lahiri Pamphlets*, Sl. No. 31, NMML.
55 *Hindu Mahasabha Papers*, File No. C-8/1934–37, NMML.
56 Editorial. *Amrita Bazar Patrika*, 19 March 1947.
57 *APCC Papers*, Pkt. No. 71, File No. 5, NMML.
58 *Ananda Bazar Patrika*, 20 August 2014.
59 *S. P. Mookerjee Papers*, II–IV Instalments, Speeches and Writings by Others No. 16, NMML.
60 Saiyad Mansur Ahmed. 2008. 'Abul Hashim: Bangali o Mussalman'. In *Abul Hashim: Tanr Jibon o Samay*, ed. Saiyad Mansur Ahmed, 305. Dhaka: Jatiya Sahitya Prakash.
61 Asim Roy. 2001. 'The High Politics of Indian Partition: The Revisionist Perspective'. In *India's Partition: Process, Strategy and Mobilisation*, ed. Mushirul Hasan, 112. New Delhi: Oxford University Press.

62 *S. P. Mookerjee Papers*, II–IV Instalments, Speeches and Writings by Others, No. 6, NMML.
63 Taj-ul-Islam Hashmi. 1999. 'Peasant Nationalism and the Politics of Partition: The Class-Communal Symbiosis in East Bengal 1940–1947'. In *Region and Partition: Bengal, Punjab and the Partition of the Subcontinent*, ed. Ian Talbot and Gurharpal Singh, 6–41. New Delhi: Oxford University Press.
64 *Star of India*, 12 May 1946.
65 I. H. Qureshi. 1970. 'A Case Study of the Social Relations Between the Muslims and the Hindus'. In *The Partition of India: Policies and Perspectives, 1935–1947*, ed. C. H. Philips and Mary Doreen Wainwright, 363. London: George Allen and Unwin Ltd.
66 *Hindustan Standard*, 26 May 1947.
67 *Star of India*, 2 May 1947; *The Statesman*, 2 May 1947.
68 *Amrita Bazar Patrika*, 21 March 1946.
69 *AICC Papers*, File No. 135, NMML.
70 Joya Chatterji. 2001. 'The Decline, Revival and Fall of Bhadralok Influence in the 1940s: A Historiographical Review'. In *Bengal: Rethinking History-Essays in Historiography*, ed. Sekhar Bandyapadhyay, 310. New Delhi: Manohar.
71 Partha Chatterjee. 1997. 'The Second Partition of Bengal'. In *Reflection of Partition in the East*, ed. Ranabir Samaddar, 46–47. New Delhi: Vikas-Calcutta Research Group.
72 *The Statesman*, 17 August 1946.
73 *S. P. Mookerjee Papers*, II–IV Instalments, Subject File No. 147, NMML.
74 *S. P. Mookerjee Papers*, II–IV Instalments, Subject File No. 155, *AICC Papers*, G-45/1946, NMML.
75 *S. P. Mookerjee Papers*, V–VII Instalments, Speeches and Writings by Him, No. 27, NMML.
76 *Morning News*, 20 October 1946.
77 *S. P. Mookerjee Papers*, V–VII Instalments, Speeches and Writings by Him, No. 27, NMML.
78 Interview with Boruddin Umor, a leftist political activist, academician and writer, taken on 28 December 2015 in Dhaka, Bangladesh.
79 *Prabasi*, Aswin 1353 BS.
80 Abu Jaffar. 1380 BS. 'Milaner Dut Nazrul'. *Academy Patrika, Sarat Sankhya*.
81 Interview with Anisuzzaman, taken on 30 December 2014 in Dhaka, Bangladesh.
82 File No. 5/17/47-Poll. (1), Political Branch, NAI.
83 *Ashoka Gupta Papers*, Subject File No. 1, NMML.
84 *S. P. Mookerjee Papers*, II–IV Instalments, Subject File No. 148, NMML, *Hindustan Standard*, Calcutta, 7 November 1946.
85 *Ashoka Gupta Papers*, Sl. No. 4, Speeches and Writings by Her, NMML.
86 Goutam Roy. 2013. 'Galam Sarwar o Noakhalir Danga'. In *Bibhajaner Paschadpat: Bangabhanga 1947*, ed. Debabrata Mukhopadhyay, 236–37. Kolkata: Readers Service.
87 *AICC Papers*, Subject File No. G-65/1946, NMML.
88 Shatindra Nath Dasgupta. 15 November 1947. *Shanti Mission Dinlipi*: Kajirkhil Camp. Bulletin No. 3, 4.
89 *AICC Papers*, Subject File No. G-45/1946, NMML.
90 *Asian Times*, 14 November 1946, *AICC Papers*, Subject File No CL-8/1946, NMML.
91 Bibhutibhusan Mukhopadhyay. 1396 BS. 'Kolikata-Noakhali-Bihar'. In *Bibhutibhusan Mukhopadhyay Rachanaboli*, Vol. IV, 273–77. Calcutta: Mitra and Ghosh Publishers.
92 Prabodh Kumar Sanyal. 1413. 'Hasubanu'. In *Prabodh Kumar Sanyal Shatabarshiki Sankalan*, 95–99. Kolkata: Mitra and Ghosh Publishers.
93 File No. 3R-44/50, Govt. of Bengal, Political Branch, List No. 118, B Proceedings, B-53, December-December 1950, BNA.
94 Abdul Karim's letter. *The Bengalee*, 11 January 1907, p. 3.
95 Tarashankar Bondyapadhyay. 1385 BS. 'Uttorayan'. In *Tarashankar Rachanaboli*, Vol. XVI, 379–80. Calcutta: Mitra and Ghosh Publishers.

96 Romapada Choudhury. 2004. 'Korunkanya'. In *Bhed-Bibhed*, ed. Manabendra Bondyapadhyay, Vol. 1, 305–6. Kolkata: Dey's Publishing.
97 Mizanur Rahman. 2005. 'Kamalalaya Calcutta, Shubhonagari'. In *Bhanga Bangla o Bangla Sahitya*, ed. Asrukumar Sikdar, 42. Kolkata: Dey's Publishing.
98 File No. B. Nov. 1952, Vol. 7, Department-Home, Branch-Political (CR), Government of East Bengal, BNA.
99 File No. 3R-44/50, Govt. of Bengal, Political Branch, List No. 118, B Proceedings, B-53, December-December 1950, BNA.
100 *Hindu Mahasabha Papers*, File No. 135, NMML.
101 Ashrukumar Sikdar. 1991. 'Rajniti o Purbabanger Kobita: Samporker Karjyakaron'. *Chaturanga* 52 (4): 285.
102 File No. L/52/6695/202, BL Branch, NAI.
103 *The Azad*, 5 January 1964; *Amrita Bazar Patrika*, 21 January 1964.
104 *Ganabani*, 30 September 1926.
105 *Ananda Bazar Patrika*, 16 January 1964.
106 File No. L/52/1322/202, BL Branch, 1952, NAI.
107 Notice dated 22 February 1965, Office of the Commission of Enquiry (on the exodus of minorities from East Pakistan), School of Women Studies, Jadavpur University, Kolkata.
108 *Commissioner Prashnamala Puron Samporke Nirdesh* (Guidelines for the Commission), School of Women Studies, Jadavpur University, Kolkata.
109 Interview with Anisuzzaman, taken on 30 December 2014 in Dhaka, Bangladesh.
110 Adhir Biswas. 2014. 'Mogurar Smriti'. In *Partition Sahitya: Desh-Kal-Smriti*, ed. Manankumar Mandal, 250–52. Kolkata: Gangchil.
111 Shahidulla Kaysar. 2005. 'Sangsaptak'. In *Bhanga Bangla o Bangla Sahitya*, ed. Asrukumar Sikdar, 38–39. Kolkata: Dey's Publishing.
112 The term *bhita* or *bhite* came from a Sanskrit word *bhitti* that means 'foundation'.
113 Rechel Weber. 2003. 'Re (Creating) the Home: Women's Role in the Development of Refugee Colonies in South Calcutta'. In *The Trauma and the Triumph: Gender and Partition in Eastern India*, ed. Jasodhara Bagchi and Subhoranjan Dasgupta, 63. Kolkata: Stree.
114 Interview with Pratiti Devi, twin sister of Rwitik Ghatak, taken on 28 December 2014 in Dhaka, Bangladesh.
115 Meghna Guha Thakurta. 2003. 'Uprooted and Divided'. In *The Trauma and the Triumph: Gender and Partition in Eastern India*, ed. Jasodhara Bagchi and Subhoranjan Dasgupta, 101. Kolkata: Stree.
116 Meghna Guha Thakurta. 2003. 'Uprooted and Divided'. In *The Trauma and the Triumph: Gender and Partition in Eastern India*, ed. Jasodhara Bagchi and Subhoranjan Dasgupta, 99. Kolkata: Stree.
117 Interview with Anjali Neogi, a retired schoolteacher by profession, taken on 12 July 2013 in Kolkata.

1
ENCOUNTERING THE 'REFUGEE'
Crafting the policies

The Partition of colonial India into the two new bordering nations—India and Pakistan—in 1947 initiated one of the largest processes of human displacements in the 20th century. Partition on the basis of religion became imminent in two provinces, Punjab and Bengal. The conceptualised division had been implemented through the recommendation of the Radcliffe Award and South Asia thus experienced its first mass migration and relocation of communities. Division of lands, properties and assets was as tough as separation of population (Sengupta 2018: 43). The emergence of a 'new community' was inevitable with the Partition. These uprooted populations were initially treated as 'Partition-displaced' people who needed to be dealt with politically (Rao 1967: 1–3). Yet, the irony of the situation was that when the rest of the masses in both countries were engrossed in the discussion and experience of freedom, the 'displaced persons' were not in a position to plan their future (Islam 2012: 24–27).[1] Contrary to popular perception, the Partition in the eastern borders or flow of refugees was not confined to West Bengal only. It affected almost the whole eastern frontier, including northeastern states like Assam and Tripura, Lusai Hills in Mizoram (bordering Chittagong), Garo Hills, Khasi and Jaintia Hills in Meghalaya (Nag 2002: 21–24).[2] It was such a disaster that demanded separate attention. A huge segment among the middle-class and upper-middle-class people who migrated in the first and second waves did not even register themselves officially as 'refugees', though they added to the population growth of post-Partition West Bengal, Assam and Tripura (Banerjee 2017: 552).

Throughout the 1940s, major political events in India like Quit India Movement, Naval Movement and worldwide economic depression gradually were pushing the Raj to make concrete decisions about its colonies. Congress, Muslim League and Hindu Mahasabha had open discussions on the numerous probabilities of the transfer of power. Surprisingly, although the political leaders and the Raj were aware of the displacement that would be an essential outcome of Partition, none of them insisted on or cared about making rules and design definite policies for the refugees and other religious minorities. They preferred to leave the issue on the administration. When Partition had been implemented, it kept the Raj busy, as all the political parties and pressure groups in England were engaged in bargaining for a better deal (Tunzelmann 2007: 160–64). Yet the expectations, contradictions, undercurrents and signs of catastrophe could be sensed in both the geographical locations, though a bit differently (Page 2002: xix). The planners of Partition and the concerned authorities never could imagine or visualise the untold miseries of the homeless refugees and minorities in both countries.[3] Initially, a definite religious identity was the dominant identity given to them in government records. Gradually, they were categorised legally as displaced persons and finally as refugees, which subsequently became the only identity for them. Both the newly created nation-states ideologically agreed to provide space, privilege and preferences to the refugee community. But in reality, the policymakers and administrators were aloof about the future of these floating groups, whose socio-political and economic position changed with the ideological shifts or by practical needs. But they did not get so perturbed by the prospect of Partition, or see this community as a positive workforce, an asset for the nation-making process. They tried to chalk out plans in papers for the refugees, stamped them after a nod to finalise it (*Partition Proceedings* 1949, 1: 182–84).

After Partition, India adopted secularism as an ideology for nation building, when Pakistan sought to build a state by laws on Islamic principles (Chatterji 2013a: 41). The Hindu leaders of Congress and Hindu Mahasabha promised the East Bengali Hindus that they would get land and a new address on the other side of Bengal. West Bengal had always been a place of attraction for them. It was urban, had modern amenities, a flourishing industrial economy and a thriving city-centred cultural ambience, and moreover, appeared more sophisticated than the overwhelmingly agrarian society of East Bengal.[4] Hence, the option of permanent migration to Calcutta was tempting for some educated, salaried middle-class families which would love to move to the 'new paradise of Hindus' (Mukhopadhyay 2013: 50). The Congress leaders promised to resolve the problems of the refugees as their primary responsibility, as they supported them throughout in the freedom struggle (Kapil Krishna Thakur 2011, 2: 18–9). But in reality, when the migrated refugee families reached the other side of the border, their identity changed as 'East Bengalis' (Mukhopadhyay 2002: 31–41). Initially, they were even bothered by difference in accent, rituals or professions. Factors like regionalism, clan, class and caste dominated their thought in making of a new identity.[5] These factors were merged later when the tendency to incorporate such issues as a barrier in constructing larger identity comparatively became lesser (Kapil Krishna Thakur 2011, 2: 30–31).[6]

This chapter actually focuses on the making of border or boundaries and defines the term 'refugee' in regional context, keeping it under the structure of 'high politics'. It tries to argue that the process of articulating a historical milieu for understanding of the term 'refugee', and alternation of their identities, should be analysed against the background of the political culture of contemporary nationalist ideology, as well as the nature of Indian state. Thus, this chapter aims to locate diverse layers of complexities that emerged out of Partition, though the chief focus is on the process of transformation of the legal and other identities of the refugees. The design of an imaginary border and its implementation had taken in hand to mobilise the masses, the refugees, in both the nation-states. On both sides of the Radcliffe Line, the nation-states began to look at interests of the state itself and withdrew from their commitment to safeguard the uprooted populace and stay back of the 'uneasy minorities' in countless numbers as 'internally displaced' (Chatterji 2013b: 273). It argues that the journey of the major Indian political parties to attain independence and the ambitions of leaders actually left the masses, their citizens, on the edge. The Partition-displaced refugees were born out of the twist and turns of political events, social unrest, economic crises and religious obscurity that accompanied the nationalist movement. The role of the state was thus crucial in their case, as the design of geographical divide finally led to human catastrophe, and the refugees became the worst sufferers.

There were several trial-and-error methods experimented with the 'refugees' in the next few decades after Partition. Both the states, India and Pakistan, rather introduced measures to check the influx and discouraged return of the evacuees for taking over properties. For the entire eastern region, India and Pakistan agreed 'there would be no state-assisted evacuation of refugees', and it decided, 'The vacant property of emigrant minorities would not be deployed for the rehabilitation of incoming refugees' (Chatterji 2013a: 41). The ordinances of 1949 had taken over all Muslim properties from 'the affected areas', excluding West Bengal, Assam and Tripura (Chatterji 2013a: 41–42).[7] The Delhi Pact (1950) was the first major step taken for checking the flow of the migrants.[8] Introduction of the passport system, or visa regime (1952), and other regulations made the refugees vocal about their rights, by not trusting the state system or the words of the statesmen. This chapter scrutinises their journey from 'border slips' and 'migration certificates' to 'citizenship'. The trail of mistakes born out of the altering policies of the nation-state and consequent miseries made the refugees vulnerable. The chapter argues that when the states failed to define their roles, they started posing threats to the state system itself. India, the first declared and practising democracy of post-colonial South Asia, had painfully fallen short of the bare minimum expectation of this hapless category of humanity, created as a by-product of a nation-state making process.

Impending Partition

Though the social and political polarisation of communities started in the late 1930s, the idea of separating people along communal lines was not seen as something feasible. The outbreak of World War II realigned world politics, impacted the nature of power relationships and reshaped attitude of governance (Chakrabarty 2002: 138). It however inaugurated 'a decisive period for national liberation movement' and the Indian political parties were finally in a position to bargain with the

Raj for involving India in the war without its consent. It imposed a huge economic burden on India for a war that was actually not theirs (Dutt 2008: 430–35). The Congress and Muslim League tried to make use of the situation when the Raj indeed was ready for a dialogue. In March 1940, Congress held an open session at Ramgarh and declared that 'nothing short of complete independence can be accepted by the people of India' (McMahon 2010: 41). The right of Congress to speak for the whole of India had been challenged after two days by the Muslim League at the Lahore Session. Jinnah stated 'Islam and Hinduism are not religions in the strict sense of the word, but are in fact different and distinct social orders, and it is only a dream that the Hindus and the Muslims can ever evolve a common nationality' (Menon 1957: 82–83). While proclaiming 'the Muslims are a nation, and they must have their homelands' and demanding 'their territory and their State', Jinnah made a pointed reference to Ireland, too (McMahon 2010: 41).

The apparent reaction to the Lahore Resolution 'was hardly comforting to the League diehards' (Ambedkar 1945: 12). The sum and substance was to create more Muslim states in the East to include the Muslims of Bengal and Assam.[9] A section of Muslim intelligentsia like Liaquat Ali Khan and Choudhry Khaliquzzaman viewed Jinnah's scheme 'consistent with the idea of a confederation, provided the Hindu and Muslim elements therein stood on equal terms' (Hasan 1990: 49). When Jinnah first spoke about separate homelands for both Hindus and Muslims by dividing India into two autonomous national states, people immediately visualised a Partition and creation of Pakistan in due course. The polarity between twin Partition myths and unquestionable assumptions locked in a symbiotic relationship were 'the League for Partition' and 'the Congress for unity' (Roy 1990: 385). World War II brought a boom period in small trading, particularly in the West. 'The Bengal Tragedy' started enormously with the Bengal famine of 1942–1943 (Bose 1944: 83–93).[10] It caused misery at every level from urban cities to rural areas of Bengal, with a death toll in the millions. The idea of 'Golden Bengal well-watered, fruitful, abundant with crops', which was 'A garden of culture and civilization for over a thousand years', became the deathbed of between 3.5 million and 3.8 million people (Greenough 1982: 299–309; Bose 1990: 699).[11] The *New Statesman* of London mentioned, 'The description of life in Calcutta reads like extracts from medieval chronicle of black death' (Sen Gupta 2007: 98). Such catastrophes pushed people to migrate to Calcutta in huge numbers. With the increasing number of immigrants, Calcutta was growing like a city of immigrants. The 'up-country' population was settling down throughout the breadth and length of Calcutta in thousands. It was more like a continuation of economic migration from rural Bengal. The allegation of bringing biases and prejudices started forming against them. A perception that 'they invited unruliness' and 'were at times an irritant for the settled population of Bengalis' got cemented (Srimanjari 2009: 5). The urban space of Calcutta transformed into a land of anguished people, with a prevailing sense of insecurity, confusion and chaos. It was often called *aporadhpuri*.[12]

Calcutta witnessed a new social construction of the city during the famine of 1943 that continued up till the late 1940s.[13] Popular phrases like 'man-made famine' and 'famine came to the land' were not appropriate to define the crises through which Bengal had passed. The socio-political and economic changes were extremely rapid, and the nature of food politics of 1942–1943 was hard to explain. In the end, it completely damaged Bengal's rural economy, and deteriorating rural life played havoc with morale of the masses (Sen Gupta 2001: 452). These migrants were not like Partition migrants, but widened the complexity of the situation. The League, Congress and Communists jointly made relief committees (Umor 2014: 33). They ran community kitchens called '*longorkhanas*' in urban, *mofussil* and rural areas, with some other charitable dispensaries (Majumdar and Dutta 2008, 2: 17).[14] Politically, the Muslim League and Communists were benefitted in rural areas by earning peoples' gratitude out of these endeavours; the Krishak Praja Party was slightly on the back foot (Mukerjee 2010: 260). The 1946 election revealed the polarisation that the war years had fostered. The League leaders capitalised on the discontent about food distribution by winning the election (Batabyal 2005: 133–36). In the international scenario, the *realpolitik* influenced differently on the mentality of the British Government (Talbot and Singh 2009: 13). The crucial issue was to decide on how long the British would keep their hold on India. A post-war independent India still had no 'natural' shape. Jinnah tried to present the proposal of Pakistan as Muslim 'nation' (Matthews 2012: 178). Also, to set forth logic for demand of a separate state for the Muslims, Jinnah proclaimed his two-nation theory (Atikur Rahman 1995: 64–65). Nehru failed to urge the Congress to recognise the Muslim League because of his ideological mindset, which was reflected in last two elections (Huque 1985: 50–51). His 'lack of touch with grassroots reality' or 'self-delusion' made his conviction strong that even if Pakistan happened, it would be compelled by its limitations to return to the greater Indian fold again. It prevented him to take convincing position against crises.[15] Nehru and Patel promptly had rejected Jinnah's proposal of 'exchange of populations' between India and Pakistan (Sen Gupta 2007: 452).

After the failure to break the constitutional deadlock in the Simla conference (1945) or the Cabinet Mission plan (1946), the anxiety to maintain peace and harmony increased (Mansergh 1970–1982, 5: 1222; Panigrahi 2004: 338).[16] His Majesty's Government declared to 'take the necessary steps to effect the transfer of power in the responsible Indian hands by a date not later than June 1948'.[17] Being 'A skilful negotiator', Lord Louis Mountbatten mentioned a separate independent state for the Muslim-majority provinces. He declared that the representatives of the Hindu majority areas in Bengal and Punjab would be at liberty to opt for Partition of these provinces (Tunzelmann 2007: 161–64; Joshi 2007: xxi). Mountbatten managed to extract a tentative promise from Nehru, Jinnah and Baldev Singh in the very first meeting on 2 June 1947 that they would go on the radio and urge their communities to support the plan (Islam 1993: 186; Mosley 1971: 144).[18] Gandhi was the only one who was always against this idea of 'Plan Balkan' (making a comparison to the division of the Balkan nations). He gave his consent for immediate transfer of power with an alternative plan of 'a unitary Government composed entirely of either Congress or League nominees should be sworn in . . . but any such decisions was to be left entirely to Indians' (Matthews 2012: 205). After negotiations and approval from every front, Mountbatten announced his plan on 3 June 1947. The British House of Commons declared it officially as the 'Third June Plan'.[19] Both Congress and League had reached the 'moment of no return' by then. When Mountbatten tried to bargain with his plan a bit and it led to 'moment of truth' that the Partition became inevitable (Roy 1996: 55). In a press conference, Mountbatten casually announced the transfer of power would take place not in June 1948, but on 15 August 1947.[20] None of the political parties was happy with its terms. Nehru and Baldev Singh had not been in favour of Partition, and Jinnah said he was given a 'truncated' Pakistan (Bhabnani 2014: 3). The masses were made to imagine a paradise where there would be no miseries, as written in newspapers. The price of rice and clothes would go down, and tax rate would be reduced, after Jinnah would take charge as the 'King of Pakistan' and 'Gandhiji for India' (Ishhak 2010: 22). Saibal Kumar Gupta, a civil servant by profession and a social worker, remembered how the 3 June declaration on radio affected the disciples of Gandhiji who was then working in Noakhali (Gupta 1994: 83).

Border in the making

In Bengal, the real challenge was to meet up demands and expectations of the masses, along with political parties for the settlement of boundary between its two parts. It was apparent that the creation of a new international border required bisection of the province.[21] Organisation of a referendum in Sylhet was comparatively less tricky for Mountbatten, as the Bengali-speaking district in Assam would decide through a plebiscite whether it would form a part of Pakistan or not. Sir Cyril Radcliffe, an eminent British jurist, who neither had any experience in the Indian administration or politics nor any in adjudicating disputes of this sort, was personally chosen by Mountbatten as the author of the Boundary Awards of 17 August 1947 for both Bengal and the Punjab. The logic was, he 'should not only be, but appear to be, free from official influence'.[22] Radcliffe was not only unfamiliar with boundary making, he was totally unaccustomed to the complexities of the territory he was assigned to divide (Kudaisya and Tan 2000: 84). A Partition Council was appointed under his jurisdiction for the transparency of the entire method.[23] The participation of all relevant political parties was ensured for the democratisation of the procedure. Mountbatten personally got hold of activities of the Council by a declared post of 'joint Chairman' with Radcliffe (Chatterji 1999: 191).[24] He claimed later that he tried his best to check with the steering committee reports concerning the progress, including verifying proceedings of this Council.[25] The proposal, however, stated: 'The Boundary Commission is instructed to demarcate the boundaries of the two parts of Bengal on the basis of ascertaining the continuous areas of Muslims and non-Muslims. In doing so, it will also take into account other factors' (Mukherjee 1947: 8–9). The criteria of demography like 'continuous areas', 'other factors' and clauses of 'majority areas' added further sources of problems (Kudaisya and Tan 2000: 85). However:

> The Boundary Committee requested all pertinent political parties to submit their memorandum with their vision of division of the areas and particular reasons with explanations to the advisory committee. The report of the non-Muslim members argued 'for the purpose of arriving at a decision on the question of partition, the whole of Bengal was 'notionally' divided into Muslim and non-Muslim-majority districts, basis of division being the census figures of 1941.
>
> *(Partition Proceedings 1950, 6: 29)*

Congress, in its memorandum, highlighted that:

> by placing 73.00 per cent of the entire Muslim population of Bengal in the Eastern part, and 70.67 per cent of the entire non-Muslim population in the Western part it fulfils, as far as practicable, the main purpose of the partition better than any other scheme.[26]

The Muslim League laid considerable stress on 'lack of maps, showing union-wise communal distribution in the Office of the Director of the Land Records and Survey's'.[27] There were debates on the definition of units. Pakistan, as postulated in 1940 by the League, was geographically vague, except specifying Muslim-majority areas in northeast and northwest of India on the basis of 'geographically contiguous' units (Khan 1986: 38).[28] Both the League and Congress agreed that 'old *thanas* in Bengal' might be the smallest available unit.[29] The Hindu Mahasabha had maintained a stable position in its claims and counter-claims throughout this phase, and demanded radical alteration of the plan designed by the Commission. The Mahasabha declared that in the notional Partition of Bengal, 'West Bengal has got a population of 1,95,88,799 and an area of 31,919 sq. miles including the Chittagong Hill Tracts', whereas 'the total population of Bengal is 60,306,525 and that of non-Muslims in Bengal is 27,301,091 according to the census of 1941'.[30] They highlighted the social relationship between the districts of Bengal and claimed that 'boundary problems are really human problems as boundary divided people, not the land'.[31] But in reality, the Mahasabha often changed parameters in the statistical definitions.

Bengal indeed experienced changes in the attitude of its inhabitants and political parties as a region, just a few months before the Partition. Representatives of independent organisations like the Municipal and Union boards; civil groups like District Bar Associations, Zamindars' Associations and local clubs; and other political parties voiced their demands in support of creating a 'homeland' for the Bengalis and on issue of building a 'dream independent state'.[32] The actual reason was 'economic interests' and to capture hold in demarcation and fixation of boundaries.[33] There were tensions in sub-layers, between 'Hindu' and 'Nationalist' India, as it continued to be a moot issue. The Partition debate got linked with critical question of space and territory (Haimanti Roy 2009: 1365). At the national level, community politics was going through a dramatic change due to the acute differences in general outlook between the Congress and the League (Hodson 1985: 274–75). The leaders agreed on the idea that, 'Bengal [is] to be an independent State. The free State of Bengal will decide its relation with rest of India' (Islam 1993: 204–6). Later, the Muslim League placed a demand to incorporate Calcutta with Pakistan, as Calcutta was the administrative and financial headquarters. Their logic was, since the major portion of the Bengal Presidency would become East Pakistan, it was fair that it got the capital city of Bengal.[34] Jinnah was enthusiastic about the united Bengal scheme (Hodson 1985: 275). He commented in a meeting with Mountbatten on 23 April 1947: 'What is the use of Bengal without Calcutta? They had a much better future if they remain united and independent. I am sure they would be in friendly terms with Pakistan' (Mannan 2007: 268–69).[35]

Liaquat Ali Khan and Chaudhuri Mahmmad Ali, the League representatives in the Partition Council, had argued, 'Calcutta is pre-eminently a city of jute. As jute comes mainly from East Bengal, Calcutta should go to Pakistan' (*Partition Proceedings* 1949, 6: 38–78).[36] Transit and other free-port arrangements might help to overcome logistics. But, even if everything worked properly development would certainly be hampered (Spate 1948: 12). They opined, 'Certain wards of Calcutta have a majority of Muslim population. Hence, if Calcutta goes to West Bengal, then one-third of the total population of the province (66.9% of the total revenue) will enjoy them only' (*Partition Proceedings* 1949, 6: 39). As a result, East Bengal— with two-thirds of the population—will have at its disposal only one-third of the revenue (*Partition Proceedings* 1949, 1: 81). The British Cabinet Delegation firmly put the case of Calcutta in a special way.[37] Pakistan would mean exclusion of 'a large part of West Bengal including Calcutta, in which Muslims form 23.6% of the population'.[38] The movement of the Muslim League for 'keeping Calcutta in Pakistan' never gained momentum. Finally, the Council exchanged Calcutta for Lahore by compensation of Rs. 330 million (Chakrabarty 2004: 161–62).[39]

There were disputes between the League, Congress and Mahasabha regarding union-wise division of the province, for determining 'majority area'.[40] There was frequent usage of terms like 'Hindu Bengal' or 'Muslim Bengal', which had never been heard before (Mukherjee 1947: 21). From the beginning, Radcliffe pointed out his personal view that it would be wrong to 'draw the boundaries on the basis of natural features [since] rivers which may appear to form suitable natural boundaries, frequently change their courses and so will not provide fixed boundaries' (*Partition Proceedings* 1949, 4: 146). Professor S. P. Chatterjee, an acclaimed geographer, identified a natural boundary line in his monograph to divide the province into 'Gour-Banga' and 'Subarna-Banga'. He provided Radcliffe with institutional-written documents, maps, diagrams, tables and all his cartographic materials, but all effort went in vain (Deb Sarkar 2009: 21–23). There was discussion on communication issues relating to railways and other such popular means of transportation.[41] Radcliffe expressed that the primary consideration in drawing the boundary should be 'to eliminate any avoidable cutting of railway communications and of river systems, which are of importance to the life of the province'.[42] He hoped that, 'arrangement can be made between two States that will minimise the consequences of this interruption as far as possible' (*Partition Proceedings* 1949, 1: 311–12).

A perfect Partition of Bengal was practically impossible; the representatives of each group had their own expectations. There were a thousand points of disagreement between them, the people and the opinion of the administrators. There were disputes over areas like Khulna, Malda, Rangpur, Dinajpur, Darjeeling and Jalpaiguri district. But the controversy over Chittagong Hill Tracts (CHT) deserves a mention. Geographically, it was an isolated region, comprising Rangamati, Khagracherri and Banderban districts. Though CHT occupied almost 10 per cent of the total area of then East Bengal, the population of these three areas together makes only 1 per cent (Choudhury 1991: 10). Four rivers—the Feni, Karnafuli, Sangu and Matamuri—created a fertile valley there.[43] Its specific geographical position and Excluded Area status became a concern for the British policy makers (Chakma 1986: 162–63). CHT was a non-Muslim-majority area comprising 5,007 square miles. The Hindu Mahasabha and Congress demanded that CHT should join Indian union, as per the ratio of the population (*Partition Proceedings* 1949, 1: 56), but the League condemned their claim by pointing out the scarcity of coal in the notional area of Pakistan. The inclusion of CHT brightened the possibility of setting up a hydroelectric plant for Pakistan. The Port of Chittagong was an essential connection with the sea in the Eastern sector.[44] The League demanded: 'It is essential for the proper upkeep of the Port of Chittagong that the Karnafuli River should be under the control of the East Bengal Government throughout its catchment basin' (*Partition Proceedings* 1950, 6: 79). Though Radcliffe recommended that CHT join India, but after few days, it was transferred to Pakistan. The logic was that it would provide a hinterland to the port at Chittagong, and Karnafuli River would provide vital commercial and strategic interest (Ali 1993: 176). The inhabitants of CHT initially hoisted the flag of India, but the Pakistani army marched in on 18 August 1947 and took down that flag (Schendel 2005: 48–49). The CHT were bounded on the north by the Tipperah Hills, on the east by the Lusai Hills and Assam, and on the south by Burma. The League thus placed claim over Tipperah, which was contiguous to CHT and had no means of travel by road or river except through Chittagong division (Roy Choudhury 1977: 127). The Chakla Roshanabad Estate of the Maharajas of Tripura was part of Comilla (*Partition Proceedings* 1950, 6: 56). Another single route from Comilla to Agartala could connect through a railway station, Akhaura.[45] There were similarities in the mode of production, *jhum* cultivation and cultural likeness. The entire area was interdependent for food supply, as this region always worked as an economic and geographical unit. Thus, the League demanded control over the whole region on the logic that 'it should not be separated only on the ground of its high percentage of non-Muslim populace' (*Partition Proceedings* 1949, 6: 81).

The Sylhet referendum

The last challenging task for the Boundary Commission in finalising the demarcation of the geographical boundary of Bengal was to deal with complexities that arose around Sylhet. Demand for a referendum like North-West Frontier Province (NWFP) left the Sylheti-Bengalis in confusion (Sengupta 2006: 214–15). They were not sure which of their identities, caste, class or religions were crucial in determining their future (Ashfaque Hossain 2012: 8). Sylhet was historically a Bengali-speaking district, and was part of Bengal until 1874 when it was separated from Bengal and attached to Assam to generate extra revenue for the maintenance of the new province (Hossain 2010: 5). Sylhet was thus cut off from the larger life of Bengal and integrated with a new province where its people could dominate the job sector.[46] In 1905, Sylhet was again removed from Assam and attached to the new province of 'Eastern Bengal and Assam'. Yet, annulment of Partition of Bengal in 1911 led to the integration of Assam and Sylhet again (Baruah 1999: 40). Sylhet had a Muslim majority but was a part of Assam, which was not planned to be partitioned. Hence, it was decided to hold a referendum there to decide the future of the district. In fact, Sylhet was the only region of British India where a referendum was held. The census of 1941 had clearly stated, 'Assam, as a whole, is not a Muslim-majority Province. The only majority region in it is the district of Sylhet, which has been numbered and shown' (Mahalonobis 1946: 499). In the 3 June statement, Lord Mountbatten placed his arguments behind the consideration of referendum in the case of Sylhet by the Boundary Commission:

> Though Assam is predominantly a non-Muslim province, the district of Sylhet is contiguous to Bengalis predominantly Muslim. There has been a demand that, in the event of the partition of Bengal, Sylhet should be amalgamated with the Muslim part of Bengal. Accordingly if it is decided that Bengal should be partitioned, a referendum will be held in Sylhet district under the aegis of the Governor-General and in consultation with the Assam Provincial Government to decide whether the district of Sylhet should continue to form part of the Assam Province or should be amalgamated with the new Province of Eastern Bengal, if that Province agrees.
>
> *(Partition Proceedings 1950, 6: 3)*

It assured that the rest of Assam would continue to participate in the proceedings of the existing Constituent Assembly.

Sylhet was always a sought-after district for several reasons (Ashfaque Hossain 2012: 13).[47] In 1871, the Muslim and Hindu population in Sylhet were at 1:1 numerical parity, but migration into the agrarian frontiers increased the proportion of Muslims in each decennial census. Between 1891 and 1931, people reportedly born in Mymensingh increased from 31 per cent to 63 per cent, along with the population of southern Assam valleys (Ludden 2003: 15–16). Interestingly, in 1920s and 1930s, the Hindu Bengali elites insistently campaigned for a 'Back to

Bengal' movement, because few 'self-confessed' nationalist leaders were afraid of losing power and social position in a new province (Ashfaque Hossain 2012: 14). The Assamese dreamt of their own homeland. They viewed the Bengali-speaking province as a major obstacle for 'Assam is for Assamese'. Hence, a natural solution for them was to 'get rid of Sylhet' by any means (Bhuyan and Sibopada 1978, 2: 292).[48] The upper-class Muslims of Assam became increasingly powerful in provincial politics. Abdul Matin Choudhury, a 'trusted lieutenant' of Jinnah and founder of Assam Provincial Muslim League, declared in 1924 that: 'Muslims of Sylhet did not want to be a part of Bengal'.[49] The emergence of Mahammad Saadulla in the politics of Assam altered the previous political equation (Ashfaque Hossain 2012: 17). They were determined to make Assam their 'future free homeland'.[50]

The referendum was scheduled to be held on 6–7 July 1947. While defending the decision for a referendum for a district, Mountbatten asserted, it would enable people to 'decide their fate themselves'.[51] The Muslims campaigned relentlessly for the inclusion of Sylhet in Pakistan to avoid remaining under minority rule.[52] The Congress branch fought hard to keep Sylhet in Assam. In the 1940s, the population of Sylhet was 60.7 per cent Muslims, 25.1 per cent caste Hindus, 11.6 per cent scheduled castes and 2.2 per cent tribals,[53] but voters in the Assam Assembly for the Sylhet district were 311,707 Muslims and 235,808 general. The rule of acquiring a voting right was by payment of at least 6 *annas* to the government as tax.[54] This decreased Muslim representation in electoral roll from 60.7 per cent (total Muslim population) to 54.27 per cent. Mountbatten was rigid in conducting the referendum 'on the basis of existing electoral rolls'.[55] Therefore, he agreed not to involve tea planters or labourers in the vote. Ashfaque Hossain argued that: 'The voice of the indigenous-mostly Hindus but partly Muslim-elites were dominant from 1874 onwards. Pro-Pakistani *dalits* (lower-caste Hindus) and *madrassa* educated pro-Indian *maulvis* emerged as crucial players in the referendum' (Ashfaque Hossain 2012: 1). Drawing a new map for East Bengal and Assam was a defining moment in the region. Newspapers were publishing reports of a rift between the local leaders and followers of Congress and the League.[56] The campaign of the League sometimes suffered an ideological rift between Bhasani and Saadullah (Sharma 1984: 218–19).[57] Sir Akbar Hydari, the then Governor of Assam, and Liaquat Ali Khan conveyed their hope that minorities would help majorities in this area, even in voting.[58]

The result of the referendum shows the verdict on amalgamation,[59] with 56.6 per cent of Sylhetis voting for joining Pakistan and 43.3 per cent preferring to remain in Assam (Dasgupta 2008: 19). Sylhet relatively had less history of communal antagonism, yet few reports conveyed incidents of violence (Bhattacharjee 2009: 77). The government reported that 'the referendum was completed fairly and peacefully'.[60] Surama Ghatak, who had been brought up in Shillong and Sylhet, remembered that Muslims voted more in comparison to Hindus (Ghatak 2010: 99–100). Sylhet was separated from Assam for the first time since 1826. For the Bengalis of Sylhet, it was the 'last betrayal'. They felt 'doubly punished' as the fate of Sylhet was 'cut into pieces' (Ashfaque Hossain 2012: 32). Following the referendum, Hindu-majority districts of Ratabari, Patherkandi and Badarpur, and half of the Karimganj thanas of the old Karimganj subdivision of Sylhet district, were brought back to join the Cachar district of Assam (Ludden 2003: 15–16). Therefore, task of the Boundary Commission turned out to be relatively easier. While demarcating the boundary for Sylhet, Radcliffe claimed it was an outcome of the voice of people (*After Partition* 1948: 30–31). The Indian national press reacted sharply, describing it as the 'departing kick of British imperialism at both the Hindus and the Muslims'.[61] For many, it was 'self-contradictory and anomalous and arbitrary'.[62] The Sylhet referendum completed the final drawing of the borders of Bengal borderland. Its separation from Assam is sometimes referred to as 'Sylhet's return to Bengal', chiefly for linguistic and cultural affinities. Amalendu Guha described the referendum as 'a lifetime's opportunity for the Assamese leadership . . . to carve out a more linguistically homogenous province' (Guha 1977: 319). The outcome was greeted with immense relief and hope, but the relief of the Brahmaputra valley was short-lived. The Assamese leaders failed to foresee the massive migration of the Hindu returnees from Sylhet and rest of East Bengal after the Partition.

Sylhet became an alien territory after the Partition. A large number of Sylheti Hindus from ceded parts of Sylhet district began relocating in the northeast, especially in the southern parts of Assam (Dasgupta 2008: 19). The southern parts of Assam consisted of three Bengali-speaking districts—Cachar, Karimganj and Hailakandi—which set the undercurrent of conflicts between 'the Assamese and immigrants . . . against each other'.[63] Their displacement was 'without experience of direct violence' (Dasgupta 2001: 343). The government had no fellow feeling for accommodating them. A Cabinet meeting decided: 'Government servants who were natives of or domiciled in Sylhet and who were posted within the Sylhet district on August 14, 1947 would automatically go over to the Government of East Bengal, irrespective of their choice'.[64] Four hundred Sylhet employees who had opted for India were discharged by the East Bengal Government and were denied employment by the state government. The cabinet was against exchanging of officers. The Government of Assam addressed a letter to its gazette officers on 25 June 1947, intimating of the decision of the Assam Cabinet:

> The Government decision is that any Government servant who is a native of or domiciled in Sylhet and is posted on 14th August, 1947 in Sylhet should remain there irrespective of his choice to serve in any dominion and not be exchanged against an officer outside Sylhet who may have opted for Pakistan. The Government of Assam will take no responsibility of such officers after 15th August, 1947. Those officers who are natives of or domiciled in the rest of Assam and who may have opted for Pakistan will not be allowed for the time being to exercise their option to join Pakistan.[65]

In a fresh circular dated 22 August 1947, the Assam Government further insisted, such optees could not be absorbed in services of Assam 'in a manner that would be in excess of their requirements or create blocks to local recruitment'.[66] Finally, 1497 Sylhet employees including 422 temporary staffs were released from Indian Government service on 1 September 1947 (Binayak Dutta 2012: 1–2). The number of Pakistan choosers in Assam rose to 1,812.[67] Another 100,000 Muslim Bengalis opted out of Assam and settled into the Sylhet Haor basin, where vast tracts of lands were laid open for new colonisation. A sharp dip in the Mymensingh population in the 1950s indicates that new migrants came into Sylhet from other parts of formerly British Assam, including Mymensingh, which continued to be the origin of many migrant settlers on agricultural land in the Barak Valley. Migration across Sylhet into Cachar and across Rangpur into Goalpara became national issues, as they appeared tinged with threats to the national security. In the 1960s, total Sylhet population rose 60 per cent as a result of migration. Both incoming and outgoing migration increased and remained high for next three decades, spurred in part by wars in 1965 and 1971 (Ludden 2003: 15–16). This transformed Sylhet as much as any other part of the former British Assam.

The Radcliffe Line raised multiple disputes. As it was hurriedly drawn, much confusion occurred when the various governments tried to impose it on the ground. Radcliffe had less than two months' time to demarcate the territories. He used rivers in certain areas to demarcate the border. These rivers soon proved to be a major source of border disputes, as the rivers in Bengal delta frequently changed their courses. The Padma and Mathabhanga, for example, formed parts of the border between the two Bengals. Radcliffe trusted the locations as placed on the map, which often did not match with their actual location (Sengupta 2012: 1–2). The Commission was confronted with unclear and contradictory terms of reference, and the task was additionally hampered by claims of political parties, a strict and restricted schedule which made their task difficult (Kudaisya and Tan 2000: 78–100). Radcliffe had followed instructions of the Viceroy quite rigorously to scalpel through the map of India. He claimed to finish his task with impartiality (Chatterji 1999: 195). The result was exactly what everyone predicted. Technically, it was a bit feasible, but in practical application, it was 'a disaster' (Lapierre and Collins 2004: 354). Radcliffe was well aware of the disaster this division could bring and himself remarked while waiting for his flight to London:

> Nobody in India will love me for the Award about the Punjab and Bengal and there will be roughly 80 million people with a grievance who will begin looking for me. I do not want them to find me. I have worked and travelled and sweated- oh, I have sweated the whole time.
>
> *(Chakrabarty 2004: 170)*

Mountbatten intentionally deferred the announcement of the reports of the Boundary Commission. He felt the situation could even be worse after the declaration. Pamela Mountbatten mentioned a letter Mountbatten wrote to Patricia on 5 July 1947, wherein he wrote mournfully that 'I have boobed' and according to her, 'It was the only time he admitted it' (Mountbatten 2008: 115). The uncertainty was everywhere until the Radcliffe Award was announced. The blow on *dhon, pran* and *man* (wealth, life and honour) of the Hindus was started on a huge scale by then in East Bengal. It could also be felt by numerous memorandums and petitions given to Babu Rajendra Prasad requesting him to include their district in the Indian Territory.[68] Two contemporary newspapers of Malda, named the *Gourdoot* and *Maldah Samachar*, published such reports of insecurities on the eve of transfer of power (Sarkar 2013: 120–21).[69]

The refugees: legal definitions

Partition gave birth to a new community of people with a unique identity called the 'refugees'. The word refugee never represents anything singular. It meant a huge cluster of diversified groups uprooted from a country, struggling in an alien environment which was unfamiliar to them, for resettlement. The refugees proved to be catalysts between the two identical phases of Indian history. The term legally first found a mention in the Partition proceedings in 1947 (*Partition Proceedings* 1949, 1: 188). After the Partition, several million Hindu and Muslim refugees crossed the new international border that cut through the deltaic plains of Bengal, looking to rebuild and recreate their lives in the 'right' nation (Chatterji 2013b: 273). After the creation of 'truncated, moth-eaten Pakistan', the League leadership was occupied with thoughts of how to generate more wealth to build a nation for 'Muslim political community' (Gilmartin 1998: 1071; Basu 2006: 110). Pakistan was never apprehensive of mass migration and staying on of communities (Singh 2006: 5). Jinnah could make out, even if both the nation-states agreed on exchange of population; the ratio would be comfortable for Pakistan. On the contrary, Nehru decided to treat the issue both rationally and sensitively, instructed all the Chief Ministers to remember 'the human aspect of this problem and not to consider it as a matter of figures and files'.[70]

Sardar Vallabhbhai Patel pointed out policy decisions on refugees before Partition. He stressed on two major factors, '(a) the safeguarding of the property and other interests of the refugees and (b) the relief of refugees should be prepared by the Steering Committee for consideration by the Partition Council'.[71] The policymakers had to concentrate on procedure of resource distribution between two countries and how to share government properties and divide assets, rather than empathise with the tragedy of refugees (*Partition Proceedings* 1950, 2: 234).[72] The Partition Council highlighted five important issues:

> (i) that the refugees of one Province, who were now in a different province of the same dominion should be the responsibility of the latter only so long as there was no sense of security in the Province to which they belonged; (ii) that no refugees should be forced to return to their own Province unless and until it was clear that security had been restored and the Province had made arrangements for their transport, and was ready to assume responsibility for them; (iii) that the expenses of management of refugees' property should be a

charge on that property; (iv) that it was possible only to give an undertaking that the question of affording relief and compensation would be considered; (v) that no undertaking could be given that collective fines already imposed would be realised in full. Different provinces had adopted different policies in the matter of the imposition of such fines. The amount of these fines would be reviewed and whatever was considered reasonable in the circumstances would be collected.

(Partition Proceedings 1950, 4: 432)[73]

While looking at legal rights, care and protection for the Partition refugees provided by the Government of India, the state never treated the refugees as per the rules and conditions determined by international bodies like UNHCR (the United Nations High Commissioner for Refugees). India has attempted to regulate the status or protection of refugees by administrative means. In the UN Convention of 1951, there were suggestions to call for a democratisation of the rights regime for refugees from top to bottom, international, nation-state and local power structures (Samaddar 2003: 23–25). The Convention suggested that the refugees should have four elemental characteristics:

(1) they are outside their country of origin; (2) they are unwilling to avail themselves of the protection of that country, or to return there; (3) such inability or unwillingness is attributable to a well-founded fear of being persecuted; and (4) the persecution feared is based on reasons of race, religion, nationality, membership of a particular social group, or political opinion.

(Goodwin-Gill 2007: 13)

India faced another category of forced displacement, named 'statelessness', which posed threat to the national and regional stability (Banerjee and Basu Ray Chaudhury 2005: 26–28). This issue was noticed internationally in 1951 with some refugee-related concerns. The Convention of 1954 defined the status of a 'stateless person' as someone 'who is not considered as a national by any state under operation of its law' and confirmed that they comprised a different category like 'internally displaced person' kinds of clusters in South Asia.[74] India is not and never was a party to the 1951 Convention, nor was it a signatory member of the 1967 Protocol relating to status of refugees. Owing to the absence of specific legislation, the laws relating to the regulation of foreigners are applied to refugees with no difference made between foreigners and refugees as a separate class. In pre-Partition days, a Foreigners Act would regulate entry, presence, departure and rights of aliens, by which the Central Government could control the rights of citizens and outsiders in India.[75] As a result, refugees who had fled persecution became subject to the same rules and regulations as other foreigners entering India for any other purpose; no legislative framework has been developed for identifying and determining refugee status (Sarker 2017: xi). Later, both the Supreme Court of India and Human Rights Commission played an important role on the policymaking front, to address issues of crises related to the refugees (Ghosh 2004: 135).

After the creation of an international border, India had chosen to deal with the refugees at the political and administrative levels. The refugees were bound to depend on the benevolence of the state, rather in a regime of rights to reconstruct dignified living in the absence of national laws. The state tried to treat the first few batches of refugees through the politics of hospitality.[76] The authority somehow believed that the Bengali refugees would return to their places of origin after everything stabilised there. In the West, the characterisation of refugee was a 'critical component of Nation building'.[77] In South Asia, refugees were seldom treated as resources; they were rather seen as an onerous liability (Samaddar 2003: 24). The argument of the state was that they never considered Partition refugees as 'aliens'; the state welcomed them as 'co-religionist, as compatriots re-entering the fold . . . integrated at once . . . their integration was moreover, a right to which they were entitled by laws introduced during and after Partition' (Vernant 1953: 740). But the refugees were actually:

> the victims of the discursive power of nationalism, human rights, and most partisan kind of humanitarianism, no doubt, but at the same time, they were 'the active agents' of their plans, desires, dreams, conspiracies, piety, folly, intrigues, revenge and spirit of reconciliation.[78]

Their place of residence changed with the Partition, and their emotional attachment or earnest wish to stay within Bengal led them to the Bengali-speaking areas. They headed to neighbouring states, where some of their relatives or neighbours already resided.[79] The Partition was 'the freedom to be a refugee' for them (Sen Gupta 2007: 167). Yet, they suffered immensely from the contradictions between ideas, plans and policies. The crises became acute when they entered into actual physical spaces, confronted material lives and tried hard to absorb in the changed environment made of diverse languages, morals, customs, economic systems and legal frameworks.

While introducing policies on the migrants, the Centre tried to place an argument on the definition of the domiciles. The chief point of the debate was 'the refugee who came from Pakistan after the division was actually a domicile of India before 15.08.1947'.[80] The government first termed the endless flow of migrants as 'displaced persons', which reflects the dilemma of the state to set concrete policy decisions on them.[81] Then they started categorising them as 'Muslim refugees' or 'non-Muslim refugees' (Zamindar 2008: 9). The earlier religious categories were consciously replaced by the universal language of legislation, like 'refugees' and 'evacuees' in the late 1940s and early 1950s.[82] The varied experience of violence in the east resulted in a different definition of the 'displaced person' from the west. One of the earliest definitions of the displaced person in the east was that it meant any person who, in the opinion of the competent authority, 'was ordinary resident in East Bengal but on account of communal disturbances occurring from 1st day of October 1946, left East Bengal and arrived in West Bengal on or before the 31st day of December 1950'; 'has no land in West Bengal of which he is the owner'; and 'has affirmed in an affidavit filed in the office of the competent authority that he does not intend to return to East Bengal'.[83] A revised definition was adopted in 1955, which was more inclusive or definite. It defined refugee as:

> a person who was ordinary resident in the territories now comprised in East Pakistan, but who on account of civil disturbances or on account of the Partition of India has migrated . . . to the territory now included in the union of India, with the intention of taking up permanent residence within such territories.

In its final words, 'no person migrating after 15th October 1952 should be recognised as a displaced person unless he produced a migration certificate'.[84] The practice of formalising identities by the issuance of a 'refugee card' (as it was popularly known) became an important first step on the road to becoming a proper citizen-subject of the new state (Kaur 2009: 434).

To obtain rehabilitation benefits, the migrant had to produce a migration certificate, citizenship certificate or any document for opting a job through the 'option system', as a tool of change in jobs. 'Optees' were certain state employees, who chose to join the other state and were entitled to get a new job across the border (Rahman and Schendel 2003: 599). In case they failed to collect legal documents, a refugee registration certificate, a border slip, a border ration slip or even a certified copy of National Census Register was accepted as evidence of migration. The third step was to determine 'their status as displaced persons on the basis of circumstantial evidences'.[85] An 'evacuee' shall be defined as a person who left the province on or after 1 June 1947 and who declares the intention to return as soon as normal conditions are restored.[86] The broader coverage of the term 'refugee' subsequently changed. To put an end to the perpetual influx, 31 March 1958 was chosen as the cut-off date, whereafter migration from East Pakistan was considered illegal. The migrants who came during the period 1 April 1958 through 31 December 1963 were considered 'illegal migrants' or 'illegal aliens', as the Indian state saw no valid reason behind migration, except economic reasons (Samaddar 1999: Introduction). It is interesting to note how particular forms of rejection developed during the post-Partition period by the new bureaucratic forms. It led to categorise the refugees in government documents as 'foreigners', 'Pakistani minorities' or 'fugitives', who would not have the right to settle (Chakravarty 2011: 134). By using these terms, the state tried to portray a picture of the official alienation of the refugees, and the refugees were also denied any kind of state aid (Dutta 2013: 13). After 1971, with the Indira-Mujib Pact, the term 'illegal infiltrator' became part of the official usage.

The refugees: common perception

The official definition of 'refugees' changed time and again in the note-sheets of government files. Their identity altered with regional variations. Its connotations were also transformed in the local languages. In Bengali, generally two words denote a Hindu 'refugee', i.e., *udbastu* and *sharanarthi*. The term *udbastu* (uprooted from home or homeland) or *bastuhara* (one who has lost his homeland) had deeper meanings, as well, reflecting the violence involved in the process of uprooting and a strong sense of attachment with their lost homeland.[87] Thus the slogan that became popular in refugee political movement in West Bengal was '*Amra kara, bastuhara*' (who are we, who have lost their homes). The 'refugee' meant a state of destitute, helplessness and the tone of this term was kind of derogatory (Chakravarty 2011: 193).[88] Later, it became an essential identity of the refugees. They proclaimed their individuality and demanded due rights by giving powerful statements and slogans in their demonstrations, as '*moder kono desh nai . . . moder kono basa nai*' (We don't have a motherland, hence we don't have a home) (Bandyopadhyay and Basu Ray Chaudhury 2014: 11). The word *sharanarthi* or *ashrayprarthi* (who seek shelter/ protection) signifies the Hindu refugees. The word *sharan* (surrender of a human being to a higher power, including God) is a typical Hindu term (Zamindar 2008: 8). Another term used to denote this community was *chhinnomul* (uprooted from homeland) that also had an emotional connotation of having severed from their roots. The particular word reflects the sense of negligence of the state and its domiciles towards the refugees (Bandyopadhyay 2013: 69). The flight, in whatever situation, from one's homeland was a tragedy that entailed a common background for all displaced people rehabilitated in different localities, with different fates. This created a new socio-cultural category named *bangal* (an unsophisticated east Bengali), the common derogatory nickname of people of East Bengal (Bhattacharya 2017: 28). However, *bangal* was the most popular term to specify the identity of a refugee in West Bengal (Bhattacharya 2014: 31–32).[89] Ajoy Gupta, a refugee himself, later attached to the publishing industry in Kolkata (the present name of the former Calcutta) interestingly denotes how the word *buddhu* (stupid) was synonymous with the term '*bangal*'. In his school days, the word 'refugee' became his only identity (Gupta 2007: 63).

The refugee camps and colonies became signs of going back to the earlier days of civilisation, and women were the worst victims. The women refugees were in such a miserable economic conditions that they could not afford to oil their hair or use powder or a *bindi*. They rather worked hand in hand with male family members to run their families and protect themselves from 'other men'.[90] Hence, they were often termed as *jyanto Kali* (Goddess Kali in her most angry, arrogant, shrewish, tough *avatar*) and *khyapa* (rude and dangerous) (Kapil Krishna Thakur 2011: 43). Samaresh Basu, in his novel *Suchander Swadesh Jatra*, argued that the women became the 'colony *bhataris*' for the police or *babus*, just to get some portion of rice for maintaining their families and livelihood. But, these *griha-laksmis* left their *desh* to keep their honour and family pride. They disconnected from their places of origin and their addresses became colonies, about which they never thought. The author posed questions about why the leaders (planners of the division) who played with the lives of millions did not get punished for their acts (Basu 2003: 27). Amalendu Guha described the migration as self-killing in his *Swadeshe Sansar*, but Amar Mitra stressed his own set of logic in *Banhanshir Desh*. He mentioned that when everything became differentiated, he asked what is the point in staying in the motherland? (Sikdar 2005: 45). Yet, after settling down temporarily, the old residents of the traditional *paras* (locality) in Calcutta and its suburbs viewed the refugees as *aschorjyo manus* (strange people). They were astonished to notice that the refugees had no fear of anything living, except the ghosts. Sometimes they even termed them *bijatio danob* (uncivilised brutes). The categorisation as *bijatio bangal refugee* led to an identity like *bhindeshi manus gulo* (uprooted populace who do not have a motherland) (Kapil Krishna Thakur 2011: 32). The implication was demeaning, as *bijatiyo* and *bhindeshi* (alien) have a connotation of otherness. The sheer challenge of subsistence compelled them to eat things like *sak-pata* (herbs and weeds), or fruits and roots, whichever they could collect from open fields and ponds in the wilderness—especially that stuff that did not sell in the market, and the West Bengalis usually could not imagine eating them. This had brought derogatory social status to the community as a whole, increased its image as inferior species, uncouth and aliens to common West Bengali psyche. Moreover, the way they agreed to do odd jobs in their struggle for existence had further degraded their social status as a desperate category in search of livelihood.[91]

The change in the identity of the refugees was better depicted in the experience of Bulbul Osman, basically a resident of Howrah. He recollected, when his father opted for Pakistan and they moved from Jhhamtia, the East Bengal Government legally termed them as refugees, and arranged refuge and basic rehabilitation measures for them. Again, they had to cross the border during the Liberation War of 1971 for shelter. The West Bengal Government renamed them as *sharanarthi* when religious identity became merged with the national one. He laughed about his fate, saying that their motherland gave them two different identities in two decades after Partition.[92] In North Bengal, the immigrant East Bengalis were often termed as *bhatias* (outsiders).[93] The refugees were educated and intelligent enough to grab jobs or cope up in new technologies of agriculture in comparison to local Rajbangshis (Das 1982: 207–8). The *bhatias* were from higher castes and became the majority in urban areas. Amidst an uneven competition, the natives started losing lands.[94] Partition helped another category called the 'without' to emerge. These people were some groups of refugees who did not have legal documents to prove their origin or country of living (Biswas 2014: 9). Partition also contributed to the emergence of institutions, social categories and specific terms to define them for common understanding in West Bengal like, 'home' (which primarily meant for raped or single women) and 'hawkers' (refugee businessman who had chosen the footpath to sell goods and run his family) (Ghosh 2011: 56–58).

The story of refugee settlement in Assam represents an interesting contradiction. While in other states, refugees were seen in terms of their religion (Hindus or Muslims), in Assam, they were seen in linguistic terms, just as Bengalis. Assam had been experiencing huge Bengali migration from the colonial period. Eighty-five per cent of the Bengali Muslim peasants had come from the district of Mymensingh. They were termed as *Mymensinghias* (Bhuyan and Sibopada 1978:

308) or popularly referred to as *pamua* cultivators (Dutta Pathak 2017: 69). The British administration employed a definite educated Bengali middle-class from Sylhet, Dacca, Mymensingh, Rangpur and other districts of East Bengal, chiefly in the 'white-collar job sector', as they had the necessary educational qualifications required for such kinds of employment, but they gradually fell in a particular social category called the *bhadraloks* and the semi-educated clerks were known as *babus* (Das 1982: 25). Another category of Bengali Muslim immigrants had begun to settle in the river island, called *char-chaporir manuh* or *miya* (people of the *char*).[95] This term meant both indigenous poor, lower-caste Assamese and a unique diasporic community from East Bengal, who used to live in *chars* temporarily, during the dry, non-rainy seasons.[96] The *char* areas are geographically alienated from the 'mainland' and psychologically 'detached' from the mainstream population groups (Chakraborty 2014: 13–14). Some of them later settled permanently on the sandbanks of the Brahmaputra. They have been collectively seen as immigrants of the non-indigenous category who were a source of competition for scarce resources in Assam (Dasgupta 2000: Introduction).

The domicile Assamese community or the *khilanjias* first referred to the Bengali refugees in Assam as *bhogonia*, which denotes someone forced to flee from their place of origin (Bhowmick 1964: 1). From the early 1950s, the refugees started acquiring wastelands, grazing forests and capturing all white-collar jobs in Assam.[97] The refugees were then termed as *bongals* or *bongali*. They were seen in the same lens as tribes like *Khamti*, *Singhpo*, *Khasiya* and *Abor*, who were not domiciles of Assam and not willing to adopt Assamese manners and habits.[98] Yet, *bongal* was the term popular even before Partition, though it was attributed to Muslim East Bengalis, which was a bit derogatory in essence. In the later stage of identity formation, there developed strong hostility towards the Bengalis who were viewed as 'other'. The term *bhogonia* changed to *bohiragato* meaning outsider. The Bengalis were seen not only as an economic threat competing for similar job opportunities, but also as a political threat when they challenged the authority as potential vote banks (Nandana Dutta 2012: 219). There was a subsequent change in attitude towards them, as was reflected in their description as simply *bideshi* (foreigners), who hailed from *Bongal Desh* (Bangladesh). It indicated the complexity of the problem; they were seen as 'uncivilised' and 'impure' people, who did not match with others in the traditional Assamese society.[99] In the Bengali-dominated Barak or Surma valley of Assam, the uprooted refugees were even compared to a plant which grows very fast and is not of any particular use. The original inhabitants of the valley named the plant 'refugee *lota*'. During the Liberation War, another spate of refugees flew into Assam, some who wanted to stay back after the war was over. As per the conditions of Indira-Mujib Pact of 1972, the cut-off date was fixed as 25 March 1971 for the refugees who would be eligible for citizenship under the Citizenship Act of 1955.[100] The absence of fencing led to 'silent migration' into Assam. The Assamese domiciles, the political parties and other voluntary organisations like that of the students categorised and termed them as *illegal immigrants*.

The refugees were seen everywhere either as 'the offshoot of nation-state formation' or 'illegitimate children of modernity', who were marginalised in different societies.[101] The pattern of settlement of the refugees in Tripura was unique compared to West Bengal and Assam. Tripuris, or Reangs, were major indigenous *jhumia* communities in Tripura, apart from 15 other tribes (Gan-Chaudhuri 1985: 40–42). The Bengalis entered as *jiratia prajas* of the Maharaja.[102] After Partition, they started grabbing lands at nominal prices from the tribals. Tribal population felt threatened with the aggressions of this land-hungry people and termed them as *wansa*. Kumud Kundu Choudhury explained that according to the etymology, the term *wansa* derived from the *Kok-barok* term *wanama chhinchha*, which means scary. After looking at a Bengali, tribals would say *wansafaika-wansafaika*. It meant, 'they should be cautious about the Bengalis' (Choudhury 2008: 43–44). In colloquial language, *wansa* means the 'son of Bengalis'.[103] The reason behind their migration was economic rather than political before Partition. But after Partition, both the reasons subsumed each other. The word 'refugee' in legal parlance meant one 'who crossed an international border' (Kanitkar 2000: 1). It often acquired new meanings and changed its essences according to the change in socio-political environments. Pakistan classified Muslim refugees as *Muhajirs* to invoke Prophet Muhammad's historic flight from Mecca to Medina (Kennedy 1991: 942; Ahmar 1996: 1031). In Urdu newspapers, there was a popular word *panahgirs* which was used to describe the Muslim refugees in Pakistan (Zamindar 2008: 8–10). *Malaun* became another very popular word to denote a bigot in both the wings of Pakistan, West and East. In Dhaka, this migratory population was simply called *refu* or *rifu*, which had a derogatory essence, an abbreviation of the term refugees (Morshed 2008: 20).

'Border slip' to 'refugee-hood'

From the day of the historic 'tryst with destiny' speech, Nehru symbolised the spirit of India as a 'free nation' and the building of a 'developmental state'. He promised to try reconstruction of the socio-political order, reorganisation of Centre-state relationships for the development of cultural pluralism and extension of democracy to the grassroots (Das 2001: 6, 31–32). The East Bengalis did not experience immediate changes in situation after the announcement of Partition. The creation of the *ansar bahinis*, as ancillary volunteer wing of police, started treating the minorities and other political groups differently (Sen 2011: 34–35). Thus, trusting the words of Nehru, the first few batches of refugees were slightly relieved after crossing the border. They believed that their entry into India would be a mark of freedom from anxiety, insecurity and fear of being persecuted and tortured. In reality, the relief officials started taking money for registration of their names, and the staffs in the check-posts cheated them, too (Kapil Krishna Thakur 2011: 18–19). During the journey, the feeling of loss of the refugees was immense. After moving out from their roots in East Bengal, they had to compromise on several issues, including negotiating with their individual identities. The middle-class refugees were desperate to get a piece of land at a low rate for building a house so that they could recreate their identity by creating an address for them (Kapil Krishna Thakur 2011: 30–31). The most challenging task for the Central Government was to prepare immediate official policies for resettling them. But the concerned authorities did not encourage the refugees to stay, as part of policy decisions. The government had failed to understand the nature of the trauma they were passing through (Bandyapadhyay 1970: 15–16). The Centre was hopeful the refugees would return to their original abodes after the troubles were over (Bandyapadhyay 1997: 22). Thus, both the Central and state governments arranged temporary measures and bestowed 'transitional powers' to the officials of the affected states (Chatterji 2008: 128).

Apart from the elite Hindu *bhadraloks* who settled down on their own, the real struggle of Bengal middle-class and lower-class refugees began with the requirement of having a chit of a paper called a 'border slip' which was issued to them by the border officials as proof of crossing borders. It was essential for every refugee family to fill up a form or inform the officials of the country of migration. The refugees had to provide information about themselves, including total numbers of family members, professions, place of origin, what they were carrying with them and addresses of relatives in the other country (if any).[104] This was as per the requirement of the Government of India rules formulated for the purpose. It sent a legal definition of the term 'displaced persons' to all refugee-absorbent states.[105] The time frame fixed to qualify the epithet of displaced persons was from 1 October 1946 to 1 June 1947. Those conforming within this time frame were entitled to get a piece of land or the right to have a permanent residence within the host territory. The next initiative was taken for classifying refugees. The 'permit system' was introduced in September 1948 for legal resettlement of the refugees. The idea was floated to facilitate travel between the two countries. But the real purpose of introducing the permit system was to restrict refugee flow, which Nehru described as 'one-way traffic'. Pakistan conversely put up the theory that thousands of Muslims were coming from India by sea, so hence, the counting of incoming and ongoing Hindu and Muslim refugees or tally a proper percentage was difficult.[106] The Indian High Commission in Pakistan used to issue five different kinds of permits, for various categories (Zamindar 2008: 98). The East Pakistani Government objected to the extension of the permit system to its borders, as for them, 'security' was not the primary concern of that system; they believed that it would 'enable better control' of migration.[107]

According to the report no 3, dated 10 January 1948, on the socio-economic strata of the Bengali refugee population, submitted by Dr B. H. Mehta, 'the total population of refugees 12.4% belong to the poor class, 45.3% belong to the lower middle class, 26.8% belong to the upper-middle-class, and 15.5% belong to the rich class'.[108] The strategy of the Central Government was to initiate procedures for discouraging Bengali refugees to migrate permanently to India.[109] Jawaharlal Nehru believed that mutual agreements over this issue in an inter-Dominion conference could settle the problem. He conveyed that: 'India would stand by them in any serious crises', but it would be 'futile to expect intervention in day-to-day problems'.[110] The High Commissioner for India in Pakistan, Sri Prakash, said 'to take upon itself the responsibility for the protection of the lives and property of the Hindus of Pakistan' was impossible for the government.[111] A month after Partition, both the Dominions agreed to maintain conditions in respective countries. This was followed by the Inter-Dominion Conferences (15–18 April 1948 in Calcutta and 6–14 December 1948 in Delhi), in which an Indo-Pakistan agreement was signed off in April 1948 (Chatterjee 1992: 33). The official statement from the Indian side was, 'the Government of Bengal with the help and guidance of Central Government is trying to solve the problem as best as possible. Both the Central and Provincial Governments are intent on tackling the problem in all earnest'.[112] This Conference formed the base of the Delhi Pact. It had been decided that temporary relief would only be provided to the refugees; the government would not be liable or extend its hands for the permanent rehabilitation of these uprooted people sheltered in Bengal.

Partition created another group of people named the 'minorities', which became an identity for a religious group. Both the nation-states were compelled to develop policies for them. Rajendra Prasad, chairman of the Constituent Assembly, assured the minorities, 'they will receive fair and just treatment and there will be no discrimination in any form against them'.[113] Pakistan issued a similar assurance, too. The communal violence of 1950 in Pakistan posed serious questions on the future of the minorities. India and Pakistan agreed upon working on a pact which should provide measures for safeguarding the rights of minorities, even for employment in civil and armed forces of the respective countries.[114] The Nehru-Liaquat Ali Khan Agreement was concluded on 8 April 1950. Both countries declared:

> The Governments of India and Pakistan solely agree that each shall ensure to the minorities throughout its territory, complete equality of citizenship, irrespective of religion, a full sense of security in respect of life, culture, property and personal honour, freedom of movement within each country and freedom of occupation, speech and worship, subject to law and morality.[115]

The two most telling provisions of the Pact were the prevention of antagonistic propaganda and guarantee of the property left by emigrants. In reality, 12 million Hindu minorities remained in East Pakistan, amidst the Muslim majority of 32 million. Numbers of the Muslim minority in India was about 40 million, out of a total population of 335 million, at the time of signing the pact (Lombert 1950: 307). Minority Boards were constituted in all refugee recipient states as an additional safeguard. There was a provision to form a minority commission:

> Each Commission will consist of one Minister of the provincial or state Government concerned, who will be the Chairman, and one representative each of the majority and minority communities from East Bengal, West Bengal and Assam, chosen by and from among their respective representatives in the Provincial or State Legislatures, as the case may be.[116]

They were expected to 'keep up the spirits' of the minorities, dissuade them from migrating to another country. India and Pakistan also promised to keep channels of communication open in this regard.[117]

There were provisions for the safe return of minorities to the country of their origin. In some cases, the rules of Indo-Pak Agreements of 1948 and 1950 were relaxed for bona fide migrants.[118] The Delhi Pact initially ignited a light of hope in both countries, but the critique of the Pact later came not only from the political leaders, the migrants themselves commented on the failure of the Pact in building confidence among the minorities.[119] Reports of the Enquiry Commission set up by the governments were never published. So, experiences of minorities in both parts of Bengal could never be documented. Shyama Prasad Mookerjee declared on 21 May 1950: 'According to official figures about 40,000 Hindus have travelled back to East Bengal'.[120] Government and society both failed to raise refugees' spirits and give them a sense of social security there.[121] Dipesh Chakraborty depicted the nature of the dilemma within the communities in this phase. The psyche revolved around 'how Islamic ideas of the sacred might have been of value to the Muslims in creating their own idea of homeland or indeed how they might have helped create a sense of home for Bengalis', in consequence, 'it became dead without a vibrant community of Hindus' (Chakrabarty 1996: 2150). The respective administrative forces of East Pakistan were not cooperating with the returnee migrants. Some of them faced assault and harassment for the second time at the hands of *ansars*, Muslim National Guards or militaries at time of crossing border stations.[122] To top it all, the returnee Hindu migrants were disappointed with the treatment they received on return to their homes; their neighbours and relatives were unhappy with their return, as they had taken possession of their properties and were unwilling to return them. Some of them were already converted to Islam and could not come out to help them.[123]

A huge chunk of Muslims left for East Pakistan, too. Some Muslim villages in Nadia were completely vacated (Kapil Krishna Thakur 2011: 29).[124] For example, Nadia remained a Muslim-majority province after 1947 with 52.65 per cent of the population compared to 45.07 per cent of Hindus. After the Delhi Pact, Hindus comprised a whopping 77.03 per cent and Muslim population was drastically reduced to 22.36 per cent in 1951. So, 'there has been a reversal of the position by the influx of Hindu population from East Bengal' (Subashri Ghosh 2008: 853–62).[125] The returnee Muslims mostly got legal right over their properties and jobs. Renuka Roy noted:

> 12320 applications were filed by the Muslims for the restoration of properties . . . Restoration was refused in 4933 cases either because the migrant had not returned in time or they had already exchanged their properties . . . 1547 applicants already got back their lands under the Evacuee Property Act and 4750 by amicable settlement.[126]

The 1961 Census shows Muslims who came back after the Delhi Pact preferred to stay in Muslim-majority districts like Malda, Murshidabad and West Dinajpur, as Muslim population increased remarkably in those districts (60, 35 and 51 per cent, respectively) (Roy 2015: 30). The Delhi Pact was framed for regulating refugee influx in the east. It ended up resulting in quite the opposite (Chakravarty 2014: 26).

Regime of certificates: passport and visa

After the riot of 1950, authorities were forced to introduce provisions for the permanent settlement of the minorities in their new country. The idea of issuance of a Migration Certificate came out of compulsions, to make procedures transparent and simple. In legal words, 'the Migration Certificate is issued only to a person who leaves the country of origin for good and with no intention of returning'. It stated:

> The Migration Certificate is delivered to the check-post of entry in the country of destination and legally has no other effect except to permit the migrant to cross the border . . . and after, therefore, be unable to return to that country, should he later wish to do so, unless he obtains a Repatriation Certificate or other permission of the country of origin to return.[127]

Carrying a travel document was made compulsory. Getting Migration Certificate was the only proof that they were 'genuine migrant', for which they used to wait for long months in queues.[128] Pakistan hence launched 'emergency certificates' for people who came to India before 1952 and wished to leave this country by authorised routes.[129] The India–Pakistan passport emerged as a new document that shifted its role from 'being a travel document' to 'a means of controlling movements'.[130] Nehru perceived the introduction of the passport system as it would 'confirm once and for all the loyalties of the national to the Nation'.[131] It established a state-recognised national identity and declared territory of the other land as 'foreign', distinguishing between 'citizens' and 'aliens' (Zamindar 2008: 162). The Pakistan Government initiated introduction of passports to stop monitoring on migration through the Permit System and Migration Certificates. Their argument was that the decision of issuing passports along with visa stamps might change the experiences of the migratory populace, their harassment in hands of intermediary classes while crossing borders.[132] The passport was not merely a travel document; it was also meant to prove one's citizenship. It gives an individual the right to go out from the nation-space of someone's origin and ensures the right to return to that territory again.

The political developments in East Bengal against West Pakistan and the fear of Bengali nationalism during the Language Movement of 1952 generated reactions and compelled the Centre to introduce the system hurriedly.[133] The Movement of 1952 was seen and projected as a conspiracy of Bengali Hindu intellectuals against the Pakistan Government, in which communists were on the prime list of suspects.[134] The authorities felt that instigation or inspiration for such seditious activities could come across the borders (Umor 2012b: 349). Hence, there was an urge to keep a closer watch on the boundary. India accepted this idea later, as it was contradictory to the provisions of the Delhi Pact, designed in favour of 'freedom of movements'.[135] The simplification of travel procedures and the relaxation of restrictions of the Foreigners' Registration Act was declared as the intention behind the introduction of the passport system.[136] Visa regulation was integral to the passport system, was designed to 'give(s) an individual the permission to enter a foreign territory for particular purposes that also legitimate "means of movement" for a specific period' (Sengupta 2012: 6). The 'Indo-Pakistan Passport and Visa Scheme' was first announced on 15 October 1952. It was reviewed at the Indo-Pakistan Passport Conference held in Delhi (January–February 1953).[137]

In April 1955, General Iskandar Mirza, then Pakistani Minister for Interior Security, and Shri Mehr Chand Khanna, Indian Minister for Rehabilitation, spoke on liberalisation of travel facilities further, by a change in issuance rule of passports or categorising several types of visas.[138] There would be no change with regard to diplomatic, non-diplomatic and official visas.[139] They kept the existing system of travel on emergency certificates or migration certificates open and declared that these facilities had to be continued for the *pardanashin* women.[140] There were allegations and counter-allegations on the handling of the passport and visa regulations. Another procedure for entering into the Indian territories after 1952 was by obtaining a Pakistani passport with an Indian visa stamp. In such cases, one had to surrender Pakistani passport once in India and would apply for Indian citizenship.[141] Later, surrendering the passports was not necessary. It was decided that they would be given indefinite extensions on visas and would be permitted to travel all over India without any hindrance until citizenship rules came into force (Chakravarty 2011: 200).[142] At the Passport Conference in 1953, the Government of Pakistan was informed that the number of visas issued by the Indian visa office, Dacca was far greater than the number of visas issued by the Pakistan visa office at Calcutta.[143] The Indian Visa Office requested the Pakistan authorities to be liberal in their visa policies. There were many applicants in India who wished to visit East Bengal to look at their properties left behind.[144]

The passport and visa regulations were not the first step towards initiating a paper regime on the border. From 16 April 1949, persons willing to leave East Pakistan had to show a certificate issued by the Income Tax Department showing that they had paid their due taxes. People who were leaving Pakistan permanently had to prove that they had cleared all their dues (Sengupta 2012: 7).[145] It complicated the procedures of legal migration, especially for those families, whereby some of the members managed to migrate but others were hoping to cross the border soon.[146] The rule to get a valid passport was 'Each application form should include a certificate from a responsible person as to the correctness of the statements made therein' along with filling up a 'Form of guarantee to be executed by persons who already hold passports'.[147] The Minority Ministers of India and Pakistan jointly suggested changes in passport rules by saying, 'you had to go behind the passport system and find out what it was that is the background of the scare'.[148] There were thousands of reports of regular harassment in getting Indian passports and visas in the Migration office at 97, Baze Kakrail, Dacca.[149] The whole procedure became complex to handle by the uneducated common villagers of rural Bengal. The cost of getting a travel document was expensive considering the economic condition of the ordinary people.[150] Thousands of rustic populace from corners of East Pakistan had to stay in Dacca in miserable conditions for again, an unprecedented period to get information about scrolling number of passports and visas.[151] Four copies of photo cost Rs. 10 in the then Pakistani currency. Besides, a class of lawyers who had an expertise in passport matters used to charge Rs. 40 per head for their services to secure a passport. Border police used to snatch at least Rs. 22 for the goods carried by the migrants.[152] After all the hardships of securing a passport and visa, if someone in a family (especially old members or children) failed to get it at the same time, the headman of the family had to apply for a repatriation certificate. Issuing a repatriation certificate was even more difficult. The Deputy High Commissioner could decide to reject it on any ground.[153] It was decided that 'repatriation certificates should be issued to applicants liberally unless Visa Officers had specific reasons for refusal, in which case, the applications should be referred to the State Governments concerned for decision'.[154]

Letters of complaint from the refugees to the authorities, including one stating:

> the present cessation of the inflow of immigrants from East Pakistan is mainly, if not solely, due to the heavy barrier created by the imposition of the passport-visa system. This is the real cause of the abrupt waning of evacuation from East Pakistan. If there be any doubt about it in any quarter, let the barrier be removed, say for a fortnight and the result will certainly dispel all doubts.[155]

On 2 November 1952, Jawaharlal Nehru proclaimed at a press conference in Delhi that 'the situation with regard to the influx of the refugees from East Bengal had improved since the introduction of the passport system, and apart from the conditions of the minority community which were not happy, the situation in East Pakistan was more or less normal'.[156] Jogendranath Mandal, the Hindu Cabinet member in East Pakistan, commented:

> The influx of refugees from East Bengal was bound to stop since the introduction of the passport system because the intending migrants, 90% of whom are poor and rural people, are not in a position to secure passport and visa for want of money and proper knowledge of passport rules. That there are not many people now coming over from East Bengal, as has been said by the PM is no indication that either the situation has improved or that confidence of the minorities has been improved. . . . The real situation is this: there is not a single Hindu in East Bengal today who feels that his life and honour are secure there. There is not a single Hindu who does not want to leave East

Bengal. But the reason that has compelled him to stay there is his apprehension to uncertain future in his new land of migration.[157]

Citizenship issues: property regulations

Regulations and changing criteria to get citizenship, and rules about the properties left by the so-called minorities or encroaching new ones to settle down the upcoming refugees, became the crucial decision for both of the new-born countries in South Asia. India became a republic on 26 January 1950. Declaration of the date led to finality in issues like nationality and determination of citizenship. Registering oneself as potential Indian citizen and rules to include someone's name in the first census or participation in the first general election got a deadline, too. Initially, it was decided that the migrants coming after independence but before 19 July 1948 were included as citizens if 'he or any of his parents or grandparents were born in undivided India (including Pakistan), and he has been ordinarily resident in India since his migration'.[158] But, 'those who migrated after that cut-off date but before 26 July 1949 (last day of distribution of refugee registration certificates) would be accepted as a citizen only if he has applied for and obtained registration as a citizen and possesses a citizenship certificate'. Finally, it was mentioned, 'No person who had migrated from Pakistan to India on or after 25 July 1949 can be an Indian Citizen'.[159] Shyama Prasad Mookerjee pointed out that the nature of migration in Bengal was a continual process; hence, fixing a deadline would be a problem. He rather insisted the 'only criteria for admission of citizenship [be] whether the migrants intend to live in Indian Territory or return to Pakistan'.[160] After crossing of the border and settling down temporarily in the other land, the next step for refugees was acquiring Citizenship Certificates. It was mandatory for the 'optees' to get a new occupation in the host country.[161] For them, a Repatriation Certificate was also a must to get a citizenship.[162]

After much deliberation, the Indian Citizenship Act of 1955 was passed and it determined, 'those who came after the prescribed date, could be granted Indian citizenship provided they had completed one year of residence in India'.[163] The Citizenship Act of 1955 came into force in India on 30 December 1955. Two assurances were given:

> (i) No fee will be charged from displaced persons from Pakistan for registration as Indian citizens under section 5 (1) (a) of the Act. (ii) Alien women married to Indian citizens will be required to renounce their original citizenship before they are registered as Indian citizens.[164]

Many Pakistani women married to Indian citizens registered as 'alien women' category and managed to get citizenship under this section.[165] These Citizenship provisions (Articles 5–9) were brought into force on 26 November 1949, in advance of the Indian Constitution itself (Zamindar 2008: 106). In 1956, documents of registration found for 3,60,000 Bengali refugees in West Bengal, Assam and Tripura fell in the category of 'eligible displaced persons'. After the Citizenship Act started working, at least 25 lakhs of Hindus came in these states.[166] Another imperative for the refugees was to deal with properties they left in the country they used to belong. From the second half of 1950, six million refugees (according to the official statistics) started to make demands on their properties valued at Rs. 4 billion left behind.[167] Six conferences were arranged until 1949, but nothing constructive came out. The last hope was getting compensation from the Government of Pakistan. The Indian Government asked for compensations either by cash or in form of bonds, if not something like an exchange of properties.[168] They started raising questions on evacuee properties, too. Their argument was that the Government of Pakistan might levy some kind of tax on the properties; so equivalent funds might be raised to give those amounts as compensation to the refugees,[169] but the pledge was rejected and no tangible result had come out until 26 June 1950.[170] The Government of Pakistan categorised differences between movable/immovable properties and defined them. They argued that all district officers were instructed (by the early 1950s) that they 'should transmit the property or the amounts, as the case may be, to the diplomatic representatives of the other country, along with a list of owners of the property'.[171] Later, they decided to treat the properties as vested property and put them all in the Evacuee Property Management Committee under provisions of Act XXIV of 1951 with effect from 14 April 1952.[172] The rule was a temporary relief for the refugees. It clearly stated, 'an evacuee in respect of vested property have been made payable to the committee alone and nobody else has the right to give a valid discharge'.[173]

The Congress and Hindu Mahasabha rejected provisions adopted by the Government of Pakistan and accepted by the Provincial Government of East Pakistan.[174] In India, the Act used for property issues and land transfers between both the countries was The Rehabilitation of Displaced Persons and Eviction of Persons in Unauthorised Occupation of Land Act, 1951. It was introduced in 1951, modified in 1958 as per requirements of the state governments and customised up to 1 April 1962.[175] With few fresh clauses, it was renamed as The Rehabilitation of Displaced Persons and Eviction of Persons in Unauthorised Occupation of Land Act, (Amendment) Ordinance, 1958, under Article 213 (1) of the Constitution of India (promulgation of Ordinance). Interestingly, 2,58,117 Muslim evacuees came back from Pakistan, before the introduction of the passport system. They got their houses back, with necessary loans provided by the state government, based on the policy of the Centre, but the rule was applicable to those Muslims who applied for homecoming before 31 March 1951. For the next stage, the cut-off time period was fixed up to 31 March 1959.[176] Pakistan argued the respondents against the Act was 'not be found absentee, evacuee or refugee from Pakistan but are foreigners in Pakistan, therefore, Evacuee Property Act is not applicable to them'.[177] It placed a similar number of cases to claim evacuee property for transfer to the other Dominion with false documents. The modification of draft notified by West Bengal, Assam and Tripura relating to the extension of conferment of rights, with regard to restoration of the property of the evacuee *bargadars*, was prepared in the Chief Secretaries Conference first in 1952, then updated in 1959 and 1963.[178] A provision was included in the West Bengal Evacuee Property Act, 1951 and then it extended to Assam and Tripura. Under this provision, 'the evacuee *bargadars* are eligible to secure the same rights in regard to restoration of property as would accrue to other migrants under that Act'.[179] In the special provision (5a), it added:

> where an evacuee who, as a *bargadar*, was in actual possession of any agricultural land on or after the 15th day of August, 1947, has returned to states in Indian Dominion before the expiry of the appointed day and makes or had made, before the expiry of one month from the commencement of the Evacuee Property Act, 1951.[180]

It became a clause in the Assam and East Bengal Act.[181]

The citizenship regimes of India and Pakistan shared remarkably significant symmetries. In 1947, they did not place restrictions on the movement of refugees on both sides of the subcontinent. After migration, the minorities from the other country, India or Pakistan, refused to be sacrificed. They claimed affective belonging to their putative homelands, demanded compensations for their displacement and loss of homes and expected to become citizens in the host societies (Sen 2018: 6). Both the states produced a new figure named 'the minority citizen'—neither citizen nor alien, but a hybrid subject of national regimes of identification and law (Chatterji 2012: 1051). From the mid-1960s, the Indian Government implemented a number of administrative measures to limit the refugees in respect to citizenship and who should be allowed to remain in India. After the Liberation War of 1971, thousands of people found themselves on the 'wrong' side of the border. The government attempted to distance itself from the idea of the 'citizen-refugee' in case of treating the 1971 refugees. Those who were not returning home and intended to stay in India, seen as 'infiltrators' or 'foreigners', could not claim a right of residence. Citizenship remained a contentious issue for an individual who crossed an international border. Therefore, the question of accommodating the refugees within the paradigm of citizenship has remained unresolved (Chowdhory 2018: 10).

Last words

The Partition had created a border, divided lands and led to major human catastrophe. In the creation of a new socio-economic–political group, with one basic take-off point, composed of different castes and class backgrounds, bracketed under the pejorative identity of 'refugees'. The newly created two nation-states were ideologically not the same, as India proclaimed to establish its image as a 'liberal, secular state' to the world, whereas Pakistan declared itself a 'Muslim state'. There were some policy decisions taken jointly by India and Pakistan, like on 'refugees' and 'minorities'. But, in practice, it fell out into diverse categories. The states were new, and they could not take concrete decisions on them. Surprisingly, they did not opt for international guidelines to deal with the problems. From 1948 onwards, the Centre in both countries attempted to discourage migration. Nehru first tried to assure the Hindus that the overall situation of East Bengal was improving, when in reality it was deteriorating (Chakravarty 2011: 193). The Nehru-Liaquat Agreement (Delhi Pact of 1950) was signed in this particular background. Interestingly, the critique of the Pact came not only from the political leaders, but the migrants themselves commented on the failure of the Pact in building confidence among the minorities.[182] It was the first step. There were many provisions and rules implemented by the Central and state governments to stop refugee inflow. The nationalist leaders who had taken part in the struggle of independence promised the masses and minorities to provide protection and care on the other side of the country. Yet, the post-Partition scenario was scary for both the states, as they could not visualise the size of the migrant populace. The Central Governments in both India and Pakistan started crafting policies for Partition-displaced refugees, as well as the problem of their resettlement. Bengal, as a state, experienced further discrimination by the politics of favouritism; it also suffered due to its geographical location. The problem of the eastern border and Bengali refugees was already there; the changing situation became the key cause of altering policies. The nature of the problems was not homogenous; it was uneven not only in different states, but also for diverse classes and caste groups.

Despite the interchangeable usage in everyday parlance, 'refugee' was more than a literal expression of homelessness and insecurity, and less than a full legal categorisation in the administration of displaced people. The identity of refugee was affixed through official registration of displaced persons as refugees. An important ritual was performed upon arrival when a refugee card with name, registration number and date of arrival was issued. This card was an essential proof in gaining a ration card, temporary and permanent housing, admission to educational institutions and employment earmarked for the Partition migrants (Kaur 2009: 434). The Centre used terms like 'refugee', 'displaced persons', 'evacuees' and 'migrants' according to their convenience, but such inconsistencies in the official definition made the relief and rehabilitation work more difficult. In the post-Partition West Bengal, Assam and Tripura, refugees were often perceived as 'other'. Interestingly, the term '*bangal*' was always used to define one's identity as 'east Bengalis', though it generally meant the inhabitants living on the other side of river Padma. But after Partition, the '*bangal*' identity got merged with East Bengali refugees and minorities. The idea of '*ghoti*' and '*bangal*' also changed its dimension. The process of 'othering' between the Hindu refugees and the unwelcomed Muslim refugees was a strategy employed to exclude them from claiming citizenship rights. But the refugees demanded that the state should drop these labels and accept them as 'citizens', as they were the victims of the 'high politics' of Partition (Dasgupta 2016: 20–21). In the historiography of Partition and refugee studies, their definition and connotations had gradually changed. Interestingly, refugees were starting to be seen as a monolithic category, and policies meant for them also altered as per the need of time in several decades. In the time of local crises and need, it again shaped up diversely in different states. In effect, the refugees, as human beings, suffered throughout within the whimsical notions of the nation-states. Unfortunately, they were not only torn from their roots, but became one of the major victims of the so-called modern statehood.

Notes

1 Though the whole crisis, the future of the Partition-displaced became the topic of discussion inside royal meetings in England, dinner parties and formal and informal meetings of the ambitious statesmen and policymakers of both India and Pakistan.
2 The tribal zones in Northeast India suffered immensely on account of Partition. It separated the Garos by dividing Garo Hills. Khasis and Jaintias suffered immensely, the Jaintias lost their capital Jaintiapur to Sylhet. Janitiapur used to serve as an entrepôt between the people of the plains and hills, where cotton, iron, ore, wax, ivory, betel leaf and clothes were traded. The tribals exchanged these articles for salt, tobacco, rice and goats. Khasis used to sell lime from quarries in the plains of Sylhet. Partition not only stopped their trade; some of the quarries fell on the other side of the border. Partition created acute economic blockade for the Mizos, as it snatched major riverine trade route to sea through Chittagong Hill Tracts down Karnaphuli. The Lushai Hills were at the extremity of an uncertain and adequate line of communications on which they depended for all essential supplies.
3 In contrast, masses were hopeful of their unforeseen future in their own ways. Later, their feeling of joy converted to insecurity. They could not handle the stress of becoming minorities overnight. *Chitra Nodir Pare* (Quiet flows the river Chitra). A film by Tanvir Mokammel. Released in 1999, Bangladesh.
4 File No. 94/47-pub (B), 1947, NAI.
5 Interview with late Tapan Roy Choudhury, an eminent historian and writer, taken on 23 December 2010 in Kolkata, West Bengal.
6 Refugees from different *paras* like Ghoshpara, Bagdipara and Shilpara from Khulna, Barishal and Faridpur with surnames related with their traditional professions, i.e., Saha, Kundu, Poramanik, used to get happily settled down in a place, when the key factor of their bonding was the place of their origin.
7 Special Evacuee Property Management Boards were set up for that purpose. The policies adopted in the east were diametrically opposite from those of the west.
8 The Nehru-Liaquat Ali Khan Agreement (Delhi Pact) was signed on 8 April 1950. The basic idea was to create conditions in both the countries where the minorities would not feel insecure and not think of migrating to the other country. It was hoped that those who had come would go back. 'The Nehru-Liaquat Ali Khan Agreement' dated 8 April 1950. File No. P (PIV) 125 (62)/65, MEA-Pak-II, P IV, NAI.
9 Initially, the idea of Pakistan included states of Punjab, North-West Frontier Province, Sindh and Baluchistan in the northwest, while dividing India into two, Pakistan and Hindustan.
10 The term used by Tussar Kanti Bose, editor of the *Amrita Bazar Patrika*, to describe the dilemma of Bengal for deciding political issues and catastrophic events it faced continuously throughout the 1940s.
11 *Biplabi*, 7 November 1943.
12 The war blackouts over the city intensified panic over food shortages, robbery, beggary and suspicion towards neighbours. The behavioural difference between the upper-class *bhadralok* (urban literate elite) and the migrant *chhototolok* (streetwise displaced non-elite) became a recurrent marker of suspicion, fear and a kind of social anxiety. Sanjukta Ghosh. 2015. 'Famine, Food and the Politics of Survival in Calcutta, 1943–1950'. In *Calcutta: The Stormy Decades*, ed. Tanika Sarkar and Sekhar Bandyapadhyay, 219. New Delhi: Social Science Press.

74 Encountering the 'refugee'

13 *Janajuddha*, 31 March 1943.
14 The communists initiated an all-party committee consisting of Congress, Muslim League, Hindu Mahasabha, Labour Party, Krishak Sabha, BPTIUC.
15 Mushirul Hasan. 2002. 'Memories of a Fragmented Nation'. In *Pangs of Partition*, ed. S. Settar and Indira Baptista Gupta, Vol. II. The Human Dimension, 172–73. New Delhi: Manohar.
16 After the failure, Amery wrote in his diary 'so ended my efforts to save a united India'.
17 *The Statesman*, 24 February 1947.
18 Mountbatten wrote, 'Nehru is most convincingly genuine about these safeguards. He has said time and again that Congress could not conceivably disregard them'; but: 'The crux is of course, to get this across Jinnah. He has never given any indication that he would be ready to trust Congress for one moment'. Quoted from Mountbatten's India Bias-CXXXI, (Plan 'WE' and Plan 'THEY').
19 File No. MSS Eur. E. 372/11, "The Role of Lord Mountbatten", a paper presented by H. V. Hodson in a seminar on the Partition of India, organised by the School of Oriental and African Studies, IOR.
20 *The Times of India*, 17 June 1947.
21 File No. 94/47-pub (B), 1947, NAI.
22 Joya Chatterji. 1999. 'The Making of a Borderline: The Radcliffe Award for Bengal'. In *Region and Partition: Bengal, Punjab and the Partition of the Subcontinent*, ed. Ian Talbot and Gurharpal Singh, 75. Karachi: Oxford University Press.
23 File No. R/30/1/9: ff. 4–7, IOR.
24 Mountbatten tried hard to protect the credibility of Sir Cyril Radcliffe. Congress initially objected to his appointment, probably on a confusion that he was a conservative and likely to favour the Muslim League.
25 The chief objective was to divide the whole province into Muslim and non-Muslim zones. File No. L/PO/6/123, ff. 90–99: 8 May 1947, "Viceroy's Personal Report No. 13", IOR.
26 *Memorandum on the Partition of Bengal, Presented on Behalf of the Indian National Congress Before the Bengal Boundary Commission*, 15 July 1947, p. 4, NMML.
27 *A Case for Partition of Bengal, Being a Memorandum Submitted to the Advisory Committee of the Constituent Assembly of India*, Calcutta, 12 July 1947, p. 9, NMML.
28 This definition was sufficiently broad to include Assam at the extreme northeast border in India, the Hindu majority area of western Bengal with its capital Calcutta, and the non-Muslim majority areas of the eastern Punjab.
29 *AICC Papers*, G-37/1947, NMML.
30 *S. P. Mookerjee Papers*, II–IV Instalments, Subject File No. 160, p. 1, NMML.
31 *S. P. Mookerjee Papers*, II–IV Instalments, Subject File No. 132, p. 1, NMML.
32 *AICC Papers*, G-54/1947, Part-1, NMML.
33 *Ashutosh Lahiri Papers*, Pamphlets, Sl. No. 30, NMML.
34 *N. C. Chatterjee Papers*, Vol. 2, Press Clippings, NMML.
35 Jinnah always wished to have a separate referendum for Bengal, along with Sylhet and NWFP.
36 *Ananda Bazar Patrika*, 18 July 1947.
37 *The Times of India*, 27 June 1947.
38 *S. P. Mookerjee Papers*, II–IV Instalments, Subject File No. 160, p. 3, NMML.
39 The chief reason was H. S. Suhrawardy; he divided League leadership and declared Dhaka as the capital of East Pakistan few months before Partition. *The Statesman*, 18 July 1947.
40 *The Times of India*, 16 July 1947.
41 *AICC Papers*, G-54, Part-1, 1947, NMML.
42 *The Statesman*, 19 August 1947.
43 Swapna Bhattacharyya. 2001. 'The Refugee-Generating Chittagong Hill Tracts: Past, Present and Future'. In *Refugees and Human Rights: Social and Political Dynamics of Refugee Problem in Eastern and North-Eastern India*, ed. Sanjay K. Roy, 321–21. New Delhi and Jaipur: Rawat Publication.

Encountering the 'refugee' **75**

44 *S. P. Mookerjee Papers*, II–IV Instalments, Subject File No. 160, p. 1, NMML.
45 File No. B/1895, Political Dept., Tripura State Archives, Agartala (henceforth TSA).
46 File No. 76/16, *General Report on Public Instructions in Assam from 1860 to 1907*, Assam State Archives, Dispur (henceforth ASA).
47 Tea estates made this district lucrative. Job facilities in administrative posts of colonial bureaucracy to professionals, appointments of clerks were more in numbers in Sylhet. It was one of the most dynamic provinces of British India by the early 20th century.
48 The President of the Assam Association publicly said that as long as Sylhet remained in Assam, it could not develop its language and literature. The leading Assamese newspapers consistently published articles regarding the necessity to exclude Sylhet from Assam.
49 Nabanipa Bhattacharjee. 'Muslim Politics and the Partition of Assam'. *The Daily Star*, 20 March 2013.
50 File No. L/PJ/9/59, p. 13, IOR.
51 File No. R/3/1/158, Mountbatten to A. K. Hydari, the Assam Governor, 18 June 1947, IOR.
52 *The Statesman*, 16 July 1947.
53 *Census of India*, Assam, Vol. IX, 1941, pp. 38–41.
54 File No. R/3/1/158, p. 55, IOR.
55 Liaquat Ali Khan, in a letter to Mountbatten on 11 June 1947, conveyed how the Muslim votes did not reflect the real strength. He suggested multiplying Muslim votes by a factor that would equate with their voting strength. File No. R/3/1/158, Liaquat Ali Khan's letter to Mountbatten, IOR.
56 Jogendra Nath Mandal, a lower-caste leader of East Bengal, campaigned in favour of the League stating, Jinnah promised to protect their rights in Pakistan. *Dainik Asomia Janambhumi*, 1 February 1947.
57 Two Sylheti politicians, Mahmud Ali and Abdul Matin Chaudhury, supported Bhasani and tried mobilising the Muslim support. The role of the Muslim guards and the League's trained volunteers was crucial. Shyama Prasad Mookerjee sent volunteers to mobilise Hindu support. The Communist Party formed a 'Joint Volunteer Core' with the Congress. They organised parades and processions in the streets of Sylhet and chanted slogans like 'don't break golden Sylhet and don't go broken Bengal'. *The Statesman*, 6 July 1947.
58 *The Statesman*, 5 July 1947.
59 The result was, valid votes for joining East Bengal totalled 239,619, while those for remaining in Assam totalled 184,041. The overall majority for joining East Bengal totalled 55,578. The percentage of the valid votes to total electorate entitled to vote was 77:33. File No. R/3/1/158, Telegram: Confidential, 2248-S, From Governor, Assam to Viceroy, 12 July 1947, IOR.
60 File No. R/3/1/158, IOR.
61 *Amrita Bazar Patrika*, 17 July 1947.
62 *Hindustan Standard*, 18 July 1947.
63 Sanjib Baruah. 2015. 'Partition and the Politics of Citizenship in Assam'. In *Partition: The Long Shadow*, ed. Urvashi Butalia, 84. New Delhi: Viking-Penguin.
64 'Memorandum on Behalf of Released Employees' Organisation, Sylhet, 21 September 1947; 'Assam Refugees'. *AICC Papers*, 1st Instalment, G3/KWI/1947–48, NMML.
65 *AICC Papers*, 2nd Installment, PB-2, Bengal, File No. 1785, 1948, NMML.
66 *AICC Papers*, 1st Instalment, G3/KWI/1947–48, NMML.
67 *AICC Papers*, 2nd Installment, PB-2, Bengal, File No. 1785, 1948, NMML
68 *Rajendra Prasad Papers Collection*. File No. 1-B/1947, Vol. 1, on Bengal Boundary Commission 1947, NAI.
69 At English Bazar, the district administration confirmed the news of union of Malda with Pakistan, and the rumour made all the inhabitants panicky.
70 To Chief Ministers, 18 December 1950, *Letters to Chief Ministers*, Vol. 2, 1950–1952, New Delhi, Jawaharlal Nehru Memorial Fund, 1986, p. 290.
71 Extract from the minutes of the Partition Council's meeting held on the 2 August 1947.
72 Appendix III to Vol. II, Assets and Liabilities (Expert Committee No. II).

73 The Agenda and Minutes of the Partition Council Meetings held between 27 June 1947 and 1 December 1947, Case No. PC/149/16/47.
74 '1954 Convention Relating to the Status of Stateless Persons'. www.unhcr.org/3bbb25729.html. Last accessed 21 February 2020.
75 B. S. Chimni. 2003. 'Status of Refugees in India: Strategic Ambiguity'. In *Refugees and the State: Practices of Asylum and Care in India, 1947–2000*, ed. Ranabir Samaddar, 443. New Delhi: Sage.
76 Joya Chatterji. 2001. 'Rights or Charity? Government and Refugees. The Debate Over Relief and Rehabilitation in West Bengal'. In *Partitions of Memory: The Aftermath of the Division of India*, ed. Suvir Kaul, 91. New Delhi: Permanent Black.
77 Ritu Menon. 2003. 'Birth of Social Security Commitments: What Happened in the West'. In *Refugees and the State: Practices of Asylum and Care in India, 1947–2000*, ed. Ranabir Samaddar, 155. New Delhi: Sage.
78 Ranabir Samaddar. 2000. 'The Cruelty of Inside/Outside'. In *Refugees in West Bengal: Institutional Practices and Contested Identities*, ed. Pradip Kr. Bose, 5. Calcutta: Calcutta Research Group.
79 File No. L/52/6568/202, Part II, NAI.
80 File No. 43/16/47-Estb, NAI.
81 In a letter No. 13-admn (21)/49 to all provincial Governments and administrations it is directed by the officer on special duty Sri Bisambar Das that Refugees shall be termed as 'displaced persons' in all Government communications and refugee camps will be designated as 'relief camps'. File No. 51/122/49, Public, NAI.
82 File No. 2/25/56-IC section, NAI.
83 'Rehabilitation of the Displaced Persons and Eviction of Persons in Unauthorised Occupation of Land Act, 1951'. This land bill introduced in the West Bengal Legislative Assembly (WBLA) as 'The Charter for the Rehabilitation of Refugees' by Harendra Nath Rai Chowdhury, *WBLA Debates*, September 1955, p. 267.
84 Ministry of Rehabilitation, *Annual Report, 1955–56*, definition as decided upon in the Conference of the Rehabilitation Ministers from the Eastern States held at Darjeeling on 20–22 October 1955, pp. 86–87.
85 The idea of 'circumstantial evidences' introduced by Renuka Roy in the WBLA. It was decided, a recommendation from the local MLA or MP would be enough to identify or accept someone as refugee and render him rehabilitation benefits. *WBLA Debates*, 28 September 1955, p. 267.
86 Both the Governments of East Bengal and West Bengal established an Evacuee Property Management Board to safeguard interests of the minorities. File No. 1147/47, West Bengal State Archives, Kolkata (henceforth WBSA).
87 Dipesh Chakrabarty. 2000. 'Remembered Villages: Representations of Hindu-Bengali Memories in the Aftermath of the Partition'. In *Inventing Boundaries: Gender, Politics and Partition of India*, ed. Mushirul Hasan, 322. New Delhi: Oxford University Press.
88 Because of such resentments, the refugee leaders often refused to term the uprooted and floated people as 'refugees'.
89 Sabyasachi Bhattacharya. 2014. 'Purono Kolkatae Bangal'. *Arek Rokom* 18–19: 31–32.
90 Achintya Biswas. 1991. 'Anupasthit Mahakabyer Chhaya: Danga, Deshbibhag o Bangla Kathasahitya'. *Chaturanga* 52 (4): 341.
91 Interview with Ashoke Mukhopadhyay, a retired professor from Presidency College, taken on 15 June 2010 in Kolkata, West Bengal.
92 Bulbul Osman. 2015. 'Sabdhan, Ora Sojneful Hoe Aschhe Go'. In *Paschim Theke Purbobanga: Deshbodoler Smriti*, ed. Rahul Roy, 60. Kolkata: Gangchil.
93 Joya Chatterji. 1999. 'The Making of a Borderline: The Radcliffe Award for Bengal'. In *Region and Partition: Bengal, Punjab and the Partition of the Subcontinent*, ed. Ian Talbot and Gurharpal Singh, 187. Karachi: Oxford University Press.
94 Soumendra Prasad Saha. 2015. 'Swadhinatar Sankot: Deshbhag o Udbastu Samasya: Prasanga Jaipaiguri Jela'. *Itikatha* III (1): 219.

95 Jyotirmay Jana. 2008. 'Erosion-Induced Displacement in Nagaon, Morigaon, Barpeta, Dhubri and Goalpara Districts'. In *Blisters on their Feet: Tales of Internally Displaced Persons in India's North East*, ed. Samir Kumar Das, 105. New Delhi: Sage.
96 Amalendu Guha (1977: 320) stated that out of the 1.1 million acres of wasteland settled with all the migrants in Assam, East Bengal farm settlers accounted for nearly half a million acres.
97 *Notun Asamia*, 13 February 1960.
98 Gunabhiram Barua, ed. 1984. *Asam Bandhu*. Guwahati: Asom Prakashan Parishad.
99 Interview with Samujjal Bhattacharyya, Chief Advisor of AASU, taken on 20 December 2012 in Guwahati, Assam.
100 Bhupen Sharmah. 2001. 'Immigration and Politics of Assam: Questions Related to Human Rights'. In *Refugees and Human Rights: Social and Political Dynamics in Eastern and North-Eastern India*, ed. Sanjoy K. Roy, 369. New Delhi and Jaipur: Rawat Publication.
101 Harihar Bhattacharyya. 1999. 'Post-Partition Refugees and the Communists: A Comparative Study of West Bengal and Tripura'. In *Region and Partition: Bengal, Punjab and the Partition of the Subcontinent*, ed. Ian Talbot and Gurharpal Singh, 325. Karachi: Oxford University Press.
102 Landless labourers used to work in *khas* lands, owned by the royal family of Tripura in the Zamindari of Chakla Roshanabad. They were sharecroppers, but the Maharajas often treated them as their own subjects, whom they could not evict.
103 Interview with Paramartha Dutta, a lawyer by profession, taken on 2 March 2013 in Agartala, Tripura.
104 *Janakalyan*, 5 January 1948.
105 Tripura Administration, *Statistical Survey of Displaced Persons from East Pakistan in Tripura (1956)*, Printed by the Superintendent, Government Printing, Tripura, p. 1.
106 File No. D-1053-PV (VI)/53, Ministry of Foreign Affairs and Commonwealth Relations, Home-Political, B Proceedings, List-118, Bundle-86, 1952, BNA.
107 File No. 14 (2)/55-BL, BL Section, 1955, NAI.
108 Diwan Chaman Lall Paper (II Installment), File No. 147, NMML.
109 *The Statesman*, 17 April 1948.
110 N. R. Sarkar, Member of the Bengal Boundary Commission, *The Statesman*, 26 July 1947.
111 *The Statesman*, 16 August 1947.
112 *AICC Papers*, 2nd Installment, PB-3 (1), Bengal, File No. 1786 (Pt. II), 1948, NMML.
113 *A. P. Jain Papers*, Articles by A. P. Jain, Sl. No. 16, NMML.
114 File No. P (PII) 125 (65)/66, (P IV), NAI.
115 File No. PCP (IV)/285 (27)/66, Pak-II Section, NAI.
116 File No. L/52/6611/1, BL Branch, NAI.
117 *The Times of India*, 9 February 1950.
118 File No. P 11/53-PSP, P VIII Branch, NAI.
119 The Mymensingh Convention passed the following resolution pointing out towards the failure of the Pact (The letter dated 13 June 1950. *S. P. Mukherjee Papers*, Subject Sl. No. 31, NMML):

> The Convention regrets to note that in spite of the Nehru-Liaquat Agreement to rehabilitate the returned migrants to their original homes, most of the migrants, on return, are getting no help from the authorities, and are living in pitiable, deplorable conditions, without any shelter, without any means of subsistence. Their own houses are under occupation of Muslim refugees from India and the arable lands of these evacuees have been distributed to them. The efforts of the members of the District Minority Board and the Minority Commission have so far been fruitless, and the indifferent attitude of the Government is causing immense hardship to the returned people.

120 *S. P. Mookerjee Papers*, 1st Instalment, Speeches and Statements by Him, Sl. No. 4, NMML.

78 Encountering the 'refugee'

121 'The Tragedy of East Bengal Hindus and How to Resettle and Rehabilitate Them' (An Examination of the Working of the Indo-Pakistan Agreement), S. P. Mookerjee Papers, V–VII Instalments, Printed Material, Sl. No. 20, NMML.
122 *Delhi Pact Has Failed*, Proceedings of the All Bengal Refugee Convention held at the Calcutta University Institute on 11 June 1950, *S. P. Mookerjee Papers*, V–VII Instalments, Printed Materials, Sl. No. 14, NMML.
123 In a personal conversation with Protul Chandra Gupta, a retired primary school teacher in Tripura, on 9 June 2008. He was a professor of mathematics in a college in Khulna, but could not find a similar job after crossing the border and settling down permanently in India.
124 Shyama Prasad Mookerjee estimated the number of Muslims going away would not be more than 1,00,000. *S. P. Mookerjee Papers*, 1st Instalment, Speeches and Statements by Him, Sl. No. 4, NMML.
125 Nadia district recorded the highest emigration of the Muslims for the whole of West Bengal: 2,23,250 Muslims left the district in the intervening years of 1947–1951.
126 Renuka Roy, *WBLA Debates*, 7 February 1953, p. 304.
127 File No. P 11/53-PSP, P VIII Branch, NAI.
128 The declaration of a provision that the migrants who came to India before 15 October 1952 or who have come on Migration Certificate, had to adopt a nationality of a foreign state but not directly liable to get a citizenship. *The West Bengal Weekly*, Vol. 1, Calcutta, Friday, 21 November 1952, No. 6.
129 File No. D 4860/55-BL, IB-BL Section, NAI.
130 R/Bengal/15, Reel No. 9, MNNL.
131 'The Real Situation in East Bengal: Shri J. N. Mandal on Nehru's Analysis'. *Hindustan Standard*, 11 October 1952.
132 *Hindustan Standard*, 19 October 1952.
133 Rounaq Jahan. 2002. 'Political Development'. In *Bangladesh on the Threshold of the Twenty-First Century*, ed. A. M. Chowdhury and Fakrul Alam, 43. Dhaka: Asiatic Society of Bangladesh.
134 *Dhaka Prakash*, 23 November 1952.
135 *The West Bengal Weekly*, Vol. 1, Calcutta, Friday, 28 November 1952, No. 10.
136 File No. 17 (1)/56 PSP, PSP Section, NAI.
137 File No. 22 (159)-PA/52, Political A Section, NAI.
138 They agreed upon granting 'A' visas to people belonging to almost every profession, including residents of enclaves, and 'B' visas to relatives of main applicants of the visa, with an intention of providing facilities for the reunion of uprooted and sprinkled families. The normal period for issuing visas of category 'B' was only four working days, but there was no scope for 'frightening' applications for those visas. However, designing a plan to grant a 'C' category visa meant that, as an object to making the visa process faster, applicants who wanted a visa within a few hours could do so. The authority termed it as 'fright applications' in East Bengal visa office, Dacca. 'E' visas were issued mainly to Pakistani nationals working with or in an establishment and bona fide business located in India. The 'E' and 'F' categories were meant only for transit visas. File No. F. 12 (3) Sec/52, *Report from Office of the Deputy High Commissioner for India in Pakistan, Dacca*, Home-Political, B Proceedings, List-118, Bundle-86, 1952, BNA.
139 D. O. No. 548/DHC, *Fortnightly Report for the Period Ending the 31st October 1952*, Indian High Commission, Dacca, in File No. L/52/1321/202, BL Branch, NAI.
140 File No. 7/52/ PSP, Part-II, NAI.
141 *Times of India*, 26 April 1952.
142 The Government of India did not encourage such surrender of passports and procedures of permanent migration later, as the official policy was to keep the minorities in the country of their origin.

143 They confirmed by statistics maintained by the Indian check-posts (and similar statistics maintained by the Pakistan check-post), from which it was clear that the number of persons travelling (on category 'B' visas) issued by the Indian Visa Office had been much larger in every fortnight than the visas issued by the Pakistan Visa Office at Calcutta. File No. F. 24 (8) Sec/53, *Report from Office of the Deputy High Commissioner for Pakistan in India, Calcutta*, Home-Political, B Proceedings, List-110, Bundle-24, 1953, BNA.

144 File No. F. 24 (8) Sec/53, *Report from Office of the Deputy High Commissioner for Pakistan in India, Calcutta*, Home-Political, B Proceedings, List-110, Bundle-24, 1953, BNA.

145 People who would able to show this document issued by the District Magistrate certifying their Pakistani citizenship or domicile status or a document of release attested by a Pakistani gazetted officer would be exempted from this regulation. Foreigners below the age of 18 would not fall under the purview of this act. Travellers who could prove that their stay in East Pakistan did not exceed 15 days would not need the papers. Some apparent concessions were granted to agriculturists; they were to show a certificate issued by the village headman or officials of the revenue department stating them to be tax-paying residents of the village.

146 *The Statesman*, 2 November 1952.

147 File No. 4040-18/55 PSP, PSP Section, 1955; File No. 25/3/57 PV 1, PV 1 Section, NAI.

148 *Hindustan Standard*, 20 October 1952.

149 Allegations of touts hovering around these office buildings to seize upon opportunity to belabour and lure innocent and credulous villagers of minority communities for the purpose of extorting money from them. File No. P (P-IV)/283 (4)/65, Pak-II Registry, NAI.

150 *Amrita Bazar Patrika*, 28 October 1952.

151 *Hindustan Standard*, 29 October 1952.

152 *Dainik Basumati*, 29 October 1952.

153 *S. P. Mookerjee Papers*, 1st Instalment, Subject File No. 41, NMML.

154 *Minutes of the Meetings of the Central Ministers*, held on the 24 October 1952, in Eden Buildings, Dacca, mentioned in File No. L/52/66113/202, BL Branch, 1952, NAI.

155 Letter from the President of All Bengal Dislodged Minorities Association, Calcutta to Nehru, dated 13 November 1952, *S. P. Mookerjee Papers*, Sl. No. 40, NMML.

156 *Hindustan Times*, 2 November 1952.

157 'The Real Situation in East Bengal: Shri J. N. Mandal on Nehru's Analysis'. *Hindustan Standard*, 11 October 1952.

158 *S. P. Mookerjee Papers*, 1st Instalment, Subject File No. 33, NMML.

159 *Enumeration Handbook Census 1951: West Bengal and Sikkim*, Government of India Press, Calcutta, 1950, p. ix; *S. P. Mookerjee Papers*, 1st Instalment, File No. 39, NMML.

160 A letter by S. P. Mookerjee to Dr. B. C. Sen dated 22 August 1950, *S. P. Mookerjee Papers*, 1st Instalment, Sl. No. 33, NMML.

161 The 'provisional optees' of Government servants in the colonial state often conditioned themselves or compromised sometimes their choices, with the availability of the citizenship to migrate permanently. File No. L/52/1321/202, BL Branch, 1952, Ministry of External affairs, File No. F 2 (37)-RC/50, RC Branch, 1950, NAI.

162 There were two conditions to be treated as 'Displaced Government Servant' in the definition given by the Central authorities in India (File No. 104/53/57, Ad-I, Administration-I Section, 1957, NAI, *The Morning News*, 6 November 1955):

> (i) persons who were employed under the Central Government of undivided India and having opted for service in India, became surplus to requirements, as a result of the constitutional changes, and (ii) persons who were employed under the Central Government of undivided India and opted for service in Pakistan, but had to return to India or could not proceed to Pakistan owing to the conditions which prevailed in Pakistan.

163 A draft of rules had been prepared in respect of other matters in consultation with the Ministries of Law, External Affairs and Rehabilitation. Pakistan adopted same sets of conditions and rules in Pakistani Citizenship Laws. File No. 10/7/56-IC, (Part-I), Indian Citizenship Section, NAI.
164 In Article 5 of the Citizenship Act, there were two important factors to consider someone's citizenship: (i) to establish that the person is a 'domicile' or (ii) 'birth in Indian territory'. File No. 40/18/55 PSP, PSP Branch, NAI.
165 In Schedule V to the Citizenship rules, 1956, it had been laid down that a fee of Rs. 50 was to be levied on 'alien women' for registration as an Indian citizen under this section of the Citizenship Act, 1955. File No. 6/11/57-IC, (Part-I), Indian Citizenship Section, NAI.
166 File No. 10/7/56-IC, (Part-I), Indian Citizenship Section, NAI.
167 *Padmaja Naidu Papers*, Printed Materials, Sl. No. 34, NMML.
168 *Parliamentary Debates*, Part-II, Vol. V, No. 2, 1 August 1950, p. 85.
169 *Shibnath Banerjee Papers*, Subject File No. 124, NMML.
170 *Proceedings of the WBLA Assembled Under the Provisions of the Constitution of India*, Fourteenth Session, February–March 1956, p. 359.
171 File No. I/21 (5)/Ben/50, NAI.
172 File No. 28/8/58 Judi, Judi-I Section, NAI.
173 Home-Political Files, B Proceedings, List-118, Bundle-86, 1952, BNA.
174 Report of the Calcutta Session of the Akhil Bharat Hindu Mahasabha, *Ashutosh Lahiry Papers*, Pamphlet No. 33, NMML.
175 *West Bengal Act of XVI OF 1951*, The Government of West Bengal, Law Department, West Bengal Government Press, 1962, p. 1.
176 According to the estimate given by Sj. Bijesh Chandra Sen, the Deputy Minister for Rehabilitation of West Bengal, *Proceedings of the West Bengal Legislative Assembly Assembled Under the Provisions of the Constitution of India*, Fourteenth Session, February–March 1956, p. 359.
177 File No. 12 (8)/4 Pak-II, Pak-II Branch, NAI.
178 A *bargadar* means a person who—under the system known as *adhi, barga* or *bhag*—cultivates the land of another person on condition of delivering a share of the produce of such land to that person.
179 *Introduction of Legislation in the Parliament to further Amend the West Bengal Evacuee Property Act, 1951 as Extended to the State of Tripura*, The West Bengal Evacuee Property (Tripura Amendment) Ordinance, 1952, No. VI, Ministry of Law, pp. 1–2.
180 The West Bengal Evacuee Property (Tripura Amendment) Ordinance, 1952, File No. 46 (2)—PPR/51, PPR Branch, NAI.
181 File No. 46 (2)—PPR/51, PPR Branch, NAI.
182 The letter dated 13 June 1950. *S. P. Mookerjee Papers*, Subject Sl. No. 31, NMML.

2
DEALING WITH THE REFUGEES
Rehabilitation, variation, discrimination

Jawaharlal Nehru, the first prime minister of India, had jubilantly welcomed the birth of a free India as a nation-state, but in reality, the picture was stained by ceaseless human sufferings caused by division of a unified territory. Nehru was well aware of 'an inherent tendency towards disintegration of India'.[1] Thus, in his fortnightly letters to the Union's Chief Ministers, he repeatedly shared his anxieties over the communal, casteist, linguistic, sectarian and regional threats to the nation's integrity.[2] The key challenge was to negotiate and balance overlapping conceptions for competing membership claims in the nation, as his vision was to provide diverse social groups a viable place by maintaining their identities (Shani 2010: 1). After the divide, the national endeavour was to reinstate the Partition victims to the other sides of the border and help them to absorb into the fabrics of the communities in India. However, the plan of evacuation of the minorities on the western side, especially in Punjab, began even before the Partition and it continued for many months after the formal divide. The state machineries in charge of making and implementing policies for refugees were instructed by the Ministry of Relief and Rehabilitation based in Delhi to get involved in the business of rehabilitation, though the job was 'dull and uninspiring' for them (Rao 1967: 2–3).

Punjab and Bengal, two partitioned states, had suffered at all levels by the dislocation caused by the Radcliffe Award. The Bengal borderland was 4,097 km long and touched three major states in the eastern and northeastern region: West Bengal, Assam and Tripura. They received maximum numbers of Bengali refugees from then East Bengal/Pakistan in many waves, of both documented and undocumented migration, for their historical links, geographical and physical proximity (Das and Ansary 2018: 159). The Punjabi refugees proved to be relatively fortunate to get care and protection, initiated by a new-born nation-state. Yet Bengal received less attention in similar situations and circumstances, primarily on the issue of relief and rehabilitation arrangements.[3] The decisions of the Central Government regarding relief, rehabilitation and resettlement of the Bengali refugees were abrupt. The first discriminatory policy towards Bengal was the decision to not opt for exchange of population in order to achieve systematic population settlement like in Punjab. The first ruling party in the Centre, the Indian National Congress, tried to justify the logic behind such discriminatory policies between Bengal and Punjab, simply by citing differences in geographical location, separate cultural identities and political ideologies (Talbot and Singh 2009: 106). Interestingly, when the general attitude and inclination towards the uprooted populace was more or less similar in the case of West Bengal and Tripura, resident Bengalis of Assam were found to have rendered all help to new displaced persons or refugees to absorb and settle them only in those localities where the Bengalis predominated (Nag 1990: 75). Though the Central Government introduced various schemes for all the refugee-absorbent states all over India, the nature of support the states could receive for refugee relief and temporary or permanent rehabilitation depended more on their personal equation with the Centre or level of negotiation of the respective state machineries.

With this background, this chapter tries to show the nature and volume of disparity or contestations experienced by the unfortunate Bengali refugees during the course of their migration and resettlement. The varied issues of discrimination began from the planning of their future and designing the policies accordingly, also from respective procedures to form the Relief and Rehabilitation Ministry by the Government of India (Rao 1967: 11). Refugees who migrated from Pakistan through the western borders had been completely rehabilitated and resettled by the late 1950s with assistance from the Central Government and steady fund allocations by the rehabilitation department of India. Keeping such premises in the backdrop, this chapter highlights the Centre's biased attitude towards these two partitioned Indian states, as also towards the Punjabi and Bengali refugees. Within a comparative framework, this chapter tries to underline that despite provisions of the Partition resolution (1947) of equal treatment in relief, resettlement and rehabilitation benefits to diverse types of refugees, some of them did not receive equal treatment. The implementation part of the rehabilitation policies was not only uneven in case of Punjab and Bengal; it was further discriminatory as far as the states of eastern and northeastern India were concerned (*Partition Proceedings* 1949, 1: 182–84). When the Bengali-dominated state of West Bengal treated the refugee issues sensitively and comparatively with better funding, the other two states, Assam and Tripura, as well as mixed refugee rehabilitation settlement areas like Andamans, Bihar, Orissa and Dandakaranya, suffered immensely from local issues.

Therefore, this chapter deals with diverse ground problems faced by the Bengali refugees in many areas. It is interesting to note that until the late 1950s, both Centre and state governments were working on only temporary solutions in case of the refugees who crossed the Bengal borderland, promising to provide permanent rehabilitation subsequently. But looking at the sharp rise in migration patterns, later the Centre decided to provide rehabilitation benefits and promised to render some kind of measures only to those refugees who would agree to settle down outside the Bengali-dominated areas. So, the chapter demonstrates this process—how the Centre gradually shifted from their earlier stands, forgot its previous commitments regarding Bengal before Partition and changed the basic policies—as the waves of refugees began to increase much more than anticipated (Chakravartty 2005: 40–41). This chapter also aims to investigate why the rehabilitation department tried to abolish itself after the riots of 1964—and by 1965, the Government of India had taken back all the facilities that were provided to the refugees earlier and even halted rehabilitation processes. The Centre finally withdrew all rehabilitation departments in states after the Liberation War of 1971 and declared 25 March 1971 as the cut-off date for classifying the migrants for consideration as 'refugees', to acquire rehabilitation facilities offered as well as facilitated by the state, and their due right to citizenship in India.[4] In this process, the Bengali refugees were naturally reduced to a 'community of dependents' and 'dole-beggars' by the state (Chatterjee 1992: 124). This chapter tries to portray the crises and consequent confrontations experienced by the refugees in recreating the socio-cultural milieu of the lost motherland in the areas where they were rehabilitated.

Tackling the crisis: Punjab versus Bengal

Looking at the bloodshed and volume of migration on the Punjab side just after Partition, the Government of India immediately realised the necessity of taking active measures for tackling problems arising from such a gigantic influx of refugees. The stream of refugees was swelling to an uncontrollable level on the Western border. The influx raised several questions, like how to bring comfort and assurance of safety to isolated pockets, how to provide adequate protection to refugees on the move, how to feed them and clothe them, how to ensure their proper rehabilitation for which they stood so sorely in need, and when they would get sanctuary in India by extending timely relief and other protections (Rao 1967: 12). For finding a definite answer to those crises, Nehru lost no time in extending an invitation to the United Nations Relief and Rehabilitation Administration (UNRRA) to provide advice on the rehabilitation of refugees. UNRRA duly dispatched two experienced officials, Molly Flynn and Evert Barger, and they spent most of their time in the Punjab; their reports emphasised the need to tackle the refugee crisis as a national emergency (Gatrell 2013: 6). Nehru initially accepted the need to circumvent normal government channels by setting up a national Rehabilitation and Development Board, but soon shut it down and created a Cabinet post instead.[5] The Relief and Rehabilitation department had been created in the Cabinet on a war footing to handle the crisis (Rao 1967: 12). Jawaharlal Nehru had selected K. C. Neogy to take charge as the very first Relief and Rehabilitation Minister of India, and he was sworn in on 6 September 1947 (*Sangothoner Ovimukh* 2008: 22). But the Western border, chiefly Punjab, remained the chief focus of the department since its formation to plan policies for refugees.[6]

The Relief and Rehabilitation division of the Ministry of Finance tried to define the terms 'relief' and 'rehabilitation' officially, and tried to convey what the Centre meant by it in their 'Note on Financial Assistance to States'. It instructed the states in 1948: 'Relief involves provision of food, clothing, accommodation, sanitation, medical treatment, administration of camps, etc.'[7] They made their position clear by stating: 'Rehabilitation is a long-term programme and it has to be borne in mind that permanent rehabilitation of refugees cannot be divorced from various Reconstruction and Developmental schemes which States have under consideration', and 'Rehabilitation involves permanent resettlement of refugees'.[8] Nehru also called upon Nikhil Sen, who worked for the successor agency of UNRRA, the International Refugee Organisation, in Italy. Sen stressed a vocational training scheme, but Nehru pointed out, 'an essential part of relief and rehabilitation is the psychological part and the building up of morale and self-reliance', and thus according to him, these efforts were all the more necessary in the light of 'psychological disturbance' and 'reason overthrown' that refugees were deemed to have experienced.[9] It was evident from the nature of rehabilitation arrangements and distribution of free clothes (like shirts, *kurta* or bush-shirts for men and *dupatta, salwar*, sweaters or jerseys for women) that the instructions and measures were meant for West Pakistani refugees; hence, the definitions of relief and rehabilitation made by the Ministry of Finance were chiefly keeping the Punjabi refugees in mind. Bengal suffered from the fuzzy nature of the eastern borders and the problem of pan-Indian policymaking, as it often ignored cultural specificity.

Sindhis, as a community, also suffered equally on account of the issues of cultural specificity, even though they migrated through the Western borders and were entitled to be treated as the Punjabis. But the Sindhis represent a community which did not avail any favour from the state, and being well-off, could get rid of the refugee tag. The Hindu Sindhis sought refuge in India a year after Partition. The Muslims from India were first to migrate to the province of Sindh that fell in Pakistan. Hence, the minority Hindu Sindhis began to be targeted for looting and encroachment. Although there were few incidents of bloodshed, the air in Sindh was filled with panic, for the possibility of an attack on them and their property. There was pressure to vacate their place and migrate to India, which was being depicted as the land of Hindus. In this sense, the Hindu Sindhis made space for Muslims by migrating to India (Bhabnani 2014: xlii).[10] Being 27 per cent of the population, two million Sindhis left Sindh to get rid of some real and imagined fear (Kothari 2004: 3888). The Sindhis 'hailing from Pakistan' became the 'linguistic minorities' in India. They were treated as 'Muslim-like' and 'untouchables' in staunch vegetarian states like Gujarat and Rajasthan (Kothari 2007: xi). But they adapted well in India as a community. About 41 per cent of displaced Sindhis were in trade and commerce, an area they controlled to a great extent. Only about 8 per cent of the rest of the Indian population was able to achieve this feat, as per census report. Yet, there was a strong sense of up-rootedness in them, when they were categorised as 'migrants' (Falzon 2005: 41). The tag of 'refugee' was associated with their identity even after decades of Partition.

Regarding Bengal, the Centre had nourished an illusion that there would be no significant displacement and distressed migration. The base of this hypothesis was their trust in the theory of traditional harmony between Hindus and Muslims in rural Bengal, as they had lived together for many centuries, except the outward symbols of religious worship, their language, culture, social traditions and usage were strikingly similar. Partition left at least 12 million Hindus stranded in East Pakistan (Rao 1967: 141). Renuka Roy, who first worked as an Honorary Adviser, Relief and Rehabilitation to the Government of West Bengal, and was later appointed as the Relief and Rehabilitation Minister in the Cabinet of B. C. Roy in the year 1952, also was an MP from Maldah, West Bengal in the Lok Sabha from 1957, pointed out that 'from October 1947, the systematic squeezing out policy of the minorities from Eastern Pakistan was apparent'.[11] It meant once the migration of Hindus started from districts of East Bengal, there were deliberate attempts to threaten and force the Hindus to leave their habitats. Yet the Centre refused to take a firm stand on the issue of forceful eviction. Jawaharlal Nehru said: 'In Eastern Pakistan the migration has been at a lower pace' (Chakrabarty 1982: 57–73). Later, when he understood the gravity of the real situation, he wrote to Dr Bidhan Chandra Roy about his feeling of insecurity and helplessness: 'Personally I think that this business of shifting millions of people is entirely beyond our capacity' (Chakrabarty 1982: 57–73).

The Government of India had taken an official evacuation policy for West Pakistan, the state treated relief and rehabilitation procedure as 'urgent' and 'immediate' (Singh 1962: 20). The Women's Section of the Ministry was formed on 24 November 1947, particularly for unattached destitute women and children, with Srimati Rameshuri Nehru as Honorary Director and Srimati Hanna Sen as Honorary Secretary. They decided to organise relief to unattached women and children, and help in the recovery of the abducted women and their subsequent training and rehabilitation.[12] In early 1948, it appointed a committee under the Chairmanship of Sri Shri Ram for promotion of cooperative enterprise amongst the refugees.[13] Rehabilitation of destitute refugee women and children were planned, by arranging vocational training and other economic rehabilitation programmes in major camps and colonies.[14] This initiative turned out to 'introduce schemes of Technical and Vocational training for displaced persons from West Pakistan' (Chakravarty 2011: 69). The evacuation procedure finished in early 1948, the refugees were settled in a new shelter with professional opportunities by 1949, relief measures were done by 1950 and permanent rehabilitation was completed by 1955 (Gopal 1987, 4: 93). In contrast, for the Bengali refugees in West Bengal, Assam and Tripura, 'In two years, 1948–49 and 1949–50', the Centre had allotted 'a little over three crores and the rest about 5 crores was given in form of a loan' for 2.6 million refugees in West Bengal. In reality, 'it actually works out at Rs. 20 per capita spread over two years' (Chakrabarti 1990: 21).

Nehru explained the reasons behind discrimination in the policy between Punjab and Bengal in the following words:

> In West Pakistan, practically all Hindus and Sikhs were driven out. In East Pakistan a very large number remained . . . which might bring about a wholesale migration . . . from Eastern Pakistan. This would have led to tremendous misery . . . which hardly any Government would have been able to face.
>
> *(Chakrabarti 1990: 21)*

Bengali refugees were entitled only repatriation, not rehabilitation. But the West Pakistani refugees received full rehabilitation, with other necessary supports from the Central Refugee Rehabilitation Department. Necessary loans or job benefits were offered.[15] Nehru was stubbornly against the proposal of 'exchange of population' in case of Bengal. His initial ideas had been transformed in later phase and it became more a question of 'India's political, economic, social and spiritual principles' rather than exchange of displaced people. He said it would be 'breach of trust' to a 'greater principle related to it' if communal exchange of population was accepted (Chakrabarti 1990: 31). But Shyama Prasad Mookerjee was of the opinion that the issue of Kashmir actually prevented him from accepting another natural solution for Bengal (two-way traffic of refugees) in 1950. He was eager to keep his reputation of a secularist image and convey this message to the world.[16]

As a result, the Bengali refugees were treated as abandoned people. There was need of huge funds for their sustenance, as their survival and livelihood had become difficult.[17] It led to a massive humanitarian crisis in the Bengal borderland areas. The available funds were too little in proportion to the increasing number of refugees (Chottopadhyay 2014: 17–18). The Rehabilitation Ministry was busy in land acquisition for resettlement of displaced people from West Punjab, Sindh and NWFP. Their argument was that the government had to give priority to migrants who came as a result of its agreement on 'exchange of population', which assured proper arrangement of relief and rehabilitation.[18] For similar problems arising from the Bengali refugees, the approach of the Centre was different.[19] Numbers of representatives from Bengal were too few to bargain with the policymakers in Delhi. M. N. Saha, N. C. Chatterjee, Tridib Chowdhury and S. P. Mookerjee were just some faces in the House of the People who remained vocal about discrimination towards the Bengali refugees.[20] N. S. Mathur, Assistant Secretary, Ministry of Rehabilitation, mentioned in a circular on 16 August 1950:

> I am directed to say that Government of India has decided that relief should not be given to East Pakistan DP's (Displaced Persons) except in camps in the Eastern States of Indian Union. The State Governments should, however, give them all the rehabilitation facilities, business loans, educational loans, housing loans, etc.[21]

Categorisation and classification

A special feature of the migration of refugees from eastern Bengal districts was their pattern of relocation in different waves. Four time spans were major in accounting for their migration, phase by phase. The first exodus started almost a year before the Partition, which continued up to the 1950 riots of Khulna and Barishal.[22] The second wave started out of the fear of introduction of passports (1952), which was accelerated by the riots of 1954. The introduction of migration certificates as compulsory travel documents confused them in the post-passport era. Adoption of an Islamic Constitution by Pakistan in 1956 spurred more migration. The final phase took place with the introduction of 'element of uncertainty', when restrictions had been imposed on mobility in the east. After a period of relative lull (1958–1963), the borderland was sealed notionally and migration of refugees without valid documents was declared illegal. The third phase of migration started with the Hazratbal incident (Chakravarty 2011: 38–39).[23] The fourth phase was in the time of the Bangladesh Liberation War in 1971. The nature of migration was diverse in comparison to the earlier ones (Luthra 1971: 2467). It witnessed the spirit of Bengali nationalism like the Language Movement of 1952 in East Pakistan that accelerated migration. The Indira-Mujib Pact stated that migration after 25 March 1971 would be considered illegal. Hence, it marked the end of legal migration between both the Bengals, and a new era of 'silent migration' began (Roy 2015: 27). The policies for the eastern states were ad hoc, visibly different from the west. The policies for them changed time and again, primarily the way the situations varied and Centre classified them into categories, to design their relief and rehabilitation procedure. It was through the 'categorisation and classification' of East Bengali refugees that the authorities differentiated them from the West Pakistani refugees.

The first phase: relief and rehabilitation (1946–1950)

In the first phase, respective state governments were supposed to provide temporary relief measures only to those refugees who were terribly in need and not capable of self-rehabilitation. When entering through the check-posts, each refugee family had to collect a slip of different colour to define the category of refugees they were before registering themselves as refugees. These slips would entitle them to rehabilitation benefits. Red slips meant those who wished to relocate permanently to Calcutta but were not expecting any help from the government. Blue slips meant those who needed help from the government to pass through Calcutta and wished to settle down in other places. White slips were provided to those who wanted to stay in government camps.[24] Few relief camps were established in each state, to give temporary relief and rehabilitation to camp dwellers (Chakravarty 2011: 142).[25]

The second phase: rehabilitation to regulation (1950–1958)

This phase marks an important change in the rehabilitation efforts in the east. After the riot of 1950, the eastern border first experienced a two-way migration. Both the nation-states indeed found the panic-stricken movement of people alarming. They realised the need for maintaining the status quo to regulate the influx and rehabilitation in the East. The Delhi Pact of 1950 was signed in this background, which emphasised the return of migrants to their respective places of origin after the turmoil was over.[26] Promises were made between the Province of East Bengal and the states of West Bengal, Assam and Tripura that they would:

> (i) continue their effort to restore normal conditions and shall take suitable measures to prevent recurrence of disorder, (ii) set up an agency with which

representatives of the minority immediately shall assist in the recovery of abducted women, (iii) not recognise forced conversions . . . if found guilty of converting people shall be punished, (iv) set up a Commission of Enquiry at once to enquire into and report on the causes and extent of the recent disturbances and to make recommendations with a view to prevent the recrudescence of similar trouble in future.

(Chakravarty 2011: 150)

The third phase: refugee regulation to dispersal (1958–1971)

From 1958, the strategy of the respective state governments was to define the problem of refugees as national problem, and thereby bring the Central Government to distribute responsibility of rehabilitation amongst different states (Chatterjee 1992: 133–35). The Centre therefore decided to resettle the refugees in Bihar, Orissa, United Provinces and Andamans in the first phase (Chatterji 2007: 1006).[27] They argued that the major states already reached a saturation point of refugee absorption and any more refugee settlement would be a burden on the states' economies (Biswas 2015: 10–11). Thus, the policy was to disperse them from the areas of concentration, to break up refugee clusters. The goal was to resettle them outside the metropolis, send them to deserted places, empty tracts and outside West Bengal, Assam and Tripura. Sending the refugees to Dandakaranya in Madhya Pradesh for permanent rehabilitation came as a next step (Chakravarty 2011: 173). The refugees found the decisions of such dispersal arbitrary and resented the separation of kinsmen from one another.

A phase-wise definition of refugees by the Centre and their subsequent categorisation based on their time of arrival was another distinct feature of the settlement pattern in Bengal. The refugees who migrated in the period beginning from October 1946 to March 1958, stayed in West Bengal, registered themselves as bona fide refugees, were eligible to get rehabilitation assistance from the government and were categorised as 'Old Migrants' (Chatterji 2007: 1002). Joya Chatterji mentioned that the 'old migrants' (1947–1958) were identified as genuine sufferers because of political unrest in East Bengal, and they became the state's burden. The government kept close watch on the refugees who were eligible for assistance. To put an end to the perpetual influx, the migrants who came during the period from 1 April 1958 to 31 December 1963 were considered 'illegal migrants', and they were not eligible for governmental help, as the Indian state saw no valid reason except economic reasons for their migration (Chatterjee 1990: 71). The Annual Report of the Year 1958–59 by the Ministry of Rehabilitation stated:

> Whereas the year 1956 marks the first major phase in the solution of the rehabilitation in the East, the year following 1957 stands out as a landmark (since after the elimination of the elements of uncertainty) the Government was able to make a detailed assessment of the size of the problem in different states.

This particular assessment revealed, for effective rehabilitation of the displaced persons who were already in India, it was essential that the size of the problem should not be allowed to grow indefinitely. This realisation led to the important decision in December 1957 to discontinue rehabilitation assistance to those who migrated after March 1958. It was only during 1958 for the first time that the magnitude of the problem in each state was finally determined.[28]

Again, after the riot of 1964, the refugee migration was seen as 'justified' by the state. They termed them 'New migrants', those who came between January 1964 and March 1971 (Chatterjee 1990: 71). The Centre had made a policy decision that the relief and rehabilitation assistance would be admissible only to those refugees who sought admission into the relief camps outside West Bengal and were willing to be resettled outside the state (Chaudhuri 1983: 18). The earlier policy of 'rehabilitation outside' was strictly implemented on them, and those who refused were denied any state aid after the distribution of an advanced dole for six months. Later, the Centre identified another category named the 'deserter refugees', who were provided rehabilitation in the states of Bihar, Orissa, Maharashtra, Uttar Pradesh and even Andaman, but who often came back because of inhospitable condition, hostile attitude of the locals.[29] The government refused to take their responsibility anymore on the grounds that they had willingly deserted the camps and were no longer considered eligible for state aid. After April 1961, the Centre instructed the closure of all camps and the resident refugees were given two options. Either they had to accept rehabilitation outside, or move out from the camps in major refugee-absorbent states, after accepting advance dole for six months. The government would stop all facilities like food, water, electricity and medical aid to these refugees. The deserter refugees who refused to move out of camps even after withdrawal of these facilities were called the 'ex-camp site refugees' (Chakraborty 2015: 28–29). Refugees were classified on the basis of their potential to be rehabilitated too. There were permanent liability group (PL), rehabilitatable group (RG) and border line cases (BLC) categories.[30]

Centre's policies on Bengali refugees

The Government of India initially had a proposal that the major refugee-absorbent states should take some responsibility to provide relief and arrange rehabilitation for the refugees, but they were given provision to ask for financial support from the Centre with proper plans designed by the state machineries. Both of the governments agreed that the amounts of loans granted to the displaced persons 'who arrived in India prior to 01.01.50' should be 'shared between the Centre and the states in the ratio of 50:50'.[31] The Rehabilitation Ministry assured, 'this formula would be revised later, if the burden proved too heavy for the state governments to bear'.[32] S. P. Mookerjee argued, instead of giving loans, refugees should be given compensation. His logic was 'If you have to compensate them, there will be at least one thousand crores of rupees worth of property belonging to Hindus which are lying in East Pakistan'.[33] The Centre refused the idea on the grounds that the

Bengali refugees would claim their property granted by clauses mentioned in the Delhi Pact. It was therefore decided that the Centre would grant assistance to the refugee-absorbent states for sharing the burden of relief and rehabilitation. Dr B. C. Roy estimated and demanded Rs. 4,75,00,000 as required expenditure for West Bengal for the year 1949–50 (Chakrabarty 1982: 57).

There were enormous discrepancies between official and census figures about the number of refugees in Bengal. S. P. Mookerjee called it a 'jugglery of figures' referring to the politics of rehabilitation of the Bengali refugees.[34] The census officials had taken into account the issuance of border slips or registration to determine their number. For example, the number of refugees in Assam had been officially shown as 2.5 lakhs, whereas the actual number was 8 lakhs in 1951.[35] Nehru's stand was 'to prevent Hindus from East Bengal from migrating' (Chakrabarty 1974: 109). He instructed Mohanlal Saxena, the then Rehabilitation Minister on 17 March 1950:

> Arrangements for the distribution of refugees to other states . . . the camps in other Provinces will not necessarily be in places where rehabilitation will take place . . . essentially they should be wholly training camps . . . it is important that the process of dispersal should start early.[36]

Following his directions, Saxena declared, 'the decision already arrived at in Delhi' that 'the migrants would not be given rehabilitation' . . . they would only get 'temporary shelter in relief camps' (Chakrabarti 1990: 31). The Centre planned to stop free doles to refugees aged between 18 to 50 years of age, as they would be handicapped by rehabilitation policies. They introduced a scheme for persons 'who are capable of doing manual and non-manual labour'.[37]

The discrimination against the East was evident and blatant in comparative figures of expenditure in the two regions even in the Report of the Ministry of Rehabilitation (1953–1954). While the total expenditure on West Pakistani refugees was 125.65 crores on heads of housing, grants, loans, establishment, etc., East Bengali refugees had received only 47.23 crores.[38] The Rehabilitation Ministry tried to justify the uneven allotment by arguing that number of refugees from West Punjab was larger than from East Bengal.[39] The annual report of the Ministry of Rehabilitation illustrated number of refugees and expenditure incurred in these two regions till the end of 1954. The report stated that for 49.3 lakhs West Punjabi refugees, the expenditure was 142 crores, but for 31 lakhs East Bengali refugees, the expenditure was 60 crores.[40] The officials in the Relief and Rehabilitation Department were aware of the allegations of discrimination in treatment of refugees between two regions.[41] They clarified their position by pointing out, 'this effort has in no sense been inferior to, or less intensive than, that applied in the Western region. But, the problems it had to grapple with were different, more complex and, therefore, very much more difficult' (Rao 1967: 146). Apart from those refugees who legally crossed the border with migration permits, some entered with forged papers and many of them had no documents.[42] There were hardly any means of keeping track of such illegal migrants, while their number was legion. The perpetual uncertainty about the magnitude of the problem was another problem. The Government of India was dependent more on policies taken by Pakistan. No definite numbers were cited for the refugees, and planning for rehabilitation was continually being thrown out of gear (Rao 1967: 146).

Ajit Prasad Jain replaced Mohanlal Saxena as the Union Rehabilitation Minister. He insisted on taking steps for speeding up of relief and rehabilitation measures for Bengali refugees.[43] He was active and politically alert, and hence could understand their reluctance to leave India. India and Pakistan agreed on employment of these refugees, and providing financial aid to states for expenditure on the relief and rehabilitation head.[44] The Centre instructed that the ratio of distribution should be 1:4.[45] A. P. Jain realised 'The absence of Evacuee Property law of the West in its application to the East made all the difference in the rehabilitation programme of the West and the East'.[46] He admitted, 'In the Western region, rehabilitation work is now in the final stage; in the Eastern region, the situation is still fluid'.[47] He encouraged establishment of industries in the Eastern region (West Bengal, Assam, Bihar, Orissa, Tripura and Manipur) to help the unemployed refugees in permanent rehabilitation.[48] He claimed in press statements in Bombay and Srinagar in December 1954 that 'the Refugee Rehabilitation in Western Region was satisfactorily solved though in the Eastern Region a little remained to be done'.[49] He recommended that the Refugee Rehabilitation Ministry should wind up soon. Meghnad Saha, a scientist by profession and founder of the organisation 'East Bengal Relief Committee'—and a member of Parliament later—was from East Bengal and immensely sympathetic to the Bengali refugees. He was 'quite struck with the enormity of the pronouncement', and termed it as 'lack of sense of responsibility implied'.[50] He protested against the decision as:

> The Government actually undertook the problem of their (East Bengali refugees) rehabilitation seriously only in 1950, but our knowledge was that the problem of refugee rehabilitation in these parts was not only not solved, but had not even started. If the Rehabilitation Ministry was wound up, the welfare of the 5 million people would have been nobody's concern [because] The success of refugee rehabilitation depends upon the co-operation between the Central Government and State Governments.[51]

A. P. Jain refuted criticisms by saying, 'our achievement in West Bengal has not by any means been negligible'.[52]

The refugee flow was enormous by the end of 1954. The Centre was compelled to open a branch office of the Rehabilitation Department in Calcutta. Mehr Chand Khanna had been given the responsibility to take care of this office, because of his good reputation as 'being the man behind the scene who has successfully tackled the problem of refugee rehabilitation in the West'.[53] The report of the Estimate Committee stated, 'It was only some time in 1955 and thereafter that the Government of India really settled down to tackle this problem of displaced persons from

East Pakistan on a rational basis' by 'shift in emphasis from relief to rehabilitation'.[54] Mehr Chand Khanna stressed the residuary problems of the refugees and focused on their grants and loans (Rao 1967: 148). Bengal experienced acceleration of work as no more files were being sent to Delhi under the new system. Perhaps his efficiency and visions had temporarily improved the refugee programme in the eastern side.[55] But it was the minority situation in East Pakistan, which determined the volume of migration in Eastern borders. *The Statesman* reported: 'The trend of the gap between numbers of upcoming refugees and the populace who wished to settle down started decreasing from the year 1956–57'.[56] The total numbers of displaced persons in India was 87.45 lakhs in 1955–1956, and out of those, 47.40 lakhs were from West Pakistan and 40.05 lakhs were from East Pakistan (Moraes 1958: 1021).

When Mehr Chand Khanna took over charge of the Union Rehabilitation Ministry in 1964, he supported the decision of A. P. Jain to wind down the Central Rehabilitation Department. The workings of state-funded worksite camps were stopped. For non-camp refugees, the Centre enabled the state governments to take over lands for resettlement by an amendment to Article 31 (on compensation for properties). Compensation rates were formulated by the Parliament and not by any court of law (Ray 1982: 161). His so-called 'clearer vision' made him initiate a move to disband the Rehabilitation Ministry on the plea that 'the gigantic task of the permanent settlement of 9 million displaced persons has been tackled and, by and large, completed'.[57] The refugee scenario in the eastern and northeastern states became so complicated that the Centre decided to convert previous loan amounts from the head of loans to grants.[58] The flood of refugees after the riot of 1964 diminished the last hope of finishing the relief and rehabilitation task.[59] This crisis made amounts of grants even insufficient.[60] The Centre imposed rigidity to maintain the classification of 'new' and 'old' migrants for receiving shelter, doles or professional rehabilitation, and made the rule strict for not settling down any more refugees in West Bengal, Assam and Tripura. The Ministry of External Affairs passed the verdict on the Delhi Pact in November 1968 that 'Pakistan has of course all along violated the agreement' (Roy Choudhury 1977: 83–87).

Jagjivan Ram, then the Union Minister for Labour, Employment and Rehabilitation, stated in the Second Rehabilitation Minister's Conference that the Centre was equally concerned for repatriates from Burma and Ceylon along with fresh influx from East Bengal. He admitted that 'the major problem is of the Displaced Persons from East Bengal . . . even the old ones . . . quite a number of them were living in camps for a long time . . . should be dispersed'.[61] He referred to the Dandakaranya scheme discussed later in this chapter, and discussed points of success and causes of failure of plans related to it.[62] The last bell on plans of the Rehabilitation Department of giving temporary relief to the East Bengal refugees had rung during those crucial months of the Liberation War of 1971. In the brief span of seven months, up to October 1971, there was an influx of 9.5 million refugees to West Bengal, Assam, Meghalaya and Tripura. It was sometimes as high as 57,000 to 102,000 persons per day, on average 1,600 refugees entering in every hour (Luthra

1971: 1970). Thus, the problem of professional resettlement or rehabilitation of the Bengali refugees remained unsettled and unsolved. Government documents and notifications often used phrases or terms like 'almost tackled' or 'by and large completed'. The process of appropriate arrangements to settle them permanently and accepting them in the mainstream with all facilities of a citizen was never completed.

The epicentre of crisis: West Bengal

West Bengal had emerged to be the epicentre of this huge humanitarian crisis. Calcutta, once a British capital termed as 'The living city' in the 1990s,[63] was 'a venue, and practically a metaphor, for survival and opportunity' for the refugees from the late 1940s.[64] Calcutta had always been migrant's city. Ever since the emergence of the colonial city of Calcutta, it had lured a large section of the rural and semi-rural populations to the city as a venue that could provide a livelihood, owing to its colonial commercial and administrative networks (Dasgupta and Chakraborti 1992: 35–48). At various stages, it attracted people from different parts of Bengal, the Indian subcontinent and beyond. Calcutta for centuries housed a significant section of poor and semi-poor migrants who came and settled there as service providers to the urban elite.[65] These labouring people were utilised in the regular civic works, though their slums were densely populated, with minimal civic amenities.[66] Yet, the migrants had been largely sustained within the economic and cultural life of the city. The residents of Calcutta were primarily non-Muslims and they owned 91.55 per cent of the residential buildings. They paid the bulk of municipal and other taxes, and owned and operated industries and educational institutes of the city.[67] Hindu migrants from Noakhali and Tipperah, as well as Muslim refugees of Bihar, began to pour into Calcutta from 1946.[68] Calcutta was almost ten times bigger than Dacca, a centre of migration in eastern India (Ludden 2011: 24, 36). The city had experienced migration during distress like famine, communal riots and calamities long before the refugee influx had started (Bhattacharya 1998: 561). The city dwellers were accustomed to new terms 'relief' and 'rehabilitation' in their vocabulary of colloquial dialogues.[69]

The first wave of Partition migrants consisted of the *bhadralok* class. Because of their class background, they organised themselves into pressure groups by their natural skills of negotiation and social status, and through their political contacts and activism. They could rehabilitate themselves comparatively easily. The middle-class refugees were in a situation of going from the frying pan into the fire. Partition had taken away their home and hearth, assets, social status and source of income, which distinguished their way of life.[70] The lower-strata were in a real miserable condition; they took shelter at Sealdah railway platform and at transit and colony camps. They were solely dependent on governmental initiatives and other social-political organisations, for protection and refuge (Datta 1984: 14). Narrating his own refugee experience, Manas Ray observed, 'The city that was affected most by this sudden and vast traffic of people, by any estimate the biggest instance of human displacement, is Calcutta' (Ray 2002: 149). Tai Young Tan and Gyanesh Kudaisya concurred: 'Among all the capital cities affected by Partition, it was Calcutta which suffered the most severe disruptions and received the largest number of refugees' (Kudaisya and Tan 2000: 172).[71] West Bengal was the most densely populated province of India before Partition, and after the advent of refugees. According to the census of 1941, the density of population per square mile was 751, and that figure had gone up to 950 in mid-1947. In occupational statistics, 50 per cent of the population was in non-agricultural occupation, as regards distribution of population in West Bengal, about 22 per cent used to live in towns, the corresponding figure for East Bengal was only 4 per cent (*Two Years since Independence* 1949: 12). The refugee influx led to several complexities. It was swelling population of towns and grappling with problems of food supply, housing, education and public health, as well as finding employment for large blocks of floating population (*Refugee Resettlement* 1948: 116). The state government, political parties and other voluntary organisers joined hands in raising funds to meet up the responsibility of feeding the refugees.[72]

The Government of West Bengal faced two major challenges. One, how to tackle the grave situation that occurred out of the migration of huge uprooted populace at least on temporary basis, and two, how to establish peace and security in riot-stricken West Bengal and spread the message of communal harmony. The Congress, as the party in power in the post-Partition West Bengal, was slightly apprehensive. The refugees were in trauma of Partition-borne violence; hence, they could easily be in a retributive mood.[73] They had to work on rehabilitative measures, keeping susceptibility in mind. The Bengal Provincial Congress Committee established transitory camps in Bally, Uttarpara, Rishra, Titagarh and Serampore, built 35 temporary shelters and planned a colony in the northern suburban area of Calcutta for a thousand cobblers and *harijans*. Jawaharlal Nehru wrote in a letter to the General Secretary of BPCC dated 27 September 1947, 'I am glad that the Bengal Provincial Congress Committee has organised a Relief and Rehabilitation Committee for this purpose'.[74] Hindu Mahasabha made available their buildings, called 'Mahasabha Bhawan', all over West Bengal for only 'bona-fide refugees', not for 'undesirable squatters'.[75] They could accommodate a thousand refugees at a time in each space.[76] Their approach was biased, chiefly in the way they defined categories of refugees, intended to protect the 'ill-fated' migrants from 'the clutches of the communal tyranny'.[77] Offices for the registration of refugees were opened in Calcutta and other districts from April 1948, as the first step of initiatives designed by the state government. The Government of India recommended the refugees should be kept in border areas through some makeshift arrangements.[78]

In the absence of necessary legislation, registration was offered on a voluntary basis and 881,461 certificates were issued to individuals. In some cases, one certificate only was issued for one family. By July 1949, 1,090,983 displaced persons were enumerated, whereas total estimated refugee families comprised nearly 10 lakh individuals (*Two Years since Independence* 1949: 16). Refugees were divided into three major classes, as per their conditions. The Refugee Rehabilitation Commissioner's Organisation created by the state government comprised of gazetted and non-gazetted officers, along with some field staffs (*Refugee Resettlement* 1948: 122). They provided relief in five steps, dispersal from railheads, accommodation in camps and outside, gratuitous relief, food and cash doles, supply of free clothing and blankets, sanitary amenities, medical attention and water supplies. A Central Advisory Board was set up in March 1948. It collaborated with district officials, recommended various loan schemes and free grant schemes including grants to educational institutions and students and cash grants for repatriation and relief against work.[79] A blueprint for building transit camps was planned, starting in Ranaghat, Bongaon and Howrah. The West Bengal Land Development and Planning Act, 1948 had been enacted for speeding up acquisition of land for rehabilitation purposes.[80] The camp population was in peak by October 1948 with 70,000 occupants (Bandyapadhyay 1970: 46). After reaching this figure, the government imposed restriction on admitting new refugees. The total number of camps in West Bengal was 37 by the end of 1949.

After the riot of 1950, the magnitude of the refugee problem had increased tremendously. The refugees were no more a homogenous category (Ghosh 2007: 16–17). There were region-based refugees, and agriculturists and professionals had started to migrate. 'About 95 per cent of the refugees are *Namasudras*' or *matuas*, reported a police report in June 1952.[81] This pattern of migration was not like an ordinary and typical 'economic migration' (Bandyopadhyay and Basu Ray Chaudhury 2014: 1–5). They were cultivators, day labourers or belonged to various skilled craft professions like washermen, fishermen, weavers, petty businessmen, small jotedars and talukdars, etc. Manohar Mauli Biswas, a *Namasudra* author as well as significant voice in *dalit* literature, wrote firmly, 'My father, grandfather, and all my illiterate forefathers are great agriculturists of Bengal. About 80 per cent of our community produced the harvest in the wet earth and fed the whole of Bengal' (Biswas 2013: xx). This peasant community used to live side-by-side with their Muslim neighbours. They migrated from all over East Pakistan, chiefly from Barishal, Faridpur, Jessore and Khulna. The Hindu caste hierarchies equally oppressed the *Namasudras* in rural Bengal. Abu Jafar Samsuddin wrote that Dakshinbag village in Bhawal Pargana comprised both Hindus and Muslims. The status of the *Namasudras* was same as the Muslim peasants. He remembered how the Brahmins always treated both these communities as 'untouchables' and used to take a dip if anyone crossed a pond while going back to their homes. Ramkumar Mandal, the headman among the *Namasudras*, was beaten up vigorously as he dared to cross a Brahmin house with shoes on (Samsuddin 1989: 3–15). Apart from the *Namasudras*, the *jatmara* classes (popularly known as *khere*) were not entitled to enjoy any religious rights or social privilege (Byapari 2013: 2728). For Hindus, they were converts by their local system of justice (*bichar*), and for the Muslims, they were like bigots, as they did not know how to perform *namaz* or other religious rituals of Islam. They comprised a class who were against Hindu upper-castes and upper-classes in rural Bengal.

The *dalits* first identified themselves with the Hindus, and cooperated with their co-religionists across class and caste lines. Later, they were compelled to become the 'other' in front of the Congress-Mahasabha combination. Debes Roy, in *Barishaler Jogen Mandal*, argued that the *Namasudras* or Rajbanshis, other *tapashilis* (scheduled castes), could never identify themselves with the Hindu society, because of social mishandling. They were against Hindu communal organisations like Hindu Mahasabha or Hindu Mission, where upper-castes tried to unite their communities to protect their hold over the society, land, politics and power. The anger and hatred reached to such a high that Jogendranath Mandal, a leader of the *Namasudras* and other Hindu depressed classes declared in 1938, 'these communities are not going to support the Hindus in Legislative Assembly or in communal conflicts' (Debes Roy 2010: 592). The Hindu leaders sought support only when the upper classes were in trouble, and hence they decided to be on the side of the Muslim peasants, as they could relate their lives and crises more with them. Jogen Mandal pointed out that the neighbouring peasants were friends, no matter whether they were Hindus or Muslims (Kapil Krishna Thakur 2011: 163). They conveyed to the Muslim and Hindu scheduled caste politicians that the upper-caste/class Hindus were their common enemy. The process of 'othering' was already there from the caste Hindus, but a new dimension was added when the Islamisation process started in Pakistan. Pakistan played this card intelligently. The Pakistani nationhood tried to impose on them a 'Hindu' identity, a category that tends to collapse differences between non-Muslim and *dalits* that was communal and discriminatory (Sengupta 2013: 95–96). The reason behind this targeting was that in most cases, the scheduled caste peasants had been granted some portion of lands from landlords for whom they worked for generations. Some of them had even bought a piece of land at minimal rates or just grabbed it after the owner left permanently.[82] When most upper-class and middle-class Hindus left East Bengal, the Pakistan administration did not want to transfer the lands to people who were Hindus. Hence, they began to change their attitude towards these scheduled caste people.

After the riot of 1950, the scheduled caste peasants became the target of the Muslims and they started migrating (Bandyopadhyay 2004b: 237). After their arrival, they were dispatched to various refugee camps in different districts like 24 Parganas, Nadia, Burdwan, Midnapore or Cooch Behar. In allocating space in the camps, caste and identity played a vital part, despite official denials. They were also rather rigid about resettlements, as they were used to in community-wise living, in particular caste-based *paras* of East Bengal (Basu 1975: 15). They declined to accept rehabilitation in places that would compel them to live away from their kinsmen or community members. The tendency of this ghettoisation derived from their experiences, as they were subjected to a process of 'othering' by the Pakistani state, as it moved towards greater Islamisation of the polity (Bandyopadhyay and Basu Ray Chaudhury 2014: 7). Sadananda Pal also pointed out in his memoir *Aka Kumbho* that when he went back to Dhaka, he saw most of the members of his community 'Pals' were leaving East Pakistan for settling down in India (Pal 2013: 86). Looking at the vigour of the 1950 refugees, the state Relief and Rehabilitation Department introduced border slips 'as an identity proof of their date and place of entry in West Bengal, to secure a shelter first and then resettlement by rehabilitation'

(Bandyapadhyay 1970: 58). As decided in the annexation of the Delhi Agreement of 1950, joint counting of passengers were introduced for those who were travelling between West Bengal and East Bengal by train via border stations of Darsana and Benapole in East Bengal and in Burnpur and Bongaon, the nearest stations in West Bengal.[83]

West Bengal was the major recipient of refugees in eastern borderlands. Dr Radha Kumud Mukherjee, the noted economist, urged to the Government of India, 'The numerical apparatus in Calcutta which had now to cater to a population exceeding 60 lakhs was breaking down under the vastly increased pressure. Government must own their responsibility of the refugees'.[84] He argued, pointing out that 'the size and resources of West Bengal had been reduced to one-third after Partition, which had now the largest density of the population in India, could afford only about an acre of land per head of its population'.[85] He identified that classification of refugees should be an indispensable step following which he advocated for occupational census, as it always seemed to be essential for planned rehabilitation. Dr Radha Kumud Mukherjee and the Bengal Rehabilitation Organisation stressed on an estimation of refugees who were planning to stay in East Bengal. Shyama Prasad Mookerjee echoed similar views, saying:

> Many of the migrants who are going back are doing so out of despair and helplessness because of opportunities for rehabilitation in West Bengal and many have already stated that they would not hesitate to embrace Islam, completely surrender themselves in case of any future onslaught.[86]

He asserted that the introduction of the passport system was a direct negation to the Delhi Pact: 'Since the enforcement of Passport the number of migrants has dwindled away'.[87] The lack of coordination and contradiction of opinions spoiled initiatives of the Central and state governments.[88] Some voluntary organisations—such as Jatiyo Silpo o Pally Binimoy Co-operative Colony Society, Lalbagan Seba Samiti and Bhatpara Emergency Relief Society—worked hard to make stop-gap arrangements for the non-camp refugees. They distributed dry doles and cooked food when lakhs of families were starving.[89] They arranged admission in schools and colleges on free tuition basis or tried to make arrangements with educational institutions in suburban and rural areas for refugee students.[90] To enable the refugees to earn a living, some organisations tried to provide them appointments in jute mills as temporary employees.[91] Some arranged places in medical camps for them with free medicines.[92] Some organised a meeting with state rehabilitation officials for better negotiations to arrange short-term loans for middle-class refugees and fought against corruption at high levels related to relief items and cash benefits in rehabilitation.[93]

The Bengal Branch of the Central Relief Committee planned relief and rehabilitation for the camp refugees (Ray 1982: 162) and surveyed the relief camps, introducing a 'Relief Through Work' campaign within camp-mates (for female refugees, crafts like spinning and knitting).[94] All India Women's Conference

(AIWC) was concerned with the security of female refugees. AIWC arranged grants for construction of dwelling sheds and distribution of cloth and woollen garments, started running vocational training centres and rendered educational relief in various categories including a monthly stipend of Rs. 200 for female refugees.[95] Renuka Ray appreciated their initiatives and pointed out that 'the West Bengal Government or the authorities of the Central Government is trying their best to help refugees' but, 'there are so many lakhs of refugees and it is not easy to provide employment to all of them'.[96] The state government advocated equal sensitive policies for refugee orphans (*They Live Again* 1954: 6). Tough negotiations with the Central Ministry for the 'Fixation of a ceiling of Rs. 32 per head per month exclusive of rent for homes of children, working mothers and orphanages' was advocated by Ashoka Gupta.[97] Since West Bengal had not been paid the 'Pre-Partition Payments' (the due amount in October 1950 was 95,00,000), which was decided earlier at the administrative level, Dr B. C. Roy hesitated in demanding additional amount of Rs. 56,41,000 for dispersal to students. However, the total number of colleges in West Bengal was 89, and over 40 colleges were in Calcutta and its environs. He informed in the Legislative Assembly that some colleges in Calcutta 'have admitted as many as 7,000 students on their rolls' and demanded, some allowance should 'be granted for expenditure under the head- Expenditure on refugees'.[98]

Sibnath Banerjee, a famous trade union leader in the 1950s, voiced in favour of establishing new colleges exclusively for refugee students. The state government claimed to rehabilitate 226,777 persons out of the total 31,700,027 registered refugees in 1950.[99] The census of West Bengal, 1951, showed 'the total number of displaced persons from East Bengal was in the order of 20.99 lakhs' (Pakrasi 1971: 22). Some refugees refused to identify and register themselves as 'refugees' in records, as it was a disrespectful term. A significant percentage of them were ignorant about the procedures of listing, and a few left halfway due to legal complexities. Others thought that it might be derogative for their future status in the new state, as they could not accept themselves into that category. The state government claimed to rehabilitate most of the refugees waiting in the transit camps and in other shelters by 1951, and decided to send the rest of them to Bihar (50,000 refugees) and Orissa (25,000), as per the policy of the Centre (Bandyapadhyay 1982: 92). The East Bengal Relief Committee became popular for working consistently on the refugee front.[100] Like Sucheta Kripalani, Dr Meghnad Saha described the 1950 Pact as 'self-delusive'.[101] He compared the situation with 'the case of West Germany where nearly one crore sixty-five lakhs of refugees poured in, in the fateful years 1945–46. Almost one man in three in West Germany was a refugee'. He asserted that 'Our figure is one in thirty-six', and pointed out: 'An invidious distinction has so far been made between Camp and Non-Camp refugees within the state of West Bengal. In fact only 10% of the total allotments have gone to Non-Camp refugees as against 90% to Camp refugees'.[102] He demanded economic rehabilitation within urban and rural (for agriculturists and non-agriculturists) schemes and provisions, with other facilities like medical assistance, proper sanitary conditions, water supply, particularly in holding opposing views against the complaint of refusal of refugees going to rehabilitation centres from transit camps.[103]

The East Bengal Relief Committee recommended that the non-permanent liability camps:

> have outlived their existence and should be abolished as early as possible' and 'those who are in these camps should at once be sent to work-site camps or rehabilitation places, new-comers should be directed to work in site camps or colony camps from the interception stations.[104]

It opposed sending refugees to Orissa and Bihar.[105] The Committee instead encouraged the refugees to settle down in 'Assam or Hill Tipperah'. Its argument was that these terrains had a similarity with East Bengal and scarcity of land was not so acute.[106] A Fact-finding Committee was appointed in 1952:

> to make a survey and assessment of the conditions in relief camps and rehabilitation colonies, in particular in housing and gainful employment provided for and vocational and technical training given to the displaced persons in West Bengal and the results of various other rehabilitation measures undertaken by Government.
>
> *(Pakrasi 1971: 30)*

The 'passport scare' had started long before the target date of execution (15 October 1952), which continued up till 1958.[107] The Committee recommended change in approach and policies. 'After taking into account the effect of the Passport System and the trends of the future migration', the broad lines of relief and rehabilitation schemes for different categories and scales of financial assistance must be different.[108] It suggested some planned rehabilitation like early liquidation of transit camps, regularisation of squatters' colonies, restructuring of urban and rural colonies, and improvement in administrative machinery.[109] The legal regime began over rights to property between private individuals and refugees (Bose 2000: 3). The main obstacle behind the regularisation of existing colonies on permanent basis was the predicament created by the issue of landlordism. They were proving hindrances in giving lands at government rates for legal purchasing and in some areas, local residents were also against such actions.[110]

West Bengal was flooding with refugees after 1952. To tackle this overcrowded populace, the state tried to adopt the model followed by West Pakistan: land acquisition for building cooperative societies.[111] The returnee Muslim refugees were another source of headache as, 'In spite of the terrible happenings in Calcutta, Raurkela and Jamshedpur', the Muslims left for Pakistan just as a temporary arrangement.[112] Some chose to come back, but their houses were already occupied in the meantime or requisitioned by the authorities. Others, who chose to remain in the city, were gradually marginalised as a vulnerable minority.[113] Actually after the riot of 1950, many Muslims either fled from the city or became internally displaced and took refuge in the camps for security. Their cultural symbols and resources were erased from the city's landscape (Sarkar and Bandyapadhyay 2015: 11). They began to lose their graveyards and *wakf* lands, and ghettoised in specific *mohallas* of the city.[114] Towards the concern over Muslim migrants, there was a wide gap between political rhetoric and actual practice. Thus, whereas the Muslims were encouraged to stay in a new secular, sovereign nation-state, those who left were being encouraged to come back. Yet, at the bureaucratic level, strong desire seemed prevalent throughout decades to prevent the return of Muslims.

In a letter dated 1 March 1953, the Deputy Secretary, Government of West Bengal wrote to the Secretary, Government of India, that:

> this Government is inclined to think that liberal extension of visas/period of stay, as proposed in the second alternative to such persons will cover all genuine cases and will enable this Government to exercise certain amount of control over undesirable elements trying to take advantage of the system . . . it will be difficult to work our passport rules in such a manner as to allow only Hindu citizens of Pakistan the facility of surrendering their passport and not the Muslim citizens who might also wish to do so.[115]

From 1954, the chief focus was on settlement of colonies for refugees, acquisition of lands, realisation of loans and re-allotment in services in West Bengal.[116] The government was planning reorganisation of colonies in suburbs, as Calcutta reached a saturation point in terms of accommodating population (*The West Bengal Independence Anniversary* 1953: 72). Meanwhile, a policy towards the 'deserters'—the refugees who had deserted from camps of other states where Bengalis were minorities—became necessary. They were in miserable condition and were literally living on the footpaths. Mr P. S. Basu, the Deputy Mayor of Calcutta, stated, the deserters had 'seriously threatened the city's health'.[117] He advocated:

> Keeping the refugees long in camps on allowances paid by the Government is indeed very demoralising. Every attempt should be made to inspire self-confidence and self-reliance by providing them with new avocations which will not only help their quick rehabilitation but will also make them more disciplined.

He also suggested alternative plans to the government like 'the formation of a Bengal army to which the younger section of this displaced persons might be recruited'.[118]

The government was well aware of the fact that it had completed almost five years since the initiatives of providing rehabilitation to the refugees (1952–1956) began, and still 56,000 refugees were left in camps of various categories, waiting for rehabilitation (*Purbo-Pakistaner Bastuhara: Punorbasoner Panch Bochhor* 1956: 6). They introduced schemes for rural and urban areas to solve residual problems, and allocation of a definite amount of grants for the refugees, with a 'cordon system' in rationing to prevent smuggling of food grains allotted for them.[119] The refugee rehabilitation programme seriously affected the economy of West Bengal.[120] The Statistical Survey Report of 1956 stated, 'the economic standard of the State has been lowered by deficiency of income of Rs. 21.9 crores per year'.[121] The report categorically mentioned, 'Every thousand migrants who have come into the State since the date of survey (July 1955) or will come in future will adversely affect the economy of the State by an additional amount of about Rs. 2.9 lakhs per year' and 'it is important to distinguish these amounts from expenditure on rehabilitation'.[122] The years 1957–1958 were crucial for decisionmaking and settling the refugees. The Centre and state governments introduced schemes of rehabilitation with five major objectives: (i) efforts for liquidation of camps; (ii) high priority for setting up cottage, small and medium industries for creating more employment for refugees; (iii) coordination of rehabilitation programmes with the plans for general economic and social development; (iv) immediate development of available land; and (v) greater emphasis on training in technical trade for the Second Five Year Plan (*A Statement* 1958: 4).[123] In 1958, there were 12,946 cooperative societies with a total membership of 638,744 and a working capital of Rs. 1387 lakh, chiefly involving the refugee population (*Report of the Administration* 1959: 37).

The Centre and Planning Commission was determined to bring changes in provision of relief and rehabilitation of incoming refugees (Chaudhuri 1983: 18). It specified, only the 'old migrants'—those who enrolled their names in the registered book of relief officers and were waiting at a border station in the hope that someday they would get a call to board the lorries which would send them to their respective destinations; generally Kaksa, Dhubulia, Coopers or Bolagarh camps—were eligible to get rehabilitation (Kapil Krishna Thakur 2011: 17).[124] The government was forced to take such a stand. There were only 30 camps in Burdwan, where 42,665 refugees were waiting for rehabilitation, apart from non-camp refugees and vagrants. The unofficial figure of refugees settled with their own accord in West Bengal in this luminal period was 2.5 lakh (Chatterjee 1990: 71). The period experienced growth of 'new towns' and urban centres due to the increase of refugee population. The 'old towns' like Calcutta were expanding and the developments of the 'new towns' were also at faster pace (Sen and Banerjee 1983: 11). Yet, by 1960, the state government was facing criticism for not utilising the total funds allotted by the Government of India in 1957–1959.[125] Renuka Ray termed it a 'partial truth', as she stated that it happened because of the late sanction of funds from the Central authorities. A 'strict instruction had been given that only such funds as could be utilised in proper manner should be disbursed', so 'it was not possible in that short space of 8 weeks to utilise the funds sanctioned so late'.[126] She confessed that incidents of allotment of funds to 'camp refugees' sometimes went to the 'non-camp refugee' families.[127] After the regularisation of colonies, the state started distributing *arpanpatras* (title deeds) to the refugee families, though it did not mean they had permanent hold over those properties.[128] The Relief and Rehabilitation Department was busy in negotiation with local pressure groups up till 1963.[129]

The next year, 1964, was a riot year and refugee migration again reached a certain high. The Centre authorities raised their grants for the 'new migrants', and the state government readjusted from other heads to provide immediate relief to the refugees. For the financial year 1965–1966, the Centre had given Rs. 1,57,17,752 as grants to refugees and Rs. 60,00,000 in loans.[130] Abha Maiti, then the Relief and Rehabilitation Minister, Government of West Bengal, complained that the amount granted in papers by the Centre was nothing, as the state had spent so much even by shifting from other allocations.[131] The Centre constituted a 'committee of review of rehabilitation work in West Bengal' in 1968 with Shri Atulya Ghosh as chairman. The committee was instructed to review the work that had already been done by the State Rehabilitation Department 'for Old Migrants', and 'to assess the nature of the problem created by New Migrants, who have remained in West Bengal' as well as 'to suggest measures for their benefit'.[132] The refugee families were not in a position to pay back the portions of loans which they had received and spent. Hence, they could not ask the remaining part of the loan to be released. The Centre instructed the state governments for 'conversion of maintenance loan[s] advanced to Displaced Persons from East Pakistan into grant[s]'.[133] Dharam Vira, then the Governor of West Bengal, was sympathetic towards the refugee cause. He tried to accelerate the whole procedure.[134] He visited almost all temporary camps and state hospitals, and he wrote lengthy reports to draw the Centre's attention. He informed that 'due to the presence of nearly 600,000 new migrants who came to West Bengal after 1 January 1964, there had been a considerable pressure on the hospitals', and thus he recommended an immediate sanction of 537 additional hospital beds only for refugees.[135]

Yet, the arrangements were not enough, considering the magnitude of crises. The number of refugees crossing through the not-yet-fenced international border every day was so massive that the government machinery could not speculate, prearrange probable groundwork or determine policies for them.[136] Trails of grave injustices were awaiting them. They became homeless, jobless and for the government employees or optees, issues related to their pensions were never resolved.[137] The last wave of mass migration was before the Liberation War of 1971. The state and the city of Calcutta had met a 'unique challenge', rather 'paid for the nation's independence' (Chaudhuri 2002: 132). The report of Working Groups, Ministry of Rehabilitation, stated, 'the number of migrants who came over, up to 25 March 1971 amounted to 52.31 lakhs, of whom 37.32 lakhs stayed on in West Bengal'.[138] Unlike other refugee tides, it was absolutely a one-way migration (*Interim Report* 1973: 1). The maximum concentration of evacuees was in 24 Parganas, West Dinajpur and Nadia, but West Dinajpur suffered enormously (Ghosh 1972: introduction). The 1971 census informs that '84,49,482 persons were found in the district of 24 Parganas, accounting for 19.1% of the total population of the State' (De 1994: 133). The Centre had allotted a total sum of Rs. 1,10,57 crores at the disposal of the state government, for meeting expenditure relating to the refugees and evacuees of 1971. They were instructed to build some basic accommodations called 'border camps' (*Annual Administrative Report* 1973: 32). The village non-medical 'doctors' had come with the refugees and continued to provide their services in the camps.[139]

Later, the refugees moved from the bordering areas and started pouring into the city. They targeted vacant places of Calcutta, like Maidan and Salt Lake (Basu 1996: 219). It resulted in the scarcity of shelter, drinking water and sanitation, and often led to epidemics like cholera. Salt Lake refugee camp was in an area which was low lying, in a partly reclaimed swampland. Construction of the permanent camp began in June 1971, before which the refugees camped out in crude shelters of grass and sticks or in huge concrete drainage pipes. The building of the camp consisted of rows of long huts—a timber and bamboo frame with mat walls and a roof of tarpaulin and rose on a brick floor.[140] The total number of evacuees in Salt Lake had crossed 1 lakh, with 'about 1/6 of the total population of the state belonging to the category of displaced persons, most of whom have never been properly rehabilitated or absorbed in the economic mainstream of the State'.[141] The refugee children were suffering from diseases or malnutrition. A report was published in July 1971, based on a survey of malnutrition among the refugee children by Dr V. Ramalingaswami and Dr B. N. Tandon, by which the government realised the importance of treating the children separately. The Ministry of Health, in consultation with the Ministry of Rehabilitation in New Delhi, planned 'lifeline alpha' and 'lifeline beta' for them.[142] In the administrative report, the state had mentioned, 'Because of the huge exodus of evacuees from Bangladesh, the task of rehabilitation of refugees in 1971–72 was not up to expectations. The main difficulty was the diversion of energies and resources for the immediate problem faced during the year' (*Annual Administrative Report* 1973: 32).

Refugee settlements in the eastern frontier: Andamans

The Central Relief and Rehabilitation Department was firm on its idea, from the beginning, of not settling the Bengali refugees only in Bengali-speaking states. West Bengal was overpopulated from the early 1940s, after speculation of Partition began. In 1949, a special enquiry committee was appointed by the Central Rehabilitation Department for finding out suitable areas for permanent settlement of refugees. The first official visit in Andamans included Nikunja Bihari Maiti, then the Rehabilitation Minister for West Bengal, with some other Punjabi members of that committee (Chakraborty 2012: 16). Dr B. C. Roy considered it a viable idea to send Bengali agriculturist refugees under the 'colonisation scheme' of the Central Government.[143] Keeping in mind the difficulty of the task to till the land, create a new settlement, the Union Ministry for Rehabilitation decided to allot 10 acres of land per family with cash doles for one year. The government was liable to supply materials of house building and basic supplies for farming.[144] But from the beginning, the East Bengali refugees were not willing in settling down in Andamans. K. C. Ganguly, from Bomrail, Barisal, wrote a letter to the then-President of the Indian National Congress on 31 January 1949, stating that:

> We find that Sri Nikunja Behari Maiti with a band of his friends and admirers is planning to make arrangements for rehabilitation of the Bengali refugees in Andaman. Please ask this Hon'ble Minister if he ever enquired of the East Bengal refugees whether they would be willing to go to the Andaman at all. We think, they would prefer going back to East Bengal and die there.[145]

But, about 199 families from Andul relief camp first arrived in the Andamans in March 1949. They were rehabilitated in Manpur, Kolinpur, Hamfrigunj, Noyashar and Andur (Chakraborty 2012: 17). 'The resettlers were established in three clusters and as far as possible the families of a district kept together' (Biswas 2009: 43). The promises and lucrative offers did not work for long, and 21 refugee families came back within six months. The key complaint was, the authorities did not fulfil assurance of providing 10 acres of land to each agriculturist family.[146] They complained that 'some of the families were given only four acres of land each, a small portion of which was arable, and the rest being full of thick jungles. Even this small area could not be cultivated for want of implements or oxen', and they pointed out, 'The cash dole of Rs. 100 per month which each family got on our arrival, was discontinued after five months, when we were given the option of returning to India or joining the local labour force'.[147]

A conflict started between the officers of two administrative bodies, as the Rehabilitation Ministry was in charge of monitoring expenditure on the colonisation scheme in Andaman, whereas the Ministry of Home Affairs controlled administration of Port Blair. The Rehabilitation Ministry sanctioned a scheme for resettlement of 200 displaced families initially, sailed by a light cargo transport ship.[148] The Government of India assisted in rehabilitation when the Ministry of Home Affairs was responsible for the policymaking part.[149] The Ministry of Agriculture was liable for further arrangements, purchase and supply of agricultural implements, including supply of buffaloes as plough cattle. Such conflicts resulted in chaotic implementation of policies, and the project became a mess.[150] Dr Kailash Nath Katju, then the Governor of West Bengal, tried to send few batches of refugees to the Andamans, but the Home Ministry introduced a 'quota system' in the early 1950s, which meant 'settlement of outsiders in the Andamans should be on the basis of equal quota from all States in India and that there should be no preference for East Bengal Refugees'.[151] Thus, 'The refusal of the Union Home Ministry to increase the quota for the refugees from East Bengal in an island environment ideally suited to a riverine people appeared to be proof of the unsympathetic attitude of the Central Government' (Ray 1982: 164–65). When the project was more or less successful, the decision had been made on exploring the Nicobar Islands. Government tried to explore possibilities of utilisation of lands over there, too.[152]

The domiciles of the Andamans and the society were not warm towards refugees. In 1954, The Andamans Indian Associations, 'old settlers', submitted a memorandum in the States Reorganisation Commission suggesting that 'refugees from East Bengal should not be settled in the Andamans where they want a homogenous community of Andaman Indians'. They stressed on the 'cultural homogeneity' with a theory of 'pressure on lands', in their argument.[153] Generally, the poor landless *Namasudra* refugee families were rehabilitated in villages by the administration (Acharya 1978: 13). Planned rehabilitation packages started with the beginning of the First Five Year Plan and: 'With a settlement of about 785 families of displaced persons from East Bengal in the Andamans from early 1949 the total Bengali population there was now a little over 4,000. The number had almost doubled in the 1951 census'.[154]

> In the first two years, 1953–1954 of the Rangat Colonisation Scheme in Middle Andaman 438 Bengali families have been settled; in South Andaman 347 families are now tilling 1700 acres of land. A total of 5000 families, 75 per cent of them Bengalis are proposed to be settled in Rangat valley by 1958.[155]

In the last scheme of rehabilitation, more than 560 families were allotted agricultural and homestead lands over the 4,100 acres of cleared forest lands in Middle Andaman, Neil Islands and little Andaman till mid-1969, and it continued till the 1970s (Kailash 2000: 2859–60).

Bihar and Orissa

After the introduction of the passport system and visa regulations, a conference for high-level talks was organised in Calcutta, chiefly with representatives of the governments of West Bengal, Bihar, Orissa, Assam and Tripura. Sri A. P. Jain, the Minister for Rehabilitation, Government of India, presided over it. The discussions at the conference mainly centred on how far Bihar and Orissa would relieve pressure on the Bengal Government by absorbing the new arrivals.[156] Though they were bona fide refugees, the Government of Bihar had offered them only relief and temporary shelter.[157] After 1950, both Bihar and Orissa governments committed to take responsibility to help the refugees. Bihar promised to accommodate 50,000 refugees and Orissa agreed on 25,000 refugees. With the change of the policy, the Centre instructed Bihar to rehabilitate 6,000 refugees, when Orissa asked to accommodate 4,000 refugees in its lands (Bandyapadhyay 1982: 92). Renuka Roy released a press statement in 1952, claiming that the government was trying to introduce new schemes for the refugees, enquiring about the condition of the transit camps in those states by 'taking a realistic view of the situation'.[158] Rehabilitation officers were complaining that it 'would harp on saying that East Bengal people could not settle down' there, because 'local climate had not suited them or they wanted exactly same water and same lands as in their original places'.[159]

A. P. Jain announced in the House of the People that the government had decided by way of helping the refugees of Bihar and Orissa to write off loans taken by them up to the extent of Rs. 300, provided the recipients of such loans had not put in any claim for compensation.[160] In the Conference of 1952, both the states, Bihar and Orissa, agreed to do their best to accommodate refugees as much as possible. The representatives of Bihar pointed out that '64.5 lakh acres of land in Bihar had been already requisitioned by the State Government for the cause of Bengali refugees, and in the Purnea district of Bihar, they could rehabilitate 3,500 people alone' (Chaudhury 1964: introduction). But in reality, many refugees left the place where they had been settled.[161] A rumour spread in all relief and rehabilitation centres for Bengali refugees that their fellow brethren were staying in temporary shelters of West Bengal and the government had allotted lands for permanent rehabilitation or they would get a job or loan as professional or economic rehabilitation.[162] The refugees of both Bihar and Orissa naturally anticipated that they might also manage to get a piece of land in the state of Bengal.[163] They started migrating to West Bengal from the camps, rehabilitation centres and refugee colonies there.[164] The refugees had huge grievances against the camp coordinators and on the management groups in both the states.[165]

The refugees of Samalpur Refugee Colony in Balasore, Orissa, complained about not getting proper loans and shelter. They affirmed such problems as: 'The officer in charge always consoling us by words not in kinds'.[166] They were apprehensive about their future as 'our dwelling huts and stalls are now in wretched condition'.[167] The same tone of resentment was heard from inhabitants of the refugee settlements in Cuttack, Orissa. They asked for help from the branch office of the Jana Sangh.[168] Out of 28,000 refugees who went to Bihar after Partition, 5,000 had been rehabilitated and other 23,000 were waiting to be rehabilitated in the transit camps in Bettiah.[169] Those transit camps in Bihar were 'divided into 9 units, some units were well-run and supplied with water and other amenities'.[170] The refugees of Binanohi Rehabilitation Centre complained of not getting doles for a long period and lack of necessary logistics like scarcity of tube wells and drinking water, along with other facilities, which was being enjoyed by the refugees in other states.[171] Approximately '10,000 refugees have come to West Bengal from Bettiah and squatted in the Howrah Maidan and railway station and Sealdah'.[172] The situation was like an epidemic. The Central and state governments decided to compel the refugees to return to their respective camps in Bihar and Orissa.[173] The state government was providing them a free train ticket with some cash doles (Rs. 5 per family and Rs. 2 per person) for travel expenses.[174]

Dandakaranya

Dandakaranya was the most ambitious project conceptualised by the Centre authorities for permanent resettlement of the East Bengali refugees. West Bengal was bursting at the seams in the second half of the 1950s. The Centre urged the neighbouring states to search for lands to rehabilitate displaced families. The Darjeeling Conference of 1955 confirmed their fate. All state Rehabilitation Ministers gave their nods to the blueprint of a plan of rehabilitating the refugees outside

'Greater Bengal' (Pal 2010: 83). Mr S. V. Ramamurthy, then adviser to the Planning Commission, presented a report with answers of few agonising questions in 1956. He suggested that an effort for integrated development would make use of the potential of this region, and it could offer ideal facilities for large-scale settlement (Rao 1967: 199). A high-level committee of the Government of India, known as the AMPO Committee, entrusted with the task of investigating the possibilities and the idea of making a 'Second Bengal' in the territories of Orissa, Madhya Pradesh and Andhra Pradesh, started shaping up (Sen 1966: 6). The Committee analysed prospects of rehabilitation, had strongly recommended that refugees from East Bengal 'should be moved into this area' (Hota 2009: 12). The Dandakaranya project envisaged the reclamation of about 1.5 lakh acres of land from Madhya Pradesh and Orissa. Initially, the government planned to include lands from Andhra Pradesh, but those lands were found unsuitable for agricultural purposes and were excluded (*The Dandakaranya Project* 1958: 4).

The region finally selected was the Koraput and Kalahandi region from Orissa and Bastar district of Madhya Pradesh, involving a total area of 80,000 square miles, though it made up a well-defined area of 30,052 square miles. The Dandakaranya Development Authority (DDA) was set up with the purpose of the integrated development of the area with special reference to the tribal population (Dasgupta 1979: 8). Thus:

> [the] wide tract of land that has been taken in hand by the Dandakaranya Authority is the field of a grand project to reclaim the land and make it habitable for the homeless people of East Pakistan and also to improve the lot of the original inhabitants.
>
> *(Devi 1974: 2)*

The preparations for making Dandakaranya a rehabilitation area started from 1954. The Centre had allocated a huge budget for the Umerkote Irrigation Dam across Bhaskal River that was expected to be completed by 1963. Dr B. C. Roy laid the foundation stone of this dam project and urged for a 'human approach' to the refugees, as he believed, 'For no fault of theirs these people had been compelled to leave their hearths and homes causing a serious psychological setback in their minds'.[175] The average cost of rehabilitating a family of five in a village in Dandakaranya was estimated at Rs. 2,500 in Umerkote, Paralkote and Pharasgaon Zone (Rao 1967: 199). The DDA fixed the future pattern of the economy of Dandakaranya. Emphasis was given to agriculture, when they paid meticulous attention to the planning of village settlements.[176] They proclaimed to have enough lands for agriculturists, planned short training courses for traders and established worksite camps for refugees with loan facilities.[177] The Authority tried to make Dandakaranya attractive by providing a supply of drinking water and making adequate provision for looking after the health issues.[178] Large schemes for irrigation and electricity were planned. After transferring few batches from different camps of eastern and north-eastern states (as fixed earlier), the Centre decided to send more refugees where rehabilitation got stopped (Ray 1982: 167). A growing discontent about land and patterns of living was emerging, as the Bengali cultivators were accustomed to semi-aquatic and plain-land agriculture; they found it difficult to eke out a living in the rugged terrain and shallow soil of Dandakaranya (Elahi 1981: 220).

The Dandakaranya scheme was perceived as 'a failed project' from 1960, and almost all political parties voiced 'Demand for Khanna's resignation' in the Lok Sabha.[179] But, the theory to highlight the contrast between 'hardy Punjabi migrant' and the 'lazy Bengali migrants' was fuelled by the Central Government. The Annual Report of the Ministry of Rehabilitation reported (1961–1962):

> throughout the year, activities in the various departments proceed smoothly and the only reason why the results actually achieved were not greater was due to the poor response from displaced persons in camps in West Bengal to move to the Project area to settlement there.
> *(Ministry of Rehabilitation-Annual Report 1961–62: 16)*

It also pointed out:

> A number of difficulties were encountered because of the poor communication in the area, absence of land records and surveys and other important data necessary for proper planning. Reluctance on the part of the staff, both technical and administrative, to serve in this inhospitable region, constituted another major difficulty in the preparation and implementation of the scheme. There were also some difficulties in regard to the release of land for reclamation and settlement of the displaced persons.
> *(Ministry of Rehabilitation-Annual Report 1961–62: 47)*

The project was never planned properly, yet the refugee families tried hard to survive. The governments of West Bengal, Assam and Tripura were sending refugee families on a regular basis, the batches consisting of both categories: the refugees who had given their consent wilfully, and others who wished not to settle there.[180] From 1958, the refugees did not have any other option but to opt for a settlement outside Bengali-populated states.[181] It was precipitated by the policy declared by the Union Ministry; some camps in Bengali refugee-absorbed states were closed down by the end of January 1962.

The riot of 1964 made the situation even worse. The West Bengal Government started sending the riot-stricken refugees directly from borders, sometimes without informing the DDA.[182] The unending flow to Mana camp with its limited accommodation had perplexed the Dandakaranya Authorities, despite round-the-clock efforts, 'With the present rate of influx, they have no other alternative than to put the new migrants straight under the sun as the flow still continues'.[183] In effect:

> Fifteen persons, mostly children, are dying daily on an average in the Dandakaranya Transit camps for new migrants. The death rate is high at Krud

Camp where over 33,000 people have been compelled to live like pigs in a sty. Four families share a tent.[184]

The Mana Groups of Transit Centres were under the charge of DDA; surprisingly, the administrative control of the camps was taken over by the Ministry of Rehabilitation from 1 July 1964 (*Reports of the 71st India Estimate Committee*: 21). The Central Social Welfare Board stated in the annual report:

> The Government machinery is providing for the basic minimum needs but the problem of missing members of families and the problem of unattached women and children have not yet been taken up by them in right earnest as they do not have adequate staff or a body to guide them.[185]

Saibal Kumar Gupta, then the Chairman of Dandakaranya Development Authority tried to find out the root cause of the problem. He stated:

> The displaced persons have not yet had their tenancy rights secured by the grants of *pattas* because the Ministry is as yet unable to decide whether the cost of reclamation and development of agricultural land should be charged to the settler.[186]

The Centre highlighted the 'occupational disease' of Bengali refugees by explaining that the refugees were more prone to write applications for further improvement of their position, instead of working hard on that soil. A local newspaper of refugees in Dandakaranya reflected a different view. It threw light on the other side of the coin by arguing: 'The fact that the Zonal Administrator of Dandakaranya Project, Umorkote, lacks that human sympathy towards the settlers who are in his charge is amply proved when reasons leading to mass desertion by the settlers are carefully analysed'.[187] The Estimate Committee Report highlighted the causes for refugee desertion. The chief reason behind the failure of the project, as pointed out by them, was 'the inability of the Bengali refugee to adapt to the rigours of hard agricultural life' (Chakravarty 2011: 176). Saibal Kumar Gupta also reported numbers of deserters, which was 1,400 persons in 1965, 2,170 persons in 1966, and 373 persons in 1967. At the same time, he cited a comment of the Chief Administrator of DDA in an official note dated 15 August 1966. The Chief Administrator wrote: 'The settlers are putting in excellent efforts in all zones' (Gupta 1994: 159). Thus, the actual reason was different. The blame placed on the Bengali refugees—that they did not wish to leave West Bengal and wanted to survive on the easy doles without doing hard work—proved wrong. Comparison between the Punjabi and Bengali refugee cultivators could not be proved as the only reason.

The Dandakaranya project was never meant to benefit the refugees. Orissa gave its consent with the view of development of these areas with the financial support from the Central Government. Madhya Pradesh was trying to be in a safe equation with the Centre, and the Agency Tracks of Andhra Pradesh finally did not give its nod, because the Centre was asking for a fertile but low plateau.[188] Mehr Chand Khanna had mentioned on 6 April 1960 that 'because of the lack of coordination between the Governments of two districts of Orissa and Bastar district of Madhya Pradesh, great deal of time and public money was being unnecessarily wasted'.[189] The state governments of West Bengal, Assam and Tripura not only reached the saturation point; they were locally criticised for helping a huge populace, and they avoided further hassles by closing up camps and state Rehabilitation Departments.[190] The Centre could realise the crisis, as it was articulated in the Report of the Estimate Committee: 'The Committee further suggests that as far as possible, migrants should be settled in compact areas and in congenial social environment and small pockets of resettlement areas in far off States may be avoided' (*Reports of the 71st India Estimate Committee*: 25). The refugees were sent to difficult terrains of Dandakaranya, deserted places in Bihar or far-flung islands in the Andaman, and they were recruited in state-sponsored developmental projects like construction of roads and dams, clearing of forests, reclamation of wastelands and other developmental projects as camp refugees. But the contributions of Bengali migrants seldom got a mention in the official documents, which rather tried to cover up flaws on government's ends by portraying the refugees as lazy and unwilling to do hard work, and placing blame for failures of proper rehabilitation on their unwillingness to perform according to the state policies (Chakravarty 2011: 303).

Summing up

After the divide, the Centre was assigned to make policies for the refugees of Western Punjab and Eastern Bengal, when they were actually not aware of either the scale or volume of the problem. The whole issue was unforeseen for both the states. The decision for Partition had been taken on the basis of some preconceived ideas and notions of the statesmen and political parties. The layers of difference emerged not only in regard to planning the exchange of population but also in handling the relief and rehabilitation policies on Punjab and Bengal. Until the 1950s, it was the chief point of debate and discussion in government documents, all correspondences and newspaper reports. In case of eastern borders, the Central Government did not find enough reasons and justifications for such large-scale migration that continued for really long. The state did not recognise the subtle form of violence was 'violent enough' to force the minorities to migrate. Violence in East Bengal was rather treated as a 'psychological fear' and the refugees were categorised as 'not genuine victims' like those of the West. The way Jawaharlal Nehru had perceived his stand on Bengali refugees was problematic from the beginning. Only during and after the colossal riot of 1950 that led to a gigantic migration of the middle-classes and lower-classes along with the professionals, Bengal somehow managed to draw some serious attention from the Centre. The process was indeed problematic in the case of West Bengal. The policymakers were never sure even about the tentative figures of the refugees, as they migrated in several waves, in and around the riot years. The policies were naturally taken on an ad hoc basis, and they varied from time to time when implemented on the local level. On top of that, there was a floating population who migrated several times and came back with the simple hope that they might get a portion of their property in East Bengal or at least some compensation back in India. When the earlier batches of the refugees were shocked and hurt by the treatment of the authorities, the later batches were not hopeful about the treatment they were supposed to get in camps of West Bengal or other rehabilitating centres. Respective states like West Bengal, Assam and Tripura were not responsible for the maltreatment the refugees received. The respective state governments accommodated and resettled refugees as much as possible, and sent the rest of them to peripheral places like the Andamans, Bihar, Orissa and Dandakaranya.

Prior to the Partition, there were promises made by the leaders assuring the people protection and warm welcome if they decided to come to the Indian side of the border. After Partition, the newborn state was suffering from many other problems; the refugee issue was one of them. The root of the problem actually lay elsewhere. Though the Centre based in Delhi had come out as the supreme authority on the policymaking front, it was nothing but a hypothetical power block in India when Delhi was just like another state, which did not have any land and other territory or facilities to accommodate the huge influx. Actually, looking at the volume of the problem regarding Partition-displaced refugees or their resettlement, the Government of India assigned the Centre to work on it, chiefly to make policies. But the Centre was not in the position to dictate to the states in the federal polity; neither did it own or possess any land. Hence, in reality, the Centre could only request and instruct the refugee-absorbent states. They placed a few viable suggestions to respective refugee-absorbent state governments on how to work for the resettlement and permanent rehabilitation of the refugees. Thus, the Centre had designed policies and requested the concerned states to share some burden, while they had to depend on the state's goodwill and effort for implementing their policies and for providing the refugees initial relief and later to rehabilitate them. The state governments used to appeal and demand required amounts and relevant policy instruction from the Centre. The political equation between the ruling government in states and the Centre was important, in which respective policies sometimes got disrupted.

While taking their responsibility, the states, in return, demanded financial support from the Centre and modified the basic policy ideas as per the regional variation and local needs. The state government did not get the required amount of money they claimed for the refugees from the Central budget. The Centre requested the states to resolve the fund crises by allotting amounts from state allocations. The key problem was that the blueprint was in the Centre's hand, while the states were supposed to play the role of implementors. The refugees gradually became aware of all these uncertainties, but while migrating, they thought of the religious affinity which would keep them safe in a country meant for them. In their imagination, being with their own people would be with the Bengali brethren. They never thought of being sent by them to deserted places outside Bengal.

Resettling in an alien land with inhospitable terrain, then getting adjusted to other ecological habitation and people from different language and culture, seemed quite a challenge for them. In spite of being an uprooted, homeless lot, destined to survive at the mercy and dole of the government, many of them again found it extremely humiliating to adjust and share life and livelihood with the indigenous forest people and local tribes. For the refugees, the shift in their own priorities had changed with the passage of time. With their limited knowledge and understanding, they were repulsed by the idea of settling in any area beyond 'Bengal' or broadly speaking, Bengali culture. The main reason behind their insecurities was a sense of fright and anger; they did not even imagine these layers and sub-layers of differences and complications awaiting them in their 'promised land'.

Notes

1 Jawaharlal Nehru, Letters to Chief Ministers 1947–1964, Vol. 3, 1952–1954, NMML, 1985, p. 367.
2 Nehru, Letters to Chief Ministers, Vol. 5, 4 June 1961, p. 433.
3 File No. RH (C)-5(2)/50 I, RHC Branch, NAI.
4 File No. 17-G (R)-49, G (R) Branch, NAI.
5 Nehru to C.M. Trivedi, 13 January 1948, in *Selected Works of Jawaharlal Nehru (SWJN)*, Series-II, Vol. 5 (1987), Part 4, 'Rehabilitation of Refugees', 140–41; and Nehru to Vallabhbhai Patel, 17 November 1948, in *Selected Works of Jawaharlal Nehru (SWJN)*, Series-II, Vol. 8 (1989), Part 5, 147–48.
6 *AICC Papers*, File No. AICC-II, Instalment 3117, NMML
7 File No. 8 (31)-GR-48, G (R) Branch, NAI.
8 File No. 8 (32)-GR-48, G (R) Branch, NAI.
9 Correspondence in *SWJN*, Series-II, Vol. 10 (1990), Part 6, 'Rehabilitation of Refugees', 267–68, 272–75; Nehru to B.G. Kher, 13 June 1949, in *SWJN*, Series-II, Vol. 11 (1991), 88–89.
10 The Muslim League became strong in Sindh from the 1940s, and started expressing resentment towards the Hindus openly. Mohammed Ayub Khuhro proclaimed during the Election of 1946:

> I am looking forward to the day when the Hindus of Sindh will be so impoverished or economically weakened that their women, even like poor Muslim women now, will be constrained to carry on their heads the midday food to their husbands, brothers and sons toiling in the fields and market places.

11 *Renuka Ray Papers*, Speeches and Writings by Her, File No. 87, NMML.
12 *Diwan Chaman Lall Papers*, II Instalment, File No. 149, 1948–56, NMML.
13 File No. 8 (83)-GR-48, G (R) Branch, NAI.
14 File No. 2 (15)-G (R)/49, G (R) Branch, NAI.
15 Samar Mukherjee. 2001. 'Rehabilitation of Bengali Refugees'. In *Refugees and Human Rights: Social and Political Dynamics of Refugee Problem in Eastern and North-Eastern India*, ed. Sanjay K. Roy, 135. Jaipur and New Delhi: Rawat Publication.
16 *S. P. Mookerjee Papers*, V–VII Instalments, Other Papers, Serial No. 155, NMML.
17 *Amrita Bazar Patrika*, 23 September 1949.
18 *Constituent Assembly of India (Legislative) Debates*, Vols. VI and VIII, 1948, p. 1052.
19 *The Statesman*, 9 December 1948.
20 *S. P. Mookerjee Papers*, V–VII Instalments, Subject File No. 12; *M. N. Saha Papers*, VII Instalments, Subject File No. 6, NMML.
21 File No. 2 (36)-RC/50, RC Branch, NAI.

Dealing with the refugees **113**

22 *Ananda Bazar Patrika*, 29 February 1949.
23 The Hazratbal incident refers to the massive riot of 1964 in East Pakistan. It sparked by an alleged theft of the Prophet's hair from the Hazratbal shrine in Jammu and Kashmir on 27 December 1963. Though, it recovered on 4 January 1964, the repercussion had taken the shape of riots in Khulna, Jessore, Faridpur, Dacca and Narayanganj and resulted in migration of another million of Hindus. They indeed brought horrified stories of violence and rioting along with them, and it led to worst communal riots again in Calcutta and other places of West Bengal, Assam and Tripura.
24 *WBLA Debates*, Vol. III, No. 1, 1951, p. 353.
25 According to the reports of Refugee Relief and Rehabilitation Department, some families lived in such camps for more than ten years; some got converted as the centre of permanent rehabilitation of refugees like Dhubulia Camp and Cooper's Camp in West Bengal.
26 Nehru stated, 'Obviously two of the most important criteria are- (i) the preservation of order and protection of people (ii) decrees in exodus'. *The Statesman*, 11 April 1950; Shyama Prasad Mookerjee mentioned that he had travelled among the refugees to gather 'first-hand knowledge from refugees in camps in West Bengal, Assam and Tripura who returned but come back frustrated, Hindu employees of Pakistan Government and Hindus who are still living there'. Undated report published in a pamphlet titled *Delhi Pact Has Failed*, issued by his organisation Bengal Rehabilitation Organisation from Calcutta (1950), *S. P. Mookerjee Papers*, II–IV Instalments, File No. 160, NMML.
27 B. C. Roy initiated this idea of sending the refugees to the infamous penal colonies in Andaman from 1948. It was an essential part of his rehabilitation scheme to move those refugees out from West Bengal.
28 *Annual Report of the Year 1958–59*, Ministry of Rehabilitation, p. 30.
29 IG Police Note dated 31 January 1956.
30 Border Line Case families were those who were willing for rehabilitation, but could not settle up their minds, whether to opt for rehabilitation or to remain as PL. The screening committee declared them as BLC. *The Screening Committee Report*, 'Problems of Refugee Camps and Homes in West Bengal', The Government of West Bengal, Refugee Relief and Rehabilitation Directorate, 1989, p. 8.
31 File No. 32/Mics./B-51 (Part-I), Rehabilitation Branch, NAI.
32 *Renuka Ray Papers*, Subject File No. 3, NMML.
33 *S. P. Mookerjee Papers*, V–VII Instalments, Subject File No. 12, NMML.
34 *S. P. Mookerjee Papers*, V–VII Instalments, Speeches and Writings by Him, Serial No. 7, NMML.
35 'Memorandum on the Rehabilitation of Refugees from Eastern Bengal' by The East Bengal Relief Committee, *M. N. Saha Papers*, VII Instalment, Subject File No. 6, NMML.
36 *S. P. Mookerjee Papers*, II–IV Instalments, Subject File No. 162, NMML.
37 There was seldom any reference to that particular scheme in contemporary documents, as the rule of 'a camp refugee is not allowed to work outside' remained for long. *S. P. Mookerjee Papers*, II–IV Instalments, Subject File No. 179, NMML.
38 *M. N. Saha Papers*, VII Instalment, Subject File No. 6, NMML.
39 *Hindustan Standard*, 20 June 1951.
40 *M. N. Saha Papers*, VII Instalment, Subject File No. 9, NMML.
41 *The West Bengal Weekly*, 23 June 1953.
42 *Hindu Mahasabha Papers*, File No. C-136, NMML.
43 *A. P. Jain Papers*, Notebook, Serial No. 3, NMML.
44 File No. 101/48-Apptt., Apptt. Section, NAI.
45 File No. 3-R/50, R Branch, NAI.
46 *A. P. Jain Papers*, Notebook, Serial No. 3, NMML.
47 *M. N. Saha Papers*, VII Instalment, Speeches and Writings by Him, Serial No. 23, NMML.
48 *Amrita Bazar Patrika*, 30 November 1954.

49 *M. N. Saha Papers*, VII Instalment, Subject File No. 6, NMML.
50 *M. N. Saha Papers*, VII Instalment, Speeches and Writings by Him, Serial No. 23, NMML.
51 *M. N. Saha Papers*, VII Instalment, Speeches and Writings by Him, Serial No. 23, NMML.
52 *The Statesman*, 29 June 1954.
53 *M. N. Saha Papers*, VII Instalment, Subject File No. 6, NMML.
54 Estimate Committee (1959–60), *Ninety-Sixth Report*, p. 8.
55 *The West Bengal Weekly*, 9 August 1959.
56 *The Statesman*, 23 September 1954.
57 *Rehabilitation Ministry's Annual Report: 1961–62*, Introduction, p. 1.
58 File No. 39-(2)/61, Rehabilitation, NAI.
59 *WBLA Debates*, Fourteenth Session, 1965, Vol. XI, No. 1, p. 205.
60 *Ananda Bazar Patrika*, 13 August 1957.
61 The policy of the Ministry of Rehabilitation was focusing on granting 'certain concessions to repatriates from Burma and Ceylon in the matter of age, educational qualifications, execution of bond and production of cash security, etc.' and 'This concession is granted for trainees and employees under various Central Government undertaking Organisations'. File No. P-II/282/24/68, Pak-II Branch, NAI.
62 File No. P-(P IV) 282 (91)/66, Pak-II Section, NAI.
63 Sukanta Chaudhury used this phrase as a book-title in his much-acclaimed edited work, '*Calcutta: The Living City*' in two volumes.
64 Nilanjana Chatterjee. 1990. 'The East Bengal Refugees: A Lesson in Survival'. In *Calcutta: The Living City*, ed. Sukanta Chaudhury, Vol. II, 70. New Delhi: Oxford University Press.
65 Sarmistha De. 2014. 'Native Labour in Early Nineteenth Century Calcutta'. In *Calcutta in the Nineteenth Century: An Archival Exploration*, ed. Bidisha Chakraborty and Sarmistha De, 354. New Delhi: Niyogi Books.
66 Partho Datta. 2009. 'Ranald Martin's *Medical Topography* (1937): The Emergence of Public Health in Calcutta'. In *The Social History of Health and Medicine in Colonial India*, ed. Biswamoy Pati and Mark Harrison, 15–30. New York: Routledge.
67 Sengupta, Anwesha. 2015. 'Becoming a Minority Community: Calcutta's Muslims after Partition'. In *Calcutta: The Stormy Decades*, ed. Tanika Sarkar and Sekhar Bandyapadhyay, 434–37. New Delhi: Social Science Press.
68 File No. 31/26/46-Ests. (S), Establishments (Special) Section, NAI.
69 Interview with Tapan Kumar Bhattacharya, an engineer by profession, taken on 16 December 2010 in Kolkata, West Bengal.
70 Joya Chatterji. 2001. 'Right or Charity? The Debate over Relief and Rehabilitation in West Bengal, 1947–50'. In *The Partitions of Memory: The Aftermath of the Division of India*, ed. Suvir Kaul, 91. New Delhi: Permanent Black.
71 They named Calcutta 'a dying city', the phrase used by the Prime Minister Rajiv Gandhi, too, to criticise the left bastion.
72 *AICC Papers*, File No. G-26, PART-II/1947–48, NMML.
73 *AICC Papers*, File No. G-5/1947–48, NMML.
74 *AICC Papers*, File No. G-61, Vol. II/1947–48, NMML.
75 *Hindustan Times*, 13 May 1948.
76 *Hindu Mahasabha Papers*, Subject File No. C-181, NMML.
77 *S. P. Mookerjee Papers*, V–VII Instalments, Subject File No. 140, NMML.
78 *Interim Report of Rehabilitation of Displaced Persons from East Pakistan*, Government of West Bengal, Calcutta, 1973, p. 2.
79 There were complaints about corruption in the criterion and procedure of enrolment of a refugee and for availing grants in the Legislative Assembly of West Bengal. *WBLA Debates*, Fifth Session (Budget), 1949, Vol. V, No. 2, p. 106.
80 File No. 17-G (R)/49, G (R) Branch, NAI.

81 Harichand Thakur organised the *Namasudras* against the caste hierarchies in traditional society of East Bengal and introduced a new name of the sect for his followers called *Matua*. The sect grew gradually. All untouchables and lower castes became his disciples. Sekhar Bandyopadhyay. 2015. 'Popular Religion and Social Mobility in Colonial Bengal: The Matua Sect and Namasudras'. In *Caste in Modern India: A Reader*, ed. Sumit Sarkar and Tanika Sarkar, Vol. 1, 392. New Delhi: Permanent Black.
82 Interview with Tanvir Mokammel, a filmmaker by profession, taken on 25 April 2014 in Dhaka, Bangladesh.
83 '*A Note on the Implementation of the Indo-Pakistan Agreement of the 8th April 1950 and Its Annexure of the 16th August 1950*' in File No. 20 (16)-R/C/50, Rehabilitation Branch, NAI.
84 *The Free Press Journal*, 14 August 1950.
85 'Summary of Plan for Refugee Rehabilitation Drawn up by the Rehabilitation Board Formed by the Bengal Rehabilitation Organisation', *S. P. Mookerjee Papers*, 1st Instalment, Subject File No. 38, NMML.
86 'Speech Delivered by Dr Shyama Prasad Mookerjee at Deshbandhu Park, Calcutta, on 3 September 1950', *S. P. Mookerjee Papers*, 1st Instalment, Speeches and Statements by Him, Serial No. 11, NMML.
87 *S. P. Mookerjee Papers*, V–VII Instalments, Other Papers, Serial No. 15, NMML.
88 *Sibnath Banerjee Papers*, Subject File No. 122, NMML.
89 *S. P. Mookerjee Papers*, 1st Instalment, Subject File No. 34, NMML.
90 *S. P. Mookerjee Papers*, II–IV Instalments, Subject File No. 179, NMML.
91 *S. P. Mookerjee Papers*, II–IV Instalments, Subject File No. 15, NMML.
92 *B. C. Roy Papers*, Subject File No. 6, NMML.
93 *Hindu Mahasabha Papers*, Subject File No. 135, NMML.
94 *AICC Papers*, File No. 3738, II Instalment, 1950, NMML.
95 File No. 34/49-Jan. 51 (West Bengal Land), Home Department, Political Branch, B Proceedings, NAB.
96 *Renuka Ray Papers*, Subject File No. 1, NMML.
97 *Ashoka Gupta Papers*, Subject File No. 2, NMML.
98 *WBLA Debates*, Second Session, September 1950, Vol. II, p. 203.
99 *The Statesman*, 2 October 1950.
100 Interview with Shefalika Pathak and Jolly Bagchi taken on 7 August 2009 in Kolkata, West Bengal. While narrating their stories of crossing the border through Bongaon and how they could reach the Indian side, they said that they noticed only the volunteers of East Bengal Relief Committee, who were helping the migrants to get border-slips, and they were also offering immediate relief measures to the refugees.
101 *M. N. Saha Papers*, VII Instalment, Writing by Others, Serial No. 9, NMML.
102 *M. N. Saha Papers*, VII Instalment, Subject File No. 6, NMML.
103 *The Statesman*, 17 September 1952.
104 *M. N. Saha Papers*, VII Instalment, Subject File No. 6, NMML.
105 The priority was to get their own people, as preference of profession, opportunities of employment might be difficult there. *Jugantar*, 3 November 1952.
106 *Hindusthan Standard*, 5 October 1952.
107 The refugee flow poured into the districts of Jalpaiguri, West Dinajpur, Cooch Behar, 24 Parganas, Nadia, Malda and other bordering areas. *Hindustan Standard*, 4 June 1953.
108 *Hindustan Standard*, 23 August 1952.
109 *WBLA Debates,* Sixth Session (Budget), 1952, Vol. VI, No. 3, p. 1617.
110 *S. P. Mookerjee Papers*, II–IV Instalments, Subject File No. 165, NMML.
111 *WBLA Debates*, Eighth Session, November 1953, Vol. VIII, p. 864.
112 *The West Bengal Weekly*, 23 June 1955.
113 *The Statesman*, 28 April 1953.
114 The population of cosmopolitan Calcutta is predominantly Hindu. Muslims form a substantial part, comprising 12.78 per cent of the total population. The area of their

concentration followed regional and linguistic affinities, although there was one area where relatively affluent groups lived. This was around Mechuabazar, Colootola and Canning Street. Other concentrations lay in the central districts around Park Circus up to Topsia and southwestern districts extending from Khidderpur to Metiaburj. Smaller pockets comprised parts of Narkeldanga, Rajabazar and a little northward in Belgachhia, B. T, Road, Cossipur and Tollygunj. M. K. A. Siddiqui. 1973. 'Caste Among the Muslims of Calcutta'. In *Caste and Social Stratification Among the Muslims*, ed. Imtiaz Ahmed, 136–37. New Delhi: Manohar.
115 File No. 11/53-PSP MEA, PVIII Branch, NAI.
116 *WBLA Debates,* Tenth Session, 1954, Vol. X, No. 4, p. 230.
117 *Basumati*, 31 October 1954.
118 B. P. Singha Roy, a leading Calcutta-based businessman and former president of the Indian Chamber of Commerce, thought that it would be difficult to rehabilitate the refugee agriculturists within West Bengal. *The Statesman*, 31 October 1954.
119 *B. C. Roy Papers*, Printed Material, Subject File No. 8, NMML.
120 File No. RHR-23 (13) 55, NAI.
121 This report was a part of 'The Rehabilitation of Displaced Persons in the Second Five Year Plan' prepared by Renuka Ray, Minister for Rehabilitation, West Bengal, and broadcast from the Calcutta Station of All India Radio on 29 November 1956.
122 File No. 20/56-AD I, Administration Section-1, NAI.
123 'Relief and Rehabilitation of Displaced Persons in West Bengal'. *Sibnath Banerjee Papers*, Subject File No. 123, NMML.
124 Getting a call to enter into a lorry was the only possible chance to get a place of settlement. It was like a lifetime solution for the refugees to get a legal step to get a legal right in a foreign land. The author mentioned a man from Barishal who left his mother, who died out of misery she faced in course of their journey, as they got a call from the official in charge of a lorry.
125 *WBLA Debates*, Twenty-Eighth Session, 1960, Vol. XXVIII, No. 1, p. 21.
126 *Renuka Ray Papers*, Subject File No. 5, NMML.
127 File No. 19 (24)/61, Rehab. 1 Branch, NAI.
128 *Arpanpatra* was a temporary deed of ownership on a particular piece of land. It did not proclaim the right of permanent ownership, but could render a security against eviction. *WBLA Debates*, Twenty-Ninth Session, 1961, Part-II, Vol. XXIX, No. 2, p. 31.
129 File No. 11/5/63, Rehab.-II Branch, NAI.
130 *WBLA Debates*, Thirty-Ninth Session, 1964, Vol. XXXIX, No. 2, p. 22.
131 *WBLA Debates*, Fortieth Session, 1965, Vol. XL, No. 1, p. 205.
132 File No. P II/282/26/68, Pak.-II Section, NAI.
133 File No. 39 (2)/66, Rehab.-B-I/RE Branch, NAI.
134 *Dharam Vira Papers*, Subject File No. 3, NMML.
135 *Amrita Bazar Patrika*, 20 April 1968; *Dharam Vira Papers*, Subject File No. 4, NMML.
136 File No. P II/277/2/68, Pak.-II Section, NAI.
137 *AICC Papers*, File No. 249 (I), II Instalment/1969, NMML.
138 *Sibnath Banerjee Papers*, Subject File No. 129, NMML.
139 *The Lancet*, 21 October 1972.
140 *The Lancet*, 21 October 1972.
141 *Sibnath Banerjee Papers*, Subject File No. 123, NMML.
142 Many voluntary agencies (Caritas, Save the Children, Brothers to All Men, Salvation Army, CARE [Cooperative for Assistance and Relief Everywhere] and Oxfam) undertook the execution of lifeline alpha, often depending on locally recruited staff who did not insist on 'on-the-spot feeding'. *The Lancet*, 25 November 1972.
143 *Hindustan Times*, 11 September 1949.
144 File No. 53/10/1949 AN, AN Section, NAI.
145 *AICC Papers*, File No. 1786 (Pt. II), PB-3 (1), Bengal, II Instalment/1948, NMML.
146 *Ananda Bazar Patrika*, 19 February 1949.

Dealing with the refugees **117**

147 *The Statesman*, 10 September 1949.
148 File No. 8/1/50-AN, Andamans (1950), NAI.
149 File No. 30 (2)/49-RHA, RHA Section, NAI.
150 'And Still They Come', An Article by Renuka Ray, M. P., Former Minister of Rehabilitation, West Bengal, *Nagpur Times*, 13 February 1950.
151 *WBLA Debates*, Twelfth Session, August–October 1955, p. 410.
152 *Renuka Ray Papers*, Speeches and Writings by Her, File No. 60, NMML.
153 *Amrita Bazar Patrika*, 29 November 1954.
154 *Hindustan Times*, 16 June 1955.
155 *Hindustan Times*, 16 June 1955.
156 *Hindustan Standard*, 23 September 1952.
157 *AICC Papers*, File No. G-37, Sl. No. 249 (1), II Installment, 1969, NMML.
158 *Amrita Bazar Patrika*, 3 August 1952.
159 *Renuka Ray Papers*, Press Clippings, Sl. No. 1, NMML.
160 File No. RHA E 18 (2)/54, RHA Branch, NAI.
161 *Amrita Bazar Patrika*, 5 October 1952.
162 *Jugantar*, 17 April 1957.
163 *Jugantar*, 16 July 1959.
164 *WBLA Debates*, Eighteenth Session, November–December 1957, pp. 23–42.
165 *The West Bengal Weekly*, Vol. 5, No. 30, 4 July 1957.
166 *Hindustan Standard*, 9 September 1954.
167 *WBLA Debates*, Ninth Session (Budget), February–April 1954, p. 1261.
168 *S. P. Mookerjee Papers*, II–IV Instalments, Subject File No. 164, NMML.
169 *Amrita Bazar Patrika*, Puja Annual, 1957, p. 32.
170 *The West Bengal Weekly*, Vol. 5, No. 22, 9 May 1957.
171 *Sibnath Banerjee Papers*, Subject File No. 123, NMML.
172 *The West Bengal Weekly*, Vol. 5, No. 52, 19 December 1957.
173 *WBLA Debates*, Eighteenth Session, November–December 1957, p. 41.
174 *Jugantar*, 12 June 1957.
175 *The West Bengal Weekly*, Vol. VIII, No. 12, 8 November 1954.
176 *Jugantar*, 6 July 1957.
177 *The West Bengal Weekly*, Vol. VIII, No. 37, 10 November 1960.
178 *Renuka Ray Papers*, Subject File No. 5, NMML.
179 *The Times of India*, 13 April 1960.
180 *WBLA Debates*, Twenty-Ninth Session, February–March 1961, pp. 34–35.
181 *Proceedings of the Tripura Legislative Assembly*, Series-I, Vol. 1–9, 1963, p. 3.
182 *The West Bengal Weekly*, Vol. IX, No. 52, 15 March 1964.
183 'Present position at Mana and the gravity of the situation'- a report written by Ashoka Gupta in 1964, *Ashoka Gupta Papers*, Subject File No. 4, NMML.
184 *Hindustan Standard*, 9 April 1964.
185 *Ashoka Gupta Papers*, Subject File No. 3, NMML.
186 *Economic Weekly*, 2 January 1965.
187 *Dandakaranya Samachar* (a bi-lingual weekly), 27 December 1964.
188 *AICC Papers*, II Instalment, File No. 732, NMML.
189 *AICC Papers*, II Instalment, Subject File No. 2958, 1960, NMML.
190 File No. 7(26)/63-P. IV, Pak-II Division, NAI.

3
CREATING A NEW REFUGEE DOMAIN

Assam and Tripura

'Surgery' is the word that often gets mentioned by historians and social scientists in academic and popular writing on the incidents that occurred during the creation of two nation-states, India and Pakistan (Ferdous 2015: 25–44). It was a point of departure for the colonial Raj, but for the religious minorities of both countries, the journey had only begun at that moment (Kabir 2013: 29). All over the partitioned landscapes, millions of minorities felt 'stranded' on the wrong side and fled to their putative homelands (Sen 2018: 2). Partition was based on the two-nation theory, and it was supposed to be implemented in the states of Punjab and Bengal only. But in the process, some of the northeastern states, which were never a part of the communal politics of mainland India, suffered immensely. The region as a whole experienced a forced vivisection and the region's economy, socio-political life has been directly affected by Partition's shadow (Sengupta 2016: 118). The northeastern states were different in many ways from the rest of India. They were politically volatile and strategically vulnerable regions of India that added a set of special concerns, problems and anxieties to its normal national share (Dasgupta 1997: 350). Partition had thus created 'new refugee domains' in northeastern India and states like Assam and Tripura were the prior victims, which are still today suffering from many crises derived out of it. Each of these states had long been crucially dependent on the geography of East Bengal to sustain and keep its identity intact, but Partition destabilised this dependency (Saikia 2016: 73). They suddenly started redefining the multi-faceted economic, cultural and ecological commonalities which they had shared with erstwhile East Bengal over the centuries.

As in Bengal, migration contributed to the making of a definite composite identity in Assam, which crystallised as 'Assamese culture' (Ludden 2003: 13–15). Geographically, Assam was situated on traditional migration routes. It was a natural refuge of migrants who shared its land, sheltered people and, in natural course, assimilated different cultures (Hunter 1998: 3437). Mobility along river routes has connected Assam to regions in the south and west, and also to the east and north. Trade routes along river routes connected Assam and Bengal with the western Gangetic basin. The formation of mixed population was composed within the culture of Assam. It was reinforced by the migration of different ethnic groups over time as a tradition (Gosselink 1994: 85–86). The domicile Assamese people welcomed the labourers and seasonal Muslim migrants, as they did not try to occupy lands. The Assamese were afraid of the settled agricultural labourers. During the colonial period, a trail of labour migration was a part of their culture. The monopoly of Bengali Hindu *babu* and *bhadralok* classes threatened the domiciles. The later batches of migrants faced fresh resentment from the older generation, who were educated and literate, in Assam and other states of northeast India. The territorial tilt of the definition of Assam as a community allowed room for the Bengalis during the crisis years, as it gave way to an ethno-linguistic Assamese exclusivism. The non-agrarian tribal population contributed more within the complexity of the migration situation and it made the nature of the community-conflict heterogeneous. Assam even had a small Muslim population in the pre-colonial period. Nevertheless, under intense polarisation of the colonial policies and within huge turmoil, the state was demanded to be ceded to the state of Pakistan. Assam had always been an Indian frontier, but it remained the cultural and political frontier of South and Southeast Asia (Ludden 2003: 9–11).

Tripura was a princely state under the tribal Maharajas, titled the Manikyas. They claimed to belong to the moon dynasty and also to define the linage, they adopted the surname 'Fa' (Pal 2013: 22). *Bishnupurana* and some other mythical texts categorically mentioned that the ancient name of the region was *Kirat-Desh* (Kilikdar 1995: 2).[1] According to *Rajmala*, a Bengali royal court chronicle of the Maharajas, about 150 Hindu kings had ruled Tripura for an uninterrupted period of about 350 years from the legendary period (Roy 2008: 31). It was a tribal chieftaindom that evolved gradually into a monarchical state. Tripura became the centre of power from the 15th century onwards, though it had started loosening possession on its own territory from the 18th century. The Mughals subdued the Maharajas in 1722, and the mighty kingdom gently submerged by turning itself into a normal province within the Mughal Empire. The idea that Tripura had always been a part of Bengal attends to a particular way of specialising homeland ideology. Thus, it was more like imagining Tripura as a part of Bengal. Apart from Tripura, other states of northeast India, like the Koch, Ahom, Kachari, Jayantia and Manipuri monarchies, consolidated their bases and power by occasional confrontations or regular negotiations with the rulers of neighbouring Bengal, within the larger state formation initiatives taken by the Mughals.[2] But their interventions had broken the isolation, which had prevailed for centuries in this region (Dutta 1981: 1–2). The revenue demand of the Mughals was so huge that their mode of production generated impact in both the hill and plains areas of northeast India (Hangloo 1984: 179). The impact was even felt in the fields of religion, culture, language and literature. Tripura tried to retain the traditional tribal norms, formations, etc., in hill areas, until the British subjugated them and forced them to accept changes. Yet,

Tripura managed to remain as a princely state outside British India. The immigration of non-tribals, chiefly the Bengalis, was not a new phenomenon in Tripura; it rather dates back to the 14th century (Misra 1976: 20). But since the last quarter of the 19th century, immigration of Bengalis was enormous and hence, Tripura got popularised as 'open geography' (Ganguli 1983: 14). The monarchical tribal family assimilated itself both linguistically and culturally with the majority community of the state. Portrayal of the migrants as 'insiders' by the Maharajas, led to a complex process of redefining the state itself, when to situate the post-1947 refugees simultaneously as 'insiders' as well as 'outsiders'.

The colonial cartography introduced a new idiom to naturalise the traditional frontiers into colonial borderlands and forged national boundaries; Partition added a new layer of contested border-making in northeast India (Zou and Kumar 2011: 165–66). Since 1947, the borderland has been entirely surrounded by international borders with five countries. The region remained connected with the rest of India only through a narrow 30-kilometre corridor (Das 2009: 7). Assam and Tripura actually fell into the 'big' Partition politics, and they became two major Bengali refugee-absorbent northeastern states. In pre-Partition days, the zones and patterns of migration used to be controlled by the need of the rulers, but the post-Partition migration was forced and determined by religious similarities. Hindu refugees from neighbouring areas of East Bengal started crossing notional borders for settling down either in Cachar districts of Assam or the princely state of Tripura. These two areas became their 'sought-after' destinations, primarily as they fell on the traditional migratory routes of the poor and landless Bengalis from certain congested districts of Bengal. The hegemonic tendency of the Bengali refugees made the domiciles insecure in both the states, and they considered it a threat to their existence.[3] The first few batches of refugees had taken shelter in relatives or neighbours' places, or stayed with their extended families. The Assamese were afraid of the prospective numerical strength and the nature of the cultural arrogance of the Bengalis, which they often showed off. Therefore, by monopolising the professional and administrative services, the Bengali migrants emerged as the most conspicuous cultural category in the eyes of the Assamese people. They tried to retaliate by asserting themselves. Tripura experienced a fluid border and refugees who migrated there were treated as the 'real subjects' or *jiratia prajas* of the Chakla Roshanabad estate.[4] It was never easy to term them as 'economic migrants' or 'refugees'.[5] Partition altered all old equations and the Manikyan discourse of 'my land' changed in the post-Partition collective discourse to 'our land'. It marked a shift from the merger of hill-ness and plain-ness towards the modern identity formation (Debbarma 2013: 10).

Partition changed the contours of Assam and Tripura dramatically. When the Radcliffe Award was trying to impose restriction on the old routes, it also opened up new corridors of migration. An existing pattern of Bengali migration was already there, but the status of the settlers had altered since 1947. The type of post-Partition refugee mobility was different, and naturally, their absorption process also became diverse. The years between 1951 and 1971 witnessed the highest-ever rate of increase of population in Assam and Tripura due to inflow of refugees. While looking at the policies and politics of relief and rehabilitation towards the refugees in this chapter, the emphasis would be on the diverse nature of ethnic conflicts that emerged between the host communities and refugee groups in both the states. The regional discrimination in implementing the policies by the Central Relief and Rehabilitation Department and their nature of negotiation with the respective state governments would be another focus. As the communitarian sentiments of pre-Partition days had changed totally in the post-1947 situation, with a shift from 'religious categories' to 'linguistic or ethnic categories', this chapter aims to discuss how local political aspiration influenced the policy decisions and implementations. The state government of Assam and the Brahmaputra valley was against further migration. and it tried not to implement relief and rehabilitation policies of the Centre on its Bengali-speaking districts of Cachar.[6] About Tripura, this chapter investigates why the tribals gradually became vocal about state policies of providing the Bengali refugees shelter and other supports in their land. It focuses on the process whereby they started demanding their legitimate rights, recognition of separate identity and status. They protested against the state's initiative to protect the interest of the Bengali refugees and tribal Chakma refugees from neighbouring Chittagong Hill Tracts (CHT). They urged the government to put emphasis on rehabilitation of the native tribals, resettlement plans and creation of the *jhumia* colonies. The chapter explores the course of incidents and procedures by which the internally displaced tribals became indirect victims of Partition in their own lands. It argues that Assam and Tripura witnessed Partition and experienced the crises derived out of the migration of Partition-displaced people to such an extent that time and again, the post-colonial politics in these states were shaped and reshaped by the presence of the Bengali refugees. The impact generated by these issues remained as an ongoing process, which is immensely significant in the present history of northeast India.

Immigrants and Assamese existential crisis

Assam was a multilingual and heterogeneous society, where a sizeable section was constituted by diverse types of migrants. The British annexation in 1826 put this area under the sway of imperialism. It was then for the first time that Assam obtained a strong regional identity. It included both the Brahmaputra and Barak river valleys, including the Surma-Kusiara river basin of Sylhet (Goswami 2012: 226). British Assam became the eastern borderland of the Empire. The political shape and composition of Assam were completely determined by them, based on colonial rationale and administrative shrewdness until the end of their rule (Dasgupta 1997: 351). It involved a process of making Assam an appendage of the colonial province of Bengal until 1874, followed by its first Partition of 1905, reconstitution as an administrative unit (Iqbal 2015: 80). The British liked to draw a distinction between what they called 'Assam proper' and 'a number of tribes and nations whose history must be separately considered' (Dasgupta 1997: 351). The redrawing of boundaries in 1906 and 1912 continued to add more trouble to the already bewildering complexity of Assam's population. Thus, the migration of Partition-displaced refugees into Assam was different from the rest of the northeastern states. They were part of the earlier flow of immigrants from the 1880s onwards, who were absorbed within the political system and socio-cultural structure of Assam, despite the difference in language and religion. But the process of adaptation stopped after the Bengali Muslim peasants from districts of East Bengal started pouring into the sparsely populated land of '*lahe-lahe*' in larger numbers.[7] Assam, at the turn of the 19th century, became a kind of extended Bengali district to the western region to take advantage of the available lands. By the 1900s, the settlers constituted 20 per cent of the border district population and possessed the land rights. They developed separate 'linguistic-cultural islands' within the larger Assamese community (Gosselink 1994: 89). Though surprisingly, the census report of 1891 was absolutely silent about them.

Before the first half of the 20th century, there was hardly any official mention of immigrants as a major social group. The official colonial policy was to encourage settlement of East Bengali peasants in Assam. The people of the deltaic region were known for their remarkable mobility; they moved frequently as rivers change course and could create new settlements. Assam came within the orbit of huge East Bengali emigration when the British began to attract settlers to make productive use of wastelands.[8] Mymensingh and Goalpara were border districts having sizeable Bengali populations. It was their first camp, where 'Muslims constituted 85 per cent of the immigrants; Goalpara with 28 per cent Muslims, the highest in the Assam Valley, was rightly the best choice to settle without much trouble and opposition on ethnic grounds', as they could assimilate with the 69 per cent Bengali-speaking inhabitants (Pathak 1984: 2). They continued moving on upwards, along the course of the Brahmaputra. Availability of land for both settlement and cultivation brought to their attention Nowgong, where 348 square miles was under cultivation out of the total 3,143 square miles of the district in 1901.[9] 'The Bengali immigrants censused for the first time on the char lands of Goalpara in 1911 were merely the advance guard or rather the scouts of a huge army following closely at their heels'.[10] Eighty-five per cent of colonists who settled with families were Muslims.

The tone of representation and the attitude of the administration that was depicted in the census report of 1921 was interesting. It stated:

> In 1911 few cultivators from Eastern Bengal had gone beyond Goalpara, those censused in the other districts of the Assam valley numbering of a few thousands. . . . In the last decade (1911–1921) the movement has extended far up the Valley and the Colonists now form an appreciable element in the population of all the four lower and central districts.[11]

Mullan observed in his census report of 1921:

> The East Bengal settlers have increased more than four-fold in the decade to their present total of 2,58,000 in the Brahmaputra Valley. There are also some

6,000 people of Mymensingh and Rangpur in the Garo Hills, Sibsagar and Lakhimpur are scarcely touched as yet.

(Miri 1993: 54)

By 1916, migration became such a central concern in Assam that, realising its consequences, the British introduced the Line System in 1920 to restrict both Hindu and Muslim Bengali immigration. It opened a discussion or a debate on segregation of immigrants from the indigenous people, 'the attempt to relieve pressure of population on land in immigrant area[s] led to the introduction of the [new] colonisation schemes'.[12] It tried to implement rules of not exchanging *pattas* of lands between domiciles and immigrants. The census of 1931 had informed further:

> Probably the most important event in the province during last twenty-five years—an event, moreover, which seems likely to alter permanently the whole future of Assam and to destroy more surely than did the Burmese invaders the whole structure of Assamese culture and civilisation—has been the invasion of a vast horde of land-hungry Bengali immigrants, mostly Muslims, from the districts of Eastern Bengal and in particular from Mymensingh.[13]

The Barpeta subdivision of Kamrup has 'fallen to their attack and Darrang is being invaded' (Miri 1993: 54). Mullan remarked in the census report of 1931 that, 'the only thing I can compare it to is the mass movement of a large body of ants'.[14]

> Their hunger for land was so great that in their eagerness to grasp as much as they could cultivate they not infrequently encroached on Government reserves and on lands belonging to the local people from which they could be evicted only with great difficulty [but] there was not much room for further expansion.[15]

Yet, the administration became firmer on the idea that 'Boundary lines had to be fixed restricting the immigrants from occupying lands near Assamese villages'.[16]

From the 1930s, the word 'immigrant' ignited debate in Assam. It was defined in Mr Thomas' standing order that immigrants 'include[ed] all persons coming from districts in Bengal and Surma Valley, but not including tea garden coolies and ex-coolies'.[17] A strong recommendation was made that 'transfers of lands between Assamese and immigrants should be prohibited' by proposing a draft bill as Amendment to the Land Revenue Regulation.[18] Abdul Hamid Khan Bhasani, the Maulana of Bhasanir Char and a great peasant leader of Assam, started campaigning against the imposition of the Line System and eviction of immigrants from 1928 (Dev and Lahiri 1979–1981: 25). He demanded complete abolition of the Line System and tried to float the idea of 'Unified Bangastan' as a solution for land scarcity in East Bengal (Guha 1976: 415–18). Bhasani stressed how the Bengali Muslim farmers contributed to Assam: 'the immigrants used to grow as many as 5 crops from the same soil and in the same year, while the indigenous cultivators could only think of two crops therefrom' (Islam 2002: 23). The central Indian leaders questioned the legality of the Line System, too. Jawaharlal Nehru observed:

> The Present Line System seems to me a traditional affair which cannot continue as such for long. To keep it as it is seems to me undesirable. The principle is bad and we cannot encourage it in India. It is also bad to continue immigrants in a particular area and so prevent them from being assimilated by the people of the Province.
>
> *(Dev and Lahiri 1979–1981: 25)*

The Muslim League was using anti-Line System movement to grab Assam. Congress agreed to provide all pre-1938 immigrants with wastelands for their political interests. The Ministry, under the Premiership of Sir Mahammad Saadullah, introduced the 'Grow More Food' campaign with other developmental schemes, and a kind of 'sponsored immigration' was started. It became a 'Grow More Muslim' campaign (Chattopadhyay 1990: 23). This campaign intensified the process of migration and settlement of Muslim agricultural labourers in Assamese lands.[19] The communal matrix changed rapidly by this process, as the Muslims became the majority by the turn of the decade (Islam 2002: 26). Saadullah opined, 'the greedy headmen or *Matabars* of the immigrant villages were acquiring large land holdings, thereby depriving other fellow immigrants of land' (Misra 1982: 59). The Assamese middle-class was not in fear of 'loss of identity'. It argued rather that 'the immigrants from across the border are not all destitute peasants toiling in the land belonging to Assamese landlords' (Misra 1982: 59).

Assam: migration and politics before Partition

In the budget session of 1940, Saadullah declared 'Assam is suffering from want of population to cultivate the vast quantity of arable land . . . what is waiting for the plough?'[20] The strategy adopted by the Saadullah government for enumeration in 1941 census operations was classifications on basis of the community, both occupational and caste groups, rather than on the basis of religion. The intention was to take the tribal population away from the fold of the larger Hindu society, enumerate them as tribals and thereby reduce the number of Hindus in the Province (Jodhani 1993: 57). This trend was not specific to the Assam situation. It became a general fear of Congress for all over India, as the *dalits* were counted outside the Hindu fold (Tejani 2007: 242–43). From the 1940s onwards, there was an awakening within the tribals to the north of the Brahmaputra valley and their understanding about the negligent attitude of the government. They became aware of the political development and assumed a major alteration in administration to deal with a changed situation.[21] The Muslim League activists and their strong immigrant base strove hard to have Assam in Pakistan. Even when the League was slightly on a back foot during the Congress-Nationalist

Coalition (1946), it campaigned for 'the settlement of Muslim encroachers from East Bengal on the soil of Assam without any consideration for the interest of the province' (Misra 1982: 59). They tried for 'vicious political exploitation of the religious sentiments of the Muslims' (Jodhani 1993: 57). The Assam Provincial Muslim League showed faith in the organisational power of Saadullah by declaring:

> Resolved that Syed Sir Md. Saadullah was authorised to explore all possibilities and submit comprehensive scheme to the working committee on how Muslims of this province can thrive in business and take their due share in the future Industrial Development of Assam.[22]

The League's Committee of Action recruited 5,000 National Guards in Surma Valley for the protection of Muslim immigrants. The Assam Provincial Hindu Sabha and Assam Provincial Congress Committee explained their stands, too.[23] The land and immigration situation reached a boiling point in 1946. Looking at 'the surrounding upheaval of the present decade' and to protect 'Assamese Culture, Prosperity and Progress of the people living in the Brahmaputra Valley', the Congress government insisted that 'the Domicile Rules and Regulations must remain in force in *toto* just as the Line System'.[24]

The term 'landless' was redefined in order to settle domiciles of lower-strata people, minorities and immigrants in planned settlement areas.[25] The Bordoloi government decided to evict new encroachers and re-encroachers of lands. It declared: 'Eviction has been carried on in various Professional Grazing Reserves in the districts of Kamrup and Darrang. The total numbers of families as reported to be evicted so far are 4140'.[26] The League initiated a campaign against the eviction policy. Even Jinnah warned the Bordoloi Government that:

> a situation would be created which would not be conducive to the well-being of the people of Assam. The resistance to eviction in the professional grazing reserves grew violent and in a number of cases the police had to report of firing.
>
> *(Jodhani 1993: 57)*

The campaign continued unabated until April 1947. The 'invasion plan' designed by Bhasani had been challenged by the Assamese Muslims and a legal ban was imposed towards his 'restriction on movements', 'with the allegation for widespread apprehension of communal conflict through his speeches and pamphlets issued over his name'.[27] Before Partition, 'Hindus and Muslims of Bengali descent accounted for more than 40 per cent of the population of Assam'.[28] The government was steadfast in its stand on eviction. The Resolution on the Land Revenue Administration for 1946–47 declared: 'the influx of East Bengal immigrants continued to be a legacy of the old Land Settlement Policy. Some immigrants encroached upon Reserves, but evicted promptly after due notice' (Kar 1990: 39). It had clearly stated that:

> the statistics for the year show a net increase of 42,208 acres in total settled areas. The increase under the same head in the previous year was 102,921 acres. The pace of indiscriminate expansion of settlement has thus slowed down remarkably, due mainly to the modification of the old land settlement policy.[29]

When there was such acrimony over the number of Bengali immigrants, Hindus and Muslims, Partition came as a relief for the Assamese leadership. The increasing number of Bengali Muslims scared them. There was already a demographic change in favour of the Muslims, which made a ground for the League to claim Assam in Pakistan. The Assamese leadership voiced vigorously and unitedly against the increase of Muslim immigrants, but they failed against the colonial design. The only option was to evict and deport them back. It became possible when Gopinath Bordoloi assumed the Premiership of Assam, but his eviction policy could not achieve much. The colonial government and the League leaders were against it. His own party, Congress, did not support this particular agenda. Under such a bleak situation, the prospect of a transfer of Sylhet to Pakistan came as a bright solution to their political survival. They supported the proposal and campaigned in a sustained manner for the transfer of Sylhet to Pakistan. *Dainik Batori*, the first Assamese newspaper, published reports under headlines like *'Shrihotto Bichhed'* (partition of Sylhet), *'Shrihotto Bichhedot Asomia Mussalman'* (role of Assamese Muslims on the separation of Sylhet), etc.[30] It took away huge numbers of the Bengali Muslim population to another country; a large chunk of immigrant Muslims could migrate to the 'new medina' of the Muslims, the sovereign state of Pakistan. This permanently altered the demographical pattern in favour of the Assamese Hindus. They assumed deserving right on their homeland, and ensured permanent socio-political hegemony in Assam. After Sylhet was transferred to East Bengal, the League leaders were compelled to shift their base on the other side of the border. The Bengali Muslims were not in a noteworthy position as per political relevance.[31] Bengali Hindus lost their numbers, and for the first time, the Assamese were the single largest majority group in Assam. Independence made the Assamese population numerically and politically stronger (Hussain 1993: 52–60). The problem of Bengali hegemony arose again like a phoenix. A large chunk of Bengali Muslims who migrated to East Pakistan in 1947 as refugees began to come back and claim their old settlements. Sylhet was gone, but the Hindu Bengalis began to pour in, in the form of refugees. The Assamese struggle for hegemony, it appeared, was far from over.

The refugees: adding fuel to fire

The Bengali population continued to increase after the Partition. The decadal growth of Bengali-dominated Barak valley was equal to the all-India average.

Goalpara was beside Mymensingh and comfortable for the refugees as they could assimilate with the 69 per cent Bengali-speaking inhabitants (Miri 1993: 53). The *Assam Tribune* commented, 'the inflow of Hindu refugees in Assam was so enormous that the Hindu refugees would apparently create a Bengal in this province'.[32] Gopinath Bordoloi was not sympathetic to the refugee cause (Jodhani 1993: 59).[33] His government was against providing shelter to the refugees and distribution of lands to them.[34] The state ministry initiated 'Schemes for planned settlement of the available arable waste lands' to safeguard the 'interests of indigenous people including Hindus, Muslims, Tribals and other backward sections of people in Assam'.[35] An amendment of the Assam Land Revenue Regulation in 1947 redefined the series of ten tribal belts and 23 tribal blocks to protect plains tribals from losing traditional lands and forests (Verghese 1996: 38). Gopinath Bordoloi was 'a cricketer in politics', as described by Hem Baruah (Jodhani 1993: 7). For him, refugees were not any special category, but another group of immigrants from Bengal. In 1948, he pointed out:

> There are persons coming into the Province, but it is not possible to say whether any of them come with the intention of settling down permanently. Government has made it plain hitherto that there is no more land in Assam for settlement of new immigrants.[36]

His government was susceptible on immigration issue and they prepared new definitions for 'indigenous' and 'domicile' categories to identify the non-Assamese people (Dutta 1993: 365–66).

The first major difference of opinion with the Centre occurred over the question of settling the Partition-displaced refugees from East Bengal. The Assam Government expressed its sheer unwillingness, and rather disapproved of the idea to continue settling refugees without limit, as 'not much more than two lakh acres of wastelands were available, leaving aside the grazing reserves' in Assam (Borooah 1990: 31). Jawaharlal Nehru wrote to Bordoloi in May 1949 that Assam was getting a bad name for its narrow approach to this problem. He threatened the Chief Minister, saying: 'If Assam adopts an attitude of incapability to solve the refugee problem, then the claims of Assam for financial help (would) obviously suffer' (Misra 2000: 112). The rift between the Centre and state had sharpened more on the issue of unchecked migration (Misra 2000: 114). The state government demanded the introduction of the 'Foreigners Permit System' for Assam as a solution. This attitude made the Centre more impervious about their stand. Sardar Patel replied on 3 July 1950: 'I am afraid, your letter betrays lack of a sense of urgency in settling the refugee problem'.[37] He cautioned, 'Everywhere, wherever we have to deal with the refugee problem, we have to give priorities even against local sentiments' (Chhabra 1992: 54). But, 'Partition did not reverse the logic of a land frontier' and the massive movement of Hindus, along with the economically induced migration of poor Muslims, intensified population pressure on Assam (Baruah 2015: 82). The upper-class refugees started crossing borders, especially those who had older ties with this land.[38] *The Assam Tribune* reported:

> a considerable number of East Bengal people flocked in Dibrugarh . . . already many refugees from Noakhali settled here permanently either taking land on lease or purchasing it . . . from the record of the Rationing department, by now the population is believed to be increased by ten or twelve thousand. This has created well-sensation amongst the Assamese population who want that these new-comers should at once be debarred from holding lands by the Government for the benefit of the indigenous people.[39]

The Assam Government was overburdened with volumes and demands of the pre-Partition immigrants. S. G. Duncan, the Secretary to the Government of Assam, informed all Deputy Commissioners of provinces on 25 July 1947 that:

> since the Partition of Bengal and succession of Sylhet to East Bengal, people from Bengal and outside provinces have been coming to Assam in great numbers, purchasing annual and periodic *patta* lands from the Assamese on speculative prices' and hence, he instructed for remedial measures 'to prevent undesirable transfer of land.[40]

Liberal Assamese groups tried to search for a reasonable solution by insisting the government allow for property exchange between refugees, so that 'this procedure will save the reserve lands of Assam from undesirable encroachments by present helpless emigrants'.[41] The Government instructed the local officers to be 'vigilant and give protections as is feasible to welfare and vital interests of the indigenous agriculturists' against the complaints placed by thousands of application of 'unauthorised squatting of land by immigrants from outside Assam Valley' who 'are trying to buy up land at high prices'.[42] The apprehension of losing lands was so acute that after only one week of Partition, the Assam Government issued a circular on 22 August 1947, stating:

> It is considered that land within two miles of district headquarter towns, one mile of all other towns and important business centres and important railway stations and bazaars (Dhekiajuli, Tangla, Chabua, Hojai, Lumding, Lanka) and other such important places should not be settled without previous approval of Government. If you think that any part of these areas should be constituted as town lands . . . you are requested to submit proposals accompanied by map, description of boundaries and draft notification.[43]

In effect, the refugees opted for settlement on their own initiatives, compelled to shift their pedestal from urban settlement regions to rural and hilly areas. Dehiram Bora, the President of the Mangaldai Tribal Conference, sent a telegram to the Revenue Minister on 26 October 1947 and informed that 'hordes of people from outside Assam [were] purchasing periodic *patta* lands within tribal belt, immediate Government intervention solicited'. Rabicharan Kachari, ex-MLA voiced for the same issue by telegramming, 'East Bengal evacuees pouring; purchasing lands; situation threatening for tribal people, pray Government intervention'.[44]

Hostility to refugee influx

The East Bengali refugees were thousands in numbers and were crossing the border on foot, and some groups were not even registering themselves as 'refugees' to receive government assistance, so restricting them on entrance and purchasing of lands in Assam was difficult.[45] Most of them had relatives in Assam, and they were purchasing property on that basis. There were little evidence of transferring annual or periodic land as an essential proof of their ownership. Assam seldom experienced incidence of land transfer legally to 'foreigners'.[46] *Surabhi*, an Assamese monthly published in the Brahmaputra valley, demanded an alteration in the government policies towards the immigrants and refugees. First, the refugees who had migrated to Assam after the 3 June declaration should be repatriated to their native place. Second, the repatriation of these refugee groups should take place simultaneously with the immigrants who came after 1938 and had been evicted from the Reserves in pursuance of the government's eviction policy. Third, government should introduce a new legislature about 'changing of hands of all kind of lands', should pass unanimously an 'emergent ordinance' to safeguard the right and interest of the indigenous population.[47] A history of Assamese hostility towards the Bengali immigrants was there right from the colonial period, but it never crystallised into any violent outburst. Within ten days of independence, there were violent attacks on the Bengalis. On 25 August 1947, Assam first experienced the flame of Bengali-Assamese hatred; some Bengali-owned shops were stoned in Gauhati. Bishnuram Medhi, Finance and Acting Home Minister of Assam, saw the conspiracy of Calcutta press behind spreading of the news and they mentioned, 'propaganda by certain interested persons to create panic'.[48] The Asom Jatiya Mahasabha requested the government to promulgate the Immigration Act and cease issuance of domicile certificates to outsiders, so that they would not be able to apply for citizenship in future.[49] It would help in keeping the explicit difference between the indigenous and non-Assamese regarding the acquisition and requisition-sale of lands, educational facilities and services.

The Government of Assam announced rules and essential criterion for a non-Assamese to get a domicile certificate in 1948.[50] Pakistan was carrying on propaganda calling for the inclusion of the Khasi States and other hill areas into her territory.[51] The Assamese newspapers published from the Brahmaputra valley used headlines like, *'Asomot Bideshi Nagorikor Tandob'* (the chaos created by the foreigners in Assam), but not at all proved as active to prevent that (Swadeshi 2015: 207). The Centre also declined to take responsibility of these so-called Pakistani infiltrators. After attending the Inter-Dominion Conference in Calcutta, Bordoloi wrote to Patel on 18 April 1948:

> I am opposed to any matter concerning my province being discussed in the Inter Dominion Conference without the consent of the Government. I could not undertake responsibility of committing my Government to a matter in which a major policy of the Government was involved.
> (Jodhani 1993: 59–61)

He was afraid of two issues. First, the tribal unrest situation in the Garo hills, where the government could not provide any special protection measures for the tribals against the settlement of land initiatives made by the newcomers (non-Garos). Second, all routes of food distribution got blocked in Assam after Partition.[52] The state government was not in favour of the refugees and the Central aid was minimal. Thus, the relief and rehabilitation situation was unbelievably poor, and further influx had created a famine situation.[53] The state government somehow realised that crisis and had:

> Resolved that the time limit for receiving a declaration from the refugees should be extended up to 31.12.48, as Government hardly gave any sufficient notice or scope to the refugees who live in larger numbers in interior or remote corners of the District to make declaration in prescribed forms, accompanied by identifiers at the appointed hour before the sub-Deputy collector.[54]

Until 1949, the government was not aware of approximate numbers or religious affiliations of the refugees, as most of them did not ask for the Centre's assistance (Sujaud Doullah 2003: 72). Bishnuram Medhi spoke in the Legislative Assembly on 31 March 1949 in quite a pessimistic tone:

> No plan in respect of relief and rehabilitation of so-called refugees in Assam has been taken up till now, as they are staying with their friends and relations who are old settlers of Assam and a large number is residing in Railway colonies with Railway employees and earning their living.[55]

The state government was not aware of this minimum expectation. Medhi stated: 'It has not been possible for Government to allot any land up till now for housing or cultivation', but the government:

> has issued instruction to the Deputy Commissioners and other Departments to make such arrangements as to allow the poorer classes of refugees such as fishermen, weavers, labourers, etc., to serve the community in the manner they were accustomed and to give them all the facilities for the purpose.[56]

He added, 'Until the refugees produce their food or develop any resources of the Province they will obviously be a burden on the Province'.[57] The refugee scenario was changing drastically. Through the embodiment of the spirit of the Nehru-Liaquat Pact of 1950, the Nehruvian non-discriminatory principle was upheld to 'maintain a kind of status quo of the population' (Singh 1984: 1059). But with the advent of large-scale migration of both Hindu refugees and Muslim returnees in Assam, the situation went completely out of hand.[58] Few social organisations became vocal on refugee rights, in comparison to the leading political parties.[59] The government was compelled to render help on humanitarian grounds.

After the 1950 riot, the Relief and Rehabilitation Department in Assam prepared an estimated budget, as gigantic exodus of new batches of refugees could be anticipated. The government decided:

> With a view to making necessary provision for funds to meet the expenditure of the Department, the present demand is laid under different sub-heads as prescribed by the Government of India. They have signified their intention to reimburse almost the entire expenditure on this account in this State owing to our strained circumstances.[60]

Gopinath Bordoloi wrote a letter to Sri Prakasa on 9 May 1950, stating how, 'they are suffering from a most pernicious propaganda by the Bengalees and the Bengal press about communal representation of the Assamese regarding government services in Assam'.[61] He wrote in another letter to Sardar Vallabhbhai Patel one month later, on 16 June 1950 that 'some of the tribal people are still suspicious of our intentions, and need very delicate and tactful handling during this critical period of transition'.[62] From the tone of these letters, it becomes quite clear that the Assamese domiciles and the state government were sceptical about two communities, local or immigrant Bengalis and the tribals. Hearing about the fallout of the refugee situation in Assam, Shyama Prasad Mookerjee communicated to Gopinath Bordoloi about his desire to visit Assam in June 1950, as he believed, 'my visit to Assam is to create an atmosphere for better understanding between Assamese and Bengalis, and also to study the problem of refugees from east Bengal and the plans for their rehabilitation'.[63] He received a reply from Bordoloi's office stating that, 'Mr Bordoloi told me to inform you that he would welcome your visit to this Province, but he would expect you not to deliver any speech that might in any way embarrass his Government which is trying its best to implement the Nehru Liaquat Ali Agreement'.[64] However, pressures from many corners compelled the state government finally to declare the total of the numbers of Hindu refugees in Assam for the first time in 1950:

> Out of the 1,20,000 'Old refugees' as per census of Refugees in July 1949 (of whom 55,000 were in Cachar and 65,000 in Assam Valley) and the 3,90,000 'New refugees' who came to Assam (of whom nearly 2 lakhs are in Cachar

and the rest in Assam Valley), it has been decided that during the year 1950–51 Assam Government would rehabilitate only about 1,25,000.[65]

Matia camp of Goalpara and other camps situated in Sidhbari, Dudhnoi, Tengabari, Dubapara and Harimura were set up to provide immediate relief and rehabilitation. Interestingly, Bonda refugee colony consisted of both Mymensinghia Bengalis and tribal refugees like Garos and Hojongs (Dutta Pathak 2017: 124).

Cachar: the centre of crisis

Cachar was overflowing with Bengali refugees from the early 1950s. Because of similarity in language and cultures with the adjacent areas along borderlands, Bengali Hindu refugees were more inclined to settle down in Cachar (Singh 1984: 31). The Assam Government first tried to deny massive refugee presence in Cachar and thus, the refugees had taken shelter 'in school and college buildings, other public and private houses, railway stations and even in open air tents' in the beginning.[66] A constant demand was raised in Cachar to conduct a special census for Assam to determine the actual refugee figure. That particular census compelled the government to acknowledge them officially in July 1949. The rehabilitation work was taken up late. It involved three separate stages for variations in migration patterns, complexities of relationships between two valleys and shift in policies between the Centre and state. The first stage was handled by the state government (1949–April 1950). But to deal with the refugee crises, the second stage was directly under the Ministry of Relief and Rehabilitation, Government of India (May 1950–1953). The third stage again fell under the supervision of the state government (1954–1958). In the first stage, 'the nominal aid in the shape of doles and loans ranging from Rs. 25 to Rs. 400 was accorded to a number of refugee families'.[67] From 1950, relief camps had to be started by public organisations to undertake rescue work for the refugees who were stranded on borders. The state government had taken charge of few camps in urban areas and distributed cash relief only. Relief camps in rural areas were dependent on initiatives and the cooperation of social work organisations. From the mid-1950s, the Central Government decided to take responsibility of refugee rehabilitation in Cachar due to the grave situation created by communal flare-ups in Silchar and other places.[68]

The state government was sceptical on land issues and was indeed sensitive towards the idea of distributing further lands to the refugees. The pre-Partition migration made them vulnerable, so the term 'rehabilitation' was redefined and it came out with a fresh idea that 'mean[t] giving a person or a family a suitable homestead and a holding economically viable and such pursuits of life as would bring them economic stability, ease and sufficiency to which they were usually accustomed before migration'.[69] The voluntary organisations working for the refugees were critical of policies. They complained about the attitude of both the Centre and state. Acquiring lands was an essential pre-requisite for rehabilitation. They stated clearly that 'Rehabilitation is not as yet aimed at'.[70] Loans amounting from Rs. 295–Rs. 5000 paid to them 'in uncertain and delayed instalments, out of which again 40–50% went to *nazranas, khazna* and even illegal gratification of some landlords'.[71] According to the facts and figures stated in the census of 1951, the total number of refugees in Assam was 'only 2,76,824 and in Cachar 93,000 and odds' (Marbaniang 1970: 123–24). The lack of collecting relevant data, failure in understanding the volume of the problem and confusion about their real number hampered the general economic development of Assam; and hence, the planning of rehabilitation for Cachar was deferred.[72] The absorption of refugees within the political framework and socio-economic system posed severe problems, too. A report of the Land Settlement Advisory Committee recommended for essential arrangements on how to use the wastelands, but it did not provide directives for refugee rehabilitation.[73]

Hem Chandra Chakravarty, President of Silchar District Congress Committee, discussed the land survey report on Cachar in the late 1940s. According to the Land Survey report, 'Total area of the district is- 29,29,650 acres and area under crop is- 6,05,733 acres'.[74] The Centre tried to assess the availability of fallow cultivable lands by a committee headed by Dorab Gandhi, who reported that 18 million acres of cultivable lands could be used for the new settlers. This figure tallied with the Assam Government's own assessment too, mentioned in 'Industrial Planning and Development of Assam (1948)' (Dutta Pathak 2017: 111). The theory of scarcity of land might not be an absolute truth. Mohanlal Sakshena, the Relief and Rehabilitation Minister at the Centre, had assertively stated that the rehabilitation policy of the Government of Assam was largely governed by political considerations. The report, which was prepared after his visit in May 1949, reflected the parochial attitude of the government to rehabilitate the displaced persons. He stated: 'The refugees who have got into the State of Assam are there, in spite of the unhelpful attitude of the State Government' (Sakshena 1950: 82). For that, Cachar came under the direct control of the Branch Secretariat of the Union Relief and Rehabilitation Ministry in Calcutta, as the Centre decided to take over the charge of the district on 1 May 1950.[75] The state had created equal difficulties in way of settling the refugees on surplus land of tea gardens. A controller as supervisor of the ITA Scheme (Indian Tea Association) was appointed with no power to requisition or acquisition lands, the soul of all rehabilitation efforts. The ITA Scheme was first made with an agreement, exclusively for Assam. ITA, 'to provide lands and the Government of India to made up funds, consequently a sum of about Rs. 22,00,000 from the public exchequer was spent, but the Scheme met a dismal failure'.[76] A report published in the journal *Rehabilitation Review* acknowledged:

> 3500 families of displaced persons who have recently come from Pakistan are to be settled on land available in tea gardens of Assam at a total estimated cost of Rs. 17,45,000. The I.T.A has been entrusted with the work and a temporary advance of Rs. 1,00,000 has been made to the Association, [but] in operation, distress of worst type overtook the refugees screened under

the ITA. Hunger, disease and death have been the fate of these unfortunate victims of Indian freedom.[77]

The government arranged lands in Veterbund and Kalinagar in Karimganj subdivision, also encroached evacuee lands in Gumrah marshes in Katigora and forest lands in Gambhira Tea Estate for them.[78]

Eighty per cent of the total refugees in Cachar were agriculturists. Some of them set up colonies by either purchasing or obtaining land on lease from landholders, both in rural and urban areas. Sri Prakasa, then the Governor of Assam, said: 'The work of rehabilitation in Assam has been divided into two parts. The work of the Assam or the Brahmaputra Valley is in the charge of Assam Government, while that of the Surma Valley, that is Cachar, is in the hands of Central Government', and also stated: 'I feel that the division of work was unfortunate: but in the circumstances, it was inevitable', as 'Cachar is a predominantly Bengali district and it is not loyal to the Government of Assam.[79] He opined, 'for their attitude may result in disaster to themselves with Pakistan pressing on them on one side and they being land-locked on all other sides as well'.[80] He tried to explain why the state government did not work much for relief and rehabilitation of the Bengali refugees:

> The Ministers told me that there was a general dislike for the settlement of Bengalis among the mass of the people and that as politicians, they have to have their eye on public opinion. Therefore, they did not want any fuss and were anxious to do all the work of rehabilitation quietly. They wanted to be trusted and deserved sympathy and understanding from all.[81]

A. P. Jain, the Union Relief and Rehabilitation Minister, had encountered similar experiences in Cachar. He wrote, 'When I first paid my visit to Silchar, I found that the atmosphere was full of tension and refugee camps replete with discontents'.[82] The numbers of refugees settling down in areas like Chandipur Tea Garden in Hailakandi were increasing, whereas procedures of granting loans became complex and the amounts were comparatively less.[83] According to him, 'The Assam Government should be asked to integrate its scheme of the rehabilitation of its own landless labourers with our scheme of the rehabilitation of refugees'.[84] But actually, 'They are always in an undue hurry to close down the Ministry of Rehabilitation long before it achieves anything to justify its foundation'.[85] The key problem was the 'open frontiers of Assam', and the refugees were migrating 'demographically in an overloaded area' for 'land, work and opportunity', primarily as the 'economic forces proved more potent than passport and visa regulations'.[86]

In 1953, the Assam Displaced Persons Rehabilitation Loans Amendment Bill was introduced and passed in favour of the repayment of the partial amount of loans to the State exchequer in instalments. It was not applicable to Cachar, as the district was under the supervision of the Central Government.[87] A provision of distribution of special relief to the returnee Muslims was there after 1950, as per the provisions of the Nehru-Liaquat Pact. The state government sanctioned Rs. 200 as a loan to those families, when the real expenditure of such loans totalled to a sum of Rs. 26,85,380.[88] After the introduction of the Passport and visas, 12,125 families migrated to Cachar, and their total numbers in various camps were 1,30,000.[89] Claims and counter-claims of not getting loans became a regular phenomenon of those camp refugees in Assam in general, and Cachar in particular.[90] On 22 November 1954, Dr Meghnad Saha had stated that he had gone 'to visit a number of permanent liability camps or destitute camps at Karimganj town itself and at Masinpur and Tarapur near Silchar town' and 'on the basis of what we have seen with our own eyes constrains us to say that the policy of rehabilitation of refugees in the district of Cachar as pursued until now has been a complete failure'.[91] The state government allotted 8,000 acres of lands for refugee rehabilitation in 1955, when the numbers of the refugees were more than 3 lakhs. So, the nature of the problem remained the same: how to accommodate these refugees in eight thousand acres of land.[92] The All India Congress Committee planned to popularise schemes like 'National Plan Loan' from the Central level from 1955. It was not introduced only for the refugees, but also for the stranded populace, IDPs (internally displaced persons), landless labourers and those distressed by other disasters and adversities like epidemics or natural calamities.[93] Among other Central schemes for rehabilitation were the long-term loans approved for the establishment of refugee markets, designed by respective municipalities at Karimganj, Silchar, Nowgong, Dhubri, Tezpur and Nalbari.[94] The Assamese were not in favour of the protective initiatives. Sri Nilmani Phookan tried to explain the Assamese psyche in this regard: 'The very word "colonialism" has been banned by world-politicians and yet "colonialism" has been established and most "colonies" are going to be established in every district of Assam'.[95] Here colonisation was used in the context of Bengali settlement in Assam, which he described as 'people somewhat different from the people of Assam; they are in our midst'.[96]

When Mehr Chand Khanna toured Assam for ten days in 1954, the state government agreed to take responsibility of refugees in Cachar. He checked with their rehabilitation endeavour and certified initiatives of State Rehabilitation Department as 'very efficiently done' and at times as 'satisfactory'.[97] By 1955, the Relief and Rehabilitation Department dispersed 25,000 refugees in the permanent government colonies. These colonies were in Kinnarkhal, Bishnunagar, Gandhinagar, Duhalin, Kalirail, Sathir-sangram, Sonbeel East and South. There were four work-cum-training centres in Ramkrishnanagar, Ghungoor, Maijgaon and Panchgram, but 'no kind of training in any gainful profession [had] yet been provided' in those training centres.[98] In June 1955, Mehr Chand Khanna, the Minister for Rehabilitation, wrote to U. N. Dhebar, mentioning that:

> You would recall the talk that you had with me regarding the condition of displaced persons in Assam, especially in Cachar. I have discussed the matter with the officers and have decided to depute a special officer to visit Cachar. He will examine the two suggestions made by you regarding the purchase of

bamboos and of rearing of Ande and Muga silk cocoons, and of manufacture of silk by displaced women on cottage industry basis.[99]

There were only two central homes in Nowgong and Cachar for destitute women and children. M. N. Saha compared the pitiful condition of the homes with the 'Nazi Enemy Concentration Camps' and stated, 'a huge number of destitute women are yet outside these "Homes," their applications for admission kept pending for indefinitely prolonged period of time'.[100]

Bishnuram Medhi, then the Chief Minister of Assam, ignored allegation of not giving enough attention to Cachar by pointing out, 'During 1st April, I visited the Sonbeel area personally and I was very glad to find there are some people who were rehabilitating themselves-they were all with smiling face and appeared to be quite happy'.[101] In 1956, to avoid delay and inconvenience, the state was instructed to 'submit complete and final district-wise schemes in so far as individual displaced families are concerned, so that we will not be approached again for granting any kind of further financial assistance to these particular families'.[102] Medhi claimed to accelerate some developmental schemes in worksite camps, refugee colonies and permanent settlement areas, 'to provide such amenities as roads, water supply, medical facilities, primary education facilities, market, irrigation and drainage, etc.'[103] The Assam Government introduced a special measure for allotment of land called 'Lankeswari Grant', which meant 'possession of land had been given to the displaced persons, group by group from time to time from 25th September 1954 to 17th March 1956', vide government notification No. RT. 29/50 dated 2nd April 1956.[104] They brought a category of 'genuine refugees' as per documents they were carrying while entering into Assam, rendered help and given loans on that basis alone.[105] The next step was passing of Land Acts in the Legislative Assembly; the State Requisition of Zamindaries Act, the Adhiar Protection Act and the Land Ceiling Act were introduced and passed to search more lands for the indigenous landless populace and the refugees, though these efforts did not prove to be enough to reach a permanent solution. The government had given an explanation that it 'cannot interfere with the land policy within the Hill Districts which are in the hands of the District Councils. In the area available in the Plains District, the density of population will be about 400 per sq. mile'.[106] The budget and allotment of funds on that head entitled 'refugees relief and rehabilitation grant' in Assam was better in the Second Five Year Plan, in comparison to the first one.[107] There were frequent reports of difficulty in road communication in Nalbari, Rangfuli, Bhelamari villages of Pacchim Barbhag Mouza and Khudia village of Bataghila Mouza, where 600 refugee families were residing in 1960. The area remained backward educationally and commercially due to the inability of transport.[108]

The final stand

The year 1960 was crucial in regard to the absorption process of the refugees in both the valleys, Assam and Cachar, as after the language movement in 1960, the old equation became more sensitive. The identity issues started shaping up differently, while the need for grants became necessary for the evacuee families.[109] Some refugee houses (made with thatch and bamboo because of the unavailability of corrugated iron sheets) were burnt down during the disturbances, making their occupants stranded again.[110] In 1961, the Muslim residents were requested to carry an identity card issued by respective *Gaonsabhas* when travelling within Cachar. The reason stated by the government was to check the influx of unauthorised Pakistanis. The rural Panchayats near Silchar, Katighora, Hailakandi, Sonaimukh, Lakipur, Hojai, Nilbagan, Murajhar and Dobokha were instructed not to harass the 'genuine refugees'.[111] From December 1963, communal disturbances in East Pakistan had pushed batches of refugees again, and their rehabilitation posed a challenge. The Centre was no longer interested in keeping the new influxes, and instructed the Department of Relief and Rehabilitation not to encourage displaced employees. Thus, the claim of restoration of these two zones again proved fruitless.[112] In 1964–1965, the trail towards Assam was similar, like the post-Partition flows when the state machineries were completely clueless about how to cope with the situation. Bamunigaon refugee camp was set up in 1964 on a sprawling 250 bighas of land at Boko (Dutta Pathak 2017: 123).[113] The exchange of *khas* lands and properties started occurring (Chhabra 1992: 24). The Government declared:

> Periodic lands can be transferred and are given effect to unless it violated lease conditions. As regards annual lands, local officers have been instructed to make *khas* following proper procedure and dispose of the same as per Land Settlement Policy barring those cases where they were exchanged and occupied by bonafide refugees [but] where however, these lands are located in tribal belts the law relating to tribal belt will operate.[114]

The boundary-making procedure between India and Pakistan started in 1965. The demarcation of the Assam-East Pakistan Boundary started in the United Khasi-Jaintia Hills-Sylhet Sector, then in Garo-Hills-Mymensingh Sector and finally in the Goalpara-Rangpur Sector.[115] The refugee influx was sturdy in Assam. For example, 'during six months ending on the 29 December 1968, 20980 migrants came to Assam from East Pakistan' (Sharma 1999: 36). The sum of loans was decreasing, while the amount of misery was increasing for the refugees. The amount of business loan used to be Rs. 3,500, but after the colossal influx of 1964, the amount fixed by the Centre was Rs. 1,500.[116] The state government made necessary arrangements to send the refugees outside Assam, like the Mana camp of Dandakaranya, in Madhya Pradesh. The Bangladesh War of 1971 was the last blow in the bordering province, and the population of Assam increased from 14.6 million to 22.9 million during the 1970s (Gosselink 1994: 90). The state government believed that 'the refugee camps would provide adequate protection against the local Assamese who do not welcome the influx of Bengalis, whether Hindus or Muslims'.[117] The government instructed the bordering police stations to take responsibility for the registration of refugees, even those who would be staying with friends and relatives.[118] It was a joint responsibility of the Centre and the state, along with the Department of Finance, to maintain relief camps opened for them. The Government of Assam had formulated a scheme named 'Operation-71' to provide arrangements for relief and shelter in Assam and Meghalaya. The scheme included inter alia opening of reception centres, relief camps, administration of improvised relief in the form of daily rations, medical facilities, etc.[119]

The state administration had sent a telegram to the Home Department, New Delhi, declaring that 'In order to ensure adequate security in connection with current influx of various categories of people from across the border, two special security camps are being set up by State Government under administrative Control of the State police'.[120] The Assam Police were concerned, as sometimes:

> it would be difficult to distinguish between an infiltrator and an evacuee coming into India as a result of Pak action in East Bengal. For, it would further complicate the scenario if the re-infiltrators would attempt to camouflage themselves as evacuees. It is therefore necessary that the check-posts meant for detecting Pak infiltrators be vigilant about Pak infiltrators and re-infiltrators.[121]

The bordering State of Assam and Tripura suffered immensely in dealing with the situation and sheltering refugees. The War of 1971 had created a second frontier in which the idea of 'effective border' became important. It tried to separate the refugees of 1947 from those of 1971, and it privileged the refugees from other ones (Dutta 2013: 13–14). After the emergence of Bangladesh, repatriation of the migrants was as per the conditions fixed by the Indira-Mujib Pact of 1972 and Bangladesh would not remain responsible for persons who had illegally migrated to India before the birth of the new Republic, prior to 25 March 1971.

Tripura: 'refugees' versus indigenous

Twipra, as in the indigenous vernacular and as the tribals of the state call it, means 'land beside water'.[122] There were two distinctive parts of the territory consisting of hilly regions and plain areas. The hilly region was named 'Parbatya Tippera' or Hill Tipperah, in which 70 per cent of the total area consisted of hills or hillocks and the rest of the area was plain land, situated in river valleys or narrow strips of land between the *tilas*, called the *loonga*-land. The five parallel hill ranges of Jampui, Sakhan, Longtorai, Atharamura and Baramura dominate this area.[123] The common people used to term it as 'Mughlan'. The land was known as 'Swadhin Tripura, Kohe Tripura, Prabat Tripura or Parbatya Tripura' and 'Hill Tipprah' (Kilikdar 1995: 4). In Tripura's day of yore, the Maharajas had control over a large territory of eastern Bengal named Chakla Roshanabad (Bhaumik 2012: 2). The territory consisted of Comilla, Sylhet, Noakhali and Dacca divisions, and a portion of Chittagong (Roy Choudhury 1977: 127). This word 'Chakla' indicates juxtaposition of three or four districts. Murshid Quli Khan divided Bengal into many such Chaklas, and named the whole area as 'Roshanabad'.[124] During the reign of Maharaja Dharma Manikya II (1714–1729), the Nawab of Bengal granted zamindari right of this area to the Manikya Maharajas. The *sanad* (royal declarations) of Indra Manikya (1743) give information about the land system, obtained in Chakla Roshanabad, which was contiguous to Hill Tipperah. From that *sanad* and a few other contemporary declarations, it is evident that the chief source of income of the Maharajas was revenue from the plains.[125] The area comprised of 600 square miles near surrounding border areas of the Tripura state (Chakravarty 1994: vi–vii). The Maharajas recognised the plain area as 'Roshonabad Tripura'.[126] Parbatya Tipperah, or Hill Tripura, was a princely land and homeland of the Maharajas; later they incorporated Chakla Roshanabad or plain Tripura. Both the areas were sustained by each other with a comfortable population density. These parts retained their distinctive features with basic utilities like collection of tax, share of produce and using the educated Bengalis as clerical staff in the administration. The integration was considered inseparable as it strengthened the economic base of the Manikyas (Pannalal Roy 2003: 59). The princely state was more or less a benevolent one, not very oppressive towards its tribal or non-tribal subjects.

Tripura, as a state, had always maintained a tradition of inviting culturally rich migrants from adjoining areas and absorbing them into its fabric to contribute to the general growth of the state. The Maharajas encouraged migration of both tribals and non-tribals. Interestingly, they encouraged immigration of tribals from other communities within the state fold much earlier than they invited the Bengalis.[127] It is important here to mention that of the tribal groups who now reside in Tripura, most do not actually fall into the category of the 'domiciles' of Tripura. W. W. Hunter described the Tipperah tribes simply as 'Mrung'. But there were many categorisations and classifications among them, too; Tripuris and Reangs were two major indigenous *jhumia* communities (Roy Choudhury 1985: 40–42). Some tribal communities such as Mogs, Halams, Chakmas, Garos and Lusais were migrants (Deb Barma 2002: 2). Out of the 19 enlisted tribes of Tripura, the Noatia, Jamatia, Chaimal, Kuki and Uchai were regarded as original inhabitants. The immigrant tribals were Khasi, Bhutia, Lepcha, Bhil, Munda, Oraon and Santal (Adhikari 1988: 10). Instead of the diversities, each tribal group could preserve their respective customs, beliefs, religion and culture, what they inherited from their predecessors (Palit 2004: 21). The Chakmas were the culturally rich group among the tribals. W. W. Hunter stated in 1874 that 'about 400 Chakmas migrated to settle down in Tripura' (Hunter 1874: 492–93). The 1901 census informed that the number of the Chakmas in Tripura was 4,501 (Sarkar and Dutta Ray 1990: 17). The Mogs also migrated from CHT and Arakan in the 18th century, as 'while *jhum* cultivation was the predominant form of economic activity among the Chakmas, a good number of Mogs took to plough cultivation as the main occupation retaining *jhum* cultivation as the subsidiary occupation' (Ganguli 1983: 16–31). Probably the population pressure on land, internal feuds and demand for land in the countryside attracted them towards the virgin soil of the state. In 1931, their population was 8,730 and 5,748, respectively (Misra 1976: 18).

The Manipuris were the next numerically significant group; 'In 1931 Manipuri population was 19,200 of whom agriculture (plough cultivation) was the main occupation of 4,171, and subsidiary occupation of 2,640 persons' (Ganguli 1983: 31). Garo, Khasi and Lushai had migrated in waves.

> The immigration of these people (the Lushais) into Tripura took place long back and as they also lived in the Lushai Hills, there had been a constant movement of these people within this area in course of their economic pursuits, that is practicing shifting cultivation.
>
> *(Ganguli 1983: 33)*

The Garos came earlier than the Khasis in search of *jhum* lands (Misra 1976: 19). In 1931, the population of Garo and Khasi tribes was 2,143 and 1,023, respectively. Easy availability of *ital* (plain land) and princely patronage through extension of facilities to immigrant settlers influenced them to migrate to Tripura. Thus, 'there had been a constant movement of these people within this area in course of their economic pursuits, that is practicing shifting cultivation' (Ganguli 1983: 31–33). But despite encouragements and offering of incentives, the immigration of tribal communities did not happen on a huge scale. Some of the tribal groups, who did not have economic and other compulsions, later preferred to stay back. *Tripuri* or *Kok-borok* was the common dialect of the tribals.[128] *Kok-borok* was a unique mixture of Tibetan and Burmese languages, though it did not have a *lipi* or script.[129] T. H. Lewin wrote 'Vocabulary of the Tipperah and of the Lushai or Kuki Languages' (Dasgupta 1997: 1–2). Some tribes, like Reang, Debbarma, Tripuri, Jamatia, Uchoi, Noatia and Koloi, used to converse in different dialects of *Kok-borok*. In a book titled *Kakbarak-ma* (*Grammar*), by Radha Mohan Dev Varman Thakur, published in 1900 in Comilla, it has been pointed out that owing to the homogeneity, most of the tribals of Tripura later accepted *Kok-borok* as their language. Regardless of other differences, they also constituted a homogeneous category (Chowdhury 1999: 15–16).

Though Tripura was a princely state headed by a Maharaja, the real power was vested in the hands of political agents and *Darbar* or the administration. Both the upper-caste/class educated Hindu Bengalis, the *bhadraloks*, started getting invitations from the Maharajas as early as 1280, to meet up administrative purposes. *Rajmala* stated that Maharaja Ratna Manikya (1464) introduced the tradition of inviting the Bengalis and encouraged their settlement (Kilikdar 1995: 5). It was not for offering jobs in fields of education and administration, but to promote plain-land cultivation that would provide them with a stable source of revenue (Sen Vidyabhusan 2013: 2–13). The Maharajas adopted Bengali culture, also declared Bengali as *Rajbhasa* (state language) and issued postal stamps bearing legends in Bengali. Culturally, they were keener to tighten their bond with the comparatively enriched, educated and enlightened Bengalis. In this context, one should mention the association of Rabindra Nath Tagore with the Maharajas, which reflects the nature of royal patronage towards Bengali art or culture.[130] Interestingly, Maharaja

Bir Chandra Manikya was proficient in Bengali; he translated texts and wrote literature in Bengali but did not know either *Tripuri* or *Kok-borok*. The decision to accept Bengali as the leading language was not taken to show their love for Bengali culture and respect for the language; the Maharajas tried to utilise the potential of the language as a *lingua franca*. Adaptation of Bengali was the only feasible option for the Maharajas. Apart from other socio-political or economic interests, they had to trust their Bengali employees for collecting revenues from tribal *Sardars* or *Khajanchis* (*Binondia* in *Kok-borok*) to run the administration (Debburma 2010: 40). During the East India Company's rule, the 'plain Tripura' became a British district. They mapped, framed the landscape and reshaped it. They started recognising the territory as 'Roshanabad Tripura' (Chakravarty 1994: vi–vii). In 1761, the British occupied alluvial plains and introduced a new boundary between hills and plains of Tripura. It constituted a disruption of old spaces of interconnection between the state-core, periphery, hills and extractive plains. In colonial discourses, the hill areas were designated as 'Hill Tipperah'. The alluvial plain that was under the sway of the Manikyas became known as 'British Tipperah' (Debbarma 2013: 10). Finally, an official change of name had taken place in 1920; the 'Hill Tipperah' was renamed as 'Tripura State'.[131]

Economics actually played the principal role in this princely state, in treatment of communities with definite socio-cultural aspects.[132] With the development of the institution of kingship, the question of surplus production arose. The shifting cultivation could not yield much surplus, which was needed for the maintenance of the ruling class, for the stability of the state (Sinha and Chakraborty 2010: 99–100). *Jhum* cultivation was the only method/indigenous technique of the production system of the domicile tribals.[133] Shifting cultivation was not a tradition of agricultural practice for the tribals; it intrinsically related to their culture and was integral to their identities (Sengupta 2013: 59). *Jhum* cultivation involves labour-intensive operation and could fit-in only in format of self-sufficient economy (Dutta 1358 TE: 3). It was a primitive form of agriculture that upsets the balance of nature (Agarwal 1985: 128). So like Assam, the Maharajas started inviting Bengali Muslim peasants to increase revenue collection for the state exchequer, through expansion of wet rice cultivation in the state (Banerjee 1998: 337). It augured the feudal economy well. W. W. Hunter mentioned of giving land grants to the upper and upper-middle-class Bengalis on fixed rentals by the Maharajas (Hunter 1874: 509). Some similar grants were given to Muslim peasants of lower-strata from Comilla, Sylhet and Chittagong of East Bengal on nominal rentals. The state was in favour of the settlement of the Bengalis for its own socio-political and economic interest. While the migration of Brahmins and upper classes was initiated to enhance the status of the state and man its administrations, the settlement of an East Bengali Muslim peasant class was for reclaiming fallow lands and multiplying revenues.

With the intervention of the British in the state administration, genuine pressure was felt to usher in designing an administrative structure capable of implementing some modernisation programmes. The Maharajas and the *Darbar* felt the need to sponsor large-scale migration of the middle-class educated Hindus and professionals, who gradually started controlling the civil, police, education, judicial and engineering jobs that created economic surplus in Tripura (Ganguli 1983: 4). In 1818, 45 per cent of the state's total population (including hills-plains) was non-tribals (Bhattacharyya 1988: 4). From this percentage, one can presume that the Bengalis were never a 'minority community' in Tripura. A resolution signed by B. K. Burman on 13 September 1909 stated: 'We should by all means encourage immigration and discourage emigration. Systematic efforts may be made to establish colonies of cultivators in the interior' (Paul 2009: 27). The migration of the Brahmins and upper-castes was initiated to enhance the status of the state and man its administrations; the settlement and encouragement to the peasant class for reclaiming fallow lands was for multiplying revenues (Banerjee 1998: 337). It came out as a one-sided demographic flow for better employment opportunities.[134] So, a surplus *bhadralok* class brought the renaissance that Tripura had experienced was rather a myth, not a reality (Bhismodeb Bhattacharyya 1989: 58). The administration was neither sympathetic to the tribals, nor initiated necessary structural reforms for them. Maharaja Bir Bikram Kishore Manikya (1923–1947) carried some processes of the modernisation initiated first by Maharaja Bir Chandra Manikya (1862–1896) and reserved half of the entire state territory to safeguard interests of the five major tribes: Tripuris, Noatias, Jamatias, Reangs and Halams. He introduced *Grama Mandali* on an elected basis. Transfer of lands to the non-tribals without prior permission of the government was strictly prohibited.[135]

Partition and assistance towards the refugees

The paramountcy of the state of Tripura lapsed when Maharaja Bir Bikram Kishore Manikya entered into a standstill agreement with the Government of India. The Partition was designed in such a way that it left the princely states with no other choices but to join one of the post-colonial South Asian nation-states, India or Pakistan. The last designated ruler of Tripura, Maharaja Bir Bikram Manikya Bahadur, was a distinguished member of the Chamber of Princes and subsequently elected as President of the Council of Rulers for the Eastern States. But, his premature death three months ahead of the formal transfer of power had changed the situation (Pannalal Roy 2003: 59). The crisis deepened in the state when on 3 November 1947, the Intelligence Bureau of India reported:

> This information is confirmed by an independent source which says that the Muslim League National Guards in East Bengal are carrying an open propaganda that Tripura State belongs to Eastern Pakistan and that preparations are made to invade Tripura. Several pamphlets inciting Muslims to conquer Tripura and annex it to East Bengal are in circulation in Eastern Pakistan.
> *(Debnath 2010: 64)*

Prior to Partition, Tripura was accessible by a rail route through eastern Bengal. After Partition, the north, west and south sides were bounded by East Bengal.

On the East, Mizoram and Cachar district of Assam bordered the state. A chain of hills obstructed the road-link with Assam across the eastern boundary (Pannalal Roy 2003: 67). 'In order to provide a railway communication for the state of Tripura, specially three divisions namely Kailashahar, Dharmanagar and Kamalpur of Tripura are left without any means of communication with the outside world except the air'.[136] Tripura was suffering from economic blockade imposed by the Pakistani Police and National Guards, internal communication connecting the capital, Agartala and other divisional towns. All necessary consumer goods and even newspapers from Calcutta were not allowed to enter into the Tripura state by railway police at Akhaura.[137] Khowai Maharajganj Bazar used to be an important business centre during pre-Partition days. The Pakistani authorities suddenly announced opening of a new bazar in Asampara in Pakistan, and they compelled the sellers not to sell their goods in Khowai bazar, which created acute crises for the local masses. Dharmanagar and Kamalpur were suffering because of the lack of internal communication and more for Pakistan's ban on exports and imports of goods from 15 August 1947 (Ghosh 2010: 235–36).

Prime Minister Jawaharlal Nehru was aware of the crisis situation and conspiracy of the Muslim League with another Islamic Party called *Anjuman-e-Islamia*, led by a rich contractor Abdul Barik alias Gedu Miah, who managed to get support from some nobles like Durjoy Karta for his plans to merge Tripura with Pakistan. The Muslim League had been bolstered by the effortless takeover of the CHT, despite strong local resistance. Nehru wrote a letter to Sardar Vallabhbhai Patel:

> You are no doubt aware of the reports that there is trouble brewing on the borders of Tripura (Agartala) State. It is said that the Muslim National Guards from East Pakistan, Tripura District, have started an agitation against accession of Tripura to the Indian Union and they may well have raids.[138]

The Centre responded 'by sending men and material to put an end to the inimical external inroads and influences' (Das 1972: 426–27). Tripura was saved from absorption by Pakistan. After much palace intrigue and political flurry, the Regent Maharani Kanchan Prava Devi, on behalf of her minor son, Kiriti Bikram Kishore Manikya Bahadur, decided to join India by exercising the Instrument of Accession. The merger with India appeared to be the only plausible way to restore traditional links with greater India (Schendel 2002: 119). She declared that:

> in accordance with the wishes of the late Maharaja Manikya Bahadur, Tripura will have a full democratic constitution and the popular representations will be associated with the Government. The interest of the people of Tripura and their economic welfare are our great concern.
>
> *(Das 1972: 434–35)*

The political parties and ethnic organisations foiled Barik's conspiracy and the Regent Maharani finally signed the agreement of merger on 9 September 1949.

Tripura became a part of the Indian Union after its administration was taken over by the Chief Commissioner on 15 October 1949 (Bhaumik 2012: 1). The Constitution of India came into force in 1950 and Tripura officially became a Part-C State (under Part-C States Act, 1950). It got a status of Territorial Council in 1956, then a Union Territory in 1963.[139] The process of state formation started with the appointment of a Lieutenant Governor on 31 January 1970 (Ray 2009: 12), and a full-fledged statehood was conferred on 21 January 1972, under provisions of the North Eastern (Reorganisation) Act, 1971 (Kumar 1996: 68–70).

Agartala, the capital of Tripura, and the state had to provide initial shelter to at least 15,000 Bengali migrants during the unprecedented Raipur/Dhaka riot of 1941 (Bhismodeb Bhattacharyya 1989: 8). Maharaja Bir Bikram Manikya treated these victims of communal conflicts as state guests and organised an administrative wing named the 'Pritibordhok Samiti'. It remained functional till the Noakhali riot, to keep communal harmony at pace (Dasgupta 2015: 54). The royal administration provided relief, planned rehabilitation measures and sheltered them in four camps around Arundhatinagar and other places near Agartala. The state offered permanent rehabilitation to them in the form of providing employment or by rendering settlement on freehold lands.[140] By this initiative, an agricultural immigrant class subsequently converted into professional people because of the liberal attitude of the administration and acceptance of the then local people of Tripura (Lodh 2002: 18–19). Agartala became an important urban space in northeast India from that time. With the variable and fluctuating incidents of accommodation of huge chunks of migrants, the spatial growth of the city became uneven and unplanned. It also led to unreal expansion of the city.[141] The major influx started from 1946, out of a communal riot in Noakhali district, Chandpur subdivision of Tipperah District (Comilla). The administration formed an official Immigration and Reclamation Department with a Relief Committee (Verghese 1996: 38). The Maharaja spared some royal buildings, arranged six shelters for refugees and created a relief fund (Sen 1970: 25). A medical camp was opened in Agartala and few voluntary groups started working with the administration in district towns. They joined hands with the Dharmanagar Hitasadhini Sabha to keep Hindu–Muslim unity intact, distributed relief materials to the migrants (Roychoudhury 1983: 59). Four thousand migrants were accommodated in the college buildings, Narsinghar Tea Garden managed to render shelter to 60 families and 1,700 migrants were put up in Ranir Bazar area. There were 6,000 unregistered migrants in private houses of old Agartala, reported in a census carried out by the relief committees.[142] The Maharaja was sensitive, generous and sympathetic towards subjects from both of his territories. The majority populations in Hill Tripura were Hindus, either tribals or Bengalis, and the *jiratia prajas* in Chakla Roshanabad estate were Muslims; yet the state could resist the communal frenzy (Mahanta 2004: 73–74).

Partition opened the floodgates of Bengali migration, which changed the demography of the erstwhile princely state (Bhaumik 2012: 1). It led to a fierce ethnic conflict that ravaged the tiny state for more than three decades. It was the only state in northeastern India in which the refugees outnumbered the original inhabitants.[143] After Partition, the situation was messy and there was confusion at every front, even on the question of succession within the royal family (Devi 2010: 178). The process of negotiations were initiated on issues like ethnic tensions, political conflicts, regional disparities, social imbalances and ideological differences within indigenous and migrant communities (Gan-Chaudhuri 1985: 52). The state stressed on making policies for beneficiaries to *jhumia* settlements.[144]

> King Bir Bikram had earmarked 1950 sq. miles as tribal Reserve, but in 1948, the Regent Maharani's Dewan A. B. Chatterjee vide order no. 325 dated 10th Aswin, 1358 Tripura era threw open 300 sq. miles of this reserve for refugee settlement. Later more of these areas would be opened to these refugees.[145]

In 1948, K. C. Neogy, the Union Relief and Rehabilitation Minister, met Sri Hari Ganga Basak and Anil Chandra Chakraborty, Secretaries of the State Congress Relief and Rehabilitation Committee. They placed a memorandum on 'miserable pecuniary conditions of the refugee numbering about 1,13,950 who have settled in different parts of the Tripura State since October 1946'.[146] Bimal Sinha, in his novel *Titas theke Tripura*, mentioned that getting relief and rehabilitation measures in terms of jobs, loans and lands were comparatively easier in Tripura. One just needed to register his/her name for getting such benefits. Apparently, essences of the warmth of the Manikya Maharajas towards the Bengalis extended to its administration; even their native subjects were generous to the first few batches of refugees. The tradition of hospitality touched the modern state system, too. The government used to give 5 *kanis* of land per family with some cash to build a house. Before their land allocations, the refugees were kept in camps with a regular supply of doles (Sinha 2009b: 43).

In October 1948, A. B. Chatterjee, then the Dewan of Tripura, submitted his first appeal for grants and a scheme to the Central Government:

> for rehabilitation of about 65,000 displaced persons from East Bengal to Tripura and asked for a total sum of Rs. 1,33,00,000' and the Centre sanctioned 'two instalments of Rs. 50,000 each, through the Adviser to the Governor of Assam for immediate relief to the displaced persons.[147]

He stated, 'Out of this amount of Rs. 1,00,000, Tripura has spent up to the end of December, 1949 about Rs. 94,000 by way of establishment, food and clothing, education and vocational training, etc'.[148] But many more batches of displaced persons were waiting in the border for rehabilitation. A shortage of food grains made their condition acute.[149] Some of them were anxious to return to East Bengal. The Government of India was ready to provide them some facilities, like bearing the cost of third-class fare for railway journeys, cost of their basic rations for two months at controlled prices in force in East Bengal, etc.[150] The Adviser to His Excellency the Governor of Assam wrote to the Regional Director of Rehabilitation in June 1949 that 'a large number of displaced persons have already left the State' because 'their economic condition has deteriorated very seriously and the discontinuance of the rice doles to all except the uncared for women and children have made the problem more acute'. He informed, 'the rough census of such persons that we have recently completed shows a total figure of only about 32,500 refugees, as against the 65,000 estimated by Mr Chatterjee in October 1948'.[151]

Such circumstances made the Centre a little apprehensive to grant further funds 'on loans' for Tripura. The Chief Commissioner instructed Manmohan Kishan, Assistant Secretary of the Ministry of Rehabilitation:

> Taccavi loans should be given only to those displaced persons who are absolutely destitute and cannot purchase bullocks, implements, seeds, etc. No loans should be granted to displaced persons who have any interest in Pakistan as such people are likely to be tempted at a later date to go back to their homes in Pakistan.[152]

Interestingly, in the Confidential Report for the period ending 15 June 1949, the Ministry of States expressed similar views: 'the stresses and strains on the present Administration of Tripura are so great that . . . it cannot continue for more than six months or a year at the utmost without a major upheaval', and however they urged 'for early orders on the Tripura scheme of refugee rehabilitation'.[153] The new Dewan, Mr Acharya was advised to implement 'institution of permit system regulating entry into Tripura'.[154] But he questioned the plan of the Ministry of Rehabilitation: 'As regards the proposal to send displaced persons to India, it would appear to be more desirable to send non-Muslims (displaced persons) rather than allow Muslims from East Bengal to squat on land'.[155] The administration pointed out real reasons, why 'they are not encouraging the displaced persons to settle down in Tripura'.[156] They primarily stressed on the complete geographical isolation of Tripura and problem of supplies for the absence of transit facilities through East Bengal, and argued: 'Apart from hill slopes and the forest areas there is no land lying waste awaiting cultivation'.[157]

Issues of complexities and contradictions

In the financial year 1949–1950, the Secretariat sanctioned Rs. 6,30,000 on the head of 'loans' for resettlement of land of 1,000 agriculturist families in Tripura. And, 'This was intended for giving rehabilitation loans for reclamation, purchasing bullocks, agricultural implements, seeds, etc.', but the Government could not utilise the whole amount during that time span. Sincere efforts for rehabilitation began from October 1950.[158] The Central Government and the Chief Commissioner of Tripura were resolute on registration of refugees: 'it was decided that details of the West Bengal Government Scheme would be furnished to the Chief Commissioner who would modify it to suit local conditions and also submit an estimate of cost for sanction by the Branch Secretariat'.[159] They agreed to build colonies for different categories of refugees at government expense, as total number of refugees dependent on doles crossed 71,479 by then.[160] They argued: 'As regards the liquidation of gratuitous relief in camps, an undeveloped state like Tripura offered practically no means of livelihood and it was not possible to stop the doles without causing misery and starvation'. They were firm on introducing 'special schemes for temporary settlement of displaced persons on Muslim migrants' land.[161] Beyond the state initiatives, Ramakrishna Mission, a renowned charitable foundation, had proposed to work collectively with the government and sanctioned financial assistance for giving basic 'amenities, like medical and sanitary arrangements, water supply, etc.'[162] A. P. Jain, the then Union Minister of Rehabilitation, agreed with suggestions made by R. K. Ray, the ex-Chief Commissioner of Tripura, after looking at the mess. They planned a scheme for sugarcane plantation, establishment of a sugar mill, in which the Centre would invest 51 per cent capital, and 'the remaining 49% would be contributed out of loans to be advanced to the displaced businessmen under the General Loan Scheme'.[163] A. P. Jain instructed the Ministry of Transport for recruitment of displaced persons on a large scale, on the construction of the Assam–Tripura road with special wage packages. In addition, K. K. Hajara, the Chief Commissioner of Tripura, proposed to establish another training-cum-work centre, in addition to the existing one in Agartala.[164]

After the disturbances of 1950, the daily average of influx was estimated at 4,500 persons and it compelled the refugees to stay in bordering areas like Dharmanagar, Kailashahar, Kamalpur and Agartala.[165] The picture was certain that the refugees would not return to their homeland. A section of the Bengal press started reporting about the slow progress of rehabilitation schemes in Tripura.[166] The State Rehabilitation Committee became active and suggested appropriate rehabilitation schemes, productive work ideas and employment. There were some cases of land exchanges between outgoing Muslims and the incoming Hindus, but the comfortable population density was saved in Tripura till 1950, as most of the refugees were agriculturists.[167] Following the refugee policies of West Bengal and Assam, the Tripura Government also introduced rehabilitation schemes of four categories in the late 1950s, which was also suggested by the Central Directorate of Rehabilitation.[168] Under the 'Colony Scheme', land was acquisitioned and loan was provided to the camp refugees, while the 'Type Scheme' targeted refugees who were staying outside the camps. In the 'Proto-type Scheme', land was given to agriculturist families. The 'Land Purchase Scheme' was meant for the professional groups. They established a total of 75 colonies and claimed to rehabilitate 1,40,598 refugees.[169] The State Rehabilitation Department had made long-term rehabilitation plans for refugees from diverse occupations. It requisitioned a large marshland area called Rudrasagar in Sonamura division, including a big lake, and tried to develop a fishery for rehabilitation of 400–500 refugee fishermen and provide smallholdings of land to agriculturist families.[170] Debaprasad Sengupta, the officer in charge of the Rudrasagar project, remembered in his autobiography that the Ministry of Rehabilitation, Government of Tripura, instructed him to finish both the works within three months. Though the fishery scheme was successful, the land settlement schemes, which were meant for the agriculturist *Namasudra* refugees, were hampered by the feudal attitude of the *jotedars* and constant opposition of the local administrative bodies (Sengupta 2003: 28–29).

Problems were actually at diverse levels and of different natures. Some refugees were carrying cash in Pakistani currency. Due to non-recognition of Pakistan exchange rates by the Central Government, they could not use their own capital and thus, were solely dependent on doles.[171] Some families were there without a male member, who had left them in camps to bring up belongings from East Bengal or rescue other family members left there, but never came back. The Centre directed the setting up of a 'Home-cum-Training Centre', chiefly 'for 250 displaced unattached women and children in Abhoynagar, Agartala', and in Narsingarh.[172] Under the old regime, the Maharaja had full powers to utilise lands for public utilities or expropriate any land for any purposes, as he desired, but in a new regime, new policies on the legal sanctions for distribution of lands became essential, as: 'Due to the lack of any proper records, the authorities found great difficulty to settle down the refugees on available lands'.[173] As per the provisions of the Delhi Pact, the state Government had spent Rs. 35,50,000 on 'head of loans' for the settlement of incoming Muslim returnees to Tripura.[174] The actual scenario was different. Forty per cent of Muslims in the 1940s exchanged their properties with the incoming Hindus; for others who left for East Pakistan, the majority Bengali Hindus occupied their land and properties.[175] They had complaints against the state machinery for occupying lands that used to belong to Muslim peasants. In a telegram to the Minister for State offices, Delhi, dated 13 February 1951, Fazlur Rahman complained, 'Paddy lands of 800 Muslim families of Bardual Chandidhapa Jamsermura Chundulmi Rudrasagar in Tripura State made *khas* for rehabilitating Hindu refugees'.[176] The situation was worsening steadily as the *jotedars* were evicting the Muslims forcibly. The Muslims felt unprotected and sent prayers for a stay order to the Chief Commissioner pending tribunal enquiries, but they were often sent for tribunal judgement, and in most of the cases, the attempted enquiry proved to be futile.

The introduction of a passport system and visa regulations impacted Tripura in a different way. It imposed a ban on crossing of the borders and overall movement of the *jiratia prajas*. The procedure of boundary demarcation restricted movement of the cultivators, and both the governments were not sure what would happen to 40,000 acres of cultivable paddy lands or houses that fell in between East Pakistan and Tripura.[177] Tripura decided to consider the matter later, but Pakistan was vocal and apprehensive on this issue.[178] The East Bengal Press was alleging persistently on 'eviction of Muslims as a result of the requisition of lands of *jiratia* tenants on border areas within the Tripura State'.[179] In 1948, it was rather decided unanimously at the first Indo-Pakistan Conference that:

> where any cultivator living in the border village of one Dominion has land in border village in the other Dominion, he should be permitted within a reasonable period after the harvest to take across the border to his residence

reasonable quantities of any controlled commodities produced by him for his domestic consumption with the minimum of restriction and formalities.[180]

For imposing an immediate restriction on smuggling of rice, the Chief Commissioner of Tripura imposed a total ban on the export of food grains across borders after the introduction of the passport and visa regulations. The second conference in 1950 declared that 'otherwise it seemed to be impossible to control the movement of the exportable limit of 40 mounds per family per annum'.[181] In 1951, the state government initiated a policy of requisitioning land and property from Muslim landowners (including *jiratias*) to rehabilitate Hindu refugees from East Pakistan. *Jiratia* tenants found it dangerous to cross the border to work, either in the forests collecting bamboo, timber or other forest products. Pakistan authorities did not support them. By the late 1950s, cross-border landholding—whether by tenure holders such as the Maharaja or by lowly *jiratias*—had come to an end (Schendel 2001: 404–5).

The refugee migration was high after the announcement of the introduction of passports. The total number of refugees in Tripura was 1,75,000, as stated by A. P. Jain in 1953.[182] The state Rehabilitation Department started encroaching *jotes*, horticultural lands and other variety of lands for paddy cultivation, in which *jotedars* used to grow thatching grass, bamboos and other valuable trees.[183] Some *khas* lands requisitioned, via 'Extra Ordinary Issue of Tripura Gazette dated 7 November 1952', in Bishalgarh and Belonia 'where original inhabitants of the villages are mostly of minority community or tribals'.[184] It was reported that 'the refugees have rendered the local people quite nervous by their hostile activities'.[185] The Ministry of States accepted 'failure to resettlement of refugees and failure to stop wanton requisitioning of the peasants', and admitted encroachment of lands in Tulakona fuel reserve.[186] A riot situation emerged at Barpather between refugees of Chandrapur colony, Udaypur and local Muslims over the issue of cutting of paddy by the Muslim inhabitants cultivated solely by them.[187] Yet, the Rehabilitation Department claimed in 1953 that:

> in spite of difficulties of transport and communication arising out of the topographical condition of Tripura, we are glad to say that we have successfully rehabilitated 57% of the total refugee population in Tripura. So the question of failure in the resettlement of refugees in Tripura does not arise.[188]

They asked for Rs. 10,00,000 on loans and Rs. 28,00,000 for rehabilitation from the Centre, in the financial year 1953–1954. The refugees who had registered themselves legally in Tripura and did not have relatives or friends there were admitted in the transit camps, dependent solely on government doles.[189]

When the difference in numbers between the registered refugees, unregistered refugees and domiciles became significant, issues related to land became more important in the then socio-cultural-political life of Tripura. Methods of distribution and transfer of lands to the refugees for their resettlement, and settling up colonies by the state, created a feeling of scare within the local tribals, landlord and *jotedar* classes. The government dealt with such issues quite sensitively by passing acts for further land reforms in Tripura.[190] In the Land Reform Bill of 1956, the Ministry of Home Affairs decided to include a provision for the abolition of intermediaries and incorporation of ceiling charges, as 'transfer or exchange by Partition' would be permitted. Concurrently, it was made mandatory that 'a transfer to a scheduled tribe when such transfer is made with the previous permission of the collector'.[191] The Ministry of Home Affairs realised the necessity for approval of an extraordinary scheme relating to the ten-year Cadastral Survey in Tripura with an estimated expenditure of Rs. 1,33,77,000. It declared that 'the survey and settlement work should be taken up immediately, the settlement officers will be responsible for settling lands in the surveyed area according to the principles laid down in the Tenancy Act'.[192] The total numbers of refugees were more or less 5 lakhs; of them 60,500 did not get any government assistance and 12,661 families failed to prove them as refugees (Debnath 2001: 39). However, a total of 3,65,000 refugees got rehabilitated from 83,000 families through colony, proto-type and land purchase schemes in 1961.[193] The lands allotted to them in the Government sponsored colonies (2 acres or more per family) consisted of *tilla* lands, which were fit for terrace cultivation. Bishu Chhatterjee, the Relief officer in charge of the projects opined that most of the lands encroached by the government with proper *khotipuron* (compensation) were either fallow lands of tribals or wastelands. The refugees made it cultivable (Debnath 2001: 40). These allotments were introduced in 1956–1957.

Education facilities for the refugees was another vital concern. The Government of India had created a category called the 'displaced students' with a definition: 'students who have either lost their parents/guardians in Pakistan or whose parents/guardians have migrated from Pakistan to India with the intention of settling down in the country permanently'.[194] They were eligible to get facilities like waiver of tuition fees, free admission in schools and other educational institutes including free books and necessities. Another extraordinary provision added by the state government was those 'whose parents or guardians yet may be in Pakistan, the student claim to have been refugees in their own right' to avail themselves of these facilities.[195] The Department of Education for Tripura was based in Calcutta and the Department of Higher Education was affiliated to the University of Calcutta. The transfer of these departments tentatively fixed in 1962 'after necessary consultation of budget provision in this regard has not therefore been made by the Ministry of Education in the Area Demand of Tripura for 1961–62'. They thought that it might prove beneficial for the tribal and refugee students.[196]

Aspects of economic rehabilitation

The nature of demand for the rehabilitation changed in every decade, and the concern of the government also shifted. The focus of the 1960s was at providing economic and professional rehabilitation to the refugees, and the government agreed on conversion from 'periodical loans' to 'grants' for generation of their collective income.[197] The state submitted a proposal of grant for 'Rural agriculturist and Non-agriculturist families, urban businessmen and small traders' to 'help the refugee families to leave the camp and start farming operations/establish their business', and advocated 'for conversion of maintenance loan amounting Rs. 55.71 lakh into grant'.[198] The administration examined some cases in which loans were irrecoverable due to death, desertion or other reasons. There were 2,469 such cases in Tripura, where the total amount of Rs. 23,61,991 had been given to refugees as loan advances.[199] The domination of the Bengali refugees and their monopoly over the land and culture changed the economy and body politic of post-Partition Tripura. It did not lead to the deprivation or crisis of the tribal domiciles only; the indigenous Muslims were losing ground, too. The legal procedures of property exchange stopped in 1960, and the Muslims were compelled to opt either for Pakistan or they were pushed to the interiors of Tripura. The state introduced a rule that immovable property of the Muslim migrants should belong to the *Gaonsabha* of the area in which it falls. And, the value of that property should be taken into consideration and added to cash balance, divided accordingly on the basis of population.[200] During the riot days of 1964, truckloads of Muslims were picked up just like animals and dumped across the border at night (Sen 2003: 125).

Yet, the tribal communities always proved themselves as the real host community of Tripura. Until the early 1960s, the Muslims were comfortably migrating from Tripura and had taken shelter in houses left by the Hindus in East Bengal. After 1965, the scenario had been totally changed. Some of the Hindu Bengalis, who experienced riot situations in East Bengal, became politically alert, socially powerful and staunch anti-Muslims. They forced the minorities to leave Tripura, compelled them to sell off their properties at very low prices and did not return the property if some of them came back. Tribal communities again proved to be their messiahs for providing temporary shelter, by not showing any communal attitude towards them (Pal 2010: 69–84). The tribal *jhumias* felt themselves detained in the transitory period and with government land settlement policies. The refugees pushed the tribals to the edge. The price of daily necessities like salt and dried fish had skyrocketed. The refugees were grabbing plain lands and targeting even the hills (Dhar 2010: 30). Bimal Sinha, in a short story '*Raima Upotyokar Upokatha*', depicted how the 'Bengali *babus*' became traumatic agents for the tribals, who could locate *jhum* lands and buy their agricultural products at a low rate. The tribals shifted their base first from locality to hillocks, from plains to hills, but the *babus* followed them everywhere. Grabbing their produce was not enough; the Bengali *mahajan*/moneylenders had taken lands and houses from the illiterate and simple tribals by false thumb impressions. The Bengalis were making laws to forbid the tribals to continue with *jhum*, their own traditional agricultural practices (Sinha 2009a: 40–53). Hence, the tribals started protesting vehemently for their right of existence and control over lands from the late 1950s. As a result of their pressure, the Tripura Land Revenue and Land Reforms Act of 1960 passed, under section 197 (by notification no. 74 [14]-Rev/60, dated the 13th April 1961).[201] The basic objective of the Act was to 'bring the cultivators of the soil into direct contact with the State and guarantee permanent heritable and transferable right over land cultivated by him' (Deb Barma 2005: 127). In tribal demography, according to the Census of 1961, tribals were only 6.87 per cent of the population, though they were about 450 communities, including sub-tribes of larger tribes.[202] From 1963, after protests, rehabilitation of *jhumias* became the concern of the government.[203] The state acknowledged in a press note that 'out of 27 thousand *jhumias*, 4000 were rehabilitated by the Government initiatives in last 10 years, 15,500 were trying to rehabilitate themselves by their own efforts and 7,000 were still to be rehabilitated'.[204]

The policies of the Centre legally stopped refugee registration for the years 1958–1964, when 8–10 families were entering the state on almost daily basis (Debnath 2001: 41). In the second Rehabilitation Minister's Conference, Shri B. Dass, the Deputy Minister for Rehabilitation of Tripura, reported to Shri Jagjivan Ram, Union Minister for Labour, Employment and Rehabilitation, after the riot of 1964, that '4,358 families migrated to Tripura only in 1964 and about 1,460 families in 1965 entered the State as a result of clashes with Muslims'.[205] During the last phase of migration (1964–1971), total numbers of the registered refugees were 32,389, but the state decided to disperse 7,065 families outside the state (Bhattacharya 1988: 40). A total of 20,198 refugees were sent to Mana camp of Dandakaranya. Few refugee colonies were established in Nalkata in Kailashahar, Amtali and Arundhatinagar in Sadar, after the leftist leaders started protesting the policy (Debnath 2001: 39). Regardless of protests from the tribal *jhumias*, the priority of the government remained the rehabilitation of refugees. The state government received 4,069 applications from *jhumias* and 4,249 from landless persons, requesting their settlement. In effect, 1,834 *jhumias* and 1,049 landless persons received rehabilitation during 1964–1966.[206] The Rehabilitation Department was providing economic rehabilitation to refugees like: 'A scheme for granting a loan for the purchase of yarn and loom to 750 skilled weavers amongst the new migrants who have come on exchange of properties has been sanctioned by the Government of India'.[207] The state introduced a policy to divide the *jhumias* into several income groups like the refugees, for providing them loans with other facilities; 6,835 *jhumias* got a loan in form of cash in 1967.[208]

From 1968, the Central Rehabilitation Ministry and Government of Tripura were desperate to finish the task of rehabilitation by establishing colonies and allotments of land for both refugees and *jhumias*. The government was encroaching new lands and de-reserving some tribal lands to settle down refugee families there.[209] It ignited flare-ups within the domiciles, as they had shown their discontentment and resentment, though the amount of land was less than 2 acres in 1969.[210] The procedures of giving citizenship cards to refugees proved to be an incessant venture, even in 1970.[211] Another category, a group of uprooted Chakma of CHT, had started migrating for refuge in Tripura (Nandy 1993: 2102). The Centre provided shelter to them and opened six camps in Kathalchari, Karbook, Pancharampara, Silachari and Tukumbari, Lebachari in the Amarpur and Subroom subdivision of the state (Basu Majumder 2003: 93). The flow of refugees was destined to be unending in the northeastern states. The Liberation War of 1971 posed the last challenge for hosting immigrant Bengalis (Sen 2003: 123). In 1971, 'the total population of Tripura was 15.56 lakh, and the number of refugees from East Pakistan was 13.42 lakh'.[212] The number of refugees further increased, and it left a deep impact upon the life and economy of Tripura. The Chief Minister stated on 25 April 1971: 'About 60,000 refugees have been registered. Of them, 40,000 were staying with relatives. Most of the refugees had come from Comilla, Chittagong, Srihatta, and Noakhali districts of Bangladesh. Every day thousands were entering Tripura through the border' (Habib 1992: 27). Most of the refugee camps were around the border police station for security reasons.[213] The inevitable dominance of the Bengalis led to an extreme demographic change in Tripura (Das 2014: 23). It made the indigenous tribals minorities, instead of Hindu and Muslim Bengalis, who used to be in that position in previous decades.

Conclusion

The northeastern states were (are) different in many ways from the rest of India. The strategic location of the region and the nature of the polity, economy and society of the neighbouring regions and countries added a set of special concerns, problems and anxieties to its normal national share. Assam and Tripura became the victims of their geographical location, as both tiny states were bordered by East Bengal and they each had a pre-existing settled Bengali population. Hence, Assam and Tripura constituted interesting cases in relation to the influx of refugees, as they became the host to Bengali refugees from East Bengal/Pakistan. Assam was rather an inextricable part of British India, whereas Tripura was a princely state ruled through a residency by the British. In Brahmaputra valley, through the colonial patronage, a steady migration of farm settlers, middle-class job seekers, petty traders and businessmen had started with the advent of British rule. The tribal state of Tripura used to invite Bengalis from the neighbouring Bengal districts and also made their settling in Tripura easy as part of effective integration with the sub-continental currents. It helped in imbibing Sanskritisation and absorbing the influence of the Bengali language and culture. Though it had succeeded in its effort, eventually Tripura turned into a Bengali majoritarian state, as the Bengalis came out as the dominant group in the polity, society and economy of the state. Initially, the Assamese middle-classes were enthusiastic recipients of the Bengali culture emanating from Calcutta—but gradually, as they found that the Bengali settlers were socio-culturally dominant, politically powerful and becoming even numerically preponderant, they began to resist the dominance and presence of the Bengalis in Assam.

This was in contrast with Tripura, where Bengalis were encouraged to bring about their progressive influence. The hostility of the Assamese towards Bengalis grew stronger as they saw there was a tacit alliance between the colonial state and the Bengali immigrants. The colonial state had downright rejected the resistance of the Assamese to further immigration of the Bengalis in Assam. What was more, the colonial state multiplied their woes by adding three new Bengali districts to the province of Assam, making the Bengalis a virtual majority, with the potential to capture political power in the future. In Assam, Bengali immigration had a religious connotation, as many of the migrants were Muslims, and in later decades, they started to pose threats to the state politics. Though during the colonial period, there was mutual admiration between the tribals and Bengalis, the hostility between the Assamese and Bengalis increased later. The Partition of India aggravated the situation beyond political imagination. Despite not being a part of communal politics, both the states were affected by the territorial division. Tripura lost its valuable possession of Chakla Roshanabad with the stroke of a pen, reducing its territorial size enormously, and Assam had to bear the brunt of losing the most revenue-generating province of Sylhet, though reluctantly. The scars of the valuable losses that both the states had to bear with seemed to have haunted them after Partition.

After Partition, both the states fell into the politics of numbers, which was later popularly named as a 'numbers game'. In pre-Partition days, the form of numbers was different; it was merely 'majority' and 'minority' communities. After Partition, the linguistic, cultural and hegemonic differences were added to the existing lines of differences. These two states experienced fallouts in more direct ways, right from the communitarian point of view to their ghettoised existence. There were differences in patterns in the nature of physical spaces, too. Assam, especially Cachar (the Surma valley) had to accommodate unlisted or unregistered refugees in huge numbers, which led to sudden population growth and naturally impacted the *mofussil* towns and villages more. Assam state and the domicile Assamese naturally tried to resist the rehabilitation and settlement of such a large number of refugees. At the same time, to safeguard their culture and politics, they tried to implement measures like making Assam a unilingual state, declaring Assamese as the state language and making the Assamese people the preferred candidates for employment. Assamese dominance led to the sparking of frequent anti-Bengali riots. All these were seen as persecution attempts. The Bengali population had to face opposition quite often, although over the years, it had grown into a force to be reckoned with. They fought back for their due rights of language, culture and employment. Hence, for the Bengali refugees in Assam, a new struggle had begun for life, culture, liberty and equality in a polity which was not meant for them.

In contrast to the scenario in Assam, the tribals in Tripura welcomed the Bengali refugees initially but, when the trickle of refugees grew into a flood, they could not resist it. Neither could the state accommodate them properly on a reduced territorial size. Agartala became the hub of post-Partition Bengali refugees. It became the gateway of all refugees, even those who had finally decided to try their luck in other refugee-absorbent states. Partition devastated the economy and altered demography, so Tripura had to withstand the impact. That was how the tribals began to lose their habitat, their land, their hills and their economy to the aggressive refugees, who were desperate for a piece of land to settle and survive. Soon the tribals lost to the refugees demographically, which in turn ensured their loss of political power to the Bengali settlers. Eventually, they had to recede back to the reserves and protected territories granted to them by the Bengalis whom they had once invited to settle in their land. Actually, the whole of the eastern border was neglected in every possible way. It neither got adequate attention in the refugee rehabilitation programme, nor did the Centre render help in planning the transformation of the geographical locale. In the case of Bengal, Calcutta was conceived as the centre of absorbing the uprooted populace or place of their shelter. Thus, the Centre did not care much to give attention to other refugee-absorbent states, primarily to the growing unplanned urban spaces like Guwahati in Assam, Silchar and Karimganj in the Barak Valley, and Agartala in Tripura.

Notes

1 In *Bishnupurana*, it is clearly mentioned that '*Purbadike Kirater Bas*' (the *Kiratas* reside in the eastern region).
2 'Tale of an Ancient Land-Tripura', in *Unwinding of Mind*, a blog with Historical Fictions, Mythology, Stories on Mystery and Travelogues, Monday, 10 September 2012. http://ananyadpal.blogspot.com/2012/09/tale-of-ancient-land-tripura.html (Retrived 27 April 2020).
3 Interview with Bodhrong Deb Burma, a *Kokborok* school teacher by profession, taken on 25 December 2014 in Agartala, Tripura.
4 Landless labourers used to work in *khas* lands, owned by the royal family of Tripura in the Zamindari of Chakla Roshanabad. Professionally, they were sharecroppers, but *Maharajas* often treated them as their own subjects, whom they could not evict. *The Law of Landlord and Tenant in the Independent State of Tripura (as Amended by Act 1 of 1296 T. E.)*, Drafted by Mohini Mohan Bardhan, Minister under Orders of His Highness Maharaja Bir Chandra Deb Barma Manikya Bahadur. Agartala: Bir Press.
5 Syamacharan Tripura. 1999. 'Tripurae Ugrapantha, Karon o Samadhan'. In *Tripurae Samaj Sanskriti Santrashbad*, ed. Saroj Chanda and Satyabrata Chakraborty, 45–46. Agartala: Tripura Darpan.
6 File No. RT-27/49, 1949, ASA.
7 Subir Bhoumik. 2005. 'India's Northeast: Nobody's People in No-Man's-Land'. In *Internal Displacement in South Asia: The Relevance of the UN's Guiding Principles*, ed. Paula Banerjee and Sabyasachi Basu Ray Chaudhury, 146. New Delhi: Sage.
8 Sanjib Baruah. 2015. 'Partition and the Politics of Citizenship in Assam'. In *Partition: The Long Shadow*, ed. Urvashi Butalia, 82. New Delhi: Viking-Penguin.
9 Bengal and Assam, File No. X/9076: Unspecific, IOR.
10 'Replies Submitted by Sjt. Nilmoni Phookan, Editor 'BATORI', to the Questionnaire issued by the Line System Committee', *APCC Papers*, Packet No. 66, File No. 17, NMML.
11 *APCC Papers*, Packet No. 66, File No. 17, NMML.
12 *Minutes of a Conference of Officials and Non-officials Held on 20th September 1928 to Discuss Colonisation and Kindred Matters*, Copy of the Census Report, 1931, Part-I, Vol. III, p. 11.
13 *APCC Papers*, Packet No. 66, File No. 17, NMML.
14 Report of the Deputy Commissioner, Nowgong on the Immigrant, 1937, p. 21. *Report of the Line System Committee*: Question of that District.
15 *APCC Papers*, Packet No. 66, File No. 17, NMML.
16 The Deputy Commissioner of Kamrup reports, 'the increase of 69% in the population of Barpeta is solely due to eastern Bengal immigrants'. *APCC Papers*, Packet No. 66, File No. 17, NMML.

156 Creating a new refugee domain

17 *Report of the Line System Committee*, Vol. III, Reply Through Questionnaire, Miscellaneous Statistics and References, Assam Government Press, Shillong, 1938, pp. 3–4.
18 *Report of the Line System Committee*, pp. 3–4.
19 *ALA Debates*, 1947, Vol. 1, No. 1, p. 266.
20 *ALA Debates*, Assam Gazette, 1940, Part VI-B, p. 117.
21 *N. K. Rustamji Papers*, Speeches and Writings by Him, Sl. No. 31, NMML.
22 'Copy of Resolution No. 9 Passed at the Meeting of the Working Committee of the Assam Provincial Muslim League, on 8th March 1946', *S. M. Saadulla Papers*, Subject File No. 9, NMML.
23 'A Note on Assam's Stand vis-à-vis British Government Statement of 6th December', *G. N. Bordoloi Papers*, Misc. File No. 5; *Hindu Mahasabha Papers*, File No. P-100, NMML.
24 *APCC Papers*, Packet No. 66, File No. 17, NMML.
25 It pointed out: 'it shall be made to include any person who holds not more than thirty bighas of agricultural land in their own names or in the names of the members of a family of five persons'. *S. M. Saadulla Papers*, Subject File No. 7, NMML.
26 *AICC Papers*, EDI/1946–47, NMML.
27 *ALA Debates*, 1947, Vol. 1, No. II, p. 124.
28 Subir Bhoumik. 2005. 'India's Northeast: Nobody's People in No-Man's-Land'. In *Internal Displacement in South Asia: The Relevance of the UN's Guiding Principles*, ed. Paula Banerjee and Sabyasachi Basu Ray Chaudhury, 146. New Delhi: Sage.
29 File No. RR-81/47, 1947, ASA.
30 Prakash Goswami. 1947. *Asomot Prothomghon Doinik Batori Kakot Doinik Batori*, p. 285.
31 File No. RRQ. 20 of 1947, ASA.
32 *The Assam Tribune*, 2 August 1949.
33 In a letter dated 3 March 1947 to Sardar Patel, Bordoloi wrote:

> Most of the trouble will arise out of the Government's policy of maintaining the inviolability of the grazing reserves which was agreed upon by all parties including the Muslim League and also by the Government's attempts to distribute the available wastelands to all, including Hindus, Muslims, tribals and immigrants themselves.

> Patel pledged his support to Bordoloi's eviction policy and wrote on 11 April 1947: 'You will have my full support in your stand on legal rights. Not an inch of land should be surrendered to the illegal immigrants and you must stand solidly and firmly on the policy you are implementing'.

34 *Dainik Assamiya*, 1 July 1947.
35 *ALA Debates*, 1947, Vol. I, p. 1220.
36 *ALA Debates*, 1948, Vol. I–II, No. 2, p. 509.
37 *ALA Debates*, 1949, Vol. I–II, p. 867.
38 File No. RT-27/49, 1949, ASA.
39 *The Assam Tribune*, 3 July 1947.
40 File No. RS-195-47/48, 1948, Revenue Department, Settlement Branch (Confidential), ASA.
41 File No. RT-27/49, 1949, ASA.
42 *Office Memorandum*. Memo No. RS.195/47/20, Instruction issued to all Deputy Commissioners of Assam Valley by Sd. S. P. Desai, Secretary to the Government of Assam, Revenue Department on 9th August 1947, in File No. RT-27/ 49, 1949, ASA.
43 File No. RS. 195/47/39, 1947, Revenue Department, Settlement Branch, Government of Assam, ASA.
44 File No. RT-27/49, 1949, ASA.
45 File No. HPT-43/49, 1949, ASA.
46 *S. P. Mookerjee Papers*, 1st Instalment, Subject File No. 34, NMML.
47 *Memorandum Submitted by a Deputation of Two Thousand Members of the Asom Jatiya Mahasabha Headed by A. G. Ray Choudhury, Its General Secretary to the Hon'ble Sri Gopinath Bordoloi on 31st August at Gauhati on Some of the Vital National Demands of the Assamese People*, File No. RT-27/49, ASA.

48 *Assam Tribune*, 31 August 1947.
49 *ALA Debates*, 1949, Vol. I–II, No. II, p. 377.
50 *Abstract of the Resolution Passed in the Public Meeting Held on 19.9.47 in the Dibrugarh College Hall, Under the Auspices of the Asom Jatiya Mahasabha with Sjt. Lokeswar Phukan in the Chair*, File No. RT-27/49, ASA.
51 Assam-Governor's Report, File No. L-PJ/5/140, IOR.
52 *Dainik Assamiya*, 18 April 1948.
53 File No. RS. 195/47/110, Revenue Department, Settlement Branch, Government of Assam, ASA.
54 *AICC Papers*, 2nd Instalment, File No. 1785, PB-2, Bengal, 1948, NMML.
55 *ALA Debates*, 1949, Vol. I–II, p. 685.
56 *ALA Debates*, 1949, Vol. I–II, p. 685.
57 *ALA Debates*, 1949, Vol. I–II, p. 685.
58 Jayanta Kumar Gogoi. 2005. 'The Migration Problem in Assam: An Analysis'. In *India's North-East: Development Issues in a Historical Perspective*, ed. Alokesh Barua, 358–60. New Delhi: Manohar.
59 Bhupen Sarmah. 2001. 'Immigration and Politics in Assam: Question Relating to Human Rights'. In *Refugees and Human Rights: Social and Political Dynamics of Refugee Problem in Eastern and North-Eastern India*, ed. Sanjay K. Roy, 367–68. Jaipur and New Delhi: Rawat Publication.
60 *ALA Debates*, 1950, Vol. I–II, p. 827.
61 *Sri Prakasa Papers*, I–III Instalments, Subject File No. 1, 1950, NMML.
62 *Sri Prakasa Papers*, V Instalment, Subject File No. 40, 1950, NMML.
63 *S. P. Mookerjee Papers*, 1st Instalment, Refugees and Minorities, Subject File No. 37, 1950, NMML.
64 *S. P. Mookerjee Papers*, 1st Instalment, Refugees and Minorities, Subject File No. 37, 1950, NMML.
65 *ALA Debates*, 1950, Vol. I–II, p. 827.
66 Editorial. *The Statesman*, 17 May 1950.
67 *M. N. Saha Papers*, VII Instalments, Refugee Problem: Its Origin and What It Is (Printed Material), Serial No. 2, NMML.
68 File No. RS-345/50, 1950, ASA.
69 *M. N. Saha Papers*, Speeches and Writings by Him, Serial No. 34, NMML.
70 *M. N. Saha Papers*, Speeches and Writings by Him, Serial No. 34, NMML.
71 *M. N. Saha Papers*, Printed Material, Serial No. 2, NMML.
72 File No. RS-T/58, 1958 ASA.
73 File No. L/52/6546/1, BL Branch, Ministry of External Affairs, NAI.
74 '*Land Not Insufficient in Cachar*', Memorandum submitted to Sri Prakash, the then-Governor of Assam and circulated by The East Bengal Relief Committee in Assam State. *M. N. Saha Papers*, VII Instalments, Printed Material, Serial No. 1, NMML.
75 *M. N. Saha Papers*, Printed Material, Serial No. 2, NMML.
76 *M. N. Saha Papers*, VII Instalment, Subject File No. 6, NMML.
77 *The Rehabilitation Review*, Vol. II, No. I, January–April 1950, p. 7.
78 *The Chronicle*, 28 May 1954.
79 Sri Prakash wrote in a personal and confidential letter (on 14 August 1951) to Jawaharlal Nehru expressing his personal views on the conflict situation within districts of Assam, *A. P. Jain Paper*, Subject File No. 1, NMML.
80 *A. P. Jain Paper*, Subject File No. 1, NMML.
81 *A. P. Jain Paper*, Subject File No. 1, NMML.
82 *A. P. Jain Paper*, Notebook, Serial No. 1, NMML.
83 *APCC Papers*, Packet No. 169, File No. 1, NMML.
84 *A. P. Jain Paper*, Subject File No. 2, NMML.
85 '*Speech on Cachar Refugees*'. *M. N. Saha Papers*, Speeches and Writings by Him, Serial No. 34, NMML.
86 File No. 48 (3)-PP & R/52, P.P. & R Section, Ministry of States, NAI.

87 *ALA Debates*, 1953, Part-II, pp. 1248–49.
88 *ALA Debates*, 1953, Part-II, p. 1632.
89 *ALA Debates*, 1953, Part-I, p. 54.
90 File No. 48-PP & R/53, P.P. & R Section, NAI.
91 Press Statement issued by Dr Meghnad Saha after his visit to Cachar with Tridib Chowdhury MP, *Meghnad Saha: Papers and Correspondences*, 1952–55, p. 126.
92 *Jugantor*, 28 March 1955.
93 *AICC Papers*, 2nd Instalment, Serial No. 2725, NAI.
94 'Governor's Address', *ALA Debates*, 1955, Part-I, p. 7.
95 *ALA Debates*, 1956, Vol. I, p. 844.
96 *ALA Debates*, 1956, Vol. I, p. 844.
97 *ALA Debates*, 1956, Vol. I, p. 850.
98 'Governor's Address'. *ALA Debates*, Budget Session, 1955, Part-I, p. 8.
99 *AICC Papers*, 2nd Instalment, Part X. (Rehabilitation), Sl. No. 4/1955, NMML.
100 *M. N. Saha Papers*, VII Instalments, Subject File No. 2, NMML.
101 *ALA Debates*, 1956, Vol. I, p. 851.
102 File No. 2 (30)/56-RHR/RHU, Rehab. Branch, NAI.
103 File No. RSG 16/55, 1955, ASA.
104 *ALA Debates*, 1958, Vol. II, No. 19–47, p. 413.
105 *ALA Debates*, 1958, Vol. I, p. 2967.
106 'A Note on Land Reforms'. *APCC Papers*, Packet No. 92, File No. 11, NMML.
107 *ALA Debates*, 1959, Vol. I, No. 1, p. 52.
108 *ALA Debates*, 1960, Vol. I, No. 1, p. 70.
109 File No. RGR 146/62, 1962, ASA.
110 *ALA Debates*, 1960, Vol. II, No. 39–50, p. 150.
111 *APCC Papers*, Packet No. 133, File No. 9, NMML.
112 File No. P. 1/107/21/67, Pak-1 Registry, NAI.
113 It was designed as permanent liability home in 1973, handed over to State Social Welfare Department by the Central Government in 1977.
114 File No. RSS/209/67, 1967, ASA.
115 File No. P. 1/107 (7)/69, Pak-1 Registry, NAI.
116 File No. RGR 61/68, 1968, ASA.
117 File No. 13/39/71-G & Q, G & Q Section, NAI.
118 *Natun Asomia*, 2 January 1971.
119 File No. 13/40/71-G & Q, G & Q Section, NAI.
120 File No. 13/53/71-G & Q, G & Q Section, NAI.
121 File No. 13/62/71-G & Q, G & Q Section, NAI.
122 *Agricultural Census*, 1970–71, State Report, Government of Tripura, Agartala, 1975, p. 3.
123 *Population Data Regarding Forestry Communities Practicing Shifting Cultivation*. Government of India: Report for India, Ministry of Agriculture, 1980, p. 32.
124 An untitled manuscript named *Tripur Desher Katha*, found in the India Office Library and Records, London.
125 H. L. Chatterji. 'Glimpses of Tripura's History'. *Tripura Review*, 15 August 1972.
126 TSA, File No. B/1920, Political Dept.
127 *Agricultural Census*, 1970–71, State Report, Government of Tripura, Agartala, 1975, p. 3.
128 *Tripurar Rabindranath: Rajtantra o Ak Ruddho Bhasa*. 1417 (Bengali year). Kolkata: Korok Sahitya Patrika, p. 46.
129 Interview with Manju Das, taken on 23 December 2012 in Agartala, Tripura.
130 *Tripura Ties with Tagore. 1969*. Agartala: Directorate of Education, Government of Tripura.
131 File No. B/1920, Political Dept., TSA.
132 *Tripura Affairs*. File No. L/PS/13/1035, IOR.
133 *A Study Over the Jhum and Jhumia Rehabilitation in the Union Territory of Tripura*. 1999. Directorate of Research, Department of Welfare for Schedule Tribes and Scheduled Castes, Special Series No. 2. Agartala: Government of Tripura, p. 10.

Creating a new refugee domain 159

134 Interview with Jana Jodh Bir Jong (niece of Rana Bodh Jong, Chief Minister and President, Mantri Parishad, 1937–46), taken on 25 December 2012 in Agartala, Tripura.
135 *A Study of the Land System of Tripura*. 1990. Guwahati: Law Research Institute, Eastern Region, Gauhati High Court, p. 9.
136 *AICC Papers*, 2nd Instalment, File No. 1786 (Pt. II), PB-3 (1), Bengal, 1948, NMML.
137 *Amrita Bazar Patrika*, 14 April 1948.
138 File No. 'A'-Year 1948–49 A.D, Political Department, TSA.
139 *A Study of the Land System of Tripura*. 1990. Guwahati: Law Research Institute, Eastern Region, Gauhati High Court, p. 9.
140 Interview with Jiten Pal, chief editor, *Janakalyan* and *Jagaran*, taken on 24 February 2012 in Agartala, Tripura.
141 File No. 8 (31)-GR-48, G (R) Branch, Ministry of States, NAI.
142 File No. R. 19–1/46-P, 1946, Political Department, I.B. Report, Secretariat Record Room, Agartala.
143 *Agricultural Census, 1970–71*, State Report, Government of Tripura, Agartala, 1975, p. 3.
144 *A Study Over the Jhum and Jhumia Rehabilitation in the Union Territory of Tripura*. 1999. Directorate of Research, Department of Welfare for Schedule Tribes and Scheduled Castes, Special Series No. 2, 26–27. Agartala: Government of Tripura.
145 Quoted in Ritonkar Mukhopadhyay. 2015. 'Onya Ak Udbastu Upakhyan', ed. Sudipta Bandyapadhyay, 54. *Charbaka* 2 (3). Popular Culture 3.
146 *Amrita Bazar Patrika*, 14 April 1948.
147 File No. 17 (1)-R/49, Rehabilitation Branch, NAI.
148 File No. 17 (1)-R/49, Rehabilitation Branch, NAI.
149 File No. 'A'-Year 1948 A.D., TSA.
150 File No. 20-R/50-1, Rehabilitation Branch, NAI.
151 File No. 17 (1)-R/49, Rehabilitation Branch, NAI.
152 File No. 17 (1)-R/49, Rehabilitation Branch, NAI.
153 File No. 17-G (R)/49, G (R) Branch, NAI.
154 File No. 20 (15)-R/50 (Secret), Rehabilitation Branch, NAI.
155 File No. 20 (15)-R/50 (Secret), Rehabilitation Branch, NAI.
156 File No. 20 (26)-RC/50, RC Branch, NAI.
157 File No. 20 (26)-RC/50, RC Branch, NAI.
158 File No. 27 (26)-Econ/53, Economics Section, NAI.
159 File No. 20-R/50 II (Secret), Rehabilitation Branch, NAI.
160 File No. 20 (12)-R/50 II (Secret), Rehabilitation Branch, NAI.
161 File No. 20 (13)-R/50, Rehabilitation Branch, NAI.
162 File No. 20-R/50 II (Secret), Rehabilitation Branch, NAI.
163 File No. 20 (6)-R/50, Rehabilitation Branch, NAI.
164 File No. 20 (17)-R/C/50, Communication Branch, NAI.
165 File No. 20-R/50 I, Rehabilitation Branch, NAI.
166 *Hindustan Standard*, 2 May 1950.
167 Interview with Jiten Pal, taken on 24 February 2012 in Agartala, Tripura.
168 *Janakalyan*, 4 May 1951.
169 Gayatri Bhattacharya. 1885. 'Refugee Rehabilitation'. In *An Anthology of Tripura*, ed. Jagadis Gan-Chaudhury, 46. New Delhi: Inter-India Publications.
170 File No. 7/12 (12)-P/51, Political Branch, NAI.
171 File No. ID/2-5-Year 1950–55 A.D., Home (ID) Department, TSA.
172 File No. 17 (1)-R/50, Rehabilitation Branch, NAI.
173 File No. ID/2-2-Year 1950 A.D., Home (ID) Department, TSA.
174 File No. 20 (5)-R/50, Rehabilitation Branch, NAI.
175 Meenakshi Sen. 2003. 'Tripura: The Aftermath'. In *The Trauma and the Triumph: Gender and Partition in Eastern India*, ed. Jasodhara Bagchi and Subhoranjan Dasgupta, 125. Kolkata: Stree.
176 File No. 7/12 (12)-P/51, Political Branch, NAI.
177 *Free Press Journal*, 13 December 1952.

178 File No. 50-P. P. & R/51, P. P. & R Branch, NAI.
179 The definition of a *jiratia* tenant was: '*Jiratia* is the term applied to Pakistan nationals who themselves live in Pakistan but own and cultivate lands in Tripura'. File No. 12 (11)-PA/53, Political A Section, Ministry of States, NAI, *The Pakistan Observer*, 19 April 1952.
180 File No. 12 (11)-PA/53, Political A Section, Ministry of States, NAI.
181 File No. 21 (22)-PA/51, Political A Branch, NAI.
182 File No. 22 (48)-PA/53, Political A Section, NAI.
183 File No. 49 (2)-P. P. & R/ (53), P. P. & R Branch, NAI.
184 File No. 34-P. P. & R/ (53), P. P. & R Branch, NAI.
185 File No. 34-P. P. & R/ (53), P. P. & R Branch, NAI.
186 File No. 48-P. P. & R/ (53), P. P. & R Branch, NAI.
187 File No. 12 (38)-PA/53, Political A Section, NAI.
188 File No. 34-P. P. & R/ (53), P. P. & R Branch, NAI.
189 File No. F. 3 (7)/57 ADM, Year 1957, Rehabilitation Department, TSA.
190 File No. F. 3 (1)/57 ADM, Year 1957, Rehabilitation Department, TSA.
191 File No. 12/18/J/II/56, J. II Section, NAI.
192 File No. 14/17/57-MT, MT Section, NAI.
193 File No. 17/6/61-MT, MT Section, NAI.
194 File No. G. 6 (18)-RDH/50, RDH Branch, NAI.
195 J. K. Choudhury. 1952. *A Dream College. Being a Report on the Origin and Working for the First Five Years, 1947–52 of the Maharaja Bir Bikram College*. Agartala: Tripura, p. 24.
196 File No. 17/16/61-MT, MT Section, NAI.
197 File No. 17/34/61-MT, MT Section, NAI.
198 File No. 17/16/61-MT, MT Section, NAI.
199 File No. 17/35/61-MT, MT Section, NAI.
200 *The Tripura Panchayet Raj Rules*, Tripura Administration, Agartala, 1961, p. 3.
201 File No. 19/51/61, Judl, II Section, NAI.
202 B. K. Roy Burman. 1972. 'Tribal Demography: A Preliminary Appraisal'. In *The Tribal Situation in India*, ed. K. Suresh Singh, 39. New Delhi: Indian Institute of Advanced Study and Motilal Banarsidass.
203 File No. 7/25/63-P IV, Pak-II Division, NAI.
204 *PTLA*, 1963, Series-I, Vol. 1–9, p. 31.
205 File No. P-(P IV) 282 (91)/66, Pak-II Division, NAI.
206 *PTLA*, 1966, Series-VII, Vol. 5–7, p. 4.
207 *PTLA*, 1966, Series-VIII, Vol. 1, p. 20.
208 *PTLA*, 1967, Series-X, Vol. 1–3, p. 73.
209 *PTLA*, 1968, Series-XIII, Vol. 1–2, p. 5.
210 *PTLA*, 1969, Series-XIII, Vol. 1–2, p. 13.
211 *PTLA*, 1970, Series-XIX, Vol. 1, p. 26.
212 K. C. Saha. 2003. 'The Genocide of 1971 and the Refugee Influx in the East'. In *Refugees and the State: Practices of Asylum and Care in India, 1947–2000*, ed. Ranabir Samaddar, 218. New Delhi: Sage.
213 File No. 13/39/71-G & Q, G. & Q Section, NAI.

4

BECOMING POLITICAL

Politicisation of refugees in West Bengal

India achieved independence with two permanent pieces of baggage: one was an insecure border, and the other was the burden of refugees. India was born within contradictions of policies. To maintaining secular credentials, Nehru's idea was to create states on the basis of language rather than ethnicity or religion. The democratic state was based on adult franchise (voting rights of the adult citizens), while the Centre-state relations had emerged within the federal structure. But the country was carrying several colonial legacies. It was maintaining hierarchy and parallel power relationships. The educated, elite, enlightened upper- and upper-middle–classes of the society were the decisionmakers, and they were in charge of the leadership of different socio-political movements (Franda 1971b: 8–13). The rise and growth of a 'party system' emerged out of it, and the politics of governance led to a culture of mass support based political parties.[1] The Constitution of India later endorsed this, too.[2] Hence, the overall perception and nature of negotiation between political parties and government remained exactly the same in the new political ideologies and equations (Brass and Franda 1973: 189). The opposition in the Centre and states tried shaping up their own separate stands (Chatterji 1985: 6–8). Within the structure of democratic post-colonial nation-state and other issues of compulsion and negotiation, one of the major tasks remained essential for the Centre and for all refugee-absorbent state governments, again for many decades: the nation-state had to include the rehabilitation of the refugees as an essential administrative target, even as the waves of influx seemed never ending. The state had not foreseen it, and as such had not prepared necessary policies regarding it.

Even though the Partition was designed on communal lines, post-colonial India avowed to be a secular state. It could not discriminate between Hindu, Muslim and Sikh refugees. There were some ideological issues and regional variations involved, too. Refugees were from Punjab, Bengal, Sindh and other Partition-affected regions. Punjabi Hindu and Sikh refugees were to be rehabilitated in and around Punjab, and Bengali refugees in and around Bengal, but neither of those states was in a position to accommodate all of them. Thus, the Centre appealed to all the states to resettle some of the refugees, yet certain regions refused to share the burden, which complicated the problem more. The leaders at the Centre had their own ideas and plans for refugee rehabilitation, which was often discriminatory and partisan (Pakrasi 1971: 19–21). Under such a situation, the refugees were caught in a dangerous crisis. On the one hand, they were displaced from their home and hearth and on the other, across the border, into the hands of safety and freedom; they were considered inferior 'others' and did not often receive a generous welcome from their fellow brethren in rehabilitating them. The refugees were found to be no longer a heterogeneous group of displaced people. They emerged in time as a cohesive political group of people who realised that they had been the victims of the formation of the nation-states; and hence, they started demanding their due rights.[3] When India opted for a multi-party democratic system and a federal setup of the polity, refugees emerged as an important player. A trend of deeper change was underway silently yet swiftly.[4] The partitioned areas—especially the states which experienced the settlement of large numbers of refugees—and the political parties could not ignore the refugee population and their grievances. Refugees formed a socio-political group with definite religious connotations (Irani 1968: 1–5). They also made serious efforts to mobilise political parties to support their demands (Biswas 2005, IV: 766). Finally, they turned to 'become political' to prove their victimhood and demanded their legitimate rights like permanent rehabilitation, a defined national identity, citizenship rights and a share in the power structure of the new nation-states.

As per the Centre's policies, the Bengali refugees were dispersed over many states like West Bengal, Assam, Tripura, Bihar, Orissa, Rajasthan, Andaman and Dandakaranya.[5] Most of the refugees were desperate to come back to West Bengal and settle down permanently in that state, where they dreamt of possessing a piece of land or procuring a job (Bandyapadhyay 1970: 258). For the time being, they accepted temporary relief and regularisation of doles, but they aimed at permanent rehabilitation with some kind of right over lands (Roy Choudhury 1977: 59–61). And, in such a process to attain their deep-rooted desire, the refugees became the chief players in political decisionmaking and an essential vote bank in West Bengal. The leftists started getting footage in the state politics by involving them into their agendas and party (Singha 1999: 18–22). The question of economic migration had created opportunities for the leftists to move in as champions of the refugees (Majumdar and Dutta 2014, XII: 265–66). The leftist parties could manage to increase their power base in post-1947 West Bengal and posed a threat to the ruling Congress by taking up the issues of the refugees, including land grabbing. They promised to introduce a policy of standing up for marginalised sections, like working and peasant class (Roy Choudhury 1985: 47). The leftist forces tried hard to show the party's commitment to unleash the spirit of redistribution of wealth and land amongst the refugees, and other marginalised and landless populace, under the principle of social and economic justice.[6]

This chapter discusses the problems the refugees encountered in their host countries and the process of their politicisation in the state of West Bengal. It tries to understand the emergence and diversification of refugee political movements in West Bengal, and also aims to explore how the refugees became a crucial factor in this changed political environment that compelled the Centre and state to negotiate with their rights and aspirations. The crucial question was: how did an entirely new form of refugee politics slowly but steadily influence—and, in some cases, wipe out—the formerly typical structure of strategy-based Congress politics? It thus attempts to investigate the nature of shift from 'policy-based' politics to 'strategy-based' politics, and indicates fissures between proclaimed secular identities of India and the Hindu identity that the refugees wanted to forge. This chapter aims to focus on these factors, especially on how the East Bengali refugee women changed their role under severe social and economic hardship. Their utter desperation compelled them to come out from the private domain of domesticity and they were gradually exposed to the outside world (Majumdar and Dutta 2008: 17). Being the torchbearers of economic freedom, they at times found themselves in conflict between 'inside' and 'outside' worlds. Despite many trials and tribulations, they emerged as the symbol of courage and determination (Basu Guha Chaudhury 2009: 66–68). Some of them participated actively in the left political movements and inspired even the traditional West Bengali families to come out from old conservative ideas (Sen 1982: 181). So, demand for resettlements was the major demand of the refugees for attaining socio-economic security, linguistic rights and religious freedom, which could erase their memory of the holocaust. In a nutshell, this chapter highlights the resulting alteration in the policies and political structures by looking at the root causes of refugee agitations, political movement strategies and change in the form of leadership in West Bengal.

The politics and policies of Congress vis-à-vis the refugees

Post-Partition India had tried a structured political system for the smooth running of administrative machineries, based on electoral democracy. Congress became stable as an institutionalised political party at the Centre. It headed most of the state ministries including West Bengal, where it ruled uninterrupted for almost two decades.[7] This period played a crucial role by the involvement of the masses in politics and also in organising new social structures. West Bengal was directly affected by Partition, had sheltered massive numbers of refugees (Ghosh 2013: 12). Yet, it helped in creating alternatives, fresh ideas and new identity formations.[8] Congress had stronghold in Bengali politics from the 1930s, but the party was plagued by the clash of interests of factions and their aspirations of acquiring more power. Partition implanted division between Congress leaders from East Bengal and West Bengal (Franda 1971b: 1). Most of the veteran leaders hailed from East Bengal, and they lost their constituencies where they were influential, just as it fell on the other side of the border.[9] The process of partitioning geographical areas, assets and population had upset old balances; it changed the standing of political parties in unintended ways. Partition tended to shift strength of factions within all political parties. Both Rastriya Svayamsevaka Sangha (RSS) and the Muslim League lost political relevance in India. The League shifted its base in East Bengal, as RSS and Mahasabha suffered for their extremist ideas, stands on the pre-Partition riots and politics (Banerjee 1969: 40–41).

The All India Congress Committee decided earlier that:

> in the Provinces that are divided, namely Bengal and the Punjab, while the Provincial Committees for the two provinces remain as at present, zonal committees for the two portions in each of two Provinces may be formed if such demand was made.[10]

But the Bengal Provincial Congress Committee decided not to divide, as 'this will seriously affect the prestige and popularity of the Congress'.[11] It argued that the 'members still hold their status', for 'the impression that Congress desires Partition to be permanent will be confirmed in the mind of the public', but in reality:

> The workers here are of opinion that it will be extremely difficult, almost impossible to work in the name of the Congress. The majority community looks upon the Congress with suspicion, while a section of the minority community also is not well disposed to it.[12]

A new political party named Pakistan Gana Samity was formed in East Bengal to replace the Congress there. Its objectives proclaimed the party's objective 'to fight for political, social and economic freedom of the masses and for a secular democratic State in Pakistan where fundamental rights of citizenship will be assured to everyone irrespective of caste, creed or colour'.[13]

With all the perplexity in the backdrop, Acharya Kripalani, then President of the AICC, nominated Dr Prafulla Chandra Ghosh, a disciple of Mahatma Gandhi, as the first Premier of West Bengal. This decision—other factions termed it appeasement—was aimed at controlling damages caused by the apparent animosity of the East Bengali leaders and retain the sympathy over miseries faced by their Hindu counterparts (Chatterji 2008: 217). They treated it as a solution against the growing unpopularity of the Congress in both parts of Bengal (Chakrabarty 1962: 6–7). But, this selection generated apathy of the West Bengalis. The Association of North Calcutta Clubs expressed their view to J. B. Kripalani thus: 'Dr P. C. Ghosh has been elected as the leader of West Bengal Congress Party. But, Dr Ghosh is more or less unpopular among the general public of Bengal'.[14] The Ghosh Ministry faced civil unrest immediately, as he chose to follow the well-trodden path like his predecessors. He introduced the Bengal Special Powers (Second Amendment) Ordinance, the Bengal Disturbed Areas Ordinance, 1947, to deal with law and order situation. The CPI and Socialist Republican Party termed it 'Black Bill' (Bandyapadhyay 2009: 73–75). He welcomed public servants and officials in significant posts from East Bengal (Chatterji 2008: 221). Within less than six months, the West Bengal Congress Assembly Party passed a vote of a 'no confidence' against him, firmly wanting a change in leadership (Ray 1982: 190).

Dr Bidhan Chandra Roy replaced Dr Ghosh on 14 January 1948. He was the Centre's key man, personal physician both to Gandhi and Nehru, and close friends with many powerful members of the Congress High Command. His stronghold over the Delhi lobby helped him in getting their unstinted support. He had also a reputation of having no factional affiliation (Sen Gupta 2002: 80). He promised to introduce 'a more dynamic administration', though the nature of his cabinet remained the same (Bandyapadhyay 2009: 73). The political scenario and the physical environment of West Bengal were rapidly changing in an environment in which the floating population of refugees posed major challenges. Apart from other crises and miseries, the state had to manage their rehabilitation and resettlement. The unending inflow of refugees in many waves increased population, leading to a virtual collapse of the state economy. Renuka Ray mentioned that 'Calcutta, the once graceful city of palaces, was now truly a nightmare city with a trebled population, mostly consisting of scavengers, street dwellers and beggars' (Ray 1982: 190). The state was aware of this new addition of population, which would soon demand the legitimate share in state resources and equitable distribution of wealth (Chakraborty 2015: 27). Dr S. P. Mookherjee acknowledged that the refugees 'were about to become a powerful force in the politics of West Bengal' (Chatterji 2008: 269).

The composition of the migrant population in form of a unitary group named the 'refugees' is indeed interesting to notice through the time, phases, diverse waves and nature of their migrations. There were three distinct categories of refugees who migrated to West Bengal. The migrants who came to Indian states in the first batches were not 'refugees' in the real sense, as in actuality, they had never asked for 'refuge' in the form of shelter. They were largely urban *bhadraloks*, rural gentry and businessmen who already had a toehold in West Bengal. In the first wave, the caste elites with education, assets and kith and kin found it relatively easy to integrate and assimilate with Bengali societies of all refugee-absorbent states. Dakshinaranjan Basu in *Chhere Asa Gram* depicted the right feature of Hindu *bhadraloks*, comprised of the economically and socially powerful elites of the then-East Bengali society. Their dominating influence over their Muslim subordinates (tenants, servants, artisans and sharecroppers) is often reflected in autobiographies and memoirs. The blow on their *dhon, pran* and *man* (wealth, life and honour) could also be clearly understood by numerous memorandums and petitions given to Rajendra Prasad by this particular class, urging him to include their districts with the Indian Territory.[15] They were not convinced to accept themselves as impending second-class citizens in an emerging and declared Islamic state named Pakistan. They had both education and connections, and thus, they had given apt leadership in refugee political movements.[16] The second category was those of the educated middle-class. They tried to settle themselves on their own efforts.[17] The third and largest category was comprised of lower-middle–class, the lower-caste refugees (Bandyopadhyay and Basu Ray Chaudhury 2014: 5). They were the ones who had actually taken shelter in government camps, while awaiting rehabilitation. The Congress Working Committee adopted a resolution on 25 November 1947, stating that 'the Congress is bound to afford full protection to all those non-Muslims from Pakistan who have crossed the border and come over to India or may do so to save their life and honour'.[18] The lower-class/caste refugees were initially firm in their belief that Congress would save them from the insecurity of the uncertain future and rescue them from the hell of Sealdah station. They would also give them back a new home and identity.

The communist and the displaced: early phase

Since the establishment of the Communist Party of India (CPI) in 1925, the left had failed to make a mark in Indian politics (Roy Choudhury 1985: 41). The end of World War II saw the beginning of waves of popular protests in Bengal, organised by the left in general and the CPI in particular (Sengupta 1997: 85). These protest movements had taken a 'spontaneous' shape, as the masses began to join in movements in great numbers, especially when they did not have any party affiliation (Basu 2012: 1). The communists and the socialists had already a small base within educated middle-classes of East Bengal.[19] Regardless of factions within the left, their activities were confined to few particular pockets; 'There were roughly a thousand party members in East Pakistan on the eve of Partition' (Chakrabarti 1990: 40). The Communists started working actively among peasants, workers and other downtrodden classes of both the Bengals in the stormy decade of the 1940s (Chattopadhyay 2014: 18–19). The communists became the beneficiaries in the changed environment, as they were able to increase their mass appeal and popularity among the refugees in the next two decades (Upadhyaya 1989: 86). The leftist parties decided to suspend party activities in Pakistan by 1948, restricting their sphere of activities within the Indian Union (Ghosh 2010: 331).[20] The leftists were well aware of the gravity of refugee crises, but they were lacking in leadership and were having some ideological conflicts (Mohit Roy 2009: 5). They could manage to consolidate them after the Second Party Congress in Calcutta in 1948. They had now been able to secure a strong foothold in the political arena of West Bengal.

The refugees could slowly identify themselves with the communists, although the party was at first suspicious of the refugees as being potentially reactionary and anti-Muslim (Chatterji 2008: 260). They incorporated the 'Bengali sentiment' in their political strategies by bringing class issues, which in a way turned the 'Hindu refugees' into 'Bengali refugees'. They argued, 'Although in the wake of Partition hordes of East Bengalis streamed into West Bengal . . . some slept in the footpath but did not leave West Bengal' (Modak and Bhatkhalkar 1997: 39). They whipped up an emotional appeal to use against Congress. The Hindu middle-class of East Bengal initially became supporters of Congress after migrating to West Bengal. Thus, the leftist communists preferred to work amongst the refugees in disguise by distributing minimal relief through charitable organisations (Chakrabarti 1990: 45). They constituted a heterogeneous group of ex-terrorists turned Congressmen and Marxist leftists. Their training and participation in nationalist struggles enabled them to speak about themselves as the Congress (Chatterjee 1992: 232). When most of the lower-middle-class refugees had taken shelter in temporary camps, the rest of the population were compelled to wait in railway stations, military barracks, slums, footpaths and in the houses left by the Muslims. The *bhadralok* refugees either bought a house or arranged a shelter on rent for they 'scorned the uncertain Government doles and did not care for any other form of Government assistance' (Chakrabarti 1990: 35). The middle-class refugees began squatting and 'took the law into their own hands and started the unauthorised occupation of land' and they 'began the process of settlement in Calcutta and its suburbs, what came to be known as squatters' colonies' in West Bengal (Chakrabarti 1990: 35). The middle-class and lower-middle–class refugees staying in camps and colonies formed committees under various political affiliations. The word 'colony' was popularised during this particular phase (1947–1950).

The concept of collective identity as against the individual had become essential. To prevent eviction either by police and local goons initiated by the zamindars, the legal owners of those lands/houses, the colony committees realised a need for a colonisation movement.[21] A joint platform was formed to demand equal treatment like that of the West Pakistanis.[22] Thus, the squatters' colonies were the first political agency of the refugees. The Centre was treating the Bengali refugee issues differently as a policy right from the beginning. Jawaharlal Nehru travelled to Dhaka and some district towns of East Bengal during 1948 to check upon the minority situation and tried hard to convey to the Hindus that they would be safe there. Hence, they should not migrate to West Bengal or any other states in India. When numbers of the refugees in 1948 reached almost 11 lakhs in West Bengal, the state did not have an official rehabilitation department. Nikunja Behari Maiti, the Minister for the relief department, had arranged small amounts of cash dole for them. Nehru refuted the claim of the sufferings of the refugees straightway (Singha 1995: 4). On 14 January 1948, Nehru visited Barrackpur for the inauguration of *Gandhighat*. The refugees, who were staying in the Sealdah station, organised a peaceful procession to inform the Prime Minister about their crisis with a memorandum 'on the curse of the refugee life' (Singha 1999: 13), but police dismissed their procession, *lathi*-charging them without valid reasons, and even women were not spared. The students of the different colleges even organised a procession against such brutal acts by police, and in order to show sympathy to these innocent refugees as they were dispersed, beaten and shot by the police.[23] This incident came out as an 'eye-opener' for the refugees, and they lost their last hope of getting assistance from the mainstream Congress leaders. In any case, the only idea of the Central Government was to send these refugees to their homes in East Pakistan.

Accordingly, an Inter-Dominion Conference was arranged in April 1948. Both India and Pakistan agreed to transfer minority properties once the refugees would return to their places of origin.[24] In connection to that agreement, India had withdrawn the system of providing 'refugee certificates' to the migrants by 25 June 1948 (Singha 1995: 5). On 4 October 1948, the state government declared in a press note that no displaced persons would be allowed to stay in West Bengal for more than one month. Only women and children would be eligible to receive assistance, though they would also not get permanent shelter in this land. The conditions of temporary shelters in *mofussil* towns were even worse than those that were in Calcutta. In Burdwan, there were 15 such shelters in 1948. While in 24 Parganas (north and south), Medinipur, Hoogli, Murshidabad, Bankura, Nadia and Howrah, the number of the temporary camps were five, three and one, respectively (Singha 1999: 9–12). The loyal Congress workers were losing hope, and they started to protest against the stand of the government. Sevok Sashi Mohon, an active Congress worker, wrote a letter to the President of AICC stating:

> The people have no confidence in Inter-Dominion Conferences for the simple reason they yield no practical results. The Hindus in East Pakistan have suffered untold sufferings and were only compelled by dire circumstances to leave their own hearths and homes. But their sufferings also in West Bengal know no bounds. Most unfortunately, they have been receiving the worst treatment in all possible ways in the hands of local officials. Is there any justification for this attitude taken by the Government with regard to the refugees?[25]

Refugees activated

The leftist leaders felt an urgent need to organise the refugees as a social group. In the Pradeshik Bastuhara Circular No. 2, directed to the party units at the district level and issued on 1 November 1950, it was mentioned that the CPI organised a *Bastuhara Andolon* Committee by the end of 1948. To strengthen its organisational root and base, it encouraged the inclusion of Congress leaders and other educated liberal members under their fold for the creation of a new forum. Amritalal Chatterjee, a veteran Congressman, convened the All Bengal Refugee Conference at Naihati in September 1948 and the *Nikhil Vanga Bastuhara Karma Parishad* (NVBKP), or All Bengal Refugee Council of Action, was established as an organisation to fight for the political and other rights of the refugees.[26] The NVBKP ensured footage of the leftists with the refugees, which later led to the rise of a united front. NVBKP prepared a 'charter of demands' and tried to submit it to AICC in the Jaipur Session of 1948. Nehru termed them as 'foreigners' and refused to look into their memorandum. He suggested that 'the Karma Parishad representatives had better talk to the Foreign Bureau of the AICC' to look at their crisis (Chakrabarti 1990: 51). Following this failure, Amritalal Chatterjee resigned from NVBKP. He realised that unless the refugees initiated a sustained struggle, they would not achieve anything related to their existence and self-respect. Ideologically, he had a different outlook towards the political strategies, too. Thus, the future leadership was transferred to Mahadev Bhattacharya, a member of the Hindu Mahasabha. Interestingly, his background also did not prevent him from forming an association with the Congress followers and a different faction of communists. His political views helped him to work with representatives from any party sincere about working with the refugees. He was flexible about political tactics and pragmatic in ideas. Bijoy Majumdar, a CPI party worker, a faithful companion and a great organiser, was the Secretary of NVBKP. He understood the value of the squatters' colony committees for both organisational work and united struggle in the cause of the refugees. The NVBKP leaders realised that the Congress High Command would not design sympathetic policies for the refugees if they continued begging. They left the methods of conducting *gherao*, meetings and processions, and decided to opt for direct action as a solution for instigating large-scale squatting. The refugees had already occupied fallow lands and garden houses of the zamindars and *jotedars* in six or seven localities and arranged settlements under the leadership of NVBKP.[27] Motivated by this initiative, the refugees built hundreds of colonies in Calcutta and its suburbs. Thousands of refugees were living without any prior support by the Centre (Biswas 2003: 249). They built their homes, schools, *paras* and clubs in those properties, designed their own communities within the structure of a larger West Bengali society. They promised to protect these creations even by fighting with the social forces, whosoever was against it (Singha 1995: 9).

The NVBKP was the first group that pressured the state government for providing relief and rehabilitation to both the camp and colony refugees. NVBKP planned to arrange a 'self-settlement movement' in Calcutta as a quick solution if both the Centre and state governments continued to ignore the refugees. The trend of organising '*andolon*' (political movement) started with the issues related to the settlement of refugees.[28] Bijoygarh colony was one of the few first squatters' colonies in West Bengal (Dutta 2001: 27–31). The name itself speaks to its legacy. '*Bijoy*' means victory and '*garh*' symbolises self-settled colony. The colony started with only 12 families in November 1947, and first named as *Jadavpur Bastuhara colony* (Chakraborty, Mandal, Roy and Ghosal 2007: 12–13). The early residents did not confine their efforts but initiated to establish schools, colleges and markets within a demarcated area. NVBKP helped to establish the Deshbandhunagar colony in Sodepur and Bijoynagar colony in Naihati in April 1949 (Singha 1995: 6). The Shahidnagar colony of Kanchrapara actually encouraged establishing refugee colonies along the railway line extending from Dum Dum in the north. The typical image of a spontaneous leftist line of protest became evident in organising a mass demonstration on 14 January 1949 for deputation to Jawaharlal Nehru (Chatterjee 1992: 234). The situation was volatile, with police using tear gas, open firing and *lathi*-charging on refugees, which continued for the next 15 days (Singha 1995: 9). NVBKP joined hands with BPSF to involve the students in organising a successful student's strike on 18 January 1949.[29] Ten tram cars and five state buses were burnt on 19–20 January 1949; later, it became a distinctive feature of violent leftist demonstration in Calcutta (Chakrabarti 1990: 54–55). They designed an organised form of political movement for the refugee cause, establishing the communists as bona fide. They indeed compelled the concerned authorities to hear their voices by pointing out:

> The victims of Partition must be given every facility and help all over the Indian Dominion for living and earning their livelihood in whatever they like if they so desire because for the independence and well-being of the rest of India, they are sacrificed and left out their fate in Pakistan. Our narrow-minded leaders forget this moral obligation when they deliver sermons to the refugees to return to Pakistan.[30]

And, a process of radicalisation had begun (Biswas 2015: 41–42).

The radicalisation of the refugees under the leftist leaders did not go unnoticed. The Congress became aware of gradual transformation in the attitude of the Congress supporters towards the uprooted populace. They decided to organise a rehabilitation bureau for the refugees to help them on 3 February 1949 (Singha 1999: 13–14). This committee, under the aegis of the West Bengal Government, held a public meeting in Girish Park, but some eminent Congress leaders like the Labour Minister Kalipada Mukhopadhyay, Atulya Ghosh and Prafulla Sen raised negative points against them. Atulya Ghosh repeated those points with further elaboration deliberately to whip up anti-refugee sentiments among the locals in Hendua Park on 5 February 1949.[31] Some refugee representatives protested against his comments and asked some basic questions like why the police charged *lathi* even on refugee women.[32] The communists criticised the Congress government in Centre and state by pointing to how they were utilising these uprooted masses against the poor Muslims by categorising them as *ansars*, an ancillary wing of the Pakistani police (Chaudhury 1964: 18). They warned them by pointing out that the East Bengali Hindus would suffer more by this policy. Incidents like driving out poor Muslims from slums and dispatching them off to Pakistan was reported in each and every newspaper of both the Bengals. The counter-effect of such atrocities made the Hindu minorities more uncertain about their future there (Majumdar and Dutta 2010: 670–71).

The communist leaders tried to organise the refugees and interpreted their grievances into the language of protest. They arranged a meeting in Shraddhananda Park on 28 July 1949 and pointed to the change in the nature of political movements. It was designed by them and supported by the refugees. They portrayed how the police in Sealdah station attacked and tortured the refugees when they were preparing to visit Nehru in Maidan to communicate their problems and ask for their due rights and for adoption of a concrete policy on them. The leftist leaders tried to convey that the refugees were becoming firmer in their demands and now they were threatening both the Governments by uttering slogans like, '*bhat-kapor-siksha dao . . . noile godi chhere dao*' (arrange for our food-cloth and basic education; otherwise, quit from the governance).[33] The refugees experienced inhumane conditions in the government camps. A refugee, working in a bank on a salary of Rs. 40 per month and staying in the Ichhapur camp with eight other family members, wrote a letter to the editor of *Manjil* on 31 July 1949, stating that the government had put up a notice in front of their camp declaring that the residents should live there at their own risk as it was not at all safe to stay anymore. He lamented by pointing out that his elder son, a student of class VI in East Bengal, became a train hawker and rest of the children remained illiterate after coming to India. He was in the refugee procession of 14 July to give Nehru a memorandum, but police had used tear gas and grenades (bombs) on them. He mentioned that death was probably the only option left for them in the Congress regime, as a solution to get rid of the camp life. Hence, he wished to welcome death at the earliest than to die in one of the epidemics, in which 4–5 persons were dying every day in their camp.[34]

The communists expressed their fear as they believed that the ruling government was trying to create a riot situation again, as the government started recruiting refugees in the factories instead of the Muslim workers. Thus, they categorically declared that their struggle was against the Nehru-Liaquat governments, not to any other organisations (Majumdar and Dutta 2010: 672). Interestingly, when the Pakistan Government had banned distribution of some major Indian newspapers like *Ananda Bazar*, *Amrita Bazar* and *Swadhinota* in East Bengal, the Congress government in West Bengal also banned the publication of *Swadhinota*, a popular declared leftist organ. They were scared of the rising popularity of the newspaper. By 1949, a portion of West Bengalis became curious about the declared ideologies of the communists and they also started buying this organ, chiefly to understand the nature of the demands conceived by the leftists' leaders and the refugees (Singha 1999: 11). Dr B. C. Roy opened regular dialogues and discussions with the Centre for consolidating government machineries.[35] He separated the Department of Relief and Rehabilitation and also appointed Hinranmay Bondhyopadhyay as commissioner of the directorate (Basu 1977: 9). He had taken some measures that proved beneficial for the fresh influx, in comparison to the earlier refugees who were waiting for a piece of land and jobs (Mandal 2011: 205). The left orientation in the political approach of the refugee organisations was visible, yet the refugees were hesitant, panicky and afraid of getting involved with the 'adventurous political forces', the leftist communists. The land-grabbing movement was in the line for establishing further squatters' colonies (Chakrabarti 1990: 6465). The refugee organisations carried on vigorous campaigns for illegal seizure of lands from the landlords or government. The NVBKP passed a resolution for unauthorised occupation of fallow lands. The government could not control such tendencies. They were aware of the strategies of the left to acquire power (Singha 1995: 9). Calcutta was marked by social fermenting or political coalescence of refugees, with other few marginalised sections. It actually created a genuine and huge opportunity for the leftist leaders chiefly to emerge as a major opposition force in state politics (Majumdar and Dutta 2010: 677).

Unification of leftist movements

By 1950, a huge influx caused not only by organised riots in every corner of East Bengal but also natural calamities like cyclones, floods and famines compelled the

Hindus to turn out to be 'economic migrants' in West Bengal (Singha 1995: 10). In addition to that, the police and *ansars* were scaring and forcing the minorities to donate large amounts of money to the Jinnah Fund. This fear somehow increased the numbers of the migrants, too. The old refugee settlers residing in West Bengal were not hopeful towards the ruling government. The Bidhan Roy government instructed the concerned officials to arrange tents to keep fresh influx in the border so that the refugees could not enter the city. The major railway stations like Sealdah, Howrah and Dumdum were overflowing with refugees. Tushar Singha, a leftist activist, mentioned in his memoir *Moronjoyee Sangrame Bastuhara* that there were days when 16,000 refugees lived in Sealdah station together (Singha 1999: 6–7). The Centre signed the Nehru-Liaquat Pact, arranged some basic relief and lived in peace with the expectation that the refugees would go back soon. A few voluntary organisations—like the Kashi Biswanath Seba Samiti, Ramakrishna Mission, Bharat Sebasram Sangha and Shriramakrishna Bedantamoth—helped the refugees by distributing food, clothes and medicine. All Bengal Relief Committee, Central Calcutta Relief and Peace Committee, Indian Red Cross, Campbell hospital, PRC and the Indian Students Federation (a student voluntary organisation of the communist party) started working among the refugees in different capacities.

Dr Kailashnath Katju, then Governor of West Bengal, formed an organisation named United Council of Relief and Welfare with other welfare societies. The state government used to provide a dole of Rs. 2 with some food per week (Singha 1999: 5–6). The refugees living in occupied fallen lands were suffering from threats of zamindars and their hired goons. Those who were residing in the temporary government camps in Dhubulia, Ghusuri, Cooper's Camp, Kashipur, Rupashri Palli, Bhadrakali, Bagjola, Ghurni, Jatragachhi, Kandi, Moholondi, Moheshdanga and Palla-road started organising protest movements against the government. Manikuntala Sen, a communist activist, pointed out distresses of the refugee children. There were 580 children younger than 5 years of age who died in the Dhubulia camp in 1950 alone. Almost 2 lakh children died between 1947 and 1950 because of the inhumane conditions of the camps.[36] Manoranjan Byapari, a caste refugee writer, remembered in his memoir *Itibritte Chandal Jiban* that there was hardly a day in his camp when he had not heard the cry of a mother who lost her child to disease like typhoid, cholera, tuberculosis or jaundice. His mother often embraced both the brothers with tight hugs, so that the *Jomraj* (according to mythology, the god of death) could not snatch them, too (Byapari 2013: 33).

Nehru visited West Bengal twice in 1950. He even went to the temporary refugee shelters in Bongaon and camps in Ranaghat to enquire about their condition in person. Yet in his next parliamentary address, he remarked that the East Bengali refugees came with assets. In his official report, he showed photos of temporary buildings where they got shelter (Majumdar and Dutta 2010, VI: 85–86).[37] In effect, the total budget allotted for refugee relief and rehabilitation in 1950 was less by Rs. 8 crores than the previous year. Mohanlal Saxena, the Union Rehabilitation Minister, met with all state rehabilitation ministers of eastern and northeastern states in a meeting at Calcutta on 2 March 1950, and unhesitatingly declared that the Government of India would not be able to take any more responsibility to rehabilitate the fresh influxes; the government could only arrange some temporary relief for them. He planned not to confine the refugees to West Bengal but send them to other provinces such as Assam, Tripura, Orissa, Madhya Pradesh and Bihar. The CPI had opined that whereas job opportunities were at stake in West Bengal, both the Centre and state governments instructed the educated middle-class refugees to arrange something by their own efforts, as they were not in a position to offer them any economic and professional rehabilitation (Majumdar and Dutta 2010: 87–88).

West Bengal Government employees, who were apparently not sympathetic towards the refugees, were also astonished to hear the solution from the Centre. This situation led to the establishment of massive numbers of squatters' colonies in the district towns of West Bengal. There was spontaneous participation of refugees in building up colonies in Jadavpur, Tollyganj, Dhakuria, Behala, Dumdum, Belgachhia, Belghoria, Baranagar, Kamarhati, Sodepur, Khardah, Panihati, Barrackpur, Titagarh, Shyamnagar, Ichhapur, Jagaddal, Naihati, Kanchrapara, Sreerampur and Mahesh (Singha 1995: 6). The colony committees realised the necessity to remain united in their struggle to save their settlements from the police or local goons. The camp refugees believed that probably it was the only way to get rid of the hell of camp life. Apart from the camps and colonies, they established primary units of the *sangram* committees in *paras*, slums, military barracks and other categories of rehabilitation centres (Singha 1995: 11–12). The CPI criticised anti-nationalist activities of Liaquat Ali Khan-Nurul Amin towards the Hindus of East Bengal. They were critical of the political stand of Nehru-Patel and Bidhan Roy, too, in tackling minority issues and refugee crisis. They pointed out that the RSS, Hindu Sabha, *Ansar* and Muslim League were the same in conducting atrocities in both the Bengals, in which the Hindu-Muslim citizens and minorities were worst sufferers. They instigated the refugees to squat on land, grab empty houses and demand economic rehabilitation.[38] By 1950, the communists felt the need to publish a weekly newspaper for popularising their activities among the refugees that might help them in building communication among party members across countries, interacting with the masses and understanding their mentality and expectations. They tried to portray the actual scenario of refugee crisis to the West Bengalis to raise an awareness that the party was favouring a social group of those who were suffering immensely, and the locals should interact with them both on ethical and moral grounds.[39]

The refugee situation became more complicated by 1950 as the numbers of refugees were multiplying every day and the state Government was struggling with limited allocation in the budget. In a letter, Dr B. C. Roy wrote to Nehru:

> Do you realise that the total grant received for this purpose from your Government in two years- 1948–49, 1949–50, is a little over three crores and the rest, above five crores was given in form of a loan. Do you realise that this sum is insignificant compared to what has been spent for the refugees from West Pakistan? . . . For months the Government of India would not recognise

the existence of the refugee problems in East Pakistan and therefore would not accept the liabilities in their account.

(Chakrabarty 1962: 20)

The refugees were often compelled to stand in the queue of some charitable organisations for hours in severe cold to obtain warm clothes (Singha 1999: 17). The CPI tried to provide medical facilities to camps and squatters' colonies. They instructed the volunteers to render these services to the refugee families on a regular basis. They organised relief squads with the help of local volunteers. The camps were epidemic-prone and huge numbers of refugees died from cholera, typhoid fever and chicken pox.[40] Their aim was to make an emotional connection with the refugees by sharing miseries from their everyday life. The strategy was to reach out to their grievances on sensitive issues related to their being and existence. The refugee movement reached momentum by 1950. The colonising movement extended to the south, and large colonies had been founded there; Bagha Jatin, Vidhyasagar and Ramgarh colonies were established. The refugees from Durganagar camp chose a strip of government land and founded Poddarnagar colony on January 28 (Chakrabarti 1990: 66). The *Dakshin Kalikata Bastuhara Sangram Parishad* (DKSBS), or the South Calcutta Refugee Council of Action, was established as a coordinated organisation of the NVBKP to weld together the isolated colonies of south Calcutta (Mandal 2011: 206). Congress and the other opponents were constantly trying to divide the refugees into groups. The government used police forces to wipe them out from the settlements like in Mahesh, Vivekananda Nagar, Jadabgarh and Char-Jodubati (Biswas 2003: 251–53). For mobilising protest against the refugees, the government even tried to create situations of communal conflict by distributing to them rooms in Muslim slums and houses. The NVBKP's aim was to unify the refugees under one banner.[41]

An organised struggle

To create a joint platform for the cause of the refugees, the NVBKP decided to incorporate primary units of the organisation. Included were seven other leftist parties and representatives from camps, colonies and refugee relief organisations to decide unanimously on the refugee front (Biswas 2003: 247). It confirmed assimilation of all leftist parties in this amalgamation with other ancillary bodies. The delegates of the organisation involved representation from CPI, Forward Bloc, Marxist Forward Bloc, Socialist Unity Centre, RCPI (Rebel), Democratic Vanguard, Bolshevik Party, Socialist Republican Party (SRP) and others like Hindu Mahasabha. NVBKP could not maintain popularity, however, due to a lack of designing relevant policies. Keeping consistency in communication was the biggest challenge that it could not manage to handle well. Like any other front, it failed to reach its goal because of an ideological and internal rift between the parties, but the background set a stage for the emergence of a central body 'which would look after the manifold needs of the refugees and take under its aegis the mushrooming squatters' colonies (Chakrabarti 1990: 67). The United Central Refugee Council (UCRC) was founded on 4 June 1950 and an 'era of refugee meetings, processions and demonstration as a mass movement began' (Mandal 2011: 206). Right from enquiring into the material condition of the refugees, this platform aimed at convincing both the governments and to make them understand their requirements. It targeted to 'co-ordinate, consolidate and direct the work to a particular end, the economic rehabilitation of refugees' (Chakrabarti 1990: 75); worked on the 'democratic consensus' of the masses including 'all political parties and democratic organisers' to move along paths of 'broad democratic front' (Chakrabarti 1990: 75); and first demanded basic amenities for survival like pure water, food and medical facilities, then later asked for permanent rehabilitation, voting rights, legalisation of colonies, etc.[42]

In the journal *Punarbasan*, the official mouthpiece of refugees, Anil Sinha, the editor and an eminent member of UCRC conveyed, 'it is necessary to work towards a united and wider refugee movement. Not only would this project require stronger linkages within the state-wise organisation of refugees, it would need a presentation of the refugee' problems to the public. UCRC urged to 'battle for resettlement' in resolving the problem of rehabilitation.[43] The refugees came out from their 'Hindu identity' by then, which was the key issue while migrating from their places of origin. They were proclaiming their refugee identity firmly and it became the 'only identity' for them to get a strong foothold in West Bengal.[44] The state government was planning to close down all temporary camps from 1950 onwards; Ambica Chakraborty and Satyapriyo Bondyopadhyay, the leaders of UCRC, protested against this decision (Singha 1999: 1822). Manikuntala Sen remembered in her memoir *Sediner Katha* that the refugees in the camps were like beggars. Some of them left camps and started living in the suburbs of Calcutta, and there was hardly any vacant space. The ruling government tried to evacuate some lands that belonged to specific owners. But, the refugees raised slogans like '*jan debo to ghor debo na*' ('we would sacrifice our lives, but not let others occupy our houses again') (Sen 1982: 181). A group of refugees demanded to the Chief Commissioner of Police, Calcutta, '*bastuharader jomi dao, bhat dao, ba kaj dao*' (give the refugees lands to till, rice to eat or at least work to survive).[45] Manoranjan Byapari mentioned that his family was given allotment in the Shirmanipur camp in Bankura and they shifted in scorching summers. The government arranged only two tube wells for thousands of refugee families. In effect, one of the members from those families was always in queues to collect a bucket of water for survival (Byapari 2013: 31). Manikuntala Sen opined that the negative attitude towards the camp and colony refugees made the Congress government unpopular within all refugees groups. Even the Muslim residents and returnees were disappointed by their apathetic stand. They were compelled to lead a life below the basic dignity level. They were poor in the East Bengali society, but in West Bengal, they became merely beggars (Sen 1982: 182).

The colony refugees were more organised; their number crossed 6,000 by 1950. UCRC floated the idea of collecting signatures to bring them into common causes, treat any adverse situations in a united manner, organise protest movements and create a fellow feeling within members of various political groups. In the circular *Pradeshik Bastuhara*, directed to all members of party units, issued on 26 November 1950, titled as '*Bastuharadiger Colony Swikar, Bastur Dabi o Bhotadhikar Dabir Abedonpatre Soi Sangraher Modhyo Dia Bastuhara Front er Bamponthi Doler Akotake Bastuhara Jonotar Akotae Porinoto Korun*', the CPI clarified the reason to unite leftist parties who used to work separately within the refugee front. The CPI's opponents were the governments and zamindars/*jotedars*, against whom a joint struggle became indispensable. The CPI started collecting mass signatures as consent to protest against the forcible evacuation of the properties captured by the refugees without arranging any alternatives. The legalisation of colonies and government dissolution of camps were points of discussion raised.[46] The CPI used those thousands of signatures in deputations. The party stressed the necessity to know about the changing nature of protest movements through meetings, organised separately by colony committees in different zones.

The strategy of the communists was mentioned in *Circular 5* published by the CPI. It pointed out that the reason behind introducing such a code of conduct was to make the party members an integral part of the refugees' lives. They felt that the importance of working within colonies, engaging in public relations to acquire trust and involving the refugees in leftist ideology. The CPI pointed out that it was the right of the masses to survive on fallow lands captured by the rich classes of society. The party realised it would be important to involve women members in units and district factions (Biswas 2003: 252). Leaders like Pranakrisna Chakrabarti, Ambica Chakraborty and Satyapriya Banerjee were converts from other political affiliations after the Partition. They had to re-establish hold from a different background to pursue their political aspirations.[47] UCRC campaigned against police action on refugees at Jadabgarh colony and claimed that the government was trying to 'resort to violence in expelling the refugees from the colonies'.[48] Ambica Chakraborty attacked the ruling party by saying, 'It was the Congress which partitioned the country and brought about the refugee problem. If Government failed to feed these people, it had no right to rule'.[49] Mahadev Bhattacharya conveyed in the *Bastuhara Parisad*'s meeting that refugees should 'face bullets for their legitimate demands and exhorted the womenfolk to encourage their sons and daughters in fighting the Congress demons'.[50] UCRC faced a blow with the establishment of the Refugee Central Rehabilitation Council (RCRC) as a rival organisation; it lacked organisational apparatus, but could establish such in that political arena. RCRC tried to take hold of the urban colonies of south Calcutta dominated by RSP, KMPP, FB (Leela Roy group), RCPI (Soumen Tagore group) and the Socialist Party (SP).[51] The state passed acts against the colonising movement under the UCRC, issued 'Gazette notification directing the squatters' to vacate lands within 15 days of unauthorised occupation or face forcible eviction.[52]

The protest continues

The squatters' colonies came out as a challenge against the inhumane policies directed toward the refugees. It became a prestige issue on the part of the Congress government; hence, they introduced an 'Eviction Bill' in the West Bengal Legislative Assembly against squatters' colonies.[53] It was impossible to fight against each and every refugee who occupied lands or properties forcefully. The total number of squatters' colonies crossed 149. It was impossible to evict 1.5 lakh people (30,000 families). In addition, there were 1.45 lakh refugees in relief camps.[54] The landowners treated the verdict as a weapon to take back their lands by raids on the colonies with help of hired hooligans or police. The *jabardakhal* (seizure and settlement) colonies became the source of conflicts.[55] The eviction was like uprooting for the second time for the refugee families. Shachin Das, in his novel *Udbastu Nagarir Chand*, portrayed how the leaders of the *jabardakhal* colonies were busy in discussing what should be the terms to get a hold on the lands they occupied (Das 2008: 190–92). UCRC condemned the Amended Refugee Eviction Bill and alleged that the Congress government had adopted 'divide and rule policy' by supporting the zamindars and local affluent classes. Refugees settled in Mahesh, and Hoogly experienced combined raids of the local landlord and police.[56] The raids in suburban colonies were sporadic in nature. The RCRC formed the Refugee Eviction Resistance Committee. Almost 1.5 lakh refugees gathered under the Martyrs Monument[57] on 18 February 1951. They marched to Wellington Square to protest against this bill. UCRC and RCRC came close in the fight against the bill, but failed to force the government to withdraw it. UCRC challenged it by pointing out, 'if a person remained in unauthorised occupation of land or premises continuously for three months, there could be no criminal proceedings against him' (Chakrabarti 1990: 80–82). In effect, the bill finally got corrected and a new amendment had been included with some protection (Singha 1995: 14–15). It, however, rectified that until and unless government provided the refugees with economic rehabilitation, no one should evict from squatters' colonies.

The Act XVI of 1951 (the Eviction Bill) transferred responsibility of eviction from the landowners to the state.[58] Dr B. C. Roy introduced a new bill called 'Eviction of Persons in Unauthorised Occupation of Land Bill'. It declared, 'Forcible and unauthorised occupation of private and Government lands and premises requisitioned by the Central and State Governments . . . could not be resolved by the normal process of legal action'.[59] The Government introduced 'The West Bengal Evacuee Property Act 1951' to protect properties of ordinary residents of West Bengal and it declared 'in case the evacuee returned to West Bengal before 31 March 1951, could reclaim and possession of the property to be delivered to the evacuee'.[60] The delegates' conference of the *Sanjukta Udbastu Sammelan* was held at Serampore Town Hall on 27 January 1951. UCRC decided to request the government to regularise the legal status of colonies and recognise their rights on lands. They realised that until the refugees got legal right over lands, nothing would change.[61] UCRC opted for the method of 'sit-in' strikes or *satyagraha* as a declared strategy, launched by Amritalal Chatterjee. Vallabhbhai Patel argued at a press conference on 15 December 1947 that the Congress Ministry was elected by the people in Bengal, 'so any attempt to launch a *satyagraha* against that ministry appeared to be '*duragraha*' (a bad or negative force or desire) (Bandyapadhyay 2009: 74–75). They developed a structure of political agitation and started the distribution of printed resolution during meetings. They also used statistical tables to make the people aware of their demands and the government's reaction to it (Chakrabarti 1990: 91). The camp refugees adopted a practice to receive instant attention of the press through *anashan* (hunger strike) in front of the State Government Rehabilitation Directorate at Auckland House, for the fulfilment of their demands. After achieving partial success against the Eviction Bill, UCRC realised the necessity to increase representation in the Assembly to be a part of decisionmaking in the political affairs on the refugees.[62] The government established Refugee Peace and Welfare Committees for allotting plots to some of the refugees. Yet, providing them with proprietary rights or regularisation of the colonies remained a distant dream.[63]

It is indeed interesting to note how the language and nature of slogans in the refugee political movement changed over the decades. In the 1950s, UCRC started addressing the Congress government with epithets such as '*dalals* of the Anglo-American imperialists' and 'friends of capitalists and zamindars', etc. They arranged *Udbastu Shibirs* (organised camps to have detailed discussion on this crisis) with posters like '*Bastuhara korlo kara? Gadi ankre ache kara? English Markin dalal jara, Bastuharader dabi mante hobe, Anna bostro siksha dao, Nijer gadi chhere dao*', etc. (Who made us refugees? Who were trying to capture power? None but the agents of Anglo-American, The demands of refugees should be honoured, provide us with food, clothing and education or step down from power, etc.).[64] These slogans were gradually merging with anti-imperialist campaigns propagated by the leftist parties in the early 1950s. They used to decorate meeting areas with flags, festoons and a gate with inscriptions '*Anukul Toron, Binapani Toron*' (in the name of refugees, killed in police firing), to keep the masses updated about their strategies of the political movements.[65] By calling for setting up representative preparatory committees in camps/colonies, UCRC tried to involve them in every layer of decisionmaking.[66] They teamed up for 'forcibly occupying the vacant houses of zamindars' after the eviction bill. The design was that 'the refugees who would be evicted should make another forcible occupation'.[67]

Before the first general election, they demanded citizenship rights, anti-eviction measures, loans and grants, and professional and economic rehabilitation for the refugees. The leftists suggested building up of small-scale industries, training centres for women, appointment of committees within camps based on democratic procedures, permanent rehabilitation within three months, return of Muslim houses and arrangement of any other viable alternatives for the refugees.[68] The Communist Party of India (CPI) had launched a mass movement for inclusion of the names of the refugees in the voter list so that they could participate directly and 'be a voice' in the first general election of 1952.[69] They started criticising the election manifesto of the ruling Congress government before the election. The Congress loudly claimed that it had initiated several measures and was successful in providing rehabilitation and resettlement to the refugees. The leftists criticised continuous brutal methods of evictions by the Congress. They pointed out that the government used bombs to clear slums owned by the zamindar of Narail in 1948. They ordered *lathi*-charge on the refugee procession and made arrests. In

'Netaji-Nagar', which was situated in Majuhat Naskarpur, the government evicted refugees from 3,000 houses. The Mahesh incident again happened in 1950 when women refugees were hospitalised following police atrocities. Cooper's camp saw more death by police attacks, and the same incidents happened in Tollyganj and Jadavpur. In 1951, the Government of India asked a team of anthropologists from the Anthropological Survey of India, led by Dr B. S. Guha and backed by experts from UNESCO (the United Nations Educational, Scientific and Cultural Organization), to look into the causes of 'social tensions' among the refugees of West Bengal. After violent demonstrations on the streets of Calcutta and a spate of forcible occupation of properties by the refugees on the outskirts of Calcutta, the state government had reluctantly been forced to recognise that 'the refugee problem' was a cause for serious concern (Guha 1959: 51).

Yet finally, in 1951, the government introduced eviction laws, by which they were empowered to evict refugees from any area without any prior notice.[70] Thus in 1952, UCRC placed their '14 point' demands, which focused on 'not [sending] refugees outside West Bengal', in which the main points were: (i) 'They should not be detained in any station, platform or transit camp more than two days'; (ii) 'They must not be removed from the places they were occupying'; (iii) 'All cultivable fallow lands in West Bengal and its contiguous districts must be distributed to them'; (iv) 'The Government must withdraw forthwith all the cases against the refugees arrested in connection with the refugee movement'; and (v) 'The Government should immediately grant rights of citizenship to all the refugees in India'.[71] They hinted, 'the anti-Bengali feeling noticed in Orissa, Bihar, Assam and other states were secretly fomented by the Centre to oust Bengalis from every sphere of life'.[72] They criticised roles of the newspapers like *Amrita Bazar Patrika*, *Ananda Bazar Patrika* and the *Jugantar* for failing to write about refugee issues.[73] When the refugees were organised politically, they tried to make an impact through the ballot box. They remarked, 'a floating population on whom the seekers of election cannot reasonably count' (Chatterji 2008: 222). The result of the general election of 1952 provided the refugees with a sense of belonging. The leftist candidates became identical with the refugee identity, working and campaigning hard for them to be a part of the opposition. The government realised their failure in sending the refugees back to their place of origin by the Delhi Pact (1950).[74] They agreed to settle them in squatters' colonies,[75] and opined that the 'refugees living in Muslim abandoned houses should not be evicted unless and until suitable houses or lands were given to them'.[76]

Leftist methods in refugee movements

The passport regulation was introduced right after the general election of 1952. There was a demand of population exchange between both the Bengals, in which, apart from Hindu Mahasabha, Congress leaders were also being supportive. Few communal incidents occurred in the Bashirhat border, Badure (regarding *Sati Ma er than*) and Canning. Many Muslims left for East Bengal, and the Hindu refugees immediately occupied their houses. There were few incidents of exchange of a whole Muslim village in Bongaon with a Hindu village in Khulna by mutual understanding (Singha 1995: 27). From 1953, the state government started acquiring thousands of acres of agricultural lands from the Muslim owners in places like Rajarhat, Bhangor, Deganga, Bashirhat and Haroa to distribute among the refugees. The local farmers and residents were agitated against it, as the government was acquiring the lands for allotting to the refugees in Bagjola, Baruipur and Sonarpur.[77] CPI protested against such abrupt activities and described it as 'another strategy' to make the West Bengalis and the minorities unsympathetic towards the refugees. They spoke for the rights of both Hindu refugees and Muslim evacuees.[78] The leftists went to the court, organised *satyagraha* for an injunction order so that the government could not acquire lands in Bagjola by this method.[79] Mohit Moitro, the chief organiser of the United Leftist Election Committee, opined that the party always stood by the minorities and protested against such acts, the leftists would try to convince the government and the government should return properties to the Muslim owners by the end of 1953 after a final settlement. The Muslim vote bank, however, was in favour of the Congress.[80] Yet, by bringing the Muslim issue to a similar platform, the idea of an economic class was formed over the religious identity of the refugees and native Muslims.

Within such an environment of constant turmoil and contradiction, the West Bengalis gradually became more unsympathetic toward the refugees and started blaming them for overpopulating and polluting their state (Asit Baran Thakur 2011: 29–31). Few nationalised banks failed in between 1952 and 1955. The West Bengalis often complained that the communist leaders organised deputation in front of bank gates to get some facilities of easy transactions, introduction of rules to transfer of amounts from East Bengal and fixing a currency exchange rate.[81] Their argument was that the leftists never addressed their crises; even the reputed newspapers had not given enough importance to their issues. They always published news related to the refugees only.[82] The refugees became accustomed to the strategy or type of UCRC agitation and its techniques of demonstration; like 200 refugees living at Howrah and Sealdah station gathered outside of the west gate of the Assembly House and demanded an interview with the Relief Minister, Mrs Renuka Ray, to discuss their grievances. Ambica Chakraborty placed a memorandum in the Assembly in 1953, while 20,000 refugee demonstrators were waiting outside.[83] They urged the formation of a District Advisory Rehabilitation Committees and restoration of Muslim properties.[84] UCRC opposed harassing the supporters aligning with leftist parties.[85] Jyoti Basu commented that 'the Government alone could not deal with this vast problem', hence they should initiate 'pilot schemes' to meet up legal difficulties regarding the acquisition of lands.[86] The report of the Ministerial Committee somehow 'brought to light in its reports about various Governmental corruptions and malpractices, and classified the different classes of refugees thus bringing in some change in the rehabilitation policy'.[87] Renuka Ray requested all leading political parties to cooperate and remain united on rehabilitation of the displaced persons. Jiban Lal Chatterji voiced against 'atrocities of a commandant of

Dhubulia camp, who was responsible for the death of some refugees in police firing and insisted on a non-official enquiry into the matter to take an adequate step'.[88]

The Mahila Atmaraksha Samity (MARS) was founded as the women's front of the leftists in April 1943, and it was later successful in organising the women refugees (Sen 2001: 117–19). MARS activist Lila Roy's group, with other voluntary organisations, worked with the women refugees in the Sealdah station. She stressed the female participation both in urban and rural areas.[89] MARS, along with 21 women's forums, submitted a memorandum to Nehru to draw the government's attention to large-scale abduction and torture of women refugees. Under their pressure, the state government rehabilitated women refugees in *Uday Villa*, Women's Co-operative Industrial Home and *Ananda Ashram* (Chakraborty 1980: 165–67). MARS integrated the women refugee concerns with the larger mainstream women's movement. They formed a sizeable section and participated in the central rallies under the banner of UCRC. In a leaflet of MARS, published on 2 April 1952, their slogan was 'Long Live Women's Movement' (Chakravartty 2005: 59–60). In Rupasree Pally, Bhadrakali camp of Nadia district, the women refugees had organised *satyagraha* movement[90] and decided to observe the 'Women's Refugee Day' on 3 April 1952,[91] and women *satyagrahis* also planned demonstrations and a mass meeting in Palashi women's camp.[92] It is interesting to notice that earlier, they used to participate in political activities passively, but from 1953, they came forward to offer active support for strengthening the refugee cause.[93]

From 1953, Union Rehabilitation Minister Ajit Prasad Jain was busy in making policies for the West Pakistani refugees; he surprisingly announced the closure of the rehabilitation department of Bengal. The communists protested against the decision and compelled the Centre and the states to deal with the crisis. UCRC demanded the legalisation of the squatters' colonies and refugee-occupied lands, arguing that the Bengali refugees were deprived in every possible way. It criticised the government schemes, as they did not prove beneficial for these refugees. Finally, in 1954, A. P. Jain recommended to give refugees some rights in his report of 1954. It was the first major victory of the leftists (Singha 1995: 16). The refugees were initially under the impression that the state of West Bengal and the West Bengalis would receive them with open arms.[94] When they built up colonies entirely with their resources, they faced resistance from the locals, and it left a psychological effect on the mentality of their displaced leaders, and they became keen to achieve powerful positions.[95] Between 1954 and 1956, the government labelled refugee rehabilitation as an administrative issue[96] and started acquisition of land in district towns and providing loans to both colony and camp refugees.[97]

The deserters from Bihar and Orissa, however, became a new respondent group.[98] UCRC tried to provide them a platform under their banner.[99] Being sympathetic, B. C. Roy requested them to go back to their camps where they availed loans earlier and instructed government officials to enquire about them.[100] He asked their leaders to submit a 'Charter of Demands'.[101] He assured them of employment in worksite camps,[102] but there were only 79 worksite camps in West Bengal, where the government was capable to keep only 92,273 persons.[103] It was already nine years after independence, so the government was not sure for how long it could keep them in transit camps.[104] The leftists demanded professional rehabilitation for the colony dwellers who were ready to pay for legal rights in lands and houses. Satya Priya Banerjee criticised:

> the direction of the Government for refusing to accept court affidavits and certificates from the M.P.s and M.L.A.s and gazetted officers as proof of the *bona-fide* refugees and calling for the production of border-slips and receipt of taxes paid in Pakistan, etc.[105]

UCRC had strengthened its base by 1955 and merged refugee issues with the labour agitation and other marginal sections.[106] The refugees gradually became a part of the 'composite group' of unprivileged people. In their joint demonstrations, marginality became the key issue.[107] The Rajarhat Krishak Samiti, Bhojerhat Union Krishak Samiti and Bhangar Thana Krishak Samiti tied up with Manicktala Refugee Bazar Samiti, Murari Pukur Bastuhara Samiti and Ultadanga Anchalik Bastuhara Samiti, and conveyed 'they were living like cats and dogs, being neglected by the rulers'.[108] The leftists fought to arrange facilities for the refugees like opening up of spinning mills, introducing cooperative, marketing centres, arranging vocational training for girls and physically challenged refugees in worksite camps, and professional rehabilitation for some specific castes.[109]

Saga of broken promises and losing hopes

Shri Mehr Chand Khanna, the next Union Rehabilitation Minister, was not at all sympathetic towards the Bengali refugees. He 'had the knowledge of all the details of the Government policy regarding claims and their compensation, and was in possession of all the official secrets in this behalf, and fully knew the shape of things to come' from the beginning.[110] He declared in 1956 that every migrant should come with a 'Migration Certificate' and this certificate was available in the Indian High Commission's Office, Dhaka. But the condition to grab a certificate was that the refugee families had to take shelter in any relative's place and they would not ask for any support from the government (Singha 1995: 6). Also, in the Calcutta Conference of 1956, both the Centre and West Bengal governments decided to send the refugees to Cachar and Tripura to minimise their numbers. It was expected that agriculture would be supplemented by the development of some small-scale industries.[111] Satya Priya Banerjee criticised Mr Khanna's statement in the Rehabilitation Ministers' Conference of 12 states in 1956 and commented, 'they would first examine the suitability of the place for refugee rehabilitation'.[112] The UCRC pointed out, 'it was a lie; a bluff to say that there was no land in Bengal. But the Government was unwilling to part with the land as the next general election was nearing'.[113] In a meeting on 28 January 1956, Satya Priya Banerjee mentioned 'there were enough lands in Bengal. In Sundarbans, there were two big landowners who possessed 70 thousand and 40 thousand *bighas* of land respectively. But the

Government would not touch them as the Government belonged to their party'.[114] He stated 2–3 other options to settle, and opined: 'The refugees had proved that the people of Bengal were not afraid of manual work or physical labour'.[115] Their demand was 'voting right for the refugees who were living in West Bengal for 3 years or more'.[116] They proposed 'In case the Government failed to rehabilitate the refugees within a particular date, they would not rely upon them anymore'.[117]

Mohit Moitro, the chief organiser of the United Leftist Election Committee, protested against illegal cultivable lands acquired in Kulgachhi from April 1956. But the Central Rehabilitation Minister Khanna announced that those lands were fallow arable lands surrounded by *hogla* leaves, and he decided to distribute these lands within 2,400 refugee families. The leftists communicated with all downtrodden classes to support the cause of the refugees, though they were not against local farmers and labourers. There was another category of refugees and local farmers who opted for the '*baynanama* scheme'. This meant that they located a piece of land and booked it with some advance notice and asked for loans as per the scheduled amount fixed by the state government—but the government did not allot any loans afterwards. Hence, the land and the amount for booking of the land mostly went in vain.[118] So the UCRC leadership felt the need to modify its demands in a changed situation. There was epidemic in camps, which the government ignored.[119] Diseases like tuberculosis were spreading in 24 Parganas, while 143 refugees died of tuberculosis and pneumonia in the Kurmitola Camp, Murshidabad. The government did not arrange any special care.[120] Some groups were staying in worksite camps and weaning tents (an improper structure to live or survive) without any permanent structures. The refugees were not getting payments against earthcutting work in the worksite camps. Ambica Chakraborty demanded in Memari on 17 January 1956 for refugees to be paid 'immediately the arrear wages due to them for earth-cutting work for the last year by the Government'.[121] They sat in demonstration on railway lines to protest against the delay in receiving doles, and complained against police pickets in camps and corruption of the officers.

More than 80 per cent of refugees were residing in the camps. In some bigger camps like Ghusuri, Kashipur and Cooper's camp, they were compelled to live in open spaces. UCRC observed an 'All India Refugee Demand Day' to highlight on *lathi*-charge and throwing of tear gas canisters on the *satyagrahis*.[122] In 1957, Congress won in the second general election, but the leftists were gaining power, winning 46 seats against total 156 constituencies.[123] They eventually started lobbying with the Muslim politicians, when Congress could not come out of caste- and class-based mobilisation patterns (Chatterji 2008: 300). Between January and March 1957, police reports were full of stories of communist leaders hobnobbing with the Muslim politicians. One such report conveyed, 'communal sentiments of Muslims were repeatedly fanned to the advantage of leftist parties'.[124] The government admitted in 1957 that some of its relief and rehabilitation policies were neither viable, nor were all of those schemes operated properly. Only 11 per cent of refugees could resume a profession in this land. Others came back from the rehabilitation centres outside West Bengal. The government had withdrawn previous recommendations to design new policies as numbers of the refugees were increasing every month. The leftists argued that government should first accept the refugee families that came in between 1947 and 1954 as citizens by including their names in voter lists before they became floating population. If so, they would feel like part of the West Bengali society, not 'outsiders'.[125]

Time and again, the government was raising the point that the nature of the influx and exodus in Bengal was not like that in Punjab, as it was not a one-time splash. But no such effort was noticed to correct their mistakes to fight against such crucial crises.[126] The Centre had not given priority to resettle the refugees to Bengal between 1947 and 1957. They provided loan amounts of Rs. 1,250 for building houses, Rs. 700 for businesses and Rs. 500 as cattle loans. These amounts were counted as crores in government's exchequer, but the refugee families hardly got benefitted. The Centre had appointed a fact-finding committee in September 1952 and a high power committee in 1954, but no reports got to see the daylight.[127] They did not implement the recommendation of the Darjeeling Convention of 1955 and could not arrange sitting of State Development Board Quarterly to check upon the real developments. The government promised to introduce diverse type of jobs for the refugees, but in practice, they encouraged only earth-cutting work in worksite camps by providing a fixed amount of test relief. It was a total loss from the government's point of view, too, as it were spending amounts in summer and it went in vain during rainy seasons. Bankim Mukherjee questioned how many teachers got salary through the Union Board Scheme, and what the total amount was. The government had given permanent rehabilitation to 4,000 businessmen in a single village in Taherpur; 2,000 came back within a month. Bankim Mukherjee wondered what business the businessmen would opt for, and who would be the seller or buyer.[128] In such messy situations, suddenly the Union Rehabilitation Ministry started using the phrase that West Bengal had reached a 'saturation point' and thus the refugees were left with no other viable option than settling down outside West Bengal.

The 'deserted' refugees

The Central Government finally had withdrawn all rehabilitation schemes for Bengali refugee-absorbent states in 1958 and instructed the refugees to resettle in Dandakaranya. This policy was implemented on the refugees who came in between 1958 and 1963 (Singha 1995: 7). Based on a resolution taken at the Ranaghat Convention of 1958, the UCRC conducted a 'Demand Week'. Yet, the government ordered some refugees be sent from the Bishnupur camp to Rajasthan. The refusal from the refugees' part led to the stoppage of the doles. The refugees had launched a civil disobedience movement. The locals became gradually sympathetic to their causes. The basic plan of the UCRC was to make a common platform of struggle by including the camp and colony refugees, and include the West Bengalis into that struggle. It was for shaping up of a united struggle against the ruling government throughout the state (Majumdar and Dutta 2013, X: 400).[129] But the Centre was determined to resettle the camp refugees first, and reiterated its plan to close down relief and transit camps in West Bengal, Assam and Tripura, and relocate them in Dandakaranya (Chatterjee 2012: 21). It added a clause; the refugees 'should be moved into this area only after their representatives visit localities to see prevailing conditions' (Hota 2009: 12), though the refugee leaders were not given the opportunity to visit the site. The option left for the refugees was an en masse desertion following the settlement. Asoka Gupta described how the unending flow to Mana and Kurud perplexed the authorities with its limited accommodation.

The Dandakaranya authority had no alternative other than to put the refugees straight under the sun. Nearly 'a thousand families are put up in single fly-tents'.[130] The refugees were crammed into some 'refugee special' trains. They were directly dispersed to the actual site of rehabilitation: Pharasgaon, Umerkote or Paralkote. For the non-camp refugees, UCRC demanded regularisation of colonies with professional rehabilitation.[131] The committees placed demand for land settlements with landowners.[132] During 1954–1958, the government was in the midst of many setbacks; Calcutta experienced the Bettiah returnees who came back seeking refuge in West Bengal. The Bettiah camp refugees marked the beginning of resistance to arbitrary rehabilitation programmes (Singha 1999: 42–49). Bettiah was the largest of many camps set up by the Centre, outside refugee-absorbent states (Chakraborty 1980: 166). The Bihar government was not concerned about them or their crises. In inhumane conditions, minimum doles were not distributed properly. Because of the police firings, along with a whole lot of other grievances and while they were dying in dozens, the refugees deserted the camps and decided to return as a final resort. The government, unfortunately, saw only political conspiracies behind the return of those absconders. Their consequent accumulation had created a volatile situation again in Calcutta.[133] The spokesperson of the Bihar Government claimed that some leftist leaders of West Bengal visited Bettiah camp, 11 days before the general election of 1957. They assured the refugees of the arrangement of their rehabilitation. The government often used to quote this statement against their hunger strikes.[134] Renuka Ray spelt out the Government's stand: 'if people do not go out of West Bengal they should expect no help from the Government'.[135]

The first batch consisted of 475 refugees sent to Bettiah with the promise that they had been taken just to give them an idea about the probable distance from Bengal. But the government never made arrangements to accommodate them back in West Bengal. They kept on sending letters and telegrams to the government office, but did not receive any reply. The same happened in some islands in Orissa and Rajasthan.[136] Leftist parties grabbed the opportunity to launch a fresh movement with a new agenda and enthusiasm after the coming of Bettiah refugees when the locals were criticising government policies.

> [as] the Congress Government and Congress, who gave an undertaking the refugee problem would be given the highest priority and it would be treated as national problem, has failed to solve the issue, rather the Congress Government is now trying to shirk the responsibility and in doing so the

Government is rehabilitating the refugees in a haphazard way and dealing with the refugee problem whimsically.[137]

For them, it was like a recurrence of old post-Partition days, with refugees forced to stay in stations and Howrah Maidan.[138] Nine thousand refugees came in the first four weeks. The Red Cross and Bharat Sevasram Sangha distributed medicine, food and other essentials,[139] but after some time, the masses became aloof because of the constant social tension around the refugees. Though the party tried to render equal importance to the crises of the middle and poor West Bengalis, like this newly emerged social class (Majumdar and Dutta 2013, X: 401).

In the meantime, the Praja Socialist Party (PSP) started an initiative with the same agenda to divide the united spirit. Jogen Mandal, a *Namasudra* leader from East Bengal, was a part of this initiative. The state government agreed not to send refugees forcefully outside West Bengal. Both PSP and UCRC agreed to withdraw the civil disobedience movement launched separately by them. From July 1958, the Government decided in a conference that: (i) only 10,000 refugees might be accommodated in West Bengal, while the rest of the 32,000 would be sent to Dandakaranya; (ii) all camps should be shut down by July 1959; and (iii) both the governments declined to take any responsibility of the non-camp refugees. The state government decided to send 31,000 refugees to Dandakaranya by checking material conditions there (Majumdar and Dutta 2013, X: 400). The conflict between the camp and colony refugees occurred for the first time in 1958, with exhibition of class differences. The colony refugees were from the middle-classes, whereas 70 per cent of the camp dwellers were from the lower orders. The camp refugees did not participate in the anti-eviction movement, while the colony refugees refused to be a part of the *satyagraha* of the camp refugees. The internal conflicts between these two categories were the chief reason for not introducing a joint movement even by UCRC (Chakravarty 2011: 210). The veteran UCRC leaders, Amritendu Mukherjee and Apurbalal Majumdar, condemned 'the apathy of Government in providing food and shelter', the refugees on 'pavements and railway platforms are now actually on the verge of death'.[140] Some refugees went back to Dandakaranya with fresh promises of getting doles, immediate loans, and arrangement of Bengali doctors in the camps, etc.[141]

The next phase was categorised by the government's decision to forward the 'Rehabilitation of Displaced Persons and Eviction of Persons in Unauthorised Occupation of Land (Amendment) Bill, 1957' for prior concurrence of the Government of India.[142] It was a temporary enactment, effective from 1 April 1958.[143] They did not support the conversion of the Cooper's Camp, Rupasree Palli and Women's camp into a township.[144] The government started abolition of transit and other camps.[145] UCRC involved the camp refugees in its struggle and stressed the distress of women refugees in Bhadrakali refugee camp.[146] UCRC decided to form *Sangram* committees in every camp and recruited 50,000 volunteers to protest against sending refugees to Orissa, Rajasthan and Dandakaranya. And, 'to raise the tempo of the agitation', they had arranged regular meeting in camps, so that they would hear grievances of the camp refugees. *Sara Bangla Bastuhara Sammelan* observed a 'Refugee Day', and 82 batches of refugee demonstrators participated.[147] The communists pointed out that the refugee political movement organised for rehabilitation of 40 lakhs Partition-displaced Bengali refugees.[148] Of them, 20 lakhs did not get government assistance. Apart from the refugees residing in the government accommodations, there were few lakhs of refugees surviving on their own in towns and villages. The government claimed to spend 95 crores until 1959, of which at least 50 crores went in vain; only a section of government employees had benefitted.[149] Both the governments did not initiate any holistic plan for these refugees. Some of them could manage a shelter in colonies, though 80 per cent of the refugees did not have any income.[150] The communists opined that the role of the state government was confusing. They were seen using the grants for other purposes like distribution of amounts to zamindars, *jotedars* and promoters as prices of the lands, captured by refugee colonies. From 1959 onwards, there was hardly any possibility to allot more refugees, and the government compelled few batches to settle down in Dandakaranya. When the result was not satisfactory, the government tried to mobilise the West Bengalis by saying that refugees were needed to be sent to Dandakaranya for the betterment of the locals and their future generations (Majumdar and Dutta 2013, X: 388–89).

Time and again, the party and UCRC had actually persuaded the Centre to declare the refugee rehabilitation problem as a 'national crisis'. They conducted protest movement against using force for stoppage of dole payments and dispatched them to Dandakaranya. They introduced a 'direct action programme' from 7 January 1959. They facilitated ideas like: (i) they were not against the refugees who wished to settle down in Dandakaranya; (ii) they were just protesting against the forcible transfer of refugees; and (iii) Bhupesh Gupta and Jyoti Basu made the point clear that the state government had to plan the rehabilitation of refugees in West Bengal, along with other landless and poor peasant categories (Majumdar and Dutta 2013, X: 333). They stated that the Communist Party never demanded an unending supply of doles for the 2.5 lakhs refugees staying in the camps of West Bengal. The UCRC believed that West Bengal could have accommodated 3 crores of refugees, if planned centrally and properly. If the same amount of money which had already been spent in the Dandakaranya plan could have been spent in West Bengal, the result would be far more fruitful (Majumdar and Dutta 2013, X: 389). The Dandakaranya plan was not a 'rehabilitation scheme' for the refugees. It was not the same as the rejected 'Andaman scheme' 6–7 years previously. They treated *punorbason* (resettlement) in Dandakaranya as *puno-nirbason* (again an exile). But, Manoranjan Byapari opined, the communist leaders played great roles in discouraging the refugees to be rehabilitated permanently there, though did not take any responsibility to feed the starving refugees (Byapari 2013: 38–39).

UCRC sought to open a dialogue with the state agencies by submitting a detailed document on 'An Alternative Plan for Rehabilitation of Camp Refugees in West Bengal' to Dr B. C. Roy. He questioned the loyalty of the communists to refugee causes and criticised the leftists for their inactiveness in the days of the

Noakhali riot.[151] He stressed the state's 'economic saturation' and said that West Bengal was too densely populated for any further settlement. Long-term projects of land reclamation in Bagjola worksite camp and Sonarpur camp came to a standstill. The earlier decisions of transforming large transit camps like Dhubulia and Cooper's camps into satellite industrial townships were abandoned (Chatterjee 2012: 21–22). Yet, the government had claimed to resettle 21 lakhs of refugees out of 32 lakhs of refugees, but the settlement of 10,000 refugees was satisfactory. According to the communists, 70 per cent of families did not get any rehabilitation, while some of the refugees settled in Orissa, Rajasthan and Bihar. A few batches migrated from Mikir hills of Assam. The floating refugees who did not have any documents got settled in Dandakaranya. The government threatened the refugees to close down the camps after giving advance dole for six months (Byapari 2013: 218). The government threatened closing down the rehabilitation department, too. The leftists suggested:

> (i) Government now should collect information about the actual scenario of the refugees, (ii) Government should use fallen lands for industrialisation schemes for the refugees, (iii) they should not shut down the rehabilitation department, (iv) they should invite all related groups, parties and other philanthropic organisations to work unanimously.
> *(Majumdar and Dutta 2013, XI: 371–72)*

Yet, most of the camps were closed down by 1959 in West Bengal, even after a rigorous campaign by UCRC (Chakravarty 2011: 174).

The food movement of 1959 gave the leftists another opportunity to consolidate their base (Das and Bandyopadhyay 2004: 160). The Partition-endured population pressure was worse in West Bengal. In 1948, the state government could reach only 50 per cent of its target regarding the procurement and distribution of food grains. The scenario further deteriorated between 1950 and 1952, and the population escalated steeply owing to the fresh flow of refugees. From 1953, an artificial scarcity had been created on the distribution of food grains.[152] The food situation worsened more by hoarding and black marketing, creating a famine situation in rural Bengal (Basu 2012: 3), so the middle-class started to be attracted to the pattern of leftist politics and their agendas. They were aware of the evil of corruption on food issues.[153] The food movement established the economic issue more profoundly. It was another eye-opener for the West Bengalis. UCRC criticised the state government for non-utilisation of budget allocations in the last two five-year plans.[154] The issues of conflicts spread beyond the political arena. The food crisis had immensely affected rural areas in comparison to the urban spaces. The involvement of the refugees in this movement could help them in identifying themselves with the crisis. They became an essential part of the mainstream West Bengali lower-classes.

1960s: the refugee front

The first half of the 1960s had seen inter-migration of Bengalis from Assam to North Bengal because of the conflict over language issues. The government refused to accept those categories as refugees and render any help to them.[155] Both the Central and state governments did not allot any budget in the third five-year plan for the refugees left. Mr Khanna declared that only some residuary works remained to be done, after completion of the rehabilitation (Singha 1999: 29). Prafulla Sen, the State Rehabilitation Minister for West Bengal, declared in 1961 that the rehabilitation problem of the East Bengali refugees had almost been sorted out;[156] it was needed to spend 21 crores more from the Centre to solve the residuary problems and resettlement of the rest of the refugees.[157] UCRC submitted a new 'Charter of Demands' on 3 August 1961 under Hemanta Basu. They criticised the 'Sweep Survey' and conveyed that out of 24 lakhs, almost 16 lakh refugees were yet to get resettlement in West Bengal.[158] They complained that regardless of their pressure and regular demands, Congress never treated the refugee problem as a 'national crisis'.[159] Even after 14 years of independence, thousands of refugees were lying in slums, barracks, roads, open fields and rail stations. Within the colony refugees, 50 per cent did not have any professional rehabilitation. Some of the families got partial rehabilitation. The refugees of squatters' colonies were still struggling with some legal issues (Singha 1995: 7). The government decided to close down the rehabilitation department in 1961. After sending all camp refugees to Dandakaranya, they had already given notice to the employees, who were in temporary posts in the state government's rehabilitation department (Majumdar and Dutta 2014, XII: 265–66). UCRC condemned Nehru's idea of closing down the Rehabilitation Department in the East (Singha 1999: 58), and demanded 'an official or non-official enquiry, for ascertaining the real cause of the desertion of the camps outside West Bengal'.[160] It affirmed Congress's failure to keep its promises of providing alternative employment to the refugees.[161] The UCRC organised an all-party delegation in January 1962, but the government maintained its previous stand. In the 1962 elections, Congress secured 157 seats.[162] The percentage of rural vote decreased by small margins. Yet 'in West Bengal, Communists have consistently secured a larger vote in urban constituencies than in the countryside' (Weiner and Field 1977: 23). The regularisation of squatters' colonies started from 1963.[163] The Centre had launched a 'Scheme for Providing Tools and Implements for Partially Rehabilitated Displaced Non-agriculturist Families in West Bengal',[164] but complained, 'we are finding it difficult to process proposals, regarding the development of colonies, in the absence of information concerning those colonies, which the state government had been asked to furnish in the pro-forma prescribed by us'.[165] The sudden influx in 1964 disrupted resettlement and rehabilitation work, which resumed after the electoral result of 1962.[166]

The refugees coming in a riot year officially were liable to get assistance from the government. But, the refugee organisations demanded due rights in a more composed way (Sengupta 1997: 53–54). The Centre allotted a budget, but the amount was not enough to get them permanently rehabilitated (Singha 1995: 7). After the major riot of 1964, the communists opined that the Congress government should allow them to cross the border without any more hassle and accept them wholeheartedly in this country (Majumdar and Dutta 2014, XIII: 535). Almost 8 lakh refugees migrated in this phase, but the state government hardly extended hands to support them (Biswas 2005, IV: 767). The 'Save Pakistan Minorities [1]'*Paschimbanga Bidhansabhae Danga Bisoye Somnath Lahirir Boktrita'*, in Manju Kumar Majumdar, Bhanudeb Dutta (ed.), *Banglar Communist Andoloner Anusandhan* (in Bengali), Vol. XIII, Manisha, Kolkata, 2014, p. 535

Committee' was formed by UCRC in the wake of the development. They emphatically reiterated the demand of 'applying economic blockade against Pakistan and safe migration of the minorities of East Pakistan to India',[167] and said that a 'strong and firm policy should be adopted by the Government against Pakistan'.[168] Political negotiations between two countries soured again from 1965, which aggravated through the conflict on 'enclaves' or *chhit-mahals* (Schendel 2002: 124). The Government of India was again forced to allow those refugees to enter India without valid 'travel documents'.[169] The state of West Bengal was actually going through a process of radicalisation. The changes in the correlation of political forces at the national level and the ideology, strategy and tactics adopted by the left finally got a response.[170] Congress failed to win a clear-cut majority for the first time in the fourth general election of 1967.[171] The upshot was the emergence of the United Front combination of 14 political parties, representing a broad ideological spectrum.[172] The United Front government came to power twice in West Bengal in the years 1967 and 1968. It: (i) supported UCRC and 'formally approved' its '18-point programme' (Irani 1968: 6); (ii) organised a 'State Rehabilitation Committee', placed a report and recommended 11 major suggestions against policies of the Congress government[173]; (iii) opposed the discriminatory approach towards the 'residuary policy' of the Centre; demanded Rs. 250 crores again for rehabilitation of all categories of refugees, having taken shelter in different establishments to complete rehabilitation (Biswas 2005, IV: 768); and (iv) placed a total of 32 demands to the Centre—the refugee crisis was one of them. The new state government had set up another 'Fact-Finding Committee' to find out the real magnitude of the problem.[174] The committee ceased to function in colonies and refugee centres of different districts. Even after the government collapsed, they recommended some modifications.

A state convention of the leftist parties was organised from 6–9 December 1968. The chief foci were on the problem of rehabilitation, and the probable role of UCRC in organising political movements for refugees. They pointed out that though the refugee situation remained almost the same, the Congress government, led by Indira Gandhi in the Centre, had declared that the problem of refugees had been solved. The Central Government claimed to have spent Rs. 260.34 crores for refugee rehabilitation in East Indian states like West Bengal, Assam, Tripura, Bihar and Orissa.[175] In West Bengal, 21.88 crores were allotted as the last instalment of the total budget. The state Congress government spent a huge amount of money in the election of 1967 and wasted the rest of the amount in such projects, which were not related to their traditional professions (Biswas 2005, IV: 766). There were 10,000 refugees staying in deserted camps. The United Front government sketched a plan for them and demanded 6.36 crores from the Centre, yet nothing happened on that front. Rather, the Centre was planning to demolish those camps. The permanent liability (PL) camps were suffering in various ways; 27,000 refugees were residing there, but the cash amount did not increase. Some refugees had been denied dole and other rehabilitation benefits in the name of screening, and 45,000 refugees were left in private accommodations as the government sent them eviction notices to leave the premises (Biswas 2005, IV: 766). Almost 50,000 applications were lying in the government rehabilitation office from different social groups and professions. The state was not initiating the establishment of small-scale industries, government-aided cooperative schemes, variant schemes, non-contributory colonies, etc.[176] The plot-holders in the squatters' colonies were facing constant harassment in tracing out their documents of possession. In the mid-term election of 1969, Congress came down from 127 seats to only 55, whereas the communists captured 110 out of 280 seats (Basu 1974: 41). The United Front government came into power and could implement some ideas. Congress pointed out that its defeat was a result of the refugee issues,[177] but the desperate state Coalition government could not save the state, as none of these governments lasted for more than 13 months. The President's rule was operative in West Bengal for most of 1968, 1970 and 1971, though it failed to arrest the deterioration of the political and economic situation (Brass and Franda 1973: 183). It became more complicated in 1971 when approximately seven million migrants crossed the borders (Samad 1983: 2). The Centre finally decided that the refugees who migrated after 25 March 1971 from Bangladesh would be treated as 'foreigners'. This trend started right from the 1970s (Singha 1995: 7). The Indira Congress ignored all recommendations made by the United Front government. The Coalition government in 1971 was not eager or ready to solve the refugee issues, either. While UCRC consistently was working on the refugee front, the communist party was looking at the crises involving other downtrodden social classes (Biswas 2005, IV: 769–70).

In 1972, Congress formed the State Ministry again under Siddhartha Sankar Ray, as Chief Minister. UCRC forced him to prepare a 'Master Plan', but the Centre was not ready to accept it.[178] Siddhartha Ray instructed that the execution of the 'Master Plan for Rehabilitation of Displaced Persons in West Bengal' should be finished within the next five years (1973–1978). The Centre set up a 'working group' to assess the magnitude of the problem, initiated by UCRC. The process of providing economic rehabilitation had started from 1981, by distributing *arpanpatras* or land titles to the refugees.[179] The correlation between the roles of UCRC behind the left orientation of the refugees and their successful organisational demands was evident. The political struggle of the refugee groups challenged the theory of systematic hegemonisation behind a slow and continuous evolution of the left political idiom (Chatterjee 2012: 20). The grievances of refugee have-nots became a major issue in leftist politics and a factor behind radicalisation of politics in West Bengal. The squatters' movement became violent, and it led to the state's armed response. The CPI increasingly invented strategies for violation of laws. The refugees became ambivalent, and they were actually not sure about which political party they should opt for or what would finally benefit them (Mandal 2011: 203–7). The Congress government had its own inherent handicap. It was suffering from resource crunch to provide Central assistance to the refugees. In urban spaces, communist strength was not based on any particular caste or community. The refugees constituted almost one-fourth of the population and they apparently voted for the communists overwhelmingly, which was a classic example of 'uprooted and declassed individuals supporting an extreme party in accordance with the model put forth by the proponents of the concept of mass society' (Ghosh 2013: 44). The failure of the rehabilitation policies proved advantageous to the CPI.

Surprisingly, after the leftist government came to power, it simply refused to recognise that the party workers contributed to their organisation (Byapari 1421: 166–67). UCRC first came up with the idea of the settlement of the Bengali refugees in Marichjhhanpi. They submitted a memorandum to Dr B. C. Roy with statistics stating that the government might offer to settle at least 6,875 families there in a total area of 65.6 square kilometres and 3,300 families of fishermen in 12,000 acres of land. Dr B. C. Roy also agreed, as the government could locate 5,000 bighas of lands in the Marichjhhanpi Island by then. At an All India Refugee Conference organised in the Mana Camp in 1975, a few communist leaders—including Ram Chatterjee, Kripa Sindhu Saha and Jomburao Dhoute from Forward Block—promised to bring the refugees back to West Bengal (Pal 2009: 35–36). Manoranjan Byapari remembered that Jyoti Basu promised the refugee leaders of Mana Camp on 25 January 1975 that if the communists rose to power in West Bengal, they would advocate settling them down to Marichjhhanpi.[180] After they came into power, a representation from Dandakaranya visited Jyoti Basu, the Chief Minister, regarding their wish to get legal permissions to be in Marichjhhanpi in the future (Bhattacharjee 2015: 212–15). Until March 1978, the leftists encouraged them with loads of promises to receive the refugees in West Bengal, if they decided to migrate (Byapari 2013: 218–19). About 30,000 lower-caste refugees of various inhospitable areas managed to sail to Marichjhhanpi, where cultivable wastelands were available. It was the northernmost-forested islands of the Sundarbans. But, the refugees were brutally evicted by the police force for violating the Forest Acts (Mallick 1999: 105). Asit Baran Thakur compared the refugee killings in Marichjjhanpi with genocide, as the innocent refugees became the recipients of the police torture (Asit Baran Thakur 2011: 12). It was a case of 'double betrayal' for them, and they were shattered (Jalais 2005: 1758). Probably it was their last sincere initiative, chiefly as a community, to settle down in West Bengal. How the left betrayed the refugees after coming into power was another story. Yet, the Marichjhhanpi incident demonstrated that the Bengali refugees had come to the dead end of their journey, and the rehabilitation work for them was never being satisfactory (Asit Baran Thakur 2011: 29–32).

The last episode

The Partition of India created refugees. 'Refugees' is a misnomer, because they were displaced people who considered their present habitat to be unsafe and insecure, and they hence shifted to the other side, which was their utopia of security and abundance. But the reality proved quite a contrast. Ironically, they were treated as 'outsiders' when they expected to be considered as brethren from the other part. They had to face discrimination and discouragement from the Central Government, and they found themselves unwelcome by their own linguistic community. Certain class-, caste- and region-based prejudices became manifest. Dominant political parties had played around with them and smaller ideologically orientated parties found a potential constituency in them. Betrayed by the nation-state they fought for and deserted by political parties, the desperate group of refuge-seeking people found themselves in an intensely helpless situation wherein they had to either perish or fight one last battle for survival. The struggle needed politicisation. Thus, the refugees organised and activated themselves politically. The leftist parties proved sympathetic, and their mode of struggle was in the right mode. Therefore, the organisation had a distinct leftist bias. UCRC had included two basic essences in the political movement of the refugees and other downtrodden classes: one, they had given birth to a political organisation comprised of all leftist, socialistic and communist parties, who used to fight separately and diversely with some common causes; and two, they declared agendas regardless of different classes and castes, provided them with a common platform, put them under one umbrella and tried to unite the whole refugee community.

UCRC started its struggle with a basic issue, relief and rehabilitation of the refugees, but shifted from these ideas and demands with the passing of time. After the gigantic influx of 1950, the Government of India set up a Commission of Enquiry 'to enquire into the exodus of the minorities of East Pakistan into India', when the purpose behind setting up of this Commission was 'to determine the causes of the influx of the refugees' (*udbastu agomonr karon nirdharon kora*), though the report never was published.[181] The leftists felt the need to organising a joint movement by including these new groups of unfortunate uprooted people, existing camp and colony refugees, to unite them. By the early 1950s, refugees of the squatters' colonies were rather stable, while the camp refugees fought with uncertainties. The colony refugees became the face of the UCRC's regular protest. They opted for anti-eviction struggle from early 1951 and compelled the government to change some of the provisions. From the mid-1950s, the UCRC and other similar refugee organisations started agitating about the legalisation of the squatted lands and colonies. They fought against the removal of the zamindari system and compelled the government to ban it in 1953, though they did not implement it strictly. Ajit Prasad Jain, the United Rehabilitation Minister, and the state government announced the legalisation of 149 colonies initially, then 175 and later 607 such colonies, out of their pressure. The city of Calcutta became a battleground in these decades, in which concepts of ownership of land played vital roles. There were many other factors behind these conflicts and undercurrents between Congress and the left, though the refugee issues often grabbed the limelight. The political trends revolved around their crises, which few political parties tried utilising to capture a foothold in the politics of Bengal. The refugees inspired the mobility of other downtrodden classes and became the key force in rehabilitation programmes planned by the Government.

The political strategy of the UCRC for conducting refugee movement was the method of *satyagraha* or *gherao*. This new pattern of protest became popular later as the 'leftist style of protest'. The refugees were gradually initiated into designing their own agenda, included their specific needs or demands, and came out with a secular outlook by the inclusion of the minority issues or Muslim returnees. They indeed set a trend of blocking roads and railway tracks, conducting the *amoron anashan* (hunger strike till death) and criticised the policy of the Congress, both in the Centre and the state. They first pointed out that the Centre did not have any plan to rehabilitate the refugee groups like they had for the West Pakistanis. They thought this community would go back once the socio-politico-economic situation in East Bengal normalised, and arranged temporary relief for them, but the communists not only united them—they made them prepared to get their due rights, though the West Bengalis later termed it as 'refugee culture' that itself had a derogatory connotation. The United Front government tried to implement all recommendations pointed out by UCRC. They asked for 179 crores from the Centre and appointed a 'Developmental Committee' for a neutral report. Looking at the leftist orientation of the refugees, the Congress supported some of their recommendations and published the report of the 'Working Group' appointed by them in 1975. The budget allocations on their resettlement in the fifth and sixth planning commissions were not significant, yet the emergence of refugees as a clear 'political force' was a bit dramatic in West Bengal. It became evident that it would be the refugee population which would determine who would capture power in the electoral politics of the state in the next decades. Since the Congress proved to be betrayer and left patronship of the refugees, it was evident that sooner or later, it was the left parties that would dominate the power politics in West Bengal. The floating refugee population supported only those political parties which had supported their cause of welfare, and in return, they helped those parties by turning into their potential vote banks to help them ascend to power, and even form the government. But on the ground level, the parties failed to land up as per their expectation at the end. The climax, however, was ironic. The left parties finally captured power in the state in 1977, which they did not relinquish for the next 35 years—but once they captured power, politics vis-à-vis the refugee cause shifted again. The Marichjhhanpi tragedy had shown that once in power, the left deserted the refugees who had voted them into power, showing some legal and environmental issues.

The portrayal of Bengali refugees as un-enterprising or lazy, and solely dependent on the government doles or initiatives had been repeatedly depicted in official documents over the next many decades after Partition, but there were huge flaws in the government policies and its implementation. The initiative of the refugees for self-rehabilitation was often ignored, too, because of their participation in state politics, through which they attempted to claim and reclaim their dues from their migrated states. The organisation of mass movement and violent protest had created their image as rebels and aggressive people as if they were anti-state, if not anti-social, and criminals. It overshadowed their constructive role in setting up colonies and other planned developmental work like the establishment of schools, colleges, libraries, health centres, parks or playgrounds within many newly built colonies and in the adjacent areas. Squatting was the first expression of their determination to create a new address in the migratory states. The government recognised the refugee colonies much later. In some cases, the third-generation refugees had to stand in the queue in the Relief and Rehabilitation Department to get a freehold title deed even in the late 1980s and for the regularisation of their colonies. But, these colonies survived as a pre-urban heart of the city where the thatched huts and bamboo-framed partitions with creeper linings were housing families yet to establish themselves in urban lives, denied of urban facilities including electricity, water, sanitation, but often sharing anti-Governmental political platforms to demand their minimum rights. So, the presence of the refugees in the city did not only ring the bell of caution against the complete breakdown of the urban system, but also added a history of cohesiveness whereby the people of completely rural backgrounds came and settled in the city, and contributed to the cultural pandemonium known as Calcutta urbanity. The refugees adopted the local language, culture and food habits, and they tried hard to create a new identity by imposing new essences on their culture and making an address in their lands of migration.

Notes

1 *Janajuddho Patrika*, 31 March 1943.
2 *Doshdishi*. 1314. A Journal in Bengali. Vol. 1, 44–45.
3 Sandip Bandyopadhyay. 2000. 'Millions Seeking Refuge: The Refugee Question in West Bengal'. In *Refugees in West Bengal: Institutional Processes and Contested Identities*, ed. Pradip Kumar Bose, 32–33. Calcutta: Calcutta Research Group.
4 Dwaipayan Bhattacharyya. 2011. 'Party Society, Its Consolidation and Crisis: Understanding Political Change in West Bengal'. In *Theorizing the Present: Essays for Partha Chatterjee*, ed. Anjan Ghosh, Tapati Guha Thakurta and Janki Nair, 226. New Delhi: Oxford University Press.
5 *Jagaran*, 23 January 1955.
6 '*Purbo Bangla Theke Agoto Bastuharader Proti Communist Partyr Dak: Basosthan, Khadhyo, Kaj o Jomir Jonyo Lorun*', 22 March 1950.
7 *AICC Papers*, File No. G-30/1947–48, NMML.
8 Prasanta Sengupta. 1985. 'The Congress Party in West Bengal: Politics, Patronage and Power'. In *Politics in West Bengal: Institutions, Processes and Problems*, ed. Rakahari Chatterji, 31. Calcutta: The World Press.
9 Interview with Shefalika Pathak, a retired headmistress from a Government school of Shahid Nagar Colony, who is from Netrokona, East Bengal. Interview taken on 27 August 2012 in Jadavpur, Kolkata.
10 *Hindustan Standard*, 31 July 1947.
11 *AICC Papers*, File No. G-62/1947, NMML.
12 *Amrita Bazar Patrika*, 27 June 1948.
13 *Amrita Bazar Patrika*, 19 July 1948.
14 *AICC Papers*, File No. CL14D-1946/Pt. II, NMML.
15 *Rajendra Prasad Papers Collection*, File No. 1-B/1947, Vol. 1, on Bengal Boundary Commission 1947, NAI.
16 Interview with Jolly Bagchi, a retired librarian by profession. Her family migrated from East Bengal just after Partition, and became involved in the leftist politics from her school days. The interview was taken on 6 September 2012 in Selimpur, West Bengal.

17 *Uchchhed Uchchhed: Dharabahik Omanobikotar Khondochitro.* 2003. Shalti Research Group, 12–13. Kolkata: Kamb.
18 *The Statesman,* 27 November 1947.
19 *Amrita Bazar Patrika,* 21 March 1948.
20 *Amrita Bazar Patrika,* 30 June 1948.
21 Interview with Bamacharan Mukherjee, the councillor of the Shahid Nagar Colony area. Interview taken on 26 November 2010 in Kolkata, West Bengal.
22 Interview with Satyajit Choudhury, a retired professor and a leftist activist. Interview taken on 13 February 2014 in Naihati, West Bengal.
23 *AICC Papers,* II Installment, File No. 1786 (Pt. II), PB-3 (1), Bengal, 1948, NMML.
24 *Ananda Bazar Patrika,* 4 October 1948.
25 *AICC Papers,* II Installment, File No. 1786 (Pt. II), PB-3 (1), Bengal, 1948, NMML.
26 Arun Deb. 2000. 'The UCRC: It's Role in Establishing the Rights of Refugee Squatters in Calcutta'. In *Refugees in West Bengal: Institutional Processes and Contested Identities,* ed. Pradip Kumar Bose, 66. Calcutta: Calcutta Research Group.
27 *'Bastuhara Karmaparishader Agami Sommelone Amader Kaj'.* A Leaflet by Pradeshik Bastuhara Kendra, Pashchimbanga Pradeshik Songathoni Committee, Bharater Communist Party, 1 November 1950.
28 *Ananda Bazar Patrika,* 17 January 1949.
29 *Hindu Mahasabha Papers,* Subject File No. C-177, NMML.
30 *AICC Papers,* II Installment, File No. 1786 (Pt. II), PB-3 (1), Bengal, 1948, NMML.
31 *Ananda Bazar Patrika,* 12 February 1949.
32 *Ananda Bazar Patrika,* 8 February 1949.
33 *Manjil,* 31 July 1949.
34 *Manjil,* 31 July 1949.
35 *The West Bengal Weekly,* 21 May 1950.
36 *WBLA Debates,* Vol. VI, 1 June 1952, p. 27.
37 *'Purbo Bangla Theke Agoto Bastuharader Proti Communist Partyr Dak: Basosthan, Khadhyo, Kaj o Jomir Jonyo Lorun',* 22 March 1950.
38 Editorial. 'Bastuharader Oikyoboddho Korun', *Swadhinota,* 6 April 1950.
39 *Pradeshik Bastuhara Kendrer Tinti Circular,* 12 November 1950.
40 *'Bastuharadiger Sebar Jonyo Protyek Colony te Relief Committee o Swechhasevobdol Gothon Korun'.* A Leaflet by Pradeshik Bastuhara Kendra. Pashchimbanga Pradeshik Songathoni Committee, Bharater Communist Party, 10 December 1950.
41 *'Bastuhara Karmaparishader Agami Sommelone Amader Kaj'.* A Leaflet by Pradeshik Bastuhara Kendra. Pashchimbanga Pradeshik Songathoni Committee, Bharater Communist Party, 1 November 1950.
42 *Agami Bastuhara Protinidhi Sammelan o Amader Kaj,* 4 December 1950.
43 *Punarbasan,* No. 1. 1984, p. 2.
44 *The West Bengal Weekly,* 3 July 1950.
45 File No. 601–603/F-6/50, NAI.
46 A Leaflet by Bastuhara Kendra. Pashchimbanga Pradeshik Songathoni Committee. Bharater Communist Party. Circular No. 2, 1 November 1950.
47 File No. RT-1483/32 (Dup.) (P.F), Part-III, IB, WBSA.
48 File No. 321/22 (1), Sl. No. 45/1922, IB, WBSA.
49 File No. 321/22 (K.W), Sl. No. 46/1922, Part-V, Folder No. 3, IB, WBSA.
50 File No. 321/22 (K.W), Sl. No. 46/1922, Part-V, Folder No. 3, IB, WBSA.
51 File No. 518B/ 26, Sl. No. 84/1926, IB, WBSA.
52 *B. C. Roy Papers,* Printed Material, File No. 5, NMML.
53 *WBLA Debates,* Vol. V, 1951, pp. 96–97.
54 *Ananda Bazar Patrika,* 31 August 1951.
55 It parodied the current terminology for government requisition of properties; *hukumdakhal* meant acquisition by order. Uditi Sen. 2015. 'Building Bijoygarh: A Microhistory of Refugee Squatting in Calcutta'. In *Calcutta: The Stormy Decades,* ed. Tanika Sarkar and Sekhar Bandyapadhyay, 406. New Delhi: Social Science Press.

56 File No. 321/22 (K.W), Sl. No. 46/1922, Folder No. 5, IB, WBSA.
57 The Shaheed Minar (Martyrs Monument) was formerly known as Ochterlony Monument, which was erected in 1828 in memory of Major-General Sir David Ochterlony. In August 1969, it was rededicated to the memory of the martyrs of the Indian freedom movement.
58 File No. 321/22 (K.W), Sl. No. 46/1922, Part-V, Folder No. 3, IB, WBSA.
59 Samir Kumar Das. 2003. 'State Responses to the Refugee Crisis: Relief and Rehabilitation in the East'. In *Refugees and the State: Practices of Asylum and Care in India, 1947–2000*, ed. Ranabir Samaddar, 146–47. New Delhi: Sage.
60 Samir Kumar Das. 2003. 'State Responses to the Refugee Crisis: Relief and Rehabilitation in the East'. In *Refugees and the State: Practices of Asylum and Care in India, 1947–2000*, ed. Ranabir Samaddar, 146–47. New Delhi: Sage.
61 File No. 321/22, Sl. No. 18/1922, Part-VI, IB, WBSA.
62 *Hindustan Standard*, 12 July 1952.
63 *WBLA Debates*, Vol. VI, No. 2, 1952, p. 792.
64 File No. 321/22 (K.W), Sl. No. 46/1922, Folder No. 3, IB, WBSA.
65 File No. 321/22 (K.W), Sl. No. 46/1922, Folder No. 1, IB, WBSA.
66 File No. 321/22 (K.W), Sl. No. 46/1922, Folder No. 1, IB, WBSA.
67 File No. 321/22 (K.W), Sl. No. 46/1922, Folder No. 1, IB, WBSA.
68 *Bastuharader adhikar o punorbason*. Pratham Sadharon Nirbachaner Dike, 1952.
69 Bharoter Communist Party, Pashchimbanga POC. *Sadharon Nirbachan Samporke Prastab*, 2 December 1950.
70 *Bastuhara Samasyar Samadhan*, 1952.
71 File No. 321/22, Part-III, Sl. No. 41/1922, IB, WBSA.
72 *Amrita Bazar Patrika*, 2 August 1952.
73 File No. 321/22, Sl. No. 18/1922, Part-VI, IB, WBSA.
74 *Hindustan Standard*, 14 July 1952.
75 *Hindustan Standard*, 15 July 1952.
76 File No. 1483/32 (Dup) (P.F), Part-1, IB, WBSA.
77 *Swadhinata*, 19 November 1953.
78 *Swadhinata*, 12 November 1953.
79 Mohit Moitra. 1957. 'Beporoa Jomi Acquire Kora r Nitir Protirodh'. In *Sammilito Bamponthi Nirbachoni Committee_r Kormosuchi*.
80 Mohit Moitra. 1957. 'Sankhaloghu Samasya'. In *Sammilito Bamponthi Nirbachoni Committee_r Kormosuchi*.
81 File No. 1483/32, Sl. No. 7, IB, WBSA.
82 Prasanta Ray. 2015. *Namer Sandhane*, 8–9. Transcription of Professor Susovan Chandra Sarkar Memorial Lecture.
83 *The Statesman*, 5 February 1953.
84 *WBLA Debates*, Seventieth Session (Budget), 1953, p. 135.
85 File No. 1483/32, (Dup) (P.F), Part-I, IB, WBSA.
86 *Amrita Bazar Patrika*, 8 March 1953.
87 File No. 165Z/24, Sl. No. 70/1924, Part-V, IB, WBSA.
88 File No. RT-1041/16, Sl. No. 44/1916, IB, WBSA.
89 File No. 218 B/26, Sl. No. 84/1926, IB, WBSA.
90 File No. 1482/32, IB, WBSA.
91 File No. 359/29, Sl. No. 144/29, IB, WBSA.
92 Mentioned in the history sheet of Amritendu Mukherjee. File No. 303/39 (No serial number available), IB, WBSA.
93 File No. 1652/2A, Part V, Sl. No. 70/1924, IB, WBSA.
94 B. S. Guha. 1959. 'Studies in Social Tensions Among the Refugees from Eastern Pakistan'. Memoir No. 1, Department of Anthropology, Government of India, Calcutta, p. x.
95 *WBLA Debates*, Vol. X, No. 1, 1954, p. 230.
96 *Hindustan Standard*, 19 November 1954.
97 *WBLA Debates*, Vol. X, No. 2, 1954, p. 118.

98 *WBLA Debates*, Vol. IX, No. 3, 1954, p. 270.
 99 File No. RHAE 18 (2)/54, RHA Branch, NAI.
100 *Hindustan Standard*, 16 November 1954.
101 File No. 321/22 (1), Sl. No. 45/1922, IB, WBSA.
102 File No. RHR 14 (2)/55, RHR Branch, NAI.
103 *WBLA Debates,* Vol. IX, No. 3, 1956, p. 419 and Vol. XV, No. 2, 1956, p. 343.
104 *WBLA Debates,* Vol. IX, No. 2, 1954, p. 1222.
105 File No. 321/22, Sl. No. 41/1922, Part-III, IB, WBSA.
106 *The West Bengal Weekly*, 22 October 1955.
107 *WBLA Debates,* Vol. IX, No. 3, 1955, p. 89.
108 File No. 1483/32, (Dup) (P.F), Part-I, IB, WBSA.
109 Mohit Moitra. 1957. 'Bastuharader Kormosangthan o Susthu Punorbason Dabi'. In *Sammilito Bamponthi Nirbachoni Committee_r Kormosuchi*.
110 *Diwan Chaman Lall Papers*, II Instalment, Papers and Correspondence Regarding Refugees and Their rehabilitation, 1946–1955, Subject File No. 5, NMML.
111 *Renuka Ray Papers*, Subject File No. 4, NMML.
112 File No. 321/22 (1), Sl. No. 45/1922, IB, WBSA.
113 File No. 321/22, Sl. No. 46/1922, Part-V, IB, WBSA.
114 File No. 321/22, Sl. No. 46/1922, Part-V, IB, WBSA.
115 File No. 321/22, Sl. No. 46/1922, Part-V, IB, WBSA.
116 File No. 321/22, Sl. No. 46/1922, Part V, IB, WBSA.
117 File No. 321/22 (1), Sl. No. 45/1922, IB, WBSA.
118 Mohit Moitra. 1957. 'Beporoa Jomi Acquire Kora r Nitir Protirodh'. In *Sammilito Bamponthi Nirbachoni Committee_r Kormosuchi*.
119 *WBLA Debates,* Vol. IX, No. 2, 1956, p. 187.
120 Mohit Moitra. 1957. 'Worksite Camp e Bastuharader Durdosha'. In *Sammilito Bamponthi Nirbachoni Committee_r Kormosuchi*.
121 File No. 321/22, Sl. No. 46/1922, Part-V, IB, WBSA.
122 *Hindustan Standard*, 2 February 1956.
123 *Report of the Administration 1957–58*, West Bengal Land and Revenue Department, p. 8.
124 File No. 321/22, Sl. No. 18/1922, Part-VI, IB, WBSA.
125 Mohit Moitra. 1957. 'Worksite Camp e Bastuharader Durdosha'. In *Sammilito Bamponthi Nirbachoni Committee_r Kormosuchi*.
126 *Rajyo Bidhansabha e Udbastu Tran Doptorer Byay-Boradder Prostaber Upor Bankim Mukherjee r Boktobyo*, 14 December 1957.
127 Samar Mukherjee. 2001. 'Rehabilitation of the Bengali Refugees in Eastern and North-Eastern India: An Unfinished Struggle'. In *Refugees and Human Rights: Social and Political Dynamics of Refugee Problem in Eastern and North-Eastern India*, ed. Sanjay K. Roy, 137. Jaipur and New Delhi: Rawat Publications.
128 *Rajyo Bidhansabha e Udbastu Tran Doptorer Byay-Boradder Prostaber Upor Bankim Mukherjee r Boktobyo*, 14 December 1957.
129 *Bastuhara Sangram*.
130 'Present position in Mana and gravity of situation' by Asoka Gupta. *Asoka Gupta Papers*, File No. 3, NMML.
131 *WBLA Debates,* Vol. XVIII, No. 2, 1957, pp. 3–5.
132 *M. N. Saha Papers*, Subject File No. 6, NMML.
133 *Jugantar*, 14 May 1957.
134 File No. 329/27, Sl. No. 13/192, Part-VII, IB, WBSA.
135 *WBLA Debates*, 24 August 1956, p. 369.
136 *Rajyo Bidhansabha e Udbastu Tran Doptorer Byay-Boradder Prostaber Upor Bankim Mukherjee r Boktobyo*, 14 December 1957.
137 File No. 854/30, Sl. No. 147/1930, IB, WBSA.
138 *WBLA Debates,* Seventeenth Session, 1957, p. 9.
139 *Jugantar*, 12 April 1957.
140 File No. 303/39, Sl. No. 1, IB, WBSA; *Ananda Bazar Patrika*, 29 July 1957.

141 *Jugantar*, 6 March 1958.
142 File No. 7/25/57 Judi 1, Judicial I Section, NAI.
143 File No. 28/8/58 Judi 1, Judicial I Section, NAI.
144 File No. 329/27, Sl. No. 13/192, Part-VII, IB, WBSA.
145 *WBLA Debates*, Vol. XVIII, No. 3, 1957, p. 462.
146 *WBLA Debates*, Vol. XVIII, No. 1, 1957, p. 41.
147 File No. 329/27, Sl. No. 13/192, Part-VII, IB, WBSA.
148 File No. 854/30, Sl. No. 147/1930, IB, WBSA.
149 *Swadhinata*, 18 March 1958.
150 *The Statesman*, 29 March 1958.
151 *B. C. Roy Papers*, Printed Material, File No. 12, NMML.
152 File No. 4/2/57, Poll-II, Political II Section, NAI.
153 File No. 165Z/24, Sl. No. 23/1924, Part-V, IB, WBSA.
154 File No. 95/40, Sl. No. 23/1942, IB, WBSA.
155 File No. 166-26 (1), Sl. No. L 1336, IB, WBSA.
156 Samar Mukherjee. 2003. 'Rehabilitation of the Bengali Refugees'. In *Refugees and the State: Practices of Asylum and Care in India, 1947–2000*, ed. Ranabir Samaddar, 138. New Delhi: Sage.
157 File No. 8/3/63-Rah-II, Reh-II Branch, NAI; *Ananda Bazar Patrika*, 13 June 1960.
158 *WBLA Debates*, Vol. XXX, No. 2, 1961, p. 32.
159 *Swadhinata*, 4 April 1961.
160 File No. 329-27, Sl. No. 131/1927, IB, WBSA.
161 File No. 329-27 (Part-XI), Sl. No. 131/27, IB, WBSA.
162 Amitava Ray. 1985. 'The Left in West Bengal: Electoral and Mobilisation Strategies, 1947–1967'. In *Politics in West Bengal: Institutions, Processes and Problems*, ed. Rakhahari Chatterji, 72. Calcutta: The World Press.
163 *WBLA Debates*, Vol. XXXV, No. 1, 1963, p. 145.
164 File No. 2 (2)/63-Rahab-II, Rehabilitation Dept., NAI.
165 File No. 20 (15)/16-Rahab-II, Rehabilitation Dept., NAI.
166 *WBLA Debates*, Vol. XXXIX, No. 2, 1964, p. 817.
167 File No. 95-40, Sl. No. 23/1942, IB, WBSA.
168 File No. 422-40, Sl. No. 203, IB, WBSA.
169 *WBLA Debates*, Vol. LXL, No. 3, 1965, pp. 637–38.
170 Apurba Mukhopadhyay. 1985. 'The Left in West Bengal: Government and Movement, 1967–82'. In *Politics in West Bengal: Institutions, Processes and Problems*, ed. Rakhahari Chatterji, 81. Calcutta: The World Press.
171 File No. P1/102/39/70, Pak-1 Registry, NAI.
172 Dharama Vira. 1967. *West Bengal: Two Years of Turmoil*, Sunday, *Dharma Vira Papers*, Printed Material, Sl. No. 4, NMML.
173 *WBLA Debates*, Vol. XLIV, 1967, p. 491.
174 *Jugantar*, 17 January 1968.
175 File No. 329-27 (Part-XI), Sl. No. 133/27, IB, WBSA.
176 *Ananda Bazar Patrika*, 1 September 1969.
177 *AICC Papers*, II Instalment, File No. 2268 Pt. II, NMML.
178 *A Master Plan for Rehabilitation of Displaced Persons in West Bengal*, Refugee Relief and Rehabilitation Department, Government of West Bengal, August 1972, p. 9.
179 *Sibnath Banerjee Papers*, Subject File No. 129, NMML.
180 Jhuma Sen. 2015. 'Reconstructing Marichjhapi: From Margins and Memories of Migrant Lives'. In *Partition: The Long Shadow*, ed. Urvashi Butalia, 103–4. New Delhi: Viking-Penguin.
181 *Commissioner Prashnamala Puron Samporke Nirdesh* (Guidelines for the Commission), School of Women Studies, Jadavpur University, Kolkata.

5
POLITICS AS DEFENCE
Activation of refugees in Assam and Tripura

The migration issues, related policies and polities were often contradictory, confusing and complex in the whole of post-1947 Northeast India. After Partition, the region became a part of the Indian confederacy. The idea of a linguistically drawn state and refugee policy was imposed upon it by the Centre (Nag 1990: Introduction), but the policies for the northeastern states were ad hoc and visibly different from those for the west. The policies changed every time, as per the altered situation. Assam had a settled Bengali population with whom the host Assamese had been engaged in a bitter socio-cultural and political rivalry for almost a century (Joyeeta Sharma 2012: Introduction). So, the transformation patterns and refugee concerns that generated tension in the post-Partition period in the Assamese society were different from other refugee-absorbent states of the eastern borders (Hussain 1993: 165). In West Bengal and Tripura, because of the cultural similarity and 'emotional bond of language', the Bengali refugees were never seen as the 'irritants' that they were in Assam (Dutta 2013: 103). In Assam, the Assamese were eager to get rid of the Bengali population and were satisfied by the transfer of its Bengali-speaking district Sylhet to Pakistan in 1947.[1] Ironically, the re-entry of the resident Bengalis in form of refugees was strongly resented by the hosts and it inflamed the conflict more.[2] The profile of the *Sylheti bhadralok* did not match with the stereotypical refugees. They were not like the other type of displaced persons; they used to have relatives both in Calcutta and Brahmaputra valley. Thus, they rather always tried to resist and deny their refugee identities (Dutta 2013: 91). The real refugees chose to settle down in Barak valley, primarily because of the linguistic bonding and cultural similarities between the two geographical locations. The 'Bengali conspiracy' theory during the colonial times in dislodging the Assamese from their rightful place gained solid ground in post-Partition Assam, chiefly among the Assamese intelligentsia (Joyeeta Sharma 2012: 290).

From the pre-Partition days, Assam was burning from the Bengali migration to such extent that the state had to pass the Foreigner Act in 1946 to prevent migration.[3] After Partition, the language issue posed further challenges to the existing issues of conflicts. It was aggravated by the resentment of the Bengalis of Cachar for linguistic intervention by the dominant Assamese domiciles in their own land. The 'official language movement' of 1960 and the 'Medium of Instruction Movement' of 1972 were used as tools to establish the hegemony of the Assamese language, which was permeated by a strong anti-Bengali sentiment. The political agitations organised by the Bengalis for their linguistic identity culminated in a long-drawn struggle to establish cultural supremacy and a community distinction between the hosts and the refugees (Dutta 2012: 218–19). In the politics, the concern around languages was not the only focal point of discussions and debates for political parties and other public forums. The Assamese claim was that ideology played a decisive role in emergence of the conflict between the two major linguistic communities.[4] They outlined the agitation by shaping it up as a social movement (Hussain 1993: 166). Culturally and linguistically, Cachar had been integral more to East Bengal than Assam. Surma-Barak valley or Srihatta-Cachar used to be mentioned together in the literary sources that represented a singular and definite Bengali identity of the region.[5] The old Bengali residents and new refugee settlers of Cachar were vehement about their linguistic and cultural rights (Kar 1999: 60–63), and this led to acrimonious political rivalries that resulted in a grave political crisis that was perpetual and unending (Das 1982: 25).

Unlike other refugee-absorbent states, the Bengali refugees never felt like 'rejected people' in the princely state of Tripura. The characteristic feature of post-Partition communitarian crisis and recurrent conflicts arose from the establishment of the political and cultural dominance of the Bengalis, in form of refugees, over the domicile ethnic tribals. The context of sheltering the Bengali migrants, the refugees, was unique in Tripura. The Royal Administration tried to accommodate them within the pre-Partition political structure. The refugees left their land, property, society and identity for such a cause of which many of them were never a part, and most of the downtrodden families were not even aware of the real reasons why they left their *desh*. So, after crossing the international border, they became desperate in grabbing a piece of land, to recreate their world in a new land. The educated middle-class refugees made use of their education, political awareness and training to exercise power in society, and they earned respectable places in the socio-cultural milieu of the state. They could situate themselves well within a new political framework and gave birth to a political structure in Tripura which was different from West Bengal or Assam. Being agriculturists, the lower-class/caste refugees used their indigenous knowledge in the production system to get a hold on the economy. But, these two categories of power and land-hungry refugees started marginalising the tribals in their own lands. The tribals were not educated or enlightened, and were not aware of their due rights. Naturally, they were not in a position to demand anything from the state. The Bengalis first grabbed plains lands and then looked at the hills for resettlement.

When the refugees started encroaching the towns, the tribals shifted towards villages. In the end, the Bengalis even targeted the *jhum tillas* at the hills. The tribals were initially confined in their societal practices, but circumspectly realised that they were pushed to the edge. Interestingly after few decades of Partition, the Bengalis established them as *jati* and the tribals became *upojati* (Bhattacharyya 2002: 17–19). The Liberation War of 1971 was the last blow on the tribals when Tripura sheltered huge numbers of *mukti joddhas* (freedom fighters) and other frightened migrants. Looking at the internal rifts between the two wings of Pakistan and their insecure socio-economic and religious positions in East Pakistan, most of the Hindus stayed back. This wave confirmed the permanent presence of Bengalis and imposition of their preferences on the agriculture, politics, economy and culture of the state.

The idea of 'refugee identity' was redefined in the federal structure of post-Partition India. As a key political party, Congress headed the Centre and most of the states after 1947, including Assam and Tripura. As per the preconditions mentioned in Partition proceedings, the nation-state had to take responsibility in helping with relocation and resettlement of the migrants. But in reality, the Centre and states bargained hard to decide who would take how much of the responsibilities of the floating population. In Assam and Tripura, the Bengali refugees had to put them in front of the domiciles, though the nature of conflict was different. Assam suffered the most because of its complicated socio-political-religious structures. It dealt with two crucial and troublesome issues over the complexities regarding religion and language. Assam had to decide how to deal with the linguistic majority and minority communities, after experiencing agitations over the linguistic identity. Both ideologically and in practice, the Brahmaputra and Surma valleys were against each other. Time and again, it was reflected in the nature of their political demands, support of political parties and techniques of conducting movements. The hill people or the tribals slowly got involved in it, too. In Tripura, the crisis was derived out of the cultural imposition of the Bengalis over the domiciles, the tribals. Communist ideologies established a strong base in Tripura long before Partition, yet the tribals had to fight with new political ideologies with the coming up of the refugees. Like in West Bengal, the refugees first tried to communicate their crisis to the Congress. Gradually, they shifted from their earlier stand, and collaborated and corroborated with the leftist parties with some local political groups, to launch a united struggle against the Congress. The communists introduced the concept of mass movement in Tripura. The leaders hailing from East Bengal convinced both the communities to trust them. The communists were vigorous in bringing political awareness within tribals and refugees (Bhattacharyya 1999: 325). But their role and contributions to address the crises was often treated as a state issue. Their efforts to highlight the demands of tribals and non-tribals could not acquire enough attention in all India politics. The alteration in the demographic pattern of the refugees and tribals led to a new power equation and control of the issue of political hegemony in Tripura. It was constantly threatened by another set of crises regarding the ownership of lands.

With this background, this chapter attempts to understand the emergence and diversification of the refugee political movements in Assam and Tripura. It seeks to explore the root causes of refugee agitations, the nature of strategies of their political movements and the forms of political leadership in both the states. Like Assam, the tradition of recruiting the Bengalis as 'colonial elites' had been a practice in Tripura, and hence, it used to have a strong control over the job market. This chapter attempts to investigate whether it was the powerful role of the colonial Bengali elites which paved the way for refugee political movements in Assam and Tripura. In the new constitutional system of India, community participation in politics or treating the percentages as potential vote banks became crucial factors—and in such format of politics and form of representation, the Bengalis could win over to be the 'ruling community' in Tripura. The popular explanation for defining the reasons behind the demographic upheaval which led to a drastic change in the princely state after Partition was putting the Bengali refugees as villains, as they had taken everything from the poor, simple, illiterate domicile tribals. Established ideas about the state through the prism of secondary sources were often simplification of the cause-and-effect version of the community relationships. The vernacular sources elaborated this theory more by arguing; the shift was because of the continual refugee influx for decades. The migrants became the deciding factor or backbone of the state, and the tribals lost their land, habitat, culture and ethnic identity, but inherent complexities behind this alteration were seldom addressed or explored, and it also failed to grab attention of the researchers. This chapter aims to interrogate the established idea that the declining position of the tribals was commensurate to the advent of the Bengalis after 1947. It argues that both the refugees and ethnic tribals were victims of Partition politics in Tripura—only the nature of their alienation and reasons for marginalisation were different. It was a parallel fight of the Bengalis and tribals to establish their claims in the same land. The state, however, supported the refugees, recognised their crisis, made policies, accommodated and rehabilitated them as they migrated from their homelands out of a compulsion created by Partition. So, it was the Bengalis within the two competing, deprived and dispossessed communities, who finally could win the race in Tripura, due to the policies of the nation-state and its vote-bank politics.

Post-colonial nation building saw the assertion of dominance by the majority community and persecution of minorities. One method of building nation-states, as an exclusive domain of the majority, was to innovate devices to convert a section of citizens into the 'other' and render them as either stateless or without rights. The northeastern part of the Bengal borderland experienced an acute form of such a crisis which continues until this date. It did not arise out of the regular conflicts between the Assamese and Bengalis or tribals and Bengalis in each of the states, respectively. The main problem was that the issues of conflicts were not confined to any particular matter in question; it rather touched every single socio-political-economic and religious concern. This chapter tries to find out how the refugees first became a decisive factor in determining the fate of the political parties and aims to examine if their huge numbers was the reason to question their identity and eliminate them later by pointing out their legitimacy. When the Centre tried to detach itself from the idea of 'citizen-refugee' in the 1950s and 1960s, there was violent dispassion between the Assamese 'nationalist' or 'ethnic hill tribes' and the Bengalis, as the refugees were seen as 'outsiders' and 'foreigners' (Dutta 2013: 92). Despite the characterisation of the Bengali refugees as being 'undeserving' of receiving the gifts of relief and rehabilitation, their position was crucial in the changed societies and in the structure of vote-bank politics. They became an important political force at the national level. Yet, the 'Bengali conspiracy' theory remained one of the favourite theories for explaining the reasons for crises, economic-political wedge locks and whipping up nationalist passions in these states; however, the role of the Indian state or major political parties in power at the Centre and the states, on catering to the crisis in Assam and Tripura, had never been categorically mentioned.

Assam: colonial policies and communities

Migration had always troubled Assam and acted as a strong force for socio-cultural, economic and political changes, wherein 'language' became the issue of conflicts and contradictions (Chakrabarty 1989: 19). Bengal had been the first region conquered by the British,[6] who annexed and ruled Assam from 1824 as a part of the Bengal Presidency (Goswami 1997: 13). Since Bengal was in contact with the British already, importing functionaries from Bengal was the easiest option for the Raj. Hence, the British administrators deprived the local eligible people in Assam (Gosselink 1994: 87–88). In 1836, Bengali was declared as 'the language of court and office' on the pretext that Assamese was nothing but a dialect of Bengali (Barpujari 1963: 266–67); the languages were closely related, but they were quite distinct from each other.[7] In spite of the provision of the Act XXIX passed in 1837 and Section 337 of the Criminal Procedure Code that conformed that the language of the soil should be used in both judicial and revenue proceedings, Bengali was introduced as the official language of Assam in 1838 (Nag 2018: 98). Under the leadership of the American Baptist Missionaries, the nascent Assamese middle-class demanded the restoration of Assamese language to its rightful place. They urged firmly for publication of textbooks in Assamese.[8] The British initiated a change in the language policy hereafter. Mills wrote, 'I think we made a great mistake in directing that all business should be translated in Bengali and that the Assamese must acquire it. Is it too late to retrace our steps?'[9]

A 'conspiracy theory' has been shaped up from the colonial period, which states that the Bengali cultural expansionists were behind the persecution of the Assamese language. It remained popular and continued to circulate for many decades (Miri 1993: 69). A general apprehension concerning the Bengalis was that they were not actuated by the desire to learn local dialects and languages. They did not send their children to vernacular schools, but somehow managed to set up their own schools, whether in Assam or Tripura. It was the first grievance against the Bengalis from the Assamese front.[10] This grievance was fomented by the competition for employment in the colonial offices where the English employers preferred Bengalis to run the imperialist administration. David Scott introduced the policy of recruiting Bengalis when the Assamese 'men of rank', who were appointed as a part of the conciliatory policy, were found to be corrupt and too inefficient to perform the duties as required by the new administrative system. Bengali clerks and officers got preference, as they were familiar with systems of the Company Administration.[11] The Assamese often put their grievances into words, whenever they encountered a Bengali script, *'Ki jani ki likshe, Mohoriye ki likshe. Bangla katha moi ki janoo?'* (How do I know what has been written. The *Mohoriye* write it. How do I understand the Bengali language?) (Nag 2018: 113–15). They started feeling deprived and marginalised in their own land.[12] From the 1850s, the tea plantation industry flourished in Assam and the indentured labourers were mostly from tribal areas of Bengal.[13] In plantation industries, too, the Bengali *babus* and *bhadraloks* dominated the white-collar job sector. The government declared that 'under the influence of these men (*amolas*), they recruited mostly from Bengal' (Gosselink 1994: 88). The real reason was the elites and upper-middle-class Bengali Hindus adopted the basics of the Western education well. In 1874, three districts of Bengal—Goalpara, Sylhet and Cachar—were cut off from Bengal and added to Assam for the increase of its revenue capability.[14] To protect the massive inflow of capital in tea gardens, it became necessary to cut off Assam from Bengal, to meet the required expenses of upgrading Assam into a full-fledged single province (Chief Commissionerate).[15]

The transfer of these districts to Assam increased the Bengali population, and concomitantly, the socio-cultural and political dominance of the Bengalis increased the insecurity of the Assamese. To accelerate the revenue generation, local zamindars or *muttabbor* and colonial government began to encourage the migration of landless migrant farmers from congested Mymensingh, Comilla, Sylhet and other adjacent districts (Guha 1997: 76–85). The trickle that started in the 1880s grew to be a massive influx of Bengali Muslim farm settlers into Assam, and this community was marked as 'a notoriously turbulent class of people' (Sujaud Doullah 2003: 72–73). They were settled in the wastelands, *char* areas, tribal lands and forest lands. They converted the province into a prosperous agricultural province, but by avoiding the terms of the Land Ceiling Act, which increased the paranoia of the Assamese.[16] As Muslims, they were prey to the contemporary communal mobilisation, and as Bengalis, they became the object of insecurity against them. *Bongal-Bongalini* (1870), a literary work by Rudraram Bordoloi, depicted the lifestyle of these outsiders.[17] The Bengalis were about to tilt the demographic structure, and the Assamese feared that it might even cause transfer of political power to them (Gohain 1997: 389). Myron Weiner tried to explain the reasons behind the psychological fear:

> The Assamese found the Bengalis in a superior and himself in a subordinate position. The teacher is a Bengali, the pupil Assamese. The doctor is a Bengali, the patient Assamese. The pleader is Bengali, the client Assamese. The

> shopkeeper is Bengali, the customer Assamese. The Government official is Bengali, the petitioner Assamese.
>
> *(Weiner 1988: 115–16)*

This strife led the Assamese middle-class to organise socio-political movements for an adequate share of employment and restoration of the ethnic culture. The Assamese people had strong roots in the rural sector of the society, as well as feudal attitude towards life, property, moorings in social relationships and behaviour (Sharma 1990: 139–41). First, they confined themselves to a linguistic or literary regeneration; later they tried to denote it as 'cultural nationalism' (Deka 2013: 36–37). They found the Bengalis as an obstacle in the path of their development.

The year 1905 is crucial in the spatial history, as the Indian nationalist opposition to the new Province of Eastern Bengal and Assam brought Indian national space into public politics for the first time (Ludden 2011: 6). It gave a taste of power to the Assamese as Calcutta ceased to be the controlling authority there (Molla 1981: 36). Sir Bamfylde Fuller, the then Lieutenant Governor of Eastern Bengal and Assam, first raised the slogan 'Assam is for Assamese' in 1909. This initiative got immense support from the Assamese middle-class. Lt. Col. Gurdon, the Commissioner of the Assam Valley, expressed apprehension about the Assamese being 'elbowed out of all Government and industrial employment by the people of East Bengal' (Kalita 2011: 48). Maniram Dewan voiced against appointing the Bengalis and Marwaris in the revenue department in Assam (Kalita 2011: 15–17). Eminent Assamese nationalist thinker Ambikagiri Ray Choudhury kept on urging the Assamese to protect their linguistic identity (Dev and Lahiri 1985: 160). He stressed 'adaptation of Assamese language as a criterion for Assamese nationality' (Baruah 1991: 62). The 'Bengali factor' made the 'educated young Assamese middle-class' insecure about getting jobs and business opportunities (Boruah 2009: xi). They expressed the need for preservation of sufficient employment scope in services and reservations in jobs. The novel *Herowa Swarga* by Muhammed Piyar made a comparative study between the outsider communities in Assam. He depicted the Bengalis as 'more dangerous' than other migrating communities like Marwaris and Nepalis, as even after staying in Assam for such a long period, they remained into their own culture and practised their language only (Nag 1990: 140).

The long history of clashes of interests between the Assamese and Bengali middle-class started from the 1930s. Culturally, the Bengalis had evolved into a strong and distinct nationality (Barpujari 1998: 43). *Apurna*, a novel by Daibo Chandra Talukdar, highlighted on the gravity of the social crisis caused by it. He categorically described '[t]he way Mymensinghias had entered Assam, plundered and exploited the villages and land of Assam and made the Assamese strangers in their own homeland'.[18] Until 1931, Assamese continued to remain the minority language as 19,92,846 declared themselves as Assamese-speaking, as compared to 39,60,712 speaking Bengali and 12,53,515 speaking tribal languages.[19] The attitude of suspicion and hatred of the Assamese middle-class had increased on account of the formation of separate organisations for the protection of the interests of the

Bengalis. In Tezpur, Bengalis demanded in a public meeting, 'the Assamese leaders must live on the terms of the Bengali settlers who have already overflown the province'.[20] The Bengali newspaper *Samachar Darpan* reported in 1931: 'The number of subscribers from Assam outnumber the subscribers in any district of Bengal'.[21] The Secretary of the Bengali Association in Assam wrote in *Natun Assamiya*: 'The Bengalis are the only majority community in Assam and the days are not far off when Bengali language would be the State Language of Assam' (Phukon 1996: 29). The Assam Domiciles and Settlers Association (Assam Citizens Association) demanded equal citizenship rights and education through the medium of one's mother tongue from the early 1940s (Barpujari 1998: 43). The idea of 'communalism' and the word 'communal' was not the same in government reports and official documents in Assam. At times, the communal conflicts meant the Hindu-Muslim conflict, but it applied mostly to denote the Assamese-Bengali rifts (Roychoudhury 2009: 46–47). The entire framework of language dispute and the crisis over linguistic identity of the then society became a major theme of the politicisation of regionalism.

Assam: refugees and politics

Post-1947 Assam experienced conflicts compounded by immigration and demographic changes, 'which have pitted indigenous Assamese against migrant Bengalis, Hindus against Muslims, and Assam against India's Central Government' (Gosselink 1994: 83). The logic of the Assamese politicians behind the agitation to expel foreigners was that it was necessary for the protection of their own language and culture and to preserve Assamese dominance in state's political arena.[22] A circular was sent to all government-aided schools, issued by the Assistant Director of Public Instruction in 1948, 'asking them not to employ any one on the staff who is not a native of or is not domiciled in the Indian dominion'.[23] The state government was pressing the Centre to introduce Immigration Acts to check the regular flow of migrants and start a process of eviction from unauthorised lands, grazing reserves, etc. There were series of arguments between Centre and state regarding the actual number of refugees (Deka and Deka 1981: 18). Almost 7 lakh Bengali refugees migrated from East Bengal to Assam, 13 per cent of the total number of refugees in India, which contributed to a relatively higher growth of the Hindu population. Nevertheless, the decadal growth of Muslims in the post-1947 period was higher than the rate of growth in the decades before Partition.[24] Hitesh Deka ushered in the crisis and challenged the authoritarian attitude of the Bengalis in his work *Mati Kar (To Whom Does the Land Belong?)*. In 1950, Prem Narayan, an Assamese author wrote a story titled '*Anchani*' in a collection of short stories named *Ashirbad*, about an Assamese lawyer who formulated plans called *Bongal Kheda*, a strategy for driving out foreigners (Bengalis) from Assam (Nag 1990: 140).

From the 1950s, the state government declared, 'no surplus land was available for settlement of outsiders' (Misra 2000: 117). Immigrants were settled in 1,508,000 acres of land between 1930 and 1950 in the Brahmaputra valley. After looking into serious conflicts between Bengali refugees and Assamese domiciles, the Centre promulgated an ordinance on 6 January 1950 to halt further immigration (Das 1982: 44). This ordinance was replaced by an act known as Immigrants (Expulsion from Assam) Act of 1950 that came into effect from 1 March 1950 (Roychoudhury 2009: 51–52). The 'Statement of object and reasons' of the Act mentioned:

> During last few months, a serious situation had arisen from the immigration of a very large number of East Bengal residents into Assam. Such large migration is disturbing the economy of the province besides giving rise to a serious law and order problem'[25]

The Act allowed migration of the Pakistanis who were displaced because of civil disturbances. It stated, 'by which the social psychology towards the outsiders came out as the homogeneity in the Assamese got disturbed by an outsider group with their different life style'.[26] It granted the Centre the power 'to remove from India or Assam, immigrants whose stay in Assam was detrimental to the economic interests of India' (Gosselink 1994: 93). But this law was repealed in 1957, as it discriminated against Muslims in favour of Hindus. The middle-class–dominated press did not support the demands of land reforms, distribution of land and grazing reserves among refugees or other downtrodden classes (Deka 2013: 45). Fresh communal disturbances occurred in Assam in the early 1950s, and the refugees living in Goalpara, Kamrup and Darrang fled to their places of origin by leaving their property behind. But the Nehru-Liaquat Pact of 1950 tried to give the minorities a sense of security and declared anyone who migrated before 31 December 1950 to be a citizen of India. The government conducted a comparative study between the incoming Hindu refugees and outgoing Muslims after 1950 to make the arguments stronger, pointing out by showing evidence that a total of 1,61,360 immigrants came back to Assam through recognised routes of travel by 31 December 1950.[27]

Apart from the general crises created by Partition, economic imbalances between East Bengal and Assam, opportunities for cultivating massive arable lands led to such migration. The 1951 Census reported that of 1,344,003 persons born outside the state, 3,88,288 were from East Bengal (Weiner 1998: 101). The population trend and percentage of the encroachment of lands scared the Assamese.[28] The Census Commissioner, R. B. Vaghaiwalla, commented in 1951:

> despite the present political, constitutional and psychological climate of Assam and despite the passport system and other difficulties many Muslim immigrants will yet run the gauntlet of these legal and administrative barriers and attempt to settle down in Assam.[29]

From Goalpara, 27,000 Muslim families had migrated after 1947, of which 24,000 came back in 1951. The question of their voting rights became complicated. During the census of 1951, a National Register of Citizens (NRC) was prepared under the directive of the Ministry of Home Affairs. The purpose was to register the census documents containing information of each and every person enumerated. The NRC ensured the names against the houses, holdings and number of persons staying therein, which would be used in detention and deportation of foreigners illegally staying in Assam. The accommodation of the refugees under the Delhi Pact remained enforced: 'no compromise in the matter of identification of foreign infiltrators as per provisions of the Constitution' continued.[30] The state ensured that humanitarian grounds might be considered at the time of deportation. The introduction of passport/visa regulation led to another massive wave of refugees.[31] The general election of 1952 made the situation more complex with citizenship issues. Alteration of some clauses of the Citizenship Act of 1955, like stress on the 'citizens by birth' instead of 'citizenship by registration', made the Bengalis vulnerable in Assam (Chhabra 1992: 58).

Cachar: Bengalis in the Surma valley

Partition made the Assamese numerically and politically stronger, as they became the single largest group in Assam (Hussain 1993: 166). The Bengalis, Hindu educated elites and Muslim peasant classes lost their proportions (Abu Naser Saied Ahmed 2011: 401–05). Cachar remained as the only Bengali district, which continued as the centre of aspiration to maintain different linguistic identity (Nath Barua 1944: 93). There were competing constructions of Cachar's past, its cultural identities. Cachar was tied to Bengal than the rest of Assam in terms of intellectual and political currents (Baruah 1999: 103). The rift in ideologies arose within the indigenous populations of the two valleys long before Partition. Leftism started attracting the student political front from 1939 in Assam; CPI and RCPI were active in Cachar from 1946. There were several eviction attempts in the 1940s under Premier Gopinath Bordoloi. The leaders of West Bengal largely inspired the ideological aegis and strategy of conducting leftist political movements in Cachar.[32] In such a state, proposals for rehabilitation of Bengalis after 1947 was like a return of the ghosts. The Assamese had been ceaselessly agitating against the continuing influx of Bengalis to Cachar. The state government tried to resist several attempts to settle refugees in Assam and Cachar, yet the Centre compelled the state to absorb the refugees. Cachar was the favourite site for refugee resettlement; it became the hub of refugee politics and resistance movements against Assamese hegemony. After the Sylhet referendum, there were serious misgivings about retaining the Cachar plains within India, and to keep the Hailakandi subdivisions in Assam. It culminated in a Bengali-Assamese riot in 1951. Yet the census of 1951 indicated that the Bengali refugee influx towards Assam had no decisive demographic impact. It is argued, however, that this was because of the return of Muslim migrants, who declared 'Assamese' as their mother tongue, primarily to legitimise the possession of their landed properties they had left behind when they migrated to East Pakistan.

The protests against Assamese hegemony in Cachar pushed both the resident and migrant Bengalis to participate in socio-political movements with definite agendas to accomplish.[33] An emergent political consciousness among the Bengali protagonists tends to question their identity (Hazarika and Baisya 2000: 19). The Bengali refugees migrated to Cachar because of the similarities in religious and linguistic identities with their place of origin (Kar 1999: 60–63). To justify their uprooted self and political consciousness, they often compared their crises with the time they got involved in the *Bhasa Andolon* (Language Movement) of 1952 in East Bengal (Choudhury 1973: 1214). Bengali intellectuals and political workers in Cachar called for their basic rights in Assam (Baruah 1999: 104). They organised political associations to claim their educational rights, economic resettlement and professional rehabilitation as primary agendas (Ghosh 2004: 54–56). The methods or strategies to organise political movements adopted by refugee leaders of Cachar were strikingly similar to those of West Bengal.[34] The UCRC leaders and other political fronts were constantly in touch with the local refugee organisations of Cachar. The blame placed on the West Bengal press was that it tried to convert Assam into a bilingual state, to make the land accessible to all sorts of 'Bengali fortune-seekers'.[35] Ambica Chakraborty of UCRC stated: 'It is duty of every refugee to learn Assamese culture and language and vice versa to derive benefit for each other',[36] yet, the chief allegation of the Assamese against the Calcutta press was that it often ignored the feeble voice of the Assamese press.

The Cachar District Refugee Council in Silchar was one of the major organisations working for the refugees from 1948. Being an official wing of the East Bengal Relief Committee, headed by M. N. Saha, it organised a conference to:

> ventilate the legitimate grievances and ameliorate the sorrows and sufferings of the refugees, arising out of the virtual failure of the rehabilitation due to the un-planned, un-scientific, hap-hazard, slow and dilatory methods of rehabilitation works done so far attended with non-allotment of suitable lands for rehabilitation in this district.[37]

It demanded extension of areas of the three big towns of Cachar: Silchar, Karimganj and Hailakandi. They urged the improvement of roads, and demanded basic amenities like water, light and educational facilities, which the state Government provided to some towns in the Brahmaputra valley.[38] The All Assam Refugee Association organised deputations to the Chief Minister for reclamation of land for the refugees.[39] The politics of resistance to refugees reinforced the Assamese desire for cultural hegemony (Choudhury 1973: 10–11). Assam's multi-ethnic landscape was the product of colonial geography; migration was an older diversity, for all intents and purposes.[40] Under the pan-Indian cultural syntax of the 'nation-province', Assam's challenge to be a part of 'language-based model' was quite exigent (Baruah 1999: 91). Both the categories of Bengalis like 'already settled' and 'upcoming refugees' had fallen in the cultural politics, which had an impact on electoral affairs (Sharma 1999: 36–37). They vehemently reciprocated policies aimed at them. This multi-ethnic tendency produced 'cultural wars' that shaped up as the 'language riots' (Baruah 1999: 91). The Assamese nationalists termed the spirit of 'little nationalism' with an inherent idealism. It asserted the essences of local patriotism,

Indian nationalism and internationalism as 'composite', and argued that the 'seeds of chauvinism' and 'Asamiya little nationalism was not a cudgel' (Guha 1980: 1703). It was 'The aggressive linguistic nationalism' degenerating into 'minority-baiting'. The Assam Pradesh Congress Committee urged for 'reorganisation of the province on a linguistic basis' (Guha 1980: 1703).

After the publication of the census report of 1951, a strategy was evolved to incorporate majority of recent immigrants into Assamese nationality (Singh 1984: 74–75). The 'number game was one of the most vital ingredients in the discourse and it not only sustained but provided some nourishment as well'.[41] There had been a fear among the Assamese Hindus of being swamped by the Bengali Muslims when they were not a homogenous community. There were four distinct categories: Asamiya Muslims, Na-Asamiya Muslims, Muslims of the Barak Valley and North Indian Muslims (Hussain 1993: 197). The number of indigenous Muslims was diminutive; many of them managed to assimilate them effortlessly with the Assamese Hindus. It never caused serious problem.[42] The census of 1951 published the total number of refugees in Assam.[43] Cachar received the highest number (93,177) of Hindu refugees, followed by Goalpara (44,967) and Kamrup (42,871) (Barua 2005: 360). The Muslims settled in Assam before 1947 had voting rights and could cast votes in the general election of 1952;[44] the census of 1951 termed them 'Bengali Muslims' (Singh 1984: 32–33). But in an altering state of affairs and to protect their acquired properties, they began to identify themselves in the category of 'Assamese Muslims' in the census report of 1961 (Weiner 1988: 94). The domiciles used to believe that this group of Muslim Bengalis might change their identity again, when needed.[45] Manirul Hussain opined that 'the entire East Bengali Muslim peasant community' adopted Assamese as its mother tongue, producing different cultural politics in Assam (Hussain 1993: 207). The superintendent of the 1961 census noted that they tried to conceal their birthplace by deflecting figures, whereas 'over 90 per cent, if not more' were Pakistanis (Das 1982: 45). The real fear of Assamese being dominated by Muslim immigrants politically was a crucial factor in post-1947 Assam. It might have led to demographic transformation and posed a challenge to Assamese language and culture.[46] The new generation Muslims of East Bengali descent claimed Assamese as their language, 'stealing away, as it were, a crucial cultural patrimony which defines the Assamese people', but it was for their own interest only (Prabhakara 1999: 9–22).

Conflicts over linguistic identities

Keeping all the complexities between the two communities of two valleys in the backdrop, the demand for 'linguistic reorganisation of states' impacted Assam directly. It restored hope to growing regional aspirations with political overtones. The state reorganisation and administrative reorganisation created political units, whereby interests of the constituent units and individuality were taken into account and had been promised to be preserved.[47] The internal decisive forces, whose extraterritorial affiliations could not be ruled out in the new framework, naturally carried away the inherent tension. In 1955, the report of the States Reorganisation Commissions had mentioned:

> We do not derive to make any recommendation about the details of the policy to be followed in prescribing the use of the minority languages for official purposes. However, we are inclined to the view that a state should be treated as unilingual only where one language group constitutes about 70 per cent or more of its entire population, when there is a substantial minority consisting 30 per cent or so of the population, the state should be reorganised as bilingual for administrative purposes.
>
> *(Kar 1999: 23)*

The Commission received two memorandums in this regard. In exchange 'for putting Cachar and Tripura within the boundaries of West Bengal', the West Bengal Pradesh Congress Committee asked that 'a connecting line should also be provided from Garo Hills to Cachar'.[48] The Paschim Banga Rajyo Punargathan Sangjukta Parishad resolved, 'as the district of Goalpara in Assam which was formerly a limb of Bengal, a Bengalee majority area and as the Bengalees there are being systematically suppressed culturally, it should be transferred to West Bengal'.[49] It drew the attention of the Centre by saying, 'Cachar and Tripura are two contiguous areas with 77% and 60% Bengali-speaking population'.[50]

> The S.R.C. suggests co-ordination of development in Cachar and Tripura as one administrative unit under a Commission of the Assam Government and recognition of Bengali for education and administration', so they argued, 'Both Cachar and Tripura have expressed in the strongest terms their disapproval of Assamese administration.[51]

But Bishnuram Mehdi opined it was 'a vital matter on which depends the future of Assam' and supported 'the maintenance of the *status quo* of the state for safety and security of the country'.[52]

During the tenure of Chief Minister Bimala Prasad Chaliha, representatives of Brahmaputra valley dominated the Assam Legislature for more than two decades.[53] From 1955, the Assamese came into conflict with the Bengali Hindus, as they perceived them as a threat to the unity of a composite Assam. There were many complex layers, dimensions and essences of community conflicts. An incident of open fire by the police on the Muslims in Howraghat Bazar, Mikir Hills, was reported as communal violence in government reports. There were also numerous incidents of clashes, ideologically or practically, to establish sole right over the land and cultural superiority.[54] It was mentioned in contemporary documents that the West Bengal press and leadership had been traditionally hostile to the idea of self-assertion in Assam.[55] Newspapers published from West Bengal like *Jugantar* wanted the intervention of the Central Government to protect Bengali interests in Assam.[56] The reorganisation of Assam by way of ceding Goalpara to West Bengal developed anti-Bengali sentiments in Dibrugarh. The Asam Jatiya Sabha raised a slogan on 27 May 1955 to the effect of 'Assam for Assamese', student bodies started demanding that Cooch Behar be included within Assam and that Goalpara be saved from being given away to West Bengal. They vehemently opposed the proposed visit of Dr B. C. Roy and Atulya Ghosh to Assam, when Hindu Bengali refugees supported the proposal of the reorganisation and merger of Goalpara with West Bengal. The Assamese organised an anti-division movement fuelled by the 'Angashed Birodhi Mancha'.[57] On 12 July 1955, an official report stated that 'a large number of non-tribals burnt out a Kalibari of the Bengali Hindu refugees'.[58] They were accommodated in the relief centres and taken to the rehabilitation officer for protection. A rumour was spread that the Bengali Hindu refugees had created this rift between the Muslim immigrants and the local populace.[59]

Some socio-political platforms, like Assam Sahitya Sabha (established in 1917) and Asamiya Samrakshini Sabha (established in 1926 and renamed Asam Jatiya Mahasabha in the 1930s), acted as pressure groups (Barua 1990: 128). It attracted the Assamese intellectuals and educated middle-class to claim a separate cultural identity through the 'state language issue'. Long before the enquiries were made by the States Reorganisation Commission and the release of the S.R.C. Report in 1955, the Assam Sahitya Sabha began its systematic campaign for the recognition of Assamese as the official language of Assam. In the Margherita Session of the Sahitya Sabha (1950), Ambikagiri Roy Choudhury referred to the Bengalis as 'the greatest enemy of the Assamese', as they were trying to exterminate the Assamese nationality by both religious and linguistic expansion in Assam (Nag 1990: 139). The Sahitya Sabha observed the 'State Language Day' on 16 July 1951 (Goswami 1997: 34). In 1955, the Sabha placed a memorandum before the S.R.C. for reconstitution of the state with a chief demand, 'no part of the state of Assam, as at present constituted, is taken away from it'.[60] Initially started as an elite movement, the Sabha broadened its scope of appeal. They stressed on 'the need of making Assamese the official state language'.[61] From September 1959, the Sabha started passing resolutions in the meetings organised just for the language cause.

The other social units and agents in organising a staunch political movement to accomplish separate identity were the student communities (Deka 1996: 132). Their organisational ability in transforming the society was a unique phenomenon in the history of Assam (Bora 1992: 1). Assam Chhatra Sanmilan, a predominant student organisation initially associated with the Congress, became affiliated with the leftist student groups of India from the 1940s (Deka 2013: 39). From 1950, the All India Student Federation became a cadre institute of the communists that had given an indication of growing influence of the leftists on their political ideologies without any influence from Bengal (Deka 1996: 104). Gail Omvedt believed that even after the communists' presence for long years, Congress had a wider base in urban and rural areas of Assam, including among the tribal peasantry (Omvedt 1980: 580). The students had launched agitations pertaining to economic issues and safeguards related to protection of their linguistic identity. The nature of their agendas underwent a sea change over the decades, and they started contributing to the political arena. Their attention manifested from national issues to regional ones (Phukan 2005: 13–14). In 1959, the All Assam Students Association 'sought to introduce a non-party line for student activities', though it was branded as 'parochial, communal and partisan in outlook' (Deka 2013: 43–44). Students of diverse backgrounds formed an organisation to unite them under a single banner, both in the hills and the plains.

The All Assam Students' Union (AASU) emerged with the idea of 'organising the students on non-party lines' (Barua 1990: 132). The lack of rootedness among the peasants and working class, and the distance from the broad left and other democratic forces in the state, rendered AASU dependent on the support of the Assamese middle-class. AASU made use of the undercurrents of Assamese middle-class politics and rising student consciousness (Hussain 1993: 106), giving it a perfect plank to re-establish its waning control in both perceived and real ways in the politics of the state. Despite the existence of oppositional political parties like CPI, RCPI, Forward Block and student wings of dominant Congress, AASU had taken the lead in a struggle launched for protection of the linguistic and cultural identity of the domiciles (Mahanta 2010: 60–61). It was reflected in the anxiety of the peasantry and Assamese middle-classes, their fear of 'loss of identity' (Baruah 2002: 191). Before the budget session of the Assam Assembly in 1960, the Sahitya Sabha came out with an appeal to all members of the Legislative Assembly to take up the issue of language in the House. The Sabha indicated a 'dateline' within which the Government was requested to take proper measures to recognise Assamese as the 'state language'.[62] The introduction of the 'Language Bill' influenced by the Sabha and ideological support from socio-political platforms led to communal violence in Assam (Hussain 2005: 1). By introducing the 'Official Language Bill', the state government moved to make Assamese the official language. The then-Chief Minister, B. P. Chaliha, had stressed:

> two important reasons which warrant enactment on a state language. First, to make the official communications easily understandable to the common man, and second, to break the barrier of language which now separates the diverse population for declaring Assamese as the state's official language.
>
> *(Chattopadhyay 1990: 57)*

His government feared that if the issue was 'decided only on basis of majority or minority, its object would be defeated'.[63]

The counter-effects

The language issues created dissension among the tribals and Bengalis. Though they were equally hostile and scared by the declaration of the state language, the tribals felt threatened by the official language debate. Numerous Bengali agriculturist refugee families were evicted from the Mikir Hills by violence initiated by the local tribals there.[64] From 1950, over 9,000 Hajongs, Kachains and Koches tribals migrated and entered in the former Garo Hill district of Assam (now Meghalaya) from Mymensingh and Rangpur district to take shelter in Assam. On 23 February 1956, *The Statesman* reported that more than 60,000 tribals 'belonging to the Christian faith have been forcibly evicted from their ancestral homes and lands' (Dasgupta 2016: 76–77). The APCC passed a resolution on 22 April 1960 stating:

> (a) That Assamese be declared by law as the official language of the State and be adopted for such purpose as may be decided by the Government, (b) That Assamese be introduced as official language in all the districts except the district of Cachar, the autonomous districts of Khasi and Jaintia Hills, Garo Hills, Mizo Hills and North Cachar Hills in which areas it may be introduced as and when they are prepared for it, (c) That the right of the minorities for protection and development as their language will be fully safeguarded, (d) That in the process of introduction and extension of Assamese as official language just claims and interest of non-Assamese-speaking people in the matter of public services and such other matter will be adequately safeguarded, (e) That Government be requested to take steps accordingly and to provide as early as possible all facilities for learning Assamese and other languages spoken in the State with a view to bring the people closer and to break the language barrier.[65]

It could not satisfy the people of the Hill Districts and Cachar. Apart from the Bengalis, the dominance of the Brahmaputra-centric Assamese led to the isolations of the hill people.

The minority tribals were scared by the political and cultural aspiration of Assamese. They mobilised themselves from the late 1950s to acquire autonomy—their own 'shares'. Passage of Assam's Language Act accelerated the thrust of tribal separation from Assam. The All Party Hill Leaders Conference (APHLC) and other tribal organisations opposed the proposal in the budget session of 1960 (Gosselink 1994: 92), anticipating that it would deprive their English-educated classes of getting a good share of administrative jobs,[66] so they affirmed Assamese as the mother tongue of less than 50 per cent of the population.[67] The logic of the domiciles was that the mother tongue of more than 60 per cent of the total population was Assamese, while the Khasis, Garos and Lusais did not even have their own scripts.[68] The Bengalis were apprehensive that if Assamese were to be declared the official language of the state, it would place the Assamese-speaking people in an advantageous position with regard to recruitment in state services, when previously the Bengalis used to dominate that sector. The Assamese intelligentsia and the press were instrumental in creating a feeling of distrust and antagonism between the Assamese, Bengalis and tribals.[69] Some students' federations and political organisations planned processions, followed by a public meeting, to protest against the resolution of the APCC at Guwahati.[70]

There was counter-propaganda carried on by the Calcutta and local press. While a logical step towards safeguarding their identity and culture was necessary for the Assamese, the 'others' were beset by the fear of being Assamised (Misra 2000: 118). Under the leadership of Shri Roghunath Choudhury, the Assam Rajyabhasa Karma Parishad submitted a memorandum and demanded that the state government should abide by the instructions and rules about national language and provisions for linguistic minorities mentioned in the Constitution.[71] The refugees and other linguistic minorities approved the anti-official language resolutions taken in Karimganj on 8 April 1960 (Sarkar 1396: 212–14). The Bengal Sangram Committee of Cachar insisted on having Bengali as the second official language of Assam, and 'the official language for Cachar' at the district level. The Calcutta newspapers reported these incidents as a result of 'fear of losing identities'. It appeared as 'a sign of Bengali chauvinism' to the Assamese community.[72] During Nehru's visit to Gauhati University, students demanded immediate declaration of Assamese as the state language (Chattopadhyay 1990: 57). It was reinforced by the resolution of the APCC on 5 May 1960. The linguistic minorities of Barak valley reacted sharply against it. The Bengalis protested and damaged Assamese signboards, hurled abuses at the Assamese in the Shillong procession of 21 May 1960. At Dibrugarh and Jorhat, students' rallies were organised by Assamese student folk. They also condemned slogans of the Shillong processions that were followed by sharp anti-Bengali slogans at Mariani, Sibsagar.[73]

The first incident of attacking Bengalis on the question of language was the killing of a boy from Sibsagar in police firing in Gauhati on 4 July 1960. C. P. Sinha, the former Chief Justice, Assam High Court, stated:

> the cause of the disturbance was the language issue, namely that Assamese should be the official language of the State, the question of unemployment in the Central Services, namely the Railways, Telegraph and in particular, the Oil Refinery in Gauhati was the main subject matter forming the cause of disturbances . . . several incidents connected with the language issue at Mariani, Lumding and Shillong contributed greatly to aggravate the situation, added to this primary cause were the press reports both in the Calcutta papers and in the Assamese papers.[74]

It was characterised by spreading panic, pelting of stones, cases of assault, looting, arson, attack on public property and violation of prohibitory orders. The official report stated:

> Scuffles took place in the Railway colony near the Don Bosco School and Cotton College. Serious disturbances at the juncture of GS Road were quelled by Police firing and no casualties were reported on the roads after the firing, but a dead body and six injured persons were found in a hostel.[75]

The situation was acute 'during the crucial days between 4 and 11 July, the whole administration in Assam had collapsed'.[76] Incidents of rioting and arson wreaked havoc in Goreswar area in Kamrup district. In the report of the enquiry commission, Justice Gopalji Malhotra stated:

> deep rooted and long lasting mutual distrust and suspicion had its connection with the ongoing language issue, the propaganda of the Calcutta press as well as Assamese press and false rumours spread regarding the happenings in Upper Assam, the Brahmaputra valley and Shillong. The exaggerated rumours about the police firing in Gauhati led to these unwarranted incidents.[77]

On 25 July 1960, Bengali railway employees compelled a cinema hall manager to stop the screening of an Assamese film *Puberan* (Miri 1993: 66). Dr B. C. Roy wrote to the Prime Minister: 'A well-thought-out programme of attacking the Bengalis alone in Assam was started, perhaps at the time of the sittings of the States Reorganisation Commission' (Chakrabarty 1984: 16).

Within this situation of conflicts, The Assam Official Language Bill was introduced in the Assembly and eventually passed on 10 October 1960, becoming the Assam Official Language Act. It declared that 'Assamese shall be used for all or any of the official purposes of the state of Assam' (Trivedi 1995: 193). The Act made a provision that:

> the English language, so long as the use thereof is permissible and thereafter Hindi in place of English, shall also be used for such official purposes of the Secretariat and the offices of the heads of the departments of the State Government.[78]

The old residents and Bengali refugees of Cachar were not comfortable with the clauses or safeguards given in the Act (Chaudhury 1961: 16). The Nikhil Assam Banga Bhasa Samity submitted a memorandum to the President of India against it.[79] In the struggle for recognition of Bengali as the 'state language', the Cachar Zilla Gana Sangram Parishad had taken the lead under the aegis of the Cachar Congress committee. Later, it transformed into Bhasa Andolan Samity.[80] In May 1961, Cachar Sangram Parishad called a strike and organised picketing in offices and transport routes. Fifteen hundred students joined in a protest procession at Karimganj. The district administration had to impose prohibitory orders on 18 May 1961 in Silchar because of continuous hartals, protests and blocking movements had reached such a height there.[81] Karimganj and Silchar became their centre of action from where the leadership had designed the pattern of agitation and general strike in other *mofussil* towns of the Surma valley like Badarpur, Bhangabazar, Kaliganj, Nilambazar, Patherkandi, Bazaricherra, Rajbari and Ramkrishnanagar. The leaders of Karimganj Sangram Parisad, Rathindra Nath Sen, Bidhu Bhusan Choudhury and others were jailed on May 19 (Chakraborty 2013: 11–14). Police used tear gas and charged *lathi* to disperse crowds in the Silchar Railway station. Bengali refugees became *satyagrahis* and *shahids* by the police fire, and many were injured.[82] On 30 May, the *Hindustan Standard* reported: 'This is the first time in free India people courted death for Bengali Language and that too at a time when India and the world have been celebrating the birth centenary of Rabindranath'.[83]

The Sangram Parishad stated that 'the movement would be resumed and carried on until the Bengali language is recognised at the state level'.[84] It organised *hartals* against regular curfews in Karimganj, Lakhipur, Badarpur, Hailakandi and other places. Five local MLAs from Cachar resigned following a police shooting incident in Silchar.[85] In 1961, nearly a million out of the whole lot of seven million people living in the Brahmaputra valley were Bengalis. The language controversy touched on the issues of employment, and it also created fear among the Assamese people, as it was accurately predicted by David Scott that the migrants would outnumber the domiciles someday.[86] When the regional identity was merging everywhere in the country, Assamese tried to separate their identity from the Bengalis. To resolve the crisis, Prime Minister of India Lal Bahadur Shastri was rushed to Assam, met with cross-section of people and came out with a formula to resolve the crisis. The Shastri Formula attempted to safeguard interests of minorities, though it bypassed the language issue. The Bengalis and tribals were not satisfied with the special section in the amendment for Cachar, saying that they would continue their education in English until it was replaced by Hindi. The legislature accepted the recommendations of Lal Bahadur Shastri and the Assembly passed the amendment to the Language Bill on 7 October 1961.[87] The fear of the linguistic minorities had not been allayed by solutions given in the Shastri Formula. Their demand chiefly was that the status and treatment of Bengali should be the same as Assamese as the official language of Assam. They rather preferred retaining English, as it had served as the official language ever since Assam passed into the hands of British East India Company (Miri 1993: 53).

Medium of Instruction Movement

Assam was suffering from political contradiction, confusion in policies and community rifts when the state was overflowing with refugees following the implementation of the Nehru-Liaquat Pact, passing of NRC and the Representation of Peoples Act 1951. The census of 1951 indicated increase in percentage of Assamese to 56.7 per cent. Even after reaching peak growth, Assamese indicated a marginal increase to 57.1 per cent in 1961 and 60.89 per cent in 1971.[88] The passport and visa regulations came into operation from October 1952, and the definition of a 'foreigner' was spelt out in the revised Foreigner's Act of 1957. During the early 1960s, seeing the conflicts around language issue, the NRC register was handed over to the police for facilitating verification of infiltrators and illegal immigrants.[89] The number of applicants in the register of employment exchange increased regularly during 1961–1971.[90] On 27 June 1962, Nehru commented:

> Infiltration by Pakistanis had been continuing since 1949 is perfectly true. I believe that much of this infiltration took place in first five years of

independence when the border was not adequately guarded . . . probably it will be difficult now to deal with illegal immigrants who came before 1952. We might therefore fix 1952 as a date of enquiry.

(Das 1982: 59)

The insecurity of the domiciles increased with coming of refugees after the colossal riot of 1964.[91] The state government was resentful, as it resettled many refugee families until 1965. But, the refugees time and again complained of maltreatment from the domiciles and the administrative front.[92] The Assamese were critical of establishing Bengali medium schools in Cachar after 1964, by using Bengali as the language of instruction and appointing Bengali teachers.[93] The Centre adopted the 'Prevention of Infiltration to Assam Plan' in 1964. Under the scheme, hundreds of border watch posts were constructed and Border Security Forces (BSF) engaged to catch infiltrators and expel them immediately. During the first three years of the plan's implementation, 190,000 illegal immigrants were identified, arrested and deported (Gosselink 1994: 93).

The Chinese aggression of 1962 and Indo-Pak conflict of 1965 complicated the situation.[94] There were incidents of hoisting of Pakistani flags in places like Thelamora, Routa and Chotiar of Darrang district by the infiltrators during the Chinese aggression in 1962 (Borhogain 2013: xiii). The Indo-China War made Assam act like a strategic front. The Centre had continued maintaining its stand of not interfering inside matters of discrepancies of any state.[95] Both the Home Ministers of India and Pakistan met in a conference in New Delhi on 7–11 April 1964 to discuss the deportation issue, but it did not yield substantial results. The general consensus was that the stoppage of deportation would affect the internal equation. Between 1961 and 1966, approximately 1,78,952 infiltrators were detected.[96] The success rate went down later. From 1968–1971, 20,800 infiltrators were detected (Gosselink 1994: 93).[97] The Liberation War of 1971 aggravated the situation. The Assam-East Pakistan border remained open for long 'to a large body of suffering humanity to ensure security of their life, honour and property'.[98] The influx was unprecedented. Within a short time, as many as 9,55,854 evacuees, including 6,27,507 in Meghalaya, were provided shelter and relief; 7,20,718 of them were accommodated in camps and 2,24,134 stayed with friends and relatives.[99] Barpeta, Nalbari, Mangaldoi and Nowgong subdivision had been affected severely, and the growth of population in Assam was 345 per cent in 1971, compared with an increase of 132 per cent for India (Sharma 1999: 37). It added a different dimension and affected electoral politics in Assam. In 1971, huge voices of protest were heard in the Legislative Assembly when the Election Commission of India instructed for 'house to house enumeration' for preparing revised electoral rolls in all of Assam, including Meghalaya, 'except in the case of the four border districts of Cachar, Goalpara, United K and J Hills and Garo Hills' for the general election of 1972.[100] The Assamese leaders were opposed to including the names of the fresh refugees, who did not have citizenship cards, in the voter list. Some of the *bhaganias* reportedly left refugee camps and were residing in villages for that particular purpose.

Amidst such turmoil, the language politics did not die out; it rather raised its head again in the form of the 'Medium of Instruction Movement' of 1972. It was the second landmark in the annals of the Assamese Movement (Weiner 1993: 1742). The linguistic aspiration of the locals in Assam was expressed during the movement of 1960. But it was consolidated by making Assamese the medium of higher education (Gohain 1983: 634). The movement initially was of an academic nature; the political disturbances linked with it rapidly made it a pivotal point of Bengali-Assamese rivalry. The question of using Assamese as the regional language at the pre-university level was a change in educational policy regarding linguistic concerns raised first by the passing of a resolution at the Dibrugarh University in 1968 which was supposed to be implemented from the academic session 1971–1972. The academic council suggested that the date of change should be introduced not later than 1975–1976 in the degree course, though the importance of English was recognised. Following this recommendation, the undergraduate board of Dibrugarh University passed a resolution on 14 December 1971 that 'the change of medium would be implemented in both Pre-university and Degree course' and the question paper should be set in Assamese and English.[101] In the early 1970s, Gauhati University decided to introduce Assamese as the medium of instruction in colleges under its jurisdiction, with few exceptions. This decision was to come into effect from the academic year 1972–1973 (Goswami 1997: 70). The Academic Council in the resolution of 6 June 1972 conceded two points to the linguistic minorities of the state. First, English was to be retained for a period of ten years, and second, students would be permitted to answer examination questions either in English, Assamese or Bengali. With Sahitya Sabha's support and under the banner of AASU, the Assamese students started demonstrations in Gauhati, against the option of taking examinations in Bengali (Chattopadhyay 1990: 66). Owing to its staunch opposition, the Academic Council withdrew its decision of 'taking examination in Bengali'. They made 'partial modification' for 'various representations from the public, teachers' and students' organisations' (Deka and Deka 1981: 19).

As anticipated, the Cachar District Congress Committee leaders and Youth Congress sought legal remedies against this decision (Chakrabarty 1984: 82). Guru Charan College of Silchar, along with three other colleges affiliated to Gauhati University, petitioned the Supreme Court against the university decision restricting the medium only to Assamese. They argued that it was violating Article 30 of the Constitution, which assured protection of minorities. The socio-political situation became volatile, and the student participants from various other universities had to leave Assam. They had taken shelter mostly in West Bengal, as they were suffering from constant threats, fear and insecurities.[102] Home Minister Shri K. C. Pant discussed with the ministers the language issue that had been raised by the Cachar people in Shillong. He communicated to the Centre that 'the University and the academicians of Cachar will be able to come to an understanding'.[103] Though the court issued a stay order, the State Assembly unanimously reaffirmed the decision of the academic councils of two universities, Gauhati and Dibrugarh (Goswami 1997: 71). The decision was made to establish a separate university with territorial jurisdiction in the Cachar district. AASU had given an ultimatum to the government to withdraw its decision; otherwise, they would launch a 'direct action' in Brahmaputra valley (Baruah 1999: 105). Nowgong experienced the worst violence; 27 houses were burnt down, and 45 houses of the Bengalis were looted in Tezpur.[104] In Talapani and Nigam village of Dibrugarh district, three Bengali inhabitants died in communal frenzy that flared out of the debate and call for a movement by AASU.[105] The Sahitya Sabha decided to widen the student agitation into a 'popular' political movement in a public meeting in Gauhati, and demand a special session in the Assembly to discuss the medium of instruction controversy and establishment of a separate University in Cachar.

The Assam Legislative Assembly adopted a resolution on 23 September 1972 stating that the medium of instruction for Gauhati and Dibrugarh universities should be Assamese, but English should also continue as the medium of instruction (Chattopadhyay 1990: 68). It confirmed that, in the spirit of the Official Language Act, a separate university would be set up with territorial jurisdiction over the district of Cachar. This resolution was rejected both by Cachar and Brahmaputra valley. AASU called for 'Assam Bandh' on 5 October 1972, demanding a withdrawal of this resolution. There were regular incidents of conflicts and violence between the Assamese and Bengalis in places like Kharupetia (Mangaldai subdivision of Darrang district), Hojai (Nowgong), Bokpara (Dibrugarh), etc.[106] The anti-Bengali riots spread everywhere, and the Centre realised the necessity to defuse tension in November 1972. Prime Minister Indira Gandhi urged an AASU deputation to call off their movement. AASU called it off when it received assurance that the state government would, besides accepting recommendations for those universities, introduce Assamese as a compulsory subject in non-Assamese secondary schools.[107] Making Assamese the compulsory language from class VIII onwards led to a massive agitation in the Barak valley, as the Bengalis analysed the statement as a step towards forcible Assamisation, with the recurrent riots being aimed 'at driving out the entire Bengali population' rather than 'at usurping the Bengali language'.[108] The Bengalis categorised it as 'cultural genocide' and complained that the Assamese 'have developed an irrational craze for cultural conquest' (Barpujari 1998: 45).

The focus of the nascent Assamese movement was to establish Assamese supremacy in state services. The ultimate target was to affirm the right of the Assamese to control resources of the state (Gosselink 1994: 100). Language has always been at centre stage of ethnic turmoil in the northeast.[109] In 1972, the Bodo tribe-led Plain Tribes Council of Assam (PTCA) complained that the plains tribes have been 'uprooted in a systematic and planned way from their own soil and the "stepmotherly" treatment of the administration, dominated by the Assamese-speaking people has reduced them to "second class citizens"' (Das 2009: 3–9).[110] The leftist forces started influencing AASU from 1973 onwards. They submitted a 21-point list of demands in 1974 and organised protest movements as *satyagraha* against the internal emergency from June 1975 to February 1977 (Gogoi 2012: 86). Assam was struggling with economic, linguistic, political and national forces; the emergence of illegal Muslim community added a religious dimension to it (Dev and Lahiri

1985: 157). After AASU successfully handled the medium movement, a qualitative change in the AASU's organisational outlook had been noticed. It shifted from economic or academic issues and started arranging *satyagraha* programmes against 'the outsiders' and inclined to the issues of foreigners' expulsion more from the year 1978 (Deka 2013: 47). From 1979–1985, Assamese subnationalism came out on to the streets with the objectives of protesting against the illegal immigration, foreigners and a de facto policy of enfranchisement of non-citizens.

Tripura: emergence of political cognisance

The emergence of political consciousness and introduction of democratic institutions took a relatively long time in the princely state of Tripura. The tribal subjects of the Maharajas were illiterate, and they used to take pride in their tribal origin as it represented monarchy and the idea of divinity. The Maharajas were patrons of Bengali language and literature, known for comprehensive development of Bengalis, but they never tried to educate their tribal subjects or initiated basic education for them.[111] The monarchy had a fear that it might influence its subjects' blind loyalty.[112] In later decades, this absolute and autocratic monarchy *Bubagra* (a Tripuri word meaning the principle of divine right of the Maharajas) became responsible for the extension of Bengali terrorism in Tripura (Bhismodeb Bhattacharyya 1989: 60). The state machinery assumed a bureaucratic pattern and the economy became monetised during the colonial period.[113] It facilitated the emergence of a non-tribal middle-class. The Maharajas tried to accommodate the tribals within the existing political structure, but they led anti-monarchical and anti-imperialist movements later.[114] They had an expectation that the monarchy would be benevolent and enlightened to introduce structural reforms, but it received divergent reactions (Dey 1998: 151). A demand for a representative form of government in Tripura was first heard in the late 1920s. The concretisation of the political movement developed in two stages. Organised political activities flourished during the nationalist struggle, and it graduated to a resistance movement against the oppressive aspects of the princely rule and its administration. Revolutionary terrorist organisations like the Anushilan group of Comilla and the Jugantar group of Bahmanbaria contributed to the development of political consciousness in Tripura. They often used Tripura as safe shelter while working underground (Roychoudhury 1983: 69). The Swadeshi Movement, followed by Khilafat and Non-cooperation Movement, added further awareness and ideological changes towards the nationalist movements (Debnath 2010: 62–63). It helped in the emergence of semi-political reformist organisations like Chhartra Sangha and Bharati Sangha (1927) under the aegis of the Anushilan Samiti.

The consolidation of modern political structure began from the 1930s (Dutta 2006: 16). It contributed to free mobility and formation of few political associations (Jamatia 2007: 206). The Act of 1935 had changed equations of Indian states with the Raj, making it the 'Crown Representative'. The duty lay in the hands of the Political Department, which was supposed to operate with local residents and political agents (Dey 1998: 154). The Tripura Rajya Gana Parishad (1935) was the first declared political organisation in Tripura to claim that ideologically it, 'would follow the line of Congress' (Sen 1970: 22). In 1939, the Parishad members organised an anti-eviction movement against the eviction order of 500 Muslim peasants of Ramnagar for the expansion of the capital. With a '20-point Charter of Demand', they conveyed public resentment against feudal privileges. They compelled the Maharaja to abolish the *ghasuri* (grazing tax) of eight *annas* in the Chakla Roshanabad estate in 1941. To establish a Congress committee in Tripura, they arranged a deputation to Gandhi.[115] In the India State Peoples' Conference, the Parishad demanded 'land reforms' (Roychoudhury 1983: 73–75). Sachindra Lal Singha, Hariganga Basak, Sukhamoy Sengupta and Umesh Lal Singha were the pioneers, yet they could not popularise the organisation among the tribals (Jamatia 2007: 206). Princely resentment against this organisation even shocked Jawaharlal Nehru. He wrote to the Maharaja enquiring about imprisonment of the members without trial since World War II.[116] In his reply on 14 December 1945, the Maharaja denied the charges.[117]

Another premier political organisation, Rajya Jana Mangal Samiti, was formed in 1939. It was a by-product of an organisation named Sabuj Samiti established by Pravat Chandra Roy. Though it had been established by constitutional means, with prior consent of the Maharaja Bir Bikram Kishore Manikya, it had roots in progressive-left associations and worked as an 'appropriate political platform' within many heterogeneous groups (Dey 1998: 177). It gave importance to stimulating consciousness of the masses and emphasised tribal issues. Some young communists like Biren Datta, Anandalal De, Bansi Thakur, Pravat Chandra Roy, Sukumar Bhowmik and Kriti Singha formed the organisation (Roychoudhury 1983: 73). They raised slogan to create responsible government under the aegis of the Maharaja with '10-point political' and '16-point social and economic' demands (Majumder 1997: 9). They identified 'indifference and unsympathetic attitude of the State officials contributed to' the miseries of tribals and non-tribals, while crises of their illiteracy, indebt condition and over-taxation were the root causes (Dey 1998: 177). Their primary agenda was to create awareness within the tribals to uplift their material condition. They started publishing an official organ named *Prajar Katha*, with Biren Datta as editor (Chakravarti 2011: 23). They actually had experimented with two political tactics: one, they were not against the Maharaja, and two, their chief propaganda and attack was against the state officials.[118]

The Tripura Rajya Jana Siksha Samiti was the first ethno-nationalist outfit in Tripura, with the mission of tribal emancipation.[119] It was established in 1945 by 11 educated tribal youths under the leadership of Biren Datta. Aghore Debbarma, a Tripuri himself and victim of such situation, voiced a campaign against illiteracy among the tribals (Debbarma 1986: 24–25). The other members were Sudhannya Deb Burma, Dasarath Deb Burma, Hemanta Deb Burma and Nilmoni Deb Burma (Debray 2008: 15). The veteran leaders of the Jana Mangal Samiti started working in the tribal hilly areas to enlighten the tribals and release them from a world of superstition and religious beliefs imposed by the *Kulpurohit* and *Kulgurus*.

The boarding hostels (for tribal students) attached to the Umakanta Academy in Agartala and *Puratan* and *Natun* boarding in Khowai became the centres of this ideological base. The students used to read newspapers like *Janajudha*, leftist leaflets and books. Their principal objectives were eradication of illiteracy, superstition and poverty (Deb Burman 2013: 10–11). Dr Nilmani Deb Burman, the first tribal doctor of Tripura, mentioned in his memoir *Gadyasangraha: Janasiksha Anddolan o Anyanya Prabandha* that the indifference and unsympathetic attitude of the state officials contributed to the crises of the misery of the tribals (Deb Burma 2005: 24–25). The Siksha Samiti questioned the tribals' absolute allegiance and faith towards the institution of kingship, and tried to organise them against social injustice and the feudal oppression of the Maharajas.

The Jana Siksha Samiti was firm on its demand of compulsory education for the tribals to uplift their society from the 'curse of illiteracy and poverty that have descended on the tribal society of Tripura during the thirteen hundred and fifty years of Princely regime in the state' (Debbarma 2013: 14). D. A. W. Brown, then the Education Minister of Tripura, was a great patron of mass education.[120] He helped the Samiti to establish 400 schools, out of which the state recognised 300 schools, founded in secluded hilly areas (Dey 1998: 188). Jana Siksha Movement acted as a window in the lives of rural tribals and non-tribals. It made them a political category, struggling within the neglected landscapes. They got hold over both hills and plains, and it laid foundation of democratic movements.[121] Tribals agitated against the feudal mandate, and became enlightened and alert about unfair demands and customary exploitations imposed by the administration of the Maharajas.[122] Nripen Chakrabarty, in his novel *Longtorai Amar Ghor*, depicted how a larger group of young tribals were interested to take part in a programme of 'renaissance', organised by the Siksha Samiti (Chakrabarty 1996: 5–7). The Reangs rose to revolt in 1942–1943 under the leadership of Ratanmani Noatia against the royal agents (Jagat Jyoti Roy 1999: 34). The royal forces suppressed the revolt ruthlessly, but it portrayed the unsympathetic attitude of the rulers towards their tribal subjects. The Reangs were compelled to move from Amarpur and Udaipur of South Tripura, the centres of the uprising, and to emigrate to north Tripura.[123]

Communal organisations like Anjuman Islamia (1945), Tripura Rajya Moslem Praja Majlish (1946) and Hindu Mahasabha became operational in pre-Partition phase (Dey 1998: 172). Anjuman Islamia founded Kamalia Madrasa, published a weekly newspaper called *Naba Jagaran*, and created influence over the high officials under the leadership of Gedu Miah (Roychoudhury 1983: 75). The Tripura Rajya Moslem Praja Majlish voiced against pro-Pakistan propaganda through two newspapers named *Whip* and *Farid*. Hindu Mahasabha established a branch in Agartala, and Shyama Prasad Mookherjee addressed a meeting in the field of Umakanta Academy (Sengupta 2006: 18). The Bengali Hindu Sammelani merged with the Tripura branch of Mahasabha in 1946.[124] The Tripura Rajya Praja Mandal was the last progressive group in pre-Partition times. It appealed to the government to treat the riot-stricken migrants as guests in 1946. The administration agreed to be generous by extending support to the distressed populace from East Bengal (Dutta

1993: 45). The Praja Mandal demanded 'responsible Government through elections' to introduce a broad-based political platform and protested against indigenous exclusions (Bhismodeb Bhattacharyya 1989: 60). They argued for a democratic system, offered strong resistance against pro-Pakistani conspirators and opposed the anti-Bengali propaganda of the Seng-Krak, the militant wing of Bir Bikram Tripura Sangha. Seng-Krak began to incite the tribals, tried to introduce the cult of 'clenched fist' against the Bengalis (Bijan Mahanta 2004: 31–32). The Praja Mandal started publishing a bulletin, *Tripura Rajyer Katha*, edited by Biren Datta.[125] Maharaja Bir Bikram was frightened by developments like this and he premeditated tri-polar politics by launching an organisation named the Tripur Sangha with help of the tribal *Sardars* (Deb and Choudhury 1996: 10–12). It had emphasised ethnic solidarity.[126] The Maharaja tried to divide the tribals and non-tribals on material interests, but the tenure of this organisation was short-lived. It was wiped out in 14 months after the sudden death of the Maharaja. Some police records mentioned the influence of Tripur Sangha was on the wane after the rise of Bir Bikram Tripura Sangha under Durjoy Kishore Deb Burma.[127]

Partition and the initial years

The impact of Partition on Tripura was a major one, though the state formally joined the Indian Union in 1949. Partition exposed the land and its people to new ideas, ideologies and a state system, and it led to a change in power relationships between the communities. Politically, the earlier equations changed with the amalgamation of Samitis and parties (Debroy 2003: 84–85). With the decision of merger in 1949, 'the second phase of the unfortunate fate' of the tribals started, for 'living in land of Bengalis' (Deb Burma 2004: 165–66). The change of demographic profiles with migration of the refugees made the question of 'right over land' a debated issue for designing settlement plans for the middle-class and lower-middle-class Hindu Bengalis (Dutta 1993: 50). The Sealing Act was introduced after 1949 and land ownership of the royal family was identified (Pannalal Roy 2003: 70). The *khas*—revenue free lands—were distributed to members of the royal families and administration as 'land grants', as preconditions of the Agreement of Merger. These lands were left out from settlement plans for the refugees. The negotiating authorities did not encourage the prior rule of not interfering in tribal forests reserves.[128] The Customary Law was the only legal mandate used by the tribals, but the land question and consequent land reforms scared them about their future and land ownership in Tripura.[129] This crisis, coupled with encroachment of tribal lands and purchasing it high prices by the Bengalis, both in urban and rural areas, aggravated the situation. The communists urged a 'fundamental social transformation of the agrarian structure' for the refugee rehabilitation.[130]

The Central Relief and Rehabilitation Department decided to encroach reserved tribal lands. Some tribal clans were forcibly evicted; the Tripura Administration, in collusion with the *jotedars*, had evicted 15–16 Mog tribal families from their lands in Baisnavpur, Sabroom. The Mogs had been cultivating those lands for more than 40 years by duly paying rent. 'Now the *jotedars* have sold out those lands to refugees keeping the peasants in total darkness. The refugee families resettled on such lands must be shifted elsewhere, preferably on other *khas* lands of the *jotedars*'.[131] The tribals were not aware of the capture of two major avenues of economy by the refugees: professional recruitments and holdover forest lands. The gravity of the crises went unidentified for a long time. The tribals were confined within their closed society, with definite social values and their traditional beliefs.[132] Like in West Bengal and Assam, the refugees were initially dependent on the Congress, as it had consented to Partition and were considered responsible for creating the refugees (Sengupta 1991: 24–25).[133] The Congress governments in Centre and state were desperate to keep their reputations (Bijan Mahanta 2004: 77). The Congress Udbastu Sahajya Samiti had been created to look after issues of refugees. The veteran leftist leaders working in the hills were determined to resist the *mahajan*–police–military nexus related to land issues and repression of the tribals (Majumder 1997: 16–17). They instigated collaboration of tribal and non-tribal refugees to exercise 'democratic rights' in hills and plains of Tripura.[134] The Tripura Rajya Mukti Parishad (1948) was established in this background. The Mukti Parishad was 'a democratic and revolutionary organisation of the Tripuris, Bengalis, Halams, Chakmas, Kukis, Manipuris, Jamatias, Reangs, all Hindus and Muslims' (Deb Barma 1952: 3). The success of the Parishad was derived from the trust acquired by activists of the Jana Siksha Samiti.[135]

The Parishad tried to convince the tribals that the kingship would never be exercised in Tripura, as the state had been handed over to the Congress. But the Congress had adopted a policy which was against the tribals and all depressed classes (Deb 1987: 23). The Parishad organised a procession in Agartala on 15 August 1948 and decided to carry out armed struggle against the state government. The government declared martial law in the entire hills to stamp out the opposition in 1949 (Chanda 1983: 11). The imposition of the military rule led to Golaghati carnage (1949) in Padmabil and Champa-haor (Deb 1987: 90; Sen 1970: 78). During the Golaghati insurgence, military targeted tribal villages of Mathambari, Damtabari, Kabaipara, Puinga Chanbari, Bishrambari, Sipaipara, Norjanpara and Chokaipara within the Jirania Thana. Atrocities were committed in Bishalgarh, Ramnagar, Sutarmura, Jompui, Takarjola and Khoniamara to combat the guerrilla *bahini* (troops) of the Mukti Parishad. Champahaor and Kalyanpur in Khowai were completely burnt down. The Padmabil incident also witnessed the death of three women communists: Madhutidevi, Rupasreedevi and Kumaridevi. The government declared military administration over the entire Khowai Division.[136] Both the incidents and the deaths of six tribals made them apprehensive about the Bengalis. They lost faith in Congress (Deb 1987: 27–30). In order to defy the atrocities, a strong volunteer corps and military organ named the 'Shanti Sena Bahini' was formed (Dhar 2012: 6). It kept close watch on feudal oppression and social evil. An anti-famine committee was established for a temporary period of the crisis (Dutta 1993: 53–54).

The Tripura Rajya Mukti Parishad was renamed Gana Mukti Parishad in 1950. It tempered its politics with compassion and espoused in favour of 'land to the landless' and ownership to the 'hand-that-tills-the-land', and most importantly, 'tribal-non-tribal friendship' (Debbarma 2017: 18). It was determined to introduce democracy by conducting election and making ministers through the citizens. It started running parallel governance in a portion of the hills inhabited by few lakhs of tribal *jhumias* and Bengali refugees. The government had taken measures against 'anti-state' activities of the communists. *The Nation* published an article on the state atrocities with the headline 'Men hunting in jungle of Tripura' (Dutta 1993: 61). Regardless of the initiatives of Gana Mukti Parishad for working uniformly on refugee and tribal fronts within a communist pattern of political movement, resentments between the communities started from the 1950s, as the policymakers were concerned about the refugees. Tribals were on the back foot; their underprivileged status was due to the traditional pattern of their living (Bhismodeb Bhattacharyya 1989: 12). When obtaining liquid cash was decisive for the poverty-ridden tribals, government distributed regular cash doles only among the refugees.[137]

With dissolution of the monarchy in 1949, a huge number of government servants lost their jobs. The Centre and state had agreed on providing alternative 'educational certificates' to the refugees in this dominion to get jobs. Some qualified Bengali refugees made the job market vulnerable and competitive, as they enjoyed fee concessions by the government to apply for and get jobs.[138] Congress was working for the refugees by targeting the vote-bank politics (Sengupta 2006: 27). The leftists spoke on behalf of all downtrodden classes, including refugees and tribals, and urged for introduction of schemes of the Centre (Bhattachayya 1991: 130–31). In 1950, the condition of refugees stationed at Agartala had been turning from bad to worse. One refugee committed suicide in Durgabari Camp near the palace (Sengupta 1991: 25). It was learnt that 'the deceased could not secure food or money from the Relief Officer concerned on the aforesaid date. On the 11th July another refugee was reported to have died as a result of starvation at Maharajganj Camp'.[139] The East Bengal Relief Committee opened a branch at Agartala in April 1950 and Dr Meghnad Saha had noticed, 'there was no organised relief work for about 2 lakhs of helpless refugees' in Tripura.[140] So, the refugees realised the need to organise themselves under political parties, as the administration was not providing them with adequate doles and they were not getting essentials from the relief office.[141]

Organisations like Purbabanga Sankhalaghu Kalyan Samiti (on the left) and Congress Udbastu Sahajya Samiti had strong political affiliations, when Bastutyagi Janakalyan Samiti, Tripura Rajya Nath Samiti and Tripura Rudrapal Samity were working for them (Mahanta 2004: 77). Shyama Prasad Mookerjee first talked about amalgamation of these groups, advising them to fight for the rights of refugees through a common political platform.[142] The Tripura Central Relief and Rehabilitation Association was formed accordingly, and it planned systematic movements for the refugees.[143] This forum raised 18 demands, including voting rights of the refugees.[144] Following the strategies experimented with by the leaders, they organised rallies, hunger strikes and *satyagraha* with demands of schemes for better living and speedy resettlement procedure. Chief Minister Sachindralal Singh failed to foresee the danger of placing the land-hungry peasants, belonging to relatively advanced Bengalis, in direct confrontation with backward *jhumias*.[145] The government provided the refugees with ration cards at Mandai, Takarjala, Jampuijala, Khowai and Kalyanpur in West Tripura (Paul 2009: 33). The refugee colonies were built in tribal lands, surrounded by tribal villages, as per the recommendation from the rehabilitation department (Debburman 2002: 61). The government had taken projects to grow cash crops in the hilly regions.[146] Tribals lost their natural rights over their forests. Sankho Subhra Debburman, a descendant of the royal family of the Manikyas, tried to explain these incidents of exploitation and gradual marginalisation of tribals from class perspectives. By comparing them with the refugee categories who came to Surma valley of Assam and West Bengal, he opined, the refugees who migrated to Tripura mostly belonged to the lower-strata of people. They lacked in education, family morals and sophistication.[147]

The rise of the leftists

After forming the government in Tripura, Congress got involved in refugee rehabilitation on a war footing. Keeping the general election of 1952 in mind, the government was extra cautious (Bhattachayya 1991: 130–31). But the leftists were successful in the end in achieving their goal in the election. Biren Dutta and Dasharath Deb were elected as representatives and Members of Parliament when they were in the underground (Deb 1987: 17–18). A National Conference was held in 1952, and Nehru visited Tripura to discuss problems of scheduled castes and tribes, after Congress was defeated in that election (Bandyapadhyay 2005: 3). Dasharath Deb emphatically stated: 'Some area or areas of Tripura shall have to be set aside for the tribal alone and no other persons belonging to non-tribal communities should be allowed to settle there'.[148] He advocated for an Advisory Board on behalf of the Gana Mukti Parishad for settlement of refugees in those areas, by issuance of an ordinance. He called for 'stopping all evictions pending proper legislation on tenancy rights'.[149] The Parishad approached the Communist Party, Kisan Samitis, Ganatantrik Sangha and Praja Socialist Party to represent the Advisory Board.[150] The tribal experience of having refugees in their lands was complex. The whole idea of an enduring peaceful life suddenly was confronted with land-hungry refugees.[151] The Ministry of States reported on the pitiable condition of the tribals in South Charilam and Khas Brajapur, Bishalgarh in 1953:

> It will be noticed that there is some trouble over the requisition of cultivable land by Government for the purpose of rehabilitating the displaced persons, with the result that the rightful owners are being deprived of the land which is the only means of livelihood.[152]

The Bengalis contributed to dislocating the tribals in every possible way. The price of daily necessities like salt and dried fish skyrocketed. The hilly terrain, considered the territory of the tribals by birth, and their sole source of survival and economic base, was the first choice of the rehabilitation department for providing lands to the refugees under various schemes proposed by the Centre (Choudhury 1991: 10). With the building up of refugee colonies, the concept of 'private property' first emerged in 'Hill Tripura'.[153] The tribals were suffering on account of land shortage and the state was insisting on the transformation of the *jhum* economy. It led to the curtailing of their freedom of choosing portions of hills for *jhum* cultivation. The scientific measures taken by the government to protect the environment and logical restrictions imposed on the tribals to give up *jhum* posed a challenge to tribal entity for the first time. The government tried to portray the plains as 'safe haven' for the *jhumias* in terms of alternative occupations.[154] The imposition of ban on *jhum* was the final blow on their life and culture. They lost their identity and romanticism of life around it (Debburman 2007: 28). They started agitating against tribal land transfer and insisted the government not allow more migration from 1954 (Dhar 2010: 30–31). Sudhanya Deb Barma, in *Hakuch-Khurich* (a novel in *Kok-barok*), stressed the psychological impact of the changes on the tribals (Deb Burma 2004: 30–31). The leftists kept on pressuring the government to pay compensation to the tribals for land acquisitions.[155]

The impact of the changes in demographic profile could be seen in the city of Agartala. Anjali Barman, a refugee herself remarked: 'In early 1950s, Krishnanagar was full of houses owned by the tribals and later, it mostly occupied by the Bengalis'. She remembered: 'I can still visualise how the tribal owners of those houses allowed the helpless refugees to stay. But, now the land and houses had permanently been taken over by those shelter-seekers'.[156] The Gana Mukti Parishad had affirmed:

> in the present scramble of land, it is not possible for the tribals, particularly for tribal *jhumias* to secure land on personal initiative. Therefore, in the area inhabited by tribal people, all *khas* lands should be reserved exclusively for rehabilitation of tribals.
> *(Bhattachayya 1991: 131)*

The communists had broadened their appeal and earned the conviction of the masses by supporting rehabilitation of the tribal *jhumias* along with the Bengali refugees (Debburma, Roy Chiran and Choudhry 2002: 343). The Mukti Parishad demanded establishment of industry, commerce and agricultural cooperatives at the conference of the Sanjukta Bastuhara Parishad in 1953, in exchange for providing jobs to the refugees and tribals (Mahanta 2004: 84–85); yet, Gobind Ballabh Pant, then the Union Home Minister, stated in Parliament in 1955 that the resettlement of refugees had reached a 'saturation point' and it would not be advisable to rehabilitate additional people in Tripura (Paul 2009: 30). The Rehabilitation Department closed down its branch office in Agartala.[157] The state government was firm in carrying out the decision of the Centre. They 'refused to accept the cooperation of Tripura Ganatantrik Samiti in providing refugee relief, inauguration of schools and industrial centres'.[158] The refugees started a hunger strike in Durgabari under the leadership of Dasharath Deb. Bisyambor Nomo Das, a caste refugee, eventually died. The situation became so volatile that Indira Gandhi was compelled to visit Tripura to inspect the conditions (Saha 2009: 119–20). The agitations forced the government to resettle the refugees at Nalkata in Kailashahar, Amtoli and Arundhatinagar (Paul 2009: 50).

Such incidents made the tribals think that the refugees were the 'pet sons of the Government' who were getting 'at least rupees one thousand a month' (Chakrabarty 1996: 6–7). The idyllic existence of the tribals in a tradition-bound society was not the sole factor responsible for their impoverishment. Exploitation by the Bengalis and well-off tribals towards the poor tribal families was significant. There was a wide gap between what tribals were earning and how much they needed to survive.[159] Small sizes of their holdings, lack of irrigation facilities, institutional credit systems, paucity of non-farm job opportunities at the localities, their ways of living and their unwillingness to adopt new means increased their indebtedness. They had a tendency to borrow money from the moneylenders by mortgaging land or households. As per the indigenous rule, if the creditor did not possess anything, he had to render labour for the moneylender and the moneylender would decide the duration of the period.[160] Some refugees started moneylending businesses, land grabbing and practicing unfair means in trading with the tribal neighbours.[161] It was an unequal economic competition with the culturally advanced non-tribals. The Bengali version was that they got settled in barren lands where no cultivation had ever been undertaken by the tribals. The Bengali peasants with their hard toil turned it into fertile, highly productive agricultural zones (Singh 1987: 265). This tendency increased the alienation of the tribals. The government tried to conduct rehabilitation of the *jhumias* and refugees with equal precedence. Crash programmes like allotting of lands; giving bullocks, milch cows, poultry birds and other subsidies were not enough as feasible solutions for them. They had to be economically rehabilitated within their own ways of living, in their geophysical and psychic frameworks.[162] The tribals had finally accepted the majoritarian presence of the refugees in their land; they tolerated their dominance in cultural issues and in other privileged sectors, like education and administrative jobs in Tripura. Manju Das, in her short story *Uttoran*, asked why the Bengalis had forgotten the contributions of the tribals in their survival and later behaved like an enemy (Das 2014: 23).

Many refugees and consequent conflicts

As compulsions of electoral politics and party system, the tribals remained on the receiving end. They became marginalised and their population was decreasing in every decade. In 1921, percentage of the total tribal population was 54.69; in 1941, it was 50.09; in 1961, it was 31.53; and in 1971, it was 28.95.[163] Such demographic explosion was attributed more to the influx of migrants than to the natural increase of indigenous people. The official figures showed that a total of 6,09,998 Bengalis migrated to Tripura between 1947 and 1971 and had taken financial assistance from the government.[164] During the 70-year period 1901–1971, while the percentage increase in population for India as a whole was 129.6, for northeastern India in general and Tripura in particular, it was 358.4 and 797.9, respectively (Sinha 1982: 59–60). Some extremist tribal organisations became vocal about it from the late 1950s. Tripuri identity politics took definite shape marked by ideological breaks that were different from the earlier discourses (Bhattacharyya 2002: 17–19, 42–44). Tripur Sangha Paharia Union, Adivasi Samiti and Tripura Rajya Adibasi Sangha started opposing Bengali dominance in the job market and state administration on ideological grounds. In 1954, all groups were merged to form Adivasi Sansad and represented modern political construction of Bengali as 'others' or 'outsiders' (Devi 2010: 179). A broad-based common platform for the tribals of Northeast India named the Eastern Indian Tribal Union was established in 1957. The organisation argued that the refugee rehabilitation had been standing in way of tribal rehabilitation in Tripura, and no unqualified support to the refugee rehabilitation was ensured from them.[165]

Introduction of new acts became necessary to check further displacement of the tribals, and an effort was needed to bring back illegally transferred lands. The Dhebar Commission Report of 1960 suggested formation of tribal development blocs in tribal compact areas as experiments. They stated:

> The influx of displaced persons from Pakistan to Tripura has been enormous and has upset the local economy. It has greatly affected the tribals and has made the tribal problem acute. The right of the tribals in land should be safeguarded.
>
> *(Deb Barma 2005: 57)*

The Government of India enacted the Tripura Land Revenue and Land Reforms Act (TLR & LR Act). The chief concern of the Act was to abolish the intermediaries and make the tillers (*raiyats*) the owners of land. Besides, for prevention of land alienation of the tribals, the Act sought to officially record title ship and to address bottlenecks in increasing agricultural production.[166] The TLR & LR Act was based on the understanding that unless the land ownership of the tribals was ensured and protected by law, illegal transfer of their land to the non-tribals would not be stopped. Yet, alienation of the tribals could not be checked effectively. The Act barred transfer of land from a tribal owner, under section 187.[167] It was a bold step to protect tribal interests from government's front, yet these '*benami*' transfers continued.[168]

In the annual report of the Commission for Schedule Caste and Tribes, it was mentioned 'the tribal people are apprehensive of their land given to the refugees'.[169] The Commissioner interacted with them to get a first-hand experience, reporting: 'I gathered that some of the refugees have purchased land from the tribals. I recommend that elimination of tribals' land inside and outside the Tribal Reserves must be stopped immediately'.[170] Between 1962 and 1966, 3 lakhs of refugees were rehabilitated in tribal areas, but the tribals were not encouraged to settle down in Shilachhori and Amarpur by the police or administration.[171] Bichitra Mohan Saha, Minister of Revenue Department, informed in the Legislative Assembly that the refugees who got land rights through exchange system, or by a valid power of attorney, did not receive any grants and loans from the government.[172] The attitude of the state and condition of the marginal communities was evident from the discussion in the Legislative Assembly: 'Large scale displacement of tribals and refugees of Bogafa, near the Block area in Belonia Subdivision due to acquisition of land for public purposes and absence of any re-settlement schemes for the displaced persons'.[173] With the enactment of Government of Union Territories Act of 1963, the Legislative Assembly was constituted in Tripura. It was empowered to make laws under section 18.[174] The Upajati Gana Mukti Parishad, which was renamed again in 1964 from Gana Mukti Parishad, was working to strengthen the tribal base and for tribal rights. They insisted on incorporation of military administration in tribal areas, treating it as a compulsion in their movement to fight with the Congress state forces and Bengali in-migration (Verghese 1996: 169).

The identity politics in Tripura was represented by three political formations: Tripura Upajati Jubo Samity (TUJS), Twipra Students' Federation (TSF) and Tripura National Volunteer (TNV). TSF's anthem '*Kusung Kusung*' (in *Kok-barok*) harps on Tripura as a mighty expensive kingdom of the tribals. Unlike previous narratives of Manikya rule as feudalistic, the past (prior to merger with India) was imagined as 'glorious' (Debbarma 2013: 15). TUJS was born with a bang under the leadership of Sonacharan Debbarma in 1967 (Paul 2009: 56). TUJS was a student organisation; gradually it entered into the political arena of the state and carried out a long and sustained campaign, focused on the decrease of tribal population from 70 per cent to 30 per cent.[175] TUJS had provided support to the agenda of the Communist Party of India (Marxist) (CPIM) in the first phase, and the party was keen to portray TUJS as its youth wing. But looking at their aims and ideas, Dasharath Deb thought that such an organisation might look communal—and that might have a negative impact on its 'democratic movement' (Verghese 1996: 172). TUJS demanded active participation of tribals in administration, self-management and adequate control over their own affairs under Autonomous District Council (ADC) for tribals, extension of the Inner Line Regulations and restoration of alienated tribal land under the TLR & LR Act of 1960. The Amendment of the Act put a ban on alienation of tribal land, but legalised all land transfers that had taken place before 1969.[176]

The Tripura National Volunteers (TNV) had targeted the Bengalis, not the state. Subir Bhaumik argued 'The TNV's anti-Bengali violence created general climate of ethnic hatred which was sharpened by the large-scale alienation of the tribal lands and actual marginalisation in jobs, professions and politics'.[177] Prior to TNV, the *Seng-krak* (Clenched Fist) surfaced as a tribal insurgent group in 1967. It was vocal in advocacy for expulsion of refugees from Tripura (Debbarma 2013: 14–15). It maintained close links with the Mizo National Front (Das 2009: 1). By 1969, TUJS floated a force of armed volunteers named *Tripura Sena*. Bijoy Kumar Hrangkhawl was selected as the chief of the new outfit. Considering the sensitive nature of inter-community relations between the Bengalis and tribals, it demanded coverage of the Sixth Schedule after 1971, as it had the potential to spark off the explosion.[178] CPM's support in its demand evoked adverse reaction from the Bengalis. They perceived it as a threat to their landholdings. The Amra Bangali, a communal outfit of the non-tribals and political arm of the Ananda Marg, launched a counter-campaign 'to protect the Bengalis' and their right to oppose the ADC. The base of TUJS got stronger with its decision to contest in the election of 1972. The TUJS logic was that the Government cannot give 68.10 per cent of its land (7131 sq. km) to 30.50 per cent of the population, depriving the 69.50 per cent majority (Paul 2009: 63). TUJS demanded ADC for tribals under the Fifth Schedule of the Constitution (Bhattachayya 1991: 134).[179] From 1974, TUJS demanded setting up of schools under the banner of Tripura Tribal Linguistic Enterprise, and demanded restoration of *Kok-barok* as one of the official languages and introduction of the same as the medium of instruction for tribal students in Roman scripts. The language and script issues engulfed Tripura for a long time, though it had hardly been addressed in proper earnest (Das 2009: 1).

In the absence of expansion of non-agricultural job opportunities, pressure on the limited land had increased. The Dhebar Commission recommended providing jobs to the scheduled caste and scheduled tribes 'not only to fill up the ratio but to give them more facility'.[180] Non-agricultural employment opportunities required expansion as alternatives. The demographic upsurge due to natural increases and influx of refugees led to overcrowding on land. In 1971, the percentage of agricultural workers in Tripura was 74.37. The non-tribals tried to come out from lower economic position. They tried their luck in new ventures, in which tribals were reluctant. So, the tribes became the natural victims of the demographic pressure on land.[181] The 1971 census stated that *Kok-barok* was the mother tongue of 3,60,654 tribals, which was 79.79 per cent of the total tribal population consisting of 18 tribes and sub-tribes of the state (Bhattacharjee 1989: 31). The emergence of Bangladesh did not fetch positive changes in the fate of ethnic communities of Chittagong Hill Tracts. From 1971, the Chakmas of CHT claimed separate homeland and independent Bangladesh was plagued by insurgency.[182] The Bangladesh Government believed in the ideology of Bengali nationalism, they rendered patronage and rapid growth of the 'outsider' Bengali settlement in CHT, especially during the reign of General Zia-ur-Rehman and General Ershad (Mutsuddhi 1992: 14–15). The Bengali Muslims were depriving the indigenous Chakmas, both by transferring lands and submerging as a community (Bhattachayya 1991: 123).

The migration of the Chakma refugees had started from the late 1950s. *Hindustan Standard* reported on 16 March 1959 that the Buddhist Chakmas were fleeing from CHT and taking shelter in Tripura (Sengupta 2016: 190). After the construction of the Kaptai hydroelectric project in 1966, about 66,000 Chakmas and Hajong refugees entered India (Choudhury 1991: 10). The Centre provided them temporary shelters and arranged relief camps for them, but the question of their rehabilitation was non-existent (Nandy 1993: 2102). There were no opportunities to get medical treatment, education or food within the camps. Despite regular grants and aid from the Centre, the state started considering these refugees to be a burden.[183] Their presence had created environmental concerns in South Tripura. The steady rise in birth rate within the camps threatened and strained the state resources (Basu Majumder 2003: 93). The area surrounding the refugee camps underwent deforestation. The local people faced shortages of natural resources like firewood, wild vegetables, bamboo shoots and wild potatoes, which constituted primary sources of their livelihood.[184] The Central Government had spent Rs. 13.5 million on the refugees. It became a reason for discontent among the indigenous tribals. They felt marginalised and harboured resentment for treating the tribal refugees as privileged.[185] It generated conflicts of interest between the local tribals and tribal refugees. Another 55,000 Chakmas entered Tripura after 1971.[186] TUJS, based in Amarpur and Subroom subdivisions, agitated on the staying on of the Chakma refugees from the CHT. It demanded that the Chakmas be shifted to other states of India.

After the Liberation War of 1971, the Government of Tripura was firm on the idea of issuing citizenship cards to all its citizens. The domicile tribals used to enjoy a quick procedure to get a citizenship card, but the Chief Minister Sukhamoy Sengupta, on behalf of the state, had given responsibility to all Panchayat offices to perform some mandatory enquiries including showing of a certificate stating one's place of birth. The domicile tribals were wary of such complicated procedures and started protesting against the idea of providing them citizenship in their own land.[187] The entire decade of the 1970s experienced a diverse identity politics that was marked by radically polarised confrontations between the state and ethnonationalist fronts in Tripura.[188] The conflicts and underlying threat perception of tribal and non-tribals reached its nadir in the 1977 election results (Das Gupta 1984: 451). With the CPIM-led Left Front in power, their demand for ADC got an impetus and it created an environment of expectation among the tribals. They urged 'expulsion of the foreigners (Bengalis) who had come to this state since October 15, 1949, the day Tripura joined the Indian Union' as a solution (Das Gupta 1986: 1665). This demand for deportation of foreigners, implementation of the Sixth Schedule (District Council), led to ethnic riots of 1980 at Mandai between tribals and Bengalis. The communal riot split the state bureaucracy, police and the Communist party along the ethnic lines. As the politics continued to play on sharply ethnic lines, the communal divide was widening fast (Karlekar 1985: 1428).

Bimal Sinha, in his novel *Titas theke Tripura*, portrayed the complexities in the mentalities of the refugees. They tried to settle down in a similar geographical location to recreate an almost identical essence, which they left in their *desh*. The *Koibortyas* had chosen a riverbank for resettlement. Some purchased lands in the border villages of Charipara, Gojaria, Joypur, Shanmura, Lonkamura and Kalikapur. Their argument was, though they left their country, they would be in touch with their land (Sinha 2009b: 45). With the colossal effect of the Bengali migration and strong cultural impact, the tribals started forgetting their own culture and language. The urban tribal population hardly could converse in *Kok-barok* or

Tipra.[189] The Bengalis became so dominant that they started changing names of the places at their convenience, as the *Kok-barok* names were difficult to spell out. In some cases, they altered the names by keeping its essence intact. At times, they introduced a word, which was either an abbreviation or similar to hear. For example, the place Lengnama (a place for taking rest) permanently changed to Jirania from the Bengali term 'jirano' (taking rest).[190] Tula Chhikok in Khowai changed to Tula Shikhor, Khuruilung in Teliamura became Koroilong, and Khumpuilung in Udaypur was reborn as Kupilong. The Bengalis never faced firm resentment for resettlement or received a treatment of being labelled as 'uncalled-for immigrants' in Tripura. Imposition of cultural hegemony by the Bengalis was disturbing for the tribals (Kundu Choudhury 2008: 30–31). Their hegemonic effect was so impactful and deep that the tribals often left their food, customs, practices and language to be like the 'civilized' educated Bengalis.[191] Meenaakshi Sen depicted insecurity of the tribals in her short story *Surjyosombhob*. The central character, a convicted terrorist named Korno Kumar Jamatia, tried to teach the technique of binding a bunch of flowers as per the tribal practice. Seeing his fellow tribal prisoners, he lamented that when Bengalis had authority to judge what is right or wrong, which conduct was punishable or not, the tribal community lost all rights and forgot their ethnic customs, norms and cultures. For him, it was the last attempt to revive the craft (Sen 1418: 111).

The fate of the peripheral refugees

Assam and Tripura experienced the creation of a borderland in northeastern India and received huge number of refugees. At the time of Partition, both of the states had settled Bengalis who used to dominate the job market, along with other working units. But unlike West Bengal, the settled Bengalis voiced the grievances of the refugee Bengalis, and some provided shelter to them. But the pattern of refugee handling was completely different in these states, situated in the same region. Right from the Partition, Assam was against their absorption, as they claimed the total percentage of Bengali Hindus and Muslims would be more than the domiciles. The policy was communicated to the Central Rehabilitation Ministry, too. Yet, the Congress High Command compelled the state to accommodate the refugees in Cachar and some areas of the Brahmaputra valley. The communal divide along religious lines was never predominant in Assamese society. There were few Hindu-Muslim rifts in the pre- and post-independence phases, which was insignificant in comparison to the number of conflicts held between the Assamese and Bengalis (Rafiabadi 1988: 28–30). Congress rather always tried to exploit sentiments of migrant Muslims and used them as vote banks. In 1960 and 1972, the Muslims supported the cause of the Assamese against the stand of the Bengali Hindus. The word community denotes two prominent linguistic groups, in which the domiciles tried to reject the birthright and due claims of the Bengalis by categorising them as *bhogania*, immigrants, Pakistanis, fugitives, infiltrators and foreigners. The politically inclined vibrant student communities, and some socio-cultural platforms like

Sahitya Sabha, played crucial roles in highlighting the regional aspirations of the Assamese within the structure of nationalism to deny the right of the Bengalis to maintain their language and culture, primarily in Brahmaputra valley and the tribal areas. It eventually hit upon the identity issues that touched the politics. The conflict on the state language or the medium of instruction ignited the separatist tendencies of the ethnic tribals, and they started protesting against the Assamese hegemony more profoundly. From the 1970s, a trend emerged in the northeastern region to create tribal-identity-centric or linguistic states, which was initiated by the creation of Meghalaya in 1972. It aggravated Assamese aggression towards the Bengali communities.

Because of Partition and coming of the refugees in waves, the ethnic tribals were wiped out by the socio-political and linguistic domination of the Bengalis. Until the mid-1950s, the Bengalis enjoyed all sorts of possible power and privileges, except facing challenges from the tribals. From the 1960s, a section of the tribals was forced to trigger new identity formation and community building for them. Like in West Bengal, political parties played a crucial role in politicising the issues of grievances of both the communities to establish their foothold in Tripura. While the Bengali refugees helped the communists to grab positions in the state ministry in 1977, the leftists corroborated their participation in each layer of the society, and they could legalise their claim over lands by passing laws and amendments. The communists had control over the tribals as they tried to educate and enlighten them. The tribals trusted the leftists, and this is the reason why the extremist tribal organisations like TUJS primarily tried to be a sister concern of the CPIM. The Congress as a sole political block failed to earn the confidence of the Bengali refugees in both Assam and Tripura. The communists and other leftist parties could establish themselves in the mainstream politics of the northeastern states with the help of the refugees. The communists used to have a hold over the large terrain of East Bengal, when the Central authorities banned the party in both pre- and post-Partition periods. The party members internally connected the whole region. Hence, the leftist leaders of the Samitis of Cachar had been designing plans for political strategy on behalf of the leaders in Tripura. The region itself facilitated the separatists' organisations and political platforms. A network was established from the CHT to Indian separatist organisations by involving all other tribal ethnic extremist groups of northeastern states, including Assam and Tripura. The refugees, as new social agents, contributed to the massive alteration of the landscape design, power hierarchies in state politics and socio-economic change. The border remained notional, as the region enjoyed open borders until the 1980s. A whole network of 'silent migration' of the underground operators continued through the porous border, termed in local language as *gola-dhakka* passage.[192] It was not demarcated or fenced. Except during the time of colossal tides, the refugees never felt that they were crossing international borders. Malaykanti Ghosh, a leftist activist writer of Barak valley, depicted the emotions of a Muslim peasant Ashraf, the central character of a short story, who came to India as an economic migrant and was deported forcibly by the police. He wonders: the lands were visually the same;

vegetation, language and food habits were not different; and he did not even notice any border—why, then, was some territory called India and other side Pakistan? The only difference he could notice was the dress of the military garrison placed in the check-posts, and they even converse in the same tones of a common language, Bengali (Dey 2014: 59–60).

Notes

1 'Viceroy's Personal Report No. 13, dated 18th July 1947'. File No. L/PO/6/123, Pt. 1, Neg 9850 (1-105), IOR.
2 File No. V/24/1033: 1942–1947, IOR.
3 *Invasion in Disguise: The Problem of Foreign Infiltration in Assam*. 1980. Gauhati: Co-Ordination Committee, Gauhati University Teachers' Association, p. ii.
4 *Nagarik*, 27 July 1978.
5 Jyotsna Roy Choudhury. 2006. 'Surma Nodir Parer Smriti'. In *Dasdishi Troimashik Sahitya Patrika*, 48–49. Kolkata: Somadrita.
6 File No. 5/1/4/1: 15 May 1900–25 June 1923, IOR.
7 B. C. Allen. *Assam District Gazetteers, Nowgong, Secretariat Administration, Record and Library Department, Assam Secretariat*, File No. Z/E/4/32/R639: 1858, p. 277, IOR.
8 File No. V/23/95, No. 22 D: 1955, IOR.
9 Letter Issued to the Government of India, Vol. 7, No. 236, *Jenkins to William Grey*, 7 December 1854, Assam Secretariat Records.
10 A. J. M. Mills. 1984. *Report on the Province of Assam*. Guwahati: Publication Board Assam, 26.
11 Anindita Dasgupta. 2004. 'Partition Migration in Assam: The Case of Sylheti *Bhadraloks*'. In *State, Society and Displaced People in South Asia*, ed. Imtiaz Ahmed, Abhijit Dasgupta and Kathinka Sinha Kerkhoff, 117. Dhaka: UPL.
12 Revenue Department, Revenue-A, November 1898, No. 128–138, Record and Library Department, Assam Secretariat.
13 Atul Goswami and Jayanta Kr. Gogoi. 1984. 'Migration and Demographic Transformation of Assam, 1901–1971'. In *Northeast Region: Problems and Prospect of Development*, ed. B. L. Abbi, 68. Chandigarh: Centre for Research in Rural and Industrial Development.
14 File No. 471, Year- 1862–73, *Assamese Language*, ASA.
15 Tilottama Misra. 1982. 'Assam and the National Question'. In *Nationality Question in India*, Seminar Papers (held in Madras), 50. Hyderabad: Andhra Pradesh Radical Students Union.
16 P. C. Goswami. 1984. 'Foreign Immigration into Assam'. In *Northeast Region: Problems and Prospect of Development*, ed. B. L. Abbi, 37–39. Chandigarh: Centre for Research in Rural and Industrial Development.
17 Satyendranath Sharma. 1967. *Ashomia Sahityor Itibritta*. Gauhati: Sahitya Academy, p. 244.
18 Daibo Chandra Talukdar. 1930. *Apurna*. Guwahati: Published by the Author, pp. 76–78.
19 R. Gopalakrishnan, K. K. Jhunjhunwala and Manasi Shailaja. 2002. 'Population Displacement and Development Dilemmas: A Reflection on Linguistic Politics in the North-East'. In *Dimensions of Displaced People in North-East India*, ed. C. Joshua, 56. New Delhi: Regency Publications.
20 *Amrita Bazar Patrika*, 20 November 1935.
21 *Samachar Darpan*, 24 September 1931.
22 L-PJ/5/140-1947- Assam Governor's Reports, IOR.
23 *ALA Debates*, 1948, Vol. I–II, No. 2, p. 1352.
24 P. C. Goswami. 1984. 'Foreign Immigration into Assam'. In *Northeast Region: Problems and Prospect of Development*, ed. B. L. Abbi, 35. Chandigarh: Centre for Research in Rural and Industrial Development.

25 *Gazetteer of India*, 24 December 1949, p. 503.
26 *White Paper on Foreigner's Issues*, Home & Political Department, Government of Assam, 20 October 2012, p. 6.
27 *Invasion in Disguise: The Problem of Foreign Infiltration in Assam*. 1980. Gauhati: Co-Ordination Committee, Gauhati University Teachers' Association, p. ii.
28 *ALA Debates*, 1950, Vol. I–II, p. 163.
29 S. M. Saadullah Papers, Subject File No. 18, NMML.
30 *Invasion in Disguise: The Problem of Foreign Infiltration in Assam*. 1980. Gauhati: Co-Ordination Committee, Gauhati University Teachers' Association, p. ii.
31 *The Foreigners Problem: An Analysis*. 1990. Gauhati, Assam: The All Assam Gana Sangram Parishad, p. 15.
32 File No. 165 z/24-1, Sl. No. 70/1924, I B Reports, WBSA.
33 R. Gopalakrishnan, K. K. Jhunjhunwala and Manasi Shailaja. 2002. 'Population Displacement and Development Dilemmas: A Reflection on Linguistic Politics in the North-East'. In *Dimensions of Displaced People in North-East India*, ed. C. Joshua, 58–59. New Delhi: Regency Publications.
34 *APCC Papers*, Packet No. 97, File No. 5, NMML.
35 *Invasion in Disguise: The Problem of Foreign Infiltration in Assam*. 1980. Gauhati: Co-Ordination Committee, Gauhati University Teachers' Association, pp. iii–iv.
36 File No. 165 z/24, Sl. No. 70/1924, IB Reports, WBSA.
37 Press Statements issued by Dr Saha after his visit to Cachar with Shri Tridib Chowdhury, MP. *M. N. Saha Papers and Correspondences*, 1952–55, VII Instalment, Subject File No. 2, pp. 124–27, NMML.
38 *Jugantar*, 25 October 1959.
39 *ALA Debates*, 1959, Vol. I, No. 1, Part-1, p. 28.
40 J. B. Bhattacharjee. 1994. 'The Pre-Colonial Political Structure of Barak Valley'. In *Essays on North East India: Presented in Memory of Professor Venkata Rao*, ed. Milton S. Sangma, 61–63. New Delhi: Indus.
41 Bipul Chaudhury. 2007. 'The Growth of Assamese Identity in Colonial Assam'. *NEIHA*, Twenty-Eighth Session, Goalpara, p. 284.
42 *S. M. Saadulla Papers*, Subject File No. 19, NMML.
43 *ALA Debates*, 1950, Vol. I, No. 1, Part-1, p. 78.
44 *APCC Papers*, Packet No. 97, File No. 2, NMML.
45 R. Gopalakrishnan. 1987. 'Stress and Response in a Socio-Economic Crisis in the Brahmaputra Valley: A Response Perception of the Assam Gana Sangram Parishad'. *NEIHA*, Eighth Session, Kohima, p. 358.
46 Bhupen Sharma. 2001. 'Immigration and Politics in Assam: Question Relating to Human Rights'. In *Refugees and Human Rights: Social and Political Dynamics of Refugee Problem in Eastern and North-Eastern India*, ed. Sanjoy K. Roy, 369. Jaipur and New Delhi: Rawat Publications.
47 R. Gopalakrishnan, K. K. Jhunjhunwala and Manasi Shailaja. 2002. 'Population Displacement and Development Dilemmas: A Reflection on Linguistic Politics in the North-East'. In *Dimensions of Displaced People in North-East India*, ed. C. Joshua, 57. New Delhi: Regency Publications.
48 Memorandum submitted to the States Reorganisation Commission by The West Bengal Pradesh Congress Committee, *Sibnath Banerjee Papers*, Subject File No. 6, 1954, p. 188, NMML.
49 *Indian Statutory Commission, Memoranda Assam 57-1033*. File No. Q/13/1/1, IOR.
50 *M. N. Saha Papers*, VII Instalment, Printed Material, Sl. No. 6, NMML.
51 Mahasammelan of Bengali-Speaking People organised by Paschim Banga Rajyo Punargathan Sangjukta Parishad at Senate Hall, Calcutta, 1956, p. 8.
52 *ALA Debates*, 1955, Vol. II, No. 25, p. 224.
53 *Padmaja Naidu Papers*, Subject File No. 9, NMML.
54 File No. 1/C-3 (1) (K), 1955, Sl. No. 20 SB Kahalipara.

Politics as defence **239**

55 *Invasion in Disguise: The Problem of Foreign Infiltration in Assam.* 1980. Gauhati: Co-Ordination Committee, Gauhati University Teachers' Association, pp. iii–iv.
56 File No. 1/C-3 (1) (E), 1952, Sl. No. 344 SB Kahalipara.
57 File No. 1/C-3 (1) 1953, Sl. No. 648 SB, Kahalipara and *Natun Asomia,* Dated Dibrugarh, 8 June 1955.
58 File No. 1/C-3 (1) 1952, Sl. No. 334 SB, Kahalipara.
59 File No. 1/C-3 (1) (N) 1955, Sl. No. 42 SB, Kahalipara.
60 Memorandum submitted before the States Reorganisation Commission by the Assam Sahitya Sabha on 10 May 1955.
61 *APCC Papers,* Packet No. 42, File No. 11, NMML.
62 'Asomor Dwitiya Lekhak Sibir: Lipi Somporkio Alochona Chokro', Report of the Assam Sahitya Sabha, *APCC Papers,* Packet No. 42, File No. 11, NMML.
63 Copy of the Resolution on 'State Language and Hill State' Adopted by the Provincial Executive of the PSP, Assam in its Meeting held at Jorhat on 23rd and 24th of September 1960. *APCC Papers,* Packet No. 97, File No. 1, NMML.
64 *Notun Asamia,* 28 February 1960.
65 Memo No. SB 40070.77, Deputy Inspector General of Police, CID, Assam Daily Situation Report No. 42, by G. C. Bordoloi, DIG of Police, Dated Shillong, the 1st July 1960.
66 *ALA Debates,* 1960, Vol. I, No. 1–10, pp. 30–31.
67 Memorandum Opposing the Declaration of Assamese as the Official Language of the State of Assam Submitted to the President of the Republic of India, by The Council of Action Appointed by the Conference of All-Party Hill Leaders of Assam Who Met at Shillong on July 6th and 7th, 1960. *APCC Papers,* Packet No. 97, File No. 3, NMML.
68 *Notun Asamia,* 17 March 1960.
69 File No. PLB 91/60, Daily Situation 1960, Language Riots.
70 *Notun Asamia,* 2 June 1960.
71 *Notun Asamia,* 24 March 1960.
72 *Notun Asamiya,* 10 October 1960.
73 'Report on the Recent Disturbances in Assam', *AICC Papers,* File No. 4063-C, NMML.
74 *Report of the Enquiry Commission into the Police Firing incident of 4th July 1960 at Gauhati by C. P. Sinha.* 3 August 1960. Chief Justice, Assam High Court.
75 *Report of the Enquiry Commission into the Police Firing incident of 4th July 1960 at Gauhati by C. P. Sinha.* 3 August 1960. Chief Justice, Assam High Court.
76 *Khandu Bhai Desai Papers,* (190 XXX), Sl. No. 57, NMML.
77 *Report of the Commission of Enquiry into the Goreswar disturbances by Justice Gopalji Mehrotra,* 1960.
78 The Assam Official Language Act, 1960, Clause 3, '*Official Language for Official Purposes of the State of Assam*'.
79 *A Case for Bengalis in Assam.* April 1960. Hojoi: Published by Nikhil Assam Banga Bhasa Samity.
80 *Padmaja Naidu Papers,* Subject File No. 8, NMML.
81 Secret Memo Bearing No. 41233.70/C, dated 17th May, 1961 from SP, Cachar to other police officials.
82 *Findings and Resolution on Assam's Language Problem by the Citizen's Welfare Committee.* Silchar, Adopted on 15th September 1960.
83 *Hindustan Standard,* 30 May 1961.
84 *Times of India,* 30 May 1961.
85 The demonstrators who lost their lives in police firing were named Sachindra Paul, Chandi Charan Sutradhar, Hitesh Biswas, Tarani Devnath, Kumud Das, Sukomal Purkayasta, Sunil Sarkar, Kanailal Neogi, Kamala Bhattacharjee, Satyendra Deb and Birendra Sutradhar. Extract copy of weekly confidential report for the week ending 24/05/1961 of Cachar District: *Report of the Non-Official Commission of Enquiry headed by N. C. Chatterjee, Barrister-at-Law,* Supreme Court of India.

86 R. Gopalakrishnan, K. K. Jhunjhunwala and Manasi Shailaja. 2002. 'Population Displacement and Development Dilemmas: A Reflection on Linguistic Politics in the North-East'. In *Dimensions of Displaced People in North-East India*, ed. C. Joshua, 54. New Delhi: Regency Publications.
87 *APCC Papers*, Packet No. 97, File No. 3, NMML.
88 R. Gopalakrishnan, K. K. Jhunjhunwala and Manasi Shailaja. 2002. 'Population Displacement and Development Dilemmas: A Reflection on Linguistic Politics in the North-East'. In *Dimensions of Displaced People in North-East India*, ed. C. Joshua, 58. New Delhi: Regency Publications.
89 *White Paper on Foreigner's Issues*, Home & Political Department, Government of Assam, 20 October 2012, p. 7.
90 R. Gopalakrishnan, K. K. Jhunjhunwala and Manasi Shailaja. 2002. 'Population Displacement and Development Dilemmas: A Reflection on Linguistic Politics in the North-East'. In *Dimensions of Displaced People in North-East India*, ed. C. Joshua, 55. New Delhi: Regency Publications.
91 *ALA Debates*, 1964, Vol. II, No. 1, p. 2065.
92 *Notun Asamia*, 6 March 1965.
93 Shri Nogen Borurai, a member of the Legislative Assembly was critical about it, like many others. *ALA Debates*, 1965, Vol. VI, No. III, pp. 4-5.
94 *Invasion in Disguise: The Problem of Foreign Infiltration in Assam*. 1980. Gauhati: Co-Ordination Committee, Gauhati University Teachers' Association, p. 7.
95 File No. RSS 58/69, ASA.
96 Cited in *White Paper on Foreigner's Issues*, Home & Political Department, Government of Assam, 20 October 2012, p. 8.
97 Only 405 persons were intercepted in 1975 and one person detained by the BSF and returned to Bangladesh in 1976.
98 *ALA Debates*, 1972, Vol. 1, No. VI, pp. 20–21.
99 *ALA Debates*, 1972, Vol. 1, No. VI, pp. 20–21.
100 Shri Atul Chandra Goswami, a member of the Assembly raised this point to the Chief Minister, Shri Mahendra Mohan Choudhury for consideration. *ALA Debates*, 1971, Vol. II, No. 1, pp. 97–98.
101 A Commission of Enquiry constituted under Section 3 of the Commission of Enquiry Act, 1952, vide Government Notification No. PLA 57/73/22 consisting of Shri G. N. Borah, Presiding Officer, Industrial Tribunal, Dibrugarh.
102 *ALA Debates*, 1973, Vol. 1, No. II, p. 51.
103 *ALA Debates*, 1975, Vol. V, No. III, pp. 107–8.
104 *ALA Debates*, 1973, Vol. 1, No. II, pp. 39–40.
105 Report of the Commission of Enquiry into the incidents that took place in certain parts of Dibrugarh district leading to the death of Ballav Ch. Dey and Jiban Ch, Dey of Telpani Block under Dibrugarh Police Station and of Promode Bora of Nigam Village under Joypur Police Station in the month of October, 1972.
106 *Report of the Commission of Enquiry* vide Government Notification No. PLA 748/77/27 dated 20.01.73 under M. C. Pathak. This Commission, however, reconstituted under Justice B. N. Sarma vide Notification dated 8 April 1974 and 29 June 1974.
107 *Amrita Bazar Patrika*, 28 December 1972.
108 *The Statesman*, 23 December 1972.
109 R. Gopalakrishnan, K. K. Jhunjhunwala and Manasi Shailaja. 2002. 'Population Displacement and Development Dilemmas: A Reflection on Linguistic Politics in the North-East'. In *Dimensions of Displaced People in North-East India*, ed. C. Joshua, 52–56. New Delhi: Regency Publications.
110 *ALA Debates*, 1973, Vol. V, No. I, pp. 130–31.
111 Ranjit Kr. Dey. 1998. 'Tripura Rajya Jana Siksha Samiti- Its Origin and Activities'. *NEIHA,* Ninth Session, Guwahati, p. 374.
112 *Jwala*, Part-2, Vol. 4.

Politics as defence 241

113 Malaya Banerjee. 1998. 'State Formation Process of Tripura: The Economic Roots'. *NEIHA*, Eighteenth Session, Agartala, p. 337.
114 Samir Kumar Das. 2011. 'Wrestling with My Shadow: The State and Immigrant Muslims in Contemporary West Bengal'. In *Minorities and the State: Changing Social and Political Landscape of Bengal*, ed. Abhijit Dasgupta, Masahiko Tagawa and Abul Barkat, 49. New Delhi: Sage.
115 Hariganga Basak. 'Tripura Rajye Praja Andolaner Gorar Katha.' *Samaj*, 15 August 1956.
116 File No. B-53/S-6, No. 2563-24.2, TSA.
117 File No. B 52, S. 9A.3, Adm Deptt. (Unpublished), TSA.
118 *Tripura Administrative Reports*, 1937–1946, File No. V/10/2109, IOR.
119 *Leaflet of Tripura Jana Siksha Samiti*, Agartala, Bhadra 29, 1356 T.E. (corresponding year 1946).
120 *Tripura Administrative Reports*, 1937–1946, File No. V/10/2109, IOR.
121 *Iapri*, 11 July 1945.
122 *Tripura District Gazetteers*, Notification No. 176-C, File No. B 52/S.9/A.3, Adm. Deptt. (Unpublished), 1945, TSA.
123 Mahadev Chakravarti. 2008. 'Internally Displaced Persons in Tripura: Past and Present'. In *Blisters on Their Feet: Tales of Internally Displaced Persons in India's North East*, ed. Samir Kumar Das, 240. New Delhi: Sage.
124 'Tripura Bengali Hindu Sammelani', A Leaflet, 18 Chaitra 1356 T. E. (1946). Manimaya Deb Burma, 'Tripura Bengali Hindu Sammelani'. *Dainik Sambad*, 2 February 1978.
125 Biren Datta. 'Prajar Dabi'. *Dainik Sambad*, 13 December 1977.
126 Kamal Roy Choudhury. 1978. 'Jana Siksha Andolan'. *Gomati Quarterly* 79, Agartala.
127 Weekly Statement of Political and Other Organisations for the Week Ending 14.09.1947. File No B-61/S-6, Pol. Deptt. TSA.
128 Collection 17: Bengal States, File No. L/PS/13/1023–1038, 1870–1950, IOR.
129 Interview with Paramartha Dutta, a lawyer by profession, taken on 24 December 2012 in Agartala, Tripura.
130 *Tripurar Katha*, No. 1, March 1951.
131 Resolutions and Report of the 5th Central Conference of the Gana Mukti Parishad, pp. 54–55.
132 N. R. Roychoudhury. 1980. 'Causes of the Tribal Uprising in Tripura in the Nineteenth Century'. *NEIHA*, First Session, Shillong, p. 108.
133 Interview with Manju Das, Professor in Bengali, taken on 24 May 2013 in Agartala, Tripura.
134 *Barta*, 4 August 1949.
135 *Tripurar Katha*, An Essay by Dasharath Deb Burma, 3rd Year, 2nd Issue, Agartala, 25 May 1953.
136 Tripura State Gazette dated the 9 March 1949, corresponding to the 26th Falgoon of 1358 T.E.
137 Ministry's Office Memorandum No. 143/51-Ests, File No. F. 8 (15)-GA/53, Home-General Administration Department, TSA.
138 File No. F. 1(48)-P/57, Political Deptt, TSA.
139 Report of the Assistant Central Intelligence Officer, Tripura State, to the Joint Secretary, Rehabilitation Department, Government of India. File No. 20-R/50 II (Secret), Rehabilitation Branch, NAI.
140 *Meghnad Saha: Papers and Correspondences*, Instalment VII, Sub. File 2, p. 153.
141 *Janakalyan*, 4 May 1950.
142 *Janakalyan*, 26 July 1950.
143 *A Leaflet*, signed by Nibaran Chandra Ghosh, President, Tripura Central Refugee and Rehabilitation Organisation and Convener, All Tripura Refugee Convention, 4 January 1951.
144 *Janakalyan*, 4 February 1951.
145 File No. F. 21(19)-PD/56, Police Deptt., Annexure A, TSA.

146 File No. F. A, Year-1950, Political Deptt., TSA.
147 Sankho Subhra Debburman. 2008. 'Tripura o Udbastu Bangalir Culture'. In *Dhormo, Samaj o Buddhijibi*, 37–38. Kumarghat: Srot Prakashana.
148 *Memorandum Submitted to the Eighth Finance Commission by Tripura Tribal Areas Autonomous District Council*, 1960, Agartala, p. 1.
149 *Memorandum Submitted to the Eighth Finance Commission by Tripura Tribal Areas Autonomous District Council*, 1960, Agartala, p. 1.
150 File No. 22 (240)-PA/53, Political A Section, Ministry of States, NAI.
151 File No. F. 8(15)-GA/53, Home-General Administration Department, TSA.
152 File No. 49 (2)-P.P & R (53), P.P.R. Section, NAI.
153 Interview with Bodhrong Deb Burma, a *Kok-barok* teacher by profession, taken in Agartala on 30 December 2012.
154 Malabika Das Gupta. 2007. 'The Impact of militancy on the Economy of the *Jhumias* of the Northeast: A Study of Tripura'. In *National Security Issues: Northeast India Perspective*, ed. Abu Naser Saied Ahmed, 166–67. New Delhi: OKDISCD and Akansha Publishing House.
155 *PTLA*, 1965, Series-IV, Vol. 1–6, p. 1.
156 Quoted in Ritonkar Mukhopadhyay. 2015. 'Onya Ak Udbastu Upakhyan', ed. Sudipta Bandyapadhyay. *Charbaka* 2 (3): 20. Popular Culture 3.
157 *Jagaran*, 10 August 1958.
158 File No. 22 (48)-PA/53, Political A Section, NAI.
159 O. S. Adhikari. 1982. *The Problem of Indebtedness Among the Tribals in Sadar Sub-Division of Tripura*. Directorate of Research, Department of Welfare for Schedule Tribes. Agartala: Government of Tripura, pp. 5–6.
160 Interview with Nityananda Das, a school teacher by profession, taken on 29 December 2013 in Agartala, Tripura.
161 *Chiniha*, 7 May 1952.
162 O. S. Adhikari. 1982. *The Problem of Indebtedness Among the Tribals in Sadar Sub-Division of Tripura*. Directorate of Research, Department of Welfare for Schedule Tribes. Agartala: Government of Tripura, pp. 34–35.
163 *Boiri*, Agartala, Sharodia Sankhya, 1993, p. 6.
164 Subir Bhaumik. 2005. 'India's Northeast: Nobody's People in No-Man's Land'. In *Internal Displacement in South Asia: The Relevance of the UN's Guiding Principles,* ed. Paula Banerjee, Sabyasachi Basu Roy Chaudhury and Samir Kumar Das, 146. New Delhi: Sage.
165 *Resolutions and Report of the 5th Central Conference of the GMP* (unpublished in Bengali), 1960.
166 File No. 6/5/69 UTL, UTL Section, NAI.
167 The Rules were made under Notification No. 74 (14)-Rev/ 60, dated the 13th April 1961, section 197. File No. 19/51/61-Judl. II, Judl. II Section, NAI.
168 Interview with N. C. Deb Burma, taken on 30 December 2012 in Agartala, Tripura.
169 *PTLA*, 1973, Series-IV, Vol. I–IV, p. 183.
170 *PTLA*, 1973, Series-IV, Vol. I–IV, p. 7.
171 *PTLA*, 1974, Series-VI, Vol. III–IV, pp. 50–51.
172 *PTLA*, 1975, Series-VIII, Vol. I–III, p. 68.
173 *PTLA*, 1965, Series-IV, Vol. 1–6, p. 35.
174 File No. 6/5/69 UTL, UTL Section, NAI.
175 Saroj Chanda. 1988. 'Tripurar Ugro Jatiyotabader Birudhye'. In *Sharodia Sankhya*, 49. Agartala: Tripura Darpan.
176 File No. 6/5/69 UTL, UTL Section, NAI.
177 Subir Bhaumik. 13–14 January 1996. 'Patterns of Minority Violence in Northeast India'. Paper presented in a Seminar on 'Minorities in Northeast India', Organised by the Department of Political Science, University of Calcutta.

178 The Sixth Schedule of the Constitution deals with the administration of the tribal areas in the four northeastern states of Assam, Meghalaya, Mizoram and Tripura as per Article 244. It allows for the constitution of Autonomous District Councils to safeguard the rights of the tribals.
179 As per the Constitutional provisions under Article 244 (1) of the Constitution of India, the Fifth Schedule of the Constitution deals with the administration and control of Scheduled Areas as well as of Scheduled Tribes residing in any State other than the States of Assam, Meghalaya, Mizoram and Tripura.
180 *PTLA*, 1965, Series-IV, Vol. 1–6, p. 35.
181 A. P. Joshi, M. D. Srinivas and J. K. Bajaj. 2005. *Religious Demography of India*. Chennai: Centre for Policy Studies, p. 39.
182 *The Chakma Profile*. 1999. Agartala: Government of Tripura, p. 18.
183 *The Daiik Sambad*, 25 January 1990.
184 *Annual Report of Voluntary Health Association of Tripura*. 1996. Agartala, Tripura.
185 Nasreen Chowdhory. 2004. 'Coping with Refugees in India: The Case of Chakma Repatriation'. In *State, Society and Displaced People in South Asia,* ed. Imtiaz Ahmed, Abhijit Dasgupta and Kathinka Sinha-Kerkhoff, 193–94. Dhaka: The University Press Limited.
186 Sajal Nag. 2002. 'Whose Nation Is It Anyway: Nation Building and Displacement in Indian Sub-continent'. In *Dimensions of Displaced People in North-East India*, ed. C. Joshua, 35. New Delhi: Regency Publications.
187 *PTLA*, 1975, Series-VIII, Vol. I–III, pp. 5–8.
188 *Document on Population State of Refugee Inmates: As on 31st December 1996,* District Administration Office, South Tripura.
189 Manos Debburman. 2001. 'Swopne Tobo Kulloksmi'. In *Uttorpurber Nirbachito Bangla Golpo,* ed. Anup Bhattacharya and Shubhobbrata Deb, 156–57. Agartala: Akshar Publication.
190 Ritonkar Mukhopadhyay. 2015. 'Onya Ak Udbastu Upakhyan', ed. Sudipta Bandyapadhyay. *Charbaka* 2 (3): 29. Popular Culture 3.
191 Subhasis Tolapatra. 2001. 'Anonkohorir Chosma'. In *Uttorpurber Nirbachito Bangla Golpo*, ed. Anup Bhattacharya and Shubhobbrata Deb, 253. Agartala: Akshar Publication.
192 Meghna Guha Thakurta. 2003. 'Uprooted and Divided'. In *The Trauma and the Triumph: Gender and Partition in Eastern India*, ed. Jasodhara Bagchi and Subhoranjan Dasgupta, 100. Kolkata: Stree.

EPILOGUE

India is scheduled to celebrate 75 years of its independence in the next two years, which means also 75 years since the Partition of the country. It would be an occasion to celebrate the achievement of freedom after a prolonged and protracted struggle against colonial rule. It would also be an occasion to remind us that India has not yet been able to solve problems like boundary demarcation, displacement, refugee inflow, illegal migration, minority issues, trans-frontier terrorism, and so on. Often these issues raise their ugly heads and political parties appropriate them according to their ideologies, agendas and opportunism. So, as has been seen, the Partition of 1947 did not solve the problem of nation-making for both countries; rather, it created more. Partition-like situations continued to be reproduced and states continued to produce displaced people who migrated to the other country in search of safety, security and livelihood. Therefore, neither the production of refugees ceased nor had their struggle for home, habitat and identity stopped. The journey of Indian nationalism started with the idea of one nation-state, but by the time it achieved its independence, it gave birth to multiple nationalities, a few nationalisms and two sovereign nation-states. Within the next 30 years, these two nations multiplied into three. It demonstrated that nation-states by themselves were not the end but the means to give rise to many spin-offs. One of these such spin-offs was the creation of a new political 'species' called the refugees. Interestingly, the so-called 'minorities' of both the countries were keen to become a part of the 'majority' community on the other side of the proposed notional border. Thus, even before the division, the upper-class Hindus and Muslims had begun to move towards their promised utopia, either India or Pakistan. But within the utopia, the nation-seekers did not plan anything concrete about how to rehabilitate and resettle the refugees. Before Partition, river Padma was a marker to define *epar Bangla* and *opar Bangla* (East Bengal and West Bengal) (Shamshad 2017: 439). The international border became the marker to denote two sides of Bengal after Partition.

The emergence of two nation-states out of one, making separate homelands for Hindus and Muslims, and consequent displacement resulted in a human tragedy of refugee-hood. The migration was for seeking refuge and a national identity. Following the decades of Partition, the refugee issue had become intertwined with conflicts with the host communities, issues related to identity politics, disputes on boundary demarcations and decisions on the final fate of the floating populace, including legal refugees, illegal migrants and ethnic tribals in many states of eastern and northeastern India. From the beginning, the Centre, based in Delhi, desperately tried to keep a liberal facade on its stands to resolve complicated issues related to legal and illegal migration, and questions of citizenship and changed identity. The nature of recurrent tension and anxiety on the core-periphery binary and the major refugee-absorbent state's relationship with the policymakers of the Central Government of India remained the same. Although the concerns of confusion and conflicts were different in West Bengal, Assam and Tripura, these states remain major theatres of anti-displaced people movements. The process of displacement in the east had continued through several waves, different cycles of violence and consequent migration for decades. The formation of a Hindu-majority India and a Muslim-majority Pakistan led to the largest mass migration in human history. Around 15 million people crossed the newly formed notional borderlands. They migrated to West Bengal, Assam and Tripura primarily for safety, but more importantly to lands where they could live with honour—but this assumption proved wrong. The refugees were not received well, at least not the way they had imagined. Shyama Prasad Mookherjee pointed out the disillusionment of the refugees in West Bengal. 'In East Bengal it is death with dishonour and in West Bengal it is death without dishonour, but death, all the same in either case'.[1]

In India, Partition lingered in the collective imagination. Since it was a cumulative result of communal politics, communalism remained a dominant consciousness in all three countries: India, Pakistan and, later, Bangladesh. Politics continued to be dominated by communal propaganda. In these nation-states, some political parties emerged which thrived on communal mobilisation and communal agenda whereby minorities were the target of their viciousness. Since India was declared a secular nation, most of the parties adhered to a secular ideology which was pitted against the communal propaganda of the non-secular parties. Secularism as an ideology was being redefined and words like pseudo-secularism and minority appeasement came to be invented. Since then, communalism and secularism became the 'other' of each in these new polities. The event of Partition became a milestone, a metaphor and a signpost. It helped to shape discourses of nation building and secularism, caste and religious identities, ideas about majority-minority relations, issues touching upon refugees and trans-border migration. Partition in the Eastern Indian context has been synonymous with the long and difficult journey of 'settlement' of the refugees generated by the event. In the case of east borders, the Central Government did not find enough reasons or justifications for such large-scale migration that continued for very long. The state did not recognise that subtle form of violence was 'violent enough' to force the minorities to migrate. Violence in East Bengal was rather treated as a 'psychological fear' and the refugees were categorised as 'not genuine victims' like those of the west. Only during and after the colossal riot of 1950 that led to a gigantic migration of the middle- and lower-classes, along with the professionals, did Bengal managed to draw some attention from the Centre. In Bengal, 'the history of violence is, therefore, almost always about context—about everything that happened around violence' (Pandey 1992: 27). In psychological terminology, the nature of that type of violence is defined as the overtly threatened or overtly accomplished application of force that results in injury or destruction of persons or reputation or illegal appropriation of property.[2]

The body blow on the *dhon*, *pran* and *man* (wealth, life and honour) of the Hindus could be clearly understood by the numerous memorandums and petitions given to Rajendra Prasad by the Hindus, urging him to include their districts with the Indian Territory.[3] The moral fibre of such clashes had grown over the years between the Hindu and Muslim political groups. The regionalisation and possessiveness to establish the community identity enhanced the rift which had already made ground through the social and cultural divide. The Hindu press had pointed out that Muslims were never influenced by the notion of geographical unity of Bengal; they had only dreamt of establishing pan-Islamisation. Later again, Hindu Mahasabha tried to popularise the idea of pan-Hinduism to establish Swaraj. So, the Partition of India was not of just a territory, as it is often supposed. It was of people. The territory was only to create a space for people who desired to be hegemonic and dominant in that part of the space. Yet people were never a consideration in the debate and discussion on Partition. That is why in the Partition negotiation, it was never speculated about the possible impact of Partition on the people. The people who were partitioned were never consulted or their consent sought before that major event. Rather, the election results and political parties were considered spokesmen for communities. Referendums were held only in NWFP and Sylhet, where majority opinion was taken as determining factor without any consideration for the minorities who were to be affected most by the Partition. In reality, people were made stateless overnight, their citizenship of one country taken away and a citizenship of a new nation conferred on them without their consent (Gera Roy 2020: 29–33).

The loss of home, hearth and habitat as a corollary of Partition was hardly ever imagined, and the impact on the minorities in respective countries was never bothered about. This is why the scale of bloodshed, displacement and refugee influx even surprised the ruling regimes of both the newly born nation-states. Prime Minister Nehru was astonished by the volume of influx from Bengal, which he did not anticipate. The violence and consequent influx from West Punjab were understandable to him, but not Bengal, where the Bengalis were such a culturally syncretic community; more so because the influx from West Punjab was immediate and prompt after the Partition. But from Bengal, it was slow and much after the Partition—and that, too, in waves and instalments. The influx from Bengal began when refugees from Punjab were almost rehabilitated and settled. Therefore, the settlement of Bengali refugees was late, unplanned, unsystematic, insufficient and contingent. The refugees of Bengal were rehabilitated, if at all, in regions other than own. Their land, language, culture and suitability were not considered. They were placed in an adverse space where they were made to face hostility of climate, landscape, livelihood and even the people. The Central and Bengal governments decided the space of rehabilitation. After the initial period, the two governments feared the enormous amount of refugees that began to pour in from Eastern Pakistan and the impact it would have on the land, livelihood and overall economy of the country and the state of Bengal. They collaborated to settle the refugees in uninhabitable regions like Andaman, Bihar, Orissa and Dandakaranya, unleashing an inhuman tragedy and bloodshed. It was like dumping the burden in a faraway place from where even their complaints need not be heard.

The lack of consensuality and consultation was found even in the process of rehabilitation. Like the refugees were not consulted about the place where they were to be settled, the host communities were not consulted about the rehabilitation of a new community in their midst. Despite the opposition of the Government of Assam and the Assamese people, the Central Government imposed a huge community of refugees in Assam, much to the anger of the Assamese people. Although the Assamese refused to take in refugees, they noticed that the stream of migration of Bengalis from East Pakistan continued. They belonged to the Islamic faith, which was a cause of terror. They complained against the migration and the threat it posed to their identity, existence and political future, but this warranted no response from the Centre. Short-term measures were taken which had no effect in controlling the illegal migration. The Assamese, therefore, had to live with Bengali Hindus, who were perceived as an economic and cultural threat, and Bengali Muslims, who were seen as a political threat in a space where they desired their complete hegemony. The state of Tripura initially welcomed the refugees, but resisted when it could not take any more; but the government allowed the stream of migration to continue uninterrupted until the 1990s, when the host population had been completely outnumbered, relegated to the hills space and dethroned from power. Here again, two hostile communities were pitted against each other by forcing them to share a space grudgingly. In Bengal, the Partition and politics over refugees soon shaped the contours of its politics. After B. C. Roy, Congress began to decline due to its anti-refugee politics. The upper-caste Bengal *bhadralok* of West Bengal was aghast at the scale of influx of refugees which soon took over not just the space, but impacted the economy adversely and shaped a subaltern culture which was not to their liking.

In this new post-colonial space, refugees played a significant role. Congress declined because the refugees saw it as a betrayer, who agreed for Partition, and a double betrayer as its initiative towards their rehabilitation was not commensurate. Taking advantage of the slipping away of the ground of the Congress, two political forces came to help the cause of the refugees. One was the Hindu Mahasabha converted to Jan Sangh, and the other was the Communist Party of India. The Hindu Party made a lot of noise without much substantive work. The communists, on the other hand, slipped into the grassroots, took up the cause of the refugees, represented them, organised them and launched a new movement. This movement was more of a political nature rather than a simple movement for rehabilitation and settlement, and it succeeded more. It would not be an exaggeration to say that the rehabilitation and settlement of refugees in West Bengal were due much to the untiring efforts of the grassroots communist workers. Refugee leaders, too, became political leaders spearheading the unending struggle of Bengali refugees for home, identity and political space. Upper-caste Bengali *bhadralok* either agreed to be the public enemy or were absorbed into the new subaltern politics, thereby appropriating the political movement and emerging as leaders of the new political climate. The demise of Congress and the rise of communists in West Bengal and Tripura was a result of the politicisation of the refugees. The communists came to power immediately and remained in power for 35 years in both West Bengal and Tripura. Only a resurgent Hindutva could dislodge them from power in Tripura and weaken the ruling regime in West Bengal. The refugees truly became the new obiters, especially in these two states.

In Assam, too, it was the same Bengali refugees, along with perceived illegal immigrants (Bengali Muslims), who remained the object of post-colonial politics. The never-ending flow of immigration of Bengali Muslims that had started from the turn of the century had not really stopped; but another type of migration, one that was inter-district and legal, had become illegal infiltration. Since the 1950s, there were complaints about continuous Muslim infiltrators in Assam. The Intelligence Bureau reported that 'the number of illegal immigrants into Assam from Pakistan over the course of the last 12 years has been very conservatively estimated about 250 thousand. Local unofficial estimates however put this figure even higher' (Gupta 1984: 201–211). The Government of Assam initially called for the introduction of a permit system as early as July 1948. As nothing came of these demands, the government of India came out with The Immigrants (Expulsion from Assam) Act, 1950, which tried to differentiate between Hindu refugees from Pakistan and deport only Muslim migrants who were seen as illegal infiltrators. In the backdrop of the Chinese invasion, the Government began to make a fresh security appraisal, whereby it found that 'the fact that such a large number of immigrants succeeded in illegally crossing the frontier and settling down unnoticed would prove that the measures so far taken have not been effective'. It, therefore, launched the Prevention of Infiltration from Pakistan Scheme (PIP) to check on them and deport infiltrators from Assam. But deportation of illegal immigrants by the B. P. Chaliha government had to be abandoned because of the allegation of harassment and human rights abuse by Muslim leaders Fakhruddin Ali Ahmed and Moin-ul-Haque Chaudhury, and organisations like Jamiat-ul-Ulama-e-Hind. It raised a debate about the threats posed to genuine citizens by illegal immigrants. The proposal for initiating the National Registration of Citizens, as a means to tide over the vexed citizenship issue was first suggested in the PIP Scheme of 1965. This scheme, drafted by the intelligence bureau officials, proposed that a National Registration System and the issue of Identity Card should be adopted for all residents of Assam and the northeastern region.

Since then, there have many laws and measures adopted to deal with the vexed foreign national issue. Among these were the Foreigners Act 1948, The Foreigners Order 1948, Permits System, PIP, The Foreigners (Tribunal) order 1964, The Foreigners (Tribunal) Amendment order 2012, The Passport (Entry into India) Act 1920, The Citizenship Act 1955, The Citizenship (Registration of Citizen & Issue of National Identity Cards) Rules 2003, The Citizenship Rules 2009, Foreigner Tribunal and illegal migrants (Determination Tribunal), Immigrants (Expulsion from Assam) Act 1950, and the Illegal Migrants (Determination by Tribunal) Act (IMDT) Act, establishing a category of 'D' (doubtful) voters was used to detect, deport and intern the suspected infiltrators. There were even carnages (Nellie massacre, 1983) in which about 3,000 Muslims were butchered. According to the government report, during 1951–1961, a total of 2,20,691 Pakistani infiltrators entered Assam, of whom 1,22,476 were detected and deported by June 1965. Between 1985 and July 2005, after the formation of IMDT, a total of 11,2791 persons were referred to as foreign nationals of which 12,846 were declared to be so and 1547 actually deported. Between 1985 and July 2012, a total of 61,774 persons were declared D voters, of which 6,590 persons were actually declared foreigners (*White Paper on Foreigner's Issues* 2012: 40–41). Evidently, there were endeavours to detect and deport foreign nationals all along. The detection of a massive increase in Muslim voters during a 1979 by-election in Mangaldoi sparked off the anti-foreigners National Movement, which ended in 1985 with the Assam Accord which agreed to confer citizenship of India to all those immigrants who came to India up to 1971 with a caveat that those who entered between 1961 and 1971, would have to complete a term of ten years before the conferring of citizenship. There was no mention of the National Register of Citizens (NRC) in the Assam Accord. Since neither the Assam Accord nor the *Asom Gana Parishad* could deport significant number of foreign nationals, the issue continued to generate passion and was used for political mobilisation.

By 1998, the foreigners issue again came to the centre stage of politics with a report sent to the President of India by the then-Governor of Assam, Lt. Gen S. K. Sinha, becoming public. Sinha, who was a right-wing ideologue, propagated that 1 crore of illegal Muslims had infiltrated into Assam with a grand design of Pakistan laying claim to this territory. Speculative claims were made that ranging from 30 lakhs to 1 crore of Bangladeshi (erstwhile East Pakistani) nationals were staying illegally in Assam who could easily reduce the indigenous Assamese into a minority soon. The rise of Muslim population to 30 per cent and of Muslim legislators in the Assam Assembly from 12 in 1952 to 24 in 1991 in a house of 126 only strengthened their conviction (Nag 2018). It was propagated that '(with the continuous increase in the Muslim population) it is only a question of time when the indigenous Assamese ethnic groups will be alien in their homeland . . . and the next step will be demand for referendum on merger with Bangladesh' (Nag 2018: 58). The real fear, however, was that if the Muslim legislators united with the tribal, ex-tea garden, Nepali and Bengali Hindu MLAs, they could easily threaten the political hegemony of the caste Hindu Assamese, which had to be prevented.

The vexed foreign national issue had resurfaced at a tripartite meeting of AASU with the government in which it agreed to upgrade the National Register of Citizens of 1951 for the first time in 2005. While debating the issue of citizenship, the then-Chief Minister of Assam, Tarun Gogoi, in the subsequent meetings of 2011 and 2013 said that the victims of Partition Bengali Hindus case 'should be considered on humanitarian grounds' (Nag 2018), but to no avail, and he had to start the NRC updating process. It was started by the Gogoi government in 2012, but had to be halted due to violent protests from the Muslims of Dhubri and Goalpara. Riots had broken out in the meantime between the Muslims and Bodo tribals in Bodoland areas in 2012 and 2014. In 2012, a massive demonstration was organised at Guwahati to re-launch the anti-foreigners agitation. A new organisation called Assam Sanmilita Mahasangha, an umbrella organisation of 'various indigenous and Tribal communities' led the movement (Nag 2018). The Mahasangha adopted a legal way by filing a petition in the Supreme Court of India to examine the constitutional position of the laws of citizenship in India and to upgrade the NRC prepared in 1951 for Assam. The judgement on this petition, delivered in December 2014, allowed the upgrading of the NRC of 1951 to settle the contest between the citizenship and illegal immigration.

The NRC was a by-product of the Census Act of 1948. This register of 1951 was prepared as a secret administrative document prepared on the basis of Census slips by the Census enumerators, who were 'unqualified or ill-qualified persons'. Moreover, it was not open to inspection. It was a casual attempt at preparing a set of data without any planning, training or organisation. The comments of the Census Superintendent, Assam, about the persons who prepared this Register are interesting to define the origin of this data:

> In filling up the sample verification forms, the tabulation officers sometimes experienced considerable difficulty in reading the names of persons and tracing their relationship to the head of the households as the National Register of Citizens was written by unqualified or ill-qualified persons.
> *(Census of India 1951: 267–68)*

The statement clearly shows many shortcomings. As admitted by the then-Census Superintendent himself, the names of the displaced were consciously not included in the Register. The Census Report of 1951 admits that:

> [a]n important innovation of this Census was the preparation of a National Register of Citizens in which all important census data was transcribed from the census slips with the exception of the Census questions No. 6 (displaced persons), No. 8 (bilingualism) and No. 13 (indigenous persons).
> *(Census of India 1951: 267–68)*

The NRC 1951 enumeration was a hurried one, having been completed between 9 February and 28 February of that year. The register of an entire nation of citizens was prepared in an impossible span of time, merely 20 days. The enumerators were grossly untrained. As is evident from the census report, the data entered into the NRC were copied into census slips contrary to the established procedure of the slips becoming the basis for the NRC. This was a gross irregularity. Its importance was also diluted over the course of time, which is evident from the fact that even the process of tallying the slips, which formed the basis for the NRC, was abandoned at the orders of the Registrar General of Census. The task was not to track the genuine citizens, but to analyse the population structure of the country on the basis of the information collected during this census enumeration. It was pointed out that:

> If due to under-enumeration in an area or otherwise the name of a person was omitted in the census, then his name was automatically excluded from the NRC also. And if a person was accidentally not enlisted, he had no opportunity to get enlisted in the NRC subsequently. He could also not file objections. As the NRC was not publicly exhibited and was not a public document, a person could not even know if his name was at all included.
> *(Extracts from the High Court Ruling 1981: 267–68)*

Therefore, the whole matter rested on the whims of the enumerators or their supervisors. It was a one-sided affair. No indication was given to the people of the terrible consequences which might overtake them at a future date if their names were not included in the National Register of Citizens, 1951.

The upgrading of the NRC first listed more than 40 lakhs people as illegal immigrants in Assam, in its draft report. The first report a showed a majority of listed people from the Muslim community, which made the people of Assam and the ruling dispensation in Delhi glad. It became evident that NRC became an essential condition to prove someone's citizenship in Assam, for the time being. Already a number of persons perceived to be illegal immigrants, mostly Hindu, were languishing in 'detention' centres established in different parts of Assam. Inhumane living conditions, likened to the Nazi concentration camps, led to worldwide condemnation of the practice. But the government was unrelenting and bent on creating more such camps, raising the fear that all the 40 lakhs people who were rendered stateless would be sent to these detention camps for life. This had sent a wave of panic not just in Assam, but the whole of India and evoked global anxiety about the prospect. The final report, published on 31 August 2019, reduced the number to more than 19 lakhs. The 19 lakhs people who were now declared illegal immigrants were now stateless and were either to be deported to Bangladesh or, on the refusal of Bangladesh to accept them, to be detained in the detention camps. The single option available to them against non-inclusion was an appeal to a State Level Foreigners' Tribunal. If their appeal did not succeed, the stateless individuals would be sent to any one of the existing six detention camps in the state, while some are yet to being constructed throughout the state, where they would be waiting for repatriation. The Centre was declared firm in detecting the foreigners and illegal immigrants. The first draft of NRC had excluded more Muslims than Hindus, which encouraged the Hinduist power at the Centre to declare a nationwide NRC to exclude more Muslims from the polity. But the final draft had more Hindus detected as illegal than Muslims. This caused embarrassment for the ruling party, as it had propagated itself to be a protector of Hindus. Hence, they backtracked and announced an amendment to the Citizenship Laws of the country by which Hindus coming to India up to 2014 could be granted citizenship. It passed the Citizenship (Amendment) Act 2019 (CAA), which legalized the conferment of citizenship to refugees belonging to all religions other than Islam if they migrated from specified countries like Bangladesh, Afghanistan and Pakistan before 2014.

The Indian Citizenship Act of 1955 and the Citizenship (Registration of Citizens and Issue of National Identity Cards) Rules 2003 require the Indian Government to maintain a 'national register of Indian citizens' and to issue a national identity cards to all. The Citizenship Amendment Bill of 2016 is supposed to face some kind of legal challenge, as it deeply violates Article 14 of the Indian Constitution. But the chief issue here is how over a period of almost 73 years since Partition, India as a nation-state is all set to return to the negation of citizenship based on religion, ethnicity, caste or race. It might again lead to the vivisection of people; mass-scale violence and another forced migration of millions of people. The debates around religion, majority-minority community, ethnic tribals and condition of the all other marginal lower-strata populace, which lay at its foundations, has made this book a timely one. It is not a problem of India or of South Asian politics alone. Refugees, minorities and denial of their basic human rights are becoming a global phenomenon now. It has become obvious that the Centre is trying to include the Hindu refugees excluded by the NRC final list through this new legislation. The Assamese who were against the citizenship of Bengalis, both Hindus and Muslims, were aghast at this backdoor endeavour and rose in rebellion, a movement reminiscent of the Anti-Foreigner Agitation of the 1980s.

It appeared peoples' faith in BJP, the party in power in both the state and Centre whom the people voted in preference to Congress, had been betrayed again. Not just in Assam, people rose in arms in other northeastern states, too, like Arunachal Pradesh, Meghalaya, Mizoram, Manipur, Nagaland and Tripura, but the Government pacified them by saying that the law would not be implemented in Inner Line Permit areas like Mizoram, Nagaland and Arunachal Pradesh, and Sixth Scheduled areas of Meghalaya, Assam and Tripura. Since Manipur did not have any of these provisions, violating all previous premises, a colonial law like the Bengal Eastern Frontier Regulations 1873 was inaugurated in Manipur. Inspired by this, the state of Meghalaya, too, demanded it, though it already has provisions of Sixth Schedule, unleashing a spate of violence and attacks from the hosts on the Bengali refugee population settled here after Partition. Nagaland reacted by extending Inner Line beyond the hills thereby making the life and livelihood of the non-Nagas in Dimapur insecure. Tripura, already overburdened by Bengali and tribal refugees, was frightened by the prospect of regularisation of more refugees, but were mute spectators under a BJP government in their state. They protested in a sustained manner, but little was listened to. In fact, in the states of Arunachal Pradesh, Mizoram and Tripura, there is a substantial non-Bengali refugee population of Chakma and Hajongs who were displaced from Chittagong after 1947. The host population had been opposing their presence among them for a long period of time. In fact, despite the efforts of the Centre and the directive of the Supreme Court of India, these two groups were not allowed to be given citizenship. Arunachal Pradesh feared that by CAA, these groups would be granted citizenship, jeopardising their fragile demography and economy. In Mizoram, the Chakma are granted an 'Autonomous Council' and the Mizos were hostile to them. In Tripura, Chakmas are in large number, in addition to the Bengali refugees. All these states were frightened by the prospect of these unwanted refugees being granted citizenship. They were given temporary reprieve by excluding them from the purview of the Act. But the insecurity and fear remains, and the small communities of Arunchali, Mizo and Tipperas live with mortal fear of refugees. An arrogant and majoritarian centre is not expected to address their fears and apprehensions. The Khasi-Jaintia and Garos are already up in arms against the Centre, and are threatening unprecedented violence against the non-tribals in their state.

The attempt of the Centre to grant citizenship to certain religious groups from certain countries evoked opposition not just from the northeastern states, but other parts of India, too. The exclusion of Muslims from the purview of the Act was seen as a deliberate violation of the secular constitution of India. There was an unprecedented number of petitions to the Supreme Court challenging the validity of the legislation and demanding its withdrawal, which the Supreme Court is scheduled to examine soon. In Bengal, Chief Minister Mamata Banerjee, who was consistently opposing both NRC and CAA, has become vocal again. The state of Bengal is the most adversely affected refugee-absorbent state. It already has a settled Muslim population which rejected the two-nation theory and did not migrate to Pakistan. It has a long border with Bangladesh, through which regular migration of both Bengals was suspected. Any enumeration for NRC would obviously detect a huge number of people, both Hindu and Muslims, as illegal immigrants, as most of these migrants do not possess documentary evidence of their citizenship in India. These migrants have chosen this part of Bengal as their home after facing discrimination or economic hardship in Bangladesh. She not only rejected the NRC initiative in Bengal, but even rejected the CAA as she believes that all the Bengalis migrating to Bengal are citizens by virtue of their long stay in India. Her opposition to the two initiatives of the Centre found immediate resonance with the people of Bengal. Threatened with losing their home and hearth again, and being deported to Bangladesh or sent to detention camps, the people immediately sided with her and rallied around her. In West Bengal, the scheduled caste populace, especially the *Matua* community, was scared of the implementation of NRC and CAA; members of that community started migrating after the riot of 1964 and most of the families stayed back in West Bengal after 1971 and generally, they do not have papers from the censuses of 1951, 1961 or 1971. Rather, the Muslims are in a better position, as most of them have some kind of original or forged documents. The Chief Minister was now seen as the new protector and saviour of the migrants in Bengal. The Trinamul Congress Party had lost a massive 22 parliamentary seats to the resurgent BJP in the recently concluded parliamentary election in the state. The opposition of the party to NRC and CAA immediately turned the tables, and it began to regain lost ground. Not only did the people of Bengal in large numbers support her cause, but the BJP lost three seats in the by-election held after the announcement of CAA.

The move of the Centre to implement NRC and CAA backfired not only in Bengal and Assam, but in the rest of the country, too. The entire country, it seemed, rose in uprising against the Act and offered stiff resistance to both NRC and CAA, which developed into a first nationwide resistance movement comparable only to JP movement of 1977–1980. A number of states passed resolutions that they would not implement the acts in their states. The rising engulfed the entire country in an unprecedented rebellion. The students and youths were the most vocal who offered vehement resistance. From Delhi to Chennai, Bengal to Bengaluru, students were at the forefront of opposition. Independent India has hardly ever seen such a massive resistance led by youth power. Universities became the seat of resistance to the ruling regime. The might of the state power was unleashed on them without succeeding in crushing the movement. An arrogant Centre went ahead with the implementation of the CAA despite the resistance. A new force had now come to the fore. Seeing the Hindus—who were supposed to be the beneficiary of the new Act—instead opposing the Act for its non-secular character, the Muslims—who since the rise of BJP in 2014 had completely resigned to their minority fate—had suddenly risen up against the CAA. Throughout the country, a large number of Muslims—mostly women—had become symbols of resistance and upholders of the secular constitution of the country. Sites like Shaheen Bag in Delhi and Park Circus in Kolkata, and universities like Jamia Milia Islamia, Aligarh Muslim University and Jawaharlal Nehru University, came out as the new soldiers of Indian democracy and secularism. The southern states of India, where there are no resettled refugee populations, experienced prolonged agitation against the acts, which demonstrated the solidarity of people against CAA and NRC. The ruling BJP has lost power in the states of Maharashtra, Jharkhand and Delhi in the aftermath of CAA. In Haryana, too, they barely managed to retain power. A 'Will Not Show Document' movement has started in different parts of India, whereby people resolved not to show any documents to the officials for verification of their citizenship. In fact, an enumeration process like National Population Register that was actually initiated by the previous government is being suspected and seen as a covert move to replace the NRC. The country is truly up in arms. In all these, the 'refugee' has become the subject and object of the new political mobilisation in India. The ruling BJP is trying to cite the 'human tragedy' of persecution of the refugees in the country of origin to obtain sympathy of the people and mobilise support for their legislation; the people want to uphold the Constitution in upholding the rights of the refugees. Similarly, the trajectory of the refugee has found a metaphor in a small village called Matia in Goalpara district of Assam. It was in Matia that camps were constructed for refugees coming from Pakistan in

1947. It was transformed into a permanent camp in 1971 for refugees pouring from East Pakistan when the Pakistan army unleashed a reign of terror there. It is in the same Matia where the largest detention camp in Asia is being constructed now for those excluded by the NRC. Thus, if Matia is the symbol of human tragedy now, Shaheen Bag is emerging as the symbol of resistance in contemporary India.

Notes

1 *S. P. Mukherjee Papers*, Subject File No. 31, NMML.
2 Sharma, Shridhar. 1989. 'Violence: A Manifestation of Social Pathology'. In *Self Images Identity and Nationality*, ed. P. C. Chatterji. New Delhi: Allied Publishers.
3 *Rajendra Prasad Papers Collection*. File no. 1-B/ 1947, Vol. 1, on Bengal Boundary Commission 1947, NAI.

SELECT GLOSSARY

Ajlafs	Muslims of lower orders
Amolas	Administrative officers of higher posts or in white-collar jobs
Anashan	Hunger strike
Andarmahal	Inner household
Andolon	Political movement
Anjuman	A Persian word meaning association
Ansar bahinis	Ancillary organisation of the Muslim League
Ansars	Volunteer wings or helping agents of the police
Aporadhpuri	Territory of crimes
Aschorjyo manus	Strange people
Ashrafs	Elite Muslims
Ashramites	Disciples or residents of an *Ashram*
Babus	The semi-educated clerks
Bahas	Religious meetings
Bandabasta	Settlement
Bangal	Unsophisticated East Bengalis
Bari	A permanent or personally owned house
Baro-Bhunias	Twelve zamindars of Bengal
Basha	A temporary or rented house
Bastu	Ancestral home
Bastubhite	The site or foundation of a house
Bastuhara	One who has lost his homeland
Bastusap	Snakes, which guard the family property
Bhadraloks	Gentlefolk, respectable folk
Bhatias	Outsiders
Bhindeshi	Alien

Select glossary

Bhindeshi manus gulo	The uprooted populace who does not have a motherland
Bhitabari	Homesteads
Bhog	Cooked food for God
Bhogonia	Someone who forced to flee from places of origin
Bichar	Justice
Bideshi	Foreigners
Bijatio danob	Group of demons who lacked proper caste or family identity
Bohiragato	Outsider
Bongal Kheda	A strategy for driving out foreigners (Bengalis) from Assam
bongals or bongali	Bengalis
Boroder boi	Books meant for the elders
Buddhu	Stupid
Char-chaporir manuh	People of the riverbank
Chhinnomul	Uprooted from homeland
Chhit-mahals	Enclaves
Colony bhataris	Prostitutes of the colonies
Dal and bhat	Staple food of the Bengalis (lentils and rice)
Dalals	Intermediaries
Dalit	Lower castes
Dargah	Tomb, shrine of a Sufi saint
Desh	Place of origin
Dhon-pran-man	Wealth-life-respect
Dupatta	Long scarf worn by women
Durgapuja	Biggest festival of the Bengali Hindus
Gaonsabhas	Village committees headed by a headman
Ghoti	West Bengalis
Halkhata utsab	A festival to celebrate the Bengali New Year
Harijans	Member of untouchable castes
Hartal	Strike, political protest
Hawkers	Refugee businessmen sell goods in footpath
Home	A house primarily meant for raped or single women
Jabardakhal	Seizure and settlement
Jhum	Shifting/slash and burn agriculture; a type of cultivation
Jhum tillas	Hillocks used for *jhum* cultivation
Jhumias	The farmers for *jhum* cultivation
Jiratia prajas	Landless labourers who worked in the *khas* lands as sharecroppers
Jomraj	According to the mythology, the god of death
Jonmabhumi/ matribhumi	Land of birth/motherland
Jotedars	Peasant farmer, usually one with large holdings

258 Select glossary

Jyanto Kali	Goddess Kali in her arrogant, shrewish, tough *avatar*
Khere or jatmara sreni	Untouchables belonging to even lower castes and classes
Khotipuron	Compensation
Khyapa	Rude and dangerous
Kulpurohit and Kulgurus	Priests in the temples owned by the Kings of Tripura
Kurta	A kind of shirt for men or women popular in North India
Lathi	Stick
Lathial bahinis	The private forces of the zamindars of villages
Longorkhanas	Community kitchens
Loonga-land	Narrow strips of plain land situated in river valleys
Madrassa	Basic educational institutes of the Muslims
Mahajans	Moneylenders
Matabars	Village headmen
Matribhasa	Mother Tongue
Maulvis	Muslim religious heads
Milad Mehfil	Religious festival of the Muslims
Mohallas	Areas
Mullahs	The Muslim religious heads
Mussalman-para	The Muslim quarter
Naba-barsha	Bengali New Year
Naebs	Finance officers of the Hindu absentee landlords
Namasudras or matuas	A lower-caste group
Namaz	Prayer; one of the Five Pillars of Islam
Nava yuga	New age
Nirbason	Exile
Ovisap	Curse
Panahgirs	'Seekers of refuge'; Muslim refugees in Pakistan
Pap and punnyo	Idea of good and bad conduct
Para	Neighbourhood or locality
Pattas	Land deeds
Pirs	Muslim saints
Prabat or Parbatya	Hill
Praja	Subjects
Punorbason	Resettlement
Rajmala	Official chronicles of the Kings of Tripura
Refu or rifu	Abbreviations of the term refugee
Ryots	Peasants
Sak-pata	Basic green vegetables
Salwar	A special type of women's trousers popular mostly in North India
Sangram	Revolt/war

Select glossary

Santanas	Children of revolution
Sanyasis	Hindu ascetics and mendicants
Satyagraha	A strategy of conducting non-violent protests
Shahids	Martyrs
Sharan	Surrender of a human being to a higher power, God
Sharanarthi	Someone who seeks refuge and protection
Shinni	A liquid sweet dish made of rice-milk
Taluk	Hereditary estate/Zamindari
Tapashilis	Scheduled castes
Tilas	Hillocks
Udbastu	Somebody who is uprooted from home/homeland
Upojati	Tribal
Wanama chhinchha	Scary
Wansa	The son of Bengalis
Wansafaika-wansafaika	Tribals should be cautious of the Bengalis

BIBLIOGRAPHY

Archival sources

Files kept in the Manuscript Section, Oriental and India Office Collection (India Office Library and Records, London).
Ministry of Home Affairs (National Archives of India, New Delhi).
Ministry of External Affairs (NAI).
Ministry of States (NAI).
Department of Post and Communication (NAI).
Ministry of Rehabilitation (NAI).
Police Records (Nehru Memorial Museum and Library, New Delhi).
Home-Political Bundle (Bangladesh National Archives, Dhaka).
Home-Police Bundle (BNA).
Home Political and I.B. Records (West Bengal State Archives, Kolkata).
Home Political and I.B. Records (Assam State Archives, Dispur).
Administrative Reports (Secretariat Record Room, Agartala).
Home Political and I.B. Records (Tripura State Archives, Agartala).

Institutional papers

All India Congress Committee Papers (Nehru Memorial Museum and Library, New Delhi).
Assam Pradesh Congress Committee Papers (NMML).
Akhil Bharat Hindu Mahasabha Papers (NMML).
Assam Provincial Hindu Mahasabha Papers (NMML).
All India Women's Conference Papers (NMML).
Bengal Provincial Hindu Mahasabha Papers (NMML).

Private papers

Papers of Earl Mountbatten of Burma (India Office Library and Records, London).
Ajit Prasad Jain Papers (NMML).
Ashoka Gupta Papers (NMML).

Ashoka Gupta Papers (School of Women's Studies, Jadavpur University).
Ashutosh Lahiry Papers (NMML).
B. C. Roy Papers (NMML).
Bisnuram Mehdi Papers (NMML).
Dharam Vira Papers (NMML).
Diwan Chaman Lall Paper (NMML).
Khandu Bhai Desai Papers (NMML).
Lokpriya Gopinath Bordoloi Papers (NMML).
M. N. Saha Papers (NMML).
Mridula Sarabhai Papers (NMML).
N. K. Rustamji Papers (NMML).
P. C. Sen Papers (NMML).
P. D. Tandon Papers (NMML).
Padmaja Naidu Papers (NMML).
Rajendra Prasad Papers (NAI).
S. M. Saadulla Papers (NMML).
Saibal Kumar Gupta Papers (NMML).
Shyama Prasad Mookerjee Papers (NMML).
Sibnath Banerjee Papers (NMML).
Sri Prakasa Papers (NMML).
U. N. Dhebar Papers (NMML).
Vallabhbhai Patel Papers (NMML).
Verrier Elwin Papers (NMML).

Census reports

Agricultural Census, 1970–71. 1975. State Report. Agartala: Government of Tripura.
Assam Census, 1961, District Census Handbook. 1964. Gauhati: Tribune Press.
Assam Census, 1972, District Census Handbook. 1972. Shillong: Director of Census Operation.
Census of India. 1941a. Assam, Vol. IX.
Census of India. 1941b. Bengal, Vol. V (Part I).
Census of India. 1951. Vol. III, Assam, Part 1-A, p. 365, cited in Roychoudhury, Anil, 'National Register of Citizens, 1951', EPW, Vol. 16, No. 8 (February 21, 1981).
Census of Un-rehabilitated Displaced Persons in Chittagong, Chandraghona and Kaptai. 1959. Dacca: Department of Works, Housing and Settlement (Housing and Settlement), Government of East Pakistan.
Census of Un-rehabilitated Displaced Persons in Dacca and Narayanganj. 1959. Dacca: Department of Works, Housing and Settlement (Housing and Settlement), Government of East Pakistan.
Choudhury, Asit Chandra, ed. 1994. *Swadhin Tripurar Census Report* (1310 Tripura Era, 1901). Agartala: Tripura Tribal Research Institute.
Extracts from the High Court Ruling. (ALR 1970, Assam and Nagaland 206, Second Appeal No. 171 of 1967), cited in Roychoudhury, Anil, 'National Register of Citizens, 1951', EPW, Vol. 16, No. 8 (February 21, 1981).
Joshi, A. P., Srinivas, M. D. and Bajaj, J. K. 2005. *Religious Demography of India.* Chennai: Centre for Policy Studies.
Minutes of a Conference of Officials and Non-officials Held on 20th September 1928 to Discuss Colonization and Kindred Matters. 1931. 2 Vols. Copy of the Census Report: Assam.
Nag, Sajal. 2002. 'Region: Minefield of Conflict'. In *The Killing Fields: Mapping Conflict and Violence in North East India.* Report Prepared for the Violence Mitigation and Amelioration Programme of Oxfam, New Delhi.

Porter, A. E. 1933. *Census of India*. Bengal and Sikkim, Vol. V (Part 1). Calcutta: Central Publication Branch.

Report of the Census of India, 1901.

Vaghaiwalla, R. B. 1954. *Census of India, 1951*. Assam, Manipur and Tripura, Vol. XII (Part-1-A). Shillong: Government Report.

Gazetteers and statistical accounts

Allen, B. C. 1912. *Eastern Bengal District Gazetteer: Dacca*. Allahabad: The Pioneer Press.

The Assam Gazette-Extraordinary. 14 August 1947. Published by the Authority, No. 18. Shillong: Government of Assam—Order by the Governor, Education Department Notification.

Assam Gazette (Part VI-B). January–June 1940.

Bakshi, S. R., ed. 2000. *Bangladesh Gazetteer*. Vol. I. New Delhi: Cosmo Publications.

De, Barun, ed. March 1994. *Gazetteer of India*. West Bengal (24-Parganas). Calcutta: Government of West Bengal.

De, Satyendra Lal and Bhattacharjee, A. K. 1972. *The Refugee Settlement in the Sundarbans, West Bengal: A Socio-Economic Study*. Kolkata: Indian Statistical Institute.

Dey, Ranjit Kr., ed. 2000. *The Statistical Account of Tripura*. New Delhi: Uppal Publishing House.

Hunter, W. W. 1871. *The Annals of Rural Bengal*. London: Smith & Elder and Co.

Hunter, W. W. 1874. *Statistical Account of Bengal*. London: Smith & Elder and Co.

Hunter, W. W. 1998. *A Statistical Account of Assam*. 2 Vols. Guwahati and New Delhi: Spectrum Publications.

O'Malley, L. S. S. 1998. *Bengal District Gazetteer*. Calcutta: Department of Higher Education, Government of West Bengal.

Rizvi, S. N. H. 1965. *East Pakistan District Gazetteers (Dacca)*. Dhaka: Government of East Pakistan, Services/General Administration Department.

Statistical Survey of Displaced Persons from East Pakistan in Tripura. 1956. Tripura Administration. Agartala: Printed by the Superintendent, Government Printing.

Tripura State Gazette Sankalan. 1965. Tripura: Printed by the Superintendent, Government Printing.

West Bengal Statistical Abstract: 1947–48. 1948. Calcutta: Printed by the Superintendent, Government Printing, West Bengal Government Press.

Government publications and reports

Adhikari, O. S. 1982. *The Problem of Indebtedness Among the Tribals in Sadar Sub-Division of Tripura*. Agartala: Directorate of Research, Department of Welfare for Schedule Tribes, Government of Tripura.

After Partition. 1948. Modern India Series-7. New Delhi: The Publication Department, Ministry of Information and Broadcasting, Government of India.

An Analysis of Expenditure of Government of Assam 1950–51 to 1973–74. 1973. Shillong: Department of Economics and Statistics.

Annual Administrative Report 1971–72. 1973. Calcutta: The Government of West Bengal.

Annual Report of the Year 1955–56. Ministry of Rehabilitation. New Delhi: Government of India Press.

Annual Report of the Year 1958–59. Ministry of Rehabilitation. New Delhi: Government of India Press.

Bibliography 263

Annual Report of the Year 1961–62. Ministry of Rehabilitation. New Delhi: Government of India Press.

Annual Report of Voluntary Health Association of Tripura. 1996. Agartala: Government of Tripura.

Annual Reports. 1948–71. Ministry of Rehabilitation. New Delhi: Government of India Press.

The Chakma Profile. 1999. Agartala: Government of Tripura.

Chakravarty, A. *A Pilot Plan for Resettlement of Refugees and Resettlement in West Bengal*. Kolkata: National Library (publication details not attached).

The Dandakaranya Project and the Resettlement of Displaced Persons from East Pakistan. 1958. Ministry of Rehabilitation. New Delhi: Government of India.

Das, Durga, ed. 1972. *Sardar Patel's Correspondence 1945–50*. 10 Vols. Allahabad: Navajiban Publishing House.

Document on Population State of Refugee Inmates: As on 31st December 1996. South Tripura: District Administration Office.

General Report on Public Instructions in Assam from 1860 to 1907. Shillong: Government of Assam.

Gopal, S., ed. 1987. *Selected Works of Jawaharlal Nehru*. Second Series. New Delhi: Jawaharlal Nehru Memorial Fund.

Govt. of Bengal, Fin. Dept., Emigration Br. Report on the Inland Emigration for the Year Ending 30–06–1916; Commerce Dept., Emig. Br., Report on Inland Emigration for the Period Ending 30–06–1917, 30–06–1918; Rev. Dept., Emig. Br. for the Period Up to 30–06–1920, 30–06–1921, 30–061922 up till 30–06–1931.

Guha, B. S. 1959. *Studies in Social Tensions Among the Refugees from Eastern Pakistan*. Memoir No. 1. Calcutta: Department of Anthropology, Government of India.

Interim Report of Rehabilitation of Displaced Persons from East Pakistan. 1973. Calcutta: Government of West Bengal.

Introduction of Legislation in the Parliament to further Amend the West Bengal Evacuee Property Act, 1951 as Extended to the State of Tripura. 1952. Ministry of Law: The West Bengal Evacuee Property (Tripura Amendment) Ordinance (No. VI). The West Bengal Evacuee Property (Tripura Amendment) Ordinance.

Khan, Saleemullah. 1993. *The Journey to Pakistan: A Document on Refugees of 1947*. National Documentation Centre, Government of Pakistan. Cabinet Secretariat, Cabinet Division, Cabinet Block. Islamabad: Printing Corporation of Pakistan.

Luthra, P. N. 1972. *Rehabilitation*. New Delhi: Ministry of Information and Broadcasting, Publications Division, Government of India.

Mahalonobis, P. C. 1946. 'Distribution of Muslims in the Population of India'. *Sankhya: The Indian Journal of Statistics (1933–1960)* 7 (4).

Millions on the Move: The Aftermath of Partition. 1948. New Delhi: Ministry of Information and Broadcasting, Publications Divisions, Government of India.

A Note on the Implementation of the Indo-Pakistan Agreement of the 8th April 1950 and Its Annexure of the 16th August 1950. New Delhi: Government of India.

Partition Proceedings. 1949–1950. 6 Vols. New Delhi: Government of India Press.

Population Data Regarding Forestry Communities Practicing Shifting Cultivation. 1980. Report for India, Ministry of Agriculture. New Delhi: Government of India.

Purbo-Pakistaner Bastuhara: Punorbasoner Panch Bochhor, 1952–56. 1956. Calcutta: Published by the Government of West Bengal.

Rao, U. Bhaskar. May 1967. *The Story of Rehabilitation*. Department of Rehabilitation. Ministry of Labour, Employment and Rehabilitation. Faridabad: Government of India.

Refugee Relief and Rehabilitation Directorate. 1989. Calcutta: The Government of West Bengal.

Refugee Resettlement: A Report of the Relief and Rehabilitation Department. 1948. A Report by Sri Nikunja Bihari Maiti, The Hon'ble Minister in Charge, Relief and Rehabilitation Department. Calcutta: The Director of Publicity, West Bengal.

Rehabilitation Ministry's Annual Report, 1961–62. Calcutta: The Director of Publicity, West Bengal.

Report from Office of the Deputy High Commissioner for India in Pakistan. 1952. Dacca.

Report from Office of the Deputy High Commissioner for Pakistan in India. 1953. Calcutta.

Report of the Administration 1957–58. 1959. Calcutta: West Bengal Land and Revenue Department.

Report of the Dacca Riot Enquiry Committee. 1942. Government of Bengal (Home Department), Political Branch. Alipur, Bengal: Bengal Government Press.

Report of the Line System Committee. 1937. Report of the Deputy Commissioner: Nowgong on the Immigrant Question of that District. Shillong: Assam Government Press.

Report of the Line System Committee. 1938. Reply Through Questionnaire, Miscellaneous Statistics and References. Shillong: Assam Government Press.

Report on the Educational Survey in Assam. 1957. Department of Education. Shillong: Assam Government Press.

Reports of the 71st India Estimate Committee 1964–65. 1965. Third Lok Sabha. New Delhi: Ministry of Rehabilitation (Reception, Dispersal and Rehabilitation of New Migrants Arriving in India from East Pakistan Since 1st January 1964).

Reports of the 96th India Estimates Committee 1959–60. 1960. Second Lok Sabha. New Delhi: Ministry of Rehabilitation (Eastern Zone), Lok Sabha Secretariat.

Reports of the Members and Awards of the Chairman of the Boundary Commissions. Partition Proceedings. 1949. 6 Vols. New Delhi: Government of India Press.

Reports of the Members and Awards of the Chairman of the Boundary Commissions. Partition Proceedings. 1950. 6 Vols. Calcutta: West Bengal Government Press.

Singh, Brig. Rajendra. 1962. *The Military Evacuation Organisation*. New Delhi: Government of India Press.

A Statement. 15 December 1958. Issued by the Government of West Bengal.

A Study Over the Jhum and Jhumia Rehabilitation in the Union Territory of Tripura. 1999. Special Series No. 2, Directorate of Research. Agartala: Department of Welfare for Schedule Tribes and Schedule Castes, Government of Tripura.

Summary of Plan for Refugee Rehabilitation Drawn up by the Rehabilitation Board Formed by the Bengal Rehabilitation Organization, 1958 (publication details not attached).

Techno-Economic Survey of Tripura. August 1961. New Delhi: The National Council of Applied Economic Research.

They Live Again: Millions Came from East Pakistan. 1954. Calcutta: Government of West Bengal Press.

Tripura Administrative Reports. 1937–1946. London: India Office Library and Records.

Tripura Prasanga, Janasangjok o Parjaton Odhikar. May 1975. Agartala: Tripura Sarkar.

Tripura State: Consolidated Administration Report for 1353–1355 T.E. 1943–1946 A.D. Compiled and Published by the Political Department: Government of Tripura.

Tripura Ties with Tagore. 1969. Directorate of Education. Agartala: Government of Tripura.

Two Years Since Independence: A Resume of the Activities of the West Bengal Government, 15 August 1947–49. 1949. West Bengal: The Director of Publicity.

Vira, Dharama. 1967. *West Bengal: Two Years of Turmoil* (publication details not attached).

West Bengal Act of XVI OF 1951. 1962. The Government of West Bengal, Law Department. West Bengal: The Government Press.

The West Bengal Independence Anniversary. 1953. Calcutta: Government of West Bengal Press.

White Paper on Foreigner's Issues. 20 October 2012. Home and Political Department, Government of Assam.

Non-governmental reports

A Case for Bengalis in Assam. April 1960. Hojoi: Published by Nikhil Assam Banga Bhasa Samity.
A Case for Partition of Bengal. Being a Memorandum Submitted to the Advisory Committee of the Constituent Assembly of India. 12 July 1947. Calcutta.
Choudhury, J. K. 1952. *A Dream College. Being a Report on the Origin and Working for the First Five Years, 1947–52 of the Maharaja Bir Bikram College.* Agartala: Tripura Darpan.
Commissioner Prashnamala Puron Samporke Nirdesh (Guidelines for the Commission). School of Women Studies. Kolkata: Jadavpur University.
Das, Samir Kumar and Basu Ray Chaudhury, Anasua. February 2011. *A Report on the State of Being Stateless: A Case Study of the Chakmas of Arunachal Pradesh.* Kolkata: Calcutta Research Group.
Extract Copy of Weekly Confidential Report for the Week Ending 24/05/1961 of Cachar District: Report of the Non-official Commission of Enquiry Headed by N. C. Chatterjee, Barrister-at-Law. Supreme Court of India.
Findings and Resolution on Assam's Language Problem by the Citizen's Welfare Committee. Silchar: Adopted on 15 September 1960.
The Foreigners Problem: An Analysis. 1990. Gauhati, Assam: The All Assam Gana Sangram Parishad.
Gatrell. 2013. *Refugees and the Doctrine of 'Rehabilitation' in the Mid-twentieth Century.* Draft of a longer paper, May 2013 (used with the permission of the author).
Husain, A. F. A. 1956. *Human and Social Impact of Technological Change in Pakistan. A Report on a Survey Conducted by the University of Dacca.* Published with the Assistance of UNESCO, Geoffrey Cumberlege. Pakistan: Oxford University Press.
The Indian and Pakistan Year Book and Who's Who: A Statistical and Historical Annual of India and Pakistan. 1951. Vol. XXXVII. Bombay, New Delhi and Calcutta: The Times of India Group.
Invasion in Disguise: The Problem of Foreign Infiltration in Assam. 1980. Co-Ordination Committee. Gauhati: Gauhati University Teachers' Association.
The Killing Fields: Mapping Conflict and Violence in North East India. 2002. New Delhi: Report Prepared for the Violence Mitigation and Amelioration Programme of Oxfam.
The Law of Landlord and Tenant in the Independent State of Tripura (as Amended by Act 1 of 1296 T. E.), Drafted by Mohini Mohan Bardhan, Minister Under Orders His Highness Maharaja Bir Chandra Deb Barma Manikya Bahadur. Agartala: Bir Press, Independent Tripura.
Memorandum for the Bengal Boundary Commission, Submitted by the Bengal Provincial Hindu Mahasabha and the New Bengal Association. July 1947.
Memorandum on the Partition of Bengal, Presented on Behalf of the Indian National Congress Before the Bengal Boundary Commission. 15 July 1947.
Memorandum on the Rehabilitation of Refugees from Eastern Bengal by the East Bengal Relief Committee. 1952.
Memorandum Submitted Before the States Reorganisation Commission by the Assam Sahitya Sabha. 10 May 1955.
Memorandum Submitted by a Deputation of Two Thousand Members of the Asom Jatiya Mahasabha Headed by A. G. Ray Choudhury, Its General Secretary to the Hon'ble Sri Gopinath Bordoloi on 31st August at Gauhati on Some of the Vital National Demands of the Assamese People. 1949.
Memorandum Submitted to the Eighth Finance Commission by Tripura Tribal Areas Autonomous District Council. 1960. Agartala, Tripura.
Oitihasik Odhikar. 1964. Published by Purbabanga Sankyaloghu Kalyan Parishad.

Sangothoner Ovimukh. September, 2008. Paschimbanga Udbastu Tran o Punorbason Kormochari Samiti, Nobom Borsho, Dwitiyo Sankha.
Recurrent Exodus of Minorities from East Pakistan and Disturbances in India. 1965. A Report to the Indian Commission of Jurists by Its Committee of Enquiry.
Refugees: The Dynamics of Displacement. 1986. London: A Report for the Independent Commission on International Humanitarian Issues.
Rehabilitation of Refugees in Angarkata Area: West Kumarikata, Kamrup, Assam. 1978. New Delhi: Association of Voluntary Agencies for Rural Development (AVARD).
Report of the Enquiry Commission into the Police Firing Incident of 4th July 1960 at Gauhati by C. P. Sinha. 1960. Chief Justice, Assam High Court.
Resolution of the Muslim League on the Communal Award, 25–26 November 1933. 1924–36. All India Muslim League Resolutions.
Sujaud Doullah, M. 2003. *Immigration of East Bengal Farm Settlers and Agricultural Development of the Assam Valley, 1901–1947.* New Delhi: Institute of Objective Studies.
The Tripura Panchayat Raj Rules. 1961. Agartala: Tripura Administration.

Assembly debates/proceedings

Ahmed, Abul Mansur. 1944. General President's Address. *Proceedings of the Pakistan Renaissance Society Conference* 17 (10–11).
Assam Legislative Assembly Debates. Official Report. Shillong: Assam Government Press.
Constituent Assembly of India (Legislative) Debates. Official Report. New Delhi: Government of India Press.
Constituent Assembly of Pakistan Debates. Official Report. Karachi: Government of Pakistan Press.
East Pakistan Provincial Assembly Proceedings. Official Report. Dhaka: East Pakistan Government Press.
Parliamentary Debates. Official Report. New Delhi: Government of India Press.
Proceedings of the Tripura Legislative Assembly. Official Report. Agartala: Tripura Government Press.
Proceedings of the West Bengal Legislative Assembly Assembled Under the Provisions of the Constitution of India. Official Report. Calcutta: West Bengal Legislative Assembly.

Newspapers

Amrita Bazar Patrika (in English).
Ananda Bazar Patrika (in Bengali).
Asian Times (in English).
Assam Bilashini (in Bengali).
The Assam Tribune (in English).
The Azad (in English).
The Bengalee (in English).
Chiniha (in *Kok-barok*).
The Chronicle (in English).
Dainik Asomia Janambhumi (in Assamese).
Dainik Assamiya (in Assamese).
Dainik Basumati (in Bengali).
Dainik Sambad (in Bengali).
Dandakaranya Samachar (a bilingual weekly).

Dawn (in English).
Dhaka Prakash (in Bengali).
Doinik Azad (in Bengali).
Doinik Ittefaq (in Bengali).
Doinik Pakistan (in Bengali).
Economics Weekly (in English).
The Free Press Journal (in English).
The Hindu (in English).
Hindustan Standard (in English).
The Hindustan Times (in English).
The Ittefaq (in Bengali).
Jagaran (weekly newspaper in Bengali).
Janajuddha Patrika (in Bengali).
Janakalyan (weekly newspaper in Bengali).
Jugantar (in Bengali).
The Morning News (in English).
The Moslem Chronicle (in English).
The Mussalman (in English).
Nagarik (in Assamese).
Natun Asomiya (in Assamese).
Ovyudoy (in Bengali).
The Pakistan Observer (in English).
Purbadesh (a leftist newspaper in Bengali published from East Pakistan).
The Rehabilitation Review (in English).
Samaj (weekly newspaper in Bengali).
The Shillong Times (in English).
Star of India (in English).
The Statesman (in English).
Swadhinata (a leftist newspaper in Bengali published from Calcutta).
The Times of India (in English).
The Tribune (in English).
Tripura Rajyo Patrika (in Bengali).
Tripurar Katha (in Bengali).
The West Bengal Weekly (weekly newspaper in English).

Books in vernacular language

Abdul Maksud, Syed. 1994. *Moulana Abdul Hamid Khan Bhasani.* Dhaka: Bhasani Foundation/Sahitya Academy.

Acharya, Durgadas. 1978. *Udbastu: Dandakaranya o Andaman.* Calcutta: Indian Progressive Publishing.

Acharyya, Anil, ed. 2012. *Sattor Dashok.* 2 Vols. Kolkata: Anustup.

Adhikari, Harinarayan, ed. 1995. *Sangrami Rupasree Palli.* Kolkata: Published by the Author.

Ahad, Oli. 1982. *Jatio Rajniti: 1945 theke 75.* Dhaka: Khoshraj Kitab Mahal.

Ahmed, Abul Mansur. 2006. *Amar Dakha Rajnitir Ponchas Bochhor.* Dhaka: Khoshraj Kitab Mahal.

Ahmed, Muzaffar. 2003. *Amar Jibon o Bharater Communist Party.* 2 Vols. Kolkata: National Book Agency.

Ahmed, Muzaffar. 2011. *Nirbachita Prabandha.* Kolkata: National Book Agency.

Ahmed, Muzaffar. 2012. *Qazi Nazrul Islam: Smritikatha*. Kolkata: National Book Agency.
Ahmed, Rafique. 2014. *Deshbibhag: Fire Dakha*. Dhaka: Anindya Prakash.
Ahmed, Saiyad Mansur, ed. 2008. *Abul Hashim: Tanr Jibon o Samay*. Dhaka: Jatiya Sahitya Prakash.
Ahmed, Sajal, ed. 2012. *Dui Banglar Nirbachita Golpe Deshbhag*. Dhaka: Madhyama.
Ahmed, Sharmin. 2014. *Tajuddin Ahmed: Neta o Pita*. Dhaka: Oitijhhya.
Ahmed, Siraj Uddin. 1997. *Hussain Shaheed Suhrawardy*. Dhaka: Bhaskar Prakashani.
Ahmed, Siraj Uddin. 2013. *Sher-e-Bangla A. K. Fazlul Haque*. Dhaka: Bhaskar Prakashani.
Akhtar Mukul, M. R. 2001. *Bhasani Mujiber Rajniti*. Dhaka: Sagar Publishers.
Akhtar Mukul, M. R. 2010. *Ami Bijay Dekhechhi*. Dhaka: Ananya.
Ali, Syed Monoar. 2013. *Satchallisher Danga, Udbastu Samay Ebong Amader Mina Paribar*. Dhaka: Sahitya Prakash.
Anisuzzaman, ed. 1969. *Muslim Banglar Samayik Patra, 1831–1930*. Dhaka: Bangla Academy.
Anisuzzaman. 2001. *Muslim-Manas o Bangla Sahitya, 1757–1918*. Dhaka: Papiras.
Anisuzzaman. 2003. *Kal Nirabadhi*. Dhaka: Sahitya Prakash.
Atikur Rahman, A. T. M. 1995. *Banglar Rajnitite Maulana Mohammad Akram Khan, 1905–1947*. Dhaka: Bangla Academy.
Azad, Salam. 1405 (Bengali year). *Hindu Samproday Kano Deshtyag Korchhe?* Kolkata: Swatantra Prakashani.
Azad, Salam, ed. 2007. *Banglsdesher Nirjyatito Hindu Somprodaya: Prekhapot Muktijuddho*. Kolkata: Ovijan Publishers.
Bandyapadhyay, Atin. 2012. *Nilkantha Pakhir Khonje*. Kolkata: Karuna Prakashani.
Bandyapadhyay, Hiranmay. 1970. *Udbastu*. Calcutta: Sahitya Samsad.
Bandyapadhyay, Hiranmay. 1982. *Dr. Bidhan Chandra Ray-er Sannidye*. Calcutta: Nabapatra Prakashan.
Bandyapadhyay, Krishna, ed. 2005. *Abiram Raktapat Tripuranarir Sangram*. Kolkata: Mahanirban Calcutta Research Group.
Bandyapadhyay, Sailesh Kumar. 1399 (Bengali year). *Dangar Itihas*. Calcutta: Mitra and Ghosh.
Bandyapadhyay, Sailesh Kumar. 1417 (Bengali year). *Jinnah-Pakistan: Natun Bhabna*. Calcutta: Mitra and Ghosh.
Bandyapadhyay, Sailesh Kumar, ed. 1997. *Swadhinotar Panchash Bochhor*. Calcutta: Mitra and Ghosh.
Bandyapadhyay, Sandip. 1992. *Itihaser Dike fire Chhechollisher Danga*. Calcutta: Utsa Manush Publication.
Bandyapadhyay, Sandip. 2001. *Deshbhag: Smriti ar Swotta*. Kolkata: Progressive Publishers.
Bandyapadhyay, Sandip. 2010. *Marichjhhanpi: Dandakban theke Sundarban*. Kolkata: Rwitakkhor.
Basu, Dakshinarajan. 1975. *Chhere Asa Gram*. Calcutta: Jigyasa.
Basu, Samaresh. 1987. *Khondita*. Calcutta: Ananda.
Basu, Samaresh. 2003. *Suchander Swadesh Jatra*. Kolkata: Anjali Prakashani.
Basu, Shyamaprasad. 2006. *Jinnah: Dharmanirapekshata Bonam Sampradayikata*. Kolkata: Dey's.
Basu, Sudhir Madhab. 1977. *Pichhan Pane Chai*. Calcutta: Manashi.
Bhaduri, Panch Gopal. 1952. *Congress-er Nirbachoni Pracharer Jobabe*. Calcutta: National Book Agency.
Bhattacharjee, Tushar. 2015. *Aprakashito Marichjhhanpi*. Kolkata: Ekti Guruchanda Prakashona.
Bhattacharya, Anup and Deb, Shubhobbrata, ed. 2001. *Uttorpurber Nirbachito Bangla Golpo*. Agartala: Akshar Publication.

Bhattacharyya, Bhismodeb. 1989. *Sekaler Agartala*. Agartala: Published by the Author.
Bhattacharyya, Bhismodeb. 2002. *Nirbachito Bhismodeb*. Agartala: Akshar Publication.
Bhattacharyya, Harihar. 1999. 'Post-Partition Refugees and the Communists: A Comparative Study of West Bengal and Tripura'. In *Region and Partition: Bengal, Punjab and the Partition of the Subcontinent*, eds. Ian Talbot and Gurharpal Singh. Oxford: Oxford University Press.
Bibhutibhusan Mukhopadhyay Rachanaboli. 1396 (Bengali year). 4 Vols. Kolkata: Mitra and Ghosh.
Biswas, Adhir. 2010. *Deshbhager Smriti*. Kolkata: Gangchil.
Biswas, Anil, ed. 2003. *Banglar Communist Andolon Dalil o Prasongik Tothyo*. 6 Vols. Kolkata: National Book Agency.
Biswas, Henmanga. 2012. *Ujan Gang Baiya*. Kolkata: Anustup.
Biswas, Kalipada. 1966. *Jukta Banglar Ses Odhyay*. Calcutta: Orient Book Company.
Biwas, Kalipada. 1996. *Julto Banglar Ses Odhyay* (in Bengali). Calcutta: Orient Book Company.Biswas, Nitish. 2014. *Bharote Bangali Dalit Udbastu* (in Bengali). Kolkata: Ekti Oikotan Nibedon.
Biswas, Nitish. 2015. *Bharate Bangali Dalit Udbastu*. Kolkata: Oikotan Gobeshona Sansad.
Bondyapadhyay, Manabendra, ed. 2004. *Bhed-Bibhed*. 2 Vols. Kolkata: Dey's.
Bondyopadhyay, Manik. 1974. *Manik Granthabali*. 8 Vols. Kolkata: Granthalaya.
Borhogain, Homen. 2013. *Nagorikor Patot Asomor Bohiragoto Samasya*. Guwahati: Students Stores.
Boruah, Chandranath. 2009. *Assamese Response to Regionalism: A Study Based on Electoral Politics*. New Delhi: Mittal Publications.
Bose, Nurjahan. 2011. *Agunmukhar Meye*. Dhaka: Sahitya Prakash.
Byapari, Manoranjan. 1421 (Bengali year). *Itibritye Chandal Jiban, 2nd Portion*. In Hatebajare Patrika.
Byapari, Manoranjan. 2013. *Itibritye Chandal Jiban*. Kolkata: Kolkata Prakashan.
Chaki, Debabrata. 2013. *Bratyajoner Brityanta: Prasanga Bharat-Bangladesh Chhitmahal*. Kolkata: Sopan.
Chakma, S. 1986. *Prasanga Parbatya Chattagram*. Calcutta: Nath Brothers.
Chakrabarty, Dipankar, ed. 2007. *Bangladesh Prasange* (Anik) Calcutta: People Book Society.
Chakrabarty, Nripen. 1996. *Longtorai Amar Ghor*. Agartala: Tripura Darpan.
Chakraborty, Bikash. 2012. *Andamane Punarbasan: Ek Bangal Officerer Diary*. Kolkata: Gangchil.
Chakraborty, Binodlal. 2013. *Samayer Satkahon*. Silchar: Srijan.
Chakraborty, Kanai Lal. 2013. *Sharanarthir Dinalipi*. Dhaka: The Royal Publishers.
Chakraborty, Mahadev, ed. 2011. *Janma-shataborshe Biren Dutta o Tar Rachanasamagra*. Agartala: Nabachandana Prakashani.
Chakraborty, Renu. 1980. *Bharotio Nari Andolone Communist Meyera, 1949–1950*. Calcutta: Manisha.
Chakraborty, Soumen, ed. 1419 (Bengali year). *Bohuswore Udbastu Sattae Bangali*. Kolkata: Muktaman.
Chakraborty, Soumen. 2013. *Udbastu Jibon o Manobadhikar*. Kolkata: Muktamon.
Chakraborty, Soumen, ed. 2015. *Bharatrastre Bangal Prabesh—Onuprabesher Rajniti*. Kolkata: Voices for Research in Social Administration.
Chakraborty, Soumen, Mandal, Tridiv, Roy, Nirupoma and Ghosal, Poulomi, ed. 2007. *Dhyonsho o Nirman: Bongio Udbastu Somajer Swokothito Biboron*. Kolkata: Seriban.
Chakravarti, Mahadev, ed. 2011. *Biren Datta o Tar Rachana Sangraha*. Agartala: Naba Chandana Prakashani.

Chanda, Saroj. 1988. *Tripura Ugro Jatiyotabader Birudhye*. Agartala: Tripura Darpan.
Chanda, Saroj. 2006. *Prekkhapot Tripura*. Agartala: Tripura Darpan.
Chanda, Saroj and Chakraborty, Satyabrata, ed. 1999. *Tripurae Samaj Sanskriti Santrashbad*. Agartala: Tripura Darpan.
Chattopadhyay, Bhabaniprasad. 1993. *Desh Bibhag: Paschat o Nepathya Kahini*. Calcutta: Ananda.
Chaudhury, Amitava. 1961. *Mukher Bhasa Buker Rudhir*. Calcutta: Gronthoprakash.
Chaudhury, Sirajul Islam. 2011. *Dui Jatrae Ak Jatri*. 2 Vols. Dhaka Pearl Publications and Anya Prakash.
Chaudhury, Sirajul Islam. 2015. *Jatiyotabad, Sampradayikota o Jonoganer Mukti: 1905–47*. Dhaka: Sanhati.
Choudhuri, Bijaya. 2004. *Sylhet Konyar Atmokatha*. Kolkata: Anustup.
Choudhury, Kamal, ed. 2009. *Noakhali o Sandwiper Itihas*. Calcutta: Dey's.
Choudhury, Kumud Kundu. 2008. *Paharer Diary: Ekti Jibon Duti Hridoy*. Agartala: Akshar Publication.
Choudhury, Narayan. 1973. *Assamer Bhasa Danga*. Calcutta: Moni Prakashoni.
Chowdhury, Kumud Kundu. 1999. *Kakbarak Bhasa o Sahitya*. Agartala: Akshar Publishers.
Das, Atin. 2012. *Biday Janmabhumi*. Kolkata: Sopan.
Das, Manju. 2014. *Chhorano Bij Prantore*. Agartala: Akshar Publication.
Das, Naresh Chandra. 1368 (Bengali year). *Namasudra Samprodae o Bangala Desh*. Calcutta: Naba Bharat Publishers.
Das, Shachin. 2008. *Udbastu Nagarir Chand*. Kolkata: Dey's.
Das, Sukumar. 1982. *Uttorbanger Itihas*. Calcutta: Kumar Sahitya Prakashan.
Dasgupta, Ananda, ed. 2008. *Swadhinata: Swodesh-Samaj-Sanskriti*. Kolkata: Gangchil.
Dasgupta, Biplab. 1994. *Jyotibabur Sange: Pratham Parbo-1967 Parjonto*. Calcutta: Nandan.
Dasgupta, Pannalal. 1979. *Dandakaranya: Notun Somajer Jonyo Prochesta*. Calcutta: Tagore Society for Rural Development.
Dasgupta, Shatindra Nath. 15 November 1947. *Shanti Mission Dinlipi*. Kajirkhil Camp: Bulletin-3.
Datta, Kanailal. 1984. *Madhyamgram-Nabarrackpore Punarbason o Haripada Biswas*. Calcutta: Jigyasa.
De, Amalendu. 1974. *Bangali Buddhijibi o Bichchhinnotabad*. Calcutta: Ratna Prakashan.
De, Amalendu. 1975. *Swadhin Bangabhumi Gothoner Porikolpona: Prayas o Porinoti*. Calcutta: Ratna Prakashan.
De, Amalendu. 1993. *Prasanga Onuprobesh*. Calcutta: Chirayata Prakashon.
Debbarma, Niranjan, ed. 2013. *Janasiksha Andolan: Itihas o Mulyayan*. Agartala: Poulomi Prakashani.
Deb Burma, Sudhanya. 2004. *Hakuch Khurich*. Agartala: Akshar Publication.
Deb Burman, Nilmani. 2005. *Gadyasangraha: Janasiksha Anddolan o Anyanya Prabandha*. Agartala: Bhasa.
Deb, Dasharath. 1987. *Mukti Parishader Itikatha*. Calcutta: National Book Agency.
Deb, Subhabrata and Choudhury, Kumud Kundu, ed. 1996. *Patabhumika Andolon Ebong Janasiksha Samiti: Sangathak Ebong Samasamoyik der Mulyaon*. Agartala: Akshar Publication.
Debburma, Narendra Chandra. 2010. *Kokborok Bhasa Sahityer Kromobikash*. Agartala: Published by the Author.
Debburma, Narendra Chandra, Roy Chiran, Goutami and Choudhury, Kumud Kundu, ed. 2002. *Tripurar Ganatantrik Andoloner Agrapathik: Prabhat Ray er Rachana Sangraha o Smritikatha*. Agartala: Tripura Darpan.
Debburman, Sankho Subhra. 2002. *Bonkuntolar Upakhyan*. Agartala: Tripura Darpan.

Debburman, Sankho Subhra. 2007. *Aranye Prem Nei*. Agartala: Tripura Darpan.
Debnath, Jayanta. 2001. *Santrasklanta Tripura*. Agartala: Dainik Sanbad.
Debnath, Tapas. 2010. *Amar Shahar Agartala: Itihas, Andolan Nagarayan*. Agartala: Book World.
Debray, Debabrata. 2008. *Janma Shatabarshe Nripen Chakrabarty Jibon o Sangram*. Agartala: Naba Chandana Prakashani.
Debray, Mrinal Kanti. 2003. *Tripurar Siksha Sanskritir Shikorer Sondhane* (in Bengali). Agartala: Tripura Darpan.
Dey, Malaykanti. 2014. *Atmoporichaoy*. Silchar: Protisrot.
Dhar, Biman. 2010. *Onno Manus Onna Rajniti*. Agartala: Tripura Darpan.
Dhar, Biman. 2012. *Tripurae Communist Party: Prekkhit Golaghati Bidroho*. Agartala: Poulomi Prakashan.
Dutta, Biren. 1993. *Nirbachito Rachona*. Agartala: Gana Sahitya Prakashan.
Dutta, Birendra Chandra, ed., 1358 (Tripura Era). *Tripura Rajyer Katha*. 45th edition, Second Year, 13th Baishakh.
Dutta, Debabrata. 2001. *Bijoygarh Ekti Udbastu Uponibes*. Kolkata: Progressive Publishers.
Dutta, Haripada. 2012. *Mohajer*. Dhaka: Bhumika.
Dutta, Kanailal. 1984. *Madhyamgram-Nabarrackpore Punarbason o Haripada Biswas*. Calcutta: Jigyasa.
Dutta, Ramaprasad. 2006. *Agartalar Itibrittya*. Agartala: Pounomi Prakashan.
Dutta Pathak, Moushumi. 2017. *You Do Not Belong Here: Partition Diaspora in the Brahmaputra Valley*. Chennai: Notion Press.
Elias, Akhtaruzzaman. 1992. *Khoabnama* (in Bengali). Dhaka: Mowla Brothers.
Elias, Akhraruzzaman. 1998. *Khoabnama*. Calcutta: Naya Udyog.
Gafur, Abdul, ed. 1987. *Bangladesher Arthaniti: Sankater Swarup*. Dhaka: Muktadhara.
Gangapadhyay, Sunil. 1997. *Aka Ebong Koyekjon*. Calcutta: Ananda.
Gangapadhyay, Sunil. 2003. *Arjuner Upanyas Samagra*. 3 Vols. Kolkata: Ananda.
Gangapadhyay, Sunil. 2013. *Purba-Paschim*. Kolkata: Ananda.
Ghatak, Samhita. 2012. *Ritwik ek Nadir Nam*. Kolkata: Dey's.
Ghatak, Surama. 2001. *Surma Nadir Deshe*. Kolkata: Anustup.
Ghatak, Surama. 2010. *Rwitik*. Kolkata: Anustup.
Ghosh, Anandagopal. 2011. *Swadhinota Shat: Prasanga Chhere Asa Mati*. Cooch Behar: Sahitya Bhagirath Prakashani.
Ghosh, Arun, ed. 2009. *Janajuddho, Deshbhag o Bharoter Communist Party, Dalil Sangraha, 1942–44*. Kolkata: Seriban.
Ghosh, Arun. 2010. *The Moments of Bengal Partition: Selection from the Amrita Bazar Patrika 1947–1948*. Kolkata: Seriban.
Ghosh, Gour Kishore. 1997a. *Jal Pare Pata Nore*. Calcutta: Ananda.
Ghosh, Gour Kishore. 1997b. *Pratibesi*. Calcutta: Ananda.
Ghosh, Nobendu. 2001. *Fears Lane*. Kolkata: Mitra and Ghosh.
Ghosh, Semanti, ed. 2008. *Deshbhag: Smriti ar Stobdhota*. Kolkata: Gangchil.
Ghosh, Semanti, ed. 2012. *Swojati Swadesher Khonje*. Kolkata: Dey's.
Ghosh, Shankar. 1998. *Hastantar* (in Bengali). Vol. I. Kolkata: Ananda Publishers.
Gogoi, Akhil. 2012. *Bideshi Samasya aru Jatiya Andulonor Poth*. Guwahati: Akhor Prakash.
Guha, Amalendu. 1977. *Planter Raj to Swaraj: Freedom Struggle and Electoral Politics in Assam, 1826–1947*. New Delhi: People's Publishing House.
Gupta, Ajoy. 2007. *Udbritter Itibritta*. Kolkata: Ababhash.
Gupta, Ashoka. 1999. *Noakhalir Durjyoger Dine*. Calcutta: Naya Udyog.
Gupta, Saibal Kumar. 1994. *Kichhu Smriti Kichhu Katha*. Kolkata: Bibhasa.

Hashim, Abul. 1978. *Amar Jibon o Bibhagpurbo Bangladesher Rajniti*. Calcutta: Chirayata Prakashan.
Hosen, Saokot Ara. 1990. *Bongio Byabosthapok Sabha 1921–36: Abibhakta Banglar Samaj o Rajniti*. Dhaka: Dhaka Biswabidyalaya.
Hossain, Selina. 2003. *Gayatri Sandhya*. Dhaka: Samay Prakashan.
Hossain, Selina. 2012. *Sonali Dumur*. Kolkata: Ananda.
Huq, Hasan Azizul. 2008. *Agunpakhi*. Kolkata: Dey's.
Huq, Hasan Azizul. 2013. *Atmoja o Akti Karabi Gachh*. Dhaka: Sahitya Prakash.
Huq, Mahmudul. 1992. *Kalo Borof*. Dhaka: Sahitya Prakash.
Ishhak, Abu. 2010. *Surjya Dighal Bari*. Kolkata: Chirayata Prakashan.
Islam, Saiful. 2002. *Assam o Mowlana Bhasani Ebong Line Protha—Bangal Kheda*. Dhaka: Bortoman Samay.
Islam, Sirajul, ed. 1993. *Bangladesher Itihas 1704–1971*. 3 Vols. Dhaka: Bangladesh Asiatic Society.
Kar, Subir. 1999. *Borak Upotyakay Bhasa Sangramer Itihas*. Calcutta: Pustak Biponi.
Lodh, Debasis. 2002. *Ei Shohor Agartala*. Agartala: Akshar Publications.
Mahanta, Dipankar, ed. 2004. *Suhasini Das: Noakhali-1946*. Kolkata: Sahitya Prakash.
Mahanta, Manas Kumar. 2010 (December). *Bibhajoner Itihas: Jatiyotabad Ityadi* (in Bengali). Brand Value Communication.
Majumdar, Manju Kumar and Dutta, Bhanudeb, eds. 2008. *Banglar Communist Andoloner Itihas Anusandhan* (in Bengali). Vol. II. Kolkata: Manisha.
Majumdar, Manju Kumar and Dutta, Bhanudeb, eds. 2010. *Banglar Communist Andoloner Anusandhan* (in Bengali). Vol. V. Kolkata: Manisha.
Majumdar, Manju Kumar and Dutta, Bhanudeb, eds. 2013. *Banglar Communist Andoloner Anusandhan*. 12 Vols. Kolkata: Manisha.
Mamoon, Muntasir. 1993. *Dhaka—Smriti Bismritir Nagari*. Dhaka: Ananya.
Mamoon, Muntasir, ed. 2009. *Chirasthayi Bandabasta o Bangali Samaj*. Dhaka: Mowla Brothers.
Mamoon, Muntasir. 2012. *Bangladesh: Bangali Manos, Rastragathon o Adhunikota*. Kolkata: Kristi.
Mandal, Manankumar, ed. 2014. *Partition Sahitya: Desh-Kal-Smriti*. Kolkata: Gangchil.
Mannan, Mohammad Abdul. 2007. *Bangabhanga Theke Bangladesh*. Dhaka: Kathamala Prakashan.
Mitra, Ashoke. 2012. *Apila-Chapila*. Kolkata: Ananda.
Mitra, Asok. 1407 (Bengali year). *Tin Kuri Dosh: Swadhinotar Pothe 1940–1947*. 6 Vols. Calcutta: Dey's.
Mohammod, Tajul. 2005. *Sylhet e Ganahatya*. Dhaka: Sahitya Prakash.
Mokammel, Tanvir. 1397 (Bengali year). *Bangali Musalman Madhyobityer Chetanar Bikash Prasange*. Anustup, Basanta Sankhya, Rajatjoyonti Borso-Dhitiyo Sankhya.
Monsur, Minar. 2012. *Dhirendranath Dutta: Jibon o Kormo*. Dhaka: Bangla Academy.
Morshed, M. S. 2008. *Bhag*. Dhaka: Banglaprakash.
Moulik, Gopal Chandra. 2011. *Deshbhag o Nanipisima r Katha*. Kolkata: Gangchil.
Mukhopadhyay, Balaichand. 1982. *Panchaparba* in *Banaful rachanabali*. 12 Vols. Calcutta: Granthalaya.
Mukhopadhyay, Debabrata. 2013. *Bibhajaner Paschadpat: Bangabhanga 1947*. Kolkata: Readers Service.
Mukhopadhyay, Kalikaprasad. 2002. *Shikorer Sondyane*. Kolkata: Bhasa o Sahitya.
Mukhopadhyay, Sirshendu. 2000. *Parapar*. Kolkata: Ananda.
Mutsuddhi, Chinmoy. 1992. *Ashanta Parbotya Chattagram o Ananya Prasanga*. Dhaka: Agami Prakashani.

Nurul Huda, Muhammad, ed. 2013. *Langal o Ganabani*. Dhaka: Nazrul Institute.
Pal, Babul Kumar. 2010. *Barishal Theke Dandakaranya: Purbabanger Krishijibi Udbastur Punarbasan Itihas*. Kolkata: Granthamitra.
Pal, Madhumay, ed. 2009. *Marichjhhanpi: Chhinno Desh, Chhinno Itihas*. Kolkata: Gangchil.
Pal, Madhumay, ed. 2011. *Deshbhag: Binas o Binirman*. Kolkata: Gangchil.
Pal, Manos, ed. 2010. *Tripurar Char Pradhan Golpokar*. Agartala: Soikat Prakashan.
Pal, Sadananda. 2013. *Aka Kumbho: Ak Udbastu Kumbhokarer Matimakha Atmakatha*. Kolkata: Camp.
Parshad, Srishti Sampadona, ed. 2001. *Rakter Nodir Theke Kollolito-Pakistan, Bangladesh o Bharater Nirbachita Golpo*. Kolkata: Sristi Prakashan.
Paschimbanga Bidhansabhae Danga Bisoye Somnath Lahirir Boktrita. 2014. In *Banglar Communist Andoloner Anusandhan* (in Bengali), eds. Manju Kumar Majumdar and Bhanudeb Dutta. Vol. XIII. Kolkata: Manisha.
Purbo Bangla Theke Agoto Bastuharader Proti Communist Partyr Dak: Basosthan, Khadhyo, Kaj o Jomir Jonyo Lorun (in Bengali). 1950 (March 22). In *Banglar Communist Andoloner Anusandhan* (in Bengali), eds. Manju Kumar Majumdar, Bhanudeb Dutta. Vol. VI. Kolkata: Manisha.
Purkayastha, Bijan Bihari. 1955. *Tripura: Atit, Bartaman o Bhabishyat*. Kolkata: Pustak Bipani.
Rahman, Atiur, ed. 2000. *Bhasha Andolener Artha-Samajik Patabhumi*. Dhaka: University Press Limited.
Rahman, Mizanur. 2012. *Bhabnar Atmakathan, Krishno sholoi*. Kolkata: Gangchil.
Rahman, Shamsur. 2004. *Kaler Dhulae Lekha*. Dhaka: Anyaprakash.
Rahman, Sheikh Mujibur. 2012. *Asamapta Atmajibani*. Dhaka: University Press Ltd.
Rakshit, Subrata Kumar. 1999. *Dalit Neta Jogendranath Mandol Padatyag Korechhilen Kano?* Calcutta: Vivekananda Sahitya Kendra.
Ray, Ajay. 1979. *Bangladesher Arthonity Atit o Bartaman*. Dhaka: Jatiya Sahitya Prokashani.
Ray, Debojyoti. 2001. *Kano Udbastu Hote Holo?* Calcutta: Vivekananda Sahitya Kendra.
Ray, Samiron, ed. 2009. *Tothyopanji o Nirdeshika*. Agartala: Tripura Darpan.
Roy, Annada Sankar. 1996. *Nobboi Perie*. Kolkata: Dey's.
Roy, Annada Sankar. 1999. *Jibon-Joubon*. Kolkata: Ananda.
Roy, Debes. 1988. *Tistaparer Brityanta*. Kolkata: Dey's.
Roy, Debes. 2010. *Barishaler Jogen Mandal*. Kolkata: Dey's.
Roy, Jagat Jyoti. 1999. *Bidroho Bibortan o Tripura*. Agartala: Tripura Darpan.
Roy, Mohit. 2009. *Anuprabes, Aswikrito Udbastu o Paschimbonger Anischito Astitwa*. Kolkata: Kamb.
Roy, Pannalal. 2003. *Tripurar Bharat Antarbhukti o Chakla Roshanabad*. Agartala: Tripura Darpan.
Roy, Pannalal. 2008. *Rajanyo Tripurar Bangla Bhasa* (in Bengali). Agartala: Pounomi Prakashan.
Roy, Prafulla. 2003. *Bhagabhagi*. Kolkata: Dey's.
Roy, Prafulla. 2007. *Keya Patar Nouka*. Kolkata: Karuna Prakashani.
Roy, Rahul, ed. 2015 *Paschim Theke Purbobanga: Deshbodoler Smriti*. Kolkata: Gangchil.
Roy, Ranajit. 1977. *Dhongser Mukhe Paschimbanga: Kendra/Rajyo Arthonoitik Rajnoitik Samporko Nie Protibedan*. Kolkata: New Age Publishers.
Roy, Sabitri. 2010. *Sabitri Roy Rachanasamagra*. Kolkata: Granthalaya.
Roychoudhury, Anil. 2009. *Asomot Bangladeshi*. Guwahati: Jagoron Sahitya Prakashon.
Roychoudhury, Subir, ed. 2001. *Jyotirmoyee Debir Rachana Sankalan*. Kolkata: Dey's.
Roychoudhury, Tapan. 2007a. *Bangalnama*. Kolkata: Ananda.
Roychoudhury, Tapan. 2007b. *Romonthon othoba Bhimrotipraptor Porochoritchorcha*. Kolkata: Ananda.

Roychowdhury, Ladli Mohan. 2004. *Kshamata Hastantar o Desh Bibhag*. Kolkata: Dey's.
Rushad, Abu. 1998. *Atmojiboni: Jibon Kramasha-Thikana*. Dhaka: Adorn Publication.
Saha, Dinesh Chandra. 2009. *Tripurae Gana Andoloner Bichitra Dhara*. Agartala: Writers Publication.
Samsuddin, Abu Jafar. 1989. *Atmasmriti*. Dhaka: Jatiya Sahitya Prakashani.
Samsuddin, Abu Jafar. 2002. *Padma Meghna Jamuna*. Dhaka: Khoshraj Kitab Mahal.
Sanyal, Prabodh Kumar. 1413 (Bengali year). *Prabodh Kumar Sanyal Shatabarshiki Sankalan*. Kolkata: Mitra and Ghosh.
Sarkar, Jatin. 2005. *Pakistaner Jonmomrityu Dorshon*. Dhaka: Sahityika.
Sarkar, Radhakanta. 1396 (Bengali year). *Atmaghati Assam*. Calcutta: K. C. Sarkar & Co.
Sen Vidyabhusan, Sree Kaliprasanna, ed. 2013. *Srirajmala (Bango-Uponibesh, Prathom Lohor)*. Agartala: Tribal Research Institute.
Sen, Amiya. 1966. *Aranyalipi*. Calcutta: Compus Publications.
Sen, Ashalata. 1990. *Sekaler Katha*. Calcutta: Farma K. L. M.
Sen, Manikuntala. 1982. *Sediner Katha* (in Bengali). Kolkata: Nabapatra Prakashan.
Sen, Manikuntala. 2003. *Sediner Katha* (in Bengali). Kolkata: Nabapatra Prakashan.
Sen, Meenakshi. 1418 (Bengali year). *Doshti Golpo*. Kolkata: Poroshpathor Prakashan.
Sen, Mukul. 2011. *Swottay Smritite Deshtyag: Somaj, Rajniti, Itihas*. Kolkata: Ababhas.
Sen, Samar. 2004. *Babubrityanto o Prasongik*. Calcutta: Dey's.
Sengupta, Amalendu. 1991. *Uttal Chollis: Asomapto Biplab*. Calcutta: Pearl Publishers.
Sengupta, Amalendu. 1997. *Joarbhantay Shat-Sottor*. Calcutta: Pearl Publishers.
Sengupta, Debaprasad. 1991. *Tripurar Ganaandolan o Communist Partyr Itikatha*. Agartala: Tripura Darpan.
Sengupta, Debaprasad. 2003. *Sankalpa Sanghat Sambhabona, Rudraprasad Prakalpo: Pratham Porber Smriti*. Agartala: Tripura Darpan.
Sengupta, Mihir. 2013. *Bishadbrikkho*. Kolkata: Ananda.
Sengupta, Sukhoranjan. 1995. *Bangla: Fazlul Huq Theke Jyoti Basu*. Calcutta: Sujan Publications.
Sengupta, Syamal. 2006. *Kichhu Smriti Kichhu Katha*. Agartala: Akshar Publication.
Sharma, Chanchal Kumar. 1984. *Sreehatte Biplobbad o Communist Andolon* (in Bengali). Calcutta: Narendra Mahapatra.
Sharma, Dwijen. 2008. *Amar Akattor o Anyanya*. Dhaka: Anupam Prakashani.
Sikdar, Asrukumar. 2005. *Bhanga Bangla o Bangla Sahitya*. Kolkata: Dey's.
Sikdar, Sunanda. 2012. *Doyamoyee Katha*. Kolkata: Gangchil.
Singha, Anil. 1995. *Paschimbange Udbastu Uponibesh*. Calcutta: Book Club.
Singha, Tushar. 1999. *Maronjoyee Sangrame Bastuhara*. Calcutta: Dasguptas.
Sinha, Bimal. 2009a. *Alor Thikana*. Agartala: Naba Chandana Prakashan.
Sinha, Bimal. 2009b. *Titas theke Tripura*. Agartala: Naba Chandana Prakashan.
Sinha, Kankar. 2007. *Sampradayikata abong Sankhalaghu Sankat*. Dhaka: Jatiya Sahitya Prakash.
Swadeshi, Mujib. 2015. *Bangla Sahitye Bangabhonga o Deshbhag*. Kolkata: Sopan Publisher.
Taj-Uddin Ahmeder Diary 1949–50. 2000. 2 Vols. Dhaka: Pratibhas.
Tarashankar Rachanaboli. 1385 (Bengali year). 16 Vols. Calcutta: Mitra and Ghosh.
Thakur, Asit Baran. 2011. *Udbastu Mukti o Mukto Samaj*. Kolkata: Mukto Samaj Prakashani.
Thakur, Kapil Krishna. 1412 BS. *Ujantolir Upakatha* (in Bengali). Vol. I. Kolkata: Chaturtha Dunia.
Thakur, Kapil Krishna. 2011. *Ujantolir Upokatha*. Kolkata: Nikhil Bharat.
Uchchhed Uchchhed: Dharabahik Omanobikotar Khondochitro. 2003. Kolkata: Shalti Research Group/Kamb.
Udbastu Front. 2005. In *Banglar Communist Andolon Dalil o Prasongik Tothyo* (in Bengali), ed. Anil Biswas. Vol. IV. Kolkata: National Book Agency.

Udbastu Punorbason. 2014. In *Banglar Communist Andoloner Anusandhan* (in Bengali), eds. Manju Kumar Majumdar and Bhanudeb Dutta. Vol. XII. Kolkata: Manisha.
Umor, Badruddin. 1470 (Bengali year). *Dharma Rajniti o Samprodayikata*. Calcutta: Chirayata Prakashan.
Umor, Badruddin. 1978. *Chirasthayee Bandabaste Banglar Krishak*. Calcutta: (Publication details not attached).
Umor, Badruddin. 2006. *Bangabhanga o Samprodayik Rajniti*. Dhaka: Shrabon Prakashan.
Umor, Badruddin. 2012a. *Purbabanglar Bhasa Andolan o Tatkalin Rajniti*. 3 Vols. Dhaka: Subarna.
Umor, Badruddin. 2012b. *Rachana Sangraha*. 4 Vols. Dhaka: Shrabon Prakashani.
Umor, Badruddin. 2013. *Bhasa o Sahitya Prasange*. Dhaka: Jatiya Sahitya Prakash.
Umor, Badruddin. 2014. *Amar Jibon*. 6 Vols. Dhaka: Jatiya Sahitya Prakash.
Wadud, Kazi Abdul. 1935. *Hindu-Mussalmaner Birodh*. Nizam Lectures (First Speech): Bisvabharati Studies No. 6.

English books

Abbi, B. L., ed. 1984. *Northeast Region: Problems and Prospect of Development*. Chandigarh: Centre for Research in Rural and Industrial Development.
Acharya, Phanibhusan. 1979. *Tripura*. New Delhi: Publication Division.
Adhikari, O. S. 1988. *Four Immigrant Tribes of Tripura- Their Life and Culture, Directorate of Research*. Agartala: Tribal Welfare Department, Government of Tripura.
Agarwal, A. K. 1985. *North-East India: An Economic Perspective*. Allahabad: Chugh Publications.
Ahmed, Abu Naser Saied, ed. 2007. *National Security Issues: Northeast India Perspective*. New Delhi: Omeo Kumar Das Institute of Social Change and Development and Akansha Publishing House.
Ahmed, Imtiaz, ed. 1973. *Caste and Social Stratification among the Muslims*. New Delhi: Manohar.
Ahmed, Imtiaz, Dasgupta, Abhijit and Kerkhoff, Kathinka Sinha, ed. 2004. *State, Society and Displaced People in South Asia*. Dhaka: The University Press Limited.
Ahmed, Kamruddin. 1967. *A Socio-Political History of Bengal and the Birth of Bangladesh*. Dacca: Zahiruddin Mahmud Inside Library.
Ahmed, Rafiuddin. 1996. *The Bengal Muslims, 1871–1906: A Quest for Identity*. New Delhi: Oxford University Press.
Ahmed, Salauddin. 2004. *Bangladesh: Past and Present*. New Delhi: A.P.H. Publishing Corporation.
Ahmed, Sharif Uddin, ed. 1991. *Dhaka: Past Present Future*. Dhaka: The Asiatic Society of Bangladesh.
Ahmed, Sufia. 1974. *Muslim Community in Bengal, 1884–1912*. Dacca. Oxford University Press: Bangladesh.
Alam, Khorshed, ed. 1985. *Planning in North East India*. New Delhi: Omsons Publishers.
Ali, Tariq. 1983. *Can Pakistan Survive? The Death of a State*. Harmondsworth: Penguin.
Ambedkar, B. R. 1945. *Pakistan or the Partition of India*. New Delhi.
Azad, Maulana Abul Kalam. 2012. *India Wins Freedom: The Complete Version*. Hyderabad: Orient BlackSwan.
Bagchi, Jasodhara and Dasgupta, Subhoranjan, ed. 2003. *The Trauma and the Triumph: Gender and Partition in Eastern India*. Kolkata: Stree.
Bahadur, Lal. 1988. *Struggle for Pakistan (Tragedy of the Triumph of Muslim Communalism in India: 1906–1947)*. New Delhi: Sterling Publishers Pvt. Ltd.

Ball, Ellen. 2000. *'They Ask If We Eat Frogs': Social Boundaries, Ethnic Categorisation, and the Garo People of Bangladesh*. Amsterdam: Eburon.
Bandyapadhyay, Sekhar, ed. 2001. *Bengal: Rethinking History-Essays in Historiography*. New Delhi: Manohar.
Bandyapadhyay, Sekhar. 2004a. *Caste, Culture and Hegemony: Social Dominance in Colonial Bengal*. New Delhi: Sage.
Bandyapadhyay, Sekhar. 2004b. *From Plassey to Partition: A History of Modern India*. New Delhi: Orient Longman.
Bandyapadhyay, Sekhar. 2009. *Decolonization in South Asia: Meanings of Freedom in Post-Independence West Bengal, 1947–52*. London and New York: Routledge.
Bandyopadhyay, Sandip. 2013. *Bengal Partition: Battered Background Broken Minds*. Kolkata: Radical Impression.
Banerjee, A. C. 1992. *The Eastern Frontier of British India, 1784–1826*. Calcutta: K.P. Bagchi & Co.
Banerjee, D. N. 1969. *East Pakistan: A Case Study in Muslim Politics*. New Delhi: Vikas.
Banerjee, Paula and Basu Ray Choudhury, Anasua, ed. 2011. *Women in Indian Borderland*. New Delhi: Sage.
Banerjee, Paula and Basu Ray Chaudhury, Sabyasachi, ed. 2005. *Internal Displacement in South Asia: The Relevance of the UN's Guiding Principles*. New Delhi: Sage.
Banglapedia (National Encyclopedia of Bangladesh). 2003. Dhaka: Asiatic Society of Bangladesh.
Barkat, Abul, ed. 2000. *An Enquiry into Causes and Consequences of Deprivation of Hindu Minorities in Bangladesh Through the Vested Property Act*. Dhaka: PRIP Trust.
Barpujari, H. K. 1963. *Assam: In the Days of Company*. Gauhati: Lawyers Book Stall.
Barpujari, H. K. 1998. *North-East India: Problems, Policies and Prospects since Independence*. Guwahati and New Delhi: Spectrum Publications.
Barrier, N. G., ed. 1981. *Census in British India: New Perspectives*. New Delhi: Manohar.
Barua, Alokesh, ed. 2005. *India's North-East: Development Issues in a Historical Perspective*. New Delhi: Manohar.
Barua, Indrani. 1990. *Pressure Groups in Assam*. New Delhi: Omsons Publications.
Baruah, Apurba Kumar, ed. 1991. *Social Tensions in Assam: Middle Class Politics*. Guwahati: Purbanchal Prakash.
Baruah, Apurba Kumar, ed. 2002. *Student Power in North-East India: Understanding Student Movements*. New Delhi: Regency Books.
Baruah, S. L. 1993. *A Comprehensive History of Assam*. New Delhi: Munshiram Manoharlal.
Baruah, Sanjib. 1999. *India Against Itself: Assam and Politics of Nationality*. New Delhi: Oxford University Press.
Baruah, Sanjib. 2015. 'Partition and the Politics of Citizenship in Assam'. In *Partition: The Long Shadow*. ed. Urvashi Butalia. New Delhi: Zubaan - Penguin/Viking.
Basu Majumder, Chandrika. 2003. *Genesis of Chakma Movement in Chittagong Hill Tracts*. Kolkata: Progressive Publishers.
Basu, Jayanti. 2013. *Reconstructing the Bengal Partition: The Psyche under a Different Violence*. Kolkata: Samya.
Basu, Jyoti. 2010. *Memoirs: A Political Autobiography*. Kolkata: National Book Agency.
Basu, Pradip Kr. 1996. *The Communist Movement in Tripura*. Calcutta: Progressive Publishers.
Basu, Sajal. 1974. *West Bengal: The Violent Years*. Calcutta: Prachi Publications.
Batabyal, Rakesh. 2005. *Communalism in Bengal: From Famine to Noakhali, 1943–47*. New Delhi: Sage.
Bayes, Abdul and Muhammad, Anu, ed. 1998. *Bangladesh at 25: An Analytical Discourse on Development*. Dhaka: The University Press Limited.

Bibliography

Bayly, C. A. 1975. *The Local Roots of Indian Politics: Allahabad 1880–1920*. Oxford: Clarendon Press.
Bhabnani, Nandita. 2014. *The Making of Exile: Sindhi Hindus and the Partition of India*. New Delhi: Tranquebar.
Bhattacharjee, S. R. 1989. *Tribal Insurgency in Tripura: A Study in Exploration of Causes*. New Delhi: Inter-India Publications.
Bhattacharya, Nandini. 2017. *East Bengal: A Lost Land of Immortal Memories*. Kolkata: Gangchil.
Bhattacharya, Sabyasachi. 2014. *The Defining Moments in Bengal 1920–47*. New Delhi: Oxford University Press.
Bhattacharya, Sambhuti Ranjan. 1989. *Tribal Insurgency in Tripura: A Study in Exploration of Causes*. New Delhi: Inter-India Publications.
Bhattacharyya, Gayatri. 1988. *Refugee Rehabilitation and Its Impact on Tripura's Economy*. New Delhi: Omsons Publications.
Bhattachayya, Suchintya. 1991. *Genesis of Tribal Extremism in Tripura*. New Delhi: Gyan Publishing House.
Bhaumik, Subir. 1996. *Insurgent Crossfire: Northeast India*. New Delhi: Lancer.
Bhaumik, Subir, Guhathakurta, Meghna and Basu Ray Chaudhury, Sabyasachi, ed. 1997. *Living on the Edge: Essays on the Chittagong Hill Tracts*. Katmandu: South Asian Forum for Human Rights.
Bhowmick, Dhirendra. 1964. *An Open Letter to Jawaharlal Nehru*. Silchar: Published by the Author.
Bhuyan, A. C. and Sibopada, De, ed. 1978. *Political History of Assam, 1920–1939*. 2 Vols. Guwahati: Government of Assam.
Bhuyan, B. C., ed. 1992. *Political Development of the North East*. 2 Vols. New Delhi: Omsons Publications.
Biswas, Manohar Mouli. 2013. *Surviving on My World: Growing up Dalit in Bengal*. Kolkata: Samya.
Biswas, Swapan Kumar. 2009. *Colonization and Rehabilitation in Andaman and Nicobar Islands*. New Delhi: Abhijit Publications.
Bora, S. 1992. *Student Revolution in Assam, 1917–1947 (A Historical Survey)*. New Delhi: Mittal Publications.
Borooah, Gopinath K. 1990. *Gopinath Bordoloi, Indian Constitution and Centre-Assam Relations*. Guwahati: Publication Board Assam.
Boruah, Chandranath. 2009. *Assamese Response to Regionalism: A Study Based on Electoral Politics*. New Delhi: Mittal Publications.
Bose, Pradip Kr., ed. 2000. *Refugees in West Bengal: Institutional Practices and Contested Identities*. Calcutta: Calcutta Research Group.
Bose, Sarat Chandra. 1968. *Whither Two Bengals?* Calcutta: Netaji Research Bureau.
Bose, Tussar Kanti. 1944. *The Bengal Tragedy*. Lahore: Hero Publications.
Brass, Paul R. and Franda, Marcus F. 1973. *Radical Politics in South Asia*. Cambridge, MA and London: The MIT Press.
Butalia, Urvashi, ed. 1998. *The Other Side of Silence: Voices from the Partition of India*. New Delhi: Penguin.
Butalia, Urvashi, ed. 2015. *Partition: The Long Shadow*. New Delhi: Viking-Penguin.
Chakrabarti, Prafulla K. 1990. *The Marginal Men: The Refugees and the Left Political Syndrome in West Bengal*. Calcutta: Lumiere Books.
Chakrabarty, Archana. 1989. *History of Education in Assam (1826–1910)*. New Delhi: Mittal Publications.
Chakrabarty, Bidyut. 2004. *The Partition of Bengal and Assam (1932–1947)*. London: Routledge.

Chakrabarty, Dipesh. 2002. *Habitations of Modernity: Essays in the wake of Subaltern Studies*. New Delhi: Permanent Black.

Chakrabarty, Saroj. 1962. *My Years with Dr. B. C. Roy (A Record up to 1962. A Documentary In-Depth Study of Post-Independence Period)*. Calcutta: A Century Volume.

Chakrabarty, Saroj. 1974. *With Dr. B. C. Roy and Other Chief Ministers (A Record up to 1962)*. Calcutta: Bensons.

Chakrabarty, Saroj. 1982. *My Years with Dr. B. C. Roy: A Record up to 1962. A Documentary In-depth Study of Post-Independence Period*. A Centenary Volume. Calcutta.

Chakrabarty, Saroj. 1984. *The Upheaval Years in North-East India (A Documentary In-Depth Study of Assam Holocaust 1960–1983)*. Calcutta: Published by the Author.

Chakraborty, Ashoke Kumar. 2002. *Bengali Muslim Literati and the Development of Muslim Community in Bengal*. Shimla: Indian Institute of Advanced Studies.

Chakravartty, Gargi. 2005. *Coming Out of Partition: Refugee Women of Bengal*. New Delhi: Bluejay Books.

Chakravarty, Mahadev, ed. 1994. *Administrative Reports of the Tripura State*. 6 Vols. New Delhi: Gyan Publishing House.

Chanda, Saroj, ed. 1983. *Two Unpublished Documents of the Party in the Period of Its Formation*. Agartala: Tripura Darpan.

Chandra, Sudhir. 2002. *Continuing Dilemmas: Understanding Social Consciousness*. New Delhi: Tulika.

Chari, P. R., Joseph, Mallika and Chandran, Suba, ed. 2003. *Missing Boundaries: Refugees, Migrants, Stateless and Internally Displaced Persons in South Asia*. New Delhi: Manohar.

Chatterjee, Nilanjana. 1990. 'The East Bengal Refugees: A Lesson in Survival'. In *Calcutta: The Living City*, Sukanta Chaudhury, ed., Vol. II (The Present and Future), 70–71. New Delhi: Oxford University Press.

Chatterje, Surendra Nath. 1984. *Tripura: A Profile*. New Delhi: Inter-India Publications.

Chatterjee, Partha. 2013. *The Partha Chatterjee Omnibus*. New Delhi: Oxford University Press.

Chatterjee, S. P. 1947. *The Partition of Bengal: A Geographical Study*. Calcutta: Calcutta Geographical Society.

Chatterji, Joya. 1995. *Bengal Divided: Hindu Communalism and Partition 1932–1947*. Cambridge: Cambridge University Press.

Chatterji, Joya. 2008. *The Spoils of Partition: Bengal and India, 1947–1967*. New Delhi: Cambridge University Press.

Chatterji, P. C., ed. 1989. *Self-Images Identity and Nationality*. New Delhi: Indian Institute of Advanced Study and Allied Publishers.

Chatterji, Rakhahari. 1985. *Politics in West Bengal: Institutions, Processes and Problems*. Calcutta: The World Press Private Ltd.

Chattopadhyay, Dilip Kumar. 1990. *History of the Assamese Movement since 1947*. Calcutta: Minerva Associates.

Chattopadhyaya, Haraprasad. 1987. *Internal Migration in India: A Case Study of Bengal*. Calcutta: K. P. Bagchi.

Chaube, S. K. 1985. *Electoral Politics in North-East India*. Madras: Universities Press.

Chaube, S. K. 2012. *Hill Politics in Northeast India*. New Delhi: Orient BlackSwan.

Chaudhri, G. W. 1963. *Democracy in Pakistan*. Dhaka: Green Book House.

Chaudhuri, Nirad C. 1951. *The Autobiography of an Unknown Indian*. New York: The Macmillan Company.

Chaudhuri, Sukanta, ed. 1990. *Calcutta: The Living City*. 2 Vols. New Delhi: Oxford University Press.

Chaudhuri, Sukanta. 2002. *View from Calcutta*. New Delhi: Chronicle Books.

Chaudhury, Binayendra Mohan. 1946. *Muslim Politics in India*. Calcutta: Orient Book Company.
Chaudhury, Monoranjan. 1964. *Partition and the Curse of Rehabilitation*. Calcutta: Bengal Rehabilitation Organisation.
Chaudhury, Saroj and Chaudhuri, Bikach, ed. 1983. *Glimpses of Tripura*. Agartala: Tripura Darpan.
Chhabra, K. M. L. 1992. *Assam Challenge*. New Delhi: Konark Publishers.
Choudhury, Bikach Kumar. 1991. *Genesis of Chakma Movement (1772–1989): Historical Background*. Agartala: Tripura Darpan.
Choudhury, Pratap Chandra. 1988. *Assam Bengal Relations: From the Earlier Times to the Twentieth Century A.D*. Guwahati and New Delhi: Spectrum Publications.
Choudhury, Sushil. 1995. *From Prosperity to Decline: Bengal in the Eighteenth Century*. New Delhi: Manohar.
Chowdhory, Nasreen. 2018. *Refugees, Citizenship and Belonging in South Asia: Contested Terrains*. Singapore: Springer.
Chowdhury, A. M. and Alam, Fakrul, ed. 2002. *Bangladesh on the Threshold of the Twenty-First Century*. Dhaka: Asiatic Society of Bangladesh.
Cohen, Stephen Philip. 2012. *The Idea of Pakistan*. New Delhi: Oxford University Press.
Dani, Ahmed Hasan. 1957. *Dacca: A Record of Its Changing Fortunes*. Dacca: Dacca Museum.
Das, Amiya Kumar. 1982. *Assam's Agony: A Socio-Economic and Political Analysis*. New Delhi: Lancers Publishers.
Das, Samir Kumar, ed. 2008. *Blisters on Their Feet: Tales of Internally Displaced Persons in India's North East*. New Delhi: Sage.
Das, Suranjan. 1991. *Communal Riots in Bengal 1905–1947*. New Delhi: Oxford University Press.
Das, Suranjan and Bandyopadhyay, Premansu Kumar, ed. 2004. *Food Movement of 1959: Documents a Turning Point in the History of West Bengal*. Calcutta: K. P. Bagchi.
Dasgupta, Abhijit. 2016. *Displacement and Exile: The State-Refugee Relations in India*. New Delhi: Oxford University Press.
Dasgupta, Abhijit, Tagawa, Masahiko and Barkat, Abul, ed. 2011. *Minorities and the State: Changing Social and Political Landscape of Bengal*. New Delhi: Sage.
Dasgupta, Bratati. 2015. *History of Tripura from Monarchy to Democracy*. Burdwan: Avenel Press.
Datta, P. S. 1993. *Autonomy Movements in Assam (Documents)*. New Delhi: Omsons Publications.
Debbarma, Aghore. 1986. *Primary Stage of the Democratic and Communist Movement in Tripura*. Agartala: Published by the Author.
Deb Barma, Dasaratha, ed. 1952. *Some Important Decisions of the GMP*. Agartala: Published by the Author.
Deb Barma, N. C. 2005. *History of the Land System and Land Management in Tripura (1872–2000 AD)*. Agartala: Published by the Author.
Deb Barma, Suren. 2002. *A Look into Tripura*. Agartala: Gyan Bichitra.
Deb Burman, P. K. and George, S. J. 1993. *The Chakma Refugees in Tripura*. New Delhi: South Asian Publishers.
Deb Burman, Suhadeb Bikram Kishore and Gan-Chaudhuri, Jagadis, ed. 1994. *Tripura: Historical Documents*. Calcutta: K.L.M.
Deb Burman, Suren. 1995. *A Look into Tripura*. Agartala: Gyan Bichitra.
Deb Sarkar, Manisha, ed. 2009. *Geo-Political Implication of Partition in West Bengal*. Kolkata: K. P. Bagchi and Company.
Deka, Mita. 1996. *Students Movements in Assam*. New Delhi: Vikas.

Deka, Usha and Deka, Devajyoti. 1981. *Background of Assam Movement*. Assam: Bani Prakash-Pathsala.
Dev, Bimal J. and Lahiri, Dilip K. 1985. *Assam Muslims: Politics and Cohesion*. New Delhi: Mittal Publications.
Devi, Aribum Indubala, ed. 2010. *Amazing North-East: Tripura*. New Delhi: Vij Books.
Devi, Maitreye. 1974. *Exodus*. Calcutta: Council for Promotion of Communal Harmony Publication.
Dey, Ranjit Kr., ed. 1998. *Socio-Political Movements in India: A Historical Study of Tripura*. New Delhi: Mittal Publications.
Dey, Ranjit Kr., ed. 2000. *The Statistical Account of Tripura*. New Delhi: Uppal Publishing House.
Dutt, R. Palme. 2008. *India Today*. New Delhi: People's Publishing House.
Dutta Pathak, Moushumi. 2017. *You Do Not Belong Here: Partition Diaspora in the Brahmaputra Valley*. Chennai: Notion Press.
Dutta Ray, B., ed. 1986. *The Pattern and Problems of Population in North East India*. New Delhi: Uppal Publishers.
Dutta, Antara. 2013. *Refugees and the Borders in South Asia: The Great Exodus of 1971*. London and New York: Routledge.
Dutta, Jyotish Chandra. 1954. *An Introduction to the History of Tripura from Monarchy to Democracy*. Calcutta: Book Home.
Dutta, Nandana. 2012. *Questions of Identity in Assam: Location, Migration, Hybridity*. New Delhi: Sage.
Eaton, Richard M. 1993. *The Rise of Islam and the Bengal Frontier 1204–1760*. Berkley: University of California Press.
Eaton, Richard M., ed. 2000. *Essays on Islam and Indian History*. New Delhi: Oxford University Press.
Falzon, Mark-Anthony. 2005. *Cosmopolitan Connections: The Sindhi Diaspora, 1860–2000*. New Delhi: Oxford University Press.
Farouk, A. 1982. *Changes in the Economy of Bangladesh*. Dhaka: University Press Limited.
Franda, Marcus. 1971a. *Political Development and Political Decay in Bengal*. Calcutta: Firma K. L. Mukhopadhyay.
Franda, Marcus. 1971b. *Radical Politics in West Bengal*. Cambridge, MA and London: The MIT Press.
Franda, Marcus. 1981. *Bangladesh: The First Decade*. New Delhi: South Asian Publishers.
Gait, Edward A. 1967. *History of Assam*. Calcutta: Thaker-Spink.
Gallagher, John, Johnson, Gordon and Seal, Anil, ed. 1973. *Locality, Province and Nation: Essays on Indian Politics (1870–1940)*. Cambridge: Cambridge University Press.
Gan-Chaudhuri, Jagadis, ed. 1885. *An Anthology of Tripura*. New Delhi: Inter-India Publications.
Gan-Chaudhuri, Jagadis. 1985. *The Political History of Tripura*. New Delhi: Inter-India Publications.
Gandhi, Mohandas Karamchand. 2012. *The Story of My Experiments with Truth*. Kolkata: Future-BPI India.
Ganguli, J. B. 1969. *Economic Problems of the Jhumias of Tripura: A Socio-Economic Problem of the System of Shifting Cultivation in Transition*. Calcutta: Bookland.
Ganguli, J. B. 1983. *The Bengal Hills: A Study of Tripura's Population Growth and Problems*. Agartala: Tripura Darpan.
Gera Roy, Anjali. 2020. *Memories and Postmemories of the Partition of India*. London and New York: Routledge.
Gera Roy, Anjali and Bhatia, Nandi, ed. 2008. *Partitioned Lives: Narratives of Home, Displacement and Resettlement*. New Delhi: Pearson and Longman.

Ghatak, Kamal Kumar. 1991. *Hindu Revivalism in Bengal.* Calcutta: Minerva India Publications.
Ghosh, Anjan, Guha Thakurta, Tapati and Nair, Janki, ed. 2011. *Theorizing the Present: Essays for Partha Chatterjee.* New Delhi: Oxford University Press.
Ghosh, Arun. 2010. *The Moments of Bengal Partition: Selections from the Amrita Bazar Patrika, 1947–1948.* Kolkata: Seriban.
Ghosh, Papiya. 2007. *Partition and the South Asian Diaspora: Extending the Subcontinent.* New Delhi: Routledge.
Ghosh, Partha S. 2004. *Unwanted and Uprooted: A Political Study of Migrants, Refugees, Stateless and Displaced in South Asia.* New Delhi: Samskriti.
Ghosh, Sankar, ed. 1972. *Resurgent West Bengal.* Calcutta: 74th Plenary Session, Indian History Congress.
Ghosh, Suniti Kumar. 2002. *The Tragic Partition of Bengal.* Allahabad: Indian Academy of Social Sciences.
Gohain, Hiren. 1985. *Assam: A Burning Question.* Guwahati: Spectrum Publications.
Goodwin-Gill, G. 2007. *The Refugees in International Law.* Oxford: Clarendon Press.
Gopalkrishnan, R. 1991. *Political Geography of India's North East.* New Delhi: Vikas.
Gordon, Leonard A. 1990. *Brothers Against the Raj: A Biography of Sarat and Subhas Chandra Bose.* New Delhi: Penguin.
Gossman, Patricia A. 1999. *Riots and Victims: Violence and the Construction of Communal Identity Among Bengali Muslims, 1905–1947.* Boulder, CO: Westview Press.
Goswami, Priyam. 2012. *The History of Assam: From Yandabo to Partition, 1826–1947.* New Delhi: Orient BlackSwan.
Goswami, Sandhya. 1997. *Language Politics in Assam.* New Delhi: Ajanta Publications.
Greenough, Paul. 1982. *Prosperity and Misery in Modern Bengal: The Famine of 1943–44.* New York: Oxford University Press.
Guha, Amalendu. 1977. *Planter Raj to Swaraj: Freedom Struggle and Electoral Politics in Assam, 1826–1947.* New Delhi: People's Publishing House.
Guha, Ranajit, ed. 1986. *Subaltern Studies: Writings on South Asian History and Society.* 4 Vols. New Delhi: Oxford University Press.
Gupta, Sekhar. 1984. *Assam: A Valley Divided.* New Delhi: Vikash, 201–211, cited in Binayak Dutta, 'The Unending Conundrum: The Story of Citizens/Foreigners between Politics and the Law in Assam'. http//pangsau.com (Retreived 31 May 2018).
Habib, Harun. 1992. *Freedom Struggle: Deadline Agartala.* Dacca: Jatiya Sahitya Prakashani.
Halder, Dilip. 2003. *Partition Forgotten Victims: The Dalits of Bengal, a Human Rights Question.* Kolkata: Sampark Academic.
Hangloo, R. L. 1984. *Studies in the Writings on History of Medieval North East India: Some Comments.* Delhi.
Hardinge, Lord. 1948. *My Indian Years, 1910–1916.* London: Charles Hardinge Baron Hardinge of Penshurst.
Hasan, Mushirul. 1979. *Nationalism and Communal Politics in India, 1916–1928.* New Delhi: Monohar.
Hasan, Mushirul, ed. 1985. *Communal and Pan-Islamic Trends in Colonial India.* New Delhi: Monohar.
Hasan, Mushirul, ed. 1995. *India Partitioned: The Other Face of Freedom.* 2 Vols. New Delhi: Lotus.
Hasan, Mushirul, ed. 1998. *Islam, Communities and the Nation: Muslim Identities in South Asia and Beyond.* New Delhi: Monohar.
Hasan, Mushirul, ed. 2000. *Inventing Boundaries: Gender, Politics and the Partition of India.* New Delhi: Oxford University Press.
Hasan, Mushirul, ed. 2001. *India's Partition: Process, Strategy and Mobilization.* New Delhi: Oxford University Press.

Hasan, Mushirul and Asaduddin, M., ed. 2000. *Image and Representation: Stories of Muslim Lives in India*. New Delhi: Oxford University Press.
Hasan, Mushirul and Roy, Asim, ed. 2005. *Living Together Separately: Cultural India in History and Politics*. New Delhi: Oxford University Press.
Hashim, Abul. 2006. *In Retrospection*. Dhaka: Mowla Brothers.
Hashmi, Taj-ul. 1982. *The Biharis in Bangladesh*. Report No. 11. London: Minority Rights Group.
Hazarika, Bolin and Baisya, Arun K., ed. 2000. *State Politics in Assam (Recent Trends in the Government and Politics of Assam)*. Jorhat: Department of Political Science, J. B. College.
Hazarika, Sanjay. 1994. *The Strangers of the Mist: Tales of War and Peace from India's North East*. New Delhi: Viking-Penguin.
Hodson, H. V. 1985. *The Great Divide: Britain-India-Pakistan*. Karachi: Oxford University Press.
Hunter, W. W. 1872. *The Indian Mussalmans: Are They Bound in Conscience Against the Queen?* London: Trubner.
Hunter, W. W. 1874. *A Statistical Account of Bengal*. Vol. VI. Hill Tipparah. London: Printed to Her Majesty's Stationary Office, Smith, Elder and Co.
Hunter, W. W. and Garret, H. L. O., ed. 1925. *Readings in Indian History*. Calcutta: S. K. Lahiri & Co.
Hussain, Imdad. 2005. *The Guwahati Declaration and the Road to Peace in Assam*. New Delhi: Akansha Publishing House.
Hussain, Monirul. 1993. *The Assam Movement: Class, Ideology and Identity*. New Delhi: Manak and Har-Anand Publications.
Ibrahim, Muhamed. 1923. *Banglar Krishak* (in Bengali). Calcutta.
Irani, C. R. 1968. *Bengal: The Communist Challenge*. Bombay: Lalvani Publishing House.
Islam, K. Z. 1993. *Mountbatten and the Partition of India*. Dhaka: Holiday Publications.
Islam, K. Z. 2012. *Glimpses of the Great*. Dhaka: Nirman.
Islam, M. Mufakharul and Mahmud, Firoz, ed. 2011. *400 Years of Capital Dhaka and Beyond*. Dhaka: Asiatic Society of Bangladesh.
Islam, Nazrul, ed. 1996. *The Urban Poor in Bangladesh*. Dhaka: Centre for Urban Studies.
Islam, Nazrul. 1999. *Urbanization in Bangladesh and the Growth of Dhaka-Land Use, Poverty and Governance*. Calcutta: K. P. Bagchi & Company.
Islam, Sirajul, ed. 2007. *History of Bangladesh 1704–1971*. Dhaka: Asiatic Society of Bangladesh.
Jahan, Rounaq. 2005. *Bangladesh Politics: Problems and Issues*. Dhaka: The University Press Ltd.
Jalal, Ayesha. 1985. *The Sole Spokesman: Jinnah, the Muslim League and Demand for Pakistan*. Cambridge: Cambridge University Press.
Jalal, Ayesha. 2000. *Self and Sovereignty: Individual and Community in South Asian Islam Since 1850*. London and New York: Routledge.
Jalal, Ayesha. 2013. *The Pity of Partition: Manto's Life, Time and Work Across the India Pakistan Divide*. New Delhi: Harper Collins Publishers India.
Jamatia, K. B. 2007. *Modernity in Tradition: A Historical Study of the Jamatia Tribe of Tripura*. Agartala: Akshar Publications.
Jodhani, Damodar. 1993. *Assam All the Chief Ministers*. Guwahati: Vicky and Shanky Jodhani Publication.
Jones, Kenneth W. 1981. 'Religious Identity and the Indian Census'. In *Census in British India: New Perspectives*, ed. N. G. Barrier, 73–74. New Delhi: Manohar.
Joshi, Shashi. 2007. *The Last Durbar: A Dramatic Presentation of the Division of British India*. New Delhi: Oxford University Press.

Joshua, C., ed. 2002. *Dimensions of Displaced People in North-East India*. New Delhi: Regency Publications.
Kabir, Ananya Jahanara. 2013. *Partition's Post-Amnesia: 1947, 1971 and Modern South Asia*. New Delhi: Women Unlimited.
Kabir, Humayun. 1943. *Muslim Politics, 1909–1942*. Calcutta: Gupta, Rahman and Gupta.
Kalita, Ramesh Chandra. 2011. *Situating Assamese Middle Class: The Colonial Period*. Guwahati: Bhabani Print and Publications.
Kamal, Ahmed. 2009. *State Against the Nation: The Decline of the Muslim League in Preindependence Bangladesh, 1947–54*. Dhaka: The University Press Ltd.
Kamra, A. J. 2000. *The Prolonged Partition and Its Pogroms: Testimonies on Violence Against Hindus in East Bengal 1946–64*. New Delhi: Voice of India.
Kanitkar, Satish. 2000. *Refugee Problems in South Asia*. New Delhi: Rajat Publications.
Kar, M. 1990. *Muslims in Assam Politics*. New Delhi: Omsons Publications.
Kaul, Suvir, ed. 2001. *The Partitions of Memory: The Aftermath of the Division of India*. New Delhi: Permanent Black.
Khan, Yasmin. 2007. *The Great Partition: The Making of India and Pakistan*. New Delhi: Viking-Penguin.
Kilikdar, Bibhas Kanti. 1995. *Tripura of Eighteenth Century with Samser Gazi against Feudalism (A Historical Study)*. Agartala: Tripura State Tribal Cultural Research Institute and Museum, Government of Tripura.
Kothari, Rita. 2007. *The Burden on Refuge: the Sindhi Hindus of Gujarat*. Chennai: Orient Longman.
Kudaisya, Gyanesh and Tan, Tai Yong, ed. 2000. *The Aftermath of Partition in South Asia*. London: Routledge.
Kumar, B. B. 1996. *Re-organization of North-East India (Facts and Documents)*. New Delhi: Omsons Publications.
Lahiri, Pravash Chandra. 1964. *India Partitioned and the Minorities of Pakistan*. Calcutta: Writer's Forum.
Lapierre, Dominique and Collins, Larry. 1997. *Freedom at Midnight*. New Delhi: Vikas.
Lapierre, Dominique and Collins, Larry. 2004. *Freedom at Midnight*. New Delhi: Vikash.
Latif, Muhammad Abdul. 1997. *Handloom Industry of Bangladesh: 1947–90*. Dhaka: University Press Limited.
Law, D. A. and Brasted, Howard, ed. 1998. *Freedom, Trauma and Continuities: Northern India and Independence*. New Delhi: Sage.
Llewellyn, Bernard. 1955. *From the Back Streets of Bengal*. London: George Allen and Unwin Ltd.
Ludden, David, ed. 1996. *Making India Hindu: Religion, Community and the Politics of Democracy in India*. New Delhi: Oxford University Press.
Mahajan, Sucheta. 2000. *Independence and Partition: The Erosion of Colonial Power in India*. New Delhi: Sage.
Mahanta, Bijan. 2004. *Tripura in the Light of Socio-Political Movements Since 1945*. Kolkata: Progressive Publishers.
Mahmud Ali, S. 1993. *The Fearful State: Power, People and Internal War in South Asia*. London and NJ: Zed Books.
Majumder, Benimadhab. 1997. *The Legislative Opposition in Tripura*. Agartala: Tripura State Tribal Cultural Research Institute and Museum, Government of Tripura.
Mandal, Monika. 2011. *Settling the Unsettled: A Study of Partition Refugees in West Bengal*. New Delhi: Maulana Abul Kalam Azad Institute of Asian Studies-Manohar.
Mansergh, Nicholas, ed. 1970–1982. *The Transfer of Power 1942–47*. 5 Vols. London: Her Majesty's Stationary Office.

Marbaniang, Iscot. 1970. *Assam in a Nutshell*. Shillong: Chapala Book Stall.
Matthews, Roderick. 2012. *Jinnah vs. Gandhi*. New Delhi: Hachette.
Menon, Ritu and Bhasin, Kamala. 1998. *Border and Boundaries: Women in India's Partition*. New Delhi: Kali for Women.
Menon, V. P. 1957. *The Transfer of Power in India*. New Delhi: Orient Longman.
Miri, Mrinal, ed. 1982. *Linguistic Situation in Northeast India*. Shillong: Northeast India Council for Social Science Research.
Miri, Sujata. 1993. *Communalism in Assam: A Civilizational Approach*. New Delhi: Har-Anand Publications.
Misra, B. P. 1976. *Socio- Economic Adjustment of Tribals*. New Delhi: People's Publishing House.
Mishra, Omprakash, ed. 2004. *Forced Migration in the South Asian Region: Displacement, Human Rights and Conflict Resolution*. New Delhi: Manak Publications.
Mishra, Sanghamitra. 2011. *Becoming a Borderland: The Politics of State and Identity in Colonial Northeastern India*. New Delhi: Routledge.
Misra, Udayan. 2000. *The Periphery Strikes Back: Challenges to Nation-State in Assam and Nagaland*. Shimla: Indian Institute of Advanced Studies.
Modak, Ashok and Bhatkhalkar, Atul. 1997. *Left Front Rule in West Bengal: Genesis, Growth and Decay*. Mumbai: Centre of Leadership Studies.
Mohanty, Satya P., ed. 2001. *Colonialism, Modernity and Literature: A View from India*. New York: Palgrave.
Molla, M. K. U. 1981. *The New Province of Eastern Bengal and Assam*. Dhaka: The Institute of Bangladesh Studies, Rajshahi University and The University Press Limited.
Mondal, Sekh Rahim. 1994. *Dynamics of Muslim Society*. New Delhi: Inter-India Publications.
Moraes, Frank, ed. 1958. *The Times of India- Directory and Year Book including Who's Who 1957–58*. Bombay: A Times of India Publication.
Mosley, Leonard. 1971. *Last Days of the British Raj*. Bombay: Jaico Publishing House.
Mountbatten, Pamela. 2008. *India Remembered: A Personal Account of the Mountbattens During the Transfer of Power*. London: Pavilion.
Mukerjee, Madhusree. 2010. *Churchill's Secret War: The British Empire and the Ravaging of India During World War II*. New Delhi: Tranquebar.
Mukherjee, Santosh Kumar. 1947. *Boundary Problem of New Bengal*. Calcutta: Published by Hindustan Socialist Party.
Mukherji, Saradindu. 2000. *Subjects, Citizens and Refugees: Tragedy in the Chittagong Hill Tracts (1947–1998)*. New Delhi: Indian Centre for the Study of Forced Migration.
Murshid, Navine. 2013. *The Politics of Refugees in South Asia: Identity, Resistance, Manipulation*. London and New York: Routledge.
Nag, Sajal. 1990. *Roots of Ethnic Conflicts: Nationality Question in North East India*. New Delhi: Manohar.
Nag, Sajal. 1999. *Nationalism, Separatism and Secessionism*. Jaipur: Rawat Publication.
Nag, Sajal. 2018. *Beleaguered Nation: The Making and Unmaking of the Assamese Nationality*. New Delhi: Monahar.
Nanda, B. R. 2014. *Road to Pakistan: The Life and Times of Mohammad Ali Jinnah*. New Delhi: Routledge.
Nath Barua, Harendra. 1944. *Reflection on Assam cum Pakistan*. Calcutta: Printkraft.
Nehru, Jawaharlal. 2004. *The Discovery of India*. New Delhi: Penguin Books.
Niaz, Ilhan. 2010. *The Culture of Power and Governance of Pakistan: 1947–2008*. Karachi: Oxford University Press.
Page, David. 2002. *The Partition Omnibus*. New Delhi: Oxford University Press.

Pakrasi, Kanti B. 1971. *The Uprooted: A Sociological Study on Refugees of West Bengal, India*. Calcutta: Editions Indian.
Palit, Projit Kumar. 2004. *History of Religion in Tripura*. Delhi: Kaveri Books.
Pande, Ira, ed. 2009. *The Great Divide: India and Pakistan*. New Delhi: Harper Collins.
Pandey, Gyanendra. 1990. *The Construction of Communalism in Colonial North India*. New Delhi: Oxford University Press.
Pandey, Gyanendra. 1999a. *Memory, History and Question of Violence: Reflection on the Reconstruction of Partition*. Calcutta: K. P. Bagchi.
Pandey, Gyanendra. 1999b. *Remembering Partition: Violence, Nationalism and History in India*. Cambridge: Cambridge University Press.
Panigrahi, D. N. 2004. *India's Partition: The Story of Imperialism in Retreat*. New York: Routledge.
Patel, Kamla. 1985. *Torn from the Roots (Mool Sotan Ukhdelan)*. New Delhi: Women Unlimited: An Association of Kali for Women.
Pathak, Lalit P. 1984. *A Seminar Paper on 'East Bengal Immigrants in Assam Valley: An Analysis of Census Data'*. Shillong: NEICSSR.
Paul, Manos. 2009. *The Eyewitness: Tales from Tripura's Ethnic Conflict*. New Delhi: Lancer Publishers.
Philips, C. H. and Wainwright, Mary Doreen, ed. 1970. *The Partition of India: Policies and Perspectives, 1935–1947*. London: The University Press.
Phillips, C. H., ed. 1967. *Historians of India, Pakistan and Ceylon*. Oxford: Oxford University Press.
Phukan, Manuj. 2005. *Students' Politics in Assam*. New Delhi: Maulana Abul Kalam Azad Institute of Asian Studies and Akansha Publishing House.
Phukon, Girin. 1996. *Politics of Regionalism in Northeast India*. New Delhi: Spectrum Publications.
Prasad, Bimal. 2001. *A Nation within a Nation: Pathway to India's Partition*. 2 Vols. Dhaka: The University Press Limited.
Rafiabadi, H. N. 1988. *Assam from Agitation to Accord*. New Delhi: Genuine Publications.
Rahman, M. A. 1999. *Assam Muslims: Fallacy and Fallout*. Hojai, Assam: Modern Press.
Rai, Vijai Shankar. 1990. *The Last Phase of the Transfer of Power in India*. New Delhi: Arnold Publishers.
Rashid, Harun-or. 1987. *The Foreshadowing of Bangladesh: Bengal Muslim League and Muslim Politics 1936–1947*. Dhaka: Asiatic Society of Bangladesh.
Ray, Rajat Kanta. 2001. *Exploring Emotional History: Gender, Mentality and Literature in the Indian Awakening*. New Delhi: Oxford University Press.
Ray, Rajat Kanta. 2003. *The Felt Community: Commonalty and Mentality Before the Emergence of Indian Nationalism*. New Delhi: Oxford University Press.
Ray, Renuka. 1982. *My Reminiscences: Social Development during Gandhian Era and After*. Bombay: Allied Publishers.
Risley, H. H. 1981. *Tribes and Castes of Bengal*. Calcutta: Bengal Secretariat Press.
Robinson, Francis. 1993. *Separatism Among Indian Muslims: The Politics of the United Province Muslims 1860–1923*. New Delhi: Oxford University Press.
Robinson, Francis. 2000. *Islam and Muslim History in South Asia*. New Delhi: Oxford University Press.
Roy Choudhury, Prafulla. 1977. *West Bengal: A Decade (1965–1975)*. Calcutta: Boipatra.
Roy Choudhury, Prafulla. 1985. *Left Experience in West Bengal*. New Delhi: Patriot Publishers.
Roy, Haimanti. 2012. *Partitioned Lives: Migrants, Refugees, Citizens in India and Pakistan, 1947–1965*. New Delhi: Oxford University Press.

Roy, Nirode Bihari. 1967. *On the Origin of the Namasudras*. Calcutta: Kriti Publishing Concern.

Roy, Sanjay K., ed. 2001. *Refugees and Human Rights: Social and Political Dynamics of Refugee Problem in Eastern and North-Eastern India*. New Delhi and Jaipur: Rawat Publication.

Roy, Tathagata. 2007. *A Suppressed Chapter in History: The Exodus of Hindus from East Pakistan and Bangladesh 1947–2006*. New Delhi: Book Well.

Roychoudhury, Nalini Ranjan. 1983. *Tripura through the Ages: A Short History of Tripura from Earlier Times to 1947 AD*. New Delhi: Sterling Publishers.

Sakshena, Mohanlal. 1950. *Social Reflections of the Problem of Rehabilitation*. New Delhi: Progressive Publishers.

Samad, Abdus. 1983. *Bangladesh: Facing the Future*. Dhaka: Bangladesh Books International Ltd.

Samaddar, Ranabir, ed. 1997. *Reflection of Partition in the East*. New Delhi: Vikas-Calcutta Research Group.

Samaddar, Ranabir, ed. 1999. *The Marginal Nation: Transborder Migration from Bangladesh to West Bengal*. New Delhi: Sage.

Samaddar, Ranabir, ed. 2003. *Refugees and the State: Practices of Asylum and Care in India, 1947–2000*. New Delhi: Sage.

Sarkar, Ashim Kumar. 2013. *Nationalism, Communalism and Partition in Bengal: Maldah 1905–1953*. Kolkata: Readers Service.

Sarkar, Jayanta and Ray, B. Dutta. 1990. *Social and Political Institutions of the Hill People of North East India*. New Delhi: Anthropological Survey of India, Ministry of Human Resource Development, Government of India, Department of Culture.

Sarkar, Sumit. 2011. *The Swadeshi Movement in Bengal 1903–1908*. New Delhi: Permanent Black.

Sarkar, Sumit and Sarkar, Tanika, ed. 2015. *Caste in Modern India: A Reader*. 2 Vols. New Delhi: Permanent Black.

Sarkar, Tanika and Bandyapadhyay, Sekhar, ed. 2015. *Calcutta: The Stormy Decades*. New Delhi: Social Science Press.

Sarker, Shuvro Prosun. 2017. *Refugee Law in India: The Road from Ambiguity to Protection*. Palgrave: McMillan.

Sarma, Ramanimohan. 1987. *Political History of Assam*. Calcutta: Puthipatra.

Sharma, Alaka. 1999. *Immigration and Assam Politics*. New Delhi: Ajanta Books.

Sattar, Abdus. 1983. *In the Sylvan Shadows*. Dhaka: Bangla Academy.

Schendel, Willem Van. 2005. *The Bengal Borderland: Beyond State and Nation in South Asia*. London: Anthem Press.

Seal, Anil. 1968. *The Emergence of Indian Nationalism: Competition and Collaboration in the Later Nineteenth Century*. Cambridge: Cambridge University Press.

Sen, Amartya. 1981. *Poverty and Famine: An Essay on Entitlement and Deprivation*. Oxford: Clarendon Press.

Sen, Manikuntala. 2001. *In Search of Freedom*. Calcutta: Stree.

Sen, Meenakshi. 2003. 'Tripura: The Aftermath'. In *The Trauma and the Triumph: Gender and Partition in Eastern India*, eds. Jasodhara Bagchi and Subhoranjan Dasgupta. Kolkata: Stree.

Sen, Sakuntal. 1964. *Inside Pakistan*. Calcutta: Compass Publication.

Sen, Shila. 1976. *Muslim Politics in Bengal, 1937–47*. New Delhi: Impex India.

Sen, Tripur Chandra. 1970. *Tripura in Transition (1923–1957 AD)*. Agartala: Published by the Author.

Sen, Uditi. 2018. *Citizen Refugee: Forging the Indian Nation after Partition*. Cambridge: Cambridge University Press.

Sen Gupta, Nitish. 2001. *History of the Bengali-speaking People*. New Delhi: UBSPD.

Sen Gupta, Nitish. 2002. *Dr. Bidhan Chandra Roy*. New Delhi: Publications Division, Ministry of Information and Broadcasting, Government of India.
Sen Gupta, Nitish. 2007. *Bengal Divided: The Unmaking of a Nation (1905–1971)*. New Delhi: Viking-Penguin.
Sengupta, Debjani. 2016. *The Partition of Bengal: Fragile Borders and New Identities*. New Delhi: Cambridge University Press.
Sengupta, Sukharanjan. 2006. *Curzon's Partition of Bengal and Aftermath: History of the Elite Hindu-Muslim Conflicts Over Political Domination Leading to the Second Partition, 1947*. Kolkata: Naya Udyog.
Settar, S. and Gupta, Indira Baptista, ed. 2002. *Pangs of Partition*. 2 Vols. New Delhi: Monohar.
Shah, Mohammad. 1996. *In Search of Identity: Bengali Muslims 1880–1940*. Calcutta: K. P. Bagchi.
Sharma, Alaka. 1999. *Immigration and Assam Politics*. Delhi: Ajanta Books.
Sharma, Joyeeta. 2012. *Empire's Garden: Assam and the Making of India*. Ranikhet: Permanent Black.
Sharma, Manorama. 1990. *Social and Economic Change in Assam: Middle Class Hegemony*. New Delhi: Ajanta Publications.
Siddiqui, M. K. A. 1973. 'Caste among the Muslims of Calcutta'. In *Caste and Social Stratification among the Muslims*, ed. Imtiaz Ahmed, 136–137. Delhi: Manohar.
Siddiqui, Rahim Uddin. 2007. *Prachyer Rahasya Nagari* (Bengali translation of F. B. Bradley Burt, *Romance of an Eastern Capital*). Dhaka: Nabadiganta Prakashani, 13.
Singh, Anita Inder. 2006. *The Partition of India*. New Delhi: National Book Trust.
Singh, Bhawani. 1984. *Politics of Alienation in Assam*. Calcutta: Ajanta Publications.
Singh, Brig Rajendra. 1962. *The Military Evacuation Organisation*. New Delhi: Government of India Press.
Singh, Deepak K. 2010. *Statelessness in South Asia: The Chakmas between India and Pakistan*. New Delhi: Sage Publications.
Singh, K. Suresh, ed. 1972. *The Tribal Situation in India*. New Delhi: Indian Institute of Advanced Study and Motilal Banarsidass.
Sinha, Amitava and Chakraborty, Kiransankar. 2010. *Reflections on Economy and Society of Tripura*. New Delhi, Guwahati and Visakhapatnam: Akansha Publishing House.
Sinha, J. P. 1982, 'Managing the Human Resources in India: Perspective and Challenges'. In *Human Resource Management in Asia Pacific Countries*, eds. Arup Verma and Pawan Budhwar, 126–149. London: Routledge.
Srimanjari. 2009. *Through War and Famine: Bengal 1939–45*. New Delhi: Orient BlackSwan.
Talbot, Ian and Singh, Gurharpal, ed. 1999. *Region and Partition: Bengal, Punjab and the Partition of the Subcontinent*. New Delhi: Oxford University Press.
Talbot, Ian and Singh, Gurharpal. 2009. *The Partition of India*. New Delhi: Cambridge University Press.
Tejani, Shabnam. 2007. *Indian Secularism: A Social and Intellectual History, 1890–1950*. Ranikhet: Permanent Black.
Trivedi, V. R., ed. 1995. *Documents on Assam*. New Delhi: Omsons Publications.
Tunzelmann, Alex Von. 2007. *Indian Summer: The Secret History of the End of an Empire*. London: Pocket Books.
Umor, Badruddin. 1987. *Politics and Society in Bangladesh*. Dhaka: Subarna.
Upreti, Sonia. 2004. *Nationalism in Bangladesh: Genesis and Evolution*. New Delhi: Kalinga Publication.
Verghese, B. G. 1996. *India's Northeast Resurgent: Ethnicity, Insurgency, Governance, Development*. New Delhi: Centre of Policy Research- Konark Publishers.

Vernant, Jacques. 1953. *The Refugees in the Post-war World*. London: George Allen & Unwin.
Weiner, Myron. 1988. *Sons of the Soil: Migration and Ethnic Conflict in India*. New Delhi: Oxford University Press.
Weiner, Myron and Field, John Osgood, ed. 1977. *Electoral Politics in the Indian States: The Impact of Modernization*. New Delhi: Manohar.
Yong, Tan Tai and Kudaisya, Gyanesh, ed. 2008. *Partition and Post-colonial South Asia: A Reader*. 3 Vols. London and New York: Routledge.
Zafarullah, Habib, ed. 1996. *The Zia Episode in Bangladesh Politics*. New Delhi: South Asian Publishers.
Zaidi A. M., ed. 1987. *The Muslim School of Congress: The Political Ideas of Muslim Congress Leaders from Mr. Badruddin Tayyebji to Maulana Abul Kalam Azad 1885–1947*. New Delhi: Publication Department, Indian Institute of Applied Political Research.
Zakaria, Rafiq. 1970. *Rise of Muslims in Indian Politics*. Bombay: Somaiya Publications.
Zaman, Niaz. 1999. *A Divided Legacy: The Partition in Selected Novels of India, Pakistan and Bangladesh*. Dhaka: The University Press Ltd.
Zamindar, Vazira Fazila-Yacoobali. 2008. *The Long Partition and the Making of Modern South Asia: Refugees, Boundaries, Histories*. New Delhi: Viking-Penguin.
Ziring, Lawrence. 1992. *Bangladesh From Mujib to Ershad: An Interpretive Study*. Karachi: Oxford University Press.
Zolberg, Aristide R., Suhrke, Astri and Aguayo, Sergio. 1989. *Escape from Violence: Conflict and the Refugee Crisis in the Developing World*. Oxford: Oxford University Press.

Articles

Ahmar, Moonis. 1996. 'Ethnicity and State Power in Pakistan: The Karachi Crisis'. *Asian Survey* 36 (10): 1031–48.
Ahmed, Abu Naser Saied. 2011. 'Revisiting a Lost Relationship: Assam and Bangladesh in Colonial Era'. *Journal of the Asiatic Society of Bangladesh (Humanities)* 56 (1–2): 239–61.
Bandyopadhyay, Sekhar and Basu Ray Chaudhury, Anasua. 2014. 'In Search of Space: The Scheduled Caste Movement in West Bengal after Partition'. *Policies and Practices* 59: 1–22.
Banerjee, Malaya. 1998. 'State Formation Process of Tripura: The Economic Roots'. *Proceedings of North East India History Association (NEIHA)*, Eighteenth Session, Agartala, 336–42.
Banerjee, Sarbani. 2017. 'Different Identity Formations in Bengal Partition Narratives by Dalit Refugees'. *Interventions: International Journal of Postcolonial Studies*, 19 (4): 550–65.
Basu Guha Chaudhury, Archit. 2009. 'Engendered Freedom: Partition and East Bengali Refugee Women'. *Economic and Political Weekly* 44 (49): 66–69.
Basu, Sibaji Pratim. 2012. 'The Chronicle of a Forgotten Movement 1959 Food Movement Revisited'. *Policies and Practices* 56: 2–18.
Bayly, C. A. 1985. 'The Pre-history of "Communalism?" Religious Conflicts in India, 1700–1860'. *Modern Asian Studies* 19 (2): 177–203.
Bhagat, R. B. 2001. 'Census and the Construction of Communalism in India'. *Economic and Political Weekly* 36 (46–47): 4352–56.
Bhagavan, Manu. 2008. 'The Hindutva Underground: Hindu Nationalism and the Indian National Congress in Late Colonial and Early Post-colonial India'. *Economic and Political Weekly* 43 (37): 39–48.
Bhattacharjee, Nabanipa. 2009. 'Unburdening Partition: The "Arrival" of Sylhet'. *Economic and Political Weekly* 44 (4): 77–79.

Bhattacharjee, Nabanipa. 2012. 'We Are with Culture but Without Geography: Locating Sylheti Identity in Contemporary India'. *South Asian History and Culture* 3 (2): 215–35.

Bhattacharya, Sabyasachi. 1998. 'Famine and the Labouring Poor: An Un-Published Manuscript of a Folk-poet of Mid-19th Century Bengal'. *The Proceedings of the Indian History Congress* 59: 561–65.

Bhattacharyya, Harihar. 1989. 'The Emergence of Tripuri Nationalism, 1948–50'. *South Asia Research* 9 (1): 5471.

Bhaumik, Subir. 2012. 'Tripura: Ethnic Conflict, Militancy and Counterinsurgency'. *Policies and Practices* 52: 4–26.

Bose, Sugata. 1990. 'Starvation Amidst Plenty: The Making of Famine in Bengal, Honan and Tonkin, 1942–45'. *Modern Asian Studies* 24 (4): 699–727.

Chakrabarty, Dipesh. 1995. 'Modernity and Ethnicity in India: A History for the Present'. *Economic and Political Weekly* 30 (52): 3373–80.

Chakrabarty, Dipesh. 1996. 'Remembered Villages: Representation of Hindu-Bengali Memories in the Aftermath of the Partition'. *Economic and Political Weekly* 31 (32): 2143–51.

Chakraborty, Gorky. 2014. 'The Demographic Question in the *Char* Areas of Assam'. *Social Change and Development* XI (2): 113–17.

Chakravarty, Nikhil. 2008. 'Day One in Calcutta'. *Mainstream* XLVI (28): 1–8.

Chakravarty, Nikhil. 2013 (November). 'Day One in Calcutta'. *Mainstream* 2: 15.

Chatterjee, Himadri. 2012. 'From Refugee to Immigrant: The Career of a Refugee Population'. *Policies and Practices* 54: 22–39.

Chatterji, Joya. 1999. 'The Fashioning of a Frontier: The Radcliffe Line and Bengal's Border Landscape, 1947–52'. *Modern Asian Studies* 33 (1): 185–242.

Chatterji, Joya. 2007. '"Dispersal" and the Failure of Rehabilitation: Refugee Campdwellers and Squatters in West Bengal'. *Modern Asian Studies* 41 (5): 995–1032.

Chatterji, Joya. 2012. 'South Asian Histories of Citizenship, 1946–1970'. *The Historical Journal* 55 (4): 1049–71.

Chatterji, Joya. 2013a. 'Secularization and Partition Emergencies: Deep Diplomacy in South Asia'. *Economic and Political Weekly* 48 (50): 42–50.

Chatterji, Joya. 2013b. 'Dispositions and Destinations: Refugee Agency and "Mobility Capital" in the Bengal Diaspora, 1947–2007'. *Comparative Studies in Societies and History* 55 (3): 273–304.

Chottopadhyay, Partha. 2014 (October). 'Udbastu Kahini'. *Arek Rokom* (in Bengali) 18–19: 17–18.

Das Gupta, Malabika. 1986. 'Refugee Influx'. *Economic and Political Weekly* 21 (44–45): 1665.

Das Gupta, Manas. 1984. 'Tribal Unrest'. *Economic and Political Weekly* 19 (11): 449.

Das, Bhaswati and Ansary, Rabiul. 2018. 'Bangladeshi and Inter-state Migrants: Differential Adaptation and Acceptance by the Locals in West Bengal, India'. *Spat Demography* 6: 159–78.

Das, N. K. 2009. 'Identity Politics and Social Exclusion in India's North-East: The Case of Re-distributive Justice'. *Bangladesh e-Journal of Sociology* 6 (1): 1–17.

Das, Suranjan. 2000. 'The 1992 Calcutta Riot in Historical Continuum: A Relapse into "Communal Fury"?' *Modern Asian Studies* 34 (2): 281–306.

Das, Suranjan. 2001. 'The Nehru Years in Indian Politics'. *Edinburg Paper in South Asian Studies* 16: 2–35.

Dasgupta, Anindita. 2001. 'Denial and Resistance: Sylhet Partition "Refugees" in Assam'. *Contemporary South Asia* 10 (3): 343–60.

Dasgupta, Anindita. 2008. 'Remembering Sylhet: A Forgotten Story of 1947 Partition'. *Economic and Political Weekly* 43 (31): 18–22.

Dasgupta, Atis and Chakraborti, Subhas Ranjan. 1992. 'Growth of Calcutta: A Profile of Dislocations in the Early Colonial Period'. *Social Scientist* 20 (3–4): 35–48.

Dasgupta, Jyotirindra. 1997. 'Community, Authenticity and Autonomy: Insurgence and Institutional Development in India's Northeast'. *The Journal of Asian Studies* 56 (2): 345–70.

Datta, Pradip Kumar. 1993. '"Dying Hindus": Production of Hindu Communal Common Sense in Early 20th Century Bengal'. *Economic and Political Weekly* 28 (25): 1305–19.

Debbarma, R. K. 2017. 'Where to Be Left Is No Longer Dissidence: A Reading of Left Politics in Tripura'. *Economic and Political Weekly* 11 (21): 18–21.

Dev, Bimal J. and Lahiri, Dilip K. 1979–1981. 'Assam in the Days of Bhasani and League Politics'. *The Journal of the Asiatic Society of Bangladesh (Humanities)* 25–26: 189–235.

Dutta, Binayak. 2012. 'Recovering Sylhet'. *Himal South Asia* 1–6.

Elahi, K. Maudood. 1981. 'Refugees in Dandakaranya'. *International Migration Review* 15 (1–2): 219–25.

Ferdous, Sayeed. 2015 (April–June). "Surgery' in Rush and Affected Lives: Make-Believe Stories in Understanding History'. *The Journal of Social Studies (The Journal of Centre for Social Studies*, Dhaka University, Dhaka) 146: 25–44.

Ghosh, Subashri. 2008. 'The Working of the Nehru-Liaquat Ali Khan Pact: A Case Study of Nadia District, 1950'. *Proceedings of the 68th Session of the Indian History Congress*, ICHR, New Delhi, 853–62.

Gilmartin, David. 1998. 'Partition, Pakistan and South Asian History: In Search of a Narrative'. *The Journal of Asian Studies* 54 (4): 1068–95.

Gohain, Hiren. 1983. 'The Labyrinth of Chauvinism'. *Economic and Political Weekly* 18 (16–17): 1386–88.

Gohain, Hiren. 1997. 'Ethnic Unrest in the North East'. *Economic and Political Weekly* 32 (8): 389–91.

Gosselink, Robert G. 1994. 'Minority Rights and Ethnic Conflict in Assam, India'. *Boston College Third World Law Journal* 14 (1): 83–116.

Guha, Amalendu. 1976. 'East Bengal Migrants and Maulana Abdul Hamid Khan Bhasani in Assam Politics'. *Indian Economic and Social History Review* 13 (1): 419–52.

Guha, Amalendu. 1980. 'Little Nationalism Turned Chauvinist: Assam's Anti-Foreigner Upsurge, 1979–80'. *Economic and Political Weekly* 15 (41–43): 1699–720.

Hasan, Mushirul. 1990. 'Adjustment and Accommodation: Indian Muslims After Partition'. *Social Scientist* 18 (8–9): 48–65.

Hasan, Mushirul. 1998. 'Memoires of a Fragmented Nation: Rewriting the History of India's Partition'. *Economic and Political Weekly* 33 (41): 263–85.

Hossain, Ashfaque. 2012. 'The Making and Unmaking of Assam-Bengal Borders and the Sylhet Referendum'. *Modern Asian Studies* 47 (1): 250–87.

Huque, Ahmed Shafiqul. 1985. 'Political Parties and the Partition of India'. *Journal of the Asiatic of Bangladesh (Humanities)* XXX (1): 50–51.

Iqbal, Iftekhar. 2015. 'The Space Between Nation and Empire: The Making and Unmaking of Eastern Bengal and Assam Province, 1905–1911'. *The Journal of Asian Studies* 74 (1): 69–84.

Jalais, Annu. 2005. 'Dwelling on Marichjhanpi: When Tigers Became "Citizens", Refugees "Tiger-Food"'. *Economic and Political Weekly* 40 (17): 1757–62.

Jassal, Smita Tiwari and Ben-Ari, Eyle. 2006. 'Listening for Echoes: Partition in Three Contexts'. *Economic and Political Weekly* 41 (22): 2213–20.

Kailash. 2000. 'Peaceful Coexistence: Lessons from Andamans'. *Economic and Political Weekly* 35 (32): 2859–65.

Karlekar, Ranajoy. 1985. 'The Tripura Riots, 1980: Problems of Marxist Strategy'. *Economic and Political Weekly* 20 (34): 5523.
Kaur, Ravinder. 2006. 'The Last Journey: Exploring Social Class in the 1947 Partition Migration'. *Economic and Political Weekly* 41 (22): 2221–28.
Kaur, Ravinder. 2009. 'Distinctive Citizenship'. *Cultural and Social History* 6 (4): 429–46.
Kennedy, Charles H. 1991. 'The Politics of Ethnicity in Sindh'. *Asian Survey* 31 (10): 938–55.
Khan, Zillur R. 1985. 'Islam and Bengali Nationalism'. *Asian Survey* 25 (8): 834–51.
Kothari, Rita. 2004. 'Hardening of Identities After Partition'. *Economic and Political Weekly* 39 (35): 3885–88.
Kumar, Radha. 1996. 'The Troubled History of Partition'. *Foreign Affairs* 76 (1): 22–34.
Lombert, Richard D. 1950. 'Religion, Economics and Violence in Bengal: Background of the Minority Agreement'. *Middle East Journal* 4 (3): 307–28.
Ludden, David. 2011. 'Spatial Inequality and National Territory: Remapping 1905 in Bengal and Assam'. *Modern Asian Studies* 46 (3): 483–525.
Luthra, P. N. 1971. 'Problem of Refugees from East Bengal'. *Economic and Political Weekly* 6 (50): 2467–72.
Mallick, Ross. 1999. 'Refugee Resettlement in Forest Reserves: West Bengal Policy Reversal and the Marichjhanpi Massacre'. *Journal of Asian Studies* 58 (1): 104–25.
McMahon, Deirdre. 2010. 'The 1947 Partition of India: Irish Parallels'. *History Ireland* 18 (4): 40–43.
Metcalf, Barbara D. 1995. 'Too Little and Too Much: Reflections on Muslims on History of India'. *The Journal of Asian Studies* 54 (4): 951–67.
Misra, Chitta Ranjan. 1996. 'Move for a Sovereign Independent Bengal: Reaction of the Provincial Congress and Hindu Mahasabha'. *Journal of the Asiatic Society of Bangladesh (Humanities)* 41 (1): 33–50.
Mitra, Asok. 1990. 'Parting the Ways: Partition and After in Bengal'. *Economic and Political Weekly* 25 (44): 2441–44.
Mukherjee, Ramkrishna. 1972. 'Social Background of Bangladesh'. *Economic and Political Weekly* 7 (5–7): 4009–11.
Mukhopadhyay, Urvi. 2008. 'Communalism, Secularism and Indian Historical Films (1940–46)'. *Economic and Political Weekly* 43 (15): 63–71.
Nag, Sajal. 2001. 'Nationhood and Displacement in Indian Subcontinent'. *Economic and Political Weekly* 36 (51): 4753–60.
Nag, Sajal. 2006. 'Two Nations and a Dead Body: Mortuarial Rites and Post-colonial Modes of Nation Making in South Asia'. *Economic and Political Weekly* 41 (50): 5183–90.
Nag, Sajal. 2018 (September). 'The NRC: Ethnic Cleansing through Constitutional Means'. *Analytical Monthly Review* 16 (6): 58.
Nandy, Chandan. 1993. 'Unwanted Migrants'. *Economic and Political Weekly* 28 (40): 2102.
Omvedt, Gail. 1980. 'Letter to the Editor'. *Economic and Political Weekly* XV (12): 580.
Pandey, Gyanendra. 1992. 'In Defense of the Fragment: Writing About Hindu-Muslim Riot of India Today'. *Representations* 37: 27–55.
Prabhakara, M. S. 1999. 'Of State and Nationalism'. *Frontline* 9–22. Chennai.
Raghavan, T. C. A. 1983. 'Origins and Development of Hindu Mahasabha Ideology: The Call of V. D. Savarkar and Bhai Parmanand'. *Economic and Political Weekly* 18 (15): 595–600.
Rahman, M. Mahbubur and Schendel, Williem Van. 2003. 'I Am Not a Refugee: Rethinking Partition Migration'. *Modern Asian Studies* 37 (3): 551–84.
Rana, Santosh. 2005 (September). 'Deshbhag o Jinnah'. *Anik*, Kolkata, 15.
Ray, Manas. 2002. 'Growing up Refugee'. *History Workshop Journal* 53: 149–79.
Ray, Rajat Kanta and Ray, Ratna. 1975. 'Zamindars and Jotedars: A Study of Rural Politics in Bengal'. *Modern Asian Studies* 9 (1): 81–102.

Roy, Asim. 1990. 'The High Politics of India's Partition: The Revisionist Perspective'. *Modern Asian Studies* 24 (2): 385–415.
Roy, Haimanti. 2009. 'A Partition of Contingency? Public Discourse in Bengal, 1946–47'. *Modern Asian Studies* 43 (6): 1355–84.
Saikia, Arupjyoti. 2016. 'Borders, Commodities and Citizens Across Mud and River: Assam, 1947–50s'. *Studies in History* 32 (1): 72–96.
Sarkar, Jagadish Narayan. 1970. 'Islam in Bengal'. *Journal of Indian History* 48 (144): 473.
Schendel, Willem Van. 2001. 'Working Through Partition: Making a Living in the Bengal Borderlands'. *International Review of Social History* 46 (3): 393–421.
Schendel, Willem Van. 2002. 'Stateless in South Asia: The Making of India-Bangladesh Enclaves'. *The Journal of Asian Studies* 61 (1): 115–47.
Sengupta, Anwasha. 2012. 'Some Stories from the Bengal Borderland: Making and Unmaking of an International Boundary'. *Policies and Practices* 54: 3–21.
Sengupta, Anwasha. 2018. 'Unthreading Partition: The Politics of Jute Sharing Between Two Bengals'. *Economic and Political Weekly* LIII (4): 43–49.
Sengupta, Mayuri. 2013. 'The Shifting Cultivation and the Reang Tribe in Tripura'. *Economic and Political Weekly* 48 (40): 59–65.
Shamshad, Rizwana. 2017. 'Bengaliness, Hindu Nationalism and Bangladeshi Migrants in West Bengal, India'. *Asian Ethnicity* 18 (4): 433–51.
Shani, Ornit. 2010. 'Conceptions of Citizenship in India and the "Muslim Question"'. *Modern Asian Studies* 44 (1): 145–73.
Sharma, Chandan Kumar. 2012. 'The Immigration Issue in Assam and Conflicts Around It'. *Asian Ethnicity* 13 (3): 287–309.
Singh, B. P. 1987. 'North-East India: Demography, Culture and Identity Crisis'. *Modern Asian Studies* 21 (2): 257–82.
Singh, Jaswant. 1984. 'Assam's Crisis of Citizenship: An Examination of Political Errors'. *Asian Survey* 24 (10): 1056–68.
Spate, O. H. K. 1948. 'The Partition of India and the Prospects of Pakistan'. *Geographical Review* 38 (1): 205–18.
Upadhyaya, Prakash Chandra. 1989. 'Is There an "Indian Form of Communism"?' *Social Scientist* 17 (1–2): 84–91.
Weiner, Myron. 1993. 'Rejected People and Unwanted Migrants in South Asia'. *Economic and Political Weekly* 28 (34): 1737–46.
Zolberg, A. R. 1983. 'The Formation of New States, as a Refugee Generating Process'. *Annals of the American Academy of Political and Social Science* 467: 24–38.
Zou, David Vumlallian and Kumar, M. Satish. 2011. 'Mapping a Colonial Borderland: Objectifying the Geo-body of India's Northeast'. *The Journal of Asian Studies* 70 (1): 141–70.

Unpublished papers and dissertations

Ahmed, Sharif Uddin. 1986. 'Dacca—A Study in Urban History and Development 1842–1921'. Ph. D. dissertation, School of Oriental and African Studies, University of London.
Chakravarty, Pallavi. 2011. 'Post Partition Refugee Rehabilitation in India with Special Reference to Bengal, 1947–1971'. Ph. D. dissertation, University of Delhi.
Chakravarty, Pallavi. 2014. 'Post-partition Rehabilitation of Refugees in India'. NMML Occasional Paper, New Series-46, Nehru Memorial Museum and Library, New Delhi.
Chatterjee, Nilanjana. 1992. 'Midnight's Unwanted Children: East Bengali Refugees and the Politics of Rehabilitation'. Ph. D. dissertation, Brown University.

Chaudhuri, Pranati. 1983. 'Refugees in West Bengal: A Study of the Growth and Distribution of Refugee Settlements Within the CMD'. Occasional Paper No. 55, Centre for Studies in Social Sciences, Calcutta.

Dasgupta, Anindita. 2000. 'Emergence of a Community: The Muslims of East Bengal Origin in Assam in Colonial and Post-colonial Period'. Ph. D. dissertation, Guwahati University.

Debbarma, R. K. 2013. 'Heroes and Histories: Making of Rival Geographies of Tripura'. NMML Occasional Paper, New Series-34, Nehru Memorial Museum and Library, New Delhi.

Deka, Kaustubh Kumar. 2013. 'The Politics of Student Movements: Limits and Possibilities with Special Reference to Assam, 1985–2010'. Ph. D. dissertation, Jawaharlal Nehru University.

Dutta, Sushil Chandra. 1981. 'The North-East and the Mughals, 1661–1714 A.D.' Unpublished Ph.D. thesis, North Eastern Hill University.

Ghosh, Partha S. 2013. 'Refugees and Migrants in South Asia: Nature and Implications'. NMML Occasional Paper, New Series-10, Nehru Memorial Museum and Library, New Delhi.

Hossain, Ashfaque. 2010. 'Historical Globalization and Its Impact: A Study of Sylhet and its People, 1874 to 1971'. Ph. D. dissertation, University of Nottingham.

Hota, N. R. 2009. 'The Dandakaranya Project'. Ph. D. dissertation, Institute of Planning and Administration, New Delhi.

Khan, Mohammed Halim. 1986. 'Muslims in India After 1947: A Study in Political Geography'. Ph. D. dissertation, Clark University.

Ludden, David. 2003. 'Where Is Assam? Using Geographical History to Locate Current Social Realities'. Ceniseas Papers, Omeo Kumar Das Institute of Social Change and Development, Guwahati.

Ludden, David. 2010. 'Rethinking 1905: Spatial Inequity, Uneven Development and Nationalism'. Distinguished Lecture Series-2, Mahanirban Calcutta Research Group, Kolkata.

Misra, Tilottama. 1982. "Assam and the National Question' in *Nationality Question in India*.' Seminar Papers (held in Madras), Andhra Pradesh Radical Students Union, Hyderabad.

Sen, Asok and Banerjee, Alak. 1983. 'Calcutta Metropolitan District in the Urban Context of West Bengal (1951–1981)'. Occasional Paper No. 60, Centre for Studies in Social Sciences, Calcutta.

INDEX

AASU 214, 220, 221, 250
abandoned houses 179
abandoned people 86
accommodate/accommodation xii, 95, 144, 162, 203
acquisition 129, 229, 232
Act XVI of 1951 177
ADC 232, 233, 234
ad hoc 200
administration/administrative 57, 181, 211
administrator 43
Agartala 50, 143, 144, 147, 148, 154, 155
agenda xv, 185
agitation/agitational politics 13, 182, 201, 202, 203
agrarian 1, 43
agreement 63
Agreement of Merger 225
agricultural/agriculturists 94, 98, 201
agriculture 108, 202
Ahmed, Abul Mansur 15
Ahmed, Muzaffar 12, 18
Ahmed, Taj-uddin 33
Ahom 119
AICC 164, 168
AIWC 97
ajlafs 1, 9, 21
Akhaura 50, 143
Ali, Chaudhuri Mahmmad 49
alien 66, 69
alienation 203
Aligarh Muslim University 254
All Assam Refugee Association 210

All Assam Students' Union 214
All Bengal Relief Committee 172
All India Congress Committee 135
All India Refugee Conference 192
All India Refugee Demand Day 183
All India Student Federation 213
All India Women's Conference 97
All Party Hill Leaders Conference 215
Amola 205
Amra Bangali 233
Ananda Ashram 181
Anandamath 13
Anashan 178, 194
ancestral home xii, 35
Andaman xvii, 82, 88, 89, 103, 104, 110, 111, 162, 187
Andamans Indian Associations 107
Andhra Pradesh 107, 109
Andolon 169
Anglo-American imperialists 178
Anisuzzaman 11, 19, 21, 26
The annual report of the Commission for Schedule Caste and Tribes 231
Ansar, ansar bahini 62, 65, 170, 173
Anthropological Survey of India 179
anti-Bengali sentiment 201
anti-eviction movement 186
anti-foreign National Movement 249
anti-India 32
anti-Partition movement 10, 11
APCC 215
APHLC 215
apprehension 204

296 Index

arpanpatras (title deeds) 101, 191
Arunachal Pradesh 252
Asamiya Muslims 211
ashraf 1, 4, 12, 20
Asom Gana Parishad 249
Asr-e-Jadid 10
Assam xii, xiv, 42, 50, 51, 60, 69, 87, 118, 162, 200, 201, 202, 206
Assam Accord 249
Assam Citizens Association 207
Assam Displaced Persons Rehabilitation Loans Amendment Bill 134
The Assam Domiciles and Settlers Association 207
Assamese xv, 118, 119, 200, 201, 204, 206, 222
Assamese leadership 126
Assamese sub-nationalism 222
Assam for Assamese xv, 52, 206, 212
Assam proper 121
Assam Provincial Congress Committee 125
Assam Provincial Muslim League 52
Assam Tribune 127
assembly 20
asset xvii, 42, 93
assimilate/assimilation 2, 3, 211
Atmasmriti 15, 19
Autonomous District Council 232
Awami League 33
Azad, Maulana Abul Kalam 21, 33

babu 3, 119, 151, 205
backwardness xv
Bag, Shaheen 254, 255
Bagjola 172, 180
Bahadur, Kiriti Bikram Kishore Manikya 143
Bahini, Shanti Sena 226
Balasore 106
bande mataram 12
Banderban 50
Banerjee, Satya Priya 182
bangal xiii, 1, 59, 72
Bangladesh xiii, 61, 103, 153, 233, 245, 249, 251
Bankura 168, 175
Baraipur 180
Barak Valley xv, 54, 61, 121, 155, 200, 201
Baranagar 173
bargadar 70
bargain 44, 202
Bari 35
Barishal 31, 33, 86, 95, 103
Baro-Bhunias 2

Barrackpur 167, 173
Bashirhat 179, 180
Bastar district 107, 110
bastu 35
Bastuhara Andolon 168
Bastuhara Parisad 176
bastuhara xiii
Basu, Jyoti 180
Bayly, Christopher 8
Behala 173
Behar, Cooch 96
Belgachhia 173
Belghoria 173
belief 34, 36
belonging 33
Benapole 33, 97
Bengal xi, xii, xvii, 2, 3, 5, 6, 8, 21, 42, 84, 153, 161
Bengal Borderland xii, xvii, 37, 82, 86, 87, 97, 203, 245
Bengal Legislative Assembly 14
Bengali/Bengalis xii, xiii, xiv, 5, 6, 12, 89, 112, 153, 200, 201, 203, 206
Bengali conspiracy 200, 204
Bengali medium school 219
Bengali Muslim 2, 6
Bengal Pact 17, 18
Bengal Provincial Congress Committee 23, 94, 164
Bengal Provincial Muslim League 22
The Bengal Rehabilitation Organisation 97
Bengal Sangram Committee of Cachar 217, 218
Bettiah camp 106, 185
Bhadrakali refugee camp 172, 181, 186
bhadralok 4, 14, 23, 36, 61, 63, 93, 119, 140, 142, 200, 205
Bhasa Andolon 210
Bhashani, Abdul Hamid Khan 33, 52, 123
bhogonia xiii, 219, 235
Bhojerhat Union Krishak Samiti 182
bideshi xiii
Bihar xvii, 82, 88, 89, 91, 99, 105, 173, 181, 185
Bihari 28
Bijoygarh colony 169
Bishnupur camp 184
Bishnupurana 119
BJP Government 252, 254
Black Bill 164
black death 45
bloodshed 84
bohiragoto xiii
Bolshevik Party 174

Index

bomb 171
bona fide refugees 88, 94, 105, 182
bond/bonding 200
Bongal kheda 207
Bongaon 95, 97, 172, 180
border xi, xii, xiv, 32, 63, 103, 132, 148, 161, 237
bordering state xviii
border line cases 89
border making 120, 137
Border Security Forces 219
border slips 44, 57, 63, 182
Bordoloi, Gopinath 126, 127, 130, 131, 209
Bose, Sarat Chandra 23
Bose group 22
boundary 2, 43, 47, 49, 123, 148, 244
boundary commission 47, 48, 51
BPCC 94
Brahmanic/Brahmanism 1, 2
Brahmaputra Valley xv, 53, 121, 122, 125, 153, 202
British 4, 5, 6, 7, 8, 11, 46, 54, 93, 119
Buddhir Mukti Andolon 16
buddhist 20, 32, 233
budget 111, 173
burden 161
Burdwan 96, 101, 168
Burma 92
Burnpur 97

CAA 252, 253, 254
Cabinet Mission plan 46
Cachar 53, 54, 121, 132, 133, 134, 135, 143, 154, 201, 209, 212
Cachar District Congress Committee 220
Cachar District Refugee Council 210
Cachar Zilla Gana Sangram Parishad 217
calamities 93
Calcutta 31, 34, 45, 48, 49 59, 67, 87, 91, 153, 155, 165, 200, 206
Calcutta Corporation 17
Calcutta killings 26, 27
camp xv, 37, 59, 87, 89, 95, 103, 131, 152, 174
campaigning 179
Campbell hospital 172
canning 179
cartographic 49
cartography 120
caste xiii, xvii, 2
catastrophe 43, 44, 45
categorisation 86
category 71, 72, 100, 165

census 6, 7, 69, 98, 123, 132, 208, 250
Central Advisory Board 95
Central Calcutta Relief and Peace Committee 172
Central Directorate of Rehabilitation 147
Central Government xii, 56, 63, 72, 82, 91, 108, 132, 245
Central National Mohammedan Association 11
Central National Muhammadan Association 8
Central Rehabilitation Ministry 152, 235
Central Relief and Rehabilitation Department 120
Central Relief and Rehabilitation Department 225
Central Relief Committee 97
central schemes 135
centre xii, xiv, 84, 89, 91, 102, 107, 110, 149, 179, 200, 202, 203, 245, 246
century 200
Ceylon 92
Chakla Roshanabad Estate 50, 120, 138, 139, 144
Chakma 121, 139, 152, 233, 234
Chakraborty, Ambica 180, 183, 210
Chaliha, Bimala Prasad 212, 214, 248
Chamber of Princes 142
Chandpur 144
char land 61, 205
charitable organisations 166, 174
charter of demands 168, 181, 189
Chatterjee, Bankim Chandra 13
Chatterjee, N. C. 86
Chatterjee, Partha 24
Chatterjee, Sarat Chandra 13
Chatterji, Jiban Lal 180
Chaudhuri, Nirad C. 17
check post 62, 66, 87
chhit-mahals 190
Chief Commissioner 144, 146, 147, 148, 149, 205
Chief Minister 81
Chinese aggression of 1962 219
Chittagong 42, 50, 138, 141, 153, 253
Chittagong Hill Tracts xvi, 47, 121, 233
cholera 174
Choudhury, Abdul Matin 52
Choudhury, Ambikagiri Ray 206, 213
Christian 20
CHT 139, 143, 152, 233, 236
citizen-refugee 71, 204
citizen/citizenship xvi, 44, 56, 57, 64, 66, 69, 129, 161, 173, 203, 245

citizens by birth 209
Citizenship Act 61, 249
Citizenship Act, The 1955 209, 249, 255
Citizenship Amendment Bill of 2016, The 252
citizenship by registration 209
citizenship card 234
Citizenship (Registration of Citizen & Issue of National Identity Cards) Rules 2003, The 249, 252
Citizenship Rules 2009, The 249
civil disobedience movement 184
class xiii, xvii
classification 86
clerk 61
Coalition Government 191
collaborated 202
collective identity 167
colonial 1, 2, 6, 7, 8, 120, 121, 203, 244
Colonial Bengali elites 203
colonial legacies 161
colonial modernity 2
colonising movement 174
colony xv, 37, 42, 59, 99, 106, 147
colony camp/refugees 99, 169, 175, 177, 186
colony committee 176
colony scheme 147, 150
Comilla 50, 138, 141, 144, 153, 205
commission 32, 54
commission of enquiry 87, 193
common 33
communal xii, 7, 15, 64, 93, 144, 245
Communal Award 20
communal harmony 144
communalism 20, 245
communicate 202
communist ideologies 202
Communist Party 179, 187, 228, 234, 247
communists 20, 46, 66, 166, 171, 173, 180, 192, 202, 236, 247
community/communities xi, xv, 1, 2, 3, 4, 5, 6, 7, 8, 42, 201, 202, 203
community of dependents 83
community relationship 16, 203
compensation 70, 182
competing 203
complexities 98, 202, 203
composite 2, 12, 118, 182
compulsion 203
concerns 200
conference 70
congress 3, 9, 10, 12, 15, 18, 42, 49, 70, 163, 202

Congress High Command 23, 165, 169, 235
Congress Udbastu Sahajya Samiti 226, 227
Congress Working Committee 166
Constituent Assembly 64
Constitution of India 70, 86, 143, 144, 161, 209, 233, 252
Constitution system of India 203
constitutional reforms of 1935 20
constitutional representation 13
contradiction 180
control 203
convention of 1954 56
cooperative schemes 191
Cooper's camp 101, 172, 179, 183, 186
cordon system 100
corroborated 202
Cotton College 216
country xvii, 35
CPI 164, 173, 174, 176, 180, 181, 209, 214
CPIM 232, 234, 236
crisis 83, 203
Crown Representative 222
cultivation 1
cultural exchange 15
cultural nationalism 206
cultural supremacy 201
culture/cultural xii, xvi, xvii, 2, 3, 19, 50, 112, 120, 132, 200, 201, 202, 203, 206, 211
custom 57
Cuttack 106
cyclone 171

Dacca 93, 138
Dainik Batori 126
Dakshin Kalikata Bastuhara Sangram Parishad 174
Dalit 52, 95, 123, 124
Dandakaranya Development Authority 107, 108, 109
Dandakaranya project 107
Dandakaranya xvii, 82, 88, 92, 106, 108, 111, 162, 184
Darbar 140, 141
Dargah 19
Darjeeling 50
The Darjeeling conference 106
Darjeeling Convention of 1955 184
Darrang 125, 208
Darshana 33, 97
Das, C. R. 17
DDA 107, 108, 109
debate 201

decades 161, 166
decision making 37, 101
decisive factor 203
defense 200
definition (legal), of refugees 55, 58
Delhi 81, 86, 111, 165, 245
Delhi Pact xii, 44, 64, 65, 67, 72, 87, 89, 179
demand/demand week 184, 201
democracy 44, 254
democratic 161
Democratic Vanguard 174
demography/demographic xv, 3, 20, 47, 134, 202, 203
demonstration 169
Department of Education 150
Department of Higher Education 150
Department of Relief and Rehabilitation 137
departure 35
dependency 118
deportation 209
Deputy Commissioner 130
Deputy High Commissioner 32, 67
deserted camps 190
deserter refugees 89
desh 34, 35, 201, 234
Deshbandhunagar colony 169
destiny xi
detention centres 251
determining 203
Developmental Committee 194
Devi, Regent Maharani Kanchan Prava 143, 145
Dewan, Maniram 206
Dhaka 28, 31, 61, 66, 144, 182
Dhakuria 173
Dharmanagar 143, 147
Dhebar, U. N. 135
Dhebar Commission Report of 1960 231, 233
Dhekiajuli 128
Dhubulia 101, 172, 180, 181
dialect 204
diaspora 61
Dibrugarh 128, 212, 216
Dibrugarh University 220
Dinajpur 31, 50, 65, 102
direct action 25, 26, 187
disaster 54
discriminatory/discrimination xii, 96, 131, 193
discussion 201
dispersal 88, 95

displaced people/persons/families xi, 42, 57, 70, 72, 86, 94, 106, 166, 200, 244
displaced students 150
displacement xi, xvi, 3, 42, 244
distinction 201
District Advisory Rehabilitation Committees 180
diversification 203
division 2, 3, 42
DKSBS 174
documents 69
dole 89, 103, 132, 147, 149, 162, 183
dole-beggars 83
domicile xv, xvii, 61, 104, 119, 127, 201, 202
Domicile Certificate 129
dominant 201
dominion 34, 64, 71, 148
double betrayal 192
doubtful voter 249
downtrodden classes/families 193, 201
Dum Dum 169, 172, 173
Durganagar camp 174
Durgapuja 24
D voter 249
dyarchy 17

earth-cutting work 184
East Bengal 118, 127, 128, 148, 163, 179, 202, 206, 208
East Bengali xii, 5, 8, 19, 43, 57, 68, 72, 85, 118
East Bengal Relief Committee 91, 98, 99, 210
Eastern xviii, 7, 44, 85, 91, 97, 142
Eastern Bengal and Assam 10, 11, 123, 206
Eastern border xii, xv, 42, 200, 245
Eastern Indian Tribal Union 231
East India Company 141
East Pakistan xiv, 31, 33, 34, 58, 63, 84, 89, 92, 107, 202, 249
easy target 31
Eaton, Richard 1, 2
ecological 118
economic blockade 190
economic migrant/migration 42, 45, 120, 162, 172
economic rehabilitation 150, 173
economy xii, xvi, 202
education xv
election 46, 69, 178, 191
electoral/electoral roll 8, 52, 230
electricity 107
elite 3, 4, 5, 6, 11, 93, 203

emergence 203
emergency certificate 66
emigrant/emigration 44, 122
emotion/emotional 33, 37, 57, 200
employee/employment 53, 99, 205, 206
enclaves 190
enlightened 201
Enquiry Commission 65
epidemic 171, 174
establishment 90
estimate committee 91
Estimate Committee Report, The 109
ethnic/ethnicity xiv, 119, 121, 203, 204, 205, 234, 252
ethnic tribes 204, 245
European 3, 17
Evacuee Property Act/Law 70, 71, 91
Evacuee property Management Committee 70
Evacuee/evacuee property 44, 58, 70, 72, 102, 103
eviction 125
Eviction Bill 177
ex-camp site refugees 89
exchange of population xii, 46, 86, 179
excluded area 50
exile 36
existence 60
exodus xii, xiii, 3
expenditure 90, 91
experience xvii, 29
export 143
eye-opener 167, 188

fact-finding committee 99, 184, 190
fallouts xi, 154
fallow land 171
family 30, 36, 37
famine 45, 93, 130, 171
Faridpur 95
fate 203
fear xvi, 3, 29
federal structure 161, 202
female refugees 98
Feni 50
Fifth Schedule of the Constitution 233
figure 55
file 55
financial aid 91
Five-Year Plan 136
floating population 179, 202
flood 171
focal point 201
food-supply 50, 94, 172

forced migrants xi
Foreigner Tribunal and illegal migrants (Determination Tribunal) 249
Foreigners Act 56, 58, 204, 218, 249
Foreigners (Tribunal) Amendment order, The 2012 249
Foreigners (Tribunal) order, The 1964 249
Foreigners Order, The 1948 249
foreign/foreigner xi, 2, 66, 71, 127, 129, 168, 191, 204, 207, 234, 235, 251
Forward Bloc 174, 214
freedom xi, 42, 57
freedom struggle 43
frontier xiv, 1, 119
fugitives 58, 235
Fuller, Sir Bampfylde 11, 206
future 42

Gandhi xv, 18, 27, 46, 47
Gandhi, Indira 221
Gandhi ghat 167
Gangapadhyay, Sunil 21
Gangetic basin 119
Garo 132, 139, 140
Garo Hills 42, 123, 215
Gauhati 217
Gauhati University 220
gazetted officers 95
gazetteers 7
gazette notification 176
gender xvii
general election 179, 183, 209, 190, 228
General Ershad 233
General Zia-ur-Rehman 233
genuine migrant/refugee 66, 136, 137, 171
geography/geographical xv, 3, 32, 43, 50, 61, 72, 81, 118, 153
Ghatak, Rwitik 36
ghettoised/ghettoisation 3, 96, 100, 154
Ghosh, Atulya 170
Ghosh, Gour Kishore 15
ghoti 72
Ghusuri 172, 183
Goalpara 54, 122, 127, 132, 205, 208, 211, 254
Golaghati carnage in Padmabil and Champa-haor 226
Golam Sarwar 28
government/governance 43, 44, 46, 99, 205
Government of India 63, 94, 131, 132, 145, 173, 193, 245
Government of Union Territories Act of 1963 232

grants 90, 92, 95, 100, 150
grazing forests/reserves 61, 125, 127
Great Calcutta Killing 23, 25
Greater Bengal 107
grenade 171
grievance 204
group xiii, 119, 140, 182
Grow More Food 124
Guru Charan College 220
Guwahati 155, 217

habitat/habitation 1, 3, 203, 246
Hailakandi 53, 134, 137, 209, 210
Halam 139
Haor 54
harijan 94
harmony 3
Hashim, Abul 23, 26
hawker 171
Hazratbal 32, 87
hearth xii, 93, 246
hegemony/Hegemonic 120, 126, 201, 202, 209
Hendua Park 170
heroic xiii
heterogeneous group 166
High Commissioner for India 63, 64
high politics 72
hill people 202
Hill Tipperah 138, 139, 141
Hill Tripura 144, 229
hilly region 138
Hindu xii, xiv, xvii, 2, 3, 4, 5, 8, 11, 14, 20, 34, 202
Hinduism 2, 45
Hindu Mahasabha 3, 21, 24, 42, 47, 49, 50, 70, 96, 164, 168, 174
Hindu majority 46, 47
Hindu symbols 12
historians 5
historiography xiv
Hojai 128, 137
Hojong 132, 214
holocaust 33, 163
Home-cum-Training Centre 148
home/homeland xvii, 24, 35, 36, 37, 45, 59, 93, 119, 139, 165, 203, 246
homeless, homelessness xi, 29, 72, 107
homestead 36, 132
homogenous/homogeneity xi, 8, 37
honour xvii, 29, 245
Hoogly 168, 177
host xiv, xvi, 201
hostility xii, 129, 153

housing 90, 94
Howrah 60, 95, 168, 172, 180
huge 203
humanitarian crisis 86, 93
humanity 31
Human Rights Commission 56
human suffering/tragedy xi, 81, 254
humiliation 30, 33
hunger 123
hunger strike 178
Hunter, W. W. 5, 6, 7, 139, 141
Huq, Fazlul 20, 22
Huq-Muslim League 21
Hydari, Sir Akbar 52

Ichhapur camp 170
identity xii, xiii, xvii, 2, 3, 8, 12, 30, 118, 165, 200, 201, 203, 245
identity card 248
ideology/ideologically 202, 209
IDP 135
illegal immigrant/immigration xv, 60, 61, 123, 252
illegal migrant/alien 58, 87, 88, 91, 245, 246
illegal Muslims 249
illiterate 203
IMDT Act 149
immediate 85
immigrant 121, 123, 125, 153, 207, 211
Immigrants (Expulsion from Assam) Act 1950 208, 249
Immigration Act 129, 154
impending 44
import 143
incident 33
independence xi, xii, 36, 45, 69, 72, 126, 129, 161, 244
India xi, xii, 5, 6, 42, 202
Indian confederacy 200
Indian Constitution 69, 216
Indian High Commission 63, 182
Indian National Congress 9, 45
Indian Red Cross 172, 186
Indian Students Federation 172
Indian Union 144, 234
India State Peoples' Conference 223
indigenous 61, 138, 201, 209, 230
Indira-Mujib Pact 61, 87, 138
Indo-China War 219
Indo-Pak Conflict of 1965 219
Indo-Pakistan Agreement 64
Indo-Pakistan Conference 148
industrial employment 206

Industrial Planning and Development of Assam 133
infiltrator/infiltration 58, 209, 219, 235, 247
influx 129, 130, 144, 147, 203
inhabitants 145
inherent xi, 203
Inner Line Regulations 232
insecure/insecurity 33, 72, 161
inside/insiders 120, 163
Instrument of Accession 143
intellectual 66
intelligentsia 200
inter-district migration xv
Inter-Dominion Conference 64, 130, 167, 168
internally displaced 44, 56
internally displaced persons 135
international 47, 72, 120
international border 201, 244
International Refugee Organisation 84
intervention 201
intolerance 3
Ireland 45
irrigation 107
irritants 200
Islamia, Anjuman 224
Islamia, Jamia Milia 254
Islamic state/principles 43, 165
Islam/Islamisation 1, 2, 45, 95, 96
Islam Pracharak 12
ITA Scheme 133

jabardakhal colony 177
Jadavpur Bastuhara colony 169, 178
jagirdars 4
Jain, Ajit Prasad 91, 105, 134, 147, 149, 181, 193
Jalpaiguri 50
Jal Pare Pata Nore 15
Jamshedpur 99
Janata Party Government xiv
jati 202
Jatin, Bagha 174
Jawaharlal Nehru University 254
Jayantia 119
jehad 25
Jessore 32, 95
jhum cultivation/tillas/economy 139, 141, 202, 229
jhumia 50, 62, 139, 151, 152, 227, 229, 230
jhumia colonies/settlements 121, 145
Jinnah, M. A. 13, 22, 45, 46, 55
Jinnah Fund 172

jiratia praja 62, 120, 144, 148, 149
job/job market 51, 60, 153, 162, 203
Jogendranath/Jogen Mandal 68, 96, 186
jotedar 4, 5, 95, 148, 150, 169, 187, 225, 226
journey 44, 245
J. P. C. Report 20

Kachari 119
Kailashahar 143, 147, 230
Kalahandi 107
Kamalpur 143, 147
Kamrup 123, 125, 208
Kanchrapara 169
Kaptai Hydro-electric project 233
Karimganj 53, 134, 135, 155, 217
Karnafuli 50
Kashipur 172, 183
Kashmir 32
Katju, Kailash Nath 104, 172
Khagracherri 50
Khaliquzzaman, Choudhry 45
Khan, Liaquat Ali 45, 49, 173
Khan, Moulana Akram 22
Khan, Syed Ahmed 13
Khanna, Shri Mehr Chand 67, 91, 92, 110, 135, 182
Khasi and Jaintia Hills 42, 140, 215
Khilafat 18, 222
khilanjia 61
Khowai 143
Khulna 28, 32, 50, 86, 95, 180
Koch 119, 214
Kok-borok 141, 233, 234
Kolkata 59
Koraput 107
Krishak Praja Party 20, 21, 46
Kurud 185

Lahore session/resolution 45, 49
Lakhimpur 123
Lalbazar control room 26
land 1, 4, 11, 34, 96, 123, 145, 149, 171, 181, 201, 203
land grabbing 162, 171, 201
land-hungry people 62
land hungry refugees 201
landless labour/labourers 8, 93, 119, 130, 134, 162, 182
landlord 96, 124, 171
Land Purchase Scheme 147, 150
land record 108
landscape 37
land settlement 125, 185

Land Settlement Advisory Committee 133
Land Survey Report 133
language 1, 57, 66, 132, 153, 195, 200, 202, 204, 214, 237
language controversy 218
Language Movement of 1952 xiii, 31, 66, 210
Language Movement of 1960 136, 201
language riot 210
large-scale migration 110
lathi-charge 167, 169, 170, 178, 217
law 57
layer 33
left demonstration 169
Left Front Government xv, 234
leftist line of protest 169
leftist organ 171
leftists/leftist parties xv, 162, 166, 193, 228
legal xii, 54, 63, 98, 99, 177, 245
Legislative Assembly 20, 96, 136, 232
legitimate right 121
liability camp 99
Liberation War of 1971 xvi, 33, 60, 82, 86, 92, 102, 153, 202, 234
Lieutenant Governor 144
line system 123
linguistic/linguistically xiii, xv, 81, 84, 119, 121, 163, 200, 201, 202, 206
Linguistic Reorganisation of States xv, 211
literature xvi
Little Andaman 105
little nationalism 210, 211
livelihood 244
loan 86, 89, 90, 95, 132, 150, 173
local xvii, 2, 144, 148, 181, 184, 204
location 153
Lok Sabha 85, 108
London 54
Long Live Women's Movement 181
longorkhana 46
looting 84
loss 30
lower caste/lower middle class 61, 63, 166, 167, 201
Lucknow Pact 14
Lumding 128
Lusai Hills 42, 50, 140, 215

MacDonald, Ramsay 20
Madhya Pradesh 88, 107, 109, 110, 173
madrassa 52
mahajan 151
Maharaja 50, 62, 119, 138, 139, 140, 141, 144, 148, 222

Maharashtra 89
Mahasabha, Asom Jatiya 129
Mahesh 172, 179
Maidan 26, 103, 106, 170
mainland 61, 118
Maiti, Nikunja Bihari 103, 104, 167
majority 3, 14, 20, 23, 64, 144, 154, 202, 203, 244
Majumdar, Apurbalal 186
malaun xiii, 62
Maldah 50, 65, 85
Mana Groups of Transit Centres 109, 137, 184, 192
Mangaldai Tribal Conference 128, 249
Manicktala Refugee Bazar Samiti 182
Manikya 119, 120, 139, 143
Manikya, Maharaja Bir Bikram Kishore 142, 144, 223, 225
Manikya, Maharaja Bir Chandra 140, 141, 142
Manipur/Manipuri 91, 119, 139, 252
Manjil 170
map 52
marginal/marginality/marginalisation xiii, 182, 203
marginalised sections 162, 171
Marichjhhanpi Island 192
MARS 181
Marxist Forward Bloc 174
Marxist leftists 167
mass displacement xi
mass movement 178
Master Plan for Rehabilitation of Displaced Persons in West Bengal 191
Matamuri 50
materials 49
Mathabhaga 54
Matia Camp 132, 254, 255
matua 95
maulvis 12, 52
Mecca 62
Medhi, Bishnuram 130, 136, 212
Medina 62
Medinipur 168
Medium of Instruction Movement xv, 201, 218, 220
Meghalaya 42, 92, 219, 252
memorandum 167, 171
memory/memories 33
merger 143
metaphor xi, 93
Middle Andaman 105
middle class xvii, 12, 21, 30, 42, 63, 96, 124, 141, 153, 186, 201

Midnapore 96
midnight xi
migrant 44, 72, 119, 137, 151, 202
migration xii, 3, 29, 34, 42, 54, 69, 84, 204, 245
migration certificate 44, 57, 66, 69, 86, 182
Mikir Hills 188, 212, 214
Milad Mehfil 19, 24
military 33, 237
military barracks 173
million 45
Ministerial Committee 180
Ministry of Education 150
Ministry of Finance 84
Ministry of Home Affairs 150, 208
Ministry of Rehabilitation 146, 147, 148
Ministry of Relief and Rehabilitation 81, 89, 108, 132
Ministry of States 146, 228
minority 14, 15, 20, 30, 33, 34, 64, 69, 142, 154, 173, 202, 203, 244
minority board 64
Minto, Lord 14
misery xi
Mizo National Front 232
Mizoram 42, 143, 252
mobility 87, 118
mofussil 23, 27, 46, 168, 217
Mog 139, 225
Mohammedan Literary Society 11
Mohammedans 11
monarchical 119, 120
monarchy 119
monolithic xiii, 6, 72
monopolising 120
Montague-Chelmsford reforms 14
Mookerjee, Shyama Prasad 24, 65, 69, 86, 131, 227, 245
moral 57
Morley-Minto reforms 14
motherland 35, 60
mother tongue 36, 211
Mountbatten, Lord Louis 46, 47, 52, 54
Mughal 1, 3, 119
Muhajirs 62
Mukherjee, Amritendu 186
Mukherjee, Bankim 184
mukti joddha 202
multi-party democratic system 162
multiple xiii, xvi
municipal 93
Murshidabad 65, 168
Muslim identity 16
Muslim intelligentsia 45

Muslim League 3, 10, 13, 16, 21, 22, 28, 42, 45, 49, 124, 164
Muslim League National Guard 143
Muslim majority 46
Muslim National Guard 65
Muslim nationalism 14
Muslim refugees 57
Muslim Sahitya Samaj 16
Muslim xvii, 2, 3, 5, 7, 12, 15, 19, 20, 205, 209
Mussalman 6, 9, 10, 20, 21, 24
Mymensingh 33, 54, 60, 61, 122, 123, 127, 205

Na-Asamiya Muslims 211
Naba-barsha 19
Nadia 65, 96, 102, 168, 181
naebs 4
Nagaland 252
Nagar, Vivekananda 174
Naihati 169, 173
Namasudra 31, 95, 96, 148, 186
namaz 95
Narail 178
narrative/narrating xi, xii, xvii
National Census Register 58
national crisis 189
national guard 125
national identity 245
national history xi
nationalism 12, 20, 206
nationalist struggle 167, 204
national language 31
National Medical School 25, 169
national/nationality 5, 6, 37, 45, 206
National Population Register 254
National Register of Citizens 208, 250
National Registration System 248
nation building/nation state xi, xii, 44, 73, 81, 100, 118, 142, 161, 193, 202, 203, 245
nation-making 43, 44
nations, nationhood xi, 3, 45, 55, 57, 96
Natun Assamiya 207
Naval Movement 42
Nawab 3
Nazimuddin 22, 23
Nazrul, Kazi 27
negotiation 161
Nehru, Jawaharlal xi, xviii, 28, 33, 46, 55, 62, 68, 246, 254
Nehru-Liaquat Ali Khan Agreement/Government 64, 72, 131, 135, 171, 207
Neil Islands 105

Nellie massacre 249
Neogy, K. C. 83, 145
neo-liberal state xi
Netaji-nagar 179
newborn nation xii, 81
new faith 1
new identity formation 163
new migrants 89, 102
new refugee domain 118
new refugees 131
newspaper 32, 47, 52, 62, 170, 173, 212
Nicober Islands 104
Nikhil Vanga Bastuhara Karma Parishad 168
Noakhali 27, 28, 47, 93, 138, 144, 153, 188
non-citizens xv
non-cooperation movement 222
non-tribal xvii, 202, 234
North Indian Muslims 211
North Bengal 60
Northeast/Northeastern xv, xviii, 42, 118, 119, 120, 153, 172, 200, 203, 236, 245
North West Frontier Province 51
nostalgia 35
notion/notional xi, 34, 50, 87, 120, 245
Nowgong 122, 135
nowhere people xii, xviii
NRC 208, 209, 218, 250, 251, 252, 253, 254, 255
number game 154, 211
numerical 120
Nurul Amin 173
NVBKP 168, 169, 171, 174
NWFP 86, 246

occupation xii
Official Immigration and Reclamation Department 144
Official Language/Bill 204, 214
Official Language Movement xv, 201
Old Migrants 88
old refugees/settlers 101, 104, 131
optees 58, 69
option system 58
oral 29
ordinary people xii
original inhabitant xv, 5, 145
Orissa 82, 88, 89, 91, 99, 105, 107, 162, 173, 181
others 3, 96, 162, 203, 216
outsiders 120, 129, 163, 184, 193, 204
ownership of land 202

Padma 54, 244
Pan-Islamisation 245

Pakistan xi, xii, 22, 24, 32, 55, 60, 84, 164, 245
Pakistani 58, 69, 83
Pal, Bipin Chandra 18
Palashi women's camp 181
Palli, Rupashri 172, 181, 186
Paralkote 107, 185
parallel 203
Parishad, Gana Mukti 227, 229, 232
Parishad, Paschim Banga Rajyo Punargathan Sangjukta 212
Parishad, Upajati Gana Mukti 232
Park Circus 27, 254
Part-C States 144
partition xi, xiii, xv, xvi, xvii, 11, 29, 33, 202, 208, 244
partition council 55
partition displaced xii, 44, 72
Partition of Bengal 12
partition politics 120
party system 161, 230
passport 44, 66, 67, 86, 97, 99, 134, 148, 209
Passport (Entry into India) Act 1920, The 249
Patel, Sardar Vallabhbhai 55, 127, 130, 131, 143, 173, 177
patriotism 12
patron xii
patterns 200, 202
peasant 2, 209
peripheral 235
permanent liability group/camps 89, 191
permanent/permanent rehabilitation 72, 88, 136, 161
permanent settlement 2, 4, 12
permit system 63, 66, 127, 249
persecution 203
Persian 1
Pharasgaon 107, 185
Phookan, Nilmani 135
picture 33
pilot scheme 180
PIP Scheme 248
pitiful xiii
Plain land/Tripura 138, 139, 140
Plain Tribes Council of Assam 221
Plan Balkan 42, 46
plight 30
plough cultivation xv, 139
Poddarnagar colony 174
police 173
policy 200
policy and politics 163

policy making/maker/decision making 43, 57, 86, 89, 110, 162
political xii, xv, 3, 12, 36, 42, 200, 201, 202
political category/discourse/aspiration xi, 32, 121
political demand 202
political economy 202
political ideologies 161, 244
political Islam 2
political leadership 203
political movements xv, 163, 202, 203
political party xiv, 3, 29, 44, 161, 180, 202, 203, 236
political structure 201
politics xv, 5, 8, 200, 202
population/populated 1, 8, 22, 42, 55, 84, 86, 93, 107, 119, 200
post-colonial xi, xvi, 37, 44, 161, 203
post-Partition xiii, 31, 200
power/power relationships/power equation 161, 201, 202
Praja Socialist Party 186, 228
Prasad, Rajendra 54, 64, 165, 246
preconditions 201
Prem Nei 16
pre-Partition 98, 120, 128, 132, 201
press 32, 148, 167, 210
prestige 30
Prevention of Infiltration from Pakistan Scheme 248
Prevention of Infiltration to Assam Plan 219
princely state 139
process of Partition xi
process of radicalisation 170
profession/professional xv, 63, 182, 185
profile 200
Progressive Coalition Party 22
prolonged xi, 244
promised land 22, 112
promoter 187
property xv, xvii, 34, 42, 55, 69, 89, 128, 167, 201
Prophet Muhammad 62
Proto-type Scheme 147, 150
province xi, 7, 50, 51, 55, 121, 130
Provincial Government 64, 69
psyche/psychology/psychological xii, 29, 30, 34, 60, 64, 83, 181, 246
PTCA 221
Punarbasan 175
Punjab/Punjabi xi, xii, xiii, 42, 81, 82, 83, 110, 118, 161, 246

Quit India Movement 42
quota system 104

Radcliffe, Cyril 47, 49
Radcliffe Award/line xi, 42, 43, 54, 81, 120
radicalisation 170
Rahman, Mujibur 33
Rahman, Sheikh Mujibur 26, 31
railway station 172
Raipur riot 144
Raj 5, 6, 42, 204
Rajarhat 180
Rajasthan 162, 184, 185
Rajbhasa 140
Rajmala 119, 140
Rajshahi 31
Ram, Jagjivan 92
Ramakrishna Mission 147, 172
Ramgarh colony 174
Ranaghat 95, 172
Ranaghat Convention of 1958 184
Rangamati 50
Rangat Colonisation Scheme 105
Rangat Valley 105
Rangpur 50, 54, 61, 123
ration 57
Raurkela 99
Ray, Renuka 85, 97, 101, 105, 165, 180, 185
Ray, Siddhartha Sankar 191
RCPI (Rebel) 174, 176, 209, 214
RCRC 176, 177
Reang 62
reception xii
reception centre 138
recognised 203
Red Cross 27, 186
refuge xiv, xviii, 37, 245
refugee xi, xii, xiii, 3, 42, 161, 200
refugee absorbent states xii, xiv, 63, 82, 89, 120, 155, 161, 184, 185, 200, 245
Refugee Central Rehabilitation Council 176
refugee certificate 167
refugee-hood xiii, xvii
refugee identity 202
Refugee Peace and Welfare Committees 178
Refugee Rehabilitation Commissioner 94
refugee special trains 185
refugee studies/students xiv, 150
regime 44, 66, 99
region/regional xii, xiii, xiv, xv, xvii, 1, 2, 30, 81, 118, 119

Regional Director of Rehabilitation 145
regionalisation 245
regionalism xiii, 29, 43
registration 137
regularisation of colonies 101, 195
regulation 69, 87, 88
rehabilitation xii, xv, 37, 44, 60, 64, 82, 83, 203
Rehabilitation and Development Board 83
rehabilitation centre 106
rejected people 201
rejection 33
relationship 2
relief xii, 53, 82, 83, 95, 166
Relief and Rehabilitation Department 90, 91, 96, 101, 131, 152, 195
relief camp 90, 132, 138
relief through work 97
religion 30, 202
religious xiii, 2, 6, 36, 120, 163, 202
relocation xi
rent 35
Repatriation Certificate 66, 69
Report of the Ministry of Rehabilitation 90
requisition 129, 149
research/researcher xii, 203
resentment 201
resettle/resettlement xii, xv, 37, 63, 82, 121, 149, 165, 175, 201
residuary policy 190
resistance xii, 181
resource 55, 61
respect xviii
responsibility 202
rights 44
riot 26, 29, 31, 86, 93, 108, 144, 149, 171
Risley, H. H. 2
rivalry 200
river routes 118, 119
Robinson, Francis 8, 10
root causes 203
Roy, Annada Shankar 20
Roy, Bidhan Chandra 85, 90, 98, 103, 165, 171, 181, 187
Roy, Kiran Shankar 23
Roy, Lila 181
royal administration 144, 201
royal buildings 144
RSP 176
RSS 164, 173
Rudrasagar project 148
ruling community 203
rumour 27, 31, 32

rural xvii, 1, 2, 9, 18, 27, 45, 84, 97, 100, 225

Saadulla, Mahammad 52, 120, 124
Sabha, Asamiya Samrakshini 213
Sabha, Asam Jatiya 213
Sabha, Assam Sahitya 213, 220, 221, 236
safety xviii, 34, 244
Saha, M. N. 86, 135, 136
Salimullah, Nawab 11, 12
Salt Lake 103
Samiti, Adivasi 231
Samiti, Anushilan 222
Samiti, Kashi Biswanath Seba 172
Samiti, Murari Pukur Bastuhara 182
Samiti, Purbabanga Sankhalaghu Kalyan 227
Samiti, Rajarhat Krishak 182
Samiti, Rajya Jana Mangal 223
Samiti, Tripura Ganatantrik 229
Samiti, Ultadanga Anchalik Bastuhara 182
Samities, Kishan 228
Samity, Bhasa Andolan 217
Samity, Mahila Atmaraksha 181
Samity, Nikhil Assam Banga Bhasa 217
Samity, Pakistan Gana 164
Samsuddin, Abu Jafar 15, 19
Sangha, Bharat Sebasram 172, 186
Sangha, Bharati 222
Sangha, Chhartra 222
Sangha, Ganatantrik 228
Sangha, Jan 247
Sangha, Rastriya Svayamsevaka 164
sangram committees 173, 186
Sangu 50
Sanjukta Bastuhara Parishad 229
Sanjukta Udbastu Sammelan 177
Sanmilan, Assam Chhatra 213
Sansad, Adivasi 231
sanskritisation 2, 19, 153
santanas 13
sanyasis 13
Sara Bangla Bastuhara Sammelan 187
Saraswati Puja 19
Sattor Bachhar 18
saturation point 184
satyagraha xv, 177, 180, 186, 217, 227
Satya Pir 19
Save Pakistan Minorities Committee 190
Saxena, Mohanlal 90, 91, 133, 172
scheduled caste 23, 96
scheduled tribe 150
schemes 100, 152
Sealdah Station 33, 106, 166, 170, 180, 181

secular/secularist/secularism 86, 100, 161, 245, 254
security xvii, 37, 54, 63, 244
seizure 171
self respect 168
self settlement movement 169
Sen, Prafulla 170
Seng-Krak 225, 232
separate electorates 14, 15
separate homelands 45, 245
separatist/separatism 5, 6
settlement xii, 107, 108
settlers 104, 120, 155
shadow 118
Shahidnagar colony 169
sharanarthi xiii, 59
Shastri, Lal Bahadur 218
Shastri Formula, The 218
Shayesta, Begum 26
shelter 167
Shia 7
Shraddhananda Park 170
Shyama-Huq Ministry 22
Sibsagar 123
Sikh 7, 85, 161
Silchar 134, 135, 137, 155, 210, 217
Silchar District Congress Committee 133
Simla Conference 46
simple 37, 203
Sindh/Sindhi 84, 161
Singh, Baldev 46
Singh, Sachindra Lal 228
Sixth Schedule 232, 252
slogan 35, 206
slum 173
small scale industries 182
social division 24
socialist 166
Socialist Party 176
Socialist Republican Party 164, 174
Socialist Unity Centre 174
society xvi, 8
Sodepur 169
soft violence 31, 32
soil 34, 204
solution 33
Sonarpur 180
source xvi
South Asia/Asian xi, 3, 42, 44, 57, 69, 142
South Calcutta Refugee Council of Action 174
Southeast Asia 119
sovereign independent State for undivided Bengal 23
sovereign nation-state 100

spatially xii
sponsor xii
sponsored migration 124
squatters' colonies 99, 167, 169, 171, 173, 175, 176, 181
Srihatta 153, 201
Sri Prakash 63, 64, 134
State Development Board Quarterly 184
State Government xv, 63, 82, 91, 132, 133
State Government Rehabilitation Directorate 178
statehood 73
stateless 203
State Level Foreigners' Tribunal 251
State Rehabilitation Committee 190
State Rehabilitation Department 147, 149
States Reorganisation Commissions 105, 211, 212, 213
state/state formation xv, 202, 204
state system xi, xv, 59, 145
Statistical Survey Report, The 101
steering committee 55
stranded 118, 132
strategy 163, 171, 174, 177, 180, 194, 203
strike 177
structure 202
struggle xi, xii, xviii, 36, 60, 201, 244
subcontinent xi, 1
suburb/suburban 97, 169
Sufi *pirs* 1
Suhrawardy, Huseyn Shaheed 22
Sundarbans 182
Sunni 7
supported 203
Supreme Court 56, 220
Surabhi 129
surgery xi, 118
Surma Valley 61, 123, 134, 154, 201, 202, 217
Surma-Kusiara river basin 121
survey 108
survival 175
Swadeshi 10, 11, 12, 222
Swadhinota 171
Swarajya Party 18
Sylhet Referendum 47, 51, 52, 209, 246
Sylhet 31, 47, 51, 53, 54, 61, 121, 126, 154, 200, 205, 246
Sylheti 200
sympathy/sympathetic 167, 182, 184, 193
syncretic 2, 19

Tagore, Rabindranath 140
taluk 25
Talukdar 95

Index **309**

tax 93, 139, 182
temporary 33, 34, 72, 172
temporary shelter 89, 155
Territorial Council 144
territory xi, xii, 35, 45, 47, 64, 245
testimonials 29, 33
Third June Plan 47
tilla land 150
Tippera, Parbatya 138, 139
Tipperah 27, 50, 144
Tipra/Tipraland movement xvii, 235
Titagarh 173
TLR & LR Act of 1960, The 231, 232
TNV 232
Tollyganj 173, 178
torture 62
tradition 2, 3, 29, 60
tragedy xi, 55
tree plantation industry 205
training camps/centre 90, 135, 137
transfer of land 149
transfer of power 142
transit camp 109, 179, 185
trans-border migration 245
trauma xvi, 3
travel document 66, 190
tribal reserves 231
tribals/tribal refugees xvi, xv, xvii, 107, 119, 121, 123, 131, 150, 202, 203, 228, 231, 234
Trinamul Congress Party, The 254
Tripura xii, xiv, xvii, 42, 69, 87, 91, 92, 138, 141, 162, 173, 201, 202, 212
Tripura Central Relief and Rehabilitation Association 227
Tripura Land Revenue and Land Reforms Act 151
Tripura National Volunteers 232
Tripura Rajya Adibasi Sangha 231
Tripura Rajya Gana Parishad 223
Tripura Rajya Jana Siksha Samiti 223
Tripura Rajya Mukti Parishad 226, 227
Tripura Rajya Praja Mandal 224
Tripura Rajyer Katha 225
Tripura Sena 232
Tripura Tribal Linguistic Enterprise 233
Tripura Upajati Juva Samiti xvi, 232
Tripur Sangha Paharia Union 231
Tripuri 62, 141
troublesome 202
TSF 232
TUJS 232, 233, 234, 236
turmoil 180
Twipra Students' Federation 232
two-nations 37
Type Scheme 147

UCRC 175, 176, 177, 178, 180, 181, 182, 184, 187, 193, 210
Uday Villa 181
Udbastu Shibir 178
udbastu xiii, 59
Umerkote 107, 109, 185
Umerkote Irrigation Dam 107
UN Convention 56
unauthorised occupation 171
underserving 204
undesirable squatters 94
undivided xi
uneasy minorities 44
UNESCO 179
UNHCR 56
unification 171
Unified Bangastan 123
Union Board Scheme 184
Union Home Ministry 102
Union Ministry 108
Union Rehabilitation Ministry 92, 184
Union Territory 144
United Central Refugee Council 175
United Council of Relief and Welfare 172
United Front Government 190, 191
United Leftist Election Committee 180, 183
United Nations Relief and Rehabilitation Administration 83
United Provinces 8, 88
united struggle 202
unity 32
UNRRA 83, 84
untouchables 3, 7, 8, 84, 95
up-country 45
upheaval 203
upojati 202
Upper Assam 217
upper caste xvii, 12, 248
upper class, upper middle class xvii, 42, 96, 127, 167
uprooted xvi, 36, 64
urban xvii, 18, 45, 93, 100, 195, 225, 234
Urdu 62
urgent 85
utopia xii, 37
Uttarpara 94
Uttar Pradesh 89

vernacular 205
veteran leaders 163
viceroy 54
victim/victimhood 29, 73, 118, 203
Vidhyasagar colony 174
villains 203
violence xii, xiii, 29, 32, 57, 59, 64, 176, 245

violent 245
virgin soil 139
visa 44, 66, 67, 134, 148, 149, 209
vocal 44
vocational and technical training 99, 182
voice xviii
volatile 118, 169
volunteers 174
vote bank 162, 203, 204
voting rights 161, 183, 211
vulnerable 118

Wadud, Kazi Abdul 17
wakf lands 100
wansa xiii, 62
warmth 37
wasteland 37, 61, 110, 122, 127, 150, 205
wealth xvii
welfare society 172
West Bengal xii, xiv, xv, 33, 34, 42, 57, 59, 60, 162, 163, 201
West Bengal Evacuee Property Act 1951, The 177
West Bengal Land Development and Planning Act, The 95
West Bengal Legislative Assembly 177
West Bengal Pradesh Congress Committee 212
West Pakistan 31, 66, 92
West Punjabi 90
Western education/educated 3, 4, 6, 94, 129, 165, 201, 205
Western xii, 23, 47, 83, 84, 85, 90
white-collar job 61, 205
women 30, 33, 67, 69, 181
Women's camp 186
Women's Co-operative Industrial Home 181
Women's Refugee Day 181
Working Group 194
worksite camp 99, 107, 181, 182, 184
world 33
World War II 44, 45, 166

zamindar/zamindari 2, 3, 5, 24, 139, 169, 177, 178, 187